William Woodruff was bor... ...of Lancashire cotton workers. Leaving sc... ...very boy in a grocer's shop. In ...orth of England, he decided to ...with the aid of a London Count... ...ford University. During the Seco... ...itish Army in North Africa and the Medite... ...1946 Woodruff renewed his academic career. He is a world historian whose work has been widely translated. Woodruff has seven children. He lives with his wife, Helga, in Florida.

Praise for *The Road to Nab End* and *Beyond Nab End*

'A terrific story with an archetypal rags-to-riches dimension. It is nostalgic, vivid and charming' *Observer*

'A combination of an almost photographic memory, a wonderful writing gift and a keen eye for personal dramas, which even Ibsen would have admired' *Spectator*

'Despite the air of near-constant struggle that runs through this beautifully crafted and very moving memoir, there's a streak of indelible optimism . . . A wonderful evocation of a vanished age' *Mail on Sunday*

'Memories pour forth with photographic clarity to make this remarkable book' *Express*

'Edifying and well written . . . Woodruff's writing is fresh, vivid, honest and intelligent . . . this is a truly inspiring story of a brain going up in the world, twenty years before post-war education made such mobility universally possible' *Sunday Times*

'As extraordinary as its predecessor . . . Woodruff's remarkable photographic memory still serves him as faithfully as ever' *Independent*

'Beautifully written, it is as quietly riveting as its predecessor . . . it is a fine read' *The Times*

'A moving and evocative picture of a world that has vanished as surely as Bakelite and ration books' *Observer*

Also by William Woodruff

Vessel of Sadness

Paradise Galore

The Rise of the British Rubber Industry
during the Nineteenth Century

Impact of Western Man:
A Study of Europe's Role in the World Economy,
1750–1960

America's Impact on the World:
A Study of the Role of the United States
in the World Economy, 1750–1970

The Struggle for World Power, 1500–1980

The Emergence of an International Economy, 1700–1914

A Concise History of the Modern World:
1500 to the Present

NAB END AND BEYOND

The Road to Nab End and *Beyond Nab End*

William Woodruff

ABACUS

Nab End and Beyond: This omnibus edition first published
in Great Britain by Little, Brown in 2003
This paperback edition published in December 2006 by Abacus
Nab End and Beyond copyright © Helga Woodruff 2003

Previously published separately:
The Road to Nab End: First published under the title *Billy Boy* by
Ryburn Publishing Ltd in 1993
First published in paperback by Eland Press in 2000
First published by Abacus in 2002
Copyright © Helga Woodruff 1993; copyright renewed in 2000

Beyond Nab End: First published in Great Britain as a paperback original
by Abacus in 2003
Copyright © Helga Woodruff 2003

Extract on p. 601 by Virgile Thomas and René de Buxeuil.
Copyright © assigned in 1958 to Sté D'Editions Musicales
Internationales (SEMI 4024), 5 rue Lincoln, Paris (8e)

The moral right of the author has been asserted.

A CIP catalogue record for this book is available
from the British Library.

ISBN-13: 978–0–349–11987–8
ISBN-10: 0–349–11987–2

Typeset in Sabon by Palimpsest Book Production Limited,
Grangemouth, Stirlingshire

Printed and bound in Great Britain by
Mackays of Chatham plc, Chatham, Kent

Abacus
An Imprint of
Little, Brown Book Group
Brettenham House
Lancaster Place
London WC2E 7EN

A Member of the Hachette Livre Group of Companies

www.littlebrown.co.uk
www.williamwoodruff.com

THE
ROAD
TO
NAB END

An Extraordinary Northern Childhood

This family photograph celebrates father coming home on leave early in 1917. I am sitting on mother's knee. Brenda stands in the middle, next to Jenny. Dan is in front.

To the memory of grandmother Bridget
who always called me Billy Boy

Prologue

They said I should not go. They said it was madness for an old man to cross the Atlantic to seek out his birth-place.

'You'll find nothing but ghosts there. Why don't you go and see the Grand Canyon?'

Others thought that anybody over seventy had every right to do as he pleased.

'Time's a-wasting,' they said, noting my faulty gait.

So I went.

And when I reached the north of England and came to Blackburn, the town of my birth, and asked the taxi driver to take me to Griffin Street, he eyed me cautiously.

'Are you sure you want to go there?'

'Oh yes, I was born there. I've come a long way to see it.'

'You're the boss,' he said, taking my bags and holding the door so that I could climb in. A cold north wind – the wind I'd long since forgotten – tugged at my coat. I began to regret having arrived in thin Florida clothing.

As we moved off, I caught sight of several high-rise apartment buildings; they were harsh to the eye.

'Council flats,' the driver said.

But then came landmarks I'd known as a child. The reddish-brown cathedral dominated the centre of town. When my great-grandfather Arne Woodruff fled from Westmorland to Blackburn more than a hundred years ago, there were cows grazing around the church. I wondered if the image of Christ crucified was still inside; the Christ with the big hands: worker's hands.

We passed Queen Victoria's statue on the Parade – it was as ugly as ever, grey with age and covered with bird dirt. The statue of Robert Peel, the famous nineteenth-century statesman and cotton manufacturer, stood, equally dirty, at the other side of the cathedral.

As we crossed King William Street, I looked for the clock tower above the Market Hall; it had been a touch of Italy in the north of England. My father, recently arrived from America in 1914, had paraded under that clock before going to war.

The King's Arms pub appeared on our left. Its marble pillars looked like potted meat. As a small child, I'd pressed my back against that 'potted meat' waiting to see the first automobile in my life. Mother had warned me that a motorcar was in town, and that I should watch out for it carefully. 'It's coming!' the crowd had shouted. As I turned, I saw a large black beetle with a shiny nose crawling across the cobblestones toward me. Its deep cough and trail of smoke added to my fears. I couldn't have been more amazed had an extinct reptile walked by.

But what was this nagging feeling? The more I stared through the taxi window, the more convinced I became that this was not the town of my birth. Had I come to the wrong place?

Of course not. The grey-roofed factories with their fortress-like walls were still there. So was Hornby's Mill – the mill of my childhood. It seemed so small; its windows were dirty and broken. As we turned a corner, I could see endless rows of weavers' cottages running across the town into the hills. The wet roofs glistened in the evening light; they seemed to be sagging. Using the local supplies of stone, slate, and clay, the cottages had been thrown together in the second half of the nineteenth century when the Lancashire cotton textile industry was booming. Whoever had built them had insisted on uniformity, if not downright ugliness. People lived and died in identical cottages that were little more than barracks.

Except that they looked older, most of the public buildings – the gas works, the chapels and the churches – were unchanged.

I asked the driver to go past the two schools where seventy years ago I had been a pupil. All that was left of St Philip's, was a gaunt, lonely church tower. It stood there forlorn, an island of stone.

'School fell down, church wasn't needed.'

My parents had walked through the cobbled streets to be married at St Philip's in September 1904, 'according to the rights and ceremonies of the Established Church.' I had approached this same tower as a small, rather frightened schoolboy of four in 1920.

My other school, St Peter's, was still standing, though propped up at the sides with metal supports. Its walls had the forbidding appearance that they had had when I looked upon them as a child.

We crossed the Blakewater river still running black.

In the far distance, from a high point, I caught a glimpse of the slag heaps on which I had fought with gangs of other children; they stood pyramid-like against the sky.

Yet the nagging feeling remained. The Blackburn of my childhood had had a forest of red brick chimneys belching great twisting coils of smoke. Where were they? The few chimneys I could see were cold and smokeless. I looked at my watch. It was 5:30. The light was fading. Seventy years ago, at this hour, Blackburn's streets would have been filled with the clip-clap sound of clogs as thousands of factory workers, the women in grey shawls, the men wearing dark caps, hastened home from work. Now there were few people about; they were better dressed – no shawls, few caps, no clogs – but there was no haste in their step. At this hour, the Blackburn into which I was born had been noisy, urgent, crowded, vibrant, alive.

The Blackburn I saw was becalmed – like a demasted ship after a storm.

We stood in what had been Griffin Street and surveyed a windswept, rubble-strewn wasteland covering many acres.

'Slum clearance,' the driver mused, picking his teeth. 'Had to do it, "Pakis" were moving in.'

I stared at a pile of broken glass and rusty wire where my cottage had been.

'It's a pity you came all the way from America to find everything gone.'

'Oh, no,' I answered. 'On the contrary, . . . everything is here.'

Chapter I

Griffin Street

The fierce rattling of my bedroom window-pane first roused me from the long sleep of birth. Mr Smalley, whom we called t' knocker-up man, came with his wire-tipped pole in the dark six mornings a week to shake our window until father stirred and shouted loud enough to be heard in the street below, 'We're up!' Mr Smalley then went next door and rattled the bedroom window of our neighbour, Mr Morgan, the coal hauler. I often lay in bed listening to Mr Smalley coming down the street. With his coming, Griffin Street began to stir. Daylight followed.

Not long after t' knocker-up had finished rattling our window-pane, a stream of wood-shodden workers began to hurry past my window on its way to the mills. In the Blackburn of 1916, more than two hundred factory and workshop chimneys were belching smoke by five a.m. Muffled voices and morning greetings flew up from the street. As the grey light grew and the night's bright stars paled, the stream of passers-by, their heads covered with shawls and caps, became a river and then a flood. The clip-clap of their clogs on the cobbles drowned out all other noises. In winter, deadened clogs meant a heavy snow; clogs that rang meant a frost. When it was raining, I looked down on a sea of glistening umbrella tops bobbing up and down on their way to the mill.

Once the flow of workers had subsided, except for the rattle of a cart in the distance, all was still again: still enough, that is, until I heard the last running steps dash by – someone trying to reach the mill before the whistle sounded and the tall iron gates were slammed to. Latecomers never failed to excite me. Sometimes, with nothing on but my grey flannel shirt, I jumped out of bed and, with my face pressed against the cold glass, watched the last workers rush by. 'Hurry,' I shouted, 'you'll make it!' Back in bed, I had visions of them squeezing through the crack in the heavy factory gates before they closed. Those shut out of the mills came traipsing back. I could tell from the ring of their clog-irons that they had failed. Time was a hard master.

I also heard the coming and going of our neighbour, Mr Morgan, the coal hauler, who left his house later than the mill workers. Mr Lambert on the other side of our house walked to his job at the gas works with Mr Morgan. About this time, the lamplighter passed down the street with his long pole with a hook on the end of it, and the street lamps were extinguished.

By mid-morning the stream of clogs had been replaced by a stream of horse-drawn carts, clippety-clopping their way to the railway station with mountains of grey cloth. Some of the cloth, which we called 'duties' – after the Indian word dhotis – was on its way to be bleached, dyed and printed in Manchester twenty-five miles to the south; the bulk of it would then go to Liverpool, thirty-five miles to the south-west, on its way to India, wherever that was. India must have been very important to Blackburn because I seemed to hear more about India as a child than I did about England.

The long columns of horse-drawn carts passed within an arm's reach of our front door. I watched the wind tugging at the tarpaulins. With marked regularity, the buckles smacked against the sides. The journey to the station was a race in which the whip was not spared. I wondered if the horses which did not move fast enough were shut out of the station as the workers were shut out of the factories.

As the day wore on, the street echoed to the call of the rag-and-bone man, who cried his wares from a donkey cart. In exchange for a handful of rags, a bare bone or two, some old medicine or pickled-onion bottles, or old newspapers, or any old piece of metal, he gave mother a donkey stone – a piece of hard chalk – with which to colour the kitchen hearth-stone and the front doorstep. Everybody knew that the rag-and-bone man was not as poor as he looked. He was followed by the scissors-grinder who, for a penny or two, sharpened scissors and knives amid a shower of sparks with a foot-driven grinding wheel. There were other peddlers, such as the thread, needles and ribbon seller, who cried their wares. My favourite was the tinker who mended pots and pans. Because Griffin Street was one of the main highways to the mills, there was no lingering in the street for man or beast until darkness came.

At the end of the working day, as the last empty carts drawn by froth-covered horses returned to the mills, the tide of workers, the women walking arm in arm, surged past our cottage door again, homeward bound. Their step was not as brisk as it had been at the beginning of the day. After that, apart from the plaintive shriek of a train in the distance, or the haunting sound of a lonely concertina being played by a passerby, silence reigned. To keep up steam, the thump of the mill engines went on all night, but that didn't bother anybody. The workers didn't notice noises that brought them bread.

Like all the other weaver's cottages, our house was one of an endless row. The outside was brick; the roof was grey slate. It had four white-washed rooms, two up and two down. They were about seven feet high. The front rooms measured nine feet by nine feet. Tall people had to dip when coming through the front door. When I was sitting on my father's shoulders, I had to watch out not to bump my head. The downstairs floors were made of large flagstones, covered with a scattering of clean sand that was swept up and renewed weekly. The sand got between our toes. In winter the stones froze to our feet. The ceilings were the wooden floor boards of the upper rooms. There was a tiny yard at the rear, where the rain sat between the cobbles. Beyond was an alley and another unbroken line of cottages.

My brother Dan and I shared a bedroom with our parents. There were two metal beds with straw mattresses resting on thin metal slats. Sometimes the slats sagged, leaving a pocket into which we sank our hips. Dan and I slept in the same bed. We slept so close to our parents that we could touch them. The nearness of our bodies made us feel safe. No one noticed the lack of privacy. I accepted my parent's love-making long before I understood it. It was as natural as somebody using the pisspot (I didn't know the word chamber-pot until I had left school). It didn't disturb me, or confuse me, or revolt me. Like father's deep snoring, I ignored it. Living in such a confined space meant everybody shared everybody else's joys and sorrows.

I think the straw mattresses must have encouraged bugs, for I recall mother sitting on the side of the bed running her fingers down the seams of blankets and sheets. I didn't find anything strange about her crushing the bugs between her thumb nails, though it did get bloody at times. It was a never-ending battle.

Our clothing, what little we had, hung on the whitewashed walls. As the walls were sometimes damp, sheets of brown paper were slipped between the clothes and the plaster. The pegmat at my bedside protected my feet from the freezing floor. In our house there was one by every bed as well as before the two fireplaces downstairs. They were made from old clothing and could be of all colours. They were not only solid and warm; they meant that no garment, however old, was wasted. The women made them at night, pulling strips of cloth with a rughook through a stiff piece of fabric. Several women would work together, chattering, singing and laughing into the night. The mats were kept clean by beating them against the outside wall.

There was not much else in the bedroom: a lace curtain, a tiny black iron fireplace and an empty orange crate scavanged from the fruit market, which served as a bedside table. The crate's two compartments were brightly painted and decorated with a linen cloth at the front. There were also two pisspots, an open-flame gas light, the flame blue at the bottom, white at the top, and a cracked wooden door with a latch.

My sisters Jenny and Brenda slept in the other bedroom, behind a paper-thin wall. When I was born in 1916, Jenny was eleven and Brenda was six. Dan was four years older than I. Because of the wooden staircase, the back bedroom was smaller than the front bedroom. There was only space for one bed and a large wooden trunk filled with linen and bedding. There was no end to what that trunk contained. My sisters' clothing also hung on the walls.

The kitchen, which was beneath the back bedroom, was the centre of family activities. There was ever a din going on there at night. The room contained a plain deal bench that served as a table, two rush-bottomed stand chairs, two foot-stools, two rocking chairs, a cupboard for groceries, hooks for pots and pans, the bread-mug (a large clay bowl with a clay lid in which we kept bread, margarine and other food), and another large clay bowl in which the bread was made. A big earthenware dish could be used for any purpose. As the kitchen was three paces one way and two-and-a-half the other, children didn't sit at table, we stood for meals.

The coal-burning open fire range had an oven at one side

and an oblong tank for heating water at the other. The water was rusty because the metal flaked off, but it could be used for cleaning jobs. In front of the fire was a top-bar on which the kettle sang. Steel fire irons stood on the hearth which had a metal surround. The whole range was kept clean with black-lead and ammonia. I don't know how much lead we consumed. Ashes from the fire fell into a stone-lined hole in the floor, and were shovelled into a bucket and thrown into the midden in the backyard. I didn't like the look or the taste of ashes, and kept well away from the hole in the floor when it was being emptied. If a mouse fell in there, it never got out again. Coal was dumped in the kitchen under the stairs, a sack at a time. It kept dry there. It was brought by our neighbour, Mr Morgan, who staggered through the front room with a hundred pound sack on his back.

The cloud of dust that flew up when Mr Morgan poured the coal – though on our behalf he was ever careful – took time to settle. The worst thing that could happen was for Mr Morgan to arrive while we were eating. With a sack of coal being shaken out almost against the dining table, it was impossible not to eat coal dust. No one grumbled. Even a child knew that we couldn't possibly manage without coal.

When done, Mr Morgan quietly folded his sack, adjusted the leather hood that protected his ears as well as his head, repositioned the studded leather guard, which prevented the coal from digging into his back, picked up his shilling and left. I never knew Mr Morgan to stand in our kitchen talking – perhaps because he was so dirty.

Above the fireplace was a gas light, which was capped with a one-penny asbestos mantle – about the size and shape of a white clay pipe. Beneath the gas light was a shelf on which sat two red and white earthenware dogs. One of my mother's brothers had given them to her as a wedding present. They came with an unfriendly look and never changed. Some said that's how pot dogs always looked; others said, he'd got them cheap. Time in the house was kept by a steel watch that hung on a hook. Father had got it from the navy, years before. To escape time in Blackburn, you had to go into the country.

Under the window was a stone sink and a slopstone, or draining board. Above the sink was the only tap in the house. Next to the fireplace was a deep, large metal basin called a setpot or copper. It was heated with free orange-box wood, and had a chimney connected to the fireplace. Clean water, water free of rust, was boiled in the setpot. My mother and my sisters washed clothes there. Washing was soaked, boiled, rotated with a wooden dolly, rinsed and starched in this small corner. The steaming wet washing was run through a wringer that stood in the yard and, weather permitting, hung out to dry on the clothesline. How forsaken the washing looked through the window when it was left in the rain. Brought inside, it was flung over a clothes rack, fixed to the ceiling in front of the range. Damp clothing usually hung from the ceiling for half the week. The grown-ups got their heads caught in it.

A single metal gas ring stood next to the setpot for cooking. For the gas there was a penny meter under the stairs. If the light gave out and we didn't have a penny, we used a candle; if we didn't have a candle we sat by the fire and told tales or went to bed.

When you opened the front door and stepped down one step you stood in the street. In winter a heavy curtain was put up to stop drafts. Some people called this room the parlour, but that was putting on airs. There was a lace curtain in front of the window, a gas light, a fireplace with a pegrug in front of it, and a rocking chair at either side. The fire-irons and metal surround were made of brass, not steel as in the kitchen. There were also some stools, and another large chest for clothing and belongings. On the Singer sewing machine in front of the window stood an aspidistra that was periodically washed with soap and water and put out for air. Mother's cut-glass punch bowl stood on a small table against the wall. On the shelf above the fireplace were several framed pictures of relatives. There also was a coloured picture of Blackpool Tower and the Big Wheel. The front room was used for entertaining, for holidays such as Christmas and, if coal was available, at weekends. When my sisters grew up, it became our dance floor. Except on the hottest days of summer, it was too cold to sit there without a fire.

For me, the cobbled yard at the back of the house was another world. It could be traversed with a hop, skip and a jump. Underneath the kitchen window was a tap over a drain where the pisspots stood after being rinsed. In frosty weather the tap froze and the pots had to be washed inside. In one corner was a tiny shelter where the cast iron clothes wringer, brushes and brooms were kept. Another corner contained a pile of cinders, picked by us children from factory tips. Our neighbour Mr Lambert sometimes added a sack of coke from the gasworks. Coke and peat sods were used in winter to keep the kitchen fire going throughout the night; we called it banking-up. Above the cinders hung a large tin tub that was carried into the kitchen when somebody wanted a bath, which wasn't very often.

There was also a petty in the backyard connected to the main sewer; there was no flushing, no lighting, no seat. We used nothing but newspaper there. In summer it stank, in winter you froze to the board. If you stayed too long, one of the family would call from the backdoor, 'Wot yer doin' in t' petty? Are yer makin' yer will?' An odd question, because the working class didn't make wills. My sister Jenny would never go out there at night without a flickering candle. If we had no candle somebody had to go out with her and stand outside the petty door until she was done.

Next to the toilet was a brick, roofed-over midden where we threw our rubbish. This was shovelled from the back alley into a horse-drawn cart. A door lead into the alley, which had a stone gutter down which rats used to scurry. They frightened me to the point of panic. The yard was enclosed by a rough stone wall.

In summer, the smell of rotting garbage was everywhere.

Flies descended in clouds; hence the upset stomachs. Indoors we had penny flypapers. In warm weather, we ate while watching the death throes of flies caught on the flypaper above the dining table. Great buzzing bluebottles were the only ones to escape, and they not often.

———◦———

I learned as a child to avoid talking about the damp and cold in our house. 'It's bad enough without having you gassing,' my folk grumped. I think the damp worried them more than the cold. There was nothing to stop it rising through the flagstones that covered the floor. It got into people's bones. The washing hanging from the kitchen ceiling didn't help either. The cold was sometimes so severe that it made us forget the damp. When the northwind was blowing and the air was smoking with snow, we went to bed with all the preparations of a military campaign. As the only heat upstairs was that which came from the kitchen through the cracks in the wooden floors, we didn't walk, we dashed to bed, taking care not to get splinters in our feet on the staircase. No praying at the bedside for us. The hot oven shelves, covered with flannel, went into bed first, our clothing followed; every garment that could be found was heaped on top. Sometimes we even used thick layers of newspaper as an extra blanket, which rustled when we turned in bed. Underneath it all, my brother and I kept each other warm.

The kitchen fire was banked up and kept alight throughout the night. That was father's job. If the man-of-the-house was about, nobody else touched the poker. I never ceased to wonder how much interest father took in the fire. You knew his mood from the way he handled the poker, or how he rearranged the coals. I think it gave him great satisfaction and saved him from talking. The house would have been unbearable without keeping the kitchen fire going. Even so, there were nights when it was too cold to sleep. On a really cold morning we had to dress quickly or freeze. We didn't linger in the bedroom, we raced to breakfast. Cold and hunger were the great persuaders.

Curiously enough, we never lit the bedroom fires except on Christmas Eve to welcome Father Christmas who entered our bedrooms by way of the chimney. Every Christmas my brother and I woke in the early hours of Christmas Day to find one or two little gifts at the foot of the bed. What magic to waken and find that Father Christmas had not forgotten us – that somebody cared! In my stocking was an apple or an orange, some nuts, and a shining new penny. Requests for fires in the bedrooms at times other than Christmas were met with: 'It isn't really cold enough for fires upstairs,' or, with the snow-flakes spinning to earth outside, 'It's going to get warmer.' The answer that settled all arguments was 'Coal's done.'

One piercingly cold night – with a thick crust of ice and snow covering the bedroom window – father woke up to use the pisspot. He must have been caught unexpectedly. Perhaps he'd been out drinking. Anyway, to his annoyance, he discovered that the pisspots had been left by the drain in the yard and were now buried under deep snow. Before mother could stop him, he'd shot up the window and was pissing into the street. All would have been well had he not pissed on somebody's head. Even better had the passerby not looked up to see who was opening the window. A great howl arose from the cobbles below. With a freezing wind entering the room, mother choked with anger at father. Father choked with fury at the passerby, whose own fury was waking the street. 'What reet have you,' father bawled, 'to be wanderin' t' streets at this hour? Why can't you watch where ye're goin'?' With that he slammed the window shut. Next morning there was an unusual tension at breakfast.

It took father a long time to live the pissing incident down. In our street such tales quickly got around. I was at a workers' meeting with father some nights later when someone shouted: 'Any more bull's eyes, Will?' Everybody roared with laughter, including father, which was not like him. When I told grandmother Bridget about the pissing business she crossed herself.

———◇———

I'd always believed that I had been born in our cottage in Griffin Street.

'Ah, no, Billy,' mother said one day, 'that's where tha wrang; tha was born in t' mill.'

'But that's not what it says on my birth certificate.'

I discovered that I was born prematurely in the carding-room of Hornby's cotton mill, which was only a few minutes from Griffin Street. Day long, mother cleaned cotton there. On the morning of my birth she had fainted before one of the cotton grinders.

'It was the telegrams.'

'What telegrams?'

'From t' War Office. Dad was in France fighting the war. The first telegram they brought to t'mill. The foreman, Patrick Murphy, read it to me. It said that your dad was killed and that the War Office regretted it. Just a line to change your life. Everybody was real nice. Told me to go home and rest, and to come back when I was ready.'

'Did you?'

'Well, when you don't have any money and your husband is dead and you've got four mouths to feed, including your own and your unborn child, you'd better be ready all the time or you'll starve.'

'But Dadda wasn't dead.'

'No, that's right, he wasn't. A week later another telegram came saying that the first telegram had been a mistake. Two hours after that you arrived. Patrick Murphy delivered you on a heap of cotton against a wall in a corner of the shed. I was in my own bed by the time Dr Grieves got there. He wrote Griffin Street in your birth certificate. With or without Grieves, it was a fine birth. No commotion. Of course,

19

there was the din of the carding machines and cotton dust falling on us, but no bother, all went well. When he'd delivered you, Mr Murphy dipped his thumb into one of the fire buckets and baptized you, "Father, Son and Holy Ghost." He wrapped you in a sheet and shouted to the other card-room hands: "Cum and look! Have you ever seen sich? It's a boy, and a sturdy one at that; worth a drink o' rum and tay, he is." They came running. "Oh, a grand bairn, a really grand bairn," they clucked as they crowded around. "It's not every day it happens in t' shed. Tha can be reet proud of thiself, Maggie, tha can. Spitten image of his dad. Lucky his dad's alive!"

'Later that morning grandmother Bridget came across from Dougdale's mill. The three of us were bundled onto one of the factory's horse-drawn carts. With you held in my arms, we rattled our way through the streets until we reached our cottage. Two days after you were born, I was back at work, slubbing in the mill; cooking, washing and cleaning at home.'

With mother in the mill during the war years, the job of caring for me fell to my sister Jenny, who was eleven years older than I. I think she brought me up more than my mother did. Staying home and keeping house meant the end of her own childhood, and the end also of whatever little schooling she had had. Nobody bothered to enforce the rule that she should have stayed at school until she was fourteen. Several times a day she took me from the wooden box that served as my cradle, wrapped me in a blanket and ran through the streets to the mill, where mother was waiting to suckle me. The suckling done, Jenny then went home again and rocked me to sleep.

Once, when Jenny was unwell and could not take me to the mill, mother ignored the factory regulations and walked out. She had the misfortune to run headlong into the time-keeper at the gate.

'Here, where t' goin'?' he demanded.

'Home, t' feed child, it's clemmin'.'

'If tha goes out now, tha stays out!'

Mother returned to the cardroom.

Being in Jenny's care didn't do me any harm; I thrived. She handled me as well as a grown woman. Indeed, one might say that I had a privileged childhood, for Jenny, whom I called Gaga, loved me and sang to me all day. She loved me even more when I began to creep about and play with her. She never thought of me as a burden. Only reluctantly did she surrender me to mother at the end of the day. Jenny was pleased when morning came and mother departed, and she could reclaim me as her own.

When in later years I suggested that I'd robbed her of her schooling, she countered: 'Playing with a baby brother was much better than going to school, especially here.' She never forgave the Blackburn children for having ripped the buttons off her brand-new American coat. After four years at school in the United States, she never forgot America. Later on in life when I met her on the streets and asked 'Where to, Jenny?' she would grin and reply, 'America.'

'I had a dream,' she told me one day, 'in which I travelled back to America alone in a beautiful gondola.'

Jenny not only looked after me; after four o'clock, when my sister Brenda and my brother Dan came home from school, she had to care for them, too. Wearing one of mother's dresses, and one of her wide-brimmed hats held on with a long hat pin, she clowned and acted for us until mother arrived. Then she helped to cook and wash and prepare for still another day.

The wonder is that mother and grandmother Bridget should have gone on working in the mill all day while the Woodruff children ran wild. With father away at war and our savings exhausted, mother had no choice. The war allowance from father was not enough to keep the family going. Her earnings as a slubber in the mill were fifteen shillings a week. Grandmother's savings had gone too and she had to work to stay alive. She had a tiny cottage not far from Griffin Street. For some reason she never lived with us or her other children – not even during the war.

There were times during the war when mother felt that the world was crazy. There'd never been such slaughter. The first casualty lists from the Battle of the Somme in 1916 stunned the whole of Blackburn. The tragedy was on such a scale that people simply couldn't understand it. 'Everybody felt they'd been kicked in the belly. You couldn't go out, without having to stop and hold somebody's hand,' mother said. 'Death was common; black clothing was everywhere. The war frayed everybody's nerves; put everybody's temper on edge. The best went to France and got killed, the rubbish stayed home. One day I bumped into a neighbour who had lost her three sons on the Somme. I held her by the hand and nearly died.' Mother wondered whether the war was a scourge sent by God. She remembered vividly the excitement when German Zeppelins first bombed London in May 1915. Innocent people had been killed asleep in bed. What was the world coming to?

Like so many of her generation, mother blamed the war for everything. Whatever misfortunes followed 1914, she put them down to the war. She was convinced that it had changed father for the worse. The man who left her to fight in France in 1914 was not the man who returned in 1918. 'My Will never really came home again,' she grieved. 'Fellow who did come home was somebody else. He'd had t' stuffin' knocked out of him.'

———◦———

When Jenny was thirteen, a job became available for her in the mill. 'No point in her going back to school for another year,' said father. 'She needs to learn a skill in t'mill.' As a result, I was farmed out to baby-sitters, first to Mrs Beddle and then to Mrs Allison, both of whom lived in the vicinity.

Mrs Beddle was a warm-hearted barrel of a woman, with

an unpleasant smell, who seemed to roll about the house rather than walk. As her skirt touched the ground, I could not decide whether she moved on wheels or feet. Her only inheritance from her husband, who had been lost at sea, was a large green parrot called Toby. Mrs Beddle spoke to the parrot as if she were talking to her dead husband.

'What do you think we should do now, Mr Beddle?'

Peering through the wires of the cage, Toby blinked a lot before answering. Scratching his head gravely, he ruffled his feathers as if he was about to say something of the utmost importance. He must have had a lot of advice to give, for once started, he squawked and screeched on and on like a cotton grinder. Toby had been to sea and had picked up words that the barrel-like woman said would have been better left behind. 'Well, damn my eyes!' threw her into fits.

One morning when I arrived, the bird was hidden beneath a cloth where he remained silent and unrepentant throughout the day. Mrs Beddle didn't tell me what he'd said.

She was always strict about my eating habits, and was ever ready to help if I was slow in eating the bread and cheese, or hot-pot, that mother had left for me.

'We mustn't overeat, must we,' she warned, as her fork repeatedly stabbed and carried off what I thought was a disproportionate part of my dinner. But then she had almost no resources of her own. Eating my dinner was the only way Mrs Beddle could stop the stomach growlings that went on all the time.

The other baby-sitter, Mrs Allison, had a strange way of running to the door while calling 'Is that you, Jack? Is that you?' In her haste, she dropped whatever she was doing. The odd thing was that Jack was never there. Nor was anybody else.

'I thow't it was 'im,' she said sadly on returning; 'I thow't it was 'im.'

Then she carried on as though nothing had happened.

The longer I stayed with Mrs Allison, whose heavy

eyebrows and large nose gave her a frightening appearance, and whose ammonia smell was no better than Mrs Beddle's, the more she ran to the door. One day I told mother about it.

'She's lost her only son,' mother explained.

'Is he dead?'

'He just disappeared. Nobody knows where. It's left her a bit queer in t' 'ead. Mrs Allison is a good woman.'

It's just as well she was, for I was left in her care for hours on end.

Chapter II

Noises in the Night

As I was the first to be put to bed, I fell asleep to the drone of voices in the kitchen below. Sometimes I fell asleep listening to Jenny singing. She twittered and chirped like a bird; she never sang a song right through as mother did. The cracks in the bedroom floor were so wide that, except when the adults took an unfair advantage by whispering, I could hear all that was going on. When the whispering had gone on too long, I leapt out of bed, and pressed my ear to a crack to listen to the scandal. In our street everybody knew everybody else's business: who was sick, who was well; who was richer, who was poorer; who had 'got on,' and who had 'gone wrong.'

The cracks were large enough to drop metal washers the size of a penny into the front room below. One night Dan outdid himself by dropping one right down the front of a visitor's dress. Convinced that it was a mouse (it was not unknown for mice to fall from the ceiling), the woman grasped her breast and gave a great scream. There was much commotion before the washer was retrieved. It all ended with father bawling at Dan through the ceiling and threatening him with his belt; though father, like the rest, went into fits of laughter once the woman had left.

If I stayed awake, I could tell what everybody was doing. I knew it was washing night because of water being sloshed about. The whole house became damp; condensation covered the windows. Next morning the plastered walls were streaked with wet.

Ironing night had its slightly burning smell. There was the tell-tale snap of the flat iron lid as a fresh red-hot iron was taken from the fire and placed inside.

Baking night was best of all; it offered titbits. Mother's knocking on the side of the bread tins to get the loaves out, and the rich smell of freshly baked bread, brought me creeping down the stairs in the hope of claiming my share. Before going to bed, I loved to watch mother and Jenny mix the flour, and (with father's help) knead the dough, roll and pat it before putting it in the bread tins which Brenda then placed in the oven. I was allowed to prick the tops of the loaves with a fork.

When I heard hot coals being pushed under the oven, I knew that baked potatoes with lots of margarine were in the offing. The most disappointing thing that could happen was to fall asleep before the feast was ready.

Many other noises reached me. I knew from the smells and the rattle of pots and pans that mother was cooking the next day's meal. For her, work was unending. When all else was done, there were clothes to be patched, socks to be darned. I heard the click of her needles, the kettle whistling on the hob, the scrape of the rockers, the squeak of chairs.

I listened to my family playing games and knew who had won. I heard the cups being tossed, the dice thrown, the dominoes clinking, the shuffling of the cards. Sometimes they would play Find-the-Thimble – giving great gleeful shouts when one of them went from warm to hot. I knew from the way that those huddled round the fire jumped back that a gust of wind had come down the chimney and had driven smoke into their eyes. Chairs being picked up and put down again meant that the family and visitors were changing places in the hope of avoiding drafts. Some found shelter where others found nothing but a gale. On a really cold, windy night everybody was entitled to scrape his chair about the floor as much as he saw fit.

For my sisters to jump and squeal at the same time meant that a mouse had run across their feet. The mice were cheeky because they were hungry. They marched out of the holes in the plaster as bold as brass. That's why most families, poor as they were, had to keep a cat. We had no fat mice and no fat people. We didn't have a cat in our house; mother said there was no room for one. We used mousetraps. They haunted me. The sharp crack of the trap would waken me at night, followed by a momentary squeaking in the corner.

Very early, from where I lay, I heard talk of a 'ship coming home.' I puzzled about that particular ship for a long time. It must have been the slowest ship on the seas because it never seemed to arrive. 'Aye! Tha'll see when it cums,' people shouted, slapping their knees. But it didn't come. The only man whose ship came home was mother's brother, uncle Eric. He was the wonder of the family and they often talked about his doings downstairs.

A thin, self-confident man, uncle Eric was head of the local Mechanics Institute. He knew all about inventions, and was always making speeches. 'Uncle Eric,' mother said, 'has the gift of the gab.' He was written up in the newspaper as one of the first in our town to have electricity installed in his house. The rest of us considered it quite an honour.

One night, I was taken to celebrate uncle Eric's triumph. Clutching mother's hand, we followed a little knot of muffled-up relatives. The wind roared over the cold rooftops. We crossed the unmarked boundary that separated the poorer from the richer parts of town. We found uncle Eric waiting for us at his garden gate with a lantern that showed up his bright eyes and the blue veins that ran down his nose. His hair was parted down the middle and shone with oil. As he jumped about with his lamp, shadows flitted among the bushes. He was very proud to have so many visitors. He led us into a dark room where we stood about wondering what was going to happen. Other people followed until the room was quite full.

I didn't share the hearty humour of these people. Even the word 'eeelectricity' sounded sinister to me. It was a word we had never used before. It didn't come easily to the adults. Perhaps, as the doom-sayers warned, we were about to be blown up! Nervously, I held mother's hand and tried not to fidget.

With a slightly tipsy uncle Eric dragging out the drama, and with everyone else shouting 'One, two, three!' the room was suddenly flooded with an entirely new and magical light. The light was soft, yet blinding; it made us blink. It reached everywhere, right into the corners of the room. It came from a glittering bulb hanging from the ceiling. There was no flame, or spluttering, or hissing; there was no smell as with gas light. From the look of astonishment on the faces around me, there might have been a thousand bulbs above our heads. The air was suddenly filled with a barrage of congratulatory 'ahs' and 'ums.'

'It's past talking,' they said, looking around; 'it beats it all.'

'Aye, Eric,' they chorused, 'tha're a one, tha're! Tha should be Mayor!'

'Nay, nay, not Mayor. Eric will have to be our mon in parliament fro' Blackburn.'

We all clapped. 'Speech!' somebody called.

Never stuck for words, a beaming uncle Eric began by saying that 'eeelectricity' was going to change all our lives. There was no telling the wonders it would bring. With the help of 'eeelectricity,' things would buck up for everybody. None of us would have to work anymore. Electricity would do it for us. In the golden age of electricity that lay ahead, we'd all be rich. Strikes and lock-outs, hunger and poverty were going to be things of the past. Progress would come if we all used our 'eads.

Uncle Eric had certainly used his. He had made a lot of money equipping hospitals with furniture and supplies. He didn't make them, he simply took them from one group of people and sold them to another. He and aunt Pearl had started out quite poor. 'Couldn't afford children,' mother told me. I hadn't met aunt Pearl before. She had blue rings round her eyes; her lips were painted firebucket red. She had a strange rasping voice. Her fat fingers were laden with jewellery. When I saw how small she was, I found it hard to believe the family story that she had once knocked uncle Eric out with a frying pan. He didn't seem any the worse for it.

As if to acclaim the coming of the golden age, uncle Eric and aunt Pearl served hot meat pies, black puddings that scalded our tongues, and great slabs of cold, potted meat. For 'afters' there was hot rhubarb pie smothered with cream. There was lots of beer. As the food was heaped onto our plates, the talking stopped. Although everyone set to with a good heart to 'brass th' guts,' it was some time before everything was gone.

When there was nothing left to eat or drink, we picked up sticks and trailed back – some a little unsteadily – to our homes by the mills. Before leaving we all sang 'For he's a jolly good fellow.' Uncle Eric stood there blinking, a contented Cheshire-cat look on his face. Everyone agreed that uncle Eric and aunt Pearl had put on a 'reet luvly do.' The talk going home was more about black puddings than about science.

Two things stick in my mind about that night: one was that uncle Eric was the only man wearing a suit and tie, the other was the large mantelpiece clock decorated with tiny colourful birds. I'd never seen such a clock before.

Many things talked about by the adults downstairs in our house mystified me. The war was one. It had changed everything for the worse in their lives. Much later, I discovered that the war was the Great War of 1914–1918 in which my father had fought. Only then did I connect the many limbless men who hobbled through our streets with the war. I'd no idea that the war had made our neighbour, Mr Beatty who lived two doors away, the gibbering idiot he was.

On fine days Mrs Beatty put Mr Beatty outside the front door to air. He lay in a long patched wicker bed on wheels on the narrow pavement, inches away from the street, jabbering and drooling at passersby. He always had a towel under his chin. When I dared to look at him, I was surprised how strong and big his head was. I didn't dare to look what was under the blanket. His eyes were like a blind man's, they looked directly ahead but didn't see. The carters called and waved their whips at him.

'Up and at 'em,' he shouted back, making his wicker bed shake. He shouted it so often that it became his nick-name.

'And how is old Up-and-at-'em?' passersby asked as they took hold of his blanket and waggled one of his stumps. Years had to pass before I learned that 'Up and at 'em' was what British soldiers shouted to each other on the Western Front before going over the top of the trenches. Mr Beatty went on fighting the Great War until he died. His great comfort was for Mrs Beatty to sit and read the Bible to him. On Jenny's orders, I crossed the street when she was reading, so as not to disturb.

Nothing in my childhood, not even downright wickedness, was as bad as the war. Everybody knew how the war had come about. The Germans had caused it. The Germans were responsible for most troubles. I think it helped a great deal to have the Germans to blame. Whatever the trouble, if the war and the sickness couldn't be held responsible, then the Germans must have done it. It came as quite a surprise later on to meet Germans who struck me as ordinary people – people who could smile and have a toothache.

The sickness was the influenza epidemic that followed the war, and from which so many people died. Whole families lay sick together. The church bells never stopped tolling; the undertakers were busy night and day. My mother, my sister Jenny and my grandmother Bridget were all stricken by it. So great was the fear of contracting the illness that even my mother's sister Alice had refused to help when father had gone to fetch her. Little did she realize that one day, when on her way to the workhouse, she would seek my mother's assistance. Help came from Dr Grieves and a good Samaritan woman who walked in off the street. She had seen us in the morning, a dejected group of children huddled in the doorway; we were still there in the late afternoon. 'Where's your mother?' she asked Brenda. 'She's sick.' So the stranger went in and took care of everything. For two or three weeks, she shopped and cooked and fed the whole family and kept the house clean until mother and Jenny could get back on their feet. Then, unpaid, she left as mysteriously as she had come and was never seen by us again.

Provided I stayed awake, not much escaped my ears at night: 'Aye, Ah'd really like a drink,' said father.

'A good glass of stout would make all the difference,' answered mother.

'How much money do we have, Maggie?'

'Fourpence.'

'Well, that will buy a glass of beer.'

'You go and enjoy the fourpence, Will, it will do you good.' I heard her put the coins on the table.

'Nay, if we can't afford a glass each, we'll share it,' father replied. 'Off tha goes t' Griffin and get it.'

I heard mother get a mug, put on her clogs and shawl, and leave the house. I heard her footsteps going down the street toward the pub and coming back again.

'Real gradely,' father said, smacking his lips, as they savoured half a glass each.

Neighbours who lifted the latch at night with a shout of 'Y'in?' were greeted with laughter. Some 'y'in's' were so loud that they startled me out of my sleep. Having shut the door behind them, because of drafts, visitors usually stood quite still, head cocked, waiting for an invitation to proceed farther. The answering shouts of the family were equally loud; 'Cum in, cum ya.' Sometimes I could tell who it was by the smell rather than the voice. Visitors were told to make themselves 'at 'ome.'

The habit of shouting sprang from a good-natured exuberance; also the constant clatter of the mill machinery had made many of the workers partly deaf. It was common for people to cup their ear with their hand and shout 'Eh?' In the mills they used lip-reading or shouted to be heard. Shouting in our house was common. It never crossed anybody's mind that I was trying to sleep above their heads. Nobody apologized for making a noise. Except for churches and funerals it was unnatural for us to be quiet.

Quiet or loud, I loved their voices: voices slow and melodious; voices sharp and quick; voices full of sorrow; voices full of joy; sweet voices, like Jenny's, which quite spontaneously could break into song and break off again just as quickly; voices which, as the night lengthened, fell silent. Once a subject had been talked to death, custom demanded that the workers should sit back and digest what had been said. I knew when they were ruminating, for the long pauses would be punctuated by isolated remarks like: 'By gum! It doesn't bear thinking about,' or 'Now, what use war that?' or just plain 'Eeees!' or 'Aiiiis,' followed by long meaningful sighs. Minutes later a galaxy of voices were at it again. My people loved talking; eloquence was their birthright. I loved them for it. I never tired of listening, even when I'd no idea what they were talking about. It was the music of the words that mattered.

It was from talk in the kitchen that I first learned about Fall River, Massachusetts, where my parents had lived and worked for some years. They had gone in 1906 as steerage passengers to America with my sister Jenny. It took a long time before talk of America made any sense to me. Blackburn was my world. It was one of the first words I learned to write at school. 'Blackburn, Blackburn, Blackburn,' I wrote all over my slate. Later on I heard about London and that the king and queen lived there.

Our neighbours took it for granted that the Lancashire cotton industry started with us, and that cotton was king. Nobody knew how to make textiles like Lancashire folk. Nobody ever would. Father had a different view than those who had never been out of England. He was always telling his fellow weavers that the cotton mills in Fall River were more efficient and that they'd better watch out. Mother said he told his trade union, the Amalgamated Weavers Association, the same story, but they didn't thank him for it. He went on about automatic looms, rings, and mules, and batteries, and goodness knows what other ingenious devices he'd seen in America. His listeners were astonished when he explained that Fall River weavers did not 'kiss the shuttle' to replenish the weft; but that a rotating hopper did it for them. Even more astonished when he told them that in Fall River six, not two, looms were common. 'By gum,' they said when dad had finished. 'It doesn't bear thinking about.' Having said that, I suspect they forgot all about it.

The other threat posed to Lancashire came from 't' niggers' who were prepared to work for less money. As far as I could discover, 't' niggers' were poor people who lived in Asia and Africa. My people were simple people, they divided most of the world into 'us and 't' niggers'; in those days racism was a common ill. As my father had been to China, he was expected to be able to talk about 't' niggers' at first hand.

The workers took 't' niggers' no more seriously than they took the challenge posed by the cotton workers of Fall River. 'T' niggers' couldn't match our skill – nobody could. Besides, they were too far away to do us any harm. The idea that 't' niggers' might have begun the cotton industry and might replace us entirely in the cotton trade didn't enter anybody's head. Even in the bleakest days of the 1920's and 1930's, when Lancashire was outcompeted, or shut out of European, American and Asian markets, Lancashire workers never stopped looking on the bright side. Things were 'allus' going to get better. There was 'allus a silver lining through each dark cloud shining.' 'You'll see,' they said, slapping their thighs and putting on a brave front, 'things are bound to buck up. It's not t' fost time we've had troubles. I mean, what dun yo think we're made of? . . . Toffee, he, he, he. Cum on, lad, it'll be aw reet!'

Chapter III

Lights and Shadows

The postwar boom in Lancashire cottons meant that there was a job for father when he returned to Griffin Street after the war. Nothing had helped the industry as much as the war. Despite the sky-rocketing price of cotton, brought on by speculators (once the United States had entered the war in 1917), the last year of the war was the most prosperous year in the industry's history.

Properous times meant that we had plenty to eat. Food was something we took seriously. You might say we had a hunger mentality. When we could afford it, we began the day by eating a bowl full of scalding hot oatmeal porridge, made with water, served with a little salt. Nothing could fill you up like porridge. 'Gives you a lining.' Even when mother was working in the mill, no morning passed but that she did not make the breakfast. Porridge was followed by chunks of home-made bread, covered with Maggy Ann (margarine), beef-dripping, syrup, or jam. Coarse fish was cheap, a week's supply for one person might cost sixpence, and we ate a lot of it. Bought just before it 'went off,' it was obtained at rock-bottom prices. Even at breakfast it was customary to gnaw upon a leftover cold haddock or kipper. We children were told to watch out for bones. Weak tea was drunk, piping hot, without sugar and milk, in great quantities. Other than mother's milk, the only milk I knew until I was in my teens was canned Nestlé's milk and blue milk (milk with the cream skimmed off), which was doled into our jug out of a churn brought on a cart from a farm. We knew when the milkman arrived because he shouted: 'Fresh milk, fresh milk,' in the street.

Dinners were the hot-pots taken to the mills and eaten between noon and one o'clock. Supper was eaten when the family came home – usually physically drained – at the end of the day. Mother decided what to cook or serve cold. Supper could be anything: left-over stew, porridge, fish and chips, toasted crumpets, boiled or baked cod, cold sausage meat, cold tripe doused with lots of vinegar, cheese, pickles – how we loved pickles and beetroot – or a sheep's head boiled in the setpot with barley and peas. The butcher mesmerized me when he split the sheep's head with his cleaver. Crash! . . . and out came the brains. If we didn't have a sheep's head, mother might make soup from fish heads and tails, or from a ham bone, or a cowheel, or bits of meat, with herbs and lots of potatoes and vegetables. There was always plenty of bread.

Sunday breakfast was a feast. There was time to cook eggs, bacon, sausages, tomatoes, sweetbreads, kidneys and anything else that could be heaped into the frying pan and onto a plate.

Sunday dinners were very special. It took the concerted efforts of mother, Jenny and Brenda to prepare them. In the affluent years, we had roast beef, or a shoulder or a leg of lamb, with several vegetables. In addition, there was pudding, fruit and balm cakes, dripping with treacle. We weren't fussy about foods that dripped. There was no table linen to be spoiled, only a newspaper. In very cold weather, mother prepared a great cauldron of broth, often with a neck of mutton. I used to watch it cooking on the gas ring, bubbling and popping like an active volcano. I was addicted to its smell; I put my head over the side and breathed it in. With a bit of luck, there was no telling what the brimming ladle might bring to the surface. Being the youngest, I got more than my share of the yellow, greasy, delicious dumplings that were fished up. They were so slippery that you had to be careful or they'd jump off your plate onto the sanded floor.

It was usually at this point that aunt Alice would come down the street and put her gaunt, hungry face around the door. Perhaps she'd smelled the broth. After mother and Alice had made friendly noises, auntie would leave with a brimming jug of hot broth. It always happened this way. I remember aunt Alice well because – except for grandmother Bridget – she was the only relative who regularly came in and out of our house.

The richer we were, the more we ate; when we could afford it, we gorged. On Pancake Tuesdays and Hot-Cross-Bun Good Fridays we children did nothing but eat. I suppose, in good times, before the bottom dropped out of Lancashire textiles in the early 1920's, that is where our money went. We even bought fancy nuts, which father cracked for us with his granite-like teeth. Nobody was accused of gluttony. Few bothered about their waistlines, not even my sisters. We didn't shy away from fatty meat. If we did, father quickly ate it. Food that the rest of us might not be able to stomach, he'd swallow at one go. All meals with us were favourite meals. There was an earthy naturalness about our eating. There was a vigour about it; ''unger's t'best sauce.' We champed and chewed with relish. The smacking of lips, belching and sucking of fingers were all ignored, so was slurping hot tea out of a saucer. To eat and drink one's fill was to be blessed.

When there was plenty of good food on the table, those who talked were hushed. 'Let food stop thi gob,' father used to say. We thanked nobody for our meals, except ourselves, silently. Mother was a good cook, but she didn't expect thanks. 'Oh, go on,' she'd say if anybody offered praise. I'm told that the rich were brought up to leave a little on their plates. For us, that would have been sinful. We were taught to polish our plates, using a handful of bread as a wiper. We needed no encouragement. We didn't need a dog in our house to eat the scraps. We ate them, even if they'd been dropped on the floor.

It was while we had money to spare that Mr Levy, the pawn-broker, who owned t' pop shop a few streets away, persuaded my father to take a large-horned phonograph off his hands. It was called a Victrola. 'American – a chance in a lifetime,' he'd told father. The phonograph was one of the first of its kind, and everyone was overwhelmed by it. Mother had her misgivings. 'It's not like father to chuck money about, I don't know what's come over him.'

The first I knew about the machine was when it startled me out of my sleep. I was spellbound by the strange, whin-ing voice singing in the room below. As the voice contin-ued to whine for most of that night and the next and the next, the spell did not last; especially as there was only one scratched cylinder with only two songs: 'Take a Pair of Sparkling Eyes' and 'Just a Little Love, a Little Kiss.' The woman who denied the singer 'Just a Little Love, a Little Kiss,' must have been pretty hard-hearted. Without a little love, the poor fellow died on father's phonograph in agony every night. Soon I knew the words by heart. In spite of Dan's contempt, I often sang myself to sleep with them. 'Just a Little Love, a Little Kiss, I'd give my whole life for this . . .'

My father took great pride in being the only owner of a phonograph in the street. Neighbours put it down to his having lived in America. It must have been unusual to own such a machine, because our house was invaded by strangely silent people all standing and listening. Others put their head round the door hoping to be asked in. There was even talk about buying a second cylinder, or a third. 'A penny from each of you will go a long way,' father told a crowded house.

There was no telling how many cylinders we might have bought if neighbours had come forward with their money. None did. They crowded into our cottage and listened to the new marvel, but declined to pay for it. The phonograph was put up for sale. Nobody bought it. At a considerable loss, it went back to t' pop shop.

We seemed to make a habit of taking things back to Mr Levy. He was good-natured about it, and never held us to the last penny. Some years later, my parents obtained a used banjo from him as a Christmas present for me. I loved it. I played 'Little Brown Jug,' the only thing I could play, from morning till night until my family was quite ready to throw me and the banjo through the door. The last time I saw it was in Mr Levy's window. I regretted losing it.

———<o>———

The prosperity of the textile industry after 1918 knew no bounds. In the early part of 1920 mill profits were higher than they'd ever been. Speculators borrowed money to buy stocks and shares which they promptly sold at a profit. Shares sold at ten pounds one day could fetch fifteen the next. The more speculation, the higher the inflated values became. Without contributing a single constructive idea to the industry's welfare, the manufacturers and the money-spinners enriched themselves. There were accounts in the newspapers of manufacturers playing dice at five pounds a throw. For a stake of £1,500, three manufacturers ran a motorcar race from Blackpool to East Lancashire. While madness reigned, some manufacturers sold out at inflated prices and became wealthy country gentlemen. Others hung on, buying up businesses with borrowed money they could not possibly repay. Much of this money came from the banks.

No matter what gains the factory owners made, my

family's wages stayed at rock bottom. Father got between one pound and thirty shillings a week.

When the crash came in March 1920, and the industry collapsed, the banks found themselves the owners of much of the Lancashire textile industry and refused to pour good money after bad. Neither the employers nor the workers recognized Lancashire's changed position. Both sides believed that they were facing temporary problems; that prosperity would return. The employers blamed the workers and the government; the workers blamed the employers. It didn't occur to anybody that Lancashire's world supremacy in cotton textile production had come to an end. The Lancashire cotton industry had got so used to the idea of industrial growth that it was mentally incapable of dealing with industrial decline. Uncertainty, misery and bankruptcy grew. Wishing, working and fighting each other changed nothing.

What the crash in March 1920 meant for the workers was not the loss of profits, but hunger. Out of hunger and social distress sprang the British Communist Party. Some months after the crash, father lost his job in the mill. It came as a great shock to him to be thrown out of work; a greater shock when mother and the rest of the family fell out of work too. Keeping a steady job in cottons in the following years became almost impossible. Life for us had always been uncertain; now it became doubly so.

Under the National Insurance Act of 1920, father received fifteen shillings a week for fifteen weeks; mother was paid five shillings for a shorter period. Children were expected to survive on one shilling per week – twelve pennies. But soon these small amounts were all gone. Any benefits father obtained from his trade union also ran out. Things became so bad that mother lost her cut-glass punch bowl to Mr Levy at t' pop shop. She called it 'my American punch bowl.' Standing on a small table in the front room against the white-washed wall to catch the eye of any visitor, its glass cups hanging on polished silver hooks, the bowl enchanted me.

The sun didn't often come into our front room, but when it did, the punch bowl magically came alive with a hundred blue-tipped twinkling lights. Although I cannot remember it being used for its true purpose, mother washed and polished it endlessly. It must have been heart-breaking when she had to surrender it. She never said anything when it was carried from the house, but I knew that with its departure she had lost a symbol of better times. I think the punch bowl was a token of the superior life that she had once lived.

It was a demoralizing blow for father to find himself on the scrapheap, especially as he felt that everybody had a duty, as well as a right, to work. 'We mun work,' he'd say. I could tell from his sighing in bed at night that the lack of work was affecting his sleep. It gnawed at his heart. It was not like him to turn and toss so. Sometimes, on a moonlit night, I'd waken to see him sitting up in bed staring at the door, muttering to himself. He simply did not understand why the mills should be standing idle. The town offered to retrain him and other unemployed weavers as shorthand-typists, but he rejected the scheme as a farce, which it was. There was any number of shorthand-typists in town looking for work.

The bottom was reached when, in exchange for a few cigarettes, which he then bartered for food, father sat in the kitchen and stitched mail bags. He had joined the navy in the age of sail and knew how to use a needle. Even with a piece of leather across his palm, I could tell from watching him that stitching mailbags by hand was a very hard job. He also tried to survive by mending the clogs and shoes of our neighbours. He bought the cokers, soles, pegs, nails and blacking from Woolworths. His bench was a three-footed last which he held between his knees. Except that he was in his own kitchen, and hungrier, he was doing exactly what the prisoners were doing in the local jail. I never heard him say it, but everybody knew that it was at times like this that he most regretted having left America.

Father refused to accept the idea that there were no jobs

available. His brand of despair was tinged with expectation. Sometimes, in the early hours, I would watch his shadowy figure slip out of the bedroom. He was a great believer in the early-bird business. For a few minutes he would shuffle about downstairs, taking a long drink from the tap. Then I'd hear him unlock and lift the latch of the front door as he went out in the dark to search for work. I heard the echo of his clogs as he hurried down the deserted street. Slowly, the night swallowed him up. By seven o'clock he would be standing with a crowd of others outside a mill in one of the surrounding towns, hoping to catch the foreman's eye. Perhaps this would be his lucky day. Many hours later, he would return footsore and hungry, chilled to the bone, a defeated look on his face. On his way home he'd pass equally exhausted workers going the other way, looking for the job that didn't exist. The next morning, wet or fine, he was off again on what mother called his 'fool's errand.'

His 'fool's errand' ended one morning in a dramatic way. He had gone off as usual into the dark night looking for work. We all thought he'd struck it lucky when he didn't return at the usual time. But we were wrong. He came back later that morning looking an awful sight. He'd got himself into a desperate fight with some pickets outside a mill at Padiham where there was a strike. They had taken him for a 'knobstick' (strike breaker), and had almost killed him. Now that was ironic because the only thing he ever belonged to was a trade union. They'd beaten him so hard that he could hardly walk. Thank goodness they didn't break his arms, which sometimes happened. Somebody must have brought him back to town and dropped him off in our street.

He arrived home his hair stiff and matted with dried blood. Jenny was horrified at the sight. She ran upstairs. 'He was still alive when he got home,' mother said, 'but only just.' His breath was shallow and laboured; his ribs were going in and out like bellows. His face was the size of a large pumpkin; he was black and blue all over where they'd kicked him with their clogs; some of his wounds were gaping.

On entering the house, he dripped blood all through the 'best room.' Brenda had to clean it up. Mother wanted him to go to the hospital or to Dr Grieves, but he refused. So mother and Brenda did what they could for him with iodine and bandages. He didn't complain when they dabbed his open wounds. It took him weeks to recover. After that, instead of going out on a 'fool's errand,' he sat by the fire, pale and glowering. I kept well out of his way. Because the wounds should have been stitched, some scars stayed with him for the rest of his days.

Unlike mother, father seemed oblivious of the famine that now stared us in the face. Tight-mouthed, he kept his thoughts to himself and went on doggedly. If anybody asked him in the street how he was, his reply was always the same, 'I'm nicely!' It was a lie, of course, but it would have shamed him to tell the truth. He never seemed to realize that his family was getting hungrier and hungrier. It was something that one was not supposed to notice. There was work and there was no work. If you worked you ate. If there was no work you went hungry. You didn't beg and you didn't steal; the unwritten code excluded both. You didn't complain, whine or whimper; it was a matter of pride. As for the rich, by his lights, it was their job to leave the poor alone. Charity from 'them' would have hurt.

Fortunately for us, it was an attitude that mother didn't share. Although she had been married to father for many years, she had a different code. Come what may, she was not going to see her children starve. Father's unemployment benefits having expired, she kept at him to apply for public relief. He refused. There was a struggle between them and a number of 'scenes.' 'Very well,' said mother, putting on her shawl and clogs, 'I'll take thi place in t' bread queue and shame thee.' Father went. He was angry at being bested. By the time he got through the door, he was black-faced.

The rest of us sat or stood around the bare table and waited. We didn't have energy for anything else. We were insensitive to anything except food. Our bellies pained for it. Jenny took it hard. Robbed of all spirit, she sat there listless.

Mother had no energy either, but she forced herself to talk about the wonderful meal that father had gone for, and how delicious it would be. She began by pretending to serve a thick, nourishing broth with many dumplings. 'Sit up,' she said, 'and eat it while it's hot.' She followed this with cutlets of veal – 'Something special. For once I didn't get the cheapest.' She served vegetables and roasted potatoes soaked in sizzling fat by the potful. She was so convincing the way she heaped our plates and pressed us to have seconds. She also dreamed up side dishes of hard boiled eggs, herrings, sausages and pig's trotters. Finally, she served cheese, fruit, nuts and dates. 'If you eat slowly, you'll make room.' My, how she made our mouths water!

Much later father returned, carrying a bulky Tate & Lyle sugar sack under his arm. He had the air of a thief. He handed the bundle to mother and left the house. She could make him bring the stuff, but she couldn't make him eat it. 'Ah won't touch it,' he said defiantly. How his body carried on without food, none of us knew. Mother worried about him.

With the rest of us watching, mother shook the contents of the sack onto the table. There were two large prison-made loaves of bread that looked as if they'd been dragged through the mud. There were several tins of corned beef, one of which had its side bashed in, a packet of tea, a pound of sugar, a can of condensed milk, some mouldy cheese, a strip of fatty bacon, some margarine that had strands of felt mixed with it, some Lyle's Syrup, a bottle of H.P. sauce and some salt.

We forgot the feast mother had promised and polished off the lot on the spot. It at least rid us of our aching hollows. The next several days we queued up at the churches and the soup kitchens in the streets. After that father was sent back for more public relief and still more. The items never varied, they were horrid, but they kept us alive. Just.

*   *   *

Perhaps it was the shame of going for 'charity bread' that made father redouble his efforts to find work. One morning, he came rushing into the house to tell us that he'd been made a town labourer and to ask for my help.

'Ah 've bin told t' wash Victoria,' he announced.

'T' queen?' my mother asked in a startled voice.

'Go on with you, girl. No, t' statue on t' Parade.'

Father and I left the house for the centre of town. He led the way carrying a long ladder. I followed with an empty bucket, brushes and rags.

''Ello! Wert'a goin' wit ladder?' neighbours shouted as we went by.

'T' wash t' queen.'

This response produced a surprised look on their faces. 'By gaw! They're goin' t' wash t' queen,' they shouted to each other.

Father got tired of satisfying people's curiosity and left it to me. I didn't tire. I loved the questions. It made me feel important. To every 'Wert'a goin'?' I proudly bawled back: 'T' wash t' queen!' and marched on, head high.

When we arrived beneath the statue we could understand why it needed a wash. Most of the head and dour face were covered with bird droppings. The marble crown, scepter and orb were all filthy. Unveiled in September 1905, in commemoration of Queen Victoria, who had died in 1901, this was the first good scrubbing the statue would have.

Pestered by a group of unemployed workers, who shouted advice from the foot of the ladder: 'Tha're a proper gobbin, tha're. Tha missing great patches of shit.' It took father and me the whole day to make an impression on the dirt. We started from the head and worked down. First we had to scrape off the muck. Then father took a hedgehog brush to the queen and scrubbed. While I carried endless buckets of water up the ladder from a nearby tap, he hung onto Victoria's head, back, front and sides, and continued to scrape, rub and scrub as if his life depended on it. Yet I knew he hated it. Like his mother Selma, who lived in Fall River, he disliked royalty.

As night came, we left Victoria glowing clean. Father still looked dour; he didn't say a word in returning the ladder and going home. It's said in the family that he never walked past that statue again. He preferred to go out of his way round the cathedral rather than relive his moment of shame. I have a suspicion that the scrubbing of Victoria was for him the blackest day of the Great Depression.

Alas, there was a limit to the number of statues that needed scrubbing, and father was soon out of work again. So were the rest of the family.

◆

During these lean times, when I was five and my brother Dan was nine, he confided to me that he was not going hungry any more. We were going to steal food together. Tom Tat's grocery shop around the corner was bursting with food. Dan's plan was simple. He told me about it in whispers when we were in bed one night. On the first really dark night he'd push me through the window above Tom Tat's shop door. The window was always left slightly ajar. I was to jump down inside the shop and open the door, so that we could help ourselves. 'What could be easier?'

I was horrified at the thought. Stealing with us was associated with going to jail. Caught stealing, you were invariably sent down. Visions of my going to jail passed before my eyes. I lay there in the dark, breathless.

'But that's stealing,' I said.

'It's not. It's the toffs that steal from us. This is taking what's ours.'

'Tom Tat isn't a toff; he's like us.'

'Ye're a coward,' Dan hissed. 'Ye're a yellow belly. If ye don't join me I'll eat yer liver. If ye tell anyone, I'll drown thee in t' canal.' He got quite worked up about his proposed raid on Tom Tat's and then fell asleep.

I was too terrified to sleep. Over and over, I asked myself what I should do? Should I tell Brenda? If I did, I might finish up in the canal. Even when I dozed, I woke up sweating. In my fevered imagination, I was already in jail. In my dream I didn't seem to have a choice between the jail and the canal.

Dan became obsessed with the idea of robbing Tom Tat's. 'What's wrang with us eating until we bust?' He kept at me for about a week, his hissing and his threats getting worse all the time. He even took me round the corner to study the fly-spotted window. It was open a crack. 'Ye don't have te steal if ye don't want to, but I can't get in unless ye help me open the door. Ye're small enough to be hoisted up there. Only ye can get through the crack.' He kept at me so hard that I began to wish that the deed was done and finished with.

The next Sunday night was pitch dark. Our parents were out. Only my sister Jenny and her boyfriend, Gordon Weall, were in the house.

'Come on!' ordered Dan, making for the door.

I was on the point of making a desperate, last-minute appeal to Jenny and Gordon; instead I slunk after my brother into the dark night.

Two minutes later we were in the shop doorway. Dan took a look up and down the empty street. All was quiet at the Tat's house next to the shop.

'Quick!' Dan ordered, offering me his back. Although I was choking with fear, I knew what to do; we'd practiced it a dozen times. I also knew from staring at them in the daytime where the lock and the two bolts were at the other side of the door. I'd made up my mind that once I'd opened the door, I'd grab my clogs and run.

I put my stockinged feet on his shoulders; he hoisted me up to the window. Reaching up, I silently pushed the window inward. Still resting on Dan's shoulders, I gingerly began to get my head and shoulders through the opening. My weight now rested on the sill. All that remained was for me to draw back the top bolt, wriggle through the open window, and drop to the floor. I could smell cheese, but couldn't see it.

'Haste!' Dan whispered impatiently. 'What are yer making?'

'I'm stuck!'

'Stuck?'

With my head and shoulders over one side of the door frame and my legs down the other, I could neither go forward nor backward. Somehow my jersey and grey flannel shirt had become twisted into a hard knot. I was held in a vice. The more I struggled, the more firmly I was held. I broke into a sweat.

'Get through!' Dan hissed.

'I can't, I'm wedged.'

'You've got to.' He reached up and pushed the soles of my feet as hard as he could.

'I can't,' I repeated, my head swimming. 'Pull me back. I'm choking.' My body trembled; beads of sweat blinded me.

After hesitating, Dan jumped up and hung onto my feet. The pain was awful. I thought he was going to pull my legs out of joint.

'Ouch, stop it!' Dan pulled harder. My body didn't budge.

'Ouch! Ouch!' I sobbed.

'Shut yer gob!' Moments later, I heard his clogs echoing down the street. He had deserted me.

Turning and twisting, I made one last panic-driven effort to break free. I expected Tom Tat to come shouting out of his house at any moment.

The next thing I knew, Gordon was standing on a small stool. He had me by the calves.

'Shush, Billy,' he whispered as he undid the knot in my clothing and gently eased me free. Once he had me out of the window, the three of us ran home, double-quick.

That night I lay in bed quaking. I swore I'd never do anything for my brother again. While Gordon and Jenny gave Dan a piece of their mind, they said nothing to father for I heard no more of it. I wonder what the Tat's said when they found their window wide open the next morning. It didn't stay ajar anymore.

———◇———

It was about this time, with things as bad as they could be, and with everybody in the house out of work, that mother and I – miracle of miracles – took the train to Blackpool, twenty-five miles away. I was baffled; I couldn't believe my luck. It was summer, the weather was warm.

I knew about Blackpool as soon as I could stand. It was a pleasure resort on the Lancashire coast. Its clean, sharp air, and its endless sands were famous. Some of the first greeting cards I ever saw came from there. Against the smoke-filled air of our town, the cards glittered with sun and colour. We had pictures of Blackpool Tower and the Big Wheel on the mantelpiece in our front room. The identical pictures were in everybody's cottage. Everybody who went to Blackpool came back chewing 'Blackpool Rock.' The very mention of Blackpool stirred the imagination of any child in Blackburn.

I don't know if father or grandmother Bridget knew what was going on. All I know is that we were on our way to Blackpool. In the train I couldn't contain myself, I hopped and jumped about with excitement. Until then I'd never seen the sea. I stuck my head out of the window most of the way to catch the first glimpse of Blackpool Tower soaring above the flat landscape. Mother was every bit as excited. I thought we might have been going to relatives, especially as we had no money – mother said we were going to friends – but I never saw relatives or friends. We did see people from Blackburn, but mother avoided them.

Mother and I shared a single bed which stood in a room the size of a cupboard on a landing in a lodging house. The place stank of cabbages and haddock. But it was, after all, Blackpool. The only person mother introduced me to was a big-breasted, fish-eyed woman who seemed to own the place. Her face was covered with paint. She wore such a tall, glossy black wig, that I kept my eye on it hoping it would fall off. She also wore a lot of artificial jewellery that hung down to her waist, and clinked as she moved about. Her earrings were long enough and large enough to swing like the pendulum of a clock. She held my hands and breathed pickled onions all over me. She grunted, but I don't think she ever spoke to me.

For the first few hours mother ran me off my feet. I was overwhelmed by the tower. It gave me a crick in the neck to stare at it, hundreds and hundreds of feet above our heads. We went to the top and looked down on the ant-like people scurrying about in the streets. Before us lay a vast expanse of sand, sea and sky, all of which ended in a far haze. I'd never seen such unending space. I'd heard about the sea – here it was stretching before me. The ships in the distance were the first I'd ever seen.

I don't know whether it was the excitement of riding in a lift for the first time, or the height of the tower, or the food we'd eaten in the street below, or my fear that anything as tall as the tower must surely fall down – whatever the cause, I felt ill. We sat down until my dizzy turn passed.

After I recovered, we raced together across the sand, at first in our bare feet and then on donkeys. Mother's donkey captured her spirit and went off at full speed careening toward the sea. My donkey wouldn't budge. The more I shouted at it, the longer it stayed and brayed and showed its teeth. By the time I got it to move, mother was on her way back, her bonny hair streaming in the wind. She was easily the winner. And so we went on, going from one thing to another until we returned to our lodgings exhausted.

The moment we got back, I began to feel uneasy. I didn't know why; I just knew that something was not right. It began when mother asked me to wait for her on the bench in front of the house. She had to meet someone inside 'on business.' I was told to stay there until she reappeared. So

I sat there alone, in the sun, swinging my legs, and wondering what it could be that kept her so long. I'd no idea whether something good or bad was happening, and it worried me. When she came out, I wondered if I should ask.

I sat there for part of the next day and the next. I became weary of sitting alone on that horrid bench. I'd never been so lonely. I was puzzled at the men who came out of the house with mother. They were strangers. They all wore suits and polished shoes. They weren't weavers, that's for sure. Some were furtive, others hearty. 'Tha're a grand lad,' they said giving me a tanner (6p) or a dodger (3p), which was a lot of money. I was at a loss to know why dodgers and tanners were being showered upon me. In Blackburn we didn't have any money. What money we had, we knew not to waste. At Blackpool everybody was chucking it about.

Mother must have been puzzled too, because after a couple of days she woke up at night and cried her eyes out, hiding her face in a towel. 'Oh Billy,' she sobbed, 'Oh Billy.' She was in real pain. I didn't know what to do. It frightened me. By then I'd come to notice strange smells in the room, and there were half-burned cigarette ends on the floor.

The next morning everything was fine again. The crying was forgotten. Once away from the lodging house, mother's natural happiness returned. She went from being sad, to being intensely happy. She skipped about, made fun, and laughed. She took me everywhere. We visited the circus, the aquarium and the fairground. We bought knick-knacks, and listened to the Punch and Judy show and the minstrels on the pier singing: 'Oh, I do like to be beside the seaside, Oh, I do like to be beside the sea . . .' We listened to the hoarse bawling of the barkers selling boat rides, and went in a boat as far as Morecombe Bay. Having done everything, we sat on top of a tram and rode up and down the sea front, mother's hair blowing in the wind.

We seemed to eat whenever the mood took us. We didn't eat with the fish-eyed woman with the clinking jewellery.

For our food we went from street cart to street cart, stuffing ourselves. There's nothing we didn't try. We had blackpuddings and Irish roasted potatoes, too hot to hold. We also had apples and oranges, Eccles cakes and lots of cups of tea. Mother fed such quantities of food into me that I could hardly stir. How wonderful it was to be rich!

We ate one meal in the Winter Gardens. Mother was excited about it, but I was nervous. Until I grew up, it was the only meal I ever shared with her in a restaurant. There was a great 'to do' before we got there. We had to get into better clothes, and wear shoes – all of which we got from a pop shop. I had to have my hair slicked down. When we were all ready, we entered this big restaurant. I've no idea what we ate. I do remember a band playing. There were many toffs there, crowds of them wearing fancy dresses and suits. I was nervous. It was a new experience for me to see so many people dressed up with nothing to do except gorge and laugh. I'd never known mother to dress so well or to be so relaxed. Her face and hair shone. She didn't talk much; she seemed to be in a dream. She only woke up when the bill came, and the waiter pressed her for a tip. When we came out we stood and watched the coloured fairy lights flicking on and off. What an exciting, colourful world it was! Why wasn't Blackburn like this?

If only we could have been free of that dreadful lodging house, mother and I would have stayed at Blackpool for ever. Instead, after an unforgettable week, we were back in the train headed for home. How drab Blackburn looked when we arrived. One could smell the poverty and the troubled times. Being summer, the smells were worse.

———◇———

Things got so bad in the early 1920s that the number of hungry-eyed tramps coming through our street grew. Dressed in rags, black with sweat, feet in the gutter, fidgeting and scratching, they'd wait until mother or other kind souls gave them butties (bread) and tea. Smells were common among the poor, but the tramps had what we called a 'ripe' smell; they reeked.

Thirst and hunger satisfied, they'd throw their string-tied packages over their shoulder and move off with the same steady slouch with which they'd come. I often wondered what their odd-shaped newspaper-wrapped packages contained.

As times got worse, the poor began to steal from the poor – something unheard of. I have reason to know. One evening as the light was fading, Brenda and I were playing with a new ball on the kitchen floor. The ball rolled into the front room where it came to rest behind a rocking chair in a corner. I ran after it, bent down, and put my hand round the back of the chair. To my horror, my fingers touched somebody's ankle; in a daze, I felt a trouser leg. Something moved. Fearful, I put my head round the chair and looked into the face of a pockmarked scarecrow of a man crouched there. A long, blue scar ran down one side of his face. His eyes and mouth had a hungry look. He smelled abominably. I jumped back as if I'd been bitten. With an oath, the man flung me aside and ran from the house into the street. Someone ran after him, but he'd gone. We never saw him again. I was left trembling and white. As we had nothing worth stealing, he must have been looking for bread, or was hoping to break into and take the pennies from our gas meter.

Somehow my family kept on weathering the storm. Aunt Alice didn't. She had got poorer, older and more ragged. Nobody gave her help. A spinster, there was no one upon whom she could make a claim. Her mother was too poor. People looked the other way, their pity for her unstirred. Either to take her mind off her troubles, or to pick up a bit of extra food, she'd started going to funerals. She never missed a good funeral and was always willing to talk about them. She'd got into the habit of sitting in the cemetery. She said she found peace there. The day came when she couldn't pay her rent. Having been thrown out of her cottage, she turned up with a bundle under her arm.

I knew that I ought to feel sorry for aunt Alice. She was going blind.

Father didn't. He wouldn't hear of her moving in with us. 'We've got all t' mouths we can feed,' he said. 'What's wrong with your brothers helping? Eric's got the money and the space. It's scandalous his turning you away.'

'He didn't,' said aunt Alice, 'Pearl did.'

'If his wife won't have you, then Eric should help with money.'

'Well, I'll tell you this,' aunt Alice wept, 'I thowt one of you would take me in. I didn't think you'd put me in t' work'ouse. You've got 'earts of stone, that's what.'

I was brought up to believe that the workhouse was a prison for the poor.

Mother cried when Alice left.

————◇————

Deep poverty introduced a degree of fear in the house. Mother worried where the next meal was coming from. We all worried about it. We went to bed hungry and slept badly.

I woke from a troubled sleep early one morning to see father going downstairs. For some reason, I crept after him. My brother and my sisters were still asleep. By the time I reached the bottom step, father's dishevelled figure was crouched before the kitchen fire. There was a tweedy smell of peat. Although the fire had been banked up all night, the house was bitterly cold. As I drew my flannel shirt closer to my body, my feet froze on the sanded floor.

Father was holding something which he was wiping with a towel. It looked like a white doll; but the doll had blood on it. Father's shadowy figure danced on the kitchen wall. 'Cum now, cum now,' he muttered.

I knew that something was wrong. Mother had been

crying in the night. Father had been downstairs several times. I had no idea that a life and death struggle had been going on; even less where the baby had come from. I had by now made up my mind that it was a baby not a doll that father was holding. I found it hard to believe that the baby had come out of the bedroom. I'd been told that storks brought them. Jenny had said they were found under flowers; Brenda believed they arrived in Dr Grieves' bag. While I watched, I heard Dougdale's factory hooter at the end of the street emit a piercing whistle. I also heard t' knocker-up man coming down the row.

'Tell t' knocker-up we're awake,' father ordered. He had not failed to see me standing in the shadows.

'Yes, Dadda.' I slipped on my clogs, which were kept at the foot of the stairs, and ran to the street door. Having turned the key, I opened the door long enough to yell into the wind: 'We're up.' Mr Smalley waved his rod and turned away.

By the time I got back to the kitchen, the gas lamp had been lit. It hissed reproachfully. The pot dogs on the mantle reflected its glow. A little wasted thing with a monkey's face lay on one of the rocking chairs. Father was standing with his back to the fire, looking at it dejectedly. ''E's a goner,' he murmured. I knew that a 'goner' meant that the baby was dead. Confused, a cold shiver running down my back, I crept away.

Father didn't go to the mill that day. Nor did mother; she stayed in bed. During the morning Dr Grieves drove up with his horse and gig, followed by his brown and white spaniel, Joy.

That afternoon, the dead baby with the monkey's face was placed into a plain box of undressed pine. Until evening the coffin stood on top of the folded sewing machine under the front window. The paper blind had been pulled down. The aspidistra that usually stood there had been placed on the floor. I tried to look into the box, but the lid was nailed down.

That evening, after the flood of homeward-bound workers had swept past the house, grandmother Bridget lifted the latch and came in. Mrs Morgan also arrived. There was loud whispering with mother upstairs. Mrs Fothergill, a woman dressed in black who cared for the chapel down the street, kept on at father about sprinklin'. 'Did you sprinkle him?' she kept asking. 'Are you sure? You know what happens to an unsprinkled soul, Will.' I'm sure that sprinklin' never entered my father's head. He didn't sprinkle my brother while I was there.

The glances and the whisperings that went on made me think that the grown-ups were hiding something. They seemed furtive. No one could tell me what had happened to my brother except that he'd 'died.' If he'd had an accident there must surely be someone in the house who could stick him together again, as I did with my toy soldiers. Instead, everybody sat there looking glum and did nothing to help.

Next morning father left with the coffin under his arm. I was desolated that my brother should have been carried off like that. Where was he being taken?

'Straight to heaven,' mother assured me.

'You'll see him again in the hereafter,' Jenny added.

'But where is heaven and the hereafter?' And if we were going to see him again, why was he put in a box and carried off? How could he find heaven in a little nailed coffin, without a name, without food, without flowers and a funeral, and all alone? It took me years to realize that, without death benefit insurance, a 'proper burial' for him was beyond our means.

His death left me afraid. Death was evidently something that neither Dr Grieves nor anyone else could fix. It was permanent as nothing else in my life had been before. It was the first time that the truth struck home. It was days before I stopped worrying about my brother. It was just as well that he was never mentioned again.

When I was a little older, I learned that a 'proper burial' was something that the workers took seriously. They knew what was proper and improper. They had a horror of being cast into a pauper's grave. It meant humiliation and disgrace. It was all very well to tell them that their spirit would enter heaven through the pearly gates; they still wanted to know what was going to happen to their bones. That is why most of them paid a penny a week death dues so that the 'proper' thing would be done when they died. We paid our pennies to a squirrel-like fellow whom we called t' bump man, but who liked to be called by his full name: Mr Charlie Hetherington.

The wonder is that the penny death dues were enough to keep Mr Hetherington in clogs. Collecting pennies for the death club, however, was only one of Mr Hetherington's occupations. His passion was to study the bumps on people's heads. 'Give me your head for a minute or two,' he would say, 'and a penny, and I'll tell you all that you need to know about yourself.' Mr Hetherington's 'reading' of bumps was more reliable than fortune telling, or tossing the cups, or cutting the cards. People said so.

One night father asked Mr Hetherington to look at our heads. Charlie didn't need persuading. He began with father. He then turned to mother, my sisters, Jenny and Brenda and my brother Dan. From the look on his face, I could tell that – as far as bumps go – my family were an uninteresting lot. Their mental faculties had not produced any unusual changes on their skulls. 'As a family, I'm afraid you're a bumpless lot,' he said to father. He expected even less of me. Yet the moment his fingers touched my head he became excited. 'Oh, look at this.' He ran his fingers through my long, fair hair, 'I say, have you ever seen anything like it?' he went on triumphantly.

The whole family crowded around. By the light of the hissing gas lamp they scrutinized my scalp. They were mesmerized by what they saw and felt. 'Well,' said father, following Charlie's fingers with his own, 'now I see what it's all about; the bumps are as plain as can be.' The family was greatly impressed when Mr Hetherington announced that with bumps like that I must surely become Prime Minister of England. 'Mm . . . mm . . .' said mother, 'if he'd been born in Fall River he could have become President of the United States.'

◄○►

The news of Lancashire's hard times in the early 1920's must have reached my grandmother Selma in Fall River, Massachusetts, for she periodically inquired if her grand-children, Jenny, Brenda, Dan and I, were alive and well. Since leaving America in 1914, there had been the odd exchange of news between Blackburn and Fall River, but I don't think grandmother Selma trusted father's letters.

One day a letter arrived saying that two of her sons were about to visit Blackburn. My American uncles, my father's brothers had emigrated to America with him in 1906. I took the letter from the postman, and it caused quite a stir in the house. My parents went into a frenzy of preparations. Crockery, cutlery, chairs and food were borrowed from rela-tives and friends. There was such a bustle. Mother planned to serve ham and tongue at the same meal, something unheard of except at a wedding. At the last minute father decided to impress his brothers by serving a two shilling bottle of 'Barrel Bottom' wine – for us a scandalous waste of money. He sent me scurrying through the streets to the vintner, a florin clasped in my hand. The vintner handed me the bottle in a brown paper bag. 'Put it under your jacket, lad.' The licensing laws were ignored. Anyway, the wine didn't impress the Americans.

Oh, what a stir the arrival of my uncles caused! Having taken one of the few taxis in town, they arrived in Griffin Street red-faced and hearty. They were full of fun and energy. They were much too florid and much too fat to be textile workers. I don't know to which class they belonged, but they weren't working class; later I discovered that Americans didn't belong to any class. They wore strange straw hats and even stranger clothing. They had shirts with attached collars and loud ties, tie-pins and highly polished shoes.

We listened wide-eyed to their talk about America as we ate. 'Richest country in the world,' they said. I didn't know we were as poor as we were until they started making comparisons. 'You've got to come to America,' they repeated. They told me that in Massachusetts they had snow right up to the roof! Jenny and I loved it when they said things like 'OK' and 'Yeah.' Later on my street gang used these words. I didn't know that the Yankees had single-handedly won the Great War until my uncles told me so. I always thought father had done that.

The meal was hardly finished when our house was flooded with people who took it for granted that my uncles knew every member of their families who had migrated to Fall River during the past generation.

On the point of their departure, my uncles pressed into my eager palm a shiny half-crown, enough to keep me in affluence for months. Before I could scuttle away with my fortune, father reached down.

'Nay, nay, Harold' he protested; as he extracted the coin from my unwilling fingers, 'tha mustn't chuck tha money at 'im like that. Tha'll be spoiling 'im. Tha can see, he wants for nothing. Tha must be reet out of tha mind, lad.' Whereupon, to my profound grief, he handed back the coin.

I knew that there wasn't a word of truth in what father was saying, and the loss of the coin hurt me deeply.

Before climbing into the taxi, my uncles warmly clasped my parents' hands. 'You must come back again, Will. Family's roots are at the other side now.'

'That's kindly, that's real kindly of thee. I can't tell thee how much Maggie and I appreciate it. Tell mother that we've just got one or two little things to arrange and then we'll be reet over. Tha'll see!' I never did work out what the little things were that he had to arrange, which he never did.

With the whole of Griffin Street gawking, my uncles shook hands all round, patted us children on the head, and tucked us under the chin. They then jumped into the rattling taxi and honked the horn repeatedly, which brought more neighbours running. The taxi swayed down the street followed by a cloud of blue smoke. After that the family and the neighbours sat around like pricked balloons. Everything in Griffin Street was ordinary again.

My parents didn't speak of it, but I wondered if the coming of my rich uncles had not given them pause for thought. After all, if father had remained a tackler in Fall River, instead of returning to Blackburn in 1914, he too could have visited his relatives in England in a straw hat, a fine suit, a loud tie, polished shoes, and a smoke-wrapped taxi.

I think the idea of returning to Fall River gradually fell out of father's reckoning. He must have been poor on coming home from the war. Moreover, the longer he delayed returning to America, the less chance he had. Beset by the severe competition of the newly-established South Carolina cotton mills, Fall River was experiencing the same decline as Blackburn and the other cotton towns in Lancashire had done earlier. Letters from his brothers in Fall River told him so. Naturally, Fall River, like Blackburn, thought the industry was suffering a temporary setback. In addition, America introduced its first generally restrictive immigration act. Emigrating to America was no longer a matter of just catching a ship.

There were other visitors from America, but I came to resent them. They left my parents more in debt than ever. Of course, our American relatives offered to pay for everything, but father wouldn't hear of it. He always put up the same humbug of 'nobody wanting for nothing.' Worse, every visit was followed by the arrival from grandmother Selma of a great parcel of children's summer clothing. Never money, never food, just clothes – clothes that were too thin for our summers. With their coloured stripes, the shirts contrasted sharply with everybody else's drab grey. Dan and I hated them. They shamed us when we wore them to school or in the streets. Other children envied us for having such rich American uncles, but they went into fits of laughter at the sight of the American shirts and dresses. Because of the stripes, the Woodruff children came to be known as the 'Zebra Kids.' Even when my uncles stopped coming to Blackburn, grandmother Selma continued to send the clothing. The ordeal went on for years. It got worse as the stripes got larger. Strangely enough the sizes never changed. Jenny, Brenda and Dan eagerly grew out of them. As I was the smallest member of the family, I regret to say that there was always something that would fit me.

Chapter IV

Family Tree

The visits of my American uncles, and the remarks my parents made about the years they'd spent in the United States, aroused in me a desire to know more about my origins. Over the years, mother tried to answer my questions. Because that kind of thing interested her, she'd made it her business to get it all in her head. Father wasn't half as good. Family history didn't interest him – he focused on the present, not the past. Sometimes mother answered my questions about family history in snatches, sometimes at great length. Bit by bit I pieced it together.

The Woodruff story began long before I was born. It began in the early part of the nineteenth century with my great-great-grandfather George Woodruff, which is as far back as the Woodruff family tree goes. He had had the misfortune to be seized by the army while he was drunk. He fought and died for Britain in Russia in 1856. Mother knew it was 1856 because there was a medal in the family with the date of great-great-grandfather George's death on it. His son Arne was my great-grandfather on father's side. He was born in the late 1840's in Westmorland.

By the time I was born, Arne had become a family legend. Mother often talked about him. She didn't tell his story as if it was dead and done with, but as something that was happening before our very eyes.

Arne had a hard beginning, mother began one day. He not only lost his father, he went and lost his mother too. She sickened and died after the death of her husband in Russia. After that Arne stood alone. Nobody came forward to look after him. As an orphan, he fell into the hands of the parish guardians who sold him to a cotton mill owner high on the moors. Fellow called Crankfit. They say he had a stone where his heart should have been.

Arne was taken by the village beadle to the village green to await the local carrier, Blethley, who would take him to Crankfit's. His few possessions were tied in a large red hand-kerchief lying at his feet. He wore a cap – from which tufts of straw-coloured hair protruded – and a long dark smock and clogs.

Presently, Blethley came along sitting on his wagon. He was a stocky figure with a clay pipe sticking out from his beard. Arne watched Lucy the bay horse leisurely pull the cart. The cart creaked to a halt.

Removing his pipe, Blethley shouted down, 'You Arne, for Crankfit's?'

'That's him,' the beadle answered.

'Well then, get up boy,' the carter gruffed. 'We can't afford to have Lucy standing here all day.'

With the beadle pushing and the carter pulling, Arne was hoisted up onto the box next to Blethley behind the horse's tail. On the point of tears, he sat there speechless, clutching his possessions on his knees.

Before the child knew what was happening, the cart with its bundles and packages had rattled around the village maypole, passed the churchyard where his mother now lay, crossed the stream where the salmon were jumping and the ravens were cawing, and left the village behind. Only then did the boy break down and cry. Blethley pulled on his pipe and studied the back of his horse's head.

The man and the boy travelled together for most of that day, passing from green meadow through plowland and pasture to fell. Prompted by a grunt from the carrier, Lucy trundled from one place to the next. In time, Blethley warmed to the child, and told him about the great world beyond the moors. It seemed that Mr James Blethley had been everywhere.

'Have you ever been to Russia?' Arne asked.

'Russia? Now let's see,' the carter answered rubbing the side of his nose.

'That's where my father fought and died in a war,' the child went on, while fishing around in his bundle to show the carter a medal.

'Oh, that Russia,' Blethley said, turning the medal over in his hand. 'Bless me, if you had told me it was that Russia that you was talking about . . . why . . .' the carter went on at great length about Russia, telling the wide-eyed boy exactly where his father had been killed. Blethley said he'd fought in the very same battle, on the very same day. And what a battle it had been! Oh, the guns, and the drums, and the flags, and the cries, and the shouts, and the smoke . . . ''Mazin',' the carter ended.

'Do you have such a medal, Mr Blethley?'

'Why, of course, but it isn't the sort of thing you carries around.'

The hedgerows and fences along which they passed gave way to dry-stone walls that climbed endlessly across the shrouded fells. Here and there greystone cottages straggled unevenly up a valley. Wild smoke blew from their chimneys. Crying curlews and peewits criss-crossed the wagon's trail. The trees gradually became thinner and sparse, the track steeper and stony, the wind stronger and fresher. In the distance a greystone peak stood out like a sentinel. Arne looked down the fells to see specks scattered like white stones which he knew were sheep. In the valley bottom a winding river glinted in the sun. Sometime during the day they stopped at a small inn where Blethley drank a glass of ale and gave Lucy a nose-bag of oats. Arne had some bread and cheese.

When they came out a whole string of pack horses were tied against the inn wall. They were loaded with textile stuff to be worked up by the handloom weavers whose cottages were farther down the slope.

The journey renewed, Blethley talked about a number of things. Yes, he had seen the queen. Yes, he had seen the new-fangled railways in whose coaches people caught their death of cold. Yes, he knew all about the dreadful accident that had occurred when one steam-driven train had crashed into another. 'Railways will never be as good as a horse and cart,' he confided to the boy. 'God never intended railways. You are God-fearin'?' the carrier questioned Arne sharply.

'Oh, yes, Mr Blethley.' His mother had reared him to be God-fearing. She used to say everything was God's will.

'Do you know the town of Blackburn? It's where my aunt Beth lives.'

'Yes, I know it. It's full of steam-driven cotton factories with tall chimneys spewing foul smoke. They say this here newfangled steam business is going to change a lot of things, but I have my doubts. The main thing is that cotton pays well. All the money-hungry people of northern England are making their way to Blackburn. God never intended facto-ries. Factories and steam-driven power looms take the work away from the cottage weavers. Fellows lost their lives for burning factories down. In 1812 at Westhoughton they hung three men and a boy of fourteen for doin' it. Lad went to the gallows calling for his mother.'

Arne shuddered. 'Couldn't she save him?'

'Not likely. Come to think of it, not long after, in the 1820's I think it was, there was a dreadful rampage at Blackburn itself. Thousands of workers armed with pikes, hammers and crowbars smashed every power loom they could find. By nightfall there wasn't one left.'

'Were there more hangings?'

'Oh my word, yes. Others were sent to Van Dieman's Land.'

'Where is that?'

'I can't actually say. All I know is that it's a long way from here and you don't come back.' There was a pause. 'Factories and power looms were soon back in Blackburn,' the carter concluded. ''Mazin'.'

The carter knew so much about everything that Arne resolved to tell everyone he met that he'd had the uncommon luck to have travelled with the world-famous Mr James Blethley.

That afternoon they met a cartload of orphans being delivered to another mill on the fells. There was a wild-eyed idiot among them who stuck his tongue out as he went by.

'Did you ever carry such?' the boy asked.

'The pity I did,' the man replied. 'They were so young – one was five, the others eight to eleven – and so tired; when I got them to the mill I couldn't waken them. They'd been on the road for days. God never intended that either.'

'Why do children have to work in factories, Mr Blethley?'

'They're cheap and nimble, there's plenty of them, and they don't have anyone to protect them. That's why. God never intended it, I'll swear.' Blethley cleared his throat and spat out of the cart.

They heard the creaking of Crankfit's waterwheel long before they got there.

'No steam here,' said Blethley.

They topped a ridge to see a mill spread out before them. The main building was solidly built in stone and slate. Oblong, it had three levels. Its narrow windows looked out across a pond. Nearby were two other buildings, both of them smaller. The windows of one of the buildings were barred. Beyond and around the mill, as far as the eye could see, stretched the lonely, windswept moors. A blue haze rested on the distant hills. There was not a tree in sight.

'Watch your step with Crankfit,' Blethley warned as they approached the building, 'whatever you say, he's bound to 'av' a fit.'

Crankfit was at the gate to meet them. He was dressed in a long black coat and a stove pipe hat. Except for the sharpest eyes, his face was lost in a thicket of beard and hair.

'You're late,' he barked at the boy as Arne jumped down from the cart and stood before him.

Remembering Blethley's warning, Arne kept a still tongue.

'Is this all there is of him?' Crankfit walked around the child, studying him from all sides. 'Fat lot of work he'll do. He's stunted, that what he is!'

'He's all I was given,' the carter explained, looking at Arne as if he was seeing him for the first time.

Crankfit sniffed at Blethley's papers like a bloodhound. 'Humph! I suppose I'd better take him. I swear they're getting smaller and smaller all the time.' He grumped and added his signature.

The dreadful conditions under which great-grandfather Arne lived and worked at Crankfit's, caused him to run away. After many adventures he found his aunt Beth in Blackburn. She adopted him and taught him how to weave. When he grew up Arne married a mill-girl called Eva Anders. They had a child who became grandfather William. Grandfather William was killed in the mill long before I was born.

———◇———

Over the years, mother also told me about her side of the family. I learned about her parents, my grandmother Bridget Gorman Kenyon, and my grandfather, Thomas Kenyon, who had died when mother was very young.

Bridget Gorman was born in County Clare, Ireland, the only daughter of a landed family. We hardly knew anything about her people. Her meeting with my grandfather, Thomas

Kenyon, was the event that was to shape the rest of her life. Bridget's relatives held that her meeting with Thomas ruined her. There was little to recommend the Englishman to them. Yet he was darkly handsome, well-dressed and dashing, with a fine moustache. Grandmother Bridget once told me, that it was the moustache that had made her fall in love. He had a good job with an English insurance company, which explains his visit to Ireland. But he was much older than Bridget's seventeen years. Worse, Thomas was a Protestant, Bridget was a Catholic.

Mother said that Bridget's father and brothers (their warnings to the would-be suitor to pack his bags having gone unheeded) had chased Thomas from the village. Bridget was in danger of making a poor marriage in an alien land. Bridget's father had forbidden her to see the Englishman again. The jovial recklessness he detected in Thomas was not to his liking. But Bridget was a wild, lawless thing; she was tired of piano and singing lessons, and going to church. She had found her Prince Charming and was eager to fly away.

There was another motive. Bridget had been 'promised' to a neighbour's son – a Catholic boy, rich by County Clare standards – whom she could not stand. The more distance she could put between him and her, the better. Fully aware that to marry Thomas was to sever relations with her family and become a social outcast, Bridget eloped and fled to England as grandfather Thomas Kenyon's Protestant bride.

Revelation followed. Bridget discovered that Thomas already had three children from a previous marriage. Also, although fairly well off, he was much less affluent than he had made himself out to be.

Having made her bed, Bridget lay in it. From the tales I've heard she had a happy life with my grandfather Thomas. He was a generous man, and easy to live with. She was a good wife and a good mother. She had four children* of her

---

*Bridget had six children, but I knew nothing about Katherine and William at that time.

own, Edward, Eric, Alice and my mother, Maggie. Maggie, the youngest, was born in Blackburn in May 1884.

Bridget's happiness lasted until Thomas died suddenly ten years later. The day after her husband's funeral, Bridget found that her total financial resources consisted of money she had in her purse. To her surprise, she was not only a widow but a pauper. Unknown to Bridget, grandfather Thomas had spent his savings; for some time he had been borrowing against his retirement and pension funds.

Time only added to her troubles. With no money coming in, she scrimped and scraped until all her resources, including her furniture, had gone. She went into cheaper housing. She appealed to her husband's relatives. Her brother-in-law, John Kenyon at Bamber Bridge, gave her some help, but he had two small daughters of his own and was not as prosperous at that time as he was to become; he couldn't go on helping Bridget forever. From Thomas' boon-companions, some of whom had helped him to spend his money, came nothing.

With no one else to turn to – her frantic appeals to her family in County Clare had gone unanswered – with no funds of her own, and with a dread that her children would finish up in the workhouse, Bridget took the only course open to her: she found foster-homes for her children with people whom she trusted. That is how my mother was 'farmed out' to friends who owned a small pasture farm on the edge of town.

Ironically, soon after that, Bridget found employment looking after the children of a local merchant. She worked hard and saved hard in the hope that she would one day be able to get her family together again. But the merchant's business failed. The merchant's wife, who had become close to Bridget, died. Within a year, Bridget had been thrown back again on her own resources.

After many unsuccessful attempts to obtain suitable work, Bridget finished up as a slubber, cleaning cotton, which was one of the dirtiest and least skilled occupations in textile manufacture. Slubbers or cardroom hands were looked down on. Coarse and degrading, was how Bridget described the work. For a woman as refined as my grandmother, it must have been a wrench to have had to enter the mill.

Yet Bridget got by. Nobody heard her complain. Brought up soft, she was as tough as steel. I never heard her say a word against the way things had turned out, or against her husband for leaving her destitute. 'How was he to know he would die when he did?' she said. 'He didn't spend the money on himself.' Anyway, my grandfather was dead and you didn't speak ill of the dead.

One day mother summed up her feelings about Bridget. 'She's quality,' she said, '. . . royal. Her trouble is, she's cum down in t' world . . . right down, I mean.'

There was a pause.

'A lot of us have.'

———◦———

On other occasions mother told me more about the Woodruffs. My father's father, my grandfather William, the child of my great-grandfather Arne and his wife Eva Anders, had been born at Witton, a sub-district of Blackburn in the 1860's. He had been a day-labourer on the land, but had entered the mills to get some ready cash to pay off a debt.

In the mill, grandfather William met a weaver, Selma Nilson, whom he later married, and who became my grandmother Selma. They had thirteen children, two of whom died in childhood. Grandmother Selma was to have a great influence on the destiny of the Woodruffs.

Mother told me that Selma's father had run foul of the law as a boy and had narrowly missed being one of the last convicts shipped to Australia in the 1840's. The injustice of the whole thing – the boy had been accused of stealing some bedding – the savagery of the sentence, coupled with the hardships he had suffered in jail, had left a deep scar on the Nilson family.

During the industrial unrest of the late 1880s, Selma had been accused of assaulting a policeman during a strike. In the witness-box she had denied assaulting anybody. She swore that she had never seen the policeman before. 'It's rotten sods like you,' she'd shouted at the magistrate, 'who make our life hell. Ah'm just as good as thi are.' Because of the uproar she caused, grandmother Selma had been sent to jail. The Nilsons were surprised she didn't get three years for carrying on as she did. Guilty or not, her experience in jail soured her of Britain and British authority for the rest of her life. On her release, she would have gladly left the country had she had the money to do so.

'You know, Billy,' mother once said, 'your grandmother Selma got her wish to escape from England in a strange and tragic way. In 1905 your dad's father, your grandfather William of Witton, was killed when a steel-tipped weaving shuttle flew out of the shuttle race and entered his chest. He had been bending down at the side of the loom when it happened. A knife could not have killed him quicker. Your grandmother Selma was left a widow with eleven children, your father was one of them. I don't know how much money Selma received from the mill-owner by way of workmen's compensation and employer's liability, but it was enough to pay for her family's emigration to America. We emigrated with her from Blackburn to Fall River, Massachusetts in 1906.'

'How old were you when you went to America?'

'I was twenty-two. Your father was twenty-three; he was born in 1883 at Witton. We sailed in the summer of 1906. We'd been married two years previously at St Philip's. Your sister Jenny was about one. Three of grandmother Selma's children remained in Blackburn. They were already married and wanted to stay. Your dad was the oldest of Selma's family to go to America. He'd already sailed with the navy around the world.'

'How old were the others?'

'Your grandmother Selma, I think, was in her late forties.

Your uncle Peter was six and your aunt Amy was thirteen. Brian, Andrew, Edward, Harold and Paul were in between. The youngest, Peter, was my favourite. They were true Woodruffs – tough as nails.'

Mother said that some of Selma's family had tried to dissuade her from going. One night she had heard Selma and Selma's brother Joshua going on hammer and tongs about it.

'You're going to a place you know nothing about,' Joshua had argued. 'It's plain madness to go off like this with seven young children. Here you've got food and a roof, and you'll have the insurance money. Over there you'll be starving in the streets before you know where you are. Anyway, why do you want to run away? England's the best country there ever was. It's plain daft to leave it as you're doing.'

'And what was grandmother Selma's answer?'

'She said "Joshua, you're prattlin' like a gobbin. You've never been the one with brains in our family. You talk about risk. William and I have slaved our guts out here, knowing nothing but risk. You talk about us becoming beggars at t' other side. Tell me any Blackburn family that's gone over and become beggars. None of them have come back with their tails between their legs. Everybody I've ever heard of who went to America became rich; you know that. Our brother Mat and his wife Hessie in Fall River have done very well, thank you. They won't see us starve. And don't give me that old buck about love of country. That kind of talk is for the toffs. You keep the country, Joshua, I'll take the money. Frankly, I don't care whether God saves our gracious king or not. I'm tired of the whole rotten lot. I'm concerned to save my family. I know where our bread is buttered and nothing's going to stop me."

'I'll tell you more about your grandmother Selma some other time,' mother said.

Chapter V

American Interlude

I was in my teens before mother told me in detail about the Woodruff migration to America.

The moment grandmother Selma knew she was going to get a lump sum in compensation for her husband's death, she set her face toward America. She'd always been talking about following her brother Mat Nilson who had gone to America years before. Now her chance had come. My father, who had learned to read and write in the navy, wrote a letter to Mat who was working in a cotton mill in Fall River. From there everything led on.

Father read Mat's reply to Selma who couldn't read. Family and neighbours came together to hear it. Mat wrote that there was plenty of work for Lancashire folk in Fall River; the living was good and the pay much higher. 'Tha can lose nothing by coming to America,' his letter ended. Mat's letter encouraged my parents to go with Selma to America, even though my sister Jenny was just a baby.

Selma then got in touch with her nephew Henry Nilson,

who worked in a shipping office in Liverpool. He came up with a June crossing on an American ship, the 'Elizabeth,' which offered the best accommodation for the lowest price. 'The only cheaper way to go to America, Auntie, is to swim.'

By borrowing money, Selma paid her deposit on the June sailing. She never doubted that the employer's liability money would come through.

Getting ready to leave wasn't much of a problem. Selma packed food in a wicker hamper, bedding in clean sacks, and the rest in straw valises. Most of the clothes the family had were already on their backs.

For two weeks, before she was due to sail, Selma basked in the sun by her front door, arms across her belly, beaming with happiness, and exchanging gossip with all who had the time to stop and talk.

'Then tha's got the death money?' passersby queried, hoping to find out what unheard-of sum had come her way. The more Selma refused to talk about it, the larger the sum became. Rumour made the figure large enough to take the whole of Griffin Street to America.

The street gave them a send-off on a Sunday afternoon when the mills were shut. As the weather was fine, tables were brought outside. Bunting and coloured streamers were hung from the houses. 'May you Prosper,' were chalked in large letters on grandmother Selma's cottage. There was lots of food and drink.

One of father's friends from the mill, Adam Sims and his wife Emily, had also decided to migrate. Although the Sims had only been married four months, Emily, a mere slip of a girl, was large with her first child. It worried grandmother Selma.

Everybody enjoyed themselves at the treat. There were lots of toasts. Nobody got Selma to her feet. She'd drunk so much that she didn't have any legs. By the time they sang 'We'll take a cup of kindness now for the sake of old lang syne,' she had to use both bench and table to prop herself up. That night she slept where she fell, in her clothes. Selma was never one for losing sleep.

Before sunrise the next day she'd stripped her cottage clean. 'It's not much to leave behind,' she said as she took a last look. All the seven Woodruff children were eager to be off. The Sims stood outside with their baggage. Alongside them were the new tenants who had turned up before first light. They sat on their boxes in the street talking in low voices.

A friend of Selma's, Joe Moss, had offered to take them the thirty miles to Liverpool in his cart. His only desire was to do a good turn. As soon as he arrived, the baggage and the bedding were loaded up. Despite the early hour, there was a lot of shouting, hugging and weeping as the migrants climbed onto the cart. 'We'll never see each other again on this earth,' grandmother Bridget sobbed, clinging to Jenny.

Selma sat next to Joe Moss, clutching a flat leather bag fastened to her waist. The women wore dark blouses and long dark skirts that wouldn't show dirt. They also had straw bonnets, a farewell gift from the pawnbroker Mr Levy. Being a warm morning, their shawls were thrown back on their shoulders.

At a shout of 'Giddup,' the cart began to rumble down Griffin Street. This was the signal for the new tenants to rush into Selma's cottage, dragging their possessions after them. As the departure coincided with the morning rush to the mills, Joe and his horse had to fight against the tide of workers going the other way.

'Lucky old devil you are, Selma,' shouted those who knew her. 'Don't forget us.' Others just stared, waved vaguely, and shouted: 'Ta, Ta!'

Relatives and friends followed the cart as far as the Griffin pub. Grandmother Bridget stood on the steps waving and weeping until the cart had passed out of sight.

The freedom to suddenly break a fixed pattern of life, to break out of the ranks of the army of workers and go their own way came as a shock to the adults. They had expected to work in the mills for ever. Until now, someone else had organized their lives. They felt easier once the canyons of brick had been left behind.

With the sun peeping over the moors, and the sounds and sights and smells of the countryside bearing in upon them, they reached the top of a hill where they looked back at the town they were leaving for good. Despite the smoke haze that hung over the valley, they were able to make out the spire of the parish church of St Mary and the railway station. The rest was a dense mass of factories, cottages and smoking factory chimneys.

The children preferred going to America to going to school. Every now and then, with great screams, they raced through a hole in the hedgerows to chase a rabbit. Once they caught a hedgehog which Selma ordered them to let go. When tired, the children came running back to the cart, climbed aboard and slept on the bedding. Sometimes the grown-ups burst into song.

Later that morning they met a labourer working by himself on the road.

'And where might ye all be goin'?' he asked as he rested on his spade and wiped his brow with his sleeve.

'To America.'

'America? That's a mighty long way to go with a horse'n cart.'

'But we're not,' the children cried. 'we're going on a ship.'

'Ye are, are ye? Well, by y'r leave, I'll be hoppin' on the cart and joinin' ye. Ah well, that's the kind of world it is; some mend the roads, others go to America. I'll be thinkin' of ye all the way. May God watch over ye.'

On looking back, they saw the man waving his cap.

They spent the night at a farm near Hesketh with the carter's relatives, the Mosses – red-faced, jovial farming people who not only gave them shelter in one of the barns, but a huge, warming evening meal as well. After everyone had washed under the pump, the stew was served with great lumps of fresh bread and a bucket of fresh milk. The children gorged.

Fussed by Adam, Emily Sims, who said grace, ate as eagerly as the rest. The meal was accompanied by the sound of thrushes singing their last song of the day.

A cock perched on one of the beams above their heads woke them the next morning. After a huge breakfast, the migrants set their backs to the rising sun and their faces to the Irish Sea. The day was cool and fresh. The Mosses walked a little way with them to wave good-bye.

After a day-long journey, the travelers were met by Henry Nilson at an inn outside Liverpool. He'd cleared their papers at the port. He struck them as a bit of a toff; he wore a suit and tie. The departure of the 'Elizabeth' had been delayed, but he'd found temporary shelter for them.

Shortly afterward they climbed a rise and saw the sea. They'd no idea that so much water and sky existed. They expected to see America in the distance.

Having avoided the town, they came to a shed by a quiet beach not far from the end of the quay. Seagulls perched on the tin roof. Farther on they could see crowds moving about. Behind the shed was a salt marsh that rang with bird song.

It took some time for Henry to open the doors, which were fastened by several locks. Tired after two days on the road, they all poured into the shed intent on finding a place to sleep. Selma and Maggie removed the shutters and threw everything open to the warm breeze. Adam and Will emptied the cart. Joe unhitched his horse and let it crop the grass. The children gathered sticks to cook the evening meal.

An hour later only Joe, Will and Maggie were awake to watch the sun slip into the sea. Swifts and swallows wove a graceful pattern in the fading light. They didn't feel like sleep; instead they sat on the steps, stretching, yawning and yarning, watching the water endlessly rising and falling and listening to the crickets. Now and again they heard the hoot of a ship.

They were wakened in the early hours by Emily's stifled cries of pain. Selma told Henry to get a doctor quickly.

'No doctor will come here at this hour, Aunt Selma.'

As the first fingers of light crept across the morning sky, Emily Sims died in childbirth. A calm stillness prevailed, broken only by Adam's sobs.

The next day city officials tiptoed in and out of the shed. 'You have our sympathy, Mr Sims.' For their services they charged several gold coins which Adam took from a drawstring pouch around his neck.

The night after the funeral, Selma took Adam aside. 'What do you intend to do, Adam? Ar' te going back with Joe to Blackburn tomorrow, or ar' te going to board the ship with us? Tha'll have to make up thi mind quick.'

'I already have. Emily wouldn't want me to turn back now.'

Later that night, Henry beckoned Selma outside. 'Listen, when you get to New York, they're going to ask you a lot of questions. They'll ask you if you've ever been in jail. You've got to watch that one. All you have to do is to say no and smile. They're not going to stop a widow with seven children.'

'I 'ope not.'

'Another thing, if they ask you about fumigation, when you reach the "Elizabeth" you'd better act daft. You've got to get on that ship. Dust everybody with the Keating's Insect Powder you've brought before you board.'

Early the next day they went down the busy quayside to where the 'Elizabeth' was moored directly opposite the Customs House. The three-masted ship was alive with activity.

Amy was surprised how small it was. 'Do you really think that's going to get us to America?'

'It's got to,' Selma said. 'They 'ave our money.'

Sheltered from the sun by a wide awning, they spent a dreary day sitting on their valises waiting to embark. The younger children fretted and cried, the older children found it torture to have to sit still.

Only when the hatches had been battened down were the passengers allowed to cross the gangplank to the main deck. First Class boarded first. 'With toffs like that aboard we should be safe,' Selma commented.

The Woodruffs were escorted by sailors to the steerage quarters. Their bunks were between the communal kitchen and the toilet, both areas already smelly. Except for sheets placed over string, there was no privacy. Baggage was stowed on the floor. Their tickets simply provided for somewhere to sleep, cook, and wash.

The sound of the ship's windlasses recovering the anchors caused everyone to rush on deck. Henry was still on the quayside. He shouted messages that no one could hear; he continued to wave his hat as the 'Elizabeth' – pushed by a battered-looking tug – threaded its way past other vessels out to sea.

Only when the land was disappearing did my mother wonder if she would ever see England again. 'I pray I've done the right thing,' she said, 'and that all our dreams will come true in America.'

It took the Woodruffs a long time to find their sea legs – longer still to get used to the confined steerage quarters and the unbelievable medley of human beings. Except when the sea was rough, they spent the day on deck. Once on board ship, Adam Sims withdrew into himself. He was often seen motionless – hands on rail – gazing across the sea. The grown-ups understood and left him alone.

Maggie used to say that it was the fine weather that saved them. There were nights when it was warm enough to take a blanket on deck and fall asleep with the wind singing in the rigging. Her most vivid memory of the journey was the night storm that terrified her and the children, and left most of the passengers prostrate. The ordeal ended with someone vomiting all over Selma's head.

Not even the storm affected Selma's appetite. Day after day, she sat on deck, at the foot of a mast, eating and hacking wedges from a loaf of bread. 'We're going to the land of the free,' she told the children. 'Once across, we'll all be rich.' She rubbed her fat hands gleefully and ate some more.

Selma had always been one for her belly. My father had come home one night when he was in his teens in Blackburn to find his siblings locked out of the house. Several of them had their hungry faces glued to the kitchen window.

'What's up?'

'Mam's eatin' our dinner.'

He had looked through the window to see his mother eating several chops.

'There just wasn't enough to go round,' she explained. 'Better a few chops for me than too little for everybody else.'

Two nights before they reached New York, Adam Sims disappeared. After a long search, all they found was his empty moleskin purse. The captain concluded that Adam had been stunned, robbed, and cast into the sea. 'It's happened before,' he said.

Although Adam's empty purse pointed to murder, he was listed as a suicide. Suicide would make it easier for everybody to avoid being held up in New York.

On the last night Selma stayed on deck. When at dawn the coast began to rise out of the sea, she rushed downstairs and brought up the children. Together they gaped at the sun-kissed city hovering on the horizon. Selma was jubilant; others just stared at the shore, tears streaming down their faces. Henry Nilson had told Selma that if they made a landfall early, they'd stand a chance of getting through to Fall River that night.

Accompanied by a growing number of other vessels, and a burst of whistles and sirens, they approached a large statue of a lady with a lamp. 'Ellis Island!' someone shouted. With much clanking and clatter the vessel docked. They'd reached the land of promise.

There followed a day of agony. After being tagged with a number, the Woodruffs joined the flood of other steerage passengers making their way to a large building. 'Everybody's afraid they're going to shut the doors,' Selma said as she urged the children to keep up.

Once through the vast doors, they climbed a long flight of stairs to a great hall, in which there was unbelievable uproar and confusion. In addition to the thousands of milling, bewildered immigrants, there were hundreds of officials bellowing out numbers and messages in every language.

The Woodruffs joined an endless line that moved between wooden rails. Doctors in blue uniforms with grave looks gave them cursory examinations. While asking questions, they examined hands, face, hair, and eyes. The Woodruffs passed the medical officials in record time; they were all good stock.

After another long wait, Selma was asked questions by a uniformed man with an impassive face.

'Where were you born?'

'England.'

'Who paid your passage?'

'I did.'

'Do you have any money? Let me see it.'

Selma fumbled in her bag. As Henry had instructed, she produced five pounds (twenty-five dollars) to prevent her becoming a public charge.

'How many dependents?'

'Seven.'

'Ever been in prison?'

'Now, what, I ask you, would a widow with seven children be doing in jail?'

'Yuh, sure. Can you read or write?'

Coached by Henry, Selma knew that there was no legal obligation to be able to do either. Nor would they test her. 'I manage,' she answered.

'Do you have any relatives here?'

'Yes, in Fall River, where I'm going.'

'What skills do you have?'

'I'm a weaver.'

'Is there a job waiting for you?' was the last question asked. For reasons which Selma never understood, to have answered 'yes' would have been fatal. Henry had told her to say 'No,' so she said 'No,' which at least was the truth. There was a law that was meant to discourage the recruiting of unskilled workers in Europe.

After several gruelling hours, the migrants' names were checked against the ship's manifest. They were given landing cards, after which they pushed open a door marked New York and emerged in the fresh air. While Maggie felt like collapsing, Selma glowed. Before leaving the building, Selma and Will changed some money. They had been warned from Fall River to make sure that they were not cheated. Selma was puzzled by the strange coins, but rattled them together in her hands to show her delight.

Will went for tickets for the ferry from Ellis Island to the mainland and the train to Boston. They saw the train long before it pulled into the station. Having sounded a deep-throated warning, it crawled toward them. It was the first train whistle that Maggie heard in the New World. She thought it sad. Years later she used to say that all American train whistles sounded sad.

There followed one of the worst free-for-alls the Woodruffs had ever experienced. To get a seat one had to push and jostle somebody else out of the way. Thanks to Selma's muscular arms and thighs, the Woodruffs obtained seats together. Mother was worn out protecting her baby, Jenny.

All the passengers cheered when at long last the train got under way. The faster it went, the more they enjoyed the breeze coming through the open windows.

My mother's first impression of America was something of a let-down. The train passed miles of dilapidated, grimy-looking tenements with people and washing everywhere. She thought the sky was larger; everything looked twice as big.

More of the houses were built with wood than brick. She was surprised at the number of negroes. Nobody had ever seen a black face in Blackburn. For hours the train hurried through a sprawling, tree-lined countryside where the farmers were still getting in the hay.

By the afternoon, the crowded coach looked as if it had been occupied for weeks. Shoes, packages, suitcases, discarded food, banana skins and orange peel, rolling bottles and crawling infants littered the floor. Despite the open windows, a heavy, rancid smell of unwashed humanity filled the swaying car.

In Boston they caught the train to Newport, which stopped at Fall River, fifty miles away. The Newport train gave them their first close look at Americans. They seemed taller; a surprising number wore suits and shiny shoes. They talked in loud voices as the train jolted along, calling across the aisles in a rude kind of way. There was nothing cowed about them. Some of them showed an interest in the Woodruff children.

The Woodruffs caught sight of Fall River as the light was fading. 'There it is,' a Fall River passenger told them, as he pointed to the town's famous landmarks, the double onion domes of St Anne's Church and the double spires of Notre Dame Church. They caught glimpses of great factory-like buildings topping the wayside trees. Quickly they got their things together. Children were wakened and ordered to hang on to each other.

As the train stopped, the Woodruffs jumped down. Selma stood in the middle of the crowded platform with her brood around her. Maggie, holding Jenny, stood next to her crying uncontrollably. Her body still swayed with the movement of the vessel left long behind.

After standing there for some time and wondering what they should do, a group of strangers approached. 'Excuse me, are you from Blackburn?' one of the men asked.

'That we are,' Selma replied.

'Well, you've cum at last,' Selma's brother Mat said as he

gave her a hug. 'This is my wife Hessie, we've been looking for you all afternoon.'

'By gum, am I pleased to see you!' Selma cried. Her face became bright red with pleasure.

There were other Nilsons there, as well as several Woodruffs. They were all eager to meet their relatives. Some of them had migrated to Fall River twenty years earlier, most had been born there. There was talk about Blackburn and the sorry fate of the Sims, but not much else. Even Selma, who had born the ordeal of the journey best of all, and who had not once been seasick, was too tired to talk. Nobody asked them if they'd had a pleasant voyage.

From family history I know that my grandmother Selma and her children prospered in Fall River. As she had predicted, America proved to be the place where most of their dreams came true.

My parents also did well. For the next eight years, my father earned more money as a 'tackler,' or overseer, at the Fleetwood Mills, than he would ever do again. His pay was much higher. For a fifty hour week – from 7 till 5 weekdays, half-day Saturday till 1 – he earned as much as $18–$20; several times his Blackburn pay of £1 to 30 shillings for almost the same hours. What he got depended on his own rather than trade union bargaining power.

My parents had their own apartment in a tenement in Country Street. It was better than anything they'd known in Blackburn. It was more spacious, it had great bay windows, hardwood floors, and high ceilings. The roof didn't leak. There also was an indoor toilet. My sister Brenda was born in County Street on 19th September, 1910. Yet Brenda's birth certificate states that she was born on 28th September. I puzzled over this until my sister explained that mother had changed the 19th to the 28th, so that it coincided with the date of her wedding anniversary. The date of mother's marriage was important to her. My brother Dan was born in the same house in January 1912.

In the early 1900's, when my parents arrived there, Fall River, which stands at the mouth of the Taunton River in southeastern Massachusetts, was the largest concentrated area of cotton textile manufacture in the United States, if not in the world. It was called 'spindle city,' or 'the Blackburn of America.' The scale of operations came as a shock to my parents. There were thousands of looms instead of hundreds. For the first time my father had to operate automatic looms and 'batteries,' a device that changed the weft in the shuttle automatically. Spinning differed as well as weaving. The Americans used the faster ring spinning process. Everything from raw cotton to the dyeing of the finished cloth was under the same roof.

Offsetting the higher rates of pay was the absence of workers' compensation. Father had one of his weavers drawn into the machinery and lose two fingers, infection spread and the girl died. Her wages were sent to her family and that was that.

To people coming from England, the ethnic variety of Fall River in the 1900's came as a shock. Most of the population must have been foreign born. There was a babel of tongues. My people were used to English, Irish, Welsh and Scots, but not to French Canadians, Poles, Russians, Lithuanians, Syrians, Armenians, Greeks, Portuguese, Puerto Ricans, Canary Islanders, Italians, Spaniards, Germans, and Swedes; all of whom they called 'foreigners.' Because they spoke English, my parents considered themselves superior. It was not uncommon for 'Anglos,' who had just got off the boat from England, to tell 'dirty foreigners' to go home.

The favourable treatment given to English-speaking workers explains why mother had no trouble getting a cardroom job as a 'doffer,' filling and emptying the carding machines. Without weaving or spinning skills, there was little else she could do. Father became a 'tackler' or overseer. The outstanding advantage he had was skill and a strong sense of pride of craft. For him nearly all the industrial processes and terms were the same. For the other migrants, many of whom were peasants, cotton manufacture was a completely alien way of life.

Mother was fascinated by the young Polish and Italian workers who sang and danced in the aisles during factory breaks. Father said that they didn't have cold English blood. Mother thought that the workers were livelier, much better dressed, and money-wise, better off.

One thing that my parents could not get over was the amount of theft in the mills. As an overseer, father found himself losing yards and yards of cloth. One thief he caught was blacklisted and run out of town. It was cheaper than sending him to jail.

To her dying day, mother remembered the breathtaking views across the Taunton River to the countryside beyond, and the visit of President Taft in 1911. She'd waved to him.

There is one thing certain, my parents didn't have to fight over pennies in Fall River. For the first time in their lives they could save. Relative to what they'd known in Blackburn, they'd become rich. So rich that they were able to pay for grandmother Bridget's crossing of the Altantic to join them. Bridget came into her own in Fall River. She became the assistant manager in one of the better hotels. It wasn't long before she had her own apartment. At long last, fortune had smiled on all of them. I don't know whether this made any of my family any happier, but it spared them the anguish over money they'd know later on.

Chapter VI

Return to England

In the summer of 1914, grandmother Bridget returned to England, travelling first-class with a party from Fall River touring Britain. She sailed on the transatlantic liner 'Carmania' – the same vessel that my parents would use later that summer. As she was extending her trip to stay with her grown-up children in Blackburn, the date of her return was left open.

By now she was in her early fifties and still attractive. My parents went to the station to see her off. They said she looked like a queen. On the 'Carmania,' Bridget danced from New York to Liverpool.

The wonder is that having visited her children in Blackburn she didn't dance all the way back again. There was nothing to stop her. All that was needed in those days was a strong stomach and money, and she had both.

I never understood why my parents followed her to England in the summer of 1914. Things could not have been going better for them in the United States. Father was earning more money as a tackler than he would ever earn again.

I was never able to get either of my parents to talk about the return journey. I can only assume that it pained them to mention it. I know that in the summer of 1914 they travelled second-class with my sisters Jenny and Brenda, and my brother Dan. My sisters remembered the fuss and bother of getting ready to leave Fall River: grandmother Selma and several uncles coming to the railway station to see them off; everybody crying; the great liner 'Carmania,' from whose bowels they hardly ever saw the sea; being met by grandmother Bridget and several Woodruffs at Blackburn in the pouring rain. My parents returned to Griffin Street, the street from which they had migrated eight years before. My sisters were put to bed that night crying their eyes out to go home to Fall River. They didn't realize that they would never see America again.

I suspect that my mother's homesickness for England was the chief reason for my family's return. Mother never became part of the New World. I think she kept at father about going back to England until he eventually gave in. It could not have been for the want of the company of Lancashire folk. Indeed, my parents talked Lancashire dialect to Lancashire people in Fall River so much that they adopted few Americanisms.

Grandmother Selma may have been another reason for their leaving – perhaps a major reason. I never heard mother express any warmth toward her. While she admired Selma's toughness in migrating as a widow with so many children, she couldn't stand her domineering ways. Selma liked to interfere. There were times when mother wondered whether Jenny, Brenda and Dan were her children or Selma's. Selma also got on mother's nerves with her criticism of England.

When Selma heard rumours of my parents' decision to return to Britain in 1914, she couldn't believe it. Having taken all the trouble to escape from what she called 'Babylon,' here was her eldest son, of his own free will, going back again.

Father knew what Selma's reactions would be. That is
why he told mother to break the news. Many years later I
asked mother what grandmother Selma had said.

'Nothing,' mother answered quietly. 'She simply took hold
of my hair with one hand and flattened me with the other.
One blow from her was enough. Then she spat on the ground
and walked away.' Selma never forgave father for taking her
three grandchildren back to England.

If it had been up to him, I'm sure that father wouldn't
have returned. More than mother, he knew at which side of
the Atlantic he was better off. 'It's better for the likes of us
at t' other side,' he said to me one day. I sensed that he had
made a mistake in leaving America; there was a touch of
conscience about it. I think that at the back of his mind, he
hoped one day to return. There would always be a job for
him in Fall River. While cotton textiles were booming, he
went on hoping to make the crossing again.

Until his death, father remained the black sheep of the
Fall River Woodruffs. As a boy, he had given his mother a
lot of trouble in running away to sea. She'd had to bail him
out of the navy because he was underage. He came home
in high feather, as brazen as could be; as soon as he was old
enough, he went off with the navy again.

I have often wondered why father ran off to war shortly
after he reached Blackburn in 1914. Of course, he acted no
more strangely than many other men at the time. In 1914
madness prevailed. Shamefaced, he had come home one day
to announce that he had joined up. Mother was dumbstruck.
She thought he was deserting her. Not so much as by her
leave, either. She argued with him; pleaded with him. How
could she manage without him? What need did he have to
get involved? The war was not for his age. Heavens name,
he was thirty-one. He had a family to think of. Instead of
his going to France they should take the first ship back to
America. President Wilson had pledged that America would
stay out of the war. Silently he had stared past her and

persisted. His silence had choked her. She had not managed to budge him. His worry was that he might not get to France in time. Like the rest of England he turned a deaf ear to Lord Kitchener's warning that the war would last three years.

A week later, in front of the Town Hall, she attended a ceremony for the men who had volunteered to go to the front. She took the three children, Jenny, Brenda and Dan. There were lots of flags and bunting. A large Union Jack flapped above their heads. The mayor, wearing an ermine-trimmed robe, a cocked hat and his chain of office, made a speech about the wickedness of the Hun, and the need to fight for freedom and liberty, for king and country. To the children's delight, a band played. And then, with orders ringing out, and with much stamping of feet and slapping of rifle butts, the men marched off to the railway station.

On the way home, the children waved small Union Jacks they had been given. Tears blinded Maggie to what was going on. The world, her world at least, had gone stark raving mad. After six weeks training in England, father was sent to France. Later, father said that when he'd got his rifle, he had felt like two men. Like being on a horse.

The war played a primary role in preventing my parents, even if they had intended it, from returning to America. In August 1914 the sea lanes around Britain were mined. In the winter, Hartlepool and Scarborough on the North Sea coast were shelled. A German submarine attack on the 'Carmania' – the ship in which they had sailed – must have come as a great shock to them. In February 1915 Germany declared that the waters around the British Isles were a war zone. To cap it all, in May 1915, the Lusitania was sunk off Ireland.

Father's running off to the war convinced mother that she had made a great mistake in returning to Blackburn. The truth struck her like someone hitting her in the face. In comparison to Fall River, Blackburn looked dowdy and run down. She found herself ensnared in the very life from which they had escaped.

'Then why,' I asked her, 'after so many years in America did you return to England?'

'I wanted to smell the lilies of the valley,' she replied, which I suppose was a symbolic way of saying that she wanted to return to her roots. I know she would not have left America had she known that father was going to run off to fight in France.

I once asked my sister Brenda how she explained father's returning to England and his running off to the war.

'Father was a gormless creature,' she said. 'He had the head and brains of a brass knob. He didn't foresee anything because he never thought about anything. He was a grand worker, nobody better, but where brains were concerned he was lost.'

Father's dashing off to war made things hard for mother. She had three children to care for. When her savings ran out, she was forced to go and work in the mills.

Mother rarely saw father for the next four years. When he came home on leave, he had changed – the old jauntiness had gone; he was thinner and there was a troubled look about him. 'There's going to be nobody left to fight,' he had said. His leave in 1916 had meant a second honeymoon for my parents. My birth on 12 September 1916, and naming me William after him, spoke of the joy they had known.

Father certainly paid a price for his actions. He fought for three years as a private with the infantry until he was gassed at the third battle of Ypres late in 1917. The Germans had released gas by shellfire which had caught the British unawares. The soldiers had panicked; clutching their throats and screaming with pain, they had fallen where they stood. Father was a great runner and had taken to his heels. He was one of the last to fall, one of the first to be picked up and treated. He was invalided out of the army in 1918.

As so many others, he came home disillusioned. His experiences had shattered any desire he might have had for change and adventure. He returned to Griffin Street a sick man.

Both body and mind were affected. For years he had a racking cough from the gassing.

When he was in a talking mood, he once told me about seeing the king in France. It was a great honour to see the king.

'You never saw such a cleaning up in the hospital as went on beforehand,' he said. 'One day, the place looked like a slaughterhouse; the next, there were flowers everywhere. They brought in a giant orderly who picked up the patients and shuffled them about like dolls. Anybody who stank or looked horrible had to go.

' "That's him," somebody called, as the king entered the ward. A long crocodile of people followed him. They moved so quickly that anybody on crutches had to hobble noisily out of the way. Here and there the king stopped, pinned a medal onto somebody's shirt, and mumbled something. He looked bewildered. At least he had the gumption not to stick his nose behind the curtains where the German wounded lay. Once he'd gone with "Three cheers for the king," the giant orderly shuffled the patients back again. The next day the ward was its usual bloody self.'

'Were you bucked up by the visit?' I asked.

'I felt the same after he left as when he came. I'm not a king's man, you know.'

By the time father left the front, a great disillusionment had settled on the battlefield. Phrases like self-sacrifice and sacred duty were not heard any more. There no longer was fraternizing with the German troops as there had been on that first Christmas in 1914. Anybody who fraternized was brought up sharp – very sharp. Bellyachers were silenced. To get a 'Blighty' – a wound that would take one home out of the carnage – or to be killed was the only escape. His regiment had come close to mutiny. They sent a staff colonel with a red band on his hat to talk them around. Gave them a good raking over, he did. 'Where is your love of country?' he asked them. Told them they were fighting for freedom. Father felt like telling him back that the only freedom they had was the freedom to get killed. First whiff of cordite, the colonel was gone.

By 1918 father was glad to be rid of his gun and uniform. After that he had to learn the hard way that the politicians' promise of a 'Land Fit for Heroes' was pie-crust thick.

I can remember nothing of my father's homecoming, or of the rejoicing that signalled the end of the war, the greatest war there had ever been. My first dim memory of father is the glee he took in throwing me against the ceiling. It was a short distance, but to me it seemed quite far. 'One, two, three, whoops!' he called out, against mother's protests. He also rasped my cheek with his coarse beard. The more I squirmed, the harder he rasped.

Having spent several months recovering from the gassing, father returned to his job in the mills. On the surface, the family life he had known before the war was resumed.

Father's recklessness in volunteering to fight for Britain in 1914 was the last straw for my American grandmother Selma. Yet she had not hesitated to encourage her other sons to fight for the United States once America had entered the war. There used to be a newspaper cutting in the family showing a picture of Selma with her sons in uniform sitting on her porch in Fall River under the stars and stripes. The accompanying article, which I read as a boy in Lancashire, declared that she had more sons serving in the United States Army and Navy than any other mother in Massachusetts.

Grandmother Selma lived into her late nineties.

Chapter VII

World Outside my Door

As soon as I was able to toddle, Jenny took me to the Morgan's next door. Later, I used to run in and out of the Morgan's house. Mrs Morgan sometimes took her daughter Annie and me to the horse trough outside the Griffin pub at the end of our street. The horses were watered there, and how deeply they drank; great draughts that I was sure would empty the trough. Withdrawing their heads, they shook their wet all over us. People drank from a dented metal cup attached by a chain to the spout from which poured a steady stream of water.

The Morgans never had more than the one child, Annie. Their house was tidy and clean and smelled as good as it looked. Mrs Morgan had a part-time job washing dishes at the Bull Hotel in town; Mr Morgan hauled coal. They could not have had much money to spare, yet I felt warm and secure there. I liked the bright red geranium Mrs Morgan kept in her window.

The Morgans were a strange contrast. He was a muscular

fellow, with strong arms and big hands. He used to stand before the mirror at the kitchen sink and, with the tap running, comb his thick, black hair until it hung in a straight line above his eyes. I used to watch him and wait for him to part his hair, but he never did. I knew Mr Morgan for years and he never parted his hair. Everybody else did. His side-whiskers luxuriated down his face like a garden gone wild. His wife was small, fair and slim. The one thing the couple had in common was their sense of humour. They were forever cheery.

In their house, I sensed the warmest love and affection. In the evening, when Mr Morgan came home, black as the coal he had carried on his back all day, Mrs Morgan used to jump up to greet him. It pleased me the way Mrs Morgan kept touching her husband. She had a way of reaching up and gently running her hand across his coal-blackened face. He responded by showing his gleaming white teeth.

Sometimes on a Sunday, Mr Morgan – his layers of coal-dust scrubbed off – took Annie and me to visit Molly, a big black horse with a star on her forehead. It was not really his horse, but he said it was. Molly lived in a dark hole in the side of a large building in town. I don't know how she put up with the dirt and the smell. She cheered up when we unlocked the door and allowed a flood of light to rush in. Mr Morgan placed his head against Molly's and soothingly asked her how she felt and told her how glad he was to see her again. He then gave her a carrot. Molly responded by rubbing her head against Mr Morgan's waistcoat. She looked at him with knowing eyes and quivering nostrils in a way that she didn't look at us. Before we left, Annie and I were allowed to sit on Molly's back and pat her neck. If it pleased her, the horse turned round and tickled us with her soft, wet muzzle. The final treat came on the moment of departure. Mr Morgan lifted us up and allowed us to take a handful of oats from Molly's bin. We were allowed to take as much as one hand could grasp. All the way home we chewed on Molly's oats.

*   *   *

When I was a little older, my parents took me to the open air market in town. Unless we went on the penny tram, and which we never used if father was in charge, we were faced by what to me was an endless march through all kinds of weather. Once, when father and I were coming home through a blizzard, which had struck unusually late in the year and had fallen upon us suddenly, I shouted to him that we should take the tram home.

He didn't even turn round. 'Tha won't melt' he shouted into the wind, as he continued to clump his way along the snow-covered pavement. With the bitter snow-laden wind stinging my eyes and pricking my face, I followed as best I could. Alongside us, steaming horses and snow-covered carts, piled high with empty beer barrels, plunged through the dirty puddles and the growing slush. My heart sank as I watched the tram, on which I had set all my hopes, lurch past. Screaming its protest at the weather, and I hoped at father too, it faded into the gloom where its yellow eye flickered and died. In desperation, I followed the snowman who trudged on before me. The usual crowds of people had vanished.

By the time we reached home, father and I were covered from head to foot with snow. The pavements had long since disappeared from view. Other than to stamp our feet and shake ourselves like dogs, we entered the cottage as if nothing had happened. Until our clothing dried, we stood on newspapers before a roaring fire drinking hot tea. My sisters had been bundled upstairs. Although we were both steaming like sheets taken out of the boiling set pot, nothing was said about our nakedness or the weather.

Every Saturday night, when they were in work, my parents went to their favourite pub. Sober from Monday to Saturday, they broke out and made up for lost time. If there was no one to look after me, I was taken along too. With other young children, mostly by myself, I wore out the night sitting in the pub kitchen, which stank of stale beer and cigarette

111

smoke. 'Sit still and keep your hands off everything,' the pub-keeper's wife ordered. Any dog or cat there fled to some hidden corner from which they hissed and growled at me for the rest of the night. Their noise was drowned only by the clash of glasses, the shouts, the wild laughter, and the snatches of song coming from the bar. 'Meet me in love's sweet garden, down where the roses grow . . .' 'Oh, you beautiful doll, you great, big beautiful doll . . .' People drank more if they sang.

Occasionally, I escaped into a picture book that the pub-keeper's wife thrust into my hands. I knew better than to say that she had given me the same book for the past three weeks. I also whiled away the hours by listening to the bar piano. When all else failed, I'd make a dream world of the fire, or watch the second hand twitch its way across the face of the Westminster Chime clock standing in the corner. It came as a relief when I heard the cry 'Time, gentlemen, please.' After that, amid muttered farewells to those who had left the pub with us, and who seemed reluctant to go home, we walked through the dark streets, my parents discussing the latest gossip. There was always something that caught their fancy. In time, as they often changed their 'favourite' pub, I came to know most of the pub kitchens in Blackburn.

One night all monotony vanished when a fight broke out in the bar. I knew from the dreadful things being shouted that somebody had run off with somebody else's wife. There was such bawling and screaming and smashing of glasses and furniture that I feared for my parents' lives. With distraught faces, they rushed into the kitchen, scooped me up and fled into the night. We never drank there again.

On occasions I was lucky enough to go with my parents to the music hall at the Theatre Royal. I peered down from the gods on the most exciting scenes. The music, the flood-lit stage, the sparkle and the glitter of the occasion intoxicated me. Everything that happened belonged to another world.

Nobody in our street talked like the actors did, nobody was so cheeky or so swaggering. They came right up to the edge of the stage and talked to us as if they'd known us all our life. Then they got everybody to sing 'Ta-ra-ra-boom-de-ay' until the windows rattled. I believed everything I saw. I felt cheated when the audience booed and threw rotten tomatoes. That's when the magic fled and I noticed the fleas.

When money was short we went to 'penny readings,' where we sat on a hard bench in a cold warehouse. The reader, Mr Peck, was a grey-haired, gaunt-faced elderly gentleman who wore a threadbare suit and a winged collar, and whose teeth kept slipping. He first told us in his own words what the story was about, and then filled in by reading from the text. I recall only the hard seat and the cold.

Some of the happiest moments I had were those spent with my sister Jenny. She looked after me, even after she started working in the mills. She was the first to take me on a community outing into the countryside. One Sunday morning we boarded a horse-drawn coal barge which leisurely made its way on the canal past the crowded housing, the mills and the slag heaps into the open countryside. We sat on newspapers to protect our clothing from the grime. The adults made light of a dog that floated by with a distended belly.

Once we had left the vile smell of the town and the black poisonous water behind, we were surrounded by meadows alive with birds and insects. The water became clear enough to watch the pike hunt their prey. Breathing deeply, we filled our lungs with fresh air. The cuckoo called from distant woods. Listless, flat-topped brown hills touched with shreds of clouds sat all around us. Wildflowers filled the banks. When we passed somebody we knew on the towpath, a shouting match occurred. A boisterous repartee was expected. The trick was to make sure you got in the last word.

It was high-spirited self-entertainment all the way. It was taken for granted that anybody who had a banjo, or a concertina, a harmonica, or a tin whistle would bring it with him. Everybody was expected to do something, even if it was just to join in the singing, or cheer and clap.

My sister's young man Gordon Weall was a proper clown. He had brought a false nose, false teeth and a wig, and in no time at all had the whole barge shaking. Once started, laughter with Lancashire people was infectious. They laughed and laughed until they gasped for breath, and tears ran down their cheeks. They laughed with a determination to wring the last bit of pleasure out of it. 'A good laugh beats all thi medicine,' they said.

We ate and drank at noon at a pub in the countryside – the horse knew where to find it. It was the first time I got a sip of beer.

The day gone, we wended our way home again, lock by lock, as the lowing cattle left the fields.

Best of all was the first 'sharabang' trip I made with Jenny and Gordon. The 'sharabang' was a long, open cart in which we sat on benches with our backs to the sides. There was a wide step at the rear. Behind us, down the length of the wagon, was a rolled tarpaulin that could be pulled over our heads in case of rain. The driver sat up on a box behind his two horses, his whip standing in its rest. It was never used. Mr Beatty in his wicker bed, this time without the wheels, was placed in the middle of the cart against our legs. Everybody had his place, nobody was neglected. With so many giving a hand, there was no trouble getting the basket in and out. When we went into a pub, Mr Beatty went with us.

We started the trip at dawn one summer's day, coming together in front of The Griffin. The younger women wore colourful dresses with wide-brimmed straw hats held on with ribbons. The older women had a kerchief wrapped tightly around their heads and fastened under the chin. Everybody brought their own food. There was a lot of shouting and laughter before we got away.

We spent the whole day in country lanes, passing through woods with the bright sun piercing the boughs; other times crossing open fields; still other times we experienced the great silence of the moors, a silence broken only by the cries of the pewits and the curlews, and the chatter of rushing streams. Once we crossed a great stone bridge that led to a sleepy village where friendly people standing in doorways passed the time of day with us. Every now and again, as we jolted through the ruts, we were bounced about, or thrown backward and forward as if we were riding a wave. 'Whoa!' everybody yelled, as we lurched forward: 'Whoa!' when we were thrown back again, while laughing ourselves hoarse. In the hilliest parts, the young got out and pushed. No setback was allowed to interfere with our merrymaking. When we struck an especially deep hole, we hung on to Mr Beatty's basket and rolled with him while he drooled. Mrs Beatty was for ever attentive to Mr Beatty, wiping his face, feeding him, and sheltering him from the sun. You'd wonder how she could have been as happy as she was.

As a result of my sister's pleading, I was allowed to sit up front on a high box next to Mr Fisher, the driver. I was proud to sit next to Mr Fisher, but I'm not sure that he had the same feelings toward me. He sat like a stone at my side, towering above me. He was the only man wearing a bowler hat. The grown-ups called it his 'badge of office.' He never took his eyes off the road, never turned round to see what was going on behind him, never acknowledged that I was there. At least he seemed deaf to anything I said to him – especially when I asked if I could hold the reins. Later on he gave me the reins and told me to start the cart. I swelled with pride at the opportunity. However, his two horses, Polly and George, both reddish-brown giants, ignored my 'Giddups!' They wouldn't budge. Finally, they looked round at me so pitifully that I could do little else but hand the reins back.

What fascinated me about Mr Fisher was his ability to

carry on a conversation with his horses and his passengers at the same time. As he never looked back, I was never sure if he was talking to the horses or the passengers.

'You're a sly one, you are, you want it your way.' And then without moving his head or his body, or even taking a breath, he went on: 'No there's been no change in Sarah's condition. One says its rheumatics, another says its water. I'll tell ye one thing, that there medicine she's got now is sheer poison. I know, because I tried a drop. If that doesn't do it, nothing will. What did I tell you,' he continued without a pause, 'I knew you'd leave it to him.' I could only think that 'you' was Polly, the horse. 'For all the good you're doing, you might as well sit up here with us.' And then without any sign that he was changing the conversation: 'No its the red, murky stuff; bottle should be marked kill or cure; can't say I'm drawn to it.'

And so the day went on until we'd visited our last pub and everyone was warm and merry back in the 'sharabang.' The horses knew when the homeward journey began – they pulled harder. Everybody took it for granted that we'd sing ourselves home. As the light faded, and the 'sharabang' rattled on, we sang:

> Come lasses and lads, get leave of your dads,
> And away to the maypole hie,
> For ev'ry fair has a sweetheart there,
> And the fiddler's standing by . . .

and

> Buy my caller herrin. They're bonnie fish and halesome
>   farin'.
> Buy my caller herrin. Just new-drawn frae the Forth.
> When ye were sleepin' on your pillows, dream'd ye aught
>   of our poor fellows,
> Darklin' as they faced the billows, all to fill our woven
>   willows? . . .

and

> In Dublin's fair city, where the girls are so pretty,
> I first set my eyes on sweet Molly Malone.
> She wheeled a wheelbarrow through streets broad
>   and narrow,
> Crying, 'Cockles and mussels, alive, alive, oh!' . . .

We sang the songs we all knew. Although it was Sunday, we sang few hymns; although when crossing a moor, we sang 'Out on an Ocean all Boundless We Ride.' Sometimes the men led, sometimes the women; sometimes there was two-part harmony, sometimes three- or four-part. Whoever was moved to sing, sang. I noticed how still everyone in the 'sharabang' became when the rich voices fell silent.

In the stillness I listened to the jingle of the harness and the whispering sounds in the darkening hedgerows and meadows around us. I watched Mr Fisher's lamps of flickering yellow patches light our way.

And then, after a mile or two, unheralded, soaring to the sky, came Patrick Mulroony's voice singing Danny Boy.

> Oh Danny boy, the pipes, the pipes are calling
> From glen to glen, and down the mountain side.
> The summer's gone, and all the leaves are falling
> 'T is you, 't is you must go and I must bide.

Out of the dusk, his brother Mike joined in from the other end of the cart:

> But come ye back when summer's in the meadow
> Or all the valley's hushed and white with snow
> 'T is I'll be here in sunshine or in shadow
> Oh Danny boy, oh Danny boy, I love you so.

> But when ye come and all the flowers are dying,
> And I am dead, as all the flowers must die,

Ye come and find the place where I am lying,
And kneel and say an ave where I lie.

And I shall hear, though soft you tread above me,
And in the dark my soul will wake and see.
For you'll bend down and tell me that you love me.
And I shall sleep in peace until you come to me.

There was no strain; no difficulty keeping the other's pace.
The two men just opened their mouths and in high, soft,
flowing voices sang like birds. Everybody joined in toward
the end. By the light of the stars I saw Mrs Mulroony and
my sister Jenny weeping, though I knew I should not have
looked. Few things can be as beautiful as a cart full of simple
people harmoniously singing their way home through the
gloaming with gladness in their hearts.

Later I watched Mr Fisher play a game in the dark with
Mr Beatty. Without moving his seat, Mr Fisher reached back
until he could grab some part of Mr Beatty. Having got hold
of him, he pretended to shake him like a terrier shakes a
rat. 'Grrrr,' he went. Mr Beatty must have known who it
was, for he gave the same squeal of delight every time it
happened.

Mrs Beatty enjoyed it too. 'Oh! Oh!' she cried every
time Mr Fisher's hand approached, 'we must stop him, Eric,
mustn't we?' Between these attacks, she wiped her husband's dribble and played with his hair.

The grown-ups said that Mr Beatty and Mr Fisher had
gone off as young men in 1914 to fight the war in France.
Mr Beatty had been hit with a shell. He would have bled to
death had Mr Fisher not scooped up what was left of him
and, risking his own life, run back through the mud looking for help. Mr Fisher, they said, had saved Mr Beatty's life.
Some said that was a good thing; others didn't seem so sure.
They looked down their noses, and studied their clogs and
said, 'Mm . . . mm,' in a serious grown-up way.

By the time we got back to the Griffin, I was fast asleep

across Mr Fisher's knees. I don't know how long I had been there. He held me up while everybody stood and sang:

> Praise God, from whom all blessings flow.
> Praise Him all creatures here below;
> Praise Him above, ye heav'nly host;
> Praise Father, Son, and Holy Ghost.

Chapter VIII

Schooling

B ecause my parents did not want to go on paying a baby-
sitter, at the age of four I was sent to St Philip's school
round the corner from where we lived. As I was to turn five
several weeks later, nobody took any notice of my age. The
law was ignored.

On my first schoolday Brenda took me by the hand and
left me in my classroom. Our caps and coats hung on hooks
on the walls. Because of the occasional outbreak of head
lice, Brenda had told me to keep my cap separate from the
others. I think I was smaller than most of my companions,
and I was afraid. I had good reason to be.

I discovered that my schoolmates were a wild lot.
Newcomers were roughed up by bullies who ran in a pack.
No sooner had I got into the schoolyard for the morning
break than several bullies knocked me down. I expected my
brother to defend me. He didn't, although he was quick with
his fists. His walking away from me on that occasion
coloured my view of him for the rest of my life.

123

With my ears ringing from the first blows, I appealed to the older children in the playground to help me. Instead they took pleasure in watching me get bashed. As I was small, I tried to seize their legs and topple them. One or two kicks in the face with steel-capped clogs put a stop to that. By then, with stars dancing before my eyes, I didn't know where I was, or where the school was. In a blind, crying rage all I could do was to hang on to one of my opponents and, in a tangle and a tussle, have the wind knocked out of me. Every time I broke free and managed to get to my feet, weeping and gasping for breath, I was thrown down again.

Only when my face was covered with blood was I allowed to scramble through the pack and run in search of my sister Brenda, who I knew was playing in the girl's yard next door. She was horrified when she saw my swollen lips and puffed-up face. 'I'll murder them for this, Billy,' she hissed as she took me home. I must have been a ghastly sight when my parents came home that night. Mother was shocked. 'Tha's been at it again,' was father's only comment.

Back to school I went the next day.

A week or so later, before my wounds had healed, three bullies grabbed me in the playground again. My earlier terror was renewed. At first I managed to break away, but they recaptured me and dragged me down. At that moment a fury landed in our midst. It was Brenda. 'I'll show you,' she shouted, 'hurting our Billy! Take that . . . and that . . . and that!' Like a wild animal she rained blows upon them until they pleaded for mercy. They got none. Everybody in the school yard was deeply impressed with Brenda. Henceforth, as long as I stayed at St Philip's, I may not have been popular, which priggish-like I sought to be, but at least no one dreamt of touching me again.

My teacher at St Philip's was Mr Manners, a small man with a thin waist. He had large, thoughtful grey eyes and a hollow face concealed behind a pepper and salt moustache. He wore a stiff, high collar and a dark suit that, like his bald head, shone with age. His nephew Joe had a swollen, misshapen face and a cast in one eye. He sat on the front row directly in front of his uncle with nothing better to do than to pick his nose. That was bad. Eating the stuff was revolting. Hardly a day went by without Mr Manners breaking off lessons to give Joe a slap on the head for his antics.

Joe and Mr Manners seemed to be tied to each other with an invisible rope. When one stood, the other stood. When one sat down, the other sat down. When one left the room, the other followed, even to the toilet. They came together in the morning; on and off they fought until noon when they sat in the classroom and had their dinner together. The battles were renewed in the afternoon. They left together at night, a weary Mr Manners muttering to himself in an absent-minded sort of way, a radiant Joe. Joe must have thought that life was a funny business, for he was always laughing. When he wasn't laughing, he looked older than his years. He was the only child there in a suit, shirt, tie and shoes. Now and again he would jab one of us with a dirty pen nib to let us know he was still about.

The decorations in Mr Manners' classroom were meager. There was a stained print of Boadicea, an ancient British queen, and a torn map of the world. Most of the map was painted red, 'The British empire, our empire,' Mr Manners assured us. I had no idea why we had such a big empire except that it was taken for granted that we were better than anybody else. On Empire Day (24th May), we sang: 'What is the meaning of Empire Day, why do the cannon roar?' The meaning to me was that we got free buns and half-a-day off school. There was also a large Lever Brother's Lifeboy Soap poster, which covered most of the wall at my side. It showed a bar of lathered Lifeboy Soap with a finger that pointed at me. Beneath the finger in great letters were the words WHERE THERE'S DIRT, THERE'S DANGER!

That poster worried me. I took it personally. Why had Mr Manners sat me there? My neck was no dirtier than the others. Nor did the poster lead me to wash my neck any more than I was doing. Washing in such a cold, wet climate didn't come easy with us. I never knew anyone who believed that cleanliness was next to godliness. I think we believed in being comfortably dirty.

Oddly enough, I got my first book with Lifeboy Soap coupons. It was a one-volume encyclopedia called the *Wonderland of Knowledge*. My letter to Lever Brothers, sending them the coupons I had saved, was the first letter I ever wrote and I haunted the postman every day after I'd posted it. I was so excited when the package arrived. It was addressed to me, personally. I wouldn't let anyone touch it. I refused to have the string cut and preferred to struggle to untie the knots. After some minutes, I extracted the book from its cardboard box and laid it on the table. It smelled so new and clean. You wouldn't believe it but it was ten-and-a-half inches long, seven-and-a-half inches wide, and one-and-a-half inches thick. I know because I measured it. It must have weighed several pounds. The cover was a treat for the eyes; it was dark blue; in the centre was a man reaching out for the sun, the moon and the stars.

I never dreamed that a book could contain so much. It not only offered knowledge, but inspiration. 'You are now standing,' it said on the title page, 'at the Gateway to the Wonderland of Knowledge . . . the key to your future and the future of the World. For you will learn by the past deeds of Men and Nations what good things to do and what bad things not to do. You will be inspired by the nobility and perseverance of those who rose from humble birth to sway by Thought or Deed the destiny of Man. And what they did, you too may do.'

I wondered why the author kept stressing the 'humble birth' bit.

'Anybody who gets a book with soap coupons, Billy,' my sister Brenda said, 'would have to be of humble birth.'

The book started by tracing the history of the world. I'd never heard about Ancient Egypt, or the Chaldeans, or the

Jews, or the Cretans, but it told me. I'd no idea How Music Began, or of the Seven Giants of Music, or the need for Mighty Music of Our Modern Age, but it told me that too.

There was nothing the book didn't tell me. Having read Music Through the Ages, I plunged into The Romance of Exploration from Marco Polo onward. I didn't realize the world was so big.

After that I tackled the Great Names in English Literature – thirty-two of them. Of the thirty-two I had heard of only two – Shakespeare and Milton, and not much of them either. Writers like the Venerable Bede and Samuel Pepys were eye-openers for me.

There followed the Marvels of Invention. There was even a section on Spinning and Weaving. Then came Wonders of the Insect World. This was the only part of the book that I couldn't get excited about, though I did enjoy the section headed Ogres of the Insect World.

I think by the time the editor had got through with the Ogres, he was ready to pitch anything in and take his pay. I suppose that next to the Bible, the *Wonderland of Knowledge* was the most important book I ever had. Being the only book I owned, I read it and re-read it until I knew it backward. I created my own adventure in learning. The book became my most treasured possession.

Mother opened her eyes with awe when I began to rattle off my knowledge: 'Imagine you knowing all that,' she said. Father was not struck by it: 'What good war all that talk?'

Anyway, back to school and Mr Manners. I think the poor man must have worked himself to death. He sat at a bare table on a platform in front of us. He stayed with us from morning till night. Behind him was the blackboard. Above his head hung an electric light bulb with a plain shade. Working on the blackboard, he taught us the alphabet, arithmetic and the names of our kings and queens from King Canute on. The moment he turned his back was the signal for students to elbow each other or fart. He also taught us the names of distinguished Englishmen and the battles they had won. We copied these things on our slates and then erased them with a rag. We rarely used ink and paper which cost more. He taught us the names of the local rivers and towns and lots of other things – like spelling – which many of us thought nobody needed to know. We learned by chanting in a sing-song voice, swaying to the letters, words, or numbers. I found it easy to learn by jingles: 'Two pints make one quart, four quarts make one gallon . . .' or, 'Thirty days hath September, April, June and November. All the rest . . .'

As Christmas approached, the school was transformed into a magic castle. A feeling of festivity filled the air. I must have been impressionable for I watched transfixed while teachers and students converted dark, crowded classrooms into glittering caves. Fluttering coloured paper streamers, pom-poms, Chinese lanterns, and decorations were hung from walls and ceilings. In the ever-present drafts, the great silver bells swung leisurely above our heads. When the gas lamps were lit in the afternoon, the magic grew.

The closer we got to Christmas, the more things changed. There was no thrashing. The cruel use of the Dunce's hat – which I feared more than anything – was temporarily suspended. Even Mr Manners and Joe took a rest from fighting. We didn't do a stitch of work. We played leap frog and had snowball fights in the school yard. We formed choirs and produced plays. For the plays we created scenery, properties and costumes out of nothing. It was great fun. I also learned something about language and elocution.

In one of the plays I was chosen to tip-toe into an artist's studio and place my head in the hole another student had made in the artist's canvas. The whole idea was that the artist would fail to notice that his canvas had been damaged and would go on touching up the face – my face – with paint. All I had to do was to put my head into the hole and keep absolutely still.

When the great night came, with most of our parents in attendance, I crept into the artist's studio. Having made sure that the artist was not there, I placed my head into the hole in the canvas. At that point the artist returned with his paints. This was the part we hadn't rehearsed. Instead of applying a dab of paint – as he had been instructed – he began to plaster me with the stuff. Howls of laughter came from the audience. When I opened my mouth to protest, he popped the paint brush right down my throat. By now the audience was uncontrollable. The play was considered a great success, but the taste of paint stayed with me for days.

Just before Christmas, the older boys carried in a Christmas tree dusted with snow. It was so high and so wide that they had difficulty getting it through the doors. I was thrilled when they hung the tree with decorations and candles. It became a mass of colour and light. I had never seen such a beautiful thing. How it contrasted with the dark day! They also brought in the crib with statues of Mary and Joseph, and the Infant Jesus, and the Three Wise Men from the East. There was a cow eating from the manger. These things brought home to me the joy and peace of Christmas for the first time.

While we were singing carols around the tree, a horse-drawn cart arrived laden with wooden crates filled with boxes of chocolates. The news spread like wildfire. Some kind soul had donated a box for every child. We shrieked with delight as box after box was extricated from the wood shavings. Each chocolate box lid was a delight in itself. My box showed a boy and a girl skating down a frozen river with snow-covered cottages lining the banks. It was sheer magic for me to possess such a prize. I kept the lid for ages.

At this time, my brother and sisters took me round the darkened streets singing carols. I carried a Chinese paper lantern with a candle inside. 'Christmas is coming,' we all chanted, 'the goose is getting fat, please put a penny in the old man's hat. If you haven't got a penny, a ha'penny will do. If you haven't got a ha'penny – God bless you.' We gave a lot of blessings and received some ha'pennies.

My school years were full of things other than learning. After school and on Saturdays, from the age of six, I ran errands for a neighbour of ours, Mr Tinworth, who had turned his front room into a grocer's shop. I also delivered groceries for him. I was so small that I found it impossible to lift the baskets off the floor. Once Mr Tinworth had helped me, I staggered off down the street, carrying the baskets on my hip. The grocer paid my parents one shilling and six-pence per week, of which I received one penny. Some customers gave me a half-penny for carrying their groceries, so I didn't do too badly.

Invariably, I spent the penny I received for my labours on a gob-stopper – a coloured ball of toffee on a stick about the size of a golf ball – which I bought at Mrs Hudson's tiny sweet shop down the street. She kept the gob-stoppers – upon which her small customers repeatedly choked when the toffee came off the stick – in a big glass jar. I felt important when the jar was brought to the counter and I was allowed to dip my grubby fingers inside to choose the colour I wanted. I liked everything about Mrs Hudson's shop. I liked the doorbell that announced my arrival, the warm, sugary, toasty smell, and all the shiny good things that were there to be eaten. Most of all I liked Mrs Hudson because hers was the only shop where my opinion counted. In Mrs Hudson's shop, the customer, however small, was in charge. Spending my penny was the most important decision of the week.

I must have shopped with Mrs Hudson for several years. We came to know each other well. She never changed. She was the same sweet, grey-haired old woman when I met her as when I left. I owe it to her that I know so much about confectionery. When I became more affluent, she introduced me to all kinds of chocolate and sugary delights. I think I must have eaten my way through her store. She also taught me to be discerning. Gob-stoppers were all very well when you were a child, but not when you were growing up. Under her guidance, I moved on through a whole gamut of liquorice delights, aniseed balls, and teeth-locking toffee, each piece of which had a different animal on the wrapper, until I reached what Mrs Hudson thought was the industry's masterpiece: colourful packets of candy cigarettes that looked just like the real thing. I never did reach the chocolate pipe and cigar stage. One Christmas I bought from her a black chocolate minstrel playing a banjo. It was a 'Christmas special,' not available at any other time. I ate it – cannibal-like, banjo and all – in one go from head to foot.

Between the ages of six and ten, I was helped in my school-work by my sister Brenda and my grandmother Bridget. Brenda was not only at her best in tough spots, she was also highly intelligent. Other than father, she was the only one among us who could handle arithmetic. Grandmother Bridget called figures 'soulless.' Mother, Jenny, Dan and I found figures equally distasteful. It mystified us how Brenda could order figures about the way she did. No matter how many she wrote down, they did exactly what she told them to do. Nor did she ever tire of doing completely dull things with them. I didn't care how long it took to fill a water-butt with a hole in the bottom. With a sum here and a sum there, she was quite happy filling the leaking water-butt for ages. I wondered why the butt should have had a hole in it in the first place. Why didn't somebody fix it? Then she worked out how many freight cars were needed on a train that stretched from London to Edinburgh? Everybody knew there couldn't be such a train. It was ridiculous.

Daft as all this seemed, she always came up with the right answers. 'You see how easy it is, Billy,' she said, arranging the figures as she wanted them. Well, it did look easy the way she did it, but, with me, the figures went crazy. The moment I touched them they stampeded in every direction; they did awful things; anarchy reigned.

'What on earth are you doing, Billy,' Brenda said, taking over. 'You've made a dreadful hash of it. It's quite simple, really.' Then she lined up the figures again and off they went. They always did what she wanted. The annoying thing was that she didn't seem to try. She was like a good collie dog with sheep. Without any fuss, all the figures finished up in the right pen. 'There's nothing to it at all, Billy,' she kept saying as she disposed of the last sheep.

There was no end to the problems she could handle. Indeed, she made problems harder than they needed to be. Once I managed to get one right. For a moment she was startled. 'Ah, but that's the answer in yards,' she gloated, 'what would it be in feet, Billy? Come on!' That floored me.

There can be no question but what Brenda was unusually bright. To everyone's surprise, she topped the state examinations for eleven-year-olds in the county. And she did it without a book in the house, and without special coaching. It was a real miracle. Her name was in the newspaper. Jenny showed it to me. It was the first time I'd seen our name in print and it had quite an effect on me. It made me giddy. The next day I expected everyone to stop me in the street and ask me if I was the brother of the girl whose name was in the paper, and who was going to go to the Grammar School in Preston. Nobody did. I became so disappointed that I stopped a number of people to tell them that I was Brenda's brother. I told them how she had won a scholarship to go to a special school for girls at Preston, ten miles away. She was going to ride the train there and back every day without paying. Nobody seemed impressed.

After several days a letter arrived from the school board about Brenda. I heard my parents discussing it in the kitchen.

'Uniforms, including stockings are provided,' said father studying a list. 'Train fare as well,' he continued. 'And books and pencils.'

'Well, imagine that,' said mother, 'I reckon they must have money cumin' out of their ears.'

There was a pause.

'What's it say about shoes?' asked mother. 'Lass can't go to college in clogs.'

'Nothing,' said father, 'nothing.'

'It must . . . look again.'

There was a longer pause.

'Mm, aye, tha reet, Maggie, it does. It says that shoes will be black, of plain design, and of good quality.'

'Um, they're fussy.'

A still longer pause. 'Where wa' it t' come fra?' mother asked. 'Her feet have long outgrown what shoes she had.'

'Well, we can borrow money to buy shoes, or we can leave her where she is,' father said finally. 'We might be making a fuss about nothing, Maggie. It's not good to put big ideas into young people's heads. What use is there in this learning when she could be doing real work?'

Although I was very young I knew that something was wrong. I wanted to shout through the cracks beneath my bed, 'Brenda's name was in the paper! You can't stop her going to Preston because she hasn't got shoes.'

But I didn't shout. Nobody did. To my knowledge, not even members of the school board. Why didn't grandmother Bridget intervene? She was, after all, the most educated among us. She was always on to us about 'larnin'.'

Brenda didn't go to Preston. One night when she came back from the lending library, I heard father tell her that they couldn't send her to school because she didn't have shoes, and they couldn't afford to buy them. Brenda didn't throw a fit, which is what I wanted her to do. Apart from a mumbled word or two, she accepted their decision. The matter was never discussed again. A brilliant career was denied her.

I think father was to blame. Somebody, somewhere would surely have paid for the shoes had he gone and asked, but he was too proud to beg. Why didn't he buy a used pair, I wondered. The truth is he wasn't interested in education for his children. It wasn't because Brenda was a girl, I think he would have done the same thing had it been my brother

Dan. He never encouraged any of us to better ourselves or to make the best of our talents by schooling. Education and keeping up the family prestige didn't matter in our lives – spinning and weaving did. The mills were our destiny. There was nothing dishonourable in that. What had been good enough for him, and for his father and grandfather, was good enough for us. It's where we belonged. It was our station in life and each should be satisfied with his station. Instead of going on to higher education, Brenda entered the mill at twelve as a half-timer. She became a piecer, an assistant to a spinner.

My debt to grandmother Bridget is even greater than that which I owe to my sister Brenda. Nightly, she taught me to read and write. I think she gave me the attention she should have given my mother when she was my age. Grandmother stood over me while I struggled to link word to word, sentence to sentence on my slate. 'Practice makes perfect,' she said as I cleaned my slate. Her wrinkled finger followed mine when I tried to read a children's English grammar she had borrowed from the public library. Work done, she would tell me about the library books she had read. She didn't go in for the classics like the Penny Reader, Mr Peck. She liked to read the novels of the time. She was fond of the books of a writer called Warwick Deeping. I suspect she liked him because he had written a book about an Irish girl called *Kitty*.

She also talked about America. She believed that America was the largest, richest country in the world. Beyond the packed cities and skyscrapers of the American eastern seaboard, she told me, were endless grasslands reaching to high mountains. Everything was big. 'One day you will go to America, Billy Boy,' she said, as if it had all been arranged. As I got older she became more concerned about what was to become of me. 'You can go a long way,' she would say, shaking her lace cap at me. 'That's if you wish to. But you won't go without "larnin'." It's the key that opens all doors.'

Chapter IX

Changing Faiths

Because mother could never make up her mind which church she belonged to – someone said she shopped for a new religion like shopping for a new hat – we children were tossed between St Philip's (Church of England) and St Peter's (Roman Catholic) schools. We started at St Philips because it was round the corner from where we lived. Later on one of the priests at St Peter's took mother to task for having her children at a Protestant school. So to St Peter's we went.

Father didn't care to which church he belonged, provided he could stay away from it. Mother said that father had believed in a God of love before the war but not after it. The slaughter in France had left him without a mooring. 'He floats,' she said. Father Prendergast of St Peter's, whom father disrespectfully called Father 'Spend-the-Brass,' once took him aside for backsliding as a Christian.

'Do you believe in God, Will?' he asked.

'I did until the war,' father answered. 'Tha'd be surprised

137

if tha'd seen what Ah've seen.' After which they shook hands. But they shook hands like two wrestlers: a touch of the hands without any warmth. I felt there was a gulf between them which neither could cross.

Mother once took father to a revival meeting in the hope that it would restore his old faith, but he was just as impassive about religion when he returned as he had been when he left the house.

Unable to get father to any more revival meetings, mother turned her attention to me. One day we took a train to a station outside Blackburn where we joined up with hundreds of other men, women and children. With banners and flags bobbing up and down above our heads, we inched our way along a narrow country lane toward a turreted church at the top of a hill. The well-trodden ground was carpeted with autumn leaves.

At the sound of a command from the front of the procession, we pilgrims repeatedly fell down on our knees in the mud (the wise ones crouched) and sang a hymn about sin. We sang loudly so that our protestations would be heard at heaven's gate:

> . . . All my sins, I now confess them,
> Never will I sin again,
> Never will I sin again.

As we shuffled forward, the more fervent among us struck their breasts, while pouring out their fears and hopes.

> Lord have mercy upon us,
> Christ have mercy upon us.

Only when I caught the eye of a girl about my own age who crouched beside me did I see the funny side of what we were doing. For a moment we had the giggles; she pinched my arm, I pulled her plaits.

Like an incoming tide, the crowd surged onward to the

church. Tightly packed, we mounted the steps and passed through the great doors. Except for the flickering red eye of the altar lamp, and the candles and tapers, the church was lit only by the dim light that filtered through the windows. The sweet smell of incense and the warm scent of burning wax was in the air. We dipped our fingers in the font of Holy Water, crossing ourselves before going forward into the church.

The building was ice-cold when we entered, but was soon 'set on fire' by a small, dark-eyed monk in the pulpit. He was dressed in a brown robe tied by a white cord at the waist. His cowl was thrown back. He wore leather sandals. His stubs of hair reminded me of a hedgehog.

The priest began by making the sign of the cross and kissing the crucifix that hung at his side. At one moment thundering, at another whispering, his powerful voice soon echoed throughout the church. Throwing his weight from one foot to the other, while stretching out his arms, he mesmerized me. He must have said some important things about our sins, for he was constantly interrupted with heartfelt cries of: 'Alleluia! Alleluia!' In their excitement, the callers seemed to try to outdo each other. The priest responded with still more thundering and whispering. It went on for a long time. It ended by our reciting the Confiteor, the Our Father and the Hail Mary. We left with the monk's blessing.

We did not have to kneel in the mud on the way back to the station. With the church bells tolling, we simply formed up outside and sang our way down the hill, now bathed in sunshine. Everybody was relaxed in the train. People were brighter-faced; they said they felt better for coming. I suppose they'd purged their sins; the wrongs they'd done were forgiven them; they'd won a new beginning.

Anyway, back to Father Prendergast and St Peter's. Father Prendergast was a fat, jolly man of undoubted sincere piety, who seemed to get fatter as times got worse. Everybody liked him, especially for his short sermons. I liked him too, but I took a dislike to St Peter's from the start. It was a forlorn building with a large bell in a belfry; the grey stone walls had blackened with age and dirt. A bare cindered yard at the side, from which dust blew most of the time, was the playground.

The best thing about St Peter's was that Rosie Gill went there. She was my six-year-old sweetheart. She always wore the same old brown woollen hat pulled down at the back, and a grey coat much too long for her. We always held hands. We didn't have much to say to each other, but we were happiest when we were together. One day she showed me an amulet of Mary and the crucified Christ, which hung on a cord around her neck under her blouse. It was a beautiful thing of the brightest colours and had been specially blessed. I knew from the way she drew it up so slowly from out of her dress that I was somebody special.

We were holding hands one afternoon on our way home from school when I had a sudden impulse to look over the stone parapet of the bridge that spanned the Darwen River. The parapet was about five feet high and was not meant to be climbed by small children. Removing my bulky woollen gloves, and disregarding Rosie's protests, I jumped and clawed my way up the wall until I was able to look down on the river rushing over boulders below.

Before I realized what was happening, one of the bigger boys took me by the heels and heaved me over the parapet into the river. Stark terror possessed me as I fell head first. I hit the water with a loud splash; my face struck the rocks.

Rosie was the only one to come to my help. Dripping with blood, I fought my way to her at the side of the river. Leaning on her, with my teeth chattering, I drunkenly made my way home. Fortunately mother was there. She nearly fainted when she saw me. She didn't console me as Rosie had done, but she washed and bandaged my wounds. When father came home, he showed no sympathy. The way he went on about it, you would have thought that I made a practice of jumping off bridges and breaking my nose. No effort was made, either by teachers or parents, to find the bully and punish him. Scores at that school were settled without the unforgivable act of running to the teachers to tell tales. Tell-tale tits got their tongues slit, or something equally dreadful.

I used to call for Rosie on my way to school. Her home was in the next street. On my arrival, Mr Gill was always standing with his back to the fire, drinking tea. 'What, eh,' he greeted me. He drank sip by sip, tasting his tea with great care before swallowing it. His bottom was so large that no heat reached any other part of the room. He wore the same oatmeal-coloured woollen undervest, with three buttons at the top, and the same balloon-like trousers. The vest and pants both looked slept in. His feet were wrapped in slippers made out of an old coat. Mr Gill must have eaten a lot of eggs, for there were egg stains from his neck to his waist. Rosie said her father was a sloppy eater and that her mother had given up worrying.

What did arouse my curiosity about Mr Gill was the strange way he kept peering down the inside of his trousers. He would push the front of his pants away from him as far as his braces would go. Then he looked down into the dark hole he'd made as if there was something moving about there. As I watched him, I wondered if he was trying to discover how much room he had to spare; or whether he had got too hot. After a while I made up my mind that Mr Gill had a pet rabbit in his pants, and was curious to see what it was up to. I would not have been the least surprised if a rabbit's head had suddenly popped up over the top of Mr Gill's trousers. I never did ask Rosie what she thought.

In time, I came to realize that there were few men as lovable, or as big-hearted as Willie Gill. He was a thoroughly good-natured man, with a good-humoured face, who was happiest when he was helping others. He had the best of intentions. Little wonder that his fellow-Catholics thought so highly of him. His size made him all the more lovable. He was so large that when he entered our house it became crowded.

In a genteel way, he had reached the last state of shabbiness. In the street he wore the same old coat, stained with snuff. It had come apart under his armpits. His trousers were so thin that his knees showed through. His cracked shoes revealed his bare feet. Above his puffy, red face, with its rheumy eyes and large whiskers, he wore a crushed hat made of wool and bits of fur. It added distinction to an already odd appearance. His hair had never seen a comb. He smelled suspiciously of urine.

Mr Gill had long since given up working for a living. Any money the Gills had came from Hessie, his thin little wife, whose weak, staring eyes didn't seem to like what she was seeing. Those eyes troubled me as a child. There was a story that Mr Gill had worked in the mills but had given it up. Some said life had been unkind to him; others said he lacked backbone. Most said he was broke because he spent his time looking after others.

Meanwhile he survived by thinking up the most preposterous schemes to make money. One of these was to sell as fresh tobacco the cigarette ends which we children retrieved for him from the gutters. After taking the paper off, he placed the tobacco in a dish in his window. It was sold as 'Fresh Virginia.' I cannot think how many diseases he must have spread. The really good cigarette ends we found, we smoked ourselves.

———◦———

Mr Gill first aroused in me the joy of going to Blackpool. It was long before my visit there with mother. One day – wonder of wonders – he suddenly proposed to take ten of us, including me, to Blackpool. Pied-piper fashion, armed with buckets and spades, we eagerly followed his waddling, fat figure to the railway station unable to believe our luck. He had our parents' consent, but we would have followed him anyway. We cheered as the train moved off. We heaped praise on Mr Gill until his cheeks shone.

We'd gone only two or three stops when Mr Gill said we had to get out. Puzzled, for we had no idea that Blackpool was so close, we leapt out of the train ready to run into the sea. But while there was plenty of sand, there was no sea. 'Tide's out,' said Mr Gill, wrinkling his nose.

'Where's the tower?' everybody demanded.

'They've just moved it,' Mr Gill said, stuffing his shirt back into his trousers.

'Where are the people?' we pressed.

'Gone home.'

'Are you sure, this is Blackpool?' I insisted.

'Eh?'

'Mr Gill, where are we?'

'Little Blackpool. Big Blackpool is farther on.'

'But you said you'd take us to Blackpool,' I protested.

'You promised us.' Some of the children began to cry. The crying got louder and louder.

What with the threatening weather, it looked as if Mr Gill was going to break down and weep too. Instead, he shuffled in place like an elephant fastened to a stake. 'Oh dear,' he kept saying, his face past hope. His good-hearted plan to take us off our parents' hands and spend the day digging in a sandpit had misfired.

Had he told us that he was taking us to a sandpit, we would have gone with him gladly. But he'd said Blackpool, and Blackpool was a very different thing. Every suggestion he made, including building sand castles – after all, we had brought buckets and spades – was rejected. By now the children were making quite a din.

Threatened by our spades, Mr Gill became desperate. 'Follow me,' he called as he shuffled off, his sail-like trousers flapping in the breeze. 'I've just remembered, Blackpool is round the corner.' Walking directly behind him, I felt the whole sky was covered by the seat of Mr Gill's trousers.

But the real Blackpool was not round that or any other corner. Turning corners only revealed more broken ground, more empty acres of sand. Tired of searching for the real

Blackpool, our protests were renewed.

A vanquished, snuff-stained Mr Gill led us back to the railway station. Some of the children cried all the way home. It was raining hard by the time we got back to Blackburn. Not knowing what to do with us – our people were still in the mills – he sat us all in his front room, half of which he occupied, and followed our movements with watchful eyes and a nervous cough. He was, after all, surrounded by ten discontented children brandishing spades. At the first mill whistle, which told him that our parents were on their way home, Mr Gill rushed us out of the house. He never played the role of Pied Piper again.

To return to St Peter's, I thought the school was as cheerless inside as it was out. The rooms were dark and had little else but rows of wooden desks and benches – the latter polished by the seats of past generations. The walls bristled with wooden pegs on which hung caps and coats. Like St Philip's, there were the same lights, the same table for the teacher; the same blackboard. Both schools shared a distinguished war record of former pupils. The Lancashire Fusiliers and the East Lancashire Regiment had won an unmatched number of Victoria Crosses in the Great War.

In addition to Father Prendergast there was a young curate called Smail. He had come from a rich parish in London, and had a hump on his back, hence his nickname 'Humpty Dumpty.' He must have wondered what he'd fallen into at St Peter's. He seemed to play no part in school life. Whenever I saw him in the streets he had his head down reading a leather-bound prayer-book. He had downcast eyes. I don't know whether he was a real priest or not. What I do know is that he had a quick temper. Give him cheek – 'Smail, Smail, ate a whale,' we used to call after him – and the prayer-book hit you like a stone. Everybody I knew gave him a wide berth. Mother said he was 'a fish out of water.'

There also were two nuns. Everybody loved the twinkling, big-boned, innocent Sister Lucy whose face was like a polished apple. I took an instant dislike to the gnarled, thin-lipped Sister Loyola, whom everyone feared. I shrank from her.

When Sister Lucy entered our room everybody looked up, everybody smiled. She had a delightful way of reaching down and gently – ever so gently – pinching your cheek. She was so sweet and cherubic that I felt like standing up and pinching her back. When Sister Loyola entered the room, the class froze. At the end of the day Sister Loyola took Sister Lucy home as though she were dragging her on a halter.

At St Peter's the teachers were forever talking about sin and hellfire, which gave me nightmares. Whereas the Lifeboy Soap poster had been my constant companion on the wall at St Philip's, at St Peter's I sat next to a large picture of Christ with hard, staring eyes, pointing to his exposed, bleeding heart. There was a Cross on the middle of the heart and a fire on top of it. I never lost my fear of the blood. Although I felt a childish loyalty to Christ – Sister Lucy had said that He had suffered terrible things to help us – I found the picture oppressive and avoided Christ's eyes and his pointing finger as much as I could. Elsewhere in the room were pictures of Christ being scourged at the pillar, and Christian martyrs being fed to the lions. The only peaceful thing was a blue statue of the Madonna that stood on a windowsill with its back to the light.

The Catholics were expected to pray all the time. We prayed and prayed. We were forever crossing ourselves and getting down on our knees. Our teacher, Miss Little – she was in fact very large – asked us to pray before class to help us in our work. Now and then, we made the Stations of the Cross in the chapel next to our classroom, to which we had a communicating door. We banged and bumped and snickered as we went down on our knees and got up again, making our way from station to station. I was too small to know

145

what it was all about. Christ's passion and death interested me, but I was bored by the time we reached the last station. Obviously, I lacked reverence and devotion.

When the door leading from our classroom to the chapel was left open, I could see as far as the altar. Compared to our drab room, it was like looking into another world. There was a ceiling studded with golden stars, gleaming metal and stone, polished wood and a mysterious, flickering red light hanging before the tabernacle. Mass was said there to a crowded congregation every Sunday.

The happiest moments were when Father Prendergast wandered into our classroom making the sign of the Cross. He was a kind man who didn't seem to have any purpose other than to tell tales in a slow mellow voice and make fun. His stories had happy endings, like Noah and the Ark, or the fellow who was swallowed by a whale. The pictures of suffering around the room didn't affect his spirits. He had a hearty laugh, which caused the folds of flesh on his neck to glisten. He laughed so much that I feared that his shaking belly would escape from beneath the black belt that held his paunch in place.

One day, during one of his visits, Father Prendergast asked us what we'd like to be when we grew up. I knew it was only meant for fun because we were all destined to work in the mills. Nevertheless, I boldly said I'd like to be a tinker. The tinkers – most of them Gypsies – who mended our pots and pans struck me as wonderfully free; they didn't work in the mills; they came and went as they wished.

For some reason my answer threw Father Prendergast into fits of laughter. Every student in the room joined in. Even Miss Little (who found Father Prendergast's visits a strain) laughed. I could tell from the trouble Father Prendergast had in adjusting his belt that his rippling belly had broken loose.

There was no laughter when Sister Loyola visited us. She was as serious as Father Prendergast was jolly. She had suffering on the brain. She was always talking about a wrathful

God. I wondered if her idea of love wasn't to thrash us all. She left me with a life-long fear of God. I didn't fear Christ. He had given His life for others, and as far as I could tell, was a good man who was now quite dead. He was the Good Shepherd: He was real; I knew Him. God was different; He was full of mystery; He was a strange figure who could pop up anywhere at any time. I never understood why God had sacrificed His son instead of Himself.

Sister Loyola did not like her views challenged, not even by Father Prendergast. Whenever he intervened: 'Oh, come now Sister, not everybody must suffer,' Sister Loyola's eyes would flash and she would withdraw into a dark, offended silence.

One had to watch out for Sister Loyola. She'd spring a question on you without warning.

'Who is God?'

By rote we answered 'God is the Supreme Spirit, who alone exists of Himself, and is infinite in all perfections.'

'Who is Jesus Christ?'

'Jesus Christ is God the son made man for us,' we chanted back.

'Why did God make you?' was one of her specials. Everybody in the class knew the answer.

'God,' we jingled, 'made me to know Him, love Him, and serve Him in this world, and to be happy for ever with Him in the next.'

'And sin?'

'Sin is an offence against God.'

Before she left the room she asked, 'What will Christ say to the wicked?'

We could jingle the answer without thinking: 'Christ will say to the wicked, "Depart from me, ye cursed, into ever-lasting fire".' Hell was final; from everlasting to everlasting.

I loved the words, I loved the imagery, the mystery and the rhythm. I loved parading my knowledge. But I didn't understand a single thing. I never worked out how three gods – God the Father, God the Son and God the Holy Ghost

– could be one. The nature of God the Father I simply could not grasp. I was especially confused about the use of the word God. To say 'God' was all right, but to say 'By God' in a loud voice was all wrong. I could tell from the distrustful look in Sister Loyola's eyes that she didn't hold out much hope for me.

'These things you must learn, child,' she insisted, 'understanding will come later.'

I have never forgotten Sister Loyola's sermon on the crucifixion and death of Christ given to the school one Good Friday. We were all assembled in the main hall. Sister Loyola stood against the plaster statue of St Michael spearing a horned serpent – the devil. Hypnotized by her words, we relived Christ's passion. We shared His agony in the garden. We saw His scourging at the pillar. We watched as a crown of thorns was pressed against His brow. Together we walked with Him as He carried His blood-spattered cross along the Street of Sorrows. Eventually we reached Calvary, where we bided while His feet and hands were pierced most cruelly. With Sister Loyola, we saw the cross being heaved up against the sky. As we looked upon the sagging figure with its bowed head, its haggard face and its stiff, outstretched arms, our sorrow was complete.

While she was talking, a storm had blown up. Papers were scattered and a cloud of dust came through the windows before we could shut them. The blackened sky was split by flashes of lightning. Sister Loyola had just cried out: 'And the curtain of the temple was rent from top to bottom,' when the whole school was shaken by a crash of thunder. I felt the building rock, my chair shake. I heard the windows rattle. I didn't need convincing that Jesus had just given up the ghost. I was too terrified to believe anything else. To me this was the God of wrath; the God of vengeance; God on the grand scale; only this God could have shaken the school down to its foundations.

Sister Loyola never let the Woodruff children forget that we had come from St Philip's. She was wary of us on that score. 'All Protestants are heretics,' she repeated with a dark look that went right through me.

I wasn't sure what a heretic was, so I screwed up enough courage to ask her: 'What is a heretic, please Sister?'

The answer was on her lips before I'd finished asking. 'A heretic,' she intoned, 'is someone who has offended God and has been abandoned by Him.' That left me more puzzled than ever.

In Sister Loyola's eyes the Woodruff heretics were lucky to have made the change from St Philip's to St Peter's. 'God is in our church,' she said proudly, 'not in their's.' I knew enough from Sister Lucy's comments that only a fool would not have God on his side. 'God,' Sister Lucy had assured me, 'is all-powerful, all-watching, all-seeing, all-vengeful. No one can fool God.' Sister Lucy's religion was simple: fear the Lord and glorify Him every day. 'Hold fast to the Cross,' she urged me. It was not only the right thing to do, it was the wise thing to do. I don't know what others thought about God, but I kept a still tongue and followed Sister Lucy.

Of course, there was more to St Peter's than the severity of Sister Loyola. As the chapel was next to our classroom, the air was sweet with incense. We heard the gentle tinkling of a bell. The colourful ceremonies and the sense of mystery overwhelmed my imagination. As long as I went to that school, I was besieged by miracles: seas parted, the dying were healed, ghosts rose, chariots of fire soared through the skies – there was no end to it. The imagery of it all sustained me. At St Peter's we were eternally being 'washed in the blood of the lamb.' At St Philip's you never saw a drop of blood; you were washed in Lever Brother's Lifeboy Soap.

The great advantage of being at St Peter's was that I could take part in the annual Easter procession. Massed Bands came from all over the district. The importance of the procession was measured by the number of bands; brass and silver bands were everything. With their leaders strutting proudly with a long silver stick with a brass ball on top, the bands thumped and pounded, blared, boomed and crashed until you couldn't hear yourself speak. Whether marking time with their polished boots on the cobbles, or on the march, the bandsmen blew their horns and beat their drums until the veins stood out on their necks and the windows rattled. The crowd made way, counted the number of bands, and crossed themselves.

I preferred the hymn:

> Oh, Mary, we crown thee with blossoms today,
> Queen of the angels and Queen of the May . . .

to the more militant 'Faith of our Fathers' with its deaths in dungeons dark.

It would take a hard heart not to be moved by the spectacle of Mary's garlanded figure rocking above a sea of wide-eyed, young girls carrying bouquets of sweet-smelling lilies of the valley. Dressed in white, stumbling along at their own pace, they contrasted sharply with the sooty walls and the grimy streets.

It was especially moving when the crowds sang their praise to Mary, Queen of the May:

> To live and not to love thee, would fill my heart
> with shame.
> When wicked men blaspheme thee, I'll love and bless
> thy name . . .

Alas, there were wicked men about who not only blasphemed Mary's name, but who did their best to disrupt the procession. Most years were peaceful, but then the fighting would break out again like a rash. To my horror, a fight did break out one day when we were passing St Philips. Protestants were touchy about the Catholics demonstrating before their church.

The fight began with a lot of shouting, which was followed by the throwing of rotten eggs and tomatoes. The throwers took care not to hit the bands, but they did hit us. While I scrambled out of the way, I saw a number of Protestants try to seize the banners. There was a free-for-all right along the street. One pole was broken over somebody's head. Nobody took any notice of the police whistles, or the shouts of the priests.

While the battle raged, the bands continued to march in place, crashing out still another hymn. Disregarding the fact that the faithful, and the not so faithful, were being beaten over the head, and little girls sent screaming, the bands played on. After all, they were being paid.

The battle over, with the Eucharist held high at the front, we all formed up again and continued the march. 'Faith of our Fathers' rang across the town.

After that, the Chief of Police always led the procession. With his medals, bright belt and his white gloves, he was out at the front looking for trouble. Blackburn Protestants had enough gumption not to knock him down.

When a wind got up, the marchers had enough trouble on their hands without protesters. As the wind rose, a shouting match developed between those holding the poles and those, front and aft, who held the guide ropes. 'Nay, nay, pull on it tha clown,' someone shouted, 'pull to t' right; can't tha see what's wanted?' It wasn't unknown for those who carried the big banners that stretched across the street to be lifted off their feet and flung aside. Because of his strength, not his religion, father was sometimes asked to help with the big banner. I knew when they'd slipped the pole into the leather holder that hung between his thighs, that that was one banner that would not blow over.

On one occasion, the wind proved too strong and the image of God Almighty, resplendent in the reddest of robes, who had been soaring above our heads and our hearts, was suddenly wrapped around somebody's head. It was a fate that could befall any of the radiant holy men and women whose portraits rode past at roof top on a full sail. Befittingly, the banner bearing the blue, glittering figure of the Virgin

Mary, with its inlaid profusion of lilies and roses, and its golden crown, never suffered such ignominy.

Following the Chief of Police at the head of the line was a resplendent figure who far outshone the arm of the law. He wore a long scarlet, gold-trimmed cloak with a fur collar, striped, sail-like trousers, an Admiral's hat, pointed fore and aft, and polished shoes covered with spats. In his right hand he carried a silver baton. This was the Grand Knight of Columbus, Willie Gill. No longer dishevelled, this was the real Willie Gill. Even his step had changed; he no longer slouched. Everybody knew him and they never failed to express their surprise at the transformation.

'My, what a toff tha are, Willie,' they called out. 'Tha're a one, tha're.'

Twirling his silver stick, Willie revelled in the praise. Such a day took years off his life. Not everything, certainly not the important things in the life of Willie Gill could be expressed in terms of money. There was happiness and dignity and glory to think about. I had to blink when I saw him the next day. It was like a mirage: the emperor had gone, the tramp had returned.

The best thing about the Easter processions, weather permitting, was the eating and drinking that followed. Some Easter picnics became a soggy, treacherous fight against the driving rain. If the weather was fine, having declared their faith to the entire town, the Catholics filed into somebody's meadow where large tents and food awaited them. Led by Mr Gill, the bands marched through the farm gate, taking care not to step in the cow dung, and then stopped playing. Chin straps were loosened, box hats removed, banners lowered and placed against the trees. For a few minutes people stood around wiping their foreheads and talking. A clap of the hands from the priests was the signal to begin eating. Accompanied by the tinkle of glass, the clatter of plates and the rattle of cutlery, it became a free-for-all.

The tents were full of refreshments. There were plates of bread and margarine. There were pies and cakes, jellies and preserves and buckets of hot water for the teapots. For those who could get to the barrels quick enough, there also was cider.

First time I ever felt tipsy was after drinking a glass of that cider. Either my mates and I had got in the wrong queue, or the people doling it out didn't realize that the drink was intoxicating. I knew something was wrong when my friends' speech thickened. It took a long time for the priests to catch on to what was happening. They thought our weaving about on the grass was funny. Not Father Prendergast. He was too old at the game. The moment he arrived, he took one shocked look at us and boomed: 'Serve no more cider! Satan is in the barrel!'

You wondered where such mountains of food for those Easter treats came from and how they could all be eaten. Despite the lean times, a lot of it was provided by the parishioners, the women trying to outdo each other. Each woman watched her own and other people's food to see which was eaten first. Pies and cakes that lingered were no honour to anybody and were quickly disowned.

We children slipped underneath the tables, hidden from sight by the tablecloths that reached to the ground. We crawled about there against the shuffling feet and ate like horses. To obtain our share, we periodically reached up and grabbed what we could.

When the serious business of eating and drinking was finished, everybody turned to gossiping or to playing games. We had races, tug-of-war and, while the fiddlers scraped, clog dances by a group called the Cloggers, who laughed shyly as they danced. And when that was done, we sat on benches or on the grass outside the tents, and sang. When the light failed, and the fiddles were stilled, my family had a way of reuniting and wandering home together.

———◇———

One day at school Miss Little sent me with a message to another teacher. It was eleven-thirty and I'd soon be off to the mills to deliver my family's midday meal. When I looked down the massive oak banisters on the main staircase, there wasn't a soul in sight. Apart from the drone of distant voices, all was still. I threw myself headfirst onto the banister and shot down toward the ground floor.

I arrived at the feet of Sister Loyola. There was no mistaking the shiny black shoes, the black gown with its black rosary hanging from waist to knees, and the wooden cross swinging pendulum-like before my eyes. Sister Loyola was a small figure but from that angle she looked enormous. I was seized with terror.

While she held me with her cold eyes, I wished I might fall through a crack. I was so frightened that I could neither move nor breathe. After one of the students had broken his arm, Sister Loyola had threatened dire consequences.

'Don't you know it is forbidden to slide down the banister?'

'Yes,' I stammered. My lips and tongue felt dry.

'So you have done it willfully?'

'Yes,' I faltered; yet I felt no remorse.

Before I could escape, she had grabbed me by the ear and was dragging me back up the stairs to my classroom. She twisted my ear so savagely that she made me cry.

The moment Miss Little saw Sister Loyola she took off her specs. 'Oh, dear,' she said. Miss Little did not like violence. If she was forced to punish us, she did so reluctantly and with a light hand. For this she was respected.

'Stop what you're doing!' Sister Loyola ordered the class, 'I am about to make an example of someone who willfully disobeys school regulations. Your cane!' she demanded of Miss Little.

'Oh, dear,' Miss Little repeated, adjusting her pince-nez.

Still held by the ear, I watched Miss Little go to the cupboard for her bamboo rod. Each teacher had such a cane and used it regularly. If you broke the rules, you were for it. No argument. The cane was administered either on the seat of the pants or on the hands. The rod on the seat of the pants was less painful. With Sister Loyola there was no choice. She went for the hands.

Having let go of my ear, Sister Loyola began to push back her wide sleeves. With my heart thumping, I stood there watching her, fearing the worst. She tested the rod, bending it with her hands. Then to get the feel of the cane, she struck the air several times. Whoosh, whoosh.

'Put up your hand!' she ordered. Her pale face had reddened. Her lips were set in a hard strength of will.

I raised one of my arms, offering my palm.

'Higher!' she ordered, lifting the hand with the tip of the cane.

Every eye was on the cane. Where thrashing was concerned, Sister Loyola had a reputation; it was something worth watching.

I waited, biting my lip.

Suddenly she brought the stick down across my palm and fingers with all her strength. There was a rattle of her cross and beads, and a sting of pain as if my hand had been laid open. I stifled a howl.

She cut me five more times on that hand, each cut worse than the last. I saw and felt the red weals. A shocked Miss Little stood there, hand over her mouth.

Breathing heavily, Sister Loyola demanded the other hand.

'No!' I screamed 'No!' Three cuts were the usual punishment. I'd already had six.

Sister Loyola reacted as if I'd struck her across the face. There was a murmur from the class.

'You wicked, wicked boy!' she called threatening me with her stick.

'No!' I repeated defiantly. Shaking with anger and shamed before the class, I felt rebellious, even violent. Before Sister Loyola could recover from her surprise, I lunged forward, struggled with her, and wrenched the cane out of her hand. I then rushed to the open window and flung it into the street. Avoiding Sister Loyola's outstretched hands, I ran from the room. I left my cap and coat behind; I didn't stop running until I reached my mother in the mill. Between tending the clattering machines, she heard me out.

'So much for St Peter's,' she said, doffing another can of cotton. Back to St Philips we went.

———<o>———

This traipsing backward and forward between St Philip's and St Peter's did not do the Woodruff children any harm. Other than to be given strange looks, and to be the subject of nods and whispers, which suggested that the Woodruffs had escaped from a zoo, we were never ostracized because of it. Father Prendergast and the Reverend Reeves of St Philip's (who was as lean as Father Prendergast was fat) probably took the view that the Woodruffs were not worth fighting over. The Reverend Reeves once asked me: 'Do you have the faith, my child?' I must have said something awful for the Reverend lapsed into shocked silence and never bothered me again.

All I cared about was how my street friends took this crossing of religious boundaries. Fortunately, they ignored it.

It says a lot about the privation of the early 1920's that we children were prepared to attend the church or chapel that offered most food. We didn't even worry about the difference between church and chapel. We cast our net widely: Catholic, Church of England, Congregational, Presbyterian, Methodist, Independent, Unitarian, Baptist; we tried them all. Dan had a nose for these things. All we had to do was to follow him. He darted from chapel to church, with a sure knowledge of who was offering what. We were completely unscrupulous about it. We sang anybody's hymns, provided tea and rock buns followed. Accompanied by the organist, and the earnest young preachers with good looks and sonorous voices, we sang 'Now thank we all our God,' or 'Count your blessings, name them one by one, count your blessings, see what God has done,' with copious insincerity.

We thundered out the words, 'I know not, Oh! I know not, what joys await us there, what radiance of glory, what bliss beyond compare,' but it meant nothing. Our sole concern was food.

I thought that some of the churches and chapels we visited were severe and dark. There was no beauty in them – no mystery. It made it easier if there were paintings on the walls. While the preacher preached, I could join Moses or some other Old Testament prophet, or lose myself in the maxims painted on the walls, such as: 'In everything give thanks,' or 'Abstain from evil,' or 'Cast all your care upon Him, for He careth for you,' and many more.

Both church and chapel smelled of hymnals, camphor, wax and carbolic soap. I don't know why, but everything had to be scrubbed, rubbed and polished. Scrubbing brushes were common; they were called hedgehogs, and would take the skin off you if you didn't watch out. If a thing didn't shine, as all doorknobs and brasses did, or smell of carbolic soap, as most floors did, it wouldn't do. The constant rubbing, scrubbing and small-tooth combing was the only way to cope with the dirt.

In our search for food, we were compelled to listen to innumerable sermons on sin, mortify ourselves in the long, polished pews, and endlessly repeat the Lord's Prayer. The sermon, usually delivered from a pulpit high above our heads, was literally and physically the price we paid for the refreshments, which at times seemed so far away. I suspected that the preacher was trying out his sermon on us before he gave it at the Sunday service. I really resented it when, on top of everything else, he announced: 'We will now lower our heads and examine our conscience.' That was all very well for a minute or two, but some of the preachers had a conscience the length of your arm. I think they were stretching it out before handing out the buns. It wasn't my conscience that was troubling me – it was my belly.

I hope there wasn't as much sin in town as the preachers said there was. According to them, the place was awash with big and little sins. The big sins were the ones to watch. If you dropped dead with one of those chalked up against you, you went straight to hell and stayed there – forever. It struck me odd that one of the big sins should have been gluttony. I didn't think my brother and I should stay awake at night watching for that one; not when we couldn't get enough to eat.

Not only did there seem to be a surfeit of sin about; there were so many ways in which the Devil could trap you – even without you knowing it. I was worried when I learned that you could even sin by silence. According to the preachers, you needed eyes in the back of your head to keep up with Satan. If you didn't watch out, he'd nab you and you'd be in hellfire before you knew it.

These sermons not only made me feel hot round the collar, they also puzzled me a lot. I didn't understand why I would go straight to hell for gluttony, but pull down a fairly light sentence for drunkenness. Nor did I understand how God and the devil could keep a proper tally of all the petty and mortal sins that were about.

I expect the preachers knew. I suspect that they also knew what we were up to. They never distributed food and drink until the sermon was over. Although the rock buns they handed out were too hard to be eaten quickly, we speeded things up by dunking them in the hot tea. One afternoon, with Dan's planning, a gang of us collected eight buns and eight cups of tea each from different places of worship. As a count was kept by the ministers and their prim wives of our comings and goings, our multiple appearances must have caused a staggering increase in church attendance.

During my school years, whether at St Philip's or St Peter's, I'm afraid I didn't learn much more than how to survive. I suspect that that is all that was expected of me. School was a holding pen until I entered the mills. No teacher ever wasted

time talking to me about the love of learning, or that education mattered. Nobody emphasized what good friends books
can be. Curiosity was not encouraged.

There were teachers other than Mr Manners and Miss
Little, but I have only dim impressions of what they taught.
Teachers at my elementary schools were interchangeable.
They taught a bit of everything. I know I must have taken
the eleven-year-old examination – the one in which my sister
Brenda had distinguished herself – but obviously my efforts
did not attract anybody's attention.

There must have been textbooks in my late years at school,
yet I cannot remember a single one – not in Mathematics,
not in English, not in Geography, not in History. No book
ever went home with me. My family never bought school
books. There was no homework and no report cards. I never
owned a school satchel. What would I have done with it?
Nor did I understand why some children went on to the
next class while others stayed behind.

I suspect I used school as a place where I could rest before
tackling the tasks that awaited me in the real world. My
teachers knew I was physically exhausted and were kind
enough to leave me alone. None of them ever asked me to
go chasing prizes. I was never put under severe mental strain.
Nor was I ever encouraged by my parents to take school
seriously. When in later years the seed of learning was planted
in me, it found a fertile, unworked soil in which to grow.

From the age of ten onward school was incidental. I was
up at five to deliver newspapers. I got to school as the bell
rang. From nine until eleven-forty-five I dozed; worse still,
I think I slept. At eleven-forty-five the teacher gave me a
signal, and I ran from school (sometimes with Dan) to deliver
my family's dinners in the mills. Dinner hour was from twelve
till one. The meal, a stew of meat, potatoes and vegetables,
had been cooked by mother the night before, filled into
basins, and taken to work in the morning. They were left
on a large stove in the mill warehouse. Before noon the
basins were hotted up, hence hot-pot. My family could, of

course, have collected their own dinners, but they had other things to do, and they were exhausted from having been on their feet for the past four hours. Besides, children were expected to help. I had to move quickly because, as spinners, my sisters did not work in the same mill as my parents. If there were groups of workers standing or squatting against the mill walls when I arrived, I knew I was late.

I collected the dinners from the stove where my family had placed them. I had a knack of distinguishing our basins from scores of others, because ours had a pretty pattern. But one day mother put father's hot-pot in a mud-brown basin. As it was the same as some of the others, I ran off with somebody else's bowl. The way the fellow chased after me through the factory, bawling out that I'd pinched his dinner, you might have thought that his life was at stake. Losing one's dinner was a serious matter.

I ran with each basin in my cap because it was scalding hot. I first went to father, then Jenny, then Brenda. Speed was essential; nobody wanted a cold-pot, not even Jenny and Brenda who seemed to be lathered with sweat from the heat and humidity of the spinning-room. Once I tripped and fell carrying father's dinner. It spilled into my cap: meat, potatoes, carrots, peas, gravy, the lot. All I could do was to scoop it out of my hat back into the bowl and say nothing. He never noticed, but my hat smelled for days. The last two basins were for mother and me. We ate our dinner balancing ourselves on an overturned round sliver can, our backs wedged against the whitewashed wall. We had to cover the hot-pot from the fine dust that fell like a gentle rain.

It wasn't difficult to know when the dinner hour was done. Precisely at one, somebody threw a lever, and with a creak, crack, thump and clatter the whole room began to tremble and shake. Once the machinery became alive and the myriad wheels began to turn, you either jumped up smartly and set about your business, or you found yourself in trouble. The machine was the boss, it wouldn't wait, and it took no excuses. Glad to escape the din, I raced back to school. From one-thirty to four I must have dozed again. After four I ran the streets with the evening edition of the local newspaper. Then I came home and ran errands.

———◦———

Running in and out of the mills daily, I could hardly fail to learn something about textile manufacture. I watched mother breaking up the bales of cotton, clean, blend, whirl and pound them until a continuous sheet of matted tufts called a lap emerged. This was called slubbing. The lap was then fed into the carder which had two rollers covered with fine wire teeth to break up the tufts and separate the individual fibres. From the carder the untwisted rope of cotton (a sliver) was coiled in tall cans. The sliver, about an inch in diameter, was then combed to remove the shorter fibres, drawn across smooth leather-covered rollers, twisted into a long, firm thread, after which it was wound onto large spinning bobbins. This was roving. The bobbins went to the spinner where the threads were blended, drawn and twisted some more. Jenny and Brenda were spinners.

The resulting yarn, both warp and weft, came in all kinds of threadcounts, or thicknesses. It was then woven. My father was a weaver. He spent his life 'kissing the shuttle.' It was called 'kissing the shuttle' because he drew the weft thread from the cop by sucking it through a small hole at one end of the shuttle.

The workers, including my own family, took pride in explaining their work. It was like being admitted to a secret society. They were serious about it. When they talked about cloth, hilarity stopped. Problems that arose in the mill during the day, such as when the weave or pattern was varied, were discussed at night until a solution was found. Men or women were not judged so much by what they did at home but by what they did in the mill. People respected skill. Pride of work meant a lot. Work was everything.

Chapter X

Blackpool Rock

I think the years from the early twenties to the mid-thirties were rather like Lancashire weather: generally awful, with bright periods. One such bright period occurred when my parents suddenly decided to take us to Blackpool.

It must have been in 1924 or 1925, when the textile industry had made a partial recovery from the crash of 1920. Anyway, my people were in jobs, otherwise we wouldn't have had the money.

We went during Wake's Week, a traditional holiday originally linked with the Church. Each cotton town had its own particular Wake's Week when everything was shut down. The mill owners spent the week doing maintenance and stock-taking. The workers – if they had the money – escaped to the hills or the sea. We hoped that the Morgans might join us, but they covered up by saying, 'No, we've decided against going away for the week. We're just going for days. There's nothing like your own bed.' We knew that talk of going away for days was humbug, but the pretence was kept up.

It was agreed by my family that we'd get away at the crack of dawn on the Saturday morning after the mills had stopped. Until then we children talked and slept Blackpool. Mother slipped me a coin to buy a new bucket and spade. When the day came we were up before dawn straining to go. We searched the sky for the sun. The family's one and only straw valise was got out and filled with food. As the price of food at Blackpool was too high, we took bread, oats, a large can of Lyle's syrup, margarine, cans of milk, fish and pineapple chunks, tea, sugar, eggs marked with our name, a jar of jam, a jar of piccalilli relish, salt and sauce. The clothes we took were on our back. Having left two shillings under the pot dogs on the mantelpiece to pay for iron rations when we returned broke, we locked the door and left the house. The week's rent we took with us to spend in Blackpool.

Father went first, carrying the valise with a leather strap round it, then mother, then us. Our first stop was the King's Arms, where our parents vanished. Jenny, Brenda, Dan and I were left to amuse ourselves on the pub step. Fortunately, the King's Arms had two marble pillars at the entrance that looked like potted meat. Jenny at once took charge. She pretended that the doorway was her shop. The rest of us lined up before an imaginary counter and placed our orders for potted meat. With an imaginary knife, Jenny (with the pub regulars stepping over us) pretended to cut slices off the pillars to feed us.

One customer, a twinkle in his eye, stopped and talked to us.

'What you up to?'

'I've opened a potted meat shop,' said Jenny.

'Oh, you 'ave, 'ave you? Where's your folks?'

'Inside.'

'Going to Blackpool, are you?' The stranger eyed our buckets and spades.

'Yis,' said Brenda.

'How much did you say your potted meat was?'

'It's very special today,' said Jenny. 'Sixpence a pound.'

'Well, I'll take two bob's worth.'

With our eyes popping, Jenny 'cut' four pounds of meat according to the customer's order. She 'weighed' it, 'wrapped' it, and 'handed' it to him carefully. The man pretended to put the packet in his pocket. After that he gave Jenny a real two shilling piece.

'That'll be a tanner each,' he said.

'Oh, thank you,' we rejoiced.

'Ta, Ta!' he said. 'Remember me when you're on't sands.'

'Oh, we will,' we chorused.

We'd 'eaten' an enormous amount of potted meat by the time our parents emerged. By now they were full of the holiday spirit. There followed further stops at the Lord Derby and The Plough. Each stop increased our fears. What if our parents drank so much that we might never get to the station? What if we had to drag them back to the house drunk? We need not have worried.

I'd noticed for some time that something was dribbling from the valise that father was carrying, but had kept a still tongue. Nothing must prevent us getting on the train. Eventually even father noticed that something was wrong. The procession was halted, the strap undone, the top of the valise lifted.

'It's the bloody syrup,' father exploded, staring at the confused heap of syrup-saturated clothes and provisions at his feet. 'You wouldn't believe it, the damned stuff's everywhere.'

With us all looking on, he separated the can and its lid from the other items in the suitcase. Staring at the empty, two pound tin in disbelief, he said the most awful things about syrup in general and Lyle's syrup in particular. Then he kicked the empty can into the street, slammed the valise shut, fastened the strap, and marched off in a towering rage toward the station. His foul mutterings could be heard yards away.

We children followed, breathing a sigh of relief.

Still dripping syrup, we climbed aboard the train. It was

an excursion train and it was packed. It was good humour all the way. Everybody had broken loose. If anybody had talked about cotton on that train he'd have been thrown out onto the track, headfirst.

On arrival in Blackpool we were told to rush past the ticket barrier. Only mother and father had tickets. 'If you're caught, act daft,' father said. Following Dan and my sisters – Jenny although fifteen was so small that she passed as a child – I dashed past the ticket collectors. They paid no attention to us. Once past the barrier, we waited for our parents at the station entrance. The rich children we saw were clean and tidy, wore respectable clothes, and had clean noses. They shouted respectability. No dashing past the ticket collectors for them.

From the station we walked to a lodging house in the back streets. Father paid for a week on arrival. The family shared one bedroom. There were lots of other Blackburn children in the house with whom we could play.

We abandoned our parents on arrival and only joined them for meals. Sitting on benches, in sand-streaked bathing suits, we ate twice a day with all the other families in a large room downstairs. Everybody squeezed in where they could. Nobody dreamed of grumbling. We'd come from the same town, some from the same street. We belonged together. There wasn't a sad face among us. Old and young, we'd promised ourselves a treat in Wake's Week, and we were not going to be done out of it. The dining-room table and benches rocked with laughter. Every meal was a joyful shouting match.

Aside from the smells, and the queuing for the toilet, everything was bliss. In the dining room the landlady's word was law; nobody answered back. She was skilled at her job, and knew how to get us out of the house when she wanted to. The only subdued person there was the landlady's husband who seemed to do most of the work.

As long as the weather was fine – and it was with us – we spent our time on the beach or paddling in the sea. We ran wild. What the adults did was their business.

A week later, with long faces, and our mouths stuffed with 'Blackpool Rock,' we caught the train home. It seemed to go faster on the return journey. There was no stopping at pubs, or pretending to eat potted meat. Our week of make-believe was over.

After Blackpool, Blackburn air hung like lead.

Chapter XI

Running Wild

I began to run wild from about the age of seven. Our house was so small that my brother and I were happier on the street. To sit around at home was to run the risk of being given a job. As I was the youngest, and Dan had a way of disappearing, I was invariably caught for these jobs. Meat scraps or a soup bone had to be obtained from the butcher. Fish heads and tails had to be collected from the fishmonger. I knew that when I went to the butcher I mustn't fail. 'Mam asks if you can let her have some scraps,' I'd say. I carried a dodger in case my pleading eyes failed to break down his resistance to part with bits of meat for nothing. I returned with my bundle of scraps wrapped in newspaper. Same with the fish heads. Printer's ink was part of our diet.

Going to the cobbler for new irons on our clogs was another job I had to do. While my family sat at home in their stockinged feet, I sat with other children by the cobbler's last. We slid along the polished bench until our turn came. Grown-ups were served first.

173

The cobbler lived a few doors away. He sat in his front room, bent over his work, with a gas lamp at his side. The lamp had mirrors around it, which gave an unusually bright light. The whole place smelled of sweaty feet and wood shavings. For front cokers (metal runners attached to the wooden sole) I paid eightpence; for heels fourpence; for a toe cap twopence. With his tools and wood in easy reach, the cobbler cut and shaped new clogs to size. They had a stout leather upper, a wooden sole and a heel strengthened with iron cokers.

I marvelled how the man filled his mouth with nails and wooden fillings, and how he seemed to fire them from his mouth at the clogs – like bullets from a gun. He never missed. When he stood up to shake the shavings off his leather apron, I noticed the stoop of his shoulders. Perhaps because his mouth was full of pegs and nails, he didn't talk much.

Chores finished, I dashed away to join a gang of boys in the often rain-darkened streets. When the paper blinds were drawn, each cottage became a shiny, orange-patched island in the dark. There were usually eight to twelve of us, huddled together in the dark in a mill shed. When it was raining outside, we sat and talked. Our favourite topic was sport. A run of victories for the town's football team, the Rovers, kept us talking for weeks. A child murder up Whalley way occupied us for a month. We were astonished at the dreadful things grown-ups could get up to.

If all else failed, we sat entranced while Shorty Cooke – one of the gang – told us a story that we all knew was a whopping lie. 'I don't think you've heard this one,' he'd begin. He told his tale so naturally and so convincingly that you wanted to believe him. One of his best tales was the visit he and his father had made to the Cup Final at Wembley in London. He had it all off pat. Yet we knew that he and his dad had never been beyond the tram ride to Whalley Bridge. Shorty ran a firewood business out of an old pram. He sold penny bundles of firewood, which he bought from a dealer in bulk, extracting a stick from each bundle and selling it again.

Often the gang shared a cigarette, passing it from mouth to mouth. Shorty Cooke always had a fag. We suspected he had pilfered them, but we never pressed him. We thought it manly to smoke and, of course, we were men. We inhaled deeply, and took pride in blowing the smoke down our noses. When the mood took us, we carried out raids on neighbouring territory. We didn't use knives; we couldn't afford them, but we did carry catapults, stones and sticks. For a few bruises, we rid ourselves of all our aggression.

Girls didn't take part in our fights; they were kept at home. Until we reached our teens, sex didn't interest us. We preyed on courting couples for the fun of it. Our flashlights were detested by them as they clung to each other against the dark mill walls.

In the nipping cold of winter I kept myself warm with a portable winter warmer – an empty Oxo beef tin, which I first perforated with a nail and then filled with slow-burning cotton waste. I carried the flat tin – half as big as my hand – inside my shirt. Periodically, to keep it nice and hot, I took it out of my shirt and whirled it around on the end of a string. I rarely set myself alight.

On Wednesday nights (market night), I'd run with several mates across the stall-covered town square snatching fruit and vegetables. There were scores of naphtha-lit stalls, selling the same produce. I didn't take the fresh stuff, I took the discarded produce thrown into the bins standing between the stalls. It wasn't as easy as you might think. I had to run, jump, hang on to the bin, reach down, sort out the rotten produce in the half-dark, fill my pockets, and make my escape before a rod descended across the seat of my pants – as it sometimes did. Successful raids ended, I'd crouch beneath a hissing gas lamp and eat enough fruit and vegetables to last the week.

Saturday morning, before I took to going to the reading room in the town library, I usually spent at the stockyards. To earn a penny or two, groups of us would struggle across a bog of steaming manure to help the farmers drive the cattle they'd bought to their farms in the surrounding hills.

When business was slow, we sat on top of a wall gaping through the barred windows of the Sumner Street Abattoir to watch the slaughter going on within. We ignored shouts of bugger off. It puzzled me how a powerful bull could be felled with a single blow to its head. One moment there was a mountain of muscle, the next moment a carcass of bones and flesh. Pigs had their throats cut, squealing all the time; after which they were thrown into great tubs of boiling water.

I agonized over the lambs and sheep. With frightened eyes they climbed a death walk in front of where I was sitting. They seemed to appeal to me for help. Instead, I watched them being stabbed through the head. Blood was everywhere. 'Look out! Look out!' I shouted, but I never saved one. I didn't understand why they died so meekly. As long as I stared through that window, I refused to accept the inevitability of death. I wanted the animals to kick and fight.

On a Saturday morning, our gang looked in on the open-air market on the town square. For a few pennies, we could buy a 'thoroughbred' puppy, or a rabbit, or a ferret (to catch the rabbit), or a singing bird, or a pocketful of tame mice, or a goldfish in a bowl. 'Real diamonds' cost sixpence each; a 'gold watch' made of brass a shilling; 'new' false teeth or spectacles, whose owners were in the graveyard, two shillings and sixpence. For nothing at all, we watched a man almost kill himself lifting heavy weights.

From the late 1920's onward, with the coming of the talking pictures, we spent many Saturday afternoons at the cinema. We paid to get in by handing over two empty, clean, two-pound jam jars. The matinee, solely for children, was a wild affair where a man kept order with a long bamboo pole. If we were caught blowing rice or rock-hard peas at the pianist, or spitting orange pips from the balcony, or whistling too long at the kissing scenes, we ran the risk of getting whacked over the head – a real hard whack.

Talking pictures opened up a new, exciting world for me. With two jam jars, I first saw Charlie Chaplin. It is impossible to convey the impression the earliest films made. It was like seeing the first electric light, or the first automobile. In exchange for two empty jam jars my spirit soared across the great plains of America as far as the Rockies. I jolted along in a covered wagon, gun on knee. There were times when, glued to my seat, I feared the red Indian warriors as much as any white settler had done.

When we children were not at the films, we were watching the town's football team, the Rovers. We got in by sliding across a neighbouring roof. Once in the ground we scattered; better one of us thrown out than the lot. I was crazy about football. The first time I heard thousands of people – caps in hand – sing 'Abide with Me' was late one afternoon at the Rover's ground. The words of the hymn appeared on a screen. To keep time with the band, one simply followed a little ball that jumped from word to word.

> Abide with me; fast falls the eventide;
> The darkness deepens; Lord with me abide;
> When other helpers fail, and comforts flee,
> Help of the helpless, O, abide with me.
>
> Swift to its close ebbs out life's little day;
> Earth's joy grow dim, its glories pass away;
> Change and decay in all around I see;
> O thou who changest not, abide with me.

The singing gave me gooseflesh.

Everybody but the dead and the dying watched the Rovers. Nothing was allowed to interfere with a game, not even a snowstorm. We'd rush off to a match with our rosettes and rattles as if our lives depended on it. When the Rovers played, the town's honour was at stake. Only Aston Villa had won the Football Association Cup more times than Blackburn – six times against our five. We spent Saturday afternoon at the game and the rest of the week arguing over the result. Next Saturday the madness began all over again. If a player left Blackburn to get better pay elsewhere, we took it as an insult. He'd put money before the game. One year, by illicitly raffling the same two pound bag of sugar over and over again, our street gang equipped our own football team with Rover colours. We played on a nearby tip, using caps for goal posts.

I was eleven when the Rovers won the Football Association Cup at Wembley Stadium in 1928. Few things have provided me with such excitement. The match against Huddersfield was broadcast all over town. My mates and I listened to every word. It was the first time the final had been broadcast by radio from London. We heard the king and queen arrive and the singing and the playing of the massed bands. It came over the radio as real as being on the field with the ninety thousand fans.

It was amazing what Blackburn did. Everybody said we were in for a licking. After all, Huddersfield had a far better record in League football that year than we had. They had a far better team. Their forward line was the best in the country; their centre forward, Jackson, was the bane of all goalkeepers. Some said he was as good as Stanley Matthews, the greatest of our football idols. But our eleven finished up beating theirs by three goals to one, just the same.

How did we do it? Well, in the first minute our centre forward, Roscamp, scored a goal by bundling Huddersfield's goalkeeper Mercer, ball and all, into the net. It took our breath away. You could hear the roar of the Blackburn fans all the way from London. After that it was our game. By half-time we had a lead of two goals to none. Huddersfield fought back in the second half, but our half-back, Campbell, bottled up their forward time and again. Only Jackson got past him to score Huddersfield's single goal. Roscamp offset that by scoring the third goal for Blackburn. Puddefoot, another of our heroes, just missed scoring a fourth.

When the final whistle blew, we all danced for joy. The town went mad. It remained mad until long after the victors came home bearing the precious trophy. It had been 37 years since we'd won the cup before. In 1928, we equalled Aston Villa's record. At the station the team was mobbed; traffic was stopped. My mates and I followed the players around the town. Where Association Football was concerned, we were top of the pile.

Most Saturday nights found us at St Philip's church hall, where they held a weekly sixpenny dance. At the interval, hot tea and meat pies were served. The dance hall had a pork pie smell. Some dancers seemed to enjoy slipping us hot meat pies as much as we enjoyed eating them. Once, when we were very hungry, we set some mice free during the spotlight dance when most of the room was in darkness. We helped ourselves during the confusion, and ran for our lives.

To escape from the murky darkness of the streets into the lighted dance hall was the highlight of my week. Unlike some of my companions, who were concerned solely to obtain meat pies, I loved the lights, the music and the air of romance. To see the mill girls prettied up with their curled hair and white dresses, and all the boys in their tight-fitting suits, raised my spirits. Everybody knew everybody else, and it was all very friendly. It was so intimate and intense that there was no room for wallflowers.

Being there every Saturday night, I knew all the dances. My two sisters danced as well as anybody; especially Jenny who danced as light as a feather. If she hadn't had a partner to hang on to, I think she might have flown round the dance hall.

The spot-dance, especially when it was a waltz, was my favourite. The moment the main lights were switched off, and the spotlight was switched on, a hush fell on the room. The ceiling became a mass of tiny twinkling stars. The girls' necklaces, bangles and earrings – all glass – winked in the flashes of light. Everything became remote. With the spotlight darting about the room, I watched the dancers swaying like a gentle wave, to the muffled tap of the drum. 'Moonlight and roses bring wonderful memories of you . . .'

Sitting under one of the tables, peeping through the table-cloth, I went on hearing the music long after the band was stilled.

It was a let-down when the lights were turned on again. The moonlight and roses, the princes and princesses had all departed; a pushing, perspiring crowd of cotton workers had taken their place.

With my mates, I also visited the music hall. As they didn't barter seats for jam jars, we either had to furtively make our way in via the endless concrete back steps, from which we tried to slip into the gods, or find a relative or friend to smuggle us in. If we failed to penetrate the theatre's defences, we'd find out where the freaks and curiosities were lodging, and carry out a vigil outside the house in order to watch them for free.

The first of such vigils I made was before a row of houses in Talbot Street several streets away from the theatre. We arrived there about forty minutes before curtain time. It was winter, dark and misty. We didn't know where The Tallest Man in the World, The Smallest Man in the World, and The Wild Man from Borneo were staying, but we knew they were there. We decided to divide our forces. Each of us patrolled several houses, ready to give a shout if anything happened. I was told to walk up and down at one end of the street.

I was staring at the front of one of the houses when I felt my hair rising. Peering through the window above the door-way was a man's face. He fixed me with his eyes. A man would have to stand on a ladder to peer through there. I was looking at The Tallest Man in the World.

Instead of raising the alarm, I froze and stared back. Moments later a taxi pulled up at the curb; it was without a roof. The door of the house opened, The Tallest Man in the World lowered his head, hurried down the stone steps, crossed the pavement without looking to the left or right, climbed into the open taxi and sat bolt upright. I could have touched him.

He was followed by The Smallest Man in the World, who

didn't reach as high as The Tallest Man's knee; yet from the way he bore himself, I knew he was a man not a child. He looked at me as if he didn't like being seen for free. Behind him came The Wild Man from Borneo, complete with skins, feathers, shield and spear. He grinned in my face, but I was too scared to laugh back.

By the time my mates had run from the other end of the street, they saw only the back of the car and the head and shoulders of The Tallest Man in the World. We went back there the next night and the next, until we had had our fill.

One day I was allowed to go on my own to a children's matinee of R. L. Stephenson's *Treasure Island*. Somehow, I'd got two pennies to pay my way into the gods. From up there it was like looking down into a magic kingdom. No man has ever frightened me as much as Long John Silver did. When it was over I rushed into the street and grabbed the first person I saw – a nice old gentleman – to tell him all about it. 'I want to warn you against Long John Silver. He's treacherous. He'll stop at nothing.' The old man must have understood children. He rested himself on his walking stick and, with a benign look, and the odd 'Well!' or 'You don't say,' heard me out. He seemed as revolted by the treachery of Long John as I.

The floodlit world of the theatre was far more real than reality to us. We entered into it, took part in it, even to the extent of shouting warnings to the heroine and hissing the villain. The audience in the gods was completely uninhibited. 'Bloody scoundrel thi are, knocking t' lass about like that,' somebody bawled. If we shouted too much, someone else yelled 'Shut thi gob!'

The trouble with some people is that they went on nursing their grievances long after the play was over. They stood outside the stage door and hissed the actors they didn't like as they left. The villain – however striking – had to watch his step when returning to his lodgings. 'Ah could teach thee a lesson or two,' they called after him. 'A thorough bad un thi are.'

181

When we'd nothing better to do, we flew our linen kites above the mill tip. The wind was always waiting for us. It could change its course so capriciously. Although I plotted and planned against it, I once lost my kite. I often wondered where the wind came from and where it was bound. I envied its freedom to come roaring over the hills and go its way.

Now and again we shared the tip with groups of unemployed workers who, desperate for something to do, played marbles or pitch and toss by the hour. Occasionally they organized a dog and rat fight. After laying bets, the dogs were matched against the rats. The man whose dog killed most rats was the winner. There was no sport in it. The rats never had a chance. From the moment they were let out of the cage, they tried to get away. When the dog went after them they crouched and squealed with fear. I never saw a dog bitten, but I saw a lot of rats killed. Those that escaped and sought refuge in the outer tip were slain by men with picking sticks. It was a cruel sport.

As we grew older, we boys took to chasing each other in and out of the town's clay pits, fighting each other with clay balls. The girls preferred to mold the clay into bread and cakes and play shop. They even made a clay currency. In summer we ran barefoot through abandoned quarries filled with nettles and dandelions, keeping a sharp look-out for broken glass. Alone, or with other gangs, we fought pitched battles along the canals and, if there were no courting couples there, or tramps setting up house, defended the railway tunnels from attack.

Oblivious of danger, we chased each other across single-line railway bridges where it was strictly forbidden to go. One winter day, three friends and I were caught on such a bridge. A coal train was upon us before we knew it, swaying toward us at an alarming speed, puffing blue smoke. We knew that the only safety bay was farther on, beyond our reach. It was too late to run back; the track was frozen and slippery. Terrified, we scrambled over a metal screen and, fully dressed, jumped into the icy canal – that is all except

Wilfred Green who fled before the train. As I fell, I felt the train thunder past above my head.

With the other two boys, I dragged myself out of the canal. Our teeth were chattering, our lips were turning blue; ice was forming on our clothing. We lay on the bank for several minutes gasping for breath. In the distance, the train rattled and rumbled on its way.

'We'd better find out where Wilf's got to,' one of us said.

We clambered up the steep bank until we reached the track again. Wilfred Green had disappeared.

'Wilf!' we shouted, 'Wilf!'

Shivering with cold, we began to walk back across the bridge, puzzled where he'd got to.

We found a lumpy object at the end of the bridge. It was Wilf. He was lying on his belly, at the side of the track. He didn't look like Wilf Green anymore; not the Wilf Green who always came out on top of our fights. He looked like a crumpled, blood-stained sack tossed out of the train. His legs had been severed at the knees. Speechless, we stood and stared.

We had the wind up too much to touch him. Instead, we backed away and fled across the bridge to a signal box. Breathlessly, we told the man in the box what had happened. Then we all ran home, slantwise across the fields.

For a long time Wilfred Green's life hung in the balance. Youth, to say nothing of medical care, pulled him through. In time he was fitted with false legs with which he began life anew. In the hospital, and in the streets later on, he avoided those of us who had been with him when he lost his legs. He wasn't blaming us – at least I don't think so – it was just that he'd begun a new life, which for reasons that he knew best, he didn't want to share with us. Mother said his pride was at stake.

After several weeks of sitting around and wondering whether Wilf would live or die, life went on as before. Undeterred by the near fatality, whole evenings were given up to playing king of the mountain on one of the slag heaps near Nig Lane. The slag heaps were pyramid-shaped piles from disused mines in the Dells End district, well outside the town. Hundreds of feet high, they were a blight on the skyline. Nobody wanted them; nobody knew what to do with them; no grown-ups went near them. Meanwhile they rotted, fumed, and fouled up the local canal and everything else in the vicinity.

The pools of stagnant water that stood at the foot of the tailings fascinated us. They were every colour of the rainbow. We were not afraid of the nettles that grew there. Reciting the words: 'Gently stroke a nettle and it will sting you for your pain; grasp it like a man of mettle and it soft as silk will remain,' we grabbed a handful and hoped for the best. Everybody had to pass the 'nettle test.'

Slipping and sliding about among the rubble, one gang defended the summit, while the others – no holds barred – tried to dislodge them. It was hard work dragging yourself up to the top and then slithering down again. It also had its dangers; landslides happened on the steep slopes. In summer, if we got too dirty and too hot, and the light was still good, we stripped off and 'One, two, three,' threw each other into the canal. When the seasons changed and winter came, we deserted the slag heaps and went sledding. Headfirst, we'd come whizzing down the hillsides, disregarding the trees and the great clods of heavy wet snow that fell upon us. The closer to the trees we came, the more exhilarating the ride.

With water everywhere – teeth-chattering cold water even in the summer – we learned to swim young. The canal was a dirty colour, but the river Blakewater or Blackwater that ran through town was worse. Its walled banks by the mills were stained with mill dyes. Although forbidden to children, we one day went wading in the black, murky river by the factories looking for fish. 'You shouldn't be in there. It's dangerous!' a woman shouted over a low wall. We took no notice of her. We turned over stone after stone without finding a fish. The river was dead.

In all our wild escapades, we seldom ran foul of the police.

For us they had a stigma; we were brought up to distrust and avoid them. We distrusted them because they defended the rich. We avoided them because they used their truncheons rather than words. We got the 'short end of the stick.'

———<o>———

The long summer school holiday was the period of greatest freedom. We fled the factories and the smoking chimneys for the hills, and empty, wind-swept moorlands outside the town. We fled like farm animals escaping from the long winter indoors. Girls and boys went together. Having been shut up, we discovered the sun, the moon and the stars again. The vast expanse of the countryside made us feel free. Our parents didn't bother that we might get lost, or drowned, or gored by a bull, or fall out of a tree, or break our necks. Children were not the focus of their life, work was. Dan avoided these outings, Jenny and Brenda were by now too old. Rosie Gill and Annie Morgan always came.

With a little food in our pockets, and accompanied by birdsong, in a straggling band, we ranged the countryside from morning to night, getting hotter as the day wore on. They were long summer days that never seemed to end. We explored the surrounding villages such as Feniscowles, Riley Green, Copster Green, Tockholes and Ribchester. Every Lancashire child knows that 'chester' means the site of a Roman camp. Ribchester was not just another village; it was the ancient crossroads of Roman communications, one arm of which went from Ilkley Moor in the east to the Fylde in the west, the other arm from Manchester, twenty-five miles to the south, to Carlisle, ninety miles to the north.

We were proud of our link with the Romans. We knew a lot about centurions, and the Roman heavy cavalry, and which legion was where. We relived our Roman history, walking the ancient roads, storming the ancient walls, stirring the pigeons out of the Roman ruins, and with exultant war-whoops, slaying the fiercest of Roman soldiers before they had time to seize their swords or sound their horns. One thing we all knew was that the Romans had built the Wall of Hadrian – seventy-three miles long across northern Britain, one hundred miles to our north. After keeping guard there for three hundred years, they got tired of our weather and went home. A lot of different people must have followed the Romans in Britain. Yet it is the Romans we remembered best.

When we were not killing Romans, we robbed birds' nests, mimicked bird calls, plucked berries, chased butterflies, fished, rabbited, skimmed pebbles across the water, and ran down the turf-clad banks to swim in the Ribble, at one time the boundary between England and Scotland. That part of our sex education which we had not already acquired in our homes we obtained by following the activities of the stallions and mares, the bulls and cows, the cocks and hens we chanced upon in the fields. Steeped in local lore, we were ever watchful for witches and fairies, especially if a mist was about. We knew that at certain times of the year witches were quite common on Pendle Hill; also that eaves-dropping elves lived in caves, or in the roots of trees, or under large rocks and were best left alone.

We knew the eerie stories connected with certain farms and buildings. Salmesbury Hall was haunted by a white lady. On dark, stormy nights ghostly horsemen rode across the moors. We took it for granted that unseen eyes were watching us as we hurried by. One field we avoided was where a milkmaid had been murdered. Some grown-ups swore that on dark nights she could be heard walking in the meadow, weeping. We knew every grim detail. We also avoided old church yards with their sloping, moss-covered stones, lest we should be caught unawares. Having run ourselves to a standstill, we made a bed on the turf and slept among the daisies.

All summer long, we ran as free as the wind. Provided we closed all farm gates behind us and didn't interfere with the grazing cattle and sheep, we were free to follow a path or a rushing beck (stream) wherever it led. Nobody bothered us. Late in the afternoons, we would look in at a farmhouse to watch them milk. I thought the way the milk squirted from the udders into the pail was magical. I loved the sloshing of milk from one pail to another. To be given a mug of warm milk with cream on top, whose sweet smell was equal to its taste, was to know what paradise was all about. Our best bet for a free drink were men milkers, not women. Naturally, we all drank from the same mug.

The only authority we recognized was that of the older children. If the oldest was a girl, she ruled; it was her job to bring us home safely. In town each child was responsible for its own acts; when roving the countryside we acted as a group. We depended upon each other. Everything had to be shared. There was no 'iffing' and 'butting,' no sticking out. You kept the rules or you didn't go next time.

Before dark we'd be home again, achingly hungry, with grazed knees and elbows, and perhaps a sunburn. We brought with us bundles of nettles for nettle-beer, cresses and docks; armfuls of flowers; and stained linen bags filled with berries. The older children knew which berries to take and which, like the baneberry, to leave alone. Sometimes we'd come home: sodden, wet through, icy-cold, and our clothes full of clinging, prickly burrs. Always our energies were spent, our instincts and our imagination satisfied. Life may have been dangerous – jagged rocks and seemingly bottomless holes in the river were the greatest hazard – but it was never dull. We lived in a world of intense activity; a world in which we didn't have enough time to fit everything in.

The sights, smells, and feelings of those long summer treks were intoxicating. Lying on our backs in the grass, we watched the cloud shadows moving smoke-like across hill and dale. Around us was the bulk of the hills, where the soil lay barren. To get to Whalley Abbey, we had to wade across a sea of bluebells, daffodils, violets, and primroses. We passed hedgerows covered with flowering currants and white hawthorn and damson trees white with blossom. Smoky-faced lambs skittered behind drystone walls that climbed endlessly across the fells into a windy sky. We never went far without smelling lilies of the valley, or new-mown hay, or the peculiar dry smell of the heather at the end of a long hot day. In our ears was the song of the pewit, the curlew, and the lark. The hills echoed to the singing streams and the shrill whistle of the shepherd calling his dogs.

If the weather went against us, we played king of the mountain in one of the cottages after the adults had gone to work. Girls were banished from these games. Armed with pillows, one gang defended the top of the staircase while the other tried to dislodge it. Repeatedly, somebody fell down the stairs without coming to any harm. More damage was done to the pillows than to us.

Sometimes foul weather was disregarded. We went out just the same. During my unfortunate, short-term career as a Wolf Cub Scout, I competed in a fire lighting contest on an island in the Ribble in the pouring rain.

When the signal to begin was given, I ransacked the island for dry twigs and dead grass. I had lit a fire in the rain before, and I knew to start with dead leaves. To the burning leaves I added a tiny stick or two. Until the fire got going, I protected it from the rain with my cap.

My fire was crackling and sending up clouds of sparks before the other fires were lit. I'd used only one of the two matches we'd been given. I must say, the Scout Master didn't like it when I gave him the other match back.

I won because I was determined to win. I wanted to show them that a stained cap, patched pants and a torn jersey had nothing to do with being the best Cub Scout.

I loved every minute I spent with the Scouts. I'd joined them not because my parents said I should, but because scouting seemed to me such a good idea. It was what I was looking for. I loved the knot-tying, the First Aid and all the rest. I really believed in it. My nemesis was the Scout master's mother who used to attend our meetings in St Alban's Church Hall at the other side of town. There was no Scout troop at

St Peter's or St Philip's. She and I didn't hit it off. She was always tidying me up, which I resented. She didn't have to keep saying how odd I looked in my ragamuffin outfit. I was tired of her treating me as an ugly duckling. It irked me so. She made it plain that I just didn't fit in, and the sooner I left the better. I suppose I'd jumped into the wrong pond.

'Oh?' was all my parents said when I asked them to buy a scout uniform 'Oh?' I did raise tenpence to purchase the Scout necktie and a leather-studded fastener, but that wasn't good enough. I was issued an ultimatum by the serious young man who led us: 'Cub Scout cap and a uniform, or out!'

I was sad and humiliated when they threw me out. I just didn't feel it was fair, especially as I was enjoying it, and I had won the firelighting contest. 'Oh,' was all my parents said when I told them that I no longer was a Cub Scout 'Oh.' For a long time afterward when moving about the town, I followed my troop's way of alternating running with walking. Run a hundred steps, walk a hundred steps, and so on. It made me feel that I was still part of the group.

On an earlier occasion, before I joined the Scouts, Harold Watkins and I had borrowed a bike and cycled down to the Ribble to camp there. I rode on the carrier with a borrowed tent, food, blankets and a pot wedged between me and the saddle. The ride was endless and bumpy. I gripped the seat springs in front of me so hard, and for so long, that I couldn't release my fingers when we got there. I also had severe cramp in my bottom and my legs. I had to run up and down the river bank, flapping my arms, trying to restore my circulation.

As we set up the tent, we watched as swallows skimmed the foaming river, feasting on clouds of gnats. Rings showed the currents' flow.

Harold and I must have been very hungry, because we ate our two day's rations during the first long twilight. Food gone, our troubles began. Unlike the warm day that had preceded it, the night became cold with a chilly breeze. The damp rose from the ground and penetrated our limbs. We sat up at every sound. One moment we were certain that someone was being strangled to death at the water's edge; the next moment somebody seemed to be crying for help from the river. Now and again, an owl hooted close by.

Shaking with cold and fear, we stuck our heads through the tent flap, and looked around. Nothing looked as it had done in daylight. The ground was a wet, misty grey. Mysterious shapes were everywhere. We had a feeling of being completely lost. I wondered out loud whose silly idea it had been for us to be there at all. Harold guardedly suggested that the idea had been mine. I really wasn't up to fighting him, so I let his silly comment pass. Blankets round our shoulders, we struggled from beneath the tent fly and walked up and down the river bank, talking to each other in strange, muffled voices. We agreed that when light came, we'd go home. Only when the blood was flowing again – we'd been walking about as stiff as posts – did we notice the starlit beauty of the sky. Our interest in stars, however, was fleeting. We crept back into our damp tent and slept.

Several hours later, before daybreak, we were wakened by a cow lowing. From the noise it was making it might have been an elephant in mortal agony. Unable to sleep with that din in our ears, we got up to investigate. It was a black and white Jersey lying on the bank closeby. With her big, sad eyes, she seemed to welcome us. While bellowing across the valley, she heaved and strained. When a calf's head popped out from her rear end, I knew why she wailed so.

I'd seen a calf born before, but this birth was no less magical. I stood there awestruck. Despite the early hour, the flies began to swarm. We tried to help the cow by driving them off with our caps. The cow didn't mind. By now she had stopped her lowing and was purring like a large contented cat. We marvelled at the way she cleaned her calf with wet, sloppy licks. Nobody had to tell the calf what to do. It struggled to its wobbly legs from a bed of buttercups and began to feed from its mother's udder. It made us feel glad that we'd come.

Though still before daybreak, I thought we should tell the farmer that he'd got a calf. With the soft light changing from grey to silver, we tramped down the misty bank in the direction of the farm house. The river sang at our side, toppling and turning in the dark shadows. Chewing their cud, other cows placidly ignored our passing. Glittering, dew-soaked cobwebs lay on the tufted grass. Across the fields a plaintive curlew called. The last bats of the night flickered by. At the house there were dogs barking, but no lights. We had to throw stones at the windows to waken the farmer. After several throws, a wild-looking head appeared.

'What's t' want?' the farmer demanded sharply.

'Tha's got a calf,' I shouted, disregarding his ugly look.

'Oh, Ah 'av, 'av Ah?'

'Tha 'as.'

'Wheer?'

'Down t' bank. He woke us up.'

'Tha's woke me up. Cudn't ya 've cum 'n told me after cockcrow?'

'We thowt tha'd want te know.'

'Ya did, did ya?'

'Ai, besides, we're goin' 'oom.'

'Well, that's summat,' said the farmer as he slammed down the window.

'Cheeky bugger,' I said to Harold. 'He doesn't seem to appreciate us tellin' 'im.'

With the sky becoming lighter, we went home, riding through the soft early morning light. As I was riding pillion again, it was as hard riding back as it had been getting there. On arrival, we shamefacedly confessed to having eaten all our food. The only thing we talked about at home was the birth of the calf. Seeing that was worth all the trouble we'd had.

Chapter XII

Siblings

Jenny's love for me grew as the years passed. By the time I was eight or nine, she was entering adulthood, and had started courting. I looked on her young men with jealous eyes. I used to think that some of them were not good enough. Whenever one of them came to the house at night, my brother and I were sent to bed. We used to spy on them through the cracks in the floor. The rest of the family went out to keep out of the way. Among the suitors there was John whose hair shone with brilliantine; there was Alec who wooed her with Black Magic chocolates or with fish and chips; and there was Mike who did nothing but sigh. I couldn't work out why Mike came at all. When the sighs became unbearable, my brother and I shouted down: 'Go and put a sock in it,' which kind of spoiled the atmosphere. Dan and I got into such fits of laughter that we had to pull the blankets over our heads. When there was nothing but silence, we felt impelled to hop out of bed and peer through the cracks to see what was going on.

I preferred it when my sisters invited their friends to dance in our front room. They were crazy about dancing. As fashion dictated, the girls had their hair bobbed, wore short skirts and gartered stockings. There wasn't a lot of space in which to dance – even though what furniture there was had been removed – but nobody worried. Somebody came with a concertina or a banjo and away we went. It was one of the occasions when Dan was willing to join in. In that confined space, we jerked, twisted, and spun to the latest tunes until it made us dizzy.

American dances were popular. I learned to dance the Charleston and the Black Bottom in that little room. The Charleston was the big hit. When the dancers got too hot, they just leaned against the walls or stepped out of the front door and cooled off in the street. Everybody was good-hearted; those were happy times.

On one occasion the dance ended in a fight. I don't know how it began. One moment all was bliss; the next the girls were screaming and the boys were knocking each other down. Dan in the middle of it. Jenny fled upstairs. I knew it was serious when I saw mother grab the rolling pin, the frying pan and the poker – the three deadly weapons in cottage fights – and run upstairs, too. My job was to open and shut the front door, lock and unlock it, as the bodies, some of them with bloodied noses and torn suits, were tossed into the street. The fight wound down with two of the boys wrestling on the sanded floor. Spoiled their shirts and trousers, they did.

Being the youngest in the family and the most readily available, I often served as Jenny's courier. It baffled me why I had to keep running with notes between Jenny and her current suitor when they were only several streets apart. I not only had to carry messages, I had to describe in detail what her young man looked like. 'Was there any last word?' she asked. There usually was: 'Tell her, I'm allus thinking of her neet and day.' If I thought a fellow was not really worthy of my sister, I stuck a dart in him whenever I could.

This courier business could go on for weeks with Jenny

going into a decline. There were times when she didn't sleep or touch her food. 'You're letting your courtin' get the better of you,' mother scolded. The courier business, as far as I could see, didn't have the slightest effect. It was just a waste of time, paper and my clog cokers.

My running stopped when Jenny decided on Gordon Weall. Nobody enjoyed life as much as Gordon. People said he laughed right down to his heels. When he walked in one day with the top of his hair shaved off, we went into fits. He must have been one of the first in town to have a crew cut. He looked just like a red Indian brave. Mother was thrilled with him. There was nobody better than Gordon. He was lucky to get Jenny; she was equally lucky to get him. I gave the romance a push whenever I could.

Jenny and he had a wonderful courtship. They were a sunny-tempered pair. When they were both in work and could afford it, they dashed off on a cheap excursion train to Blackpool to dance all night in the Tower Ballroom. They came back at dawn and went straight to work. Fifty miles for a dance! Now that was really living it up. Poor they may have been, but none so joyful.

Like Jenny, Gordon was a giver. In return for my help in his job as a painter, he was generous to a fault. One Easter, when he was in work, he took me to the Easter Fair. The night before I'd watched the long convoy entering the town. The lorries, carts, one-horse caravans (with dogs tied underneath), the animal cages, and the massive steam engines piled high with scaffolding excited me. In no time, the whole square was covered with tents, canvas booths, roundabouts and lookers-on. People came in such numbers that they had to lock arms and jostle their way through the crowds. All was din and bustle.

Gordon spent a whole three shillings on me. Thirty-six pennies! I rode on everything. I think I ate everything too: ice-cream, roasted potatoes, sticks of sugar. We went on the Big Dipper, the Cakewalk, the perilous chairboat swings and the Big Wheel, and shrieked like everybody else. I waved to

Gordon excitedly, as my papier-maché horse rose and fell to the accompaniment of piped music from the elaborately decorated steam organ. All was happy shouting and lovely disturbance.

Gordon considered the sideshows of freaks and caged wild animals a real 'swiz' so we avoided them. Instead we watched the contortionists, and listened to the black-faced pill and potion sellers who for tuppence would cure you of the most dreadful illnesses. We tried to avoid the roll-down-the-penny men, who stood ready to pick the pennies from our pockets. To the light of a naked flame, we tried to dislodge a coconut or knock down a wooden effigy of a woman.

We almost went into a booth marked: MODERN AMERICAN ENTERPRISE. REFINED ENTERTAINMENT, but decided against it. We didn't know what 'refined' meant.

At the end of the day, there was the added joy of going home through the littered, crowded streets hanging on to a coconut and a large balloon. A day or two later, with equal bustle, the fair disappeared as quickly as it had come. With it went the wet, trodden paper and the orange peel. Watercarts washed the cobbles free of sweat and stale beer. Normality returned.

Paradoxically, the fair got bigger, better and brighter as times got worse. The bleaker our world, the greater our need of diversion. No depression in trade and industry was allowed to mar it.

<hr />

It was Gordon who introduced me to speed. One day he roared up to our front door on a motorcycle he'd just bought. The big buckskin gloves and goggles he was wearing made him look very daring.

'I was lucky to get it,' he said, his face flushed and happy. 'It was already sold to a chap who couldn't take delivery. The coppers had other plans for him. I got it just at the right moment.'

I must have been somebody special, for I was the first to be invited to ride on the pillion seat. Jenny wouldn't go near the machine. It terrified her.

'What's that strange knocking sound?' I asked, as I clambered aboard.

'Nothing, Billy. Minor adjustment of the carburetor is all it needs. Goes like a bird.'

This flying like a bird past houses and park railings was an entirely new experience for both of us. The faster we went, the happier we were. Gordon went so fast that things became a blur. I learned to hang on with my knees and hands as we roared round the bends. We raced across town; we thundered down quiet country lanes leaving a cloud of dust behind. On occasions Gordon avoided obstacles by whizzing around them at the last moment. Another 'minor adjustment,' this time to the brakes, was obviously needed. Meanwhile the strange knocking sound got louder.

Gordon was not satisfied just with speed; he had to do antics. With me off the pillion, and the bike in motion, he hung on to the handlebars while jumping from one side to the other – as he had seen cowboys do with horses in western films. He also rode while standing on the seat. It was hair-raising. He became known as the daredevil of the district. It was Jenny's belief that he would finish up killing himself and her brother. With the potholes and ruts that pitted the roads, she had every reason to be afraid.

The knocking sound, which Gordon was always going to fix, but never did, one day brought our wild riding career to a close. Giving a particularly explosive knock, the engine died. Later the bike was sold for scrap.

———◇———

Brenda took after father, she was a Woodruff: stocky, silent, tough. She didn't flutter about like Jenny, she stomped. She didn't have Jenny's good looks. She had a Woodruff face: strong, square, with the broad brow and thoughtful eyes.

She didn't indulge in fairy stories like mother; she dealt with immediate problems. Nor did she sing. She could no more sing than father. One thing certain: she was utterly reliable.

Her joining the Salvation Army at seventeen came as a great surprise to my parents. Father was not against the Salvation Army, no working man was, but he didn't like her going off like that. There were words in the kitchen between Brenda and father. The dispute started innocently enough, but one thing led to another. Neither could bear to hear the other one out. The shouting match ended with father bawling: 'Goddamit, go 'n join t' Army if tha must, but stay theer. Ah've 'ad enough of thee.'

'Ah will,' Brenda flared defiantly. Then she burst into tears, ran upstairs, and slammed her bedroom door. It was so tense and quiet in the kitchen that I could hear father's watch ticking on the fireplace. Moments later, Brenda came storming down the stairs clutching her belongings. Mother tried to grab her as she crashed through the kitchen, but Brenda pushed her aside and was gone.

'See what tha's dun,' mother screamed at father, tears running down her face. 'Ah 'ope tha satisfied.'

Some days later, driven by mother, father went in search of Brenda. I think he bitterly regretted having thrown her out. He found her and they made their peace.

Brenda came home with father carrying her brown paper package, and we all sat together again in our stockinged feet in the kitchen and ate baked potatoes.

'It's like old times,' said mother. It wasn't. Everybody was tense. But time passed and wounds healed. Brenda joined the Salvation Army.

With her scrubbed face, her black bonnet and her red sash, Brenda now attacked sin as fiercely as she had attacked the bullies who had knocked me down at school when I was four.

I found her conversion overwhelming. 'Billy,' she said to me one day while pressing my hand against her bosom. 'Billy, you must declare yourself. Are you for God or for Satan?'

More than anything else, I was for Brenda, so the first thing I did was to stop the harassment our street gang had been giving the Salvation Army. Keeping our distance, so as to avoid being clouted by an overzealous Soldier of Christ, we urchins used to march after the Salvation Army band and parody the Army's favourite hymns:

> You won't go to heaven when you die, Mary Ann,
> Yes you will, no you won't, yes you will,
> Mary Ann . . .

We also mocked them with the lines:

> Sally Army sells fish,
> Three-half-pence a dish.
> If you don't like it, don't try it.
> If you don't want it, don't buy it.
> Sally Army sells fish.

We ended with:

> Oh, you're in the Sally Army
> And safe from sin.
> You'll all go to heaven,
> In a corn beef tin.

The worst kind of nonsense, yet we indulged in it repeatedly. Odd that we should have picked on the Salvation Army which did so much to help the poor. Our conduct was a mixture of mischief and hooliganism. Anyway, largely because of me, these attacks ceased after Brenda joined up.

One of the first things Brenda did – to the obvious discomfort of father – was to launch a holy war against drink. The trouble was she went overboard. Unlike her usual steady self, she worked herself up into a frenzy against alcohol. She was indefatigable in persuading people to sign the pledge of abstinence. She also was expert at working the crowd for copper and silver. She was brave the way she stood with her group under the flag in front of the Griffin pub at the end of our street, rattling her tambourine, and selling the Salvation Army newspaper *The War Cry*.

Those drinking in the Griffin took a different view. The pub was one of the few places where the workers could relax. Drink meant conviviality and friendship. For some it meant oblivion from a bleak existence; their only armour against despair. They didn't want anybody spoiling it by reminding them of sin, or by singing temperance songs in the bar.

At first the pub-keeper was good-hearted about it. He saw the funny side. But then he came round to the view that Brenda was trying to rob him of his living; especially with her talk about banishing barmaids. It was embarrassing to father. The pub-keeper was especially sore with her when the Army brought in other contingents from Preston, where the English temperance movement had begun.

Yet Brenda made many converts. She did, after all, labour in a fertile field. At some weddings and funerals people used to drink so much that they forgot why they'd come. Money that should have gone into people's bellies, or on their backs, went down their throats. I often saw shawl-covered mothers, with infants in their arms and toddlers hanging on to their skirts, trying to get their husbands out of the pub late on a Friday night before the weekly earnings had all gone.

One man Brenda saved was Mr Lambert who lived with his wife next door. Until Brenda got at him, Mr Lambert spent most of his time working as a labourer at the Gas Works or drinking in the pub. He was known as an irredeemable tosspot. Mrs Lambert, a bright-eyed badger of a woman, was forever throwing her shawl over her head and running to his rescue. Having picked him up off the pavement, she reeled to and fro with him, doing her best to get him home. She came up the street, staggering under his weight, propping him against the wall while she took a breather. The ordeal was habitual.

It was just as well that Mr Lambert was a silent rather than a fighting drunk, otherwise, being drunk so often, he would have been killed. We children were rather cruel about it. If Mrs Lambert had not got to the pub in time, we followed the old man through the street as he struggled home, teasing him, and going into gales of laughter when he clung to one of the gas lamps. He rewarded our unforgiveable behaviour with a gurgle or two and a silly grin. He never harmed anybody and was far better than a lot of nasty people I knew.

I've forgotten how long Brenda worked on him before he agreed to sign the pledge. But sign it he did, and a different man he was. He became one of the stalwarts of the Nazarene Chapel. He was one of Brenda's favourite redemptions. She used to say that if she could save Joe Lambert, she could save anybody. 'Ate out of my hand, he did.'

As long as she remained a Soldier of Christ, Brenda never relaxed in the battle against alcohol. Yet she didn't succeed in converting my parents. Despite her unending call for penitence, they remained faithful to the pub.

———◇———

There were others who took the fight against drink into their own hands. My friend Harold Watkins and I one day witnessed his mother being beaten by his father for being drunk. Somebody had run in to tell Mr Watkins that his wife was coming up the street, tipsy. He ran to meet her and beat her on the head and shoulders until, with a bleeding face, she struggled through her door.

Nobody would have dreamed of intervening; they might have intervened had he not done something about it. 'If I wor in your place . . .' they would start. In such a close society, trollops and drunks among the women had to be contained. What you did in your own cottage was your business; what you did in the street – especially what a woman did in the street – was something else. I knew the Watkins family as well as my own, and I know that Mrs Watkins didn't get drunk again.

I never did learn all the unwritten laws that told you what you could and could not do with alcohol, or anything else. There were fine lines which you must not cross, and about which you could learn only over time. You simply had to watch for the signals. I found them conflicting. Why did we react so harshly to a drunken trollop in the street, but did little, if anything, to stop two drunken women beating each other to death? I could watch two men fighting and have little reaction; a man and a woman fighting didn't upset me much; but two women fighting, their mouths full of anger and foul words, filled me with disgust. Not so for many people; such a fight had a laughing, jeering crowd around it in no time. It was the only time I would have been happy to see a copper in our street. One day I asked grandmother Bridget what she thought of women fighting in the street. 'It's not a subject for "dacent" conversation,' she silenced me.

———◦———

I was closer to my sisters than to my brother Dan. He was a real Woodruff, with all the looks of father. Trouble attracted him like a magnet. He was tough and aggressive, and had something of the rebel in him. For all the attention he gave me, I might not have existed. In the house he could be difficult. I never knew whether or not I was going to get a 'lander' to the head from him. But for Brenda who used to take my side, he might have bullied me more.

Sometime in the mid-twenties, when he was twelve or thirteen, he'd had brushes with the police. They'd been to the house twice with complaints. Once they flushed him out of the indoor market in town after it had been locked up for the night. Fortunately he had not broken into the premises, nor by the time they got to him, had he had time to eat anything. He was let off with a warning. Next time they picked him up in the railway clearing yard. Again they could not pin anything on him except trespass which wasn't worth pressing.

With his headstrong nature there was no telling what trouble Dan might cause. On an earlier occasion, when he was eight or nine, he had gone on strike against food and school. He had sat in a corner of the house where father left him, his face contorted with rage. Nothing shifted his obstinacy. Mother was out of work at the time. Dan's teacher was grey-headed Miss Grieves who passed our door daily. I don't know how long his hunger strike continued, and under what terms it was settled, but daily bulletins were issued to Miss Grieves as she went by.

'He hasn't eaten his porridge from yesterday,' mother called from the front door.

'Give it to him tomorrow,' Miss Grieves called back, hardly breaking her stride.

Mother worried about Dan. She worried about him so much that she sometimes burst into tears. He caused her the most sorrow, yet Dan was her favourite.

On leaving school at fourteen, Dan became a tenter (helper) to father in the mill. His destiny was to be a weaver. He had been reared on cotton; cotton was in his blood, but he had no love for it. He hated weaving; he hated the mill; he hated being tied to a machine; he hated being trapped for fifty hours a week; he hated the discipline.

Whenever I ran into the weaving shed with the dinners, father was always on to him.

'That's not the way to put cob on t' shuttle, you gobbin,' he scolded.

Dan bristled.

'Look,' he went on, 'tha's got a mash. That's because tha wasn't watchin'. Tha's goin' to break warp the way tha goin' on. Nah, tha'll have to start afresh. See, pull t' cloth back. Comb it out gently, there's nothing to it. Piece it from t' back and pull it through. Titivate it. All it needs is for thee to use tha gumption.'

Dan usually gave as good as he got. 'Ah didn't touch cob,

it all happened on its own,' he bawled back. The last thing he wanted to do was to please father.

I think Dan was right. Perhaps he was wooden-handed and clumsy as a weaver, but sometimes these things happened on their own. Dan got mashes like nobody else; really interesting mashes that caught everybody's attention. They crossed the weaving shed to see them. I've stood with him awestruck before his loom as the threads went wild before our eyes. In no time at all, hidden gremlins had torn them right across the loom. Dan and I were too mesmerized by the growing rent to know what to do. Eventually dad came across to see what we were staring at. Appealing to the Holy Trinity, he leaped to stop the loom.

'Tha goin' to get a prize for this one, Dan, tha are,' father shouted, eyeing the damage.

Dan sulked.

'Nobody can weave cotton and hate it at the same time,' muttered an old weaver. 'Loom won't stand for it.'

From what father told mother, I knew that Dan was always being 'fetched up' in the warehouse and fined for bad work by the 'cut looker,' the cloth inspector. As weaving was paid by the piece, it meant a cut in pay. It made Dan sullen and angry.

After my brother had suffered about a year of purgatory, father one day found the weft and warp threads on Dan's loom a tangle of mashes. Dan was nowhere to be seen.

'He's buggered t' job up,' father told mother that evening. To mother's growing concern there was no sight or sound of Dan. He didn't come home that night, or the next. Days later we discovered that he had run all the way from the mill to the army recruiting sergeant. Having lied about his age, Dan said that he was sixteen (the minimum recruiting age) whereas he was only fifteen, the sergeant enlisted him and despatched him within hours to a remote part of Scotland. A day or two later Dan entered the barracks of the Argyle and Sutherland Highlanders Regiment in Inverness. It was about as far from Blackburn as the recruiting sergeant could have sent him. As distances went in those days, he might as well have sent him to the moon.

When I heard about this, I secretly hoped that Dan had found his niche, and that I might never see him again. I hardly knew what to do with a bed to myself. I went searching among his things for the tin soldiers he'd extorted from me over the years.

My hopes were soon dashed. An impassioned, scrawled note we received from Dan told us that he was desperate to come home. However badly written, the note revealed the mind of a confused boy who had been jailed for insubordination. He was too wild to submit to army discipline. He told us how cold his cell was, and that he could see a great loch and empty mud flats from his window.

The more time passed, the colder it got, the more frantic the messages became.

Father's first letters to Inverness, asserting that his son had been recruited under age and under false pretenses, were ignored. But, urged by mother, he kept at it. Eventually he received a reply:

'I have to inform you,' the adjutant of the Argyle and Sutherland Highlanders wrote, 'that your son, Dan, has willingly undertaken to serve His Majesty for the next twenty years. This is where the matter now stands. It is purposeless to discuss it further.' There was a handwritten postscript about Dan having crablice.

Mother became excited when the letter arrived. She kept turning it over in her hand, trying to decipher it. When father came home he sat down to read it. He read it to himself several times.

'Well,' said mother, tapping her foot, 'for goodness sake, stop dilly-dallying. What does it say?'

'It says, he's got crablice,' said father, refusing to be bullied.

Prodded by mother, who seemed to have forgotten all the trouble Dan had given her before he disappeared, father continued to besiege the regiment with letters. There had never been so many letters to and from our house.

Worn down by both father and son, the colonel of the regiment began to have second thoughts about Dan. If father would send thirty pounds, the colonel wrote, he would send Dan home. Thirty pounds was two-thirds of father's annual wage when he was in work.

Shortly afterward another letter came saying that the colonel would settle for twenty pounds. Dan, he said, was giving them a lot of trouble.

'They've bitten off more than they can chew,' said father, studying the letter. 'If we hang on long enough, Maggie, they'll pay us to take him back.' It must have occurred to father that his son had turned out exactly like himself. (His mother, my grandmother Selma, had had to bail him out of the navy because he was underage.)

But mother was not prepared to wait. She took her troubles to Dr Grieves. Failing Grieves, she intended to approach uncle Eric, or the moneylender. As always, Dr Grieves helped. He knew what he was doing. The army didn't try any snotty business with him. Mother said the army's reply to Grieves when he sent the twenty pounds was all 'please and thank you, and here's your money back.'

A week later, Dan came home. It was a Saturday. Mother was busy taking freshly baked bread out of the oven. She stood speechless with emotion when the latch was raised and he entered the house. He'd lost weight; he was thinner; his head was shaven; he looked crushed. With a hoarse cry, mother dropped the loaf on the kitchen floor and ran to Dan. They hugged each other and cried.

Instead of Dan's luck taking a turn for the better, he began to tread an even harder path. A friend of father's at the Bank Top Boiler Works hired Dan as a 'devil.' A 'devil' was a boy who tightened and untightened the bolts inside mill boilers when they were being repaired. Dan was lowered through one of the boiler openings – usually too small for a man – carrying a wrench and a lamp. Except for a loincloth, he went naked. While his mates shouted and pounded on the outside, he struggled with the wrench on the inside. When he emerged, he was covered with soot. The only thing white about him were his teeth and his eyeballs.

Whether he was working locally, or for weeks at a time in other towns, he always came home as black as coal, and dead beat. He came through the back alley to our backyard. Here, wet or fine, he stripped off. With his dirty clothes lying on the cobbles, he stood naked while mother rubbed him with a cloth and scrubbed him with a brush, trying to get him clean. It was as well that water was free, for she poured dozens of warm and cold buckets of water over him. Then she lathered him again and again with soap until all the soot was driven from his rippling body and had settled on his feet. The rubbing and the scrubbing went on until Dan's skin gradually changed from black to grey, grey to pink. Mother never tired. By then the backyard was awash with clothing, soapsuds and soot. Apart from catching his breath when the cold water was thrown over him, Dan never murmured. He was too tired to talk. I felt truly sorry for him and said so.

'Tha gets used to it,' he answered me.

Chapter XIII

Bamber Bridge

I spent some of my summers with my mother's kinsfolk, my two maiden aunts, Betsy and Grace, who lived in a rambling old converted farmhouse in a quiet country lane at Bamber Bridge, near Preston. They were Kenyons, and except for heaping love onto my sister Brenda and me, assiduously avoided the Woodruffs. The only link my family had with them, as far as I knew, was through the mail. Brenda, who had spent some time with them recovering from a sickness, was the one who made the arrangements for me to go there. I knew from Brenda that their father had helped grandmother Bridget after the death of grandfather Thomas.

Betsy was the hearty, red-faced, fat one. The folds of flesh on her face almost concealed her small nose and her ever-merry eyes. She was sheer bulk and moved slowly. When she walked across the room the floor creaked. Her feet left an imprint wherever she walked. I was apprehensive that she might step on me. To a child's eye she had a gigantic bosom. When she hugged me, I felt myself smothered

213

between her breasts. She had large powerful hands; the largest I had seen among the Kenyons and the Woodruffs.

Aunt Grace was just the opposite. She was Grace by name and grace by nature. She was shy, pale and slim. Her small, fine head, wispy fair hair, pale blue eyes and tiny hands and feet gave her a delicate look. Whereas Betsy flattened everything that got in her way, Grace seemed to float above it. She was sprightly. She enjoyed life just as much as Betsy, but was restrained. Betsy was forever going into fits of laughter which shook her whole frame; which in turn shook the room. Grace never went beyond a sweet smile. Betsy was what you saw. With aunt Grace you felt she was holding back on you. If a pig, or a hen, or a duck fell sick, Grace was the one who nursed it. Betsy said that Grace had had many suitors when younger, but had neglected her own interests in favour of their widowed father whom, together, they had cared for. When I knew them, I suppose they were both in their forties.

Regardless of their different traits, my aunts loved each other deeply. They were never apart. I came to love them with all my heart.

The third member of the family at Bamber Bridge was Whiskey, a salt and pepper, wire-haired fox terrier. I cannot imagine why they called him Whiskey for my aunts were strict teetotalers. It didn't take me long to realize that Whiskey was the boss of the house. I never knew a dog that took less notice of his mistresses. Regardless of my aunts' cries of 'Oh Whiskey this' and 'oh Whiskey that,' unperturbed, the dog went his own way. He knew exactly how to handle them. Battles of will between the women and the dog always ended up with Whiskey lying fast asleep on their knee. When the four of us came home from our daily walk, ignoring aunt Betsy's loud protests, Whiskey took the big upholstered chair by the fire. They'd long since given up any attempt to dislodge him. Any effort to bother him was answered with a low growl.

Whiskey must have tired of female company. From the moment I arrived at Bamber Bridge he attached himself to me. He took my arrival as sufficient excuse to avoid his weekly bath, which he hated. He slept across the foot of my bed. A large Bible lay on a heavy table in my room. Inside was a steel roller with spikes on it. There also was a tiny key, which when turned caused the book to play 'Faith of our Fathers.' Whiskey and I played it so often that my aunts feared we'd wear it out. He took great interest in the long stories I told him before sleep claimed us both. When he fell asleep before me, I watched my candle flicker and splutter. Moths came through the open window and charged the flame before I had the chance to blow it out. Because of the dog and the kindness of my aunts, I rarely missed my gang once I left Blackburn for Bamber Bridge.

Betsy and Grace Kenyon were well off. Mother told me that their father, a builder, being a shrewd man in all his under-takings, had left them enough money to more than last them the rest of their lives. Mr John Kenyon's portrait hung in a gilded frame above a marble-encased clock in the parlour. He obviously had dressed up for the occasion. He wore an old-fashioned, black, Prince Albert coat that reached down to his knees. He had a high collar with the corners turned down and a black tie. He didn't look at ease, yet his face and his long white beard exuded kindness and good will. His life had evidently been successful. I suppose he must have been the brother of my grandfather Thomas who had left my grand-mother Bridget destitute. His daughters were the only link the Woodruffs had with the Kenyons and that a tenuous one.

He had bequeathed to my aunts the large house, with its flagstone corridors, and its heavy oak furniture, in which they lived. It had several levels with a sharply pitched, red tiled roof, a permanently locked attic at the top of the stairs, and large, bright windows which had recently been added. It must have been an old building because I could scratch out the crumbling mortar from between the bricks with my fingers. At the front – part of which was plastered – was a large white-painted doorway with a roof above it. On the

215

door was a huge, black knocker with a lion's head. One reached the front door by way of a heavy wrought iron gate that gave access to a front garden awash with flowers.

Most exciting of all, the house had a secret door built into the side of one of the steep panelled staircases. The thin, flat piece of wood that served as a door was opened by sliding a piece of the beading on the panelling. This released a bolt and allowed the panel to swing inward. Behind the panel was a hiding place, what was called a Priest's hole, where Catholic priests had taken refuge when fleeing their Protestant persecutors in earlier times. Once I was allowed to hide in the Priest's hole while aunt Betsy, pretending to be an Elizabethan soldier, tried to find me. The hullabaloo she put up when climbing the stairs would have terrified any priest.

Aunt Betsy was funny about religion. She thought that everybody in the world, at least those in their right minds, was Catholic. That's because Bamber Bridge and nearby Preston were chiefly Catholic. But I knew that Blackburn was chiefly Protestant. She refused to listen to me when I tried to put her straight. I don't know what she would have said if I'd called her a 'Cat-licker,' or had repeated the parody: 'Catholic, Catholic, quack, quack, quack. Go to the devil and never come back.'

Compared with life in Blackburn, my aunts lived in the best of worlds. Whereas in Blackburn we trod on each other's toes, Betsy and Grace had enough room to rattle around. Whereas our house smelt of cotton and fish, my aunts' house was alive with bright, sweet-smelling blooms picked from the garden at the rear of the house. Grace used to spend lots of time each morning cutting and arranging the flowers she placed throughout the house. She also cared for innumerable indoor plants. When she wasn't messing about with the flowers and plants, she was dusting the heavy furniture that shone like a polished apple. Once a week, she changed the lace covers on the backs and arms of the chairs. Because of the large windows, there was light everywhere.

The dark, serious faces staring at me from brown photos hanging on the walls didn't bother me. I presumed they were Kenyons, but I had no interest in finding out. I knew from the flowing dresses, the tight suits, and the hair styles that those Kenyons, like Mr Kenyon who kept his eyes on everything from above the clock in the parlour, were long since dead.

My aunts were lucky because they didn't have to worry about money. We worried about nothing else. Mill whistles didn't bother them. They ate regularly and well. Biscuits, dates, grapes, oranges, apples, or bananas were kept on the sideboard waiting to be eaten. I was allowed to eat as much as I wanted. Most of what we ate came from an orchard, several hen coops, and a duckpond at the end of a field. I used to throw a stick in the pond in the hope that Whiskey would retrieve it, but he spurned the idea. Some of the produce they grew was given to a middle-aged couple, Jim and Effie Bairns, who came in to help every day. Some of it was sold in Bamber Bridge and Preston. More to keep themselves busy than to earn money, for which they had no real need, my aunts also fattened a pig or two.

In the evenings they read to each other, played their gramophone with its large green horn, sewed, cut out table mats, played Snakes and Ladders with me, or made stockings on a stocking frame, which they sold to a dealer in Preston. If the gramophone became too loud, Betsy would stuff a stocking into the horn. Grace spent a lot of time at night pressing flowers in a large book on the parlour table. She was a collector like her father. As he had collected stuffed birds, she collected flowers. Sometimes my aunts chose to do nothing more than rock in their chairs. Slowly the hush of night deepened. When they were rocking, they avoided talking. Their lives were as regular, secure and stable as my family's life was haphazard, uncertain, threatening. They might have been living in a castle with a drawbridge.

Every afternoon, wet or fine, we all went for a walk. Betsy was in charge and the procedure never varied.

'Grace,' aunt Betsy yelled, 'have we got the sticks?'

'Yes, sister,' Grace answered, unperturbed.

'Billy, you ready?'

'Yes, aunt Betsy.'

'Grace, do we have the coats?'

'Yes,' Grace responded, her arms full of them.

'Grace! Where's Whiskey?'

Only when everybody had the right stick, the right coat, the right shoes – clogs were not worn – the right umbrella and the right hat did the procession begin. Betsy went first, grasping a heavy cane, moving slowly. She bore herself like some large animal venturing into perilous territory. I walked immediately behind her, carrying the umbrellas, followed by Grace. On these occasions my aunts wore poke bonnets. Wet or fine, I wore a Sou'wester.

Once in the fields, Whiskey streaked off as if he'd seen a rabbit.

'Come back! Come back!' Betsy bawled, raising her stick. 'Oh, that dog, he'll be the death of me.'

Ignoring Betsy's calls, Whiskey by now had wriggled through the hedgerow. Betsy shouted after him as if he were misbehaving himself for the first time, 'You bad dog; you bad dog!' she complained. 'We never want to see you again.'

Covered with mud, Whiskey always reappeared when we were on the homeward stretch. He fell in line with us as if he hadn't been away. Nothing was said. By then, aunt Betsy only had wind enough to trundle home.

Summer after summer, the walks took the same route. Nothing changed – not even the demonstration that Betsy put on daily by a deep pond where boys sunbathed and swam in the nude. Betsy always got worked up about the nude bathers long before we reached the pond.

'Just look at that, Grace,' she shouted in a shocked voice over her shoulder, while pointing with her stick. 'Did you ever see such? What are we coming to? That's what I ask you, what are we coming to? There's no shame.'

On and on, she went, her moist face becoming scarlet. By

218

the time we reached the pond, her stick was raised like the sword of an avenging angel. By then, the swimmers had slithered down the muddy bank into the water. Betsy marched to the water's edge to deliver her usual sermon about shame and immodesty. She ended on the same note: 'You're a bunch of hooligans, that's what you are; you brazen, disgusting ragamuffins. There's no decency in you. You're a disgrace to Bamber Bridge.'

All of which sent the swimmers into fits of laughter.

'Silly old bugger!' they shouted back, while splashing water at her. 'Why don't you fall in?'

After a summer or two I took all this in my stride. Aunt Betsy didn't mean what she said. It was her way of enjoying herself. She would have been mortified if the hooligans had suddenly worn pants. Quiet, gentle aunt Grace never intervened – she stood at some distance, her face wrapped in smiles. She enjoyed her sister's daily tirade more than the swimmers did.

Aunt Betsy was obviously destined to run into male nudes. She once took me to the Natural History Museum in Preston where she was halted in her tracks at the entrance by a bronze statue of an ancient Greek male. 'Well,' said Betsy, staring at the metal penis and testicles, 'I'll be blessed; if this is what we get at the door, Billy, what will we get inside?'

Each summer, I used to fret until my parents gave me the ten pennies for the train ride to Bamber Bridge. The fare was all I needed. I went just as I stood, wearing a jersey, a thick flannel shirt, corduroy trousers, stockings, clogs, coat and cap. Apart from a penknife and some string and one or two other odds and ends in my pockets, I didn't take another thing. I took no underwear, no change of clothes, not even a toothbrush or a handkerchief. Everything awaited me in the heavy wardrobes and drawers in my room at Bamber Bridge.

First time I ever went there, I went alone. I was told where to find and leave the train; I was given an address and ten pence for the fare, and that was that. I had no idea what prior arrangements were made. I'd met my aunts once in Blackburn, and I'm sure my father had sent them a note before I left. Nothing was said about my return. It was all done in such an off-hand way that I was neither confused nor frightened. Nobody at the station thought it odd that I should be travelling alone. I was much too concerned to stick my head out of the carriage window, and drink in all that I could see than to worry whether I should get lost or come to any harm. The journey was only a few miles, but I was as excited as if I were going to the moon. Nobody at Bamber Bridge mentioned Blackburn until the summer was done and it was time to go home.

My aunts were always at home, fussing about in the field, or in one of the out-houses with their livestock. They were never ill, or had gone away. Each time I arrived they were exactly as I had left them the time before. If they were working in the fields they'd be wearing the same funnel-like hats, the same fingerless gloves and the same clogs. Aunt Grace always wore a white lace collar; aunt Betsy a black bow on a white shirt that crackled with starch and was as hard as rock. The aprons and the heavy skirts were always the same. My room, which looked down to the duck pond, was kept ready. As if I'd arrived from an epic journey, on the first night I was expected to give them an account of what I'd seen out of the carriage window. At Bamber Bridge nothing changed.

Whiskey invariably warned everybody. With piercing yelps he flung himself against the back of the door. Then he jumped up to the glass panel to make quite sure it was me. The moment I got the door open he'd be all over me, licking my face and behind my ears. Then he howled his way through the house and across the field announcing my arrival.

Because of an unspoken agreement between us, my aunts ignored my approach. They went on fussing with their ducks and hens as if Whiskey and I did not exist. Meanwhile I crept up silently behind aunt Betsy's enormous figure and suddenly shouted out as loudly as I could, 'Auntie, Ah've cum!' Whereupon Betsy dropped whatever she was holding, pretending that she'd had the shock of her life. She slowly swung her immense figure around. Her hands shaking, she stared at me with laughing eyes. 'Why, so tha has, luv,' she said. 'He's cum, he's cum, Grace,' she bawled across the field as if Grace didn't already know. Then she took me in a tight embrace, crushing me against her crackling, starched bosom.

Continuing to hug me warmly, Betsy ran her hands over my frame.

'Oh, Grace,' she shouted, 'Grace, the poor bairn's starving. His bones are sticking out, Grace. Come and feel.'

By now, Grace had come running. 'Why, so they are,' she said, running her fingers over my arms and legs, while clucking her tongue disapprovingly.

At that point Betsy looked at me as if I were a lost cause. 'They've let him go too far this time,' she said, darkly. 'They've left it too late. He's skinnier than last time, you know. There's nowt we can do.'

'We can but try, Betsy,' Grace sighed, her fingers running over my spine. 'The skeleton's there; we've got the frame to work on.'

This talk never bothered me. I knew I wasn't dying. It was my aunts' way of preparing themselves for the challenge that lay ahead. If I looked undernourished when I arrived, they were determined that I would not leave in the same condition. The challenge was to get as much fat on my bones as possible before my summer holiday came to an end. As eating was my possessing passion, I could hardly complain.

For weeks on end, they stuffed me with food. No matter how I protested, 'seconds' and 'thirds' were piled onto my plate. I was encouraged to gobble. I lost count of the many hens and ducks I consumed, or how much fresh milk I drank. I ate so much at noon that I could hardly stand. If I didn't respond to the treatment, I was given a second dinner at night. There were occasions when I found myself almost too taut to totter to bed. The more flesh I put on – and it was impossible not to gain weight with that care – the greater their satisfaction. I was weighed nightly and they beamed at every extra ounce. Even Whiskey seemed to take a delight in it.

When the time came for my departure they weighed me for the last time. By the look on their faces, that last weighing was a life and death matter. If the figure was not to Betsy's liking, the weighing was repeated. 'Now, Billy, tha must try a little harder this time, luv,' she said, surreptitiously putting her hand on my shoulder.

The weighing having been brought to a satisfactory conclusion, the women ran their hands over me once more to make quite sure they'd done their job. They told the platform man at the railway station what miracles they'd worked on me during my stay. 'Billy's still on the skinny side,' they said, looking at me critically, 'but he'll pass. He might just last the winter. We couldn't do more in the time.' At that point they lifted my cap and ruffled my hair.

It was expected of me that I would weep when leaving them at the station, and I did. They wept too. They took turns hugging me till the last moment before letting me go. With my pockets full of apples, and my arms full of food – all of which I was ordered to consume during the half-hour's journey home – and my hot hand clutching a shining half-crown, which was pressed on me at this point, I somehow managed to clamber aboard.

As aunt Betsy was too large to climb into the train after me, she beckoned me down again so that she could give me one last squeeze. She used to squeeze me so long and so hard that it took the platform man, with his neb cap and his shining buttons, to get me back into the carriage. To forestall any further squeezes, he quickly slammed the door behind me. I barely got in before the train began to lurch out of the station. Brushing my tears aside, I waved goodbye until the two bonneted faces, handkerchiefs to noses, passed out of sight. Then I settled down and began to gorge as I had been bidden.

*   *   *

Few summers passed without my spending some time with my aunts at Bamber Bridge. They never came to our house in Blackburn. If I didn't arrive, they sent the whole of my railway fare to mother, so that there could be no excuse for my not coming. Every visit was joyful. Always they were happy and unchanged. I felt that nothing could affect their world. Yet something did.

One summer's day a stranger came to my aunts' house. The stranger had a large cardboard folder under his arm tied with a bow. I met him at the front door talking to Betsy. He was such an odd-looking fellow that I could not help staring at him. He wore a dark-blue suit with faded grey stripes. The garment was threadbare; the arms and legs were far too short. His shirt and tie were equally worn but clean. On his head he had a blue trilby that shone with grease at the sides. He had cracked shoes laced with hooks instead of eyes.

'This is Mr Simon Gripper, Billy,' my aunt said, introducing me. I jerked my head in greeting.

Mr Gripper put a cold, wet hand around mine, while observing me sharply. Neither of us spoke. I felt an instinctive dislike for him. Whiskey must have felt the same, for he growled. The hair along his back stood up, which was a bad sign.

Mr Gripper was the nearest thing to a gorilla in a suit that I could imagine. He had wide shoulders, a flat face, fish eyes, a flat nose, a protruding bottom lip, and a wet, steamy brow. When he left, he walked like a gorilla rocking from side to side. I decided to forget all about him.

Imagine my surprise, a week or two later, when running into the living room with Whiskey for tea, I found him sitting on Whiskey's favourite chair talking to my aunts. His suit seemed to have shrunk since the last visit. Apart from a grunt and a wave of the hand, he wasted no time on me. With several cucumber sandwiches and some sticky fruitcake, I chose a chair among Mr Kenyon's stuffed birds as far away from the visitor as I could. Whiskey sat under my chair with a baleful eye on the stranger. We had never been unhappy at tea before.

While eating as much as he could, Mr Gripper never stopped talking. As far as I could make out, he was telling my aunts how he had come by his present job; which, of all things, was selling religious pictures from door to door. Hence the large folder he carried.

'It's the Lord's will,' he intoned, in what I thought was a slushy voice; then he paused and gave a long sigh. Whiskey growled; I felt like growling too.

Meanwhile Mr Gripper drew from his folder one vivid picture after another. There was Jesus as a child, Jesus as a man, Jesus crucified. There was the sacrificial lamb. There was the Holy Mother Mary, dressed in silks. Pictures of the Sacred Heart and the Saints followed. Some of the Saints wore halos and floated through the sky, others were covered with blood and gore. There was no end to the pictures. The furniture in the living room was covered with them.

'One cannot make a living this way,' Mr Gripper conceded, 'but it gives me the chance to earn my daily bread and spread the gospel of love at the same time. What better task?'

I shall never understand why my aunts allowed Mr Gripper to cross their threshold. Perhaps he didn't look as ugly to them as he did to me. Perhaps it was downright jealousy on my part that made him seem so greasy and servile. I felt threatened by him. What I found really objectionable was the way aunt Grace had eyes and ears only for Mr Gripper. Aunt Betsy, Whiskey, and I might never have existed.

One week later, Mr Gripper was back. The next week he was back again. Once, out of the corner of my eye, I saw him take aunt Grace's hand, which really upset me.

Later that night, when I was on my way to join my aunts in the kitchen, I heard the only cross words that I ever heard between them. They must have been arguing for some time, for they were both worked up.

'Grace,' said Betsy, who had been plucking and trussing

some ducks for the church, 'I don't know what's come over you, luv. We've come this far. Let's go on together. I'm not happy, luv, for your sake.'

I was shocked at Grace's reply.

'You're not happy,' Grace responded in an unusually hard tone, 'the truth is, Betsy, you don't want me to be happy. You'd rather boss me for the rest of my life.'

Those words made me catch my breath. How unfair to aunt Betsy! She worshipped her younger sister. I was not surprised to hear aunt Betsy burst into tears. Her sobbing shook the room.

'May you be forgiven, Grace Kenyon,' she sobbed. 'You know, I don't want anyone to hurt you.'

'No one's going to hurt me, Betsy. I'm not marrying Simon. There's nothing going on between Simon and myself if that's what you're hinting at. We're just friends. He's a good man out on his luck who needs help.'

The next thing I knew was that aunt Grace had also burst into tears. 'Oh Betsy,' she cried as she flung herself into her sister's outstretched arms. I crept away with a heavy heart.

The next day I decided to have it out with aunt Betsy about Mr Gripper. 'I don't like him, aunt Betsy,' I said. 'Nor does Whiskey. We hate him.'

'You shouldn't talk like that, Billy. You're jumping to conclusions. You don't know anything about him. As Christians we must love Mr Gripper, forgive him from our hearts, and pray for him.' But her voice betrayed her. She obviously didn't like Mr Gripper any more than I did.

When I returned the following summer, I was dumbfounded to be met by Mr Gripper. I ran right into him. Whiskey was nowhere to be seen.

'Oh, it's you again, is it,' he said, holding my arm tightly and staring through me.

When I went down the field to give aunt Betsy a surprise she hardly responded to my creeping up on her. She seemed a bit thinner and tired. Her eyes were worried, even haunted-looking. Aunt Grace looked better. She had twice the life she had had previously. Instead of following Betsy's moves as she had done in the past, she seemed to be leading. I hadn't been there several hours before I realized that Grace had transferred her affections from me to Mr Gripper. On her suggestion, he had moved into the house; worse, he had taken my room. Whiskey now had a kennel at the back of the house. Grace seemed to have lost her head over Mr Gripper. Nothing was too much trouble. Mr Gripper was in charge.

That summer was the only unhappy one I spent at Bamber Bridge. With Mr Gripper giving orders through Grace, the peace and laughter went out of the place. Gripper's shrewd, mottled brown eyes seemed to follow me everywhere. He showed no interest in fattening me up as my aunts had done in the past. He'd given up selling holy pictures. Instead he marketed the stockings my aunts made. Each now had her own stocking frame. When they weren't looking after the livestock and the orchard they knitted stockings; the house-keepers, Jim and Effie no longer came. While Mr Gripper didn't do any work himself – he had a chest complaint that demanded rest – he was forever on about wasting time. 'The Lord never wastes time,' was one of his favourite sayings. Even our afternoon walk had been sacrificed to Simon Gripper's need for more stockings.

Yet Mr Gripper didn't bully them. 'I quite understand,' he would say when Betsy objected to something. 'How fool-ish of me. You are right and I am wrong. I was only trying to do what is best for us all.' I used to watch Betsy's reac-tions. Her face went from red to scarlet. Then it set on fire. Yet she managed to hold her tongue.

Every evening Mr Gripper told his rosary. He kept it in an old snuff box which he carried in his waistcoat pocket. It was a poor thing compared to the one aunt Grace had. Hers was made of ivory beads with a silver chain and a golden cross. As my aunts were devout Catholics, they joined him in saying a few Hail Mary's and Our Father's – something they'd never done before. Whenever we could, Whiskey and

I fled the house for the fields. We were both heavy-hearted.

Although I attended a Protestant school at that time, my aunts insisted on my going to St Augustine's Catholic Church with them on Sundays. The church was the centre of their life; there was always something being 'got up' by them for the church. Open-handedly, they gave innumerable hens and ducks to the church bazaars.

What I could not stand about Mr Gripper was his behaviour in church. When he genuflected before the altar, I thought he would never get up. He struck his breast three times during the Confiteor, hitting himself hard enough to break his ribs. 'Through my fault,' thump. 'Through my fault,' louder thump. 'Through my most grievous fault,' crash! The half empty church echoed to the thumps. At the elevation of the Host, he groaned. He relished the words 'miserable sinner,' and beat himself as he repeated them. When he grovelled before the altar rails to receive communion, I wished that the vaulted ceiling would fall on him.

To my aunts' obvious displeasure I couldn't help staring at him. 'Aunt Betsy,' I whispered, 'why does Mr Gripper have to beat himself like that? You don't.'

'Sh-sh. Stop talking, Billy, you can't talk here. What will people think?'

Not only did Mr Gripper thump himself in church more than anybody else; when the congregation recited the eight Beatitudes – blessed are the poor; blessed are the meek . . . Mr Gripper's voice was louder than the rest. At Benediction one Sunday evening he sang a solo 'The day that Thou gavest, Oh Lord, now is ending' which almost took out the windows. Grace thought it was marvelous. I thought it awful. Only Betsy's shushing stopped me from saying so.

I have reason to remember that particular summer. It was the summer Mr Gripper robbed me of a tooth. I'd had the misfortune to develop toothache. The pain was awful.

'Simon, take lad beyond t' bridge to Henry's,' aunt Betsy had asked Mr Gripper. 'He's a young man just starting out. He'll put it right. They say he's got a new-fangled American drill that does the job in half the time. Tell him to do a good job on t' lad. Mustn't lose tooth at his age. I'll pay when you tell me how much it is.'

So off we went to Henry's. Mr Gripper didn't have to tell me that I and my tooth were a complete nuisance and that he wasn't enjoying the excursion one bit.

Our arrival at Mr Henry's was announced by a large doorbell. A threateningly, ominously empty chair stood in the middle of the surgery. There were no other patients. Mr Henry emerged from a back room.

'He's got a bit of a toothache,' Mr Gripper grumped at Mr Henry. 'Can yo put it right?'

I was put in the chair. With a light, Mr Henry studied the offending tooth. His poking made it worse.

'He needs a small filling,' he concluded. 'Take a few minutes, that's all. He won't feel a thing. It'll take out all the pain.'

I watched Mr Gripper eye the dentist slyly. 'Wot's cost?' he asked.

'Three and sixpence.'

There was a pause. 'Wot's an extraction cost?'

'Two shillings.'

'Take it out,' said Mr Gripper.

'But I can save the tooth,' Mr Henry said. 'It's a straightforward job. A perfectly good tooth.'

'Take it out,' said Mr Gripper.

'But . . .' the dentist faltered.

'Young man,' said Mr Gripper, 'yo're wasting my time. Dost t' want to earn two shillings or dostn't thee?'

Mr Henry made a pathetic gesture. 'All right,' he said. 'I've heard yer.'

I returned to aunt Betsy without my tooth.

'Had to come out,' said Mr Gripper. 'Nothing else for it.'

The next time I went to Bamber Bridge, I was surprised to find my aunts' house occupied by strangers. The door was locked and I had to use the knocker. A tall oldish couple came to the door.

'Ah've cum te stay with my aunts,' I said. 'Ah cum every year.'

'Tha won't be staying this year,' the man said.

'Why not?'

'Because thi aunts don't live here any more. They sold t' house. It's an old folks' 'ome now. Didn't ye know? Thi aunt Grace has got herself wed.'

'To Mr Gripper?' I asked, my heart sinking.

'The same,' the woman said. She was about to go on, but the man gave her a reproachful glance, whereupon she fell silent.

I stood looking vacantly from one to the other. 'Where are they now?'

'They're running a general store with Mr Gripper in Preston.' He went back into the house to find the address, which he wrote on a slip of paper for me. He also gave me instructions on how to get there. His eyes told me that I was in for a shock.

An hour later I found a grocer's store in one of the back streets of Preston. The shop faced an ancient aqueduct, the black, greasy stones of which ran with moisture. All around was a bleak industrial area with the railway and factories only yards away. Dirt and peeling paint were everywhere. If anybody had told me a year earlier that I should find my aunts living in such an awful place, I would have thought them mad.

The shop was empty of customers when I entered. With their backs to the entrance, Betsy and Grace were busy unwrapping and emptying boxes. They got such a surprise when they saw me. They flapped their hands to show their discomfort.

'Oh, Billy,' they said, 'why did you come here?'

They hugged me, but it was in an absent-minded, apprehensive sort of way. They didn't have the life and strength of earlier times. Betsy moved stiffly. I was startled at aunt Grace's appearance. She looked crushed. She had great black rings under her eyes. She could hardly breathe from asthma – something she had never had at Bamber Bridge. She told me Whiskey was dead.

While we were talking, Mr Gripper came up from the cellar. He looked extremely well and prosperous. He'd got himself a better suit. His hair glistened with oil. He wore a gold watch-chain. From the moment he saw me, he was hostile.

'Oh, it's you is it?' he said as he came forward. 'Thought we'd got rid of you, we did. Well, you've come to t' wrong place for a free summer this time. Tha'd better go back where tha cum fra. Can't have thee interferin' with our business.'

'Simon!' Grace said angrily.

But Simon was not to be put off. He pointed to the door through which I had just entered. The message was clear. He wanted me back in the street. My aunts stared at me with empty eyes. There was time only to squeeze their hands. We didn't speak. We just clung to each other pathetically. None of us cried, but our eyes were wet. I knew in my heart that we all wanted to sob and sob.

I never saw my aunts again. I did write a letter to them when I got home asking them if I could help them in any way, but it was returned to me by Mr Gripper. Mother came in one day and told me in a sad voice that Grace was dead. The news gave me a lump in my throat. My eyes welled with tears. Betsy had gone to live with friends in Scotland. I thought mother was going to go on about Mr Gripper – all the Kenyons and Woodruffs knew about Simon Gripper by now – but she didn't. I don't know what became of him. I hope he did ill. He left me with a life-long distrust of unctuous people.

Chapter XIV

Grandmother Bridget

When I was about ten, I became closer to grandmother Bridget than to my own family. Hardly a day went by when I was not in her house. With Jenny and Brenda in the mills, it fell to me to help her keep it clean. I chopped the sticks for the fire that heated the washtub standing in an alcove of the downstairs room. I ran errands. When things were especially bad, I'd bring a shilling or a half-crown from mother to buy food. Grandmother didn't take charity easily and was difficult to help.

I cannot remember her sharing our house or our board, yet working-class families were usually close. For whatever reasons, she clung to her privacy. I was the only one – other than mother – who could reach out to her. Father, Dan, Brenda, and even sweet Jenny found grandmother remote. She simply didn't welcome attention. Except from me, she never accepted help gracefully. Apart from my visits, she kept herself to herself. I think she did so because fate had cast her into a society for which she was ill-suited. Maggie was right when she said her mother had 'cum reet down.'

In the mid-twenties grandmother fell on bitterly hard times. Having lost her job in the mills; she tried to survive by doing people's washing, never satisfied until it was whiter than snow. It used to infuriate me the way some of the workers robbed her. 'Tell her I'll give her the money next week,' they said when I delivered the laundry beautifully wrapped in clean newspaper. I knew they were lying; there were times when I felt like telling them so. I knew how desperately grandmother needed the money; sixpence, ninepence, or a shilling would have kept her going.

'These people don't speak with a plain tongue, Grandma,' I complained.

'They're poor too, Billy Boy,' she said, clasping her wasted hands, 'they don't know which way to turn.'

At that time, she was living in a doll-like house at the end of a row of cottages in Astley Street – five minutes walk from Griffin Street. The house was shaped like the tip of a flat iron. It had one tiny room downstairs and an equally small room upstairs. Apart from the street door, two windows (one up, one down), a corner in which to cook and another in which to wash, a broken rocking chair, two stools, a rough, bench-like table, a fireplace and a bed with a wooden chest at its foot, there was little else. Anything of value had long since gone to the pawnshop.

Next door to grandmother's cottage was a high-walled cobbled yard. At one time, grandmother had kept her brooms, tin bath and laundry tub there. When I knew it, the lock grandmother had put on the door had been broken and the yard had become a steaming manure dump used by the town's street cleaning crews as well as by several horse stables in the vicinity. Although the wall hid the manure, there was no mistaking the smell. Because of it, her two windows and her door were kept shut. The final irony was that the police had told grandmother to get rid of the manure.

Desperate, she asked me to go to the police station to get them to stop people dumping manure outside her door. I wasn't happy about going. I'd been raised to fear and avoid the police, but I went.

Having run through the streets, I reached the station and began to lay grandmother's troubles before the sergeant-on-duty. He was a tall, burly man with a clipped moustache. From the word go, he left me in no doubt that my sudden ragged appearance to discuss steaming manure was not to his liking. He had more important things to do.

'The coppers have complained to grandmother about the manure in her yard. But she's not the one who puts it there,' I said.

'Who has complained?' His face reddened.

'The coppers.'

'And who might the coppers be?'

'You're a copper, aren't you?' I said, my eyes glued to the stick he was holding.

'Bert, Charley,' the sergeant called to two policemen who were listening from the other room, 'There's a young gentleman here who thinks we're coppers. Not officers, not sergeants, not constables, just plain coppers.'

'Well, you are, aren't you?'

From that moment on, the topic of manure was forgotten. Instead, I was given the worst dressing down of my life. I was threatened with a fate worse than that suffered by the Christian martyrs. The sergeant said he would have the whole Blackburn police force down on my head and I believed him. I'd be in the 'clink' for the rest of my life. He put the fear of hell into me. With my eye on the stick, I edged back to the door and fled.

'Well?' asked grandmother, when I returned, breathless from running. 'What are they going to do about it?'

'Nothing, Grandma, they didn't want to talk about manure.'

Grandmother not only had to tolerate the manure, directly opposite her house lived the town executioner. I was horrified when she told me about the hangman. Not that I ever heard anyone speak against hanging. I spent hours gingerly peeping through her curtains in the hope of catching a glimpse of the hangman hurrying off with his rope to an execution. I tried to draw out of her the fine details of how the poor wretches died. 'It's not a subject for "dacent" conversation,' she silenced me. Father knew the hangman; he often met him in the pub. He spoke highly of him. He said he was the happiest of men. The only strange thing about him was his ice-cold hands.

◦

As grandmother got older she often talked about Ireland; about her birthplace, County Clare, with its ruined castles and the ghosts that haunted its broken walls. She also spoke of her life as a girl before she met grandfather Thomas. She told me about the balls she'd been to. She had had a passion for dancing. No matter how much she tried to conceal it, I detected a wistfulness, if not a downright sadness.

What I know about the feud that has raged between Ireland and England for centuries, I learned from her. 'The trouble with the English,' she said one day, 'is that they can never remember what the Irish can never forget.' In a quiet but rich voice, she sang a haunting song about Robert Emmet, the Irish martyr:

> The struggle is over, the boys are defeated,
> Old Ireland's surrounded with sadness and gloom;
> We were betrayed and shamefully treated,
> And I, Robert Emmet, awaiting my doom.

She sang it as a dirge, not as a call to arms. She was never bitter: not against fate, not against the British. Grudges were no part of her.

She also told me about the great famine in Ireland in the 1840's, in which millions had died or fled to America. 'It was not a famine, Billy Boy,' she said. 'It was a great "starvin'." And it was to England's shame!'

She taught me to be courageous, loyal and honest. Falseness she couldn't abide. 'If you give your word, Billy Boy, keep it.' Especially did she teach me to be upstanding. 'You must never grovel, Billy Boy. And never beg. Stand on your own feet. And don't whine.' Whatever manners and courtesies I learned, I learned from her.

She never mentioned God. The only concession she made to the saints was to wear a large sprig of shamrock on the 17th March, St Patrick's Day. In her opinion St Patrick was a 'foin Saint, a very foin Saint,' and that was good enough for me. One of her favourite ballads was about St Patrick's Day:

O Paddy, dear, an' did ye hear the news that's goin'
   round?
The shamrock is by law forbid to grow on Irish
   ground!
No more St Patrick's Day we'll keep, his colour can't
   be seen,
For there's a cruel law agin the wearin' o' the Green!

One night when we were sitting before the embers, she told me how in 1920, thousands of Irish had gathered outside a London jail where almost two hundred Irish political prisoners were fasting unto death. As darkness fell, someone called for silence. Faintly they heard the sound of voices singing inside the jail. Then a great thunder rose from the square into the night sky as the Irish – in and outside the jail – sang 'The Wearin' o' the Green.' 'It stunned everybody who heard it,' grandmother said. 'Papers were full of it. Not long afterward the prisoners were freed.'

Grandmother lived to see southern Ireland become the Irish Free State.

When my lessons were done, she turned down the glass-funnelled paraffin lamp and relapsed into quiet contentment before the fire. Often she gently rocked, while humming a tune or gravely sipping a cup of tea. She didn't touch alcohol.

Although she had few visitors, she tidied herself up at night. By the time I reached her cottage, she had changed into a long, dark garment that contrasted with the lace cap which came down to her shoulders. Sometimes she wore a blouse with big, shiny buttons. Usually I found her before the fire, her feet on a stool, her hands on her knees. There was always an open book – her escape from wretchedness – on the cornice next to her wire-framed spectacles. I often wondered how she could sit there by herself for hours on end staring at the flames. I'd catch her carrying on a conversation with the embers and her memories.

On occasions, I managed to persuade her to take a short walk. With her hat and her jacket and her silver-topped cane and her cracked shoes, all of them relics of her better days, she looked quite a toff. Even when she had been a slubber in the mills, she had refused to wear a weaver's shawl and clogs. Poor or not, she retained her dignified bearing, the Kenyon air of gentility. There were times when her neighbours found her difficult to understand, but they all called her 'royal.'

'And where do you think you're going?' she asked if I walked too fast. 'I can't keep up with you.'

Only once did I see her truly worried and sad. Regardless of her growing poverty, she was usually happy and cheerful. Shortly before I arrived, a hog of a rent collector had threatened to throw her into the street. I don't know what had happened; father usually helped her with the rent. Tears were rolling silently down her wrinkled face. Her long, thin neck seemed to have contracted. She wasn't crushed – she was too tough for that – just badly wounded. The hardness of her lot never hardened her soul.

By the time she was in her early sixties, about the time of the General Strike in 1926, she was destitute. She had no income at all. I cannot believe that some of the Kenyons did not try to help her, but I saw little evidence of it. Everybody was desperately trying to survive. Also I suspect that grandmother put them off in her own innocent, refined way, as she did the offers of help from her neighbours.

For a period at least, grandmother was eligible for outdoor relief from the town. She could have queued up for one of the Lord Mayor's parcels, which every now and again were distributed in front of the Town Hall. But the idea of queuing with hundreds of others seeking public charity was an anathema to her. She refused to make an exhibition of her need. The churches provided food – in helping to stem the tide of want, Blackburn churches and clergy had a long and honourable tradition – but some churches adhered to the maxim 'support only those that are of the faith.' It grieved mother that grandmother had not applied for the dole. To refuse the dole was refusing good money. Nor did she resort to the Poor Law Guardians. That would have been the final blow to her self-respect. Grandmother preferred to keep her pride and to genteelly starve to death. Pride was all she had left.

Living from hand to mouth ourselves, there was little we could do for her. I couldn't give her anything from what I earned running errands; my people took it. I sometimes brought her a basin of broth from the street kitchens run by the Salvation Army, or the Catholic Sisters of Mercy and Charity. Some of the Protestant churches also handed out free soup or a piece of potato pie. Grandmother wasn't easy. She ate the food I brought her, but she refused to go and get it; that was begging.

The trouble came when she began to lose interest in food altogether; not only in food but in life as well. She became increasingly listless. Etched by a nest of lines, her deep-set blue eyes became deeper still. The light in them was lowered. She didn't seem to care what happened to her. She got so weak that I began to do all her cleaning. That's how, one Saturday evening when grandmother had gone to mother's, I came to open the box that stood at the foot of her bed. I lifted the lid gingerly knowing that I was prying. I was astonished to find a whole lot of fine clothes there. Among them was a beautiful blue ball dress decorated with imitation pearls. There also was a little book headed 'Carmania' with a list of names in it.

As the clothes meant food, I brought up the subject when grandmother returned. I confessed I'd been prying into her trunk.

'You didn't tell me about all the fine clothes you're hiding. That's money. Why don't you pawn them?'

'They're not for pawning, Billy Boy. Not my best feathers,' she added with a bright, quick smile. 'Not those!'

After a long silence, she spoke up. 'Would you like to see me in my best feathers?' There was a note of mischief in her voice.

'Yes,' I said, for I knew it would please her.

Before I could stop her, she had jumped up, taken the glass-funnelled lamp from the cornice, and was on her way upstairs. I was left with the firelight.

After a few minutes she called down: 'Are you ready, Billy Boy?'

'Yes, I'm ready.'

I looked up as I heard her feet on the stairway. What I saw made me catch my breath. Grandmother was wearing the ball dress I'd seen in the trunk. The pearls glowed softly as they caught the firelight. Around her neck she wore a long fluffy boa made of feathers and delicate fabric. On her feet were the elegant slippers. A tiny patch of lace covered her hair. From her wrist hung the little book. Her face was lit by the paraffin lamp she held before her. I noticed that the deep lines and wrinkles had gone. Her face seemed much younger.

'Grandma,' I gasped.

As she stepped lightly onto the sanded floor she pretended to consult her little book. 'I believe you asked me to dance this one with you,' she said as she extended her hand toward me gracefully.

Kicking off my clogs, I hurriedly pushed whatever furniture there was out of the way. Resting her hands on my shoulders, for she was taller than I, we began to turn slowly in the confined space. The lamp on the cornice, which she had replaced, flickered a dim light. It threw our shadows against the wall. Increasing our speed, we danced round and round, grinding the grit with our feet. Grandmother's eyes were almost shut.

In time, I tired. She didn't. She moved effortlessly, like someone possessed; she didn't want to stop.

'Oh, Billy Boy,' she scolded when I stumbled, and then we were off again, faster than ever. My head spun.

I don't know how long we danced. The dance ended when I fell over a stool and could go on no more.

I didn't know what to do when I got up off the floor, so I stood there breathless and clapped as I'd seen dancers do. 'Grandma, you danced beautifully.'

She smiled, made a slight bow, and went upstairs. Shortly afterward, she came down again, coughing harshly. She wore her usual black dress, with her lace cap hanging to her shoulders. The flushed cheeks had paled; the deep lines had returned; dark rings surrounded her reddened eyes; she was strangely cast down; there was a tiredness in her voice – a grating in her throat. She had difficulty breathing. When she stepped into the room I could hear her bare feet on the sand. Her step was halting and unsteady.

I didn't see anything of grandmother the next day. Two nights later I entered her darkened cottage. There was no sign of her. Having struck a light, I saw her empty purse on the table. It lay there wide open as if it had been thrown from the door. My eyes took in the faded pictures on the wall, the setpot, the frayed curtains, the broken rocking chair, the glass-funnelled lamp on the mantelpiece and the gutted candle on the table. I knew something was wrong. I ran upstairs. There was no one there. When I lifted the lid of the trunk at the foot of her bed, it was empty. I ran home and told mother.

Two days later uncle Edward walked into our house to tell us that grandmother Bridget was dead and buried.

Wearing her ball dress, she had stumbled all the way to

the workhouse, and had died there a few hours after being admitted. She had declared herself 'without next of kin,' which had made it all the more difficult for the workhouse authorities to get in touch with us. It was the police who had informed uncle Edward.

A week or so later, Mr Hetherington, t' bump man who had studied my head years before, told us he'd seen grandmother on the day she was missing. She was sitting on a bench at the edge of town. He'd walked past her and had wondered what she was up to dressed like that. 'She was like something on t' parade. Ah've never seen anythin' like it. She was sat straight up, back like a ramrod, head held high, oh, so high, feathers aflutter. She had her silver-topped cane in her outstretched right hand. Her t' other hand lay on her lap. Cheeks were sunken, but t' nose and chin were out there. I could have sworn t' eyes were closed. Well, I didn't know what to say. I felt right bamboozled. I almost stopped and asked her what she was up to. But then I had second thoughts. It was none of my business. It was summer, and t' old lady was known for taking walks. As for t' funny dress and scarf and slippers, who was I to judge? There's no telling what an old woman will get up to. So, I doffed mi cap, held mi tongue, and went mi way.'

Several days later, the workhouse returned grandmother Bridget's belongings. There was the silver-tipped cane, the dress, the scarf, the lace cap and the now torn slippers. They also sent a faded photograph of grandfather Thomas, and the little book that contained the list of dancing partners.

Out of it all, came my first great heartbreak. For the first time in my life I knew what it was to be scalded with grief. I was more upset than when I heard aunt Grace was dead. On and off, I wept for days. Several times I cried myself to sleep. I not only wept, I loathed myself for not having done more. I loathed the grown-ups, especially uncle Eric and uncle Edward, when they came together in our house to brood over stewed tea, while they accused and mocked each other for having 'driven t' poor owd woman in t' workhouse.' Silently,

I listened to their mealy-mouthed words. Rage possessed me; they were all to blame. Grandmother had had to die before they recognized her existence. For the first time, the idea of running away from Blackburn and Lancashire entered my head. With all their fine talk, they had managed to drive Bridget Gorman Kenyon 'over t' hill.'

Chapter XV

Strike!

S omething must have been sadly wrong with Britain when people had to 'genteelly' starve to death as grandmother Bridget had done. Living through the 1920's was like sitting in a boiling pot of broth. There was no peace. By 1926 things had got so bad that the workers began to talk of bringing the country to a standstill through a General Strike. The working class was going to make one last big effort to set everything right. In April 1926 the mine owners posted new wage offers that were so low that they were tantamount to a lockout. When the miners refused the terms offered and stayed out, matters were brought to a head. On 1 May 1926 the government declared a State of Emergency. The fight was on.

I'd almost no idea what was going on, but I was thrilled at the prospect of a decisive fight with the bosses. Not for a moment did I doubt the complete justice of the workers' cause.

Before the strike there was to be a meeting in the

Blackburn Trade Hall. Father's trade union had asked him to attend. Everyone talked about it – even at school. I was so excited that I asked father to take me with him to the Trade Hall meeting.

When we entered the crowded hall you could feel the sparks. People were worked up. The place hummed with voices. Delegates from all the major industries: mining, transport, railways, engineering and textiles were present. They all had their banners. To loud applause, the meeting began with one of the miners' delegates taking the platform and appealing to his 'brothers and sisters' to come to the miners' aid. 'The hour of decision has struck!' he shouted to wild applause. 'Defend us in our fight for a living wage.'

What followed came as a surprise. I thought the weavers, the spinners and the twiners would all line up behind the miners, the railway and other transport workers to fight the bosses. Instead, a shouting match began between the textile people in which all order broke down. Nobody seemed to know if we were going to have a General Strike or a National Strike, though I couldn't see the difference. Tall, angular Patrick Murphy – the foreman who had delivered me when I was born – thought that a General Strike would make matters worse, and he advised against joining the miners. He was shouted down as 'a capitalist lackey and a running dog.' Those who wanted a General Strike were shouted down as 'bolshies and "reds" in the pay of Russia.'

'Revolution's out of the question,' Mr Murphy argued, jumping up on his chair. 'It's purposeless to talk about a workers' state. The country is not with you. Of course we must continue the struggle, but there is a right way of going about it and a wrong way. Why come out now, when you've already lost so much through strikes and lockouts? I ask you, what can you gain? Nothing. On that you have to agree. Half a loaf is better than none.'

While many workers booed Mr Murphy, half a dozen other speakers stood on their chairs bawling at each other at the top of their voices. One of them shouted, 'Half a loaf rubbish. Next thing you'll be telling us that a crumb is better than nothing. What I say is not a penny off the pay, not a second on the day! One out, all out!' By now everybody was clamouring and uneasy.

As far as I could make out, all the speakers were proposing different things. Some were calling for revolution; some were calling for peace; some wanted to support the miners; others wanted to leave the miners to their fate. Everybody was rude to each other. 'Hold thi trap,' 'shut thi gob,' and 'shut up,' were hurled across the room.

Once the meeting got out of hand, the chairman's shouts of 'Gentlemen, please! Gentlemen, recognize the chair!' were ignored. So were the appeals of many others who called for 'Silence, please. Silence!' The drum beat of the chairman's gavel only added to the din. I'd never been to a workers' meeting as unruly as this. Father's trade union meetings were all solemn affairs, like going to church.

As the noise got worse, father said, 'Let's go home. Too many crackpots.' Until then he hadn't opened his mouth. Others must have agreed with him, for lots of people were streaming out of the hall. They smelled danger. I looked back as we left: there were more people standing on chairs.

The next day father read from the paper that 'Because of the lively differences of opinion expressed at the Trade Hall meeting, a decision to join the other unions calling for a General Strike, has been deferred.' Later that week, another meeting was convoked, but that didn't get anywhere either.

Two days after that father came home looking glum. 'We're coomin' oot,' he said, 'a sympathy strike, and a damned lot of good it will do; especially as the TUC (Trade Union Congress) doesn't want us out yet. Anyway, the decision has been made. It is only the timing that's in t' air.' Murphy and other moderates had been overruled; the crackpots had won. Father was obviously worried. He began to talk about what was at stake; who would finish up having to give up what. He wanted to get it off his chest. Then he relapsed into silence.

I was with mother in the mill when the strike began. 'Where t' going?' mother asked workers who were streaming past her.

'Going? Why, on strike, of course. Didn't you hear the call "All out?" Why, you must be deaf? Y' either starve outside in t' fresh air with us, luv, or starve in here covered with cotton dust. Which dusta want?'

Mother was bewildered. Reluctantly she threw her shawl round her shoulders, shut down her machine, and walked out. The strike was on. It was 3 May 1926.

'Fight! Fight! Action! Action!' people were shouting in the streets. A river of workers was streaming home. There were bursts of cheering. Mother had a deadly fear of violence. We hurried on.

The whole world fell silent the next day. Even the factory engines stopped. It was the deep, strange silence of the high moors. There was no shouting, no roughness, no disorder, no lawlessness in Blackburn. Soldiers guarded public offices. The newspapers went off the streets. Trains, buses and trams were still. The iron and steel industry was brought to a halt. The mills, mines and engineering shops for miles around were shut down. Some merchants shuttered their stores. For all the work we did, the schools might as well have been closed too.

My family sat in silence in our kitchen in Griffin Street, holding their breath, waiting for the revolution to begin. The streets were full of rumours. In Blackburn, special constables were sworn in; extra police were brought from Burnley and Preston; the mails were censored; the telegraphs were controlled. There was arson at Bank Top Mill. A police spy was taken out of the canal near Whalley Bridge with his throat cut; at Walton-le-Dale, near Preston, the police baton-charged strikers interfering with the buses. In Manchester, demonstrators were fired on. The docks at Liverpool were paralyzed. From John o' Groats to Land's End the workers were answering the call. Troops were in charge of all main roads; there were clashes between them and groups of 'reds.'

No tale lost anything in the telling. Uncle Eric was the only one we knew who owned a radio. He could have told us what was going on, but I don't think we asked him.

After eight days the papers were back on the streets with banner headlines: GENERAL STRIKE BROKEN. ENGLAND STANDS FAST. Prime Minister Stanley Baldwin and the bosses had won. There wasn't going to be a revolution after all.

The first general strike in the history of the country had failed. Oh, what a let down! The workers cried. If they had been beaten, it would have been one thing. But they hadn't. The strike had been abandoned. Leaders like Jimmy Thomas of the Railway Workers' Union had betrayed us. Father said the Labour Party had played with fire and then run for cover.

The workers didn't starve after the General Strike, but they were humiliated. Conditions became worse. Despite all the honeyed words, victimization was common. Ringleaders were blackballed. Little pity was shown. The bosses did what they liked. They kept those they wanted and threw out those they didn't. Hours were increased, wages cut. The factory owners had never shared the good times with us. When there was cake, they ate it; when there was sorrow, they lumped it onto us. Under the Trade Disputes and Trade Union Act of 1927, which was passed almost overnight, many rights that the workers had fought for over long periods were abolished. General strikes and sympathetic strikes were outlawed. New laws were introduced against picketing. Using any excuse, workers were jailed: 'The accused was lurking in a doorway.' 'The accused had his foot over the factory threshold' during a lockout. Labour Party finances – and hence the strength of the Labour Party – were deliberately undermined. Political activity of the trade unions was curtailed. The policy of fining workers also became harsher. In 1928, Nelson (it was called 'Red Nelson') was brought to a standstill for seven weeks because of what the workers felt was an unjust weaver's fine. In Nelson a lot of families went hungry. Henceforth, you toed the employers' line or you were for it.

What the textile workers suffered was nothing compared to the miners who had started the row. The miners stayed out on strike for seven more bitter months. 'We'll starve before going back,' they said. By the time they went back they were starving. They took a heavy beating: hours, wages, the lot. Over one million mineworkers, together with their womenfolk and children, were abandoned to the mercy of the mine-owners. It was soulless capitalism at its worst. Mother's only comment, when father told her of the miners' plight was, 'Why do people have to be so cruel to each other?' She never realized that her God of mercy was not widely known; it was the God of wrath, the vindictive God that ruled.

So bad did conditions become that a proposed visit of the king to Lancashire was cancelled.

The ever-darkening scene in Lancashire after the General Strike of 1926 prompted a shift in the labour movement from trade union to political action. There was a new interest in winning seats on the town council and in parliament. If the workers could replace the toffs in parliament a new day might dawn.

Blackburn began at the local level. We tried to get Patrick Murphy onto the town council. His sunken, snub-nosed face was well-known in town politics. His fairness and candour made him well liked. The workers trusted him. His honesty was apparent. His opponent was an absentee conservative factory owner, Henry Hen, whose slogan was: 'Vote for Hen, the man who lays the golden eggs.'

I was ten at the time. With Harold Watkins, Rosie Gill, Annie Morgan and others, I gladly helped Mr Murphy by distributing handbills in the streets and at the factory gates. I got cross at workers who called him an Irish mongrel. Murphy had been kind to me since I was born. What did being Irish matter? Grandmother Bridget was Irish.

Anyway, as was to happen time and again, Labour lost the election. Despite all our shouts of 'Vote, vote, vote for Mr Murphy, Murphy's sure to win the day . . .' most

252

workers preferred to vote for the Tory bosses, who, with the Anglican Church, were all-powerful in our town. The very people Labour wanted to help proved to be their worst enemies. Too many of the workers didn't want change. They had a mental block that prevented them from putting their own people in charge. Like father, they were not radical at heart. Also, the mill bosses were generous in doling out free beer in a round about way.

All Patrick Murphy could afford to give his election helpers – when his predicted defeat was announced – was twopenny worth of fish and chips in a white paper bag with as much vinegar as we wanted. Mr Murphy stood at the fish and chip counter – the strain of the election showing on his face – doling out twopence for each of us. When we'd finished eating we all sang 'For he's a jolly good fellow!' It must have touched him for he had difficulty holding back his tears.

—◦—

As the contraction of the cotton industry continued and wage levels fell, industrial action came to the fore again. Strikes and lockouts became endemic. There was no stopping them. From the General Strike of 1926 until the mid-thirties, two-thirds of all working days lost in strikes in Britain were in textiles. Things got so bad that agitators worked on people's feelings to bring about a clash between the workers and the police at the factory gates. For boys of my age, the prospect of such clashes offered excitement. Mother told me to stay away from these meetings. 'They're dangerous,' she warned, gently rubbing the sides of my head with her hands.

I ignored her warning. Riotous meetings before factory gates drew Harold Watkins and me like a magnet. The more dangerous, the more we were drawn. I'd never heard such fiery speakers. Harold said they'd been brought in specially. One day we were in the middle of such a crowd when somebody shouted 'Coppers!' Panic-stricken, Harold and I fled with the rest. Suddenly, I tripped and fell. A tidal wave of workers passed over me. I caught a glimpse of the horses and the raised batons. I struggled to my feet. The horses were almost on top of me when I felt a stunning blow to the head. There was no 'In the name of the law, I order you to disperse,' just a crack on the skull. Stars jumped before my eyes. I suddenly felt dizzy and weak. I nearly fell again. Somehow we got away. Despite my thick woollen cap, I had an egg on my head, which I tried to conceal for weeks.

Father didn't turn up at these factory gate meetings. He was suspicious of anybody letting off steam. It embarrassed him. Yet he was ever loyal to his union. When the union said 'Strike!' he struck; when they said 'March!' he marched – though like a lot of factory folk he didn't enjoy it – if they asked him to carry a banner, he carried it. When his fellow unionists sang: 'You should rally round our banner in a true and loyal manner, And be eager in the fight that's being waged . . .' he sang as loud as the rest. He had his reservations about strikes, which he shared with the family, but he never let the union down. The trade union was the only thing my father ever joined and he remained loyal to it.

———◦———

Father's staunch loyalty to his trade union almost proved to be his undoing. The occasion was a strike meeting before the Town Hall. The time was the late 1920's. Almost everybody in town was on strike. There were to be a number of speakers including Patrick Murphy. There wasn't a 'red' on the programme. Like many others, just for the fun of it, Harold Watkins and I decided to go with father to hear what the speakers had to say. The rest of the family showed no interest.

It all began peacefully enough. Handfuls of people on their way to the meeting became a stream; the stream became a river. No one expected the crowd to become as large as it did. Drums, flags and banners came from nowhere. Some said we were going to the Town Hall, others said the meeting had been changed to the Trade Hall, and that's where we should go. Still others didn't care; they'd seen a crowd and joined it; they loved a parade. Some even brought their children and dogs.

Drawn along by the drumbeats, the procession wound its way toward the centre of town. Caps pulled down, most of the men were buttoned up to the neck. Here and there, the women had thrown their shawls back onto their shoulders. Some wore woollen hats and scarves. There was mist in the air; the leaden sky had not yet turned into rain. With the factories stopped, the air was free of soot. Odd shouts and snatches of song echoed in the street. Children skipped in and out of the crowd.

The farther we got, the more people joined in. When we got to The Royal there was a crowd standing in the door-way trying to find out what was up. There were lights inside and glints of glassware. They didn't respond to our shouts to join in. They stood there wordless, looking on.

It was just beyond The Royal, that a column of mounted police slowly emerged from a side street and blocked our path. A silence fell upon the crowd; there was a confused murmur; the dogs at the front began to bark. Harold and I thought it was just another group of police going about their business. They'd nothing to do with us. Ours was an entirely peaceful demonstration.

I was impressed by the horses. I'd never seen so many police horses in Blackburn before. They must have been brought in from outside. They were spotlessly clean and groomed as on parade. The silver pieces on the harness glinted.

I continued to be fascinated as the horses jingled toward us in a slow canter, their hoofs ringing on the stones. There were shouts: 'Get out of our bloody way! It's our bloody street!' Boos followed. Everyone began to talk at once. For a moment the column slowed down, but people pushed from behind causing the procession to sway forward again.

Only when the canter changed to a gallop, and the police drew their long batons, did I become afraid. The terror I'd felt once before, when I'd fallen in the middle of a mob, returned.

As the crowd turned to flee, a shot rang out. Pop! it went. It sounded like a firework. Somebody shouted 'They're firing on us! It's bloody murder!' Panic seized the crowd, which now tried to fall back, screaming in fear. People ran in all directions to get out of the horses' way.

Running along the pavement, father, Harold and I clashed with a group running the other way. They were led by a man who was still carrying a banner UNITED WE STAND. DIVIDED WE FALL. A group of us was swept into a furniture shop doorway. The door was locked. With the battle going on all around, we huddled there.

Baton-swinging riders repeatedly swept past our shelter. Lashed now by cold gusts of rain, the horses galloped, turned, reformed and galloped again. They were led by an officer who rode at great speed, shouting commands. The street was full of cries for help. The windows of the bakery across the street were smashed. The sound of batons on flesh – a dull whack – made me wince. Flags, clothing, food were scattered all over the cobbles.

A few feet from where we were crouching, Patrick Murphy lay on the ground. One of the horses pranced all around him. Telling us to stay where we were, father and another man ran out and, with blows raining down on their backs, dragged Mr Murphy from under the horses' hooves into the doorway. Mr Murphy had blood on his bald head. His eyes were glassy and unseeing, his face pallid. 'They've cracked his skull like an eggshell,' father said. He was calm, as firm as a rock, Harold and I were shaking.

Once the police had moved farther down the street, the shopkeeper opened the door and offered us an escape through the back alley. He was obviously on the workers' side. 'Bloody murderers,' he called the police. He refused to have Mr Murphy carried into his store, but promised to call an ambulance. We'd be sure to be arrested if we tried to carry him through the streets.

Leaving Mr Murphy on the step, the shopkeeper led us through several rooms piled high with merchandise. As he'd turned off the lights, we bumped into each other. From the rear entrance we hurriedly made our way home. Father had a nasty welt across his back. 'What a gobbin you are,' mother scolded. 'Might have got the child killed.' The experience left me shaken.

The town was in an uproar after the police attack. No one had the right to drive law-abiding people off the streets. It was a disgrace. Some preachers made sermons about it.

'It will all die down,' father grumped. 'Nothing will come of it. You'll see.'

Which is what would have happened had Mr Murphy's condition not deteriorated. Vigils were held outside the hospital. Carrying lanterns, church choirs sang hymns. Murphy became a symbol of the town's troubled conscience.

I came home one day to find mother crying. 'Patrick has gone,' she said. We were all stunned.

There followed one of the greatest funeral processions our town had known. Mother and I joined in; we felt we owed it to him. We got to the church service at St Michael's too late. It was crowded out. Willie Gill, with his cocked hat and his long robe, was up front with the Knights of Columbus. The coffin was carried on a horse-drawn hearse. The horses wore black velvet capes and black waving plumed headdresses. There were several bands. Everybody tightened up when they played Handel's Dead March. The dirge mingled with the grinding of the carriage wheels, the clink of the horses' hoofs, and the shuffling of the crowd. There were so many flowers that they had to be carried on carts. The whole route to the cemetery was lined with sad faces. Not all were hushed. 'It's a fine funeral,' someone said. 'He deserves it,' said another. 'Pity he can't see it. Upright in 'eart he was. Ah well, pray for his soul.'

Mother and I couldn't get near the grave. Father

Prendergast said a few words. He used the text 'Blessed are they which do hunger and thirst for righteousness.' He said that Patrick had led a blameless life and had gone to his reward. We saw the flowers and the piles of sods. We saw Father Prendergast reach down and scatter earth over the coffin.

'Ashes to ashes, and dust to dust, to the consummation of the world.'

Then Mrs Murphy bent down, her white hair blowing in the wind, her face marked with grief. We heard the click of spades. We waited until the solemn crowd dispersed along the cemetery paths. As their voices died away, we went forward to pay our last respects and to see the mountain of flowers. In time, except for the harsh note of the raven, the graveyard fell silent again.

Chapter XVI

Parents

My parents couldn't have been more unlike each other. One was dull and grey, the other was brightly flashing. Whereas father was placid, mother was mercurial; he was a plodder, she was a romantic.

I learned early in life that my father was a man of routine. He was a man you could count on. Whatever hour of the day, we all knew where he was and roughly what he was doing. He was the first up in the house. When there was work, he was the first to reach the mills. I think he loved the mills; he loved the humming, clattering machinery, the oil and the dirt. He started each week with a clean, collarless cotton shirt, buttoned at the neck, and cheap, blue overalls. The sleeves of his shirt were rolled up to the elbow. When he was a tackler, he wore a natty red neckerchief and a fustian waistcoat, which we thought dandy. When he went drinking, he exchanged his red neckerchief for a white crisscrossed scarf. He scorned English braces for his American belt. He would threaten us children with his belt, but never used it. There were no brutal beatings in our house.

I was proud of my father when he was a tackler. I felt it important to take his dinner every day. The way he set up a loom fascinated me. He first brought the heavy beam holding the warp threads on a two-wheeled sled to the back of the loom. Alone, he then manhandled the beam into the loom, threading hundreds, if not thousands, of warp ends through the eyes of a heald board, which was as wide as the loom. From the heald board he passed the warp ends through the teeth of a fine comb called a reed, after which he came to the front of the loom and tied all the new warp ends to the ends of the previous warp. Then he made various adjustments, which tacklers called tuning. Sometimes the warp threads were arranged by a 'drawer-in;' usually he plodded on thread after thread, by himself. I never saw him get rattled. I suppose that's where I learned about patience long before I knew what the word meant.

Day done, he'd come home, fifteen minutes after the five o'clock whistle, and put his empty basin in the same place on the sink. He also brought the *The Blackburn Telegraph*, which he read to mother. He had no interest in books, but borrowed one now and again to read to her. He read it as if he was reading a funeral notice. One night a week he'd give a hand with the heavier washing. Another night he'd get down on his knees to pummel a large bowl of dough in preparation for mother's baking. I marvelled at the way in which, with one blow, he could bury his arm up to the elbow. Plop! plop! went his fists. It sounded like something heavy being dropped into water.

When the mood took him he shaved at the kitchen sink before a small looking-glass. One day he broke the mirror. 'Mm . . . mm,' the grown-ups said in a dark way, 'seven years bad luck!' Father didn't speak, and he didn't look happy either. I think my people feared the breaking of mirrors. They knew that their spirit was reflected in the glass as well as their face. Sometimes father forgot his beard. Among the workers, nobody took any notice of an unshaved face.

Each Friday night father came through the door and placed his pay packet on the table in the front room. Quietly, mother picked it up; money matters were left to her. Other than to pay his trade union fees and shop for groceries with mother, he never handled cash. Even his cheap Woodbine cigarettes – which he called coffin nails – were bought by mother. She stacked them on the mantelpiece above the kitchen fire. Day by day, the stack was reduced until it was renewed the following Friday night. Despite all the trouble he had had with his lungs as a result of being gassed, he never stopped smoking.

The only time he showed an interest in his pay was when a co-worker cheated him. The joint earnings of father and two other men had been placed on the kitchen table awaiting division. The three of them had been working together in the factory on a special job, for which they'd been paid a handful of silver. With my head the height of the table, I saw Mr Lamp flick half-a-crown under a fold of the newspaper that covered the board. He did it so quickly that father and Mr Clay didn't see it happen, but I did.

Why would Mr Lamp want to do that, I wondered? I was doubly puzzled when I watched Mr Lamp secretly retrieve the coin before he left the house. His eyes met mine; he looked troubled. Later that night I asked father why Mr Lamp had played such a game. He paled. 'Are you sure, he did that, Billy?'

'Oh, yes, Dadda, I'm quite sure.'

Father put on his cap and went out and came back clutching ten pennies.

Sunday was a day of rest. It was the only day when the factory clocks could be ignored. Sport and entertainment were forbidden inside the town. Woe to those who disregarded this unwritten code!

One Sunday morning I and other heathens were playing football behind St Philip's Church hall when a group of black-clad women, wielding umbrellas attacked us. Until I received a whack across the head, I thought they were making fun. Far from it, the wrath of God was in their eyes. We'd fouled the Holy Day and they were after blood. We never played football on a Sunday morning in town again. Outside the town, in the hills, we could play to our heart's content.

Father and the other grown-ups had long since learned this unwritten code. When he went wrestling on a Sunday, he did so on the moors. Men and boys met at a site 'up top.' My brother and I rarely missed a match. We knew the jargon of wrestling, and could talk about chips and back-heels, hanks, clicks, hypes and hitches just like anybody else. With us it was wrestling for its own sake. Kicking, gouging, biting and tripping were all forbidden. The procedure was always the same: a ring was formed, small bets were placed. Father and his opponent stripped to the waist, rolled up their trouser legs, took off their clogs and stockings, squared up to each other, gave a touch of the hands, and the fight was on. The fight ended when both shoulders of one of the wrestlers touched the ground, or when one of the men conceded defeat.

Father was an outstanding wrestler. He knew all the holds and falls. He was all muscle. For a man in his thirties he stripped well. His arms were tattooed with a mermaid on one and an anchor on the other. On the moors I saw him as a man rather than my father. He was about medium height, had a barrel chest covered with hair, a massive ox-like neck, widespread shoulders, a well-muscled body and hairy legs like the trunk of trees. He had a large head covered with straight, brown hair, a Roman nose, a firm mouth, the strongest teeth, the dark blue eyes of his mother, and a healthy-looking skin. I was proud of him because physical strength was admired by us. For his age, having recovered from his wartime wounds, he must have been one of the fittest men about. He could lift, push, or pound anything. Few wrestlers managed to floor him. I never understood how anyone who could fight for hours on end could be as gentle with flowers and birds as he was.

Usually the wrestling contests went on until the smell of
Sunday dinner wafted across the moor. At that point the
fighting stopped, bets were settled, and everybody hurried
off for the best meal of the week. Often father was congrat-
ulated by the other workers. It made no difference to him;
he was neither elated nor downhearted. He'd had a good
'punch-up' and that's all that he cared about. It must have
been a wonderful escape from what seemed to me a monot-
onous life. Having struggled into his shirt and jacket, he left
the field as calmly as he had entered it.

Father's quiet ways didn't deceive me. I learned early in
life when to keep out of his way; lurking beneath that still,
quiet nature was what we called his Viking temper. It was
that same Viking temper that had sent his mother Selma to
jail. When aroused it was an anger that would stop at nothing. One Sunday morning on the moors I saw it almost kill
two men.

It happened like this. Father had wrestled and beaten one
of the Calvert brothers fairly and squarely. It was the brother
who always boasted about his strength and prowess. He was
then challenged by the other brother, an equally solid man.
In this match father was tripped from behind by the first
Calvert, and was sent sprawling. The movement had been
so quick that most of the onlookers didn't catch it. As father
got up the first Calvert called him a half-breed Yank. At
that, dad suddenly went wild – this time with his fists. I
heard the click as he struck his opponents' jaws. Suddenly
there were three men rolling on the ground.

I'm convinced that father would have killed the two
Calverts had the crowd not rushed in to separate them. The
three men were dragged to their feet: gasping for breath,
heads down, wet foreheads almost touching, pale with anger,
they glowered at each other through bloodshot eyes. His
arms gripped firmly from behind, father made several efforts
to break free. In a display of self-destructive fury, he twisted
and turned, reeled and staggered, dragging the three men
who were hanging on to him across the turf. Everybody was

shouting at the top of their voices and falling over each other.

With a superhuman effort, father shook off those who held him. Hitching up his trousers, he walked away. I knew from the way he walked that he was in a fearful rage, and that the brawl might be renewed. With the crowd in uproar, the Calverts followed him, but then had second thoughts. Father may not have had many brains, but when it came to fearlessness and brawn he was up front.

Except for the intensity, a fight like this was normal. People used their fists to settle disputes all the time. There was nothing wrong in punching someone on the nose, or threatening to 'knock yer bloody 'ead off.' Other workers intervened only when there was danger of someone being killed. That would complicate matters.

Oftentimes, supper over and the light still good, my brother and I accompanied father to the cindered wasteland outside the walls of Dougdale's factory where he had a small plot. He grew flowers there and kept a shed with a score of homing pigeons. It was five minutes walk from our house. Ritual-like, Dan and I trudged behind father who carried a bucket of water in each hand. The allotments, of which there were many, were rented from the mill for a minimal sum. They were used for growing vegetables.

Usually Dan and I released the pigeons. We undid a catch and raised a wooden screen. With a frantic, noisy flapping of wings, the birds were gone. Occasionally, as a special treat, we were allowed to hold one. They pecked each other, but never pecked us. Having scraped the hut clean of muck, we sat on the upturned buckets to watch the birds in flight. Father didn't sit on a bucket; he could squat on his haunches for hours on end.

Cooped up all day, the pigeons expressed great joy at being free. Endlessly, they banked and turned, wheeled and whirled. The wonder is they never collided. They watched us from neighbouring roofs, but mostly they stayed aloft, dancing in the evening sky. They had an uncanny way of knowing when their food was ready. The moment the grain was put in their trough they returned with the same eagerness they'd shown on departure. Supper done, they fluttered up noisily to the rooftops. Father seemed to fly with them.

Mother said that father talked to the pigeons more than to us. So he did. He talked to them the whole time he was there. When the time came for the birds to be fastened up for the night – not he but they decided when that was – they glided down from the roofs. He used to lure those nodding and strutting about on the shed roof by rattling the food can or calling their names from inside the cote. He went on muttering at the birds until the last one was in and the safety hatches had been dropped into place.

He also talked to his flowers, which he grew behind protective wire against the pigeon-shed. Bending over his blooms, he was deaf to whatever was said to him. Mother would have preferred 'greens' to flowers, but 'greens' to father meant 'rabbit food.' He had no interest in growing them.

How he grew anything at all was a miracle. Every ounce of soil had to be carried in and enriched with diluted pigeon droppings. The climate with its flooding and its heavy frosts presented a constant challenge. One vicious hailstorm could devastate his garden. In thirty minutes magnificent blooms became broken stalks. Yet for years he had the best chrysanthemums for miles around. Some years they were ridiculously large and reminded me of Jack and the Beanstalk.

Time and again, I watched him rebuild his garden after it had been washed away. On his hands and knees, with a trowel, he'd replant everything that had been lost. As the light faded, he'd go on tilling, mulching and watering until his garden was restored.

Father was not alone in clinging to nature and a bit of earth. All across the wasteland, workers struggled to grow potatoes, cabbages, carrots, radishes, beets, turnips, peas and beans. They needed the vegetables; even more, they needed to be out of doors, close to the earth, growing things. A cinder tip could not have been the healthiest soil in which to grow vegetables, but nobody died of it.

With the light almost gone, father banged the empty buckets together to signal that it was time to go home. No words. He marched off, with a bunch of flowers in his hand and several pigeon eggs in his overall pockets. We followed, carrying the empty buckets. On arrival home, he put the eggs into a basin on the sink. Awkwardly, almost abruptly, he handed the flowers to mother. No words, no glances, just a muffled grunt that seemed to say all that needed saying.

———◦———

The only occasion when father threw all routine to the winds was at the time of the annual pigeon race from France to Britain. Every year the family lived on the edge of a precipice until the race was over. Madness would reign. The chosen birds, as many as six, were placed in a special box, which was taken to the railway station and, with dozens of other such boxes, sent to France. I used to go with father to see the birds onto the train and to wish them farewell and good luck. He never stopped talking to the pigeons.

'Tha mustn't loiter this year, 'Arry,' he told one of his favourites, as we went along. And to another: 'Bernie, if tha finishes up in t' wrong cote this time, tha goes in t' pot.'

Silently, with other somber bird fanciers, we stood together on the platform until the train departed.

Because of his war service, father knew every station the train stopped at in France until the birds reached their destination. He kept a list of the stations on the cupboard door at home.

Once it was time for the birds to be released in France, the tension in the house became unbearable. A great excitement swallowed up all other activities. So that the whole family could be free to search the sky, meals were forgotten, baking was postponed, clothes stayed dirty. Everybody went onto the tip to watch.

The moment a tiny dot was spotted darting in and out of the low clouds, a cry went up from the crowd occupying the hilly ground. Then came the sweating: was it our pigeon or somebody else's? Only father could recognize a pigeon at that distance. With everybody frozen to the spot, the pigeon fell out of the sky onto one of the shed roofs. A sigh of relief went up. In a race like this seconds counted.

One year father's favourite bird, Charlie, had raced from France to the north of England leaving the other pigeons behind. Father saw him long before he was visible to the rest of us. In time, we spotted the bird swooping through the clouds, tacking this way then that; breaking his heart to get home first. There wasn't another pigeon in the sky. Blessedly, the wind had died down. We all knew Charlie and we swelled with pride. Father was inside the hut waiting to clock in the winner. Everybody in the surrounding pens and on the hillside kept so still they might have been carved of stone. We were certain that, for the first time in the history of the race, Charlie and Blackburn had won the coveted prize.

Hypnotized, we watched as a flapping, fluttering Charlie came in low over the house tops toward the shed roof. He flared, braked and was down.

To our horror, instead of hurrying inside as he had been trained, Charlie strutted about on the roof. The more he bowed and cooed, the louder the oaths coming from father inside the hut. While we resorted to prayer, father swore, whistled and rattled the feed can. All to no avail.

The reason for Charlie's delinquency was not long in finding. Against all rules, a female bird was strutting about on Mr Pindle's shed roof next door. In a moment, Charlie had hopped across and joined her. With everybody holding their breath, Charlie began to make little pretended dashes at Mr Pindle's pigeon. He hopped and bowed and cooed and puffed up his chest and spread his tail. What on earth was Charlie thinking about? Didn't he realize he was on the edge of fame? Obviously, he had forgotten the race.

When father realized what was going on, he came roaring out of the shed like a mad bull. 'What the bloody hell,' he shouted. He was so infuriated that he ran to Mr Pindle's fence shaking his fist. Seizing the fence, he almost wrenched it out of the ground. Mr Pindle and father began to hurl insults at each other. 'Tha's dun it on purpose,' father accused Mr Pindle. From Mr Pindle came a cry of outraged innocence. 'Ah've never heard sich.' Father must have said something dreadful, for the next thing I knew Mr Pindle had climbed the fence and was aiming blows at father's head. 'Take that! And that!' Father exploded with anger. Before anyone could stop him, he had grabbed Mr Pindle by the scruff of the neck and the seat of his pants and hurled him back over the fence. Mr Pindle sailed through the air, arms and legs outstretched, an astonished look on his face, to fall with a great bone-shattering bump at the other side. The wonder is he wasn't killed.

I saw a great deal of my father when I was a child, but I rarely got close to him. Other than mother, nobody did. But when he did talk to me, he had strange tales to tell. As a sailor, he'd visited lands where there were lions and tigers and giraffes and elephants. He'd seen a volcano erupting; he'd seen whales and seals and many creatures of the sea. In far-eastern waters he'd seen ships scattered by a typhoon. The effect upon me when he told me that we go to bed when the Chinese are waking up was electrifying. The Chinese intrigued me. It pleased me when people pointed at him and said: 'Will Woodruff's been to China and to America.'

As the years passed, he became ever more silent and heavy of mood. I've trudged miles with him through the streets of Blackburn without exchanging a word. I always wished it would happen, but I can't remember him holding my hand or carrying me on his back or patting my head. Although he kissed mother good night before going to sleep, he never kissed me or anyone else in public. Kissing was not a Woodruff trait. Even when he stood me on a box in front of one of his looms to show me how to weave, he didn't say much.

I was five or six when I first took father's hot-pot to him in the weaving shed. It was a long, low, stone-flagged, glass-roofed building. Getting through the great metal-plated door that gave access to his workplace was a nightmare. To keep the humidity in the shed, and render the cotton soft and pliable, the door had to be kept shut. Lancashire's damp climate was one of the reasons why the mill was there at all. To open it you had to haul great weights on chains. It was too heavy for me, and I had to wait until somebody came to my help. Once through the door, the weights came crashing down behind me as the door slammed to. I thought I was about to be crushed.

Inside, I was overwhelmed by the steam, the heat, the clatter, the smell of gas and the shattering din of the machines. Too frightened to move, I froze where I was. Hundreds of looms stretched as far as I could see – all of them crashing frantically. Most of the workers were women and young girls. I was mesmerized by the army of picking sticks jerking backward and forward, ready to give me a crack on the head. The sticks hit the shuttles across the loom faster than I could watch: Lat ti tat. Lat ti tat. Lat ti tat. A forest of black driving belts hummed up and down between the overhead shaft and the looms. I would have stayed frozen on the spot had father not caught sight of me. Sleeves rolled up, he came across the sanded floor and took his hot-pot from me. He didn't thank me, or make fun. 'Don't stand theer, gawkin',' was all he said. Yet his fellow workers thought well of him. 'Yo dad's aw reet,' they shouted as I tried to get away. I could hardly hear them above the racket. I couldn't get through the door fast enough. I was quite deaf when I got outside.

Mother was the youngest of Bridget Gorman Kenyon's six children. She had grandmother's fine features: the lovely blue eyes, the long eyelashes, the fine hands, the lovely, thick, dark-brown hair, the soft, sensuous oval face, the warm unaffected gaze. Of medium height, she was neither thickset nor slim; she was in between.

The early death of her father, and her being orphaned off as a child to foster parents, explained her life-long feeling of insecurity. 'No' and 'yes' were followed by 'but-er-I . . .' Although Bridget had assumed that the farmer, who had 'adopted' Maggie, while rough-mannered, was kind and honourable, there is a mystery about what happened. I suspect that she was brutalized. She definitely was neglected. She does not seem to have been sent to school. Eventually, in desperation, she fled back to her mother. The farmer didn't come after her. Bridget said he would not have dared.

Her childhood experience left mother with a fear of not being wanted. She must have been glad to marry the strong and resolute young man that by all accounts father was before the war. The marriage gave her a feeling of security, which she so badly needed. My sister Jenny told me that mother had once said that only after her marriage did she recover the sense of belonging she had known before her father's death. That's why father's running off to war in 1914 came as such a shock to her. She felt vulnerable again.

I was at a loss to understand Maggie's relations with her mother. For someone who had been orphaned off and neglected at an early age, it is a wonder that Maggie had any relations with Bridget at all. How could Maggie be so illiterate when Bridget was so schooled? Why did Bridget spend all the time educating me, when she had neglected her own child? Mother was ever tight-lipped about it. Bridget was equally silent. In all the time I knew grandmother Bridget, I cannot remember a single occasion when she talked about her daughter's early life. The only comment that Bridget ever made about mother's life-long illiteracy was that

'Maggie was not one for "larnin'".' Mother never did over-come her lack of schooling.

With mother you didn't know what she would get up to next. Father was concerned with each day; with getting by, with the immediate and the present; mother was concerned with change, with eternity. She was a stargazer; she not only knew there was life after death, she looked forward to it. Father didn't give a thought to the unknown; she never stopped thinking about it. He didn't expect much of life; mother knew that sooner or later it would be glorious. She had visions and hopes. 'No 'arm in 'opin',' she would say.

Her God was a merciful God. She was a firm believer in the 'Kingdom come' idea, 'of the glory there's to be'; of a world where everybody would be judged and punished or rewarded. She never mentioned the punishments; she stressed the rewards, and the peace and rest there was to be. She expressed herself with such conviction that you got carried away.

Mother was forever vibrant and passionate. She was spontaneous, expansive, impulsive. She needed to touch, to pat, to kiss. Nobody ever doubted her warmness of heart or generosity of spirit. Her talk was 'up in t' air,' but she was never dull. On the contrary, she crackled with life, living each moment intensely; laughter and tears were never far apart. Sad or glad, she was always singing. She had a fine, melodious voice. I never heard father sing, except at his trade union meetings. She was forever doing something different; she had to; she was easily bored. She tired when father read the newspaper to her at night. Although she couldn't read or write (the only time she had written her name was on her wedding certificate, and that with father's help), whatever father read to her, she wanted to jump to the end. He droned on monotonously reading every single word, with no sign of tiring; or for that matter, of interest either, unless perchance he came across some news from America.

When the newspaper bored her, she stopped listening and told us children a story. In one story a bird came to our rescue at the last moment. She really believed in luck. I liked best the story in which she was the queen and I the king. She had lots of coloured ribbons and dressed herself up with elaborate care. Halfway through the story I ceased to be the king and, much to my delight, became the villain. A dab or two of soot on my face from the back of the chimney, and a hat, which mother quickly made out of a newspaper, turned me into a marvelous-looking scoundrel.

Mother thought and spoke in terms of imagery. With her it was a gift. She could create magic with scissors and paper; she could snip people or animals into existence in no time. With a clay pipe filled with soap and water she did even more astonishing things. With her, we sailed away inside a bubble to a shining new world in the sky. One of my earliest memories was blowing bubbles with her, while she sang:

I'm forever blowing bubbles, pretty bubbles in the air;
Oh they fly so high, nearly reach the sky,
Then, like my dreams, they fade and die.
Fortune's always hiding. I've looked everywhere.
I'm forever blowing bubbles, pretty bubbles in the air.

She sang the words lightly, skipping about. She would suddenly grab my hands and dance me off my feet. When she played 'Ring-a-ring-o'-roses, all fall down,' she didn't pretend to fall, she fell as a child does: 'all fall down' – bump. She fell among the daisies and the bluebells, her lovely, dark hair streaming in the wind.

Mother was deaf, dumb and blind to details. To talk about ends and means to her was to take an unfair advantage. I remember the look of dismay on father's face one day when mother threw money into a beggar's cup. While father was worrying how to find enough money to feed the family, mother was chucking it away. One day, with little money to spare, she went and bought a new hat for which she could have had no use. 'Why did you buy it?' father asked incredulously. 'Because I laked it,' she answered innocently. Father almost had a fit. Usually, she didn't respond to his anger.

Money baffled her. On one occasion I stood at her knee while she emptied her purse on her lap. She made several little heaps of coins to meet her bills. I watched while she moved the piles from one knee to the other. It was like moving pawns on a chessboard. Except that the more she moved her coins, the more bewildered she became. Fear entered her eyes. Then she broke down and cried. The sobs were heartfelt; they conceded total defeat. There was no way that she could manage.

She did not have any idea of the nature of the industrial changes going on around her. Strikes and lockouts frightened her. They not only introduced violence into her life, the outcome was always the same: less to eat. 'What's the use of fighting?' she would ask. At heart she was a pacifist.

The Kenyon pacifism almost cost her her life. One afternoon she and I were coming home from the market. We'd almost reached our door when our path was suddenly blocked by a giant of a woman who wore a black shawl fastened tightly at the neck. Neither of us had noticed her approach. Although I assumed that the woman was an acquaintance of mother's, I was repelled by the pockmarked face, the bloodshot eyes and the strong smell of drink.

Before anyone could stop her, the woman had seized mother by the throat and had begun to shake the life out of her. Mother's screams were stifled by one of the woman's hands; my shouts were ignored. Mother's shawl and parcels were on the ground; her long, dark hair had come undone and was hanging down her back. Deep, bloody scratches marked her face. She didn't strike back or struggle. She was too terrified. 'Oh my God,' was all she said. I stood there paralyzed. All I managed to do was to drag the woman's shawl off her head.

Having struck mother in the face several times, the woman picked her up and tossed her onto the cobbles as if she were a rag doll. Mother lay there groaning. With every kick from the woman's steel-capped clogs her groans grew. 'Oh, my

God,' she kept saying. By now bright red blood was on the stones. Every time mother tried to get to her feet, the woman knocked her down again with a vicious kick. Screaming with pain, mother recoiled from each blow, twisting and turning like an eel trying to escape.

Panic-stricken, I ran into the house. Brenda was the only one at home. 'Mother's being murdered!' I screamed. 'She's being kicked to death in the street!'

Brenda's response was to grab the long broom and dash out. I ran after her.

A jeering, shouting ring of passersby had formed. The woman was on top of mother pummelling her for all she was worth.

Brenda dashed through the spectators' legs dragging the broom. I followed. Before anybody could stop her, she had swung the broom head into the air and brought it down on the woman's head with a sickening thud. The blow was so hard that it broke the broom handle. Squealing like a stuck pig, the woman slid off mother's chest onto the cobbles where she lay unconscious.

With the help of a neighbour, we got mother to her feet. Head down, face covered with blood, she tottered toward our door. I picked up her shawl and the torn packages. Nobody interfered. Had they done so, they would have been impaled on the splintered shaft that Brenda held spear-like before her.

I never discovered why mother was attacked.

———◦———

Maggie seemed to attract trouble. Her simple, unaffected, credulous outlook was just not up to life. It landed her in one pickle after another. The gold coin episode was one of them.

It began with a knock on the door. There was just mother and I in the house. She was ironing. She had just clicked the iron's trap door shut when there was a rap on the door. As it was unusual for people to knock, we peeped through the curtains to see who it was. We couldn't see anyone. When we opened the door, a small, dark-eyed stranger stood there, grinning. He had long, black, curly hair that fell down the sides of his face. I could not help noticing the gold rings on his fingers. He also had several gold teeth. In a twinkling he had his foot in the door. Mother thought him a Gypsy. There were always Gypsies about. My people feared them. From missing children to missing washing, it was the Gypsies who got the blame.

'We want no Gypsies here,' mother said, as she struggled to get the door shut.

'Do Gypsies come as well dressed as I?' the man asked in a hurt tone. He was wearing a dark suit – a little worn and greasy, but still a suit. He also wore a collar and tie, a black trilby and shoes. Whatever he was, he didn't look like a Gypsy.

'What do you want?' mother asked.

'I want to make you rich.'

'And how do you think you're going to do that?'

'It's easy, you give me your gold and I'll give you more money than you've ever had.' At this point the man produced a role of bank notes such as neither of us had seen before. Holding the bundle before our eyes, he flipped his thumb through the notes several times. It was enough to make our eyes pop.

'We don't have any gold,' mother said, making to shut the door again.

'You know that's not true,' the man said in an oily voice. 'There's always a ring somewhere, or a trinket, or a coin that you're hanging on to. Now I ask you, what good are you doing locking them away in the house, gathering dust? Use your gumption, woman, get rid of your dust catchers and get some real money. You can't buy food with dust catchers, but you can buy food with these.' He flipped through the bundle of banknotes again. The notes made a comforting, swishing sound. 'This is your one and only chance. For your gold I will give you enough money to pay all your debts. Think what your husband will say when he comes home: enough money to pay all the bills, and some to spare!'

I could tell that mother was dithering. She started her 'but-er-I . . .' business.

'Well, that's it.' He stuffed the money in his jacket pocket and took his foot out of the door. 'You don't know a good thing when you see it. Ta, Ta!' He touched his trilby. His gold teeth flashed a smile.

I knew that, in addition to mother's wedding ring, there was one piece of gold in the house. It was a gold coin, an heirloom from father's side. Mother said it had belonged to great-grandfather Arne. Thus far, it had survived all the ups and downs of the family fortune. It was hidden in a crack of the wall upstairs.

'Hang on a tick,' said mother, as she ran from the door, through the house and up the stairs.

In seconds she had returned with father's heirloom.

The moment the gold coin was in the man's hand he was all business. There was no more laughter, no more chatter about making mother rich. Ignoring mother's 'but-er-I,' remarks that she had decided against selling the coin, after all, he popped a piece of glass over one of his eyes and studied the gold piece carefully.

'Oh well,' he said, 'if this is all you've got, I suppose it will have to do. It's inferior, that's what it is. I'm in two minds to take it.'

He then counted out some paper money, placed it in mother's palm and was gone. Before mother could shut the door, the man was half-way down the street. 'But-er-I,' said mother, 'Ah do hope Ah've dun t' reet thing.'

I shall never forget the look on father's face when he came home and mother told him what she had done. He stood and grasped the back of a chair, his face inflamed with anger. His knuckles were white. 'Tha's done what?' he murmured. 'Tha's done what?' He couldn't grasp it. Then, flinging the chair aside, he exploded. 'Tha's a gobbin! A damned fool gobbin, that's what thi are!' That was as close as father ever came to striking mother. We children stood there, helpless, wide-eyed.

Mother having stammered out a description of the man, father put on his cap and went in search of him. 'Ah'll kill him! Ah'll kill him!' he yelled, as he banged the front door behind him with enough force to shake the house. I silently hoped he wouldn't find him. I knew that in a temper like that father would beat him to a pulp.

Father was gone for hours. We sat around waiting, imagining all kinds of horrible things. Eventually he came home still looking like black thunder.

It was a long time before we learned what had happened. He'd traced the fellow across town as far as the station. By the time he'd got there and made inquiries, the man had been and gone. Just left to catch the Manchester train, they told him. Dad had rushed off to the Manchester platform only to see the peddler leap into the last coach of the already moving train. In a towering rage he'd watched as the train whistled its way into the dark tunnel, its tail lights glowing.

He never saw his coin again.

———◇———

Father was never sure what surprise mother would spring on him next. As mother handled the money, the only thing about which he could be fairly certain was that she would pay the rent. Rent was sacred. If you didn't pay it, you finshed up in the street. Every Friday night, before any other spending was done, three shining half-crowns (seven shillings and sixpence) were placed in a little coffin-shaped box that hung on a nail behind the front door. There had to be three coins – it made it easier for the collector. You didn't argue. You paid the lot in three half-crowns. I'd reach up and shake the box to make quite sure the money was there. It made me feel better when I heard the coins clinking.

The rent was collected every Saturday afternoon by a burly, red-faced chap who burst into the house from the street. He never knocked, he never took off his cap, he rarely spoke. When he did, he was surly and abrupt. If you said that the roof leaked, and would he please ask the landlord to fix it, he'd give a grunt and leave. Complaints got us nowhere. Most times he simply pocketed the three coins, made an entry in the blue, penny rent-book that stuck out of the box and left. We feared the rent collector; we also despised him. The dislike we felt for our landlord, who was unknown to us, we turned on to him.

There were occasions when mother's romantic nature caused her to violate the all-important rent-rule. The danger signals were a penitent look on her face or new hats on my sisters' heads. When she had money, she spent her last penny on dressing up her children. I knew from the growing tension in the house as the time for the rent collector's visit approached, that the rent had gone.

The first occasion when the coins didn't roll into the collector's hand, he stood on the doormat, clutching the empty box, an incredulous look on his face. I was hypnotized. Mother, who believed in miracles, kept her eyes glued to the box. She wouldn't have been the least surprised to see a little bird fly in and three shining coins roll out.

Alas, the little bird that saved her in her fairy stories didn't arrive. The collector began to shake the box like a terrier shakes a rat. Finally, he threw it and the rent-book down. 'Well, tha knows what it means,' he said, scowling, 'three times and ye're oot.' Then he slammed the door behind him so hard that mother's punch bowl tinkled.

My parents feared the rent collector because of the power he wielded. He could not only put us in the street, he could ruin our credit. We bought 'on tick' at Tom Tat's grocery store round the corner. I ran for different things during the week, mother and Tom Tat made a reckoning every Friday night. What she couldn't pay she would 'carry over' until the following week. What the bank-book was to the toffs,

the rent-book was to the working class. Uncle Eric actually
showed us his bank-book to impress us. A rent-book without any red entries meant that you could get a loan from a
moneylender, or do business with the pawnbroker. It gave
the poor respectability as nothing else did. A 'clean' rent-
book without delinquencies could be the difference between
eating and going hungry. No wonder my parents put the
rent in the box behind the door on a Friday night before
they bought food or went drinking.

Mother's protest about living conditions came from the heart
rather than the head. Because her sensitivity and her imagination were so strong, the ugly surroundings in which we
lived hurt her more than the rest of us. The saying 'where
there's muck, there's brass,' made no impression on her. She
simply hungered for the decent life she'd known while her
father was alive. Like her mother, she didn't blame anybody
for the way things had turned out. She just wanted to live
decently. She vowed that she would find a better place to
live.

'And how will you do that, pray?' father asked.

'I'll follow a rainbow,' mother answered. Which is
precisely what she did.

One night, father came home, tired out, to learn that we
were moving.

'Will,' she announced, her face alight, 'I've taken a house
on Livingstone Road close to Eric. It's where the toffs live.
We're going to leave the grime behind. We've lived too long
in a house in which you can't swing a cat. The rent collector can keep it.'

Father was dumbfounded. He stood there and blew out
his cheeks as if recovering from a blow. He had difficulty
breathing. Mother didn't give him a chance to recover. 'It's
a champion house. There's room for everybody, four
bedrooms.' Ignoring father's 'but' and 'in heaven's name'
and 'have you taken leave of your senses, woman?' she raced
on.

Mother suddenly became wonderfully eloquent. The dykes burst. There was no stuttering, no 'but-er-I,' no hesitation about what she wanted to say. She described the new house better than any rental agent could have done. 'There's an indoor petty,' she said, 'one that flushes, and a bathroom; a bathroom; now think of that, Will – a whole room to wash in with a sky-light and a gas water heater. There's a proper kitchen, a proper dining room and a proper sitting room. A real sitting room, Will, with places to sit and no smoke or drafts. And it's all lit by electricity. That makes us as good as Eric. Can you imagine it?' She went faster still. I suspected that she was adding rooms that were not there.

With father waving his arms like a drowning man, and the rest of us standing around gaping, mother described the garden. 'Just think, Will, a proper garden. Not a pen on a cinder tip.' She pummelled him with the garden. 'Think what you could do with a garden like that, Will – front and back! Have you ever thought of the difference a hot-house would make to your plants? Have you ever thought what it would be like to go out of your front door and for the first time in your life step into a garden instead of into the street?'

Father just stood there. 'I want you to see the changing colours of the hills against the sky, Will. I want you to look up . . .' here she paused about to cry, 'instead of looking at this sanded floor and these greasy stone flags.'

She'd got it all worked out: my sister Jenny, who was about to marry Gordon Weall, would rent the front rooms overlooking the hills. Gordon, a painter, would paint and repaper the rooms. On and on she went. Then half-way through a sentence, tears rolling down her cheeks, she faltered. 'Well?' she said, brushing the tears aside and looking at father.

We all held our breath. Surely, he couldn't say no to all that. But he did.

'Tha off thi 'ead, woman,' he shouted. 'How can we afford to live with toffs? We're 'and to mouth as 'tis.'

'That's war ye're wrang,' she sobbed, hiding her face in

her hands. 'That's war ye're wrang. Don't you understand? We've got to do summat or we're goin' te dee in this dirt.'

Then Jenny joined in. 'We can do it dad, we can do it. Mother wants to move up, and you've got to help her. Your trouble is that you're not listening. You've got to listen to what she's saying. She's worn her feet off looking for a better place and all the thanks she gets from you is to say it's madness.'

By now the three women were crying; the kitchen echoed to their sobs. I'd never heard the three of them at it together. Father stared at them with glazed eyes, slowly wiping the sweat off his brow.

My sisters needn't have cried so hard. Mother had no intention of being done out of the house. She knew that father didn't want to change houses. He didn't want to change anything. There was no ambition in him. But the new house was mother's rainbow and she wasn't going to let anybody take it away. Producing all kinds of papers from her blouse, she delivered the final blow. 'Look at these,' she said.

Father looked at the papers. 'Oh Maggie, tha's really done it this time, lass.'

Of course, he could have repudiated the estate agent's contract. Mother could not read and had signed with a cross. But he didn't.

It took father some minutes to recover from shock. 'Hmm . . . hmm . . .' he kept saying to himself while staring at the floor.

'Well, hasta made up thi mind?' mother prodded him.

'Aw reet,' he answered, with a nod. 'Aw reet, provided tha'll promise no more shocks and no more fancy houses. A promise, mind?'

Maggie nodded, as she danced around the room, her eyes streaming.

'Aw reet' took us to Livingstone Road.

We all became excited about the move. We kept going up to Livingstone Road and sitting on the floor of our new house to see what it felt like. It was a substantial two-story brick and stone house next to the last in a row. It was surrounded by duck and hen farms and open pastures. Its great bay windows looked out across the valley to the hills beyond. It must have been several times the size of our Griffin Street cottage. The first night we went there, we were standing at the door of the tall, narrow bathroom wondering what it would be like to have a whole room in which to wash, when father joined us.

'Too much washin' isn't good for you,' he muttered.

We loved the wrought iron gate and railings, the front garden and the stone steps that led up to the front door. In Griffin Street we could stand at the front door and touch the horses and carts going by. We also loved the surrounding fields and farms. What a treat it was to breathe fresh air.

Everybody agreed that the house was 'Champion!'

'Oh,' said mother, striking further fear into father's heart, 'wouldn't it be luvly if this was really ours.' After which she gave a long sigh.

Chapter XVII

Livingstone Road

We moved from Griffin Street to Livingstone Road one Friday after midnight. We used a flat-topped hand cart with iron-shod wheels, which father had hired overnight for one shilling. Onto the cart we piled three beds and bedding, pisspots, four broken rocking chairs, four stools, a stand chair, a bench for sitting, a rough table and several orange boxes. We also loaded the peg rugs, pots and pans and cutlery. Personal belongings and clothing were packed in straw valises. All was tied down.

We took the rent-book with us. We also took the seven-and-sixpence. All we left in the little box behind the door was the key. Late as it was, Gordon Weall gave us fits pretending to be the rent collector taking down the empty box the next day. He took off the collector to a T: the cap and the turned-up collar, the shaking of the box, the sudden freezing, the dreadful frown, the terrier and the rat bit, the throwing down of the box and the book. His antics missed nothing. He glared at us and threatened us with the box, but then he broke down and laughed as much as everybody else.

Despite Gordon's clowning, it took little more than an hour in which to load the cart and make ready to leave. Other than turning off the gas, and taking the penny asbestos gas mantle from the kitchen, there was not much else to bother about. Anyway, gas came at a penny a time and our penny's worth was almost done.

Father was the last out. He didn't look back. Having spat on his hands, he got between the shafts and began to push the cart along the cobbled street. I ran behind to ensure that nothing fell off the cart and was lost. My brother Dan was not there to help; for several months now he had been travelling northern Britain with his work crew cleaning and repairing mill boilers.

Despite the clatter, no neighbours' curtains moved. They knew perfectly well what was going on and deliberately kept out of the way. Without blinking, they could tell the rent collector the next day that they had no idea that the Woodruffs had gone. As for the police, they didn't interfere with moonlight flits.

This was the first move in my life. It was a cold starlit night. I was ten at the time. It gave me a glorious feeling. With our belongings piled high, and the chair legs pointing to the stars like masts, I saw the cart as a tall ship in which we were setting out on a voyage around the world.

It took less than an hour to get the cart up the hills to Livingstone Road. At the worst points, Gordon and I had to put our shoulders to the wheels to get the cart out of the ruts and to keep it moving. Father held on to the shafts. The only sign of strain he showed was to wipe his forehead, adjust his cap, and spit on his hands.

We drew up outside the house on Livingstone Road. It looked to me – accustomed as I was to a tiny cottage – like a glorious castle standing against the stars. We'd reached the shores of another land.

Mother and my sisters awaited us. They had lit the fires

and were quick to give us a hand. Everybody worked with a will. To celebrate, we had hot tea on arrival. We hugged each other at our triumph, all talking at once. 'We've done it!' we laughed. Our hearts were grateful. By four or five in the morning we were all in bed and fast asleep. By then the first pale streaks of light coming through the uncurtained windows were probing our unopened bundles lying about on the floor.

I woke the next morning for the first time in a room of my own. It smelled of fresh paint. I couldn't get used to the space and the amount of light. Going downstairs was like entering a ballroom. I was amazed at the distance between things – like how long it took to walk down a corridor from one room to another. I found mother making breakfast and singing. She was in high spirits. 'You see,' she said, 'it can be done.' She'd won. She wasn't going back to squalor anymore.

With breakfast burning on the stove, she dragged everyone into Jenny's part of the house to look at the distant, sun-lit hills. 'Look, look,' she cried, pointing through the large bay windows: 'Did you ever see anything so beautiful?' The sun was streaming in. With her hands under her breasts, her eyes soared across the valley, over the mills, the smoking chimneys, the mud and decay, until they came to rest on the coloured fells and the long straight line of the hills standing stark against the sky. A dark tide of heather lapped the summit. The surge of emotion she felt when a rainbow lit the distant hills brought her to the edge of tears. 'Well,' she said to father, who was standing by her, 'do you still want to go back to Fall River?' Having drunk it all in, she gave a great sigh and went back to the kitchen. She couldn't have enough of it. For days she kept running through the house to see the hills, looking at them as if she were seeing them for the first time.

There was no stopping mother now. Unknown to us, and despite her promise to father, she was planning further shocks. We came home one night to find the house transformed into a palace. There were rugs on the floors. They were not new – later we noticed holes in them – but they were our very first rugs. We took off our clogs and stockings, and danced about in our bare feet. It tickled our toes. There were curtains instead of newspapers on the windows. There was furniture in every room. Dining room furniture, living room furniture, kitchen furniture, bedroom furniture. There were great upholstered couches and chairs such as none of us, except mother, had ever dreamt of having. I found it an extraordinary experience to lie on a couch. I felt I ought to be ill. None of the furniture was new, but it looked new. Forgetting money, mother had tastefully furnished the whole house. This was Maggie on the grand scale. If ever she had a moment of glory, this was it.

Father nearly fell down when he limped in from work. He was tired out. For a moment he thought he was in the wrong house. He couldn't believe it. With a stunned look on his face, he went from room to room, his eyes getting larger and larger. In a state of shock, he gingerly sat down on the edge of one of the chairs in the sitting room, but on second thoughts he got up and covered it with a sheet of newspaper.

Mother just stood there silently, avoiding his gaze. With her hands across her apron, she looked a picture of abject guilt.

'Maggie, lass,' father asked in a funny quaking voice, 'where did you get all this stuff?'

Gradually the awful truth came out. She'd gone shopping for one or two little items of furniture, in the course of which she'd met such a nice man. He'd persuaded her that it was cheaper to hire furniture than to buy it. Buying furniture was out of date. For just a few shillings a week they could live as they ought to live. After all, they were living on Livingstone Road. He had delivered the furniture the same day, and had worked hard putting it exactly where mother wanted it to give the family a great surprise. He had done that all right.

'But you promised . . .' father stammered.

'Ah didn't promise I wouldn't get a chair to sit on,' mother shot back. 'Ah promised I wouldn't get any more fancy houses. And Ah 'aven't.'

Money aside, as mother would say, the next three years were the best years we would ever know together. We lived in splendor. 'Better than America,' she said. She joked that we'd joined the middle class because she now stayed at home to look after the family instead of toiling in the mill. The pity that grandmother Bridget could not have seen us – such a sight would have pleased her.

With Jenny and Brenda, mother transformed the house into a comfortable home. This is where Jenny showed her talents. She sat in a corner, giving a little chirp now and again, while stitching the most marvellous curtains and cushion covers. Her needle flew as swiftly as the shuttle in the loom. Jenny could do wonders with needle and thread.

Outside, both around the house and at the back, father created an oasis of flowers. They grew so high and so thick that you had to hunt for him. I think there were moments when even he thought mother had done the right thing. He began to talk about building a hot-house. He came up with such wild ideas about growing red currents, gooseberries and raspberries in the back garden – ideas that would have cost a mint of money – that even Maggie became alarmed. I think she felt he was appropriating her role as the squanderer of the family.

———◦———

We knew that in joining the toffs we'd jumped the class barrier, but that didn't bother us. The rest of the working class would have jumped it too if they had had the chance. Father was mentally confined to a class; he was loyal to it. Mother wouldn't have known what to say about classes. She knew, as we all did, that there were classes within classes. 'Loyalty to class,' 'Standing firm,' or 'Closing the ranks,' meant nothing to her. She didn't use the terms 'them' and 'they' as other workers did. She knew that some people were rich and others were poor. If the working class meant dirt and poverty, she was glad to be out of it.

It was our new neighbours, the Peeks, who did the worrying about class. They were hoity-toity. They had feared for their lives when we arrived. Wakened by the din, Mr Peek had seen us approaching the house in the moonlight with the flatcart. 'Agnes, my dear,' he had said to his wife, as he peeped through the bedroom curtains, 'we are not only condemned to live in a slum, we are about to be overrun by savages.' Clogs and shawls had not been seen on Livingstone Road before. It took a year for Mrs Peek to tell me this, but eventually she did. Mr Peek had been a factory owner who had gone broke. As we'd gone up in the world, the Peeks had come down.

Our new neighbours were quite different from those on Griffin Street. They dressed differently, talked differently, and were standoffish – but decent just the same. The Peeks talked to us, as if we were inferior. There was a gulf between them and us; you could see it in their eyes. Brenda asked me if I'd noticed it. I said I had. It was a long time before we 'savages' were accepted. Thanks to Roger Peek, who became my close friend, I led the way. Gradually, the barriers fell.

The Peeks influenced me greatly in the three years that I knew them. There were five of them: Terence Peek, his wife Agnes, their sons Roger and John, and their daughter Millicent. Roger told me how well off they'd been before his father went bankrupt. They had lived in a large house set in spacious grounds, with servants, ponies, everything. Then it had all gone.

Roger's only drawback was that every time he had a fall, he broke a bone. I became quite expert at handling these emergencies. The brittleness of his bones, however, did not stop him from having the most dreadful fights with his younger brother John. Fortunately, when the fighting was over, it was all love and sunshine again.

Millicent, sixteen, was the eldest. She was just out of school. Like her mother, she was pretty in a doll-like way. She went in for flowery dresses and big frothy hats. I think she found our presence jarring. It didn't help when my parents told her they'd been to America. We thought she was stuck-up. She was always putting on airs; being 'Lah-de-dah' we called it.

Our relations with Millicent were marred from the start. One bright moonlit night shortly after we had moved into Livingstone Road there was the most frantic knocking on the Peek's front door. Something was dreadfully wrong for anyone to knock like that; there was a note of panic about it. Putting on the outside light, all the Woodruffs, including Jenny and Gordon, rushed to the front door to see what was going on. Imagine our surprise to find Millicent pissing in the bushes, hiding underneath her frothy hat. The poor girl must have made a desperate dash up Livingstone Road only to fail at the last moment. When Agnes Peek put on the light and opened the door, Millicent was still squatting among the shrubs.

'Milli!' Mrs Peek shrieked in a shocked tone, before quickly switching off the light.

'I don't believe it,' said mother, who was as stunned as Agnes, 'not in Livingstone Road;' after which she quietly switched off our own light, gently pushed us all back inside, and shut the door. We left Millicent out there, trying her best to merge into the shrubbery.

Once inside, we looked at each other for a moment. 'Milli!' mimicked Gordon, and we all exploded. He made us rock with laughter. We laughed so hard that we could no longer speak. That night we laughed our way to bed.

We never met Millicent after that without her blushing like a peony.

Agnes Peek was my favourite. I thought of her as plump, warm and friendly. It may have been more as a result of sickness than of good health, but she had the loveliest round face. There was a haunting beauty about it. She was never without her pearls and elegant shoes. Her fine fingers were covered with jewels. I used to look at them and think what Mr Levy at t' pop shop would give for them. Other than her wedding ring, mother had no jewellery. Grandmother Bridget's jewellery had long since been pawned. Strange, I thought, that the Peeks should call themselves poor.

Agnes had such a toff's way of talking that there were times when I couldn't tell what she was saying. But I knew her heart was good. Roger said she'd had tuberculosis, and had been treated in Switzerland. She gave me the impression of being lonely, of being cut off from former friends. She just couldn't adjust to her changed condition. It showed in her eyes and at the corners of her mouth. There were times when she looked non-plussed. She had a delightful way of fluttering her soft, white hands at problems that became too much for her. Mr Peek could escape from his troubles into books. There was no escape for Agnes. Little wonder that she had fits of moodiness.

If Agnes Peek was my favourite, Terence Peek was the man who changed the course of my life. He was as kind as any man I had met; as kind as Willie Gill but in a different way; I never saw tears in Mr Peek's eyes as I had seen them in Willie Gill's. To me he was all brain. He had a large forehead, yellowish skin, grey eyes, a little nose out of proportion to his face and the largest ears. His hands fascinated me. They were nothing like father's hands. The palms were soft, the fingers long and delicate with broadish tips. I used to watch them as they drummed the table or the arms of his chair when he was talking to me. He wore an odd-looking pince-nez, and had his hair parted down the middle. He was forever shaking hands. We only shook hands after playing football or wrestling. He never worked – not as we understood the word. He spent most of his day either in his study or walking to and from the library in town.

I was astonished when, having won entrance to the house, I discovered that he had a whole library to himself. It was a darkish room with a long table, cluttered with books, papers, maps and prints. It smelled of stale tobacco. He smoked with an elegant cigarette holder. He had a framed picture on the wall of the factory he had owned. It looked an enormous place, bigger than Hornby's. In a corner of the room stood a silent grandfather clock that he was always going to fix.

After several months, Mr Peek began to take a deep interest in me; even though he continued to call me 'the young savage.' I think he talked to me more than he did to his own children. I knew I'd won his confidence when he allowed me to borrow books. I think he looked upon me as a young disciple.

One day Mr Peek explained to me how it was possible for a man to be rich one day and poor the next. I thought that, outside America, where according to grandmother Bridget anything could happen, to be rich or poor was something you couldn't change; at least not as quickly as Mr Peek had done. I thought you were born poor and you died poor, or you were born rich and you died rich. Uncle Eric was the only man I knew who had started poor and had become rich. No matter what reason Mr Peek gave for his coming down in the world, most of which I failed to understand, his talk about being poor baffled me. By our standards, he was well-off.

I learned early on that Mr Peek shared uncle Eric's belief in science. Like uncle Eric, he was a leading member of the local Mechanics Institute. He was convinced that science was going to improve the workers' lot. He was writing it all down in a book upon which he worked every day. He never stopped talking about it; it would change the world; at least it was the only hope for Lancashire. I didn't understand half of what he said, but I had no difficulty following him when he argued that what the world needed was more money. Every cotton weaver knew that. Money was the one thing we lacked. Mr Peek had worked out a scheme whereby we could have all the money we needed. He was so sure of this that even I thought him a little mad.

When I told him that I intended to follow my father as a weaver, he warned me to look elsewhere. He was the first to convince me that there was something irretrievably wrong with the Lancashire cotton industry. He knew that it had been dealt a fatal blow.

'Thank God,' he said to me, 'that I'm not younger. I couldn't stand to see a great industry die again.'

'Rubbish,' said father when I told him. 'Cotton isn't dying. Peek is tapped, that's what he is. There will always be cotton.'

Mr Peek taught me much of what I came to know about the cotton industry. 'It's one of the greatest accidents in history that it's here at all. At one time Blackburn was just a village in the Ribble valley. Nobody predicted that a pastoral backwater would become the workshop of the world.'

As the weeks and months passed, I began to learn how cotton had come to Lancashire in the 1600's, and how great textile inventions, such as the Spinning Jenny and the Spinning Mule had fostered its growth. 'The older weaving traditions in linens and woollens helped it. We had all the land, coal, stone, clay, slate, iron and other building materials that we needed. Canals and railways were built. English and Irish workers came here in their thousands. In Liverpool we had an ideal port; in Manchester an ideal market place. There was a time,' he went on, his voice ringing with pride, 'when Manchester challenged London. In 1913 Lancashire exported seven billion yards of cloth. Imagine that, Billy, seven billion yards! We clothed England before breakfast, and the world after breakfast.'

'But the people of the world must have had clothes before we sold them cottons, Mr Peek.'

'Of course they did. Most of the fine cottons came from India and China. But the weavers of those countries, who used handlooms, were no match for the masters and men of Lancashire. Despite Asia's cheaper labour, our steam-driven machines and our inventions beat them every time. Profits were ploughed back; we took the long-term view. Absentee ownership was unheard of. Factory owners and their sons were known to every worker in the mill. This way we got bigger and bigger. Countries like America, India and Egypt couldn't keep up with our demands for raw cotton. In the United States the growing of cotton with slave labour led to a terrible civil war.

'But then came the Great War, which gave the other people the chance to industrialize and take Lancashire's markets away. By the 1920's, India, China and Japan were taking our trade. We sold them the textile machinery to do it. The machinery is still out there, Billy, working 24 hours a day to take our bread away. We only have ourselves to blame.'

On still another occasion, he explained how, since 1921, the course of the Lancashire cotton industry had been all downhill. 'Since then many parts of the world have shut out our goods, especially the low-count products upon which Blackburn depends. When the Indians can't compete they find a political reason to boycott our goods, Billy. Gandhi was in Darwen yesterday. That fellow is costing England half a million jobs. For the cloth upon which we depend, we simply can't match the Japanese, Indian and Chinese prices. I know, because I've tried. America is hitting us from the other side. She's miles ahead of us now. Foreigners are killing us, Billy.'

At this point, tracing a line with his cigarette holder, he showed me on his globe where most of our raw cotton came from in America, 4,000 miles away, and where Blackburn sent most of its woven cloth, to India, 12,000 miles away. 'Any industry that gets all its cotton from abroad and sells four-fifths of its cloth to foreigners, as we've been doing, is asking for trouble.'

One day Mr Peek was particularly down-hearted. 'Nobody recognizes what is happening to cotton. Nobody cares. Everybody tries to make a killing and get out. Those who plough their profits back into the industry and hang on get wiped out. There's no loyalty to the industry any more. Those who run it are either daft or greedy. They still cling to the idea that Lancashire will go on leading the world. Yet they know as well as I do that our markets are disappearing and our factories are being shipped to Japan.' I watched his fingers restlessly drumming the desk. 'Something is missing,' he went on, 'we're not pioneers any more; we're hangers-on. Smugness and self-satisfaction rule. The money-spinners do the rest, they make a quick profit and get out. For us, Billy, the glory is over.'

'Sounds serious, Mr Peek.'

'It is. There's only one thing the industry understands,' he went on, tapping the surface of his desk. 'Dog eat dog. Soon there will be no dogs to eat.'

'What about the workers? Where do they come in?'

'They're just as blind as the bosses. They're sheep led by the nose.'

'That's not fair, Mr Peek, it was not the workers but the bosses that caused the General Strike.'

'Nonsense,' he replied puffing on a cigarette, 'the General Strike was labour gone mad. There wasn't a chance of the strike succeeding. English workers aren't revolutionaries; they like to tinker, not to smash. They don't believe in tidal waves and big ideas like a General Strike; they believe in muddling through. They prefer to be haphazard. They're happier when they're arguing over price lists and pay lists. As a boss, I know. In 1926 they squabbled among themselves and got what they deserved. They fought for a share of a cake that is fast disappearing. Without recognizing it, what they're squabbling over is the death of the Lancashire cotton industry.'

My family's only comment when I told them what Mr Peek had been saying was 'Poor devil's barmey. If he goes on like that they'll lock him up.'

In some things, I think, Mr Peek probably was a little barmey. In other things he was practical and down to earth. I have to thank him for clearing up one great problem about which I had been complaining to my parents for years. To pass water had become agonizing for me; instead of flowing, it leaked out drop by painful drop. It was a crippling defect. Roger told his father of my plight.

Mr Peek was appalled, even horrified at my parents' primitive view of medicine, and their refusal to resort to surgery. He told them so. He came bouncing into our house one night determined to change their point of view. He became as committed to having them take me to a doctor as he was in providing the world with money. For him, it became another cause and he kept at my parents until they gave in. They took me to Dr Grieves who decided upon immediate surgery.

Getting rid of the problem was as simple as Mr Peek had predicted. Two mornings later, Dr Grieves arrived with an assistant. Fearful, I climbed onto the kitchen table, over which mother had spread a clean sheet. The table had been carried into my sister Jenny's room at the front of the house where there was more light. I could see the hills. A gauze cup was placed over my nose and mouth. 'Give him a whiff,' said Grieves to his aide. 'All over in a tick,' he said to me reassuringly. I can only remember a sickly smell. When I came to I was on the couch still facing the hills. I was dazed from the chloroform. Dr Grives and his helper had gone. Mother was at my side hushing me. Mr Peek came every day, sometimes with a book. Apart from a week or two of agony, the cure was complete. It confirmed my confidence in Dr Grieves; also that Mr Peek was an ally worth having.

———◇———

The reluctance to call in Dr Grieves stemmed more from father than from mother. Although father had recovered from gassing in France during the war, he had no faith in either doctors or hospitals. Unless he was forced to, he avoided them. Once he had collapsed at work with what Dr Grieves diagnosed as acute appendicitis requiring immediate surgery. Mother had been warning father for years that the peanuts, which he ate by the pound, would land him in hospital with appendicitis. The ambulance was sent for. Against father's protests, he was bundled into the ambulance and despatched to the Royal Infirmary. But he never arrived. Somewhere en route he managed to persuade the ambulance driver, who was a mate of his, to take him home. His mate had great difficulty explaining the empty ambulance when he got to the infirmary. Meanwhile father had put himself to bed. He resorted to folk medicine: fistfuls of steam-heated bread placed between sheets of brown paper and applied to the inflamed area. Mother continued the treatment when she came home from the mill.

All that can be said is that father survived.

Dr Grieves was not informed about his patient's escape. Meeting father later on, he asked him how he felt after the operation.

'Couldn't be better.'

'You're a lucky man, you are. It was touch and go with you, you know. A few hours later and you would have been a goner.'

'I can believe that.'

Father believed that if he ever entered a hospital he would die. It was a deep superstition he held. Many years later his fears were fulfilled precisely as he had foretold.

Father may not have appreciated Dr Grieves' skills, but there were many others who did. He was a legend in the community. Everybody knew him and his spaniel Joy. Joy always jumped into the gig and sat on guard while the doctor made housecalls. The housecall ended, the dog happily took to the street again. Everybody admired Dr Grieves. Not least because he sometimes forgot to send bills. House visits, when he remembered to charge, were two shillings and sixpence. His stock soared after it got about that he had risked his life in a collapsed mine gallery tending injured miners.

While any kind of illness was considered shameful by my people, there were occasions when we were persuaded to take a bottle of his cure. Invariably, it was I who was sent to the surgery to pick up the medicine for sixpence a bottle. I knew if I'd got the right bottle by the colour. Coughs and chest problems were treated with a blue liquid. (If goose grease and a home-made concoction of lemon, glycerin and cod-liver oil had failed.) Aches in the head, eyes, ears and nose were dosed with yellow; joint troubles with red; troubles in the belly – there being no response to the usual doses of prune and fig juice – with a black, tar-like substance. I wondered what would happen if somebody confused the colours.

The only reservation I ever heard about Dr Grieves was that he dabbled in veterinary medicine. There was the catch. People swore that there had been occasions when Dr Grieves got his medicines mixed up and that he gave to humans what was meant for horses. Nobody in his right mind ever followed his instructions to the letter and swallowed a tablespoon at one go. They first wet their tongue or took a small sip to make sure they were not going to be knocked flat.

———◇———

Soon after we moved to Livingstone Road, Jenny married Gordon Weall. That was when I got my first pair of long trousers. Father took me to a shop called Weaver to Wearer where I was measured for a suit of dark brown worsted wool. Weaver to Wearer was the cheapest tailor in town. Their cloth was thought to be better than that sold by the workers' Cooperative Store. Also, Weaver to Wearer gave me two fittings, at the Co-op I'd have got only one.

When I took the suit home in a big cardboard box, I felt like a millionaire. At last, I had stopped being a boy and had become a man. I explored all the pockets and found the sixpence, which the tailor always hid in a boy's first suit. That night I put the suit on and paraded before the family. There were many 'ooohs' and 'aaaahs.' It was the first time in my life that I had ever worn anything over my knees. It made them itch.

The wedding itself was the most elaborate affair in the family's history. Mother was not prepared to settle for second best, not in Livingstone Road. It was one of the high points of her life. That's how she thought life should be.

At great expense, we went the whole way. Everybody had new clothes. Mother was in her seventh heaven deciding what everyone should wear. Jenny wore white. Her dress had a low neck with a tight waist and sleeves all puffed up. She had a veil and carried lilies of the valley. Beautiful she looked. She also had two little girls as train bearers. Gordon wore a hired frock coat, pin striped trousers and a special grey waistcoat with a watch chain. He looked like the Lord Mayor. Nobody would have guessed he was a painter's apprentice. Like the rest of us, he got a new suit and new shoes for the wedding but kept them for going away on his honeymoon.

As it was a June wedding and the weather was kind, family and friends stood outside the church for a moment to say hello and wave greetings before going in. It's amazing what clothes will do to people when they are wearing their best. Everybody held themselves stiffly and spoke in funny voices. I never saw such a change; they weren't the same folk at all.

When we went in, the organ was playing quietly. We had organ, choir and soloist. There were six little flower girls. Gordon and a fellow-painter were waiting near the altar rail – white gardenias in their buttonholes. There were a lot of people there whom I'd never seen before. All the Wealls were present, Mrs Weall constantly wiping her eyes. Mr Weall, a little red-nosed man, who looked as if he had just stepped out of a hot bath, steadily supplied his wife with clean handkerchiefs. Mother put our neighbours, the Peeks, including Millicent, well up front. 'Savages, are we!' I could hardly recognize mother and Brenda in their flowing pink dresses and enormous wide-brimmed hats.

Then father arrived with Jenny and the train-bearers in a shining limousine. What agony father must have suffered having to pay for that car with its chauffeur and its white ribbons and orange blossom! Jenny looked an angel; she glided down the aisle with her tiny toes peeping out of her white slippers. She had the easy motions of a good dancer. Mother had seen to it that Jenny wore 'Something old, something new, something borrowed, something blue.' Father walked at her side as if he had just fallen off a wall. It was one of the few times I ever saw him wearing a tie. If the organ hadn't been thundering, 'Here comes the bride,' we could have heard his new suit creaking.

Then Jenny joined Gordon. We all stood and sang: 'Rejoice and be glad.' Then we sat down while a young woman sang, 'Love divine, all love excelling.' Then the preacher came forward and talked about matrimony, and what a serious business it was. He went on and on about loving and being faithful to each other, and bringing up children. 'The fear of the Lord,' he stressed, 'is the beginning of all wisdom.'

Then they got on with the marriage, with Bertha Weall crying so hard that she could be heard throughout the church. Then the preacher asked Gordon if he would marry Jenny, and Jenny if she would marry Gordon – which is what I thought we'd come for. You could hardly hear Jenny's reply, but Gordon's 'I do' was strong. Then the preacher gave them his blessing. 'What God hath joined together, let no man put asunder.'

While Jenny and Gordon were in the vestry, the choir sang, 'Blessed be the tie that binds.' Then everybody together, including the married couple and the choir, sang, 'God the creator, God the good.'

After pictures had been taken outside the church, Jenny and Gordon and the parents of both sides went off in the limousine. The rest of us – relatives, friends, and those who hung on in the hope of a free meal – walked down town to Harper's where the reception was to be held. It wasn't far, the weather was good, and we made fun all the way.

Jenny told me later that both mothers cried in the limousine. Mrs Weall blubbered most. She kept saying, 'I've lost my only son, Maggie, I've lost my only child.'

In response to which mother sobbingly replied, 'Aye, but tha's got a good daughter, Bertha.'

'Hisht, women,' father had scolded.

At Harper's we first had family pictures taken and then sat down to a proper ham and tongue wedding breakfast. Trifle followed, and there was lots to drink. Gordon made a speech in which he couldn't help being a clown.

While everyone was stuffing themselves and having a good time, Jenny and Gordon changed to go away. Then we all got up in our best clothes and trooped off behind the married couple, who went hand in hand, across town to the railway station. Gordon had already dropped off a suitcase there. We were a happy, laughing throng of about twenty or thirty people. Several excited children brought up the tail end.

'God bless you,' passers-by called to the bride and groom.

'All the best.'

'Never grow old.'

'Here's to your health and wealth.'

On reaching the platform we rained confetti and streamers upon the happy couple. The women hugged and kissed the bride. The men were more restrained. They patted the bridegroom on the shoulder as if he was going to war. Father stood stiffly to one side, preoccupied with his thoughts. I'm sure he was still worrying about the cost of the ribbon-bedecked limousine that awaited him in the street.

It must have taken father a long time to pay for that wedding. He must have spent the family's savings on it, and gone into debt. It will always remain a mystery to me how a man who resented paying a penny on the tram, and who was not known for giving his children anything, could suddenly spend like a profligate. The money for all the clothes must have come out of his pocket, for none of us belonged to a clothing club in which garments were bought by payments made over time.

I can only think that marrying off a daughter was something special. Of course, mother was the driving force. She didn't let price interfere. Besides the Wealls were a cut above the Woodruffs and it was up to us not to let the side down. Pride demanded that we should impress them. Also, we lived in Livingstone Road. A threadbare marriage from such an address would have been unthinkable.

In any event, money was never better spent. We had a wonderful time, we all got stuffed with food and drink; and everybody finished up with new clothes. Father's suit lasted him the rest of his life. We'd never spent like that before, and we never did again. 'Everybody is entitled to go mad once,' mother said. Mother saw to it that the wedding got into the paper. She kept asking father to read it to her over and over again. I think she often relived Jenny's wedding in her dreams.

Several months after Jenny's wedding, Brenda became engaged to Harry Entwistle. They were both members of the Salvation Army. The Army thought the world of them. Harry was a Derbyshire man. Twice the size of Brenda, he had a ruddy, well-weathered face, a mass of blond hair combed back, hands like shovels, and a body like an ox. He was one of the boilermen at Dougdale's mill. He'd been in Blackburn about a year. Not much was known about him. He didn't seem to have any family. When I first met him, he had two passions: Brenda and the Salvation Army. Brenda at this time was about twenty.

With all the tenderness of possession, Brenda brought him home one night to show him off to the family. Harry's big, bright eyes and his infectious, happy laugh exuded warmth. We took to him at once. He was so open, friendly and genuine that we were drawn to him instinctively. In an ox-like way he was also good-looking; handsome would be the right word. There were not many young men in town with as rich a blond beard as Harry's; his eyebrows were equally splendid.

Mother thought them a good match. Harry was four years

older than Brenda. He had a job, and he obviously loved her. Brenda couldn't have enough of him. Without a dissenting word, the family came down on Harry's side.

Henceforth, Harry became a member of the Woodruff household. He was always coming up to Livingstone Road; always eating with us, always engaging us in jolly laughter. Brenda and he often went off to Salvation Army meetings, their faces glowing.

One night they came back and announced to the family that they were going to get married. Harry didn't formally ask father for Brenda's hand, but then members of the working class rarely did. The couple just said they'd made up their mind.

Everybody was delighted. The date was set. According to Salvation Army tradition, they were to be married under the flag, which meant that the Army took responsibility for the service and the reception. The wedding breakfast had all been arranged; two bands had agreed to play. Brenda and Harry were to lead a short demonstration march, to be followed by prayers and massed singing. Nothing was going to be left out for the couple who had won everybody's heart.

None of us will ever forget the wedding day. There was such hustle and bustle in the house on Livingstone Road. Other than Brenda, who wore her Salvation Army uniform, we all put on the new clothes we'd obtained for Jenny's wedding and hurried down to the Salvation Army headquarters where the marriage was to take place. We took umbrellas because the weather looked bad. Father and Brenda were to follow in a taxi. The Army captain received us and made us all welcome. Scrubbed, glowing faces, black hats and red bands were everywhere. Resting against the wall in the hall were the flags to be used in the march. Harry stood waiting with a Soldier of Christ as best man.

While one of the bands was playing, Brenda and father arrived. They were just walking up to Harry when a young woman hurried toward them from one of the side doors and blocked their path. Her face was grey and drawn. Brenda stopped. She looked flummoxed. Everybody stared at the intruder.

'What can I do for you?' Brenda asked the stranger who seemed distraught.

'It's more what can I do for you,' the intruder gasped.

'Who are you?' said Brenda, her face darkening.

'Mrs Harry Entwistle,' the woman sobbed. 'Thank God I got here in time.'

Brenda's face became distorted; her lips quivered and throbbed. She looked at the woman with stony eyes.

Mother pushed past me and threw her arms around Brenda. 'Come home child,' she pleaded. Everybody in the hall was so still, they might have been struck by lightning.

Brenda turned on Harry. 'Harry Entwistle,' she asked, 'is this your wife?'

Harry shifted his feet uneasily; he was trembling; his face was flushed; he was staring at the floor. After a moment or two he looked up. 'Yis,' he stammered.

Snatching the umbrella from father's hand, Brenda struck Harry across the face. A red weal appeared. 'You scum!' she screamed, as she delivered blow after blow. Harry didn't move. Didn't flinch. Nor did anybody else. The crowd just stared. 'You rotten devil!' Brenda went on hitting him until the umbrella broke. So did her spirit. With a sob she collapsed onto a chair. With all the women weeping, the family somehow managed to get her home.

For days, Brenda didn't speak to anyone. When she did come downstairs her face was a frightful sight. She looked twenty years older. A vague sadness had replaced her distress.

She never wore the Salvation Army uniform again.

In time the wounds healed. She married a good man called Richard Paden. He was a clerk at a store in town with little money and fewer prospects. In contrast to Jenny's wedding – it was an in-and-out-of-church affair with no trimmings. Nobody said it, but I think everybody felt that the ghost of Harry Entwistle was there, mocking us with his hearty laughter. Somehow Brenda and Richard weathered the hard times.

Like my sister Jenny and most other workers who had little to eat, they only had one child. Brenda remained with her spouse until death intervened.

———◇———

It was shortly after Brenda's wedding that Agnes Peek was struck down with tetanus. She cut her finger on a piece of glass that was lying on her kitchen floor. I was standing next to her at the time. It was only a prick, which she sucked clean. That night there was a commotion next door. The ambulance came and carried her off. Mrs Peek lay at death's door in the infirmary for weeks. I often went with Roger to see her. She was never the same when she came home.

Chapter XVIII

Earning my Keep

While we were living at Livingstone Road I really began to earn my keep. I took pride in doing so. I started delivering morning and evening newspapers for George and Madge Latham, a young, childless couple in their thirties, who ran a sweets, tobacco and newspaper business on Revidge Road. The Lathams were an honest, hard-working couple. They were Lancashire folk: active, tough, resourceful. They were always cheerful. I was a year below the minimum age, but they took me on just the same; no one enforced the law. They paid me the princely sum of two shillings and sixpence per week, of which I kept a dodger. Mother took the rest. That was my contribution to help pay for the house.

I came to love the Lathams and looked upon their home as my own. They treated me as their son, which meant that Madge periodically put my head over the kitchen sink to scrub my neck. She also insisted on my taking a weekly bath in their bathroom. For the first time I started wearing woollen underclothing, which she bought. It made me feel hot. I loved

Madge because she was so kind, but when she asked me to part my hair on the other side, I pretended not to hear. When I left the shop to go to school she always tucked a bag of shortbread into my jacket pocket.

Several times the Lathams tried to adopt me. My father was agreeable; my mother, conscious of her own childhood, refused. I would have been happy to join them. In George Latham I found the companionship of a father I had never really had.

I came to spend so much time with the Lathams that home and school fell into the background. Winter and summer, wet or fine, I got myself up at five to meet George at the newspaper depot in the centre of town about a mile and a half away. I had to run through the dark, hushed streets for half an hour or so. I'd find him waiting for me with his bicycle. On cold mornings his teeth were chattering. Together, we then fought our way in and out of an ill-lit warehouse that served as the newspaper depot. It was a daily hand-to-hand battle with other men to get our newspapers. It was bedlam there.

Once we'd got the warm, damp bundles under our arms, we loaded them and George's bike onto the first tram to Revidge Road at six o'clock. Kneeling on the ribbed floor, we sorted the papers as the tram lurched along. When the floor was wet with melted snow off people's clogs, we used the seats. At Revidge Road, George helped me off the tram. With a bag of newspapers on either shoulder, I began my round. Depending on the weather, I'd be running through the streets for the next hour, or hour and a half. I found it wonderful to have the world to myself.

I had no difficulty knowing which paper went where. Labour people took the *Herald* or *News Chronicle*, conservatives the *Mail* or the *Telegraph*, liberals the *Guardian*, the toffs took *The Times*. A switch in newspaper usually meant a switch in political allegiance. I knew how my customers would vote.

Delivering newspapers taught me a lot about human

nature. I learned to recognize the news addicts and the insomniacs. In summer, these chaps paced up and down their lawns awaiting my arrival. The way they snatched the paper out of my hand, made me feel important. I knew by the way they rushed to the financial pages that, like most of the rich, they were fearful of losing their money. I'd nothing to lose so the financial crashes left me unmoved. I decided it must be worrying to be rich.

In bad weather, the kind-hearted awaited my arrival with a cup of tea and a bun. The not so kind angrily waved the paper in my face as if I were responsible for the success of Labour at the polls, or the assassination of the head of a foreign state. I felt like saying: 'Look, Mister, I don't write these papers, I just deliver them.' Usually, I kept my mouth shut. One thing I did learn was never to give a man the wrong paper. You've no idea how touchy some people can be. They'd bawl me out as if I'd permanently committed them to the wrong religion.

In time I came to have a large family of newspaper readers. I knew them more closely than they realized. I knew them by the way their houses stared, sat and slept. I closely followed my customers' births, weddings, divorces and deaths. I knew who had gone broke, and who was doing very nicely. I knew when a move was underway. I delivered Dr Michael's paper. He was the great ear, nose and throat specialist who was unable to save his own daughter from a fatal ear infection. 'And how is the Michael child?' some customers asked me as if I were a consulting physician.

With a passion for the printed word, I not only delivered newspapers, I read them too. I started every day eager to see what the world was up to. One morning in 1927 I was thrilled to read about Lindbergh's solo flight from the United States to France. My friends and I didn't stop talking about Lucky Lindy. The only aeroplanes we had seen were three single-engine aircraft flown by a group of American rough riders who came for three days to barnstorm from a field on the edge of town. They charged five shillings for a ten minute ordeal. My mates and I saw the whole show and were awestruck. The planes were thumped and banged about so much that we expected them to fall apart. When we saw people getting out and throwing up, we concluded that it was just as well that nobody was pressing a free ride on us.

The newspapers were full of politics. That's how I first heard about Mussolini in Italy and Stalin in Russia. I cut their pictures out of the paper and lined them up like a rogue's gallery on my bedroom wall. With the world depression in trade and industry at its height, the papers also had a lot to say about commercial crises, strikes and lockouts.

Sometimes the news was so arresting that I stopped under a street light to read it. Banner headlines greeted the formation of a second Labour government in 1929. We believed that Labour would put things right this time. Ramsay MacDonald was to be Prime Minister.

With the further collapse of trade and industry, equally large headlines announced the fall of the Labour government in 1931. The man upon whom all our hopes had been pinned – Ramsay MacDonald – then deserted the Labour Party to work with the Conservatives and the Liberals. My family couldn't believe that the Labour government had gone to pot.

One thing I did learn, was the way newspapers contradicted each other – that truth is not as straight-forward as I thought it was. A disaster in politics in one paper was a victory in another. I asked myself how could that be? I also learned to be suspicious of the writers who had a simple answer for everything. Every day I read the column by Hannan Swaffer in the *Daily Herald*. Why, if they'd have put Mr Swaffer in charge, the country and the world would have been on its feet again in seven days. I found it confusing.

I asked George Latham what he made of it; after all, he had newsprint all over his hands as I did, and he was much older.

'I'd never deliver the news, Billy, if I tried to make head or tail of it,' he answered. 'We're businessmen, Billy. We have our work cut out delivering papers without worrying about what it all means.'

Being a businessman did not deter me from reading the news as I ran through the streets. By the time I reached the Lathams, where a wash, and a hearty breakfast awaited me, I knew pretty well where the world was going. After school I read the evening paper as avidly as I had read the morning edition. At the end of the day, after George, Madge and I had eaten together, I was allowed to plunder the magazines and books from the Lathams small two-penny lending library. I must have read them all. I read Edgar Wallace's detective stories one after the other as they came off the press. In Latham's lending library I continued the education that grandmother Bridget had begun. When I got tired of reading, I'd play table tennis either with Madge or with George. Before I went home, I had tea and cake with them.

Each Christmas the Lathams raffled a box of chocolates – the largest and most extravagant box available. It contained several pounds of the finest confectionery. A ticket cost a dodger. Everybody who visited the shop bought one. People came from miles away to join in the raffle. As it was my first Christmas with the Lathams, I decided to have a go.

Two days before Christmas, with hundreds of tickets sold, I stood in a packed shop waiting for George to draw the winning ticket. The crowd was so large that it spilled out onto the street. With a lot of shouting going on, 'Cum on now, lad, don't keep us in suspense,' George dipped his hand into the box of tickets held by Madge. In a loud voice he called out: '283!'

I couldn't believe my ears. 'A've got it!' I shouted. I was speechless with excitement; it was the first thing I had ever won. I hurriedly pushed my way through the crowd to claim my prize.

'Oh, not you, Billy,' George said. He gave me a sickly

smile. 'Billy,' he leant over and whispered, 'would you like to sell your ticket? I'll make it right with you. We could raffle the chocolates again. It would look better.' There was a desperate look in his eye.

'No!' I shouted; I was aghast at the thought of being robbed of my trophy.

An embarrassed George had to declare me the winner. Reluctantly he placed the box in my outstretched arms. After making one or two veiled comments about shops winning their own prizes – some of them good-humoured, some not so good – the crowd dispersed. I expected the customers to slap me on the back and congratulate me; nobody did.

The box of chocolates caused a sensation in my family. They'd never seen anything like it. Nor had I. The colourful lid depicted a scene from St Mark's Square, Venice. The wrapper said so. It was all ancient buildings and lots of gondolas and glistening water. There was gold ribbon round every corner of the box. It was an adventure to raise the lid. There was a box within the box. There were several layers, drawers and hidden corners. There was even a secret drawer at the bottom, so that when you thought the feast was ended, you could start all over again. Neighbours came and admired and fingered the box. It was left to me to decide who could have a chocolate and who couldn't. And what chocolates they were! Great delicious, hand-made things wrapped in bright tinsel. Some of them actually contained liqueur, which disturbed my sister Brenda who had become a rabid drink hater.

When the next Christmas came round, I had my three pennies ready. But I was not to be given the chance to repeat my victory. 'Billy,' George begged, 'do me a favour and don't buy any more of my raffle tickets. It would ruin me, if you won it again! You are, after all, part of the business.' I put my three pennies away.

Some months after I had joined the Lathams I found a collie dog. Well, really, she found me. She came from nowhere one day when I was delivering evening papers, and adopted me on the spot. In a transport of joy, she suddenly leapt all over me, licking and fussing me. She made real loving sounds at me. She was black and white, with bright eyes and the most beautifully shaped head. She bestowed herself upon me there and then, as if she'd been looking for me all her life. We became inseparable companions. I called her Bess.

After Rosie Gill, Bess was the second great love affair of my life. Morning till night, we were never apart. Although she was allowed in the house, she was not allowed to go upstairs. Every morning she greeted me by the kitchen fire writhing and leaping around as if I'd been absent for months. She ran through the streets delivering papers with me in the dark every morning. She slunk onto the first tram with us. With her cold nose, she supervised the sorting of the papers on the ribbed floor. She knew where I had to get off, and where we had to deliver. She only got mixed up – as I did – when people stopped and started their papers. When I had to go to school or inside the mills, she waited for me outside. She was always there, lashing her tail with affection. She gave me a little bump with the side of her head to tell me that she had missed me; other times she rubbed her head against my knees. No one could have had a more good-natured or more loving companion. I paid no attention to my family's complaints that she smelled – she did, beautifully. Nor did I listen when they said that there was no room or food for her. Together, Bess and I overcame all opposition, solved all problems. We lived our own lives; the rest of the world did not exist.

One day when we reached home, a big red-faced farmer with black leggings and a check cap was waiting for us. He had a collar and a leash in his hand. His angry mottled brown eyes spelled trouble.

'Tha cumin' with me,' the farmer said to the dog.

317

I was horrified. I got as far away from the man as I could and clung to Bess in a corner.

'Doesn't ta know that stealin's a sin?' he asked me with an unblinking stare. 'Tha'll finish up in jail, th' will. And then, by gum, tha'll go t' 'ell.'

Bess and I trembled. Her head was down, her tail tucked in.

''As t' told boy this?' he turned on father.

'Dust ta expect me t' look after all t' bloody stray dogs in town?' father grumped.

'Wot dus t' think a dog like this costs?' the man said, turning to me. 'Well wot dust t' think? Ah'm waitin' fur an answer.'

'Ah don't know.' I said. I was shaking. Bess and I clung closer still. I could feel her heart thumping; she was as terrified as I was.

'Well, if Ah'd got nothin' better to do, Ah'd tell thee. As it is, Ah'll just take me dog and go.'

The farmer reached across and grabbed Bess by the neck. With Bess squirming to be free, he put the collar on her. He then attached the leash and began to drag the dog across the floor to the door. I didn't know what to do. Father just sat there as if nothing was happening. So I burst into tears. I sobbed as if my heart would break.

'You can't take Bess away from me,' I spluttered. 'She's the only thing Ah've got.' Over her shoulder, Bess pleaded for my help. I cried harder. Much harder.

The man stopped at the door and looked back. Shifting his weight from one foot to the other, he seemed embarrassed and uncertain what to do. 'Tha needn't bawl thi 'ead off,' he threw at me. 'Anybody'd think Ah'd murdered thee.'

Bess began to whine. In tears, I threw myself on the floor.

'Now, tha should stop that at once. It sounds as if tha being murdered. Ah've never seen sich. Tha could make thiself ill.'

While father looked on in a disinterested sort of way, Bess and I kept it up.

'A fine pickle,' the farmer said, 'Ah've not only had me dog robbed, Ah'm goin' t' lose me 'earin' as well.' After that he stood there bewildered, opening and shutting his mouth. 'Ah'll tell thi what Ah'll do: rather than 'avin' thee cater-waulin' like that, Ah'll give thee t' dog.' He bent down to remove the collar.

Bess was with me in a flash. I put my arms around her and together we went on crying and shaking.

''Tis been a bad day,' the big man muttered as he left the house. 'A very bad day,' he said, still shuffling his feet. 'Yo two have just wasted mah time.'

The moment the door was closed, Bess ceased whining and licked my face and hands. She declared our victory by thumping her tail on the floor.

The man never returned, and Bess and I lived happily ever after. Well, almost. One winter's day an angry neighbour entered our house:

'Would ya remove yor dog from my kennel!' he demanded. 'My own dog's in t' snow.' Early in the morning, Bess had wandered down the street, found a warm kennel, tossed out its occupant, and taken possession.

319

Chapter XIX

A Grocer's Lad

At fourteen I'd come of age and felt I ought to make my own decisions. It was tacitly agreed with the Lathams that if I couldn't find a full-time job I'd continue to work for them.

Had times been better, I'd have had no difficulty in finding a job. I'd have joined father in the mills. There had always been a place in cotton textiles for cheap child labour. A child could easily be thrown out later on. But the depression was at its height and most of the mills were shut. Nor was there hope of becoming an apprentice to a plumber, or a carpenter, or a machinist, or a glazier, or a boilermaker, or a painter. They were all looking for work themselves. People were fighting over pick and shovel jobs.

The best thing I could find was to become a shop assistant to Charles Grimshaw.

Mr Grimshaw owned a large grocery store in the wealthier part of town. He lived above the shop. Everything about the building was pretentious: it had pseudo-Tudor beams across the front; the entrance was flanked by hollow wooden pillars. Apart from himself, his wife and his daughter, there were two other assistants, Cyril and Arthur. The shop had a bakery, and was licensed to sell wines, beer and spirits. It also sold fresh fruit and vegetables. Its doors opened precisely at eight and closed at six – later on Saturdays. It catered only for the rich.

I was interviewed by Mr Grimshaw at six one evening as the store was closing. I don't think I'd ever seen anybody who looked more like an eagle. Tall, grey, with closely clipped hair and moustache, Mr Grimshaw had the eagle's ever-watchful, baleful eyes, and its strongly carved, beak-like nose. I waited at the shop door for at least thirty minutes until he had finished struggling with a large ham. Having wiped his hands thoroughly on a towel, he recognized my existence and came over to question me.

'What's your name?'

'William Woodruff.'

'Where do you live?'

'Livingstone Road.'

Mr Grimshaw paused. 'What does your father do?'

'He's a weaver, but he's out of work.'

'How many of you in the family?'

The questions went on and on. They were sharp and precise. There was no end to what he asked. After I had finally assured him that I was a God-fearing boy, he took me on at ten shillings a week. Of the sum, I received tenpence from my parents. The rest was needed at home. Mr Grimshaw's last words before dismissing me were: 'Watch thi P's and Q's and tha'll be aw reet. Don't sing in t' shop and don't whistle. Give me trouble, and tha're out on thi ear. Remember,' he warned, 'jobs these days are not two-a-penny.'

The next day I stood with the other two assistants Cyril and Arthur waiting for Mr Grimshaw. On the dot of eight, which he checked with his watch, Mr Grimshaw emerged from the house and entered the store. He looked as sharp as a razor. He wore a stiff, stand-up collar, a well-pressed grey suit, a gold watch chain across his ample chest, and highly polished shoes. We assistants froze into place holding out our hands, palm up, for inspection. Nobody talked until the inspection was done. For a moment or two, watch still in hand, he looked around, taking everything in. After which he repeated his Five Commandments, which I soon knew by heart: work hard; be humble; don't waste; be punctual; be clean. Then he snapped the watch lid to with an air of finality.

The snapping of the lid was the signal for everyone to start work. Until the shop shut at six in the evening, Mr Grimshaw didn't spare himself or others. I never saw him waste a moment. I never knew anyone as hard-working or as efficient as he.

It didn't take me long to realize that there was nothing anyone could teach Grimshaw about groceries; nothing anyone could do, as far as I could see, to improve the Grimshaw business. He had spent his working life getting everything right. He had built his business up from nothing. He knew every nook and cranny of the store. Better still, he had a first-class mind for figures. He could trace every penny that came and went. No wholesaler dared to take advantage of him. He could smell a rotten basket of fruit at ten yards. No one embroidered accounts when he was about.

As a salesman, he had no match. Ticklish customers were his speciality. He'd have them eating out of his hand in no time. He was a marvel on the telephone. People had to be sharp or he'd sell them the shop. He never lost a sale. I think he felt an obligation to succeed. I once heard him sell a number of chests of tea to a customer who came into the store looking for something for his poor relatives for Christmas. Grimshaw was poetic. 'Why sir,' he said, 'in the circumstances, I can think of no better Christmas present than a chest of tea. Think of the cheer it will bring. Think with what gratitude they will remember you daily . . .' He was as good at selling tea as anything else. I learned later that there was a high profit on tea.

One day I heard him sounding off to one of his customers about the strikes going on in cottons. 'They're spoiled, that's what they are. Yes, sir, downright spoiled. It's not good for the likes of them to be molly-coddled. Only makes them lazy and ungrateful. They'll ruin any business. They'll ruin the country with their demands. Having got a penny, they want a pound. If you don't keep them down, you won't get a thing done. I know them – they have to be threatened: hunger in this world, hellfire in the next. Strikes can't take the place of hard work and the certainty of the Lord. Shoot 'em,' was Mr Grimshaw's final word on the matter. He said these things with such heat that I expected flames to shoot out of his mouth. 'Any man who strikes on me goes through the door.'

It was taken for granted from the day I arrived that the other assistants, and members of the family, would be free to take their frustrations out on me. 'Billy, give a hand!' 'Billy, why are you standing there?' 'Billy, you're loafing.' 'Billy, look what a mess you've made!' 'Billy, you'll never learn.' 'Billy, it's a wonder we pay you.' Every crisis was solved, every problem explained, by somebody bawling at me.

Mildred, Grimshaw's daughter – a large woman who lacked all the aggressive traits of her father -- was the exception. She didn't bully me. Often she defended me from her parents. She taught me to be silent. In the early days when I was just about to get my blood up at Grimshaw and answer him back, I'd catch sight of her face. 'No!' she'd warn me with her lips and eyes and a slight shake of the head. She later told me that I'd got the job because I came from Livingstone Road.

Mildred was in love with the Reverend Black who lived a street away. For such a young man, Mr Black had unusually gaunt eyes. He used to carry a tin round with him in which he collected donations for foreign missions. 'Don't forget the poor souls of the West Indies,' he'd say, shaking the can vigorously under someone's nose. I'm sure there was no connection between his name and his avidity to save black souls. The look he used to give me suggested that white souls were boring and beyond redemption anyway. Mildred put one of his collection cans on the counter, but her father removed it. 'Nay, nay, mustn't mix religion and business.'

I think Mildred's love affair made her brood. I'd catch her, elbows on the till, lost in thought. On occasions, I had to cough to make my presence known. The only odd thing about Mildred was the way she paid us from the till on a Friday night. It was like receiving communion. She raised the money before our eyes before placing it in our eager hands. When everybody else had left, she slipped me a package of bacon ends and other scraps for my family. 'Faith, hope and charity,' she said, emphasizing the charity. 'Hide it under your jacket, Billy,' she cautioned, with an eye out for her father.

Mildred was kind to Bess, who followed our movements from across the road. Occasionally she slipped out with a bone. They were conspirators together. I cannot imagine how these things escaped her father's notice, especially as he was always going on about how businesses failed because people didn't watch the little things.

'Take care of the pence,' he kept saying to anybody who would listen, 'and the pounds will take care of themselves.' He was always shooting off remarks such as 'A stitch in time saves nine,' or 'Penny-wise and pound-foolish . . .'

'Oh father,' Mildred would respond, 'you are a one. You'll wear yourself out.'

Mildred had a sister, Nancy, who was married to the Reverend Spick, a bright-eyed, vigorous young curate, with a scrubbed face, who seemed to be running a race. Nancy was not like Mildred, loving and warm. Despite her shapeless dress and footwear, she was imperious. Whenever she visited the shop she threw me a stiff, 'And how do you do?' to which I replied, 'Quite nicely, thank you.' Her husband didn't waste time on me. A half nod or an oblique glance was the best I ever got out of him. The shop assistants never called the Reverend Spick anything else but 'Spick and Span.'

It was while I was at Grimshaw's that the notorious Rector of Stiffkey in East Anglia, the Reverend H.F. Davidson, was defrocked. There had been a sexual scandal, following which the rector, with an apparent disregard for doctrinal orthodoxy or the interests of the Church of England, proceeded to air his differences with the church in public. His case was heard before the Privy Council. The press wrote editorials about him under the heading 'The Stiffkey Scandal.' Questions were asked in the House of Commons, his picture was in all the papers, his church was inundated by a multitude of sightseers who came by special buses from neighbouring towns. When he climbed into the pulpit the church was packed to the nave, and hundreds of men and women stood outside.

Once defrocked, the rector fell on hard times. To make ends meet, he finished up sitting in a barrel on the fairground at Blackpool, side by side with an exhibition of performing fleas, where people peeped at him through a hole at twopence a go. It was all in the papers and it didn't do the Church of England any good. Mildred, her sister Nancy and the reverends Spick and Black were appalled at the rector's conduct. Mildred shook her head sadly when the unhappy details of the rector's broken life were related to her – not without certain relish – by a customer in the shop. 'Oh dear,' Mildred said, 'those who test the Lord's patience do so at their peril.' (The peril proved to be more serious than Mildred realized. In 1937 the ex-rector appeared as a modern Daniel in a lion's cage at Skegness Amusement Park, where he was mauled to death.)

I didn't like Mrs Grimshaw. She was a small woman with a hard face, deep grey eyes and a prominent nose. There was a crushed look about her. She usually wore a black blouse with a white lace collar, a string of coloured beads, and a thick black skirt. She had an unpleasant high-pitched voice, and croaked and wheezed all the time. A large pair of scissors dangled from her waist. I never saw her use them. Except when customers entered the store, when she suddenly became all smiles and friendliness, Mrs Grimshaw sat on her stool like a moulting hen. She was stiff with me and the other shop assistants.

Of the other two assistants, Arthur and Cyril, I liked Arthur best. Several years my senior, Arthur was a handsome fellow with roguish grey eyes and thick, wavy black hair parted down the middle. He had the best teeth in the shop when he laughed. He was a born mimic, and loved to impersonate the Reverend Black shaking his collection can for the foreign missions.

Nobody got the better of Arthur, he had an answer for everything. Nobody guarded his flanks like he did. Nobody could handle the butter paddles or cut bacon like him. He'd get through a job in no time. 'I gave it a lick and a promise,' he'd say. It amazed me the way he made excuses for jobs not done.

Like his boss, Arthur could mould the customers like clay. Difficult customers who were forever tasting the cheese, or saying that the bacon had been cut too thick, were his speciality. He had them smiling in no time. No trouble at all. Only Mrs Grimshaw saw through him. She was cool toward him. Yet women customers preferred him to anybody else. Grimshaw would have sacked him long ago had Arthur not been useful.

I ate my lunch with Arthur in the dimly-lit, dank cellar under the shop floor. It was the only room in the building where Mr Grimshaw did not have a peep-hole. For the thirty minutes lunch break we sat on soap boxes down there. We had to sit, the ceiling was too low to stand. Throughout lunch, Arthur was always laughing. He took nothing and nobody seriously.

What astonished me was how well he ate. After cheese sandwiches, he ate chocolate, fresh fruit and cake, which he fished out of a giant pocket at the front of his black apron. He'd then lie back and blow rings from an expensive cigarette. While he smoked, I ate what was left.

One day I asked him how he could afford to eat as he

did. For a moment or two he looked at me quizzically. Then he beckoned me over and placed his lips against my ear. 'Ye 'elps yerself, that's 'ow,' he whispered, giving me a sly wink.

'But that's . . .' I began.

'Tommyrot!' He laughed uproariously at the effect his words had had upon me.

I was too shocked to know what to say, especially as for weeks now I'd been sharing the spoils. Good God, I'd been eating stolen goods! My mouth went dry.

'Cut yer throat if ya tell,' Arthur warned in a low voice, while he held me with his eyes.

Not knowing what to say, I laughed nervously. I suddenly realized that I was in danger of losing my job. I was scared.

I came to the conclusion that Arthur's philosophy was simple: it was for the poor to rob the rich.

'Not 'alf,' was his only comment when I asked him.

Mr Grimshaw's chief assistant, Cyril, was a different fish. I couldn't stick him. He seemed to me to be full of malice and calculation. He had a funny little face, which he hid behind large spectacles. He had black eyes and black hair. At first I feared him as much as I feared Mr Grimshaw. He pushed and shoved me about as if I were a piece of merchandise. He hated Bess. He would have stopped Mildred feeding her if he could. What put me off more than anything else, were his damp, fishy hands.

Cyril had no real skills, other than monumental servility. I think Grimshaw had bullied him for so long that there was nothing left. He must have been paid a pittance. One day, when Cyril was away at a relative's funeral, I was sent by Mr Grimshaw to deliver a message to Cyril's father who lived in the woods on the outskirts of town. I was astonished how poorly they lived. I lived in a substantial house in Livingstone Road, all Cyril had was a leaking wooden hut and a bicycle.

His father was terrified that his son might lose what little income they had. A white-haired, bent old man, he clutched my hand on parting. 'Look after my Cyril,' he begged. 'Tell

Mr Grimshaw that Cyril's a hard worker.' He said much more about the merits of his Cyril, while moving bowls around to catch the rain coming through the roof.

Instead of fearing him, I came to pity Cyril. I knew from her eyes that Mildred felt the same. When he was not calling out: 'Yes, Mr Grimshaw. No, Mr Grimshaw. Right away, Mr Grimshaw,' he was worrying himself to death what on earth he would do if Grimshaw fired him. There were simply no other jobs to be had. Terrified at the thought, he clung to Grimshaw as a drowning man clings to a raft. His wildest dream was to marry Mildred and inherit the business.

Arthur roared with laughter when I told him of Cyril's hallucination. He kept slapping his thighs as if it was the funniest thing he'd ever heard.

I happened to enter the shop one day at the moment that Grimshaw was sacking Arthur. He must have caught him helping himself. Or perhaps Cyril, who looked oilier than ever, had betrayed him. The only thing that surprised me was that Grimshaw had not got on to Arthur's pilfering sooner. 'There's a week's wages,' Grimshaw snapped. 'Now get out!' Arthur was his usual cool self. He didn't seem rattled, not even when he was being fired. He knew from the shocked look on my face that I'd had nothing to do with it. 'Ta, Ta! Woody,' he said as he sauntered off, hands in pockets, trying to look casual. He whistled as he left. That takes some doing when you've just been sacked. I never saw or heard of him again.

Most of the time while I was working for Mr Grimshaw, I was too busy to worry about other people's troubles. My day began when Mildred let me into the store at seven-forty-five. My first job was to carry out the rubbish and ashes from the house and the store from the day before. I then carried innumerable buckets of coal from the cellar up several flights of stairs to the rooms above. I also lit the fire in the living room behind the shop. The room was richly carpeted. Almost covering a wall was a glass cupboard containing fine china and silverware. There were double curtains on the windows and a clock on the mantelpiece faced with black marble.

In winter my progress was speeded up by shouts from the rooms above. When the grates were cleaned and the fires lighted – the so-called house cleaning woman-cum-cook arrived later – I carried wood, coal and flour to the bakery. I learned not to stand about in the bakery talking to the cook. One morning when we were chattering away, a small wooden door slid back and Mr Grimshaw's eagle head appeared. 'I'm not paying you two to stand there gassing,' he threw at us.

Having finished the house chores, I swept the shop, first sprinkling the splintery floor with used tea leaves. Then I washed the shop windows and the pavement in front of the store. That done, I turned to my day's work, which was to deliver groceries. Cyril and Arthur had been round the district on bicycles earlier taking orders. I was never allowed to serve behind the counter.

I delivered Mr Grimshaw's groceries from a two-wheeled hand-cart – a large tray on enormous iron-clad wheels – which I pushed and pulled through the streets. On both sides of the cart were advertisements of Mr Grimshaw's merchandise. The cart had a tarpaulin cover in case of rain. My only cover was a fustian cap pulled well down and a muffler wrapped round my neck. I could get wet, the groceries never. I also had an oil lamp, which I used at night.

On the outward journeys, in order to keep my eye on the stacked boxes before me, I pushed the cart. Returning to the shop, I ran in front between the shafts like a donkey. Some passers-by asked me if I was a donkey. I doubt if a donkey could have handled some of the heavy loads. There were times when Cyril and Arthur had to help me make a wobbly start down the cobbled street. The pushing and pulling left me stiff and sore, but there was nothing like it for developing the back and shoulder muscles.

Wet or fine, I went out. Once on the road, Bess joined me. Rain, it seemed, was an almost permanent condition. I became accustomed to all kinds: dreary rain, slanting rain, driving rain; viciously cold rain that beat against my face, blinding me until I yielded; rain that soaked me to the skin, and oozed in my clogs; rain that on occasions I found exhilarating and sang to.

Often the wind held me up, trying to drive me back. I became expert at waiting until the gust had passed and then pushed on. When sleet and snow hit me, I held my head to one side. Bess was smarter; she ran along underneath the cart. Sometimes in winter a lighted tram would pull alongside us and the passengers would look lazily down at the strange apparition on the road. Bess and I were careful to yield to all other vehicles. We were at the bottom of the heap; nobody gave way to us.

It didn't take me long to realize that Mr Grimshaw's customers were living off the fat of the land. It was the same with their houses and their gardens. Everything they had was solid and prosperous. It puzzled me that while my family were fighting to make ends meet, others were eating sides of bacon, legs of lamb, whole hams, quantities of fish, eggs, milk, fruit including fresh grapes, vegetables, drink, fresh bread, pies, confectionery and whole tins of Peak Frean biscuits. It didn't seem fair. The bad times meant self-denial for the workers, self-indulgence for the rich.

I was not alone in thinking thus. One day a gang of locked-out weavers stopped me and, despite my protests, began to rummage through my boxes. Bess barked at them and ran between their legs, threatening to bite. I had trouble keeping her down.

'Just look at this,' they shouted as they uncovered one choice item after another. 'Pigs at trough! Greedy buggers!' Then they turned on me. 'What kind of a lackey are you? Pandering to the gluttony of the rich. Tha working class and tha ought to be shamed.'

Fortunately the demonstrators confined their anger to

words. They didn't steal anything. After being pushed and shoved I was allowed to go my way. One of them shouted after me: 'Tha'll get nowt but crumbs from t' rich man's table.'

True, I thought as I went along. At ten shillings a week that's all I was getting. But to anyone who was hungry, the crumbs from Mr Grimshaw's table were worth having. For my family they were indispensable. It was the crumbs from the rich men's tables that kept Bess and me going. There was hardly a house where the servants didn't feed us. They were working-class people speaking my dialect. They knew that there were a lot of hungry people about. I wouldn't be pushing a cart through the streets in the pouring rain if I wasn't poor. Besides, I was only fourteen and I think they felt for me.

'Tha must sit thiself down, lad,' they said, 'and have a bite; tha looks clemmed.' Servants and maids came cheap and were everywhere. There were maids dressed in starched white, black, or brown; maids with fine aprons and pretty caps perched on their heads; maids with a rich Irish brogue.

And so, with a roaring fire in the grate and the pots spitting, Bess and I sat among the maids in the kitchens, and tasted the food we'd just delivered before the rich could get to it. Many's the piece of hot pie or tart I had; many's the scrap that Bess got. There were so many of us eating the food downstairs that I wondered if there'd be any left to go upstairs.

During the year I worked at Grimshaw's the servants of the rich were my guardian angels. I couldn't have survived without them. They not only fed me and my dog, and dried my wet clothes before the great kitchen fires – they even provided me with cast-off clothing – they also covered up for me if I accidentally damaged some of Grimshaw's goods. They were so kind to me that I would stay in the kitchens too long. Realizing that I was late, I raced back to the shop like a mad horse, dragging the empty, bouncing, clattering cart over the cobble stones after me. Bess led, barking. Sure enough, as we approached the shop, I caught sight of

Grimshaw waiting for me on the pavement, red in the face, watch in hand. 'Wher's ta bin?' he snapped.

One of my special guardian angels was a sweet old lady called Mrs Sand who lived in a large, gabled house surrounded by trees. She was a tiny, grey creature, with grey eyes, and a long grey dress. I sometimes thought she was a ghost. The only other occupant was her sick husband who lay upstairs, making all kinds of choking noises. When he needed something he rang a bell. The moment the bell rang, Mrs Sand dropped what she was doing and rushed upstairs, calling out to her husband as she went. I couldn't understand why she had to keep running upstairs when there were so many empty rooms downstairs.

Mrs Sand's loneliness was so great that I could touch it. She welcomed our arrival by feeding Bess. Then she sat and drank tea with me while telling me all the family business. The way the words came pouring out, I wondered if she had anyone else to talk to. In all my visits, I saw no one else entering or leaving the house, not even a gardener, or a maid, or a physician. Mrs Sand told me how her son's wild life had caused her husband to have a stroke. Somehow the boy had got hold of their money and spent it on gambling and women and drink. They hadn't seen or heard of him since her husband's collapse. He had dropped out of their lives.

'Wouldn't it be awful,' she said to me one day, talking more to herself than to me, 'if he were to die in some God-forsaken place with no one to comfort him?'

'Yes,' I said, 'it would.'

'He is our only child, you know.'

She must have said this a dozen times.

Her troubles did not seem to have undermined Mrs Sand's faith in God's goodness.

The tears rising freshly in her eyes, she vowed not to leave the bell-ringer as long as he lived. She said it as if I'd made the suggestion, or she was beating back a wrong thought. Staring through her window at the garden, she wistfully talked of the coming of spring.

In return, I told her all about the worlds I intended to conquer. I told her that I was thinking about getting a big job in Manchester or London. I also told her that grandmother Bridget had once urged me to go to America.

'Yes, yes, you must,' Mrs Sand encouraged me. 'You must go at once. How exciting,' she exclaimed, jumping up. 'How I envy you.'

And then, suddenly realizing that Grimshaw was waiting, I drank my tea, swallowed my cake, and rushed off.

When Christmas came she asked me in a faltering voice to drink a toast with her. There was a miniature fir tree on the table. The two small glasses were ready. She insisted on pouring the drink, though I noticed how badly her hand shook.

'Merry Christmas,' I said, raising my glass and bowing slightly.

'Merry Christmas,' she answered smiling, 'and may all your dreams come true.'

I stood in silence, not knowing what to say.

———◇———

It was while I was working for Grimshaw that I fell in love with Betty Weatherby, the daughter of one of Grimshaw's customers. Of course, it was ridiculous. One can't have a fourteen year-old errand boy running off with a manufacturer's daughter. But nobody intended it that way. It was as much of a surprise to me as it was to everybody else, including Bess, who sat and stared at me as if I'd gone out of my mind.

It began one night at the town's indoor swimming pool where all the schools were competing. I'd learned to swim in that pool. The first time I let go of one side of the pool in the deep end and struggled to the other side, I nearly drowned. After that swimming became an obsession.

The meeting was packed and noisy. The shouting in the confined space was deafening. I was swimming for St Philip's.

I'd taken up my job at Grimshaw's a couple of weeks earlier but I was still officially allowed to compete. I was pitted against the best in the town. Luck had brought me through several heats to the finals for my age group. Now I faced the ultimate test.

'Come on Woody,' my supporters yelled. 'You can do it.'

As I stood poised, waiting for the starter's gun, I suddenly made up my mind to win. I felt a sudden urge to come out on top. It was a funny feeling that came from inside like a flash of anger. It said: 'You've got to win.'

At the crack of the gun, I and five others dived in. Dimly, I heard the thunder of voices. In the green, shimmering water I saw the black line on the bottom snaking away in front of me. To my left was another boy; at first I was level with his thighs, then he drew ahead and I caught glimpses of his feet. Gasping for breath, I chased after him.

He was still leading when we turned for the eighth and last lap; the other swimmers had fallen behind. With my lungs bursting, I ordered my arms and legs to go faster. I strained until I was level with the other fellow's head. I heard the constant thump of his arms and legs. I wondered if I had strayed out of my lane. With one last frantic effort I hit the wall. When one of the judges touched me on the shoulder, I knew I'd won. I was more exhausted than elated.

The girl's final heat for my age group followed immediately. A short, small-waisted, dark-haired girl was the winner. I had no idea who she was. Together we stood in our dripping swimsuits before the judges to receive our silver medals. Real silver. The town's poverty was forgotten. Amid all the shouting, she and I stole side-long glances. I noticed the full cheeks, the well-shaped mouth and the rounded chin. She gave me the warmest smile. I smiled back. She smiled again. It was enough to make my face burn – enough to make me forget all about the judges and the medal around my neck.

While I wouldn't have dreamt of talking to her, I tried to follow her with my eyes after we left the dais. She was soon lost in the crowd. My friends pressed around me to see my medal; I dressed in a daze.

I slept badly that night. I didn't know what had come over me. I felt pierced from top to bottom. Rosie Gill, or Annie Morgan, or any of the other girls I'd met had never affected me like that. The next day I got up without any appetite.

Several days later, while delivering Grimshaw's groceries, I was amazed to see the same girl in a blue school uniform entering the Weatherby's driveway. Ahead of us lay the Weatherby mansion, standing among wide lawns and park-like shrubs. I was too flabbergasted to know what to do. I didn't want to bump into her; not pushing a handcart.

Instead of yielding to my immediate reaction, which was to flee, I slowed down and entered the driveway well behind her. As she walked ahead of me, crunching the gravel beneath her feet, her doe-like body looked lovelier than ever. I hoped she wouldn't turn round. I think Bess knew what was going on, for she ran to the girl, wagging her tail, whining. The girl petted the dog but ignored me. Then she skipped through the front door. Shamefaced, Bess and I went round the back.

In a round-about way I asked Mrs Pegg, the head cook at Weatherby's, who the girl was.

She stopped what she was doing and looked at me curiously. 'Tha not gettin' any fancy ideas in thi 'ead, ar' ta?' she asked jovially.

'Oh no, Mrs Pegg,' I protested, blushing.

'Tha'd better not, lad. That's Betty, the apple of Mr Weatherby's eye. Mustn't throw thi cap at 'er.'

'Oh no, Mrs Pegg,' I said. 'Ah've got some gumption.'

All the kitchen hands laughed.

A week later, when Bess and I were leaving the Weatherby's drive, the same girl stepped out from behind the small, open pavilion that stood at the edge of the tennis court. She was wearing her school uniform, but was without hat. Her silky black hair was blowing in the wind. I reddened, she smiled. Bess ran to her, wagging her tail.

'I just wanted to congratulate you on your win at the swim meet,' she said in a delightful voice. 'I thought you were pretty good.'

'Well, thanks,' I stammered. I felt my face redden. 'You were pretty good yourself.'

She gave the gayest laugh and petted Bess. I saw the first blush on her face. How could anyone have such pretty, bright brown eyes, I wondered.

Every week after that, wet or fine, I met Betty Weatherby in the pavilion by the tennis court. For me, the whole week was simply the prelude to our meeting. I couldn't get her out of my head. My feelings went from utter joy, to utter sorrow, to utter joy again. It's a wonder my nerves stood up to it. I could not conceal my delight each time we met. Nor could she. She always ran toward me, arms outstretched, her face shining with delight and happiness.

With the handcart parked next to the pavilion out of sight of the house, Betty and I entered an imaginary world. It was a world without past or future, containing only the two of us. Holding each other's hands, we were deaf, blind and dumb to everything except ourselves. Instead of talking about my job, or about Grimshaw, or about her family or mine, we teased each other light-heartedly. We lived only to be together.

The time came when I told Betty that I loved her. I followed this declaration by giving her an ill-contrived peck on the cheek. To my astonishment, she responded not by pecking me back again, but by nibbling my ear. For some odd reason, she became obsessed with my ears. But surely, ears are a small price to pay for boundless delight. As the weeks passed, we began to love each other without reservation. We would have loved each other with even greater abandon had we known what was coming.

The Weatherby's housekeeper, Mrs Shaw, was our undoing. I'd seen her in the kitchen once. She had cold, rebuking eyes and a tight mouth. She had talked as if she was a cut above the rest. Her tall, thin body, with its funny little head sitting ill on her neck, suddenly appeared at the entrance of the pavilion where Betty and I were rolling about on the tennis nets. She was scowling. Bess had not warned us of her approach.

'Betty!' Mrs Shaw shrieked, as if Betty's delirious eating of my ears was the work of the devil. 'Betty! I am surprised at you.'

She was not half as surprised as we were. Suddenly, Bess came bounding up, growling.

'Young man,' Mrs Shaw pierced me, 'you will take yourself and your dog off Mr Weatherby's property.' She looked grim enough to throw me, my cart and my dog through the gate.

Betty and I squeezed hands. Then, head down, lips trembling, red-faced, she went with Mrs Shaw up the drive. Dazed, I made my way back to Grimshaw's. Bess ran alongside, wearing a contrite look.

'Tha some use,' I scolded her. 'Tha's got us into real trouble, tha 'as.' She knew she'd let us down, she ambled along, her tail tucked in.

Mrs Shaw must have telephoned Grimshaw. He was waiting for me outside the shop. Even though there were customers about, he didn't hesitate to have it out with me.

'Tha 'ere to deliver groceries,' he told me in a biting tone, 'not to go courtin'. Tha deserves to be sacked.' He really got himself worked up. The veins on his forehead protruded. I stood there between the shafts, with Bess cowering at my feet. He went on and on. 'If tha must go courtin',' he stamped his foot, 'go in thi own time, not at my expense.'

I was too dazed to make any response. For all the impact his ranting and raving had upon me, he might as well have blown smoke. I was more fascinated with the globule of sweat hanging from the tip of his nose. Had he run me through with a sword, I wouldn't have cared. My thoughts were still with Betty, romping on the tennis nets. All I cared about was seeing her again.

The next week, when I pushed my cart up the Weatherby's

drive, Betty was not there. I thought I'd die. I tried to pump Mrs Pegg in the kitchen, but she kept a tight tongue. She'd obviously had orders. A week or so later, while watching the other servants closely, she whispered that Betty had been sent to a boarding school outside London. No one seemed to know where the school was. The news made me sick for days. I became convinced that I was going to die. Bess seemed to sense my feeling of complete hopelessness. She rubbed her nose against my hand, trying to gain attention.

Mrs Pegg shared my sorrow. Every time I entered the kitchen she looked at me and sighed. 'Tha just too young to 'ave anything in t' 'ead,' she said to me one day. 'Tha'll 'ave to learn that life can be very troublesome.' She then relieved her frustration by pounding a lump of dough. Later, in great secrecy, she undertook to get a note from me to Betty. 'They'd have me 'ead if they knew.'

I returned the same day with my letter. I told Betty that I was dying without her; that I loved her; and that I'd wait for her for ever. I also gave her my address. For weeks after that, Bess and I used to trail the postman through the streets to see if he had a letter for me. Nothing came. 'Tha're out of luck, they've taken thi letter out of t' post at t' other end,' Mrs Pegg concluded after some reflection. 'Tha'll have to wait,' she counselled. 'Others do. Tha not t' only one round 'ere with a broken 'eart.'

It was about the time of Betty's departure that tragedy overtook the Grimshaws. I arrived one morning to find the shop in darkness. Grimshaw had had a stroke in the night, and was paralyzed down his left side. His speech and hearing had been affected. Although I continued to carry coal for the fires upstairs, he never spoke to me again. He lay on his bed, his face twisted beyond recognition, his ugly, shrunken body like half a sack of flour on the counterpane. To catch his saliva a towel lay under his chin. One morning while I was sweeping the hearth, the sack-like figure flapped its hands at me and grunted. I dropped the hand brush and fled in horror.

For the business, hard times followed. The family did their best, but, without Grimshaw, the shop was a ship without a rudder. Wrong accounts were sent out. Some wholesalers took advantage of Mildred and her mother. The women were just not as sharp. Cyril used the occasion to worm his way into the family business, but he didn't have the brains to help. Without Grimshaw on his back, he was at a loss to know what to do.

Grimshaw knew that his business was dying. He made heroic, if futile, efforts to get out of bed. One day he managed it. Mrs Grimshaw, Mildred and Cyril dressed him and dragged him downstairs as far as the shop floor. Held upright, he managed to get across the threshold. After each step he paused to gain strength for the next. For a few moments he stood in the shop shaking, his hands fluttering, his wild, bloodshot eyes taking everything in. What he saw must not have pleased him, for his twisted face underwent further contortion. Gasping for breath, he began to make unfriendly, unintelligible noises. Then he wobbled around and turned his back on the store. With Cyril and Mildred lifting his stricken leg at every step, he was slowly dragged back up the stairs.

The final straw for Grimshaw was to fall into the hands of a charlatan couple from Manchester who pretended to be physicians. There had been some difference of opinion between Mrs Grimshaw and the family doctor, as a result of which he was passed over. Alas, in the care of the Manchester couple, Grimshaw's condition became worse. Mrs Grimshaw suspected nothing until the police came to the shop. By the time a warrant had been issued for their arrest, the birds had flown. Everyone was dumbfounded when the story got around. Imagine Grimshaw being hood-winked like that! It put Mrs Grimshaw in a towering rage.

The shock of being diddled was too much for the old

man. I heard Mrs Grimshaw tell a customer how he'd sighed deep enough to break his heart. Mercifully, three days later, he had a second stroke and died. We put black ribbons on the shop door and on my cart. Two days later he was buried. Wearing black armbands, Cyril and I went to the funeral. It was a bitter day. The wholesalers and most of the customers had sent flowers. There was a mountain of them. I was too busy pushing cartloads of wreaths from the shop to the cemetery to attend the church service. I carried the flowers through a great crowd to the edge of the grave.

In deepest mourning, Mildred, Nancy, Mrs Grimshaw and the Reverend Black, stood by the graveside. The Reverend Spick read the funeral service for his father-in-law. It was the usual one about 'the resurrection and the life.' I was at the back of the crowd and heard only snatches. He spoke of my boss as a father, as a merchant, as a citizen and as a God-fearing, church-going man. He said he was convinced that Mr Grimshaw was already enjoying his heavenly reward. We were all the poorer for his passing.

I must confess that despite the Reverend Spick's moving oration, my thoughts were not so much concerned with the whereabouts of Mr Grimshaw's soul as with the whereabouts of Betty Weatherby.

My stay at Grimshaw's did not long outlast the death of my employer. One day, on turning a corner with a heavily laden cart, Bess and I ran slap-bang into another workers' demonstration. There were more of them this time. They were led by a man beating a drum. It struck a sinister note. A sea of hungry faces approached me, some of which I remembered from my earlier encounter. Inwardly, I groaned. They marched straight at me with their banner emblazoned with the words: WORKERS OF THE WORLD UNITE! No one else was about. The policeman who occasionally trudged along at the side of demonstrators was absent.

'Would you believe it,' somebody bawled, 'he's still serving the bloody rich.'

'Bloody lackey.'

'Disgrace to his class, that's wot 'e is.'

Barking loudly, Bess ran from me to the men.

In panic, I tried to turn the cart round, but someone grabbed one of the wheels. Several of my boxes fell over. As I reached down to secure them, a demonstrator wearing a long, black coat seized me by the collar in a violent manner. Bess attacked him; someone kicked her off. Another worker made a menace of striking me with the back of his hand.

The crowd shouted encouragement. 'Why should he help them to eat while we go hungry?'

Shaking off the man who held me by the collar, I tried to stop the pillaging of the groceries.

'Leave bloody stuff alone,' I bawled. I was hotted up by now and ready for a fight; so was Bess. Realizing that if I didn't escape there would not be a thing left, I clutched the shafts, put down my head and charged. 'Fetch them, Bess!' I shouted.

The cart hit several bodies as I fought to break the encircling ring. My clogs stomping the cobbles, I hurled myself forward again and again. With Bess nipping their heels, the line began to give way. To my great relief, I broke through the crowd and began to run down a steep hill. Several of the men came after me. I heard their footsteps behind me.

Panting and crying, with Bess at my side, I rattled away faster and faster. I ran so fast that I could neither guide nor stop the cart. I knew that if I didn't let go, it would drag me along the ground. With a cry of despair, I let go.

Transfixed, I watched the cart lurch away from me, stand on its end and then flip over, wheels spinning in the air. Groceries flew in all directions. Trickles of vinegar, wine, milk, flour, eggs and hot rhubarb pie began to ooze into the gutter. My heart sank into my clogs.

With several of the demonstrators, I ran to see what might be salvaged. Together, we got the cart back onto its wheels. Helpless, I looked at the pile of food lying on the ground. It was a terrible, chilling sight. There were pickles and jam and broken glass everywhere. With Bess barking furiously,

I stood there staring at the mess, not knowing what to say or do.

By the time I recovered my wits, the men were already helping themselves. They were like locusts. Hungrily, they rummaged through the packages. Whatever could be eaten, was eaten on the spot; the rest was carried off. In no time, all that was worth taking had gone. I was too bruised and shaken to intervene.

Distraught, I watched the crowd line up again in a quiet and orderly manner, raise their banner against the wind, beat their drum, and march off up the hill eating as they went. Boom! Boom! went the drum. With my heart thumping, I sat in the gutter wondering what to do next. Bess sat beside me, whining and licking her wounds. Without really intending to, I broke into a passion of crying. I wished that the earth might open at my feet. 'Oh Bess,' I sobbed, throwing my arms around her neck, 'what are we going to do?'

Eventually I got as much of the broken glass off the road as I could. Then I threw the empty boxes back into the cart and, with a silent, downcast Bess, slowly made my way back to the shop where, with Cyril listening to every word, I told Mrs Grimshaw what had happened. Clutching at the beads around her neck, she nearly choked. Her face became contorted. In her croaking voice, she sacked me on the spot. Not far from tears, I went home and announced to the family that my ten shillings had just been stopped. Ten shillings was a small sum, but it was the only earnings coming into our house. The rest of the family had been sitting about waiting for work for ages. My ten shillings and Mildred's bacon scraps had been an indispensable part of our welfare. The loss of that money, and those scraps, worsened an already desperate situation.

A few days later I had a note from Mildred Grimshaw, which made me feel better. She was sorry for what had happened. She asked me to go to Lady Fielden's estate on the edge of town where I might get a job as an assistant gardener. She had spoken for me. Lady Fielden, I knew, was one of the town's richest widows. I wasted no time in getting there. I arrived breathless. I simply had to get this job.

The house itself was a beautiful place surrounded with wrought-iron railings. Lilac trees and beds of peonies faced the street. I made my way through archway of roses, past an artificial rock garden and bright borders of flowers, to the back of the house. From there I was sent to the front.

To my surprise, it was not the head gardener but Lady Fielden herself who awaited me. Having been admitted to the house by a maid in starched white apron and pretty cap, I was ushered into a side room rich with tapestries and curious figurines. There I found a short, hard-faced woman in her seventies sitting perfectly upright on a high-backed chair. She was dressed in black lace from head to foot. A skein of pearls was around her neck. She smelled faintly of lavender. She had an unusual amount of hair on both sides of her face and almost a beard on her chin. I put on my best smile, 'I'm William Woodruff,' I said.

'I know, child,' she said stiffly. She then smoothed her dress while looking over her wire spectacles; her searching look went right through me.

'Sit there,' she commanded, pointing to a chair opposite her.

I did so quickly, but with a sinking feeling. I was intimidated by Lady Fielden. I felt that if I moved I might break one of her treasures.

Lady Fielden proceeded to question me. The way she pursed her lips told me that I was giving all the wrong answers.

'Which church does your family attend?' she asked finally.

'My people don't go to church,' I said, attempting to smile. She shook her head deprecatingly, while fingering her pearls. I shifted uncomfortably inside my clothes. I began to revolve my cap in my hands. From the stern look she gave me, I knew I'd said the wrong thing.

Curtly Lady Fielden made a dismissive gesture. 'That will be all,' she said. 'I will write to you.' I gave a stiff little nod.

She never did write. Another gardener there told me later that I had failed the 'religious test.' I should have boasted membership of the Church of England, he said. Instead, I'd given her the impression that my family were heathens, which they were. She wasn't going to have any heathen touch her flowers.

The last thing I heard about Grimshaw's came from Mrs Sand, whom I visited one day. She was delighted to see me again. I heard the bell still ringing upstairs. She told me that the errand boy who had replaced me had told her that Cyril had also left Grimshaw's. There'd been a storm between Mildred and Cyril and he'd been thrown out.

Weeks later, I saw a notice in the paper saying that Grimshaw's was up for sale.

Chapter XX

To Nab End

While I'd been earning my living, our neighbour, Mr Peek, had been working at his book that would save the world. He was always on about it. The more talk in the papers about a world depression, the more time he spent in his study. 'The workers don't know what's coming,' he muttered darkly one day when we were talking about the growing problems of the cotton industry. My family didn't thank Mr Peek for his warnings. Things were bad enough without listening to him.

Alas, Mr Peek's gloomy predictions gradually came true. In the summer of 1929 the cotton industry took another nose dive. The spinners were locked out to enforce wage reductions. In 1930 the weavers were locked out to enforce the increase in the number of looms from two to six, or even eight. But that only affected father and the lockout was lifted. We breathed freely again for several weeks. One way or another, my family got along. We hung on for our dear lives to the house in Livingstone Road.

In 1931, when stoppages and wage reductions became general, Mr Peek's dire warnings could no longer be denied. By then there were three million people without a job, and perhaps a similar number under-employed. Most of my family were now out of work, working part time, or double shifts, or working for less. In late 1931 the industry reached a state of collapse. By 1932 Britain slipped into the depths of a world depression. At the workers' expense everything was done to keep the industry alive: wages were cut, the hours of work increased. For the same pay workers were forced to man six, even eight, instead of two or four looms. The fight against six and eight looms went on mill by mill, Todmorden and Burnley weavers leading the way. The workers could do nothing but surrender or fight back – and go hungry.

At the beginning of 1932 my family was surviving on little more than Gordon's dole and my ten shillings from Grimshaw's. When I got the sack that left us with Gordon's money only.

One week when Gordon went to pick up his dole, the lines outside the Labour Exchange were longer than ever. There were so many people standing about, it was like after a football match. It took him ages to push his way through the shabby, hungry-looking crowd and join one of the queues shuffling toward the counter. When he got there he was faced by an unfamiliar clerk.

''Ow t' be?' the clerk said.

'Nicely,' Gordon lied, expecting to sign his name, take his money and push his way out again.

'I've got a job for thee,' the clerk went on, shuffling some papers.

'Tha 'as?'

'Yes.'

'Wher' is 't?'

'Cornwall.'

'Where's Cornwall?' asked Gordon. 'It sounds a long way.'

'That it is. A very long way.'

'What kind of painting is it?'

'It isn't painting.'

'It isn't?'

'No.'

'What is't then?'

'It's digging tin down a mine.'

'Ah'm not a tin miner, Ah'm a painter.'

'Does t' refuse to go to Cornwall?'

'Ah do.'

'Then tha's just lost thee dole.'

'Tha can't mean it.' Gordon didn't just need the money; he needed it desperately.

'Aye, but I do. If tha not "genuinely seeking work," and obviously tha not, benefits have to be stopped.'

Gordon returned to Livingstone Road dumbfounded. He couldn't understand how anyone could be so mean. The fellow didn't even say he was sorry; he just stopped Gordon's dole and that was that. We wanted him to go and fight it out, but his pride wouldn't let him. For Gordon and Jenny it wasn't love on the dole, it was love without the dole.

Somehow or other, by pinching and scraping, by using up our joint savings, and by pawning whatever was left, we continued to pay for the furniture, and hang on to the house in Livingstone Road. Mother was prepared to fight to the death to stay there. We went on living day by day, watching our resources dwindle, knowing that disaster threatened. As winter gave way to the spring of 1932, and spring to summer, we sat around for hours trying to come up with schemes to make a few shillings, or discover ways to spend less.

Armed with a sledgehammer, father earned a few pounds smashing looms that earlier he had tuned with all the skill of a piano-tuner. I watched him destroy his idols – some of them a hundred years old, and thanks to people like him, still in first-class condition. I cannot imagine what went through his head as he tossed the broken pieces through the open window. I think it took a lot of meaning out of his life. A hundred years earlier in Lancashire they'd hung people for smashing the first power looms. Now they paid them to do it.

Mother and my sisters did odd jobs like washing up and

peeling potatoes for club dinners in town, and for the hotels. Gordon – now that his dole was stopped – for the shame of it, put on a false nose and moustache and carried a sandwich board on his shoulders through the streets advertising Harper's lunches and dinners. Harper's was the restaurant where Gordon and Jenny had had their wedding breakfast. He kept his eyes on the pavement as he walked along and he didn't try to make anybody laugh. I think they paid him twenty-five or thirty pennies a day, plus a bowl of soup. And that job didn't last long either. I added little to the kitty. I did some ditch-digging for the Town Council, but after several weeks that fell through.

So much for our income. As for our outgoings, after I'd been fired from Grimshaw's and my indispensable ten shillings had been lost, we fell behind on rent and furniture payments. We spent less and less on food. We got charity bread where we could; for the rest we went hungry. Stealing was never considered. The local Public Assistance Committee refused help on the grounds that we were 'living on a scale disproportionate to [our] position.' It was their way of saying that poor people do not live on Livingstone Road. Bess and I didn't do badly because the Lathams fed us, as they would continue to do as long as I had need. Also, many were the parcels of food they sent home with me at night. For the shame of it, we revealed none of these things to our neighbours, the Peeks, or for that matter, to anybody else. Certainly not to old friends such as the Watkins, the Gills and the Morgans. They had troubles of their own.

With almost no money coming in, and everything going out, our resources continued to vanish before our eyes. Hanging on to Livingstone Road was like trying to bale out a boat with an egg cup. As each member of my family was thrown off the dole, and we struggled to hang on to a house and a way of life that was obviously beyond our means, we found ourselves with no resources at all. No amount of paring and scheming could help us. Whatever funds we still had were sacrificed in the struggle. Even father's war medals and Jenny's wedding dress were pawned for food. We would have given up earlier had we not been used to a roller-coaster existence. We were hardened to it. But now our resources and wits were finally used up.

Meanwhile mother continued to postpone the inevitable. Time and again she'd find a way to get by. She was brilliant in fending off creditors. She had no trouble at all with the thin, insignificant men who came with fly-marked paper-files from the rental agency and the furniture store. She gave them a cup of tea and charmed them out through the door again. But they were the decent types who didn't want to hurt anybody. They were followed by the muscle men who knew exactly what was needed. They were impervious to mother's charms.

'Have you read your contract, Mrs Woodruff?' the muscle men asked, knowing full well that she couldn't read. 'It states clearly . . .'

'But we've nowhere to go,' mother countered, fear in her eyes.

'That doesn't give you the right to occupy a large house rent free. The contract is quite clear and must be upheld.'

'Even if it throws my family in the street?'

'The truth is harsh, Mrs Woodruff, but it must be stated and upheld.'

'We'd pay you tomorrow, if we had the money, you know that. We've always paid.'

'Mrs Woodruff, we've already lost six weeks' rent on this house. Others are prepared to pay a higher rent than the one you paid. They're waiting for you to get out. The papers have been signed. Do you want me to get the sack?'

'How long do we have?'

'Two weeks.'

The muscle men from the furniture store didn't waste time talking. I came home to Livingstone Road one day to find all the furniture gone. I found mother sitting on a stool, looking through the rain-washed windows. Streaks of snow marked the summit of the bare hills. The curtains (Jenny's curtains) had been drawn back. She didn't notice my coming.

The muscle men must have caught her while she was washing her hair, for she wore a hand-towel wrapped round her head like a turban. Her head was lowered as if someone had struck her a blow. Tears streamed down her hollowed cheeks. I looked at her sad figure and thought how often she'd sung:

I'm forever blowing bubbles, pretty bubbles in the air;
Oh they fly so high, nearly reach the sky,
Then, like my dreams, they fade and die.
Fortune's always hiding. I've looked everywhere.
I'm forever blowing bubbles, pretty bubbles in the air.

Poor Maggie, so many of her bubbles had burst. She had lost her father as a child; neglect had become her lot. The war had changed her man; the depression had ruined their livelihood. Tied to an industry of boom and bust, she'd lived on a precipice, always uncertain, fearful that our living might disappear altogether. Now the Livingstone Road bubble – the best bubble of all – was to die too. No wonder she sat there looking totally vanquished.

I wept with her.

———◇———

Two weeks later we put our scant possessions on a flatcart and, in the middle of the night, pushed it to a lodging house in Nab End. Out of shame we didn't want the neighbours on Livingstone Road to see us go. I'd been avoiding Mr Peek and Roger for days. I didn't want their sympathy. Now, when it came time to go, I couldn't face them. I didn't say goodbye. Yet I have never forgotten the man who shared his knowledge with me; I shall feel indebted to him for ever.

The midnight flit from Griffin Street to Livingstone Road had been a triumphal march. The journey through the streets to Nab End was like a funeral. We were all too miserable to talk. We'd been robbed of the only really decent living conditions we'd ever known. There wasn't one of us who didn't feel sad and shamed. 'Who cares what people think,' mother had said when we were rising. I knew in my heart that she cared deeply what people thought now that we were falling. She walked arm in arm with Jenny and Brenda with a guilty look on her face. Even the family clown, Gordon, held his tongue.

Although Gordon's parents took in Jenny and Gordon later on, no other relative offered help. Most of them didn't have anything to give.

Nab End was a come-down after Livingstone Road; about as far as we could fall. It was worse than Griffin Street. At least we'd had our own cottage there. Nab End was chiefly lodging houses – all of them long past their prime and seedy looking – with vacant faces peering through dirty windows.

Six of us – mother and father, Jenny and Gordon, Brenda and I – occupied one room. Bess was kept outside. It was the cheapest thing we could get. Stacked with lodgers from cellar to roof, the place reeked. It wasn't the usual haddock and cabbage reek; it was a funny dead, musty smell. In Livingstone Road, which out of shame I never visited again, I had had a room to myself and a garden to sit in. In Nab End there was foul, crowded shelter, nothing more. Without the Lathams to flee to, Bess and I would have been lost.

I was so offended by the move, that I couldn't think straight. By then I was about fifteen and I had a lot of pride. It was a bad dream from which I felt I would waken. Thank goodness grandmother Bridget was not alive to see us in such squalor: the damp bricks, the dust-covered, broken windows, the sputtering gaslight, the peeling plaster and paint, the faded wallpaper, the crowded, greasy rooms, the dim landings where we washed and the shaky banisters. Toilets were shared in the yard. After Livingstone Road, the noise of the place was deafening. Everybody spoke at a higher level – almost in a hoarse shout. There was an incessant clamour throughout the building. Doors were always being banged to. There was no such thing as privacy. Everybody's business came through the walls. Outside, the shouting of children went on all day. There was no end to it.

An enormous, one-eyed man, with tattooed arms and a bullock's neck ran the place – chiefly by bawling orders from the bottom of the stairs. Gross and unclean, he looked as if he never took his clothes off. Like the ceilings and the walls of the lodging house, his bald head was covered with sweat. He had a bad limp – 'the war' everybody said – and was forever accompanied by a small, black Boston terrier. It had pricked ears and bulging eyes. It was so silent and kept so close to the man that one could mistake it for one of his boots.

Periodically the landlord and his mouse-like wife had fights to the death; usually when we were about to go to sleep. As our room was directly above theirs, we could hardly avoid the din. The fights began with shouting and name-calling; there followed the throwing of dishes, which led to a free-for-all. There were such bangs and crashes that mother feared for the woman's life. It did sound as if the brute was throwing his wife against the wall. There was a thud, followed by a deep groan, followed by silence; then another thud, followed by greater groans, followed by silence. Eventually, presumably when the combatants were lying on the floor unconscious, we were allowed to go to sleep.

As long as we were there, the woman and the dog survived. Sometimes the woman had a black eye, a split lip, or a puffed-up face, but nothing bad enough to stop her going about her daily business. The wounds on her husband's face showed that she was giving as good as she got. I couldn't make head or tail of them. Having fought half the night, they'd spend the next day cooing, laughing and chatting together like young lovers. Mother said it was ridiculous. 'Rubbish,' said father, 'they're having the time of their lives.'

The one redeeming feature about that dark hole was the sense of community among the poor wretches who lived there. They were like members of a great noisy family. They understood and sympathized with each other's hunger and desperation. They willingly shouldered each other's burdens.

With nothing to lose, these people should have been revolutionaries and thieves. On the contrary, they were the most law-abiding people one could meet. Their luck was out; like ourselves, they'd gone on the dole; they'd then endured the Means Test, which – having assessed their non-existent resources – had either reduced or removed state aid altogether. There was no work to be had. Their reserves had been used up. Their families and friends either couldn't afford to help them, or had deserted them. Beyond the workhouse, which they all feared, there was no one else to whom they could turn. 'But don't worry,' they said, 'times will change. We maun bide His will till work coom again.' With childlike innocence, they honestly believed that they would climb back to the level from which they'd fallen. Against all the misfortunes of their earthly lot they clung to the promise of heavenly salvation. God was their only balm.

Every night, the Catholics among them went down on their knees on the sanded floor in one of the rooms to implore the Virgin to intervene on their behalf. We heard the drone of voices throughout the house:

> Remember, O most gracious Virgin Mary, that never was it known that anyone who fled to thy protection, implored thy help, or sought thy intercession, was left unaided. Inspired with this confidence we fly unto thee, O Virgin of Virgins, our mother. To thee we come, before thee we stand, sinful and sorrowful. O mother of the word incarnate, despise not our petition, but in thy mercy hear and answer. Amen.

They showed infinite patience. Nothing got better; nobody seemed to hear or answer them; the world remained pitiless. Yet they always made their nightly appeal: 'Remember, O most gracious Virgin Mary . . .' They answered the skepticism they detected in my eyes with: 'Mary can't be expected to answer every supplicant at once.'

A spindly, bright-faced Irishman with silver hair led them

in prayer. He'd been the 'boots' at the local railway hotel and, having spent his life working for a pittance, had fallen about as far down the ladder as he could. I don't know how he got to Nab End. All I know is that it seemed wrong for a good man to end his life in such circumstances. I didn't know what a saint was supposed to look like, but every time I saw the Irishman in the house or on the street, he made me think of a saint. He radiated serenity and peace. When later in life, I learned about 'abiding grace and inner peace,' I thought about him. Mother had a beautiful face, but it wasn't a saint's face. There was agony on it and the agony stayed there until father got a job and she escaped from Nab End to Polly Street by the railway line. Polly Street wasn't much better than Nab End, but at least we had a small weaver's cottage to ourselves.

It was while we were at Nab End that my brother Dan married Christine Bailey. It was a quiet wedding.

Christine had met Dan while he was working away from Blackburn as a 'devil.' She didn't seem to object to soot, and fell deeply in love with him.

Mother was not happy about Christine at first. She was not prepared to have her Dan marry somebody just because the girl said she was pregnant.

'If he's put her in t' family way, then he's got to marry her,' said father.

'How do you know she's in t' family way?' mother retorted.

'Grieves will tell you,' father answered.

He did.

Christine was about two months pregnant. Mother bowed to the inevitable. The wedding took place.

Against all odds, Dan and Christine lived happily ever after.

About this time I was pulled in at the Darwen Brick Works by friends as a junior labourer. I was just sixteen. It was a temporary job, which I was glad to get. With a gang of others, my job was to stack the bee-hive shaped kilns with unbaked bricks ('green bricks'). The bricks were cut automatically, loaded onto pallets, and then dried before being fired with gas. Days later we'd take out the finished product. We used sacking to cover our hands; the alternative was suppurating blisters.

We also helped at the grinders, where the clay was crushed and forced through holes in the pan bottom, or at the pugmills, where a column of clay was forced through a die onto the cutting table. I learned early on not to hustle. At the Darwen Brick Works, slow and steady was the rule.

After several months there wasn't much I didn't know about bricks. Day after day, morning, afternoon and night, I handled the bricks. Bricks that went into kilns, bricks that came out of kilns. It wasn't the sort of thing I wanted to do for the rest of my life. Yet, by the standards of those days, I had a good job. I could keep Bess with me. I had young, enjoyable work mates, who roared at each others' jokes and the accounts of their weekend escapades. The foreman, soft-voiced Arthur Dimbleby, was a pleasant change after Mr Grimshaw. For a foreman he had unusually pleading eyes.

Best of all, I loved the moors where – because of clay – the works were sited. Most of the time, I worked out of doors where I could hear the birds and see the fells. Every morning and every night, wet or fine, with Bess running alongside, I rode for the best part of an hour across the moors to and from Blackburn on a borrowed bike. I'd stop to give Bess a chance to swim in a water-filled clay pit. In the spring and summer, the evening colours were so captivating that I often regretted it when the outskirts of Blackburn came into sight.

It's amazing what you'll do when you're poor. It was across those moors, at the end of a day's work, that I brought a kitchen sink all the way to Blackburn. I got a faulty one from the brickworks at a give-away price. The trouble began when I tried to take my give-away sink home. With Bess at my side, I trudged the whole six miles from Darwen to Blackburn, up and down hills, fighting to keep the slippery, forty-pound basin on the handle-bars. It was an ordeal. On more than one occasion, I was tempted to abandon the wretched thing by the wayside. I was drenched with sweat when I got home.

Arthur Dimbleby was a quiet father figure whom we all respected. Well-built, tough, skilled, he had a benign face that was often crinkled in a huge grin. He'd join us for a game of cards, or pitch and toss, at midday, or he'd sit with us on a plank supported by trestles, and yarn. He was always ready to join us in placing a small bet on the horse races at Aintree. One day he got talking about London where he'd worked when he was younger. His stories excited us. 'It's the place for young uns like you,' he said. 'I'd be off to the South like a shot if I was your age.'

Mr Dimbleby's talk about London put all kinds of ideas into my head. It fired me up. I knew that my job at Darwen was insecure. I never knew when I got there in the morning whether I'd still be working for them at night. It kept me on edge. Later on, I talked to Mr Dimbleby about London again. I didn't mention Betty Weatherby.

'It'll do you no harm to try to get a job there,' Mr Dimbleby said. 'You can always come home. I still know one or two people down there. I might be able to give you a hand.' A few days later, he showed me a letter he was about to send to a Mr Dent at the Bow Bridge Iron Foundry in Bow, East London. It said that I was a good labourer who needed a job, and could he help? Weeks passed without hearing anything from Mr Dent.

'Give him a chance,' was all Mr Dimbleby said when I asked him if he'd had any news.

Chapter XXI

Politics

As I did not work Saturday mornings at the Darwen Brick Works, I kept in touch with the world by spending some time reading the newspapers and magazines in the Blackburn Public Library reading room. One had to get there early because it was always full. Some of the unemployed workers just sat there with vacant, watery eyes daydreaming, killing time, glad to be off the cold streets. Others stared blankly at the ceiling or leafed aimlessly through the magazines. Still others stood before the high reading stands to which the newspapers (minus the sporting pages to discourage betting) were fastened. Few readers studied the 'Vacancies' column any more. A real job didn't have to be advertised; it was fought over.

The only woman there was the mousy librarian with eyeglasses who invariably had a cold. She always wore a blue pullover and a pleated, blue skirt. In really cold weather she put on a quilt-sized shawl that covered everything except her head. She was usually hidden behind a glass partition. On the polished counter at which she sat stood a large unneeded 'No Smoking' sign. Even when cigarettes were selling at five for twopence, few of the workers had money to smoke. Other notices demanded 'Silence.' One gained the librarian's attention by rapping hard on the glass. Earlier encounters and raised eyebrows had taught me that this was a foolish thing to do. The wise thing was to get a seat with your back to the hot pipes, keep your head down, and ask for nothing.

On one particular Saturday morning I was lost in my reading when I became aware of a thin, gaunt man standing behind me.

'After you with the *Herald*,' he said.

I began to yield my place.

'No rush,' said the stranger. 'I can read something else while I'm waiting.'

At that moment the sound of a band drifted in from the street as a procession made its way to the square. To satisfy our curiosity, we both hurried to the door to see what was afoot. It was cold out there and we wasted no time in getting back. We talked some more together in hushed tones. The man introduced himself as Peter Shad. He was in his thirties. He had a plain, pasty face with a small nose. His eyes protruded slightly; they had an intense look. He was dressed like the rest of us: cap, muffler, coat, clogs. He was an unemployed weaver.

I next saw Peter Shad one Sunday evening when I was wandering across the half-darkened town square. One could pick up a copy of left-wing newspapers there, such as the *Daily Worker*, the *Labour Leader* and the *Daily Herald*. There were little knots of people standing about, talking politics. Many of them were at a loss for something to do. To my surprise, Mr Shad was standing on a box haranguing a large crowd. His excited face was lit by an acetylene lamp hanging above his head. Behind him, flapping in the breeze, was the Red Flag bearing the hammer and sickle. I simply couldn't believe it. As most of what he was saying was being drowned out by the drums and cornets of the

Salvation Army band, which blared its way back and forth across the cobbled square, I pushed through the crowd until I stood directly in front of him.

For the next hour I stood there while Mr Shad hurled thunderbolts into the crowd. 'Theft! Theft!' he shouted. He really got hotted up. Everything he said rang with conviction. There was so much fire in him that no one dared interrupt him.

He opened my eyes to what was going on in Lancashire. 'Those who say that things will buck up, those who tell us to wait and see are fools,' he yelled. 'Capitalism has taken whatever profits it can out of Lancashire, and has gone elsewhere. Fortunes have been made here, but we've never enjoyed them.'

Mr Shad took a deep breath. 'That's what free enterprise is all about,' he went on, 'to make a fortune and then clear off, leaving the dirt behind. The problem is not cotton, it's capitalism. It will let Blackburn rot. It will let you rot. If more profit can be made in China, the capitalists will drop you and sweat the Chinese. They'll eat each other for gain.'

There followed another thunderbolt. 'Capitalism can never be changed. It can only be destroyed. To say that the rich have an obligation to the poor is tripe. Love does not make the world go round, money does. To the capitalist, making money is the only virtue. Drive the money changers from the temple!' he yelled. 'The enemy is greed. You work for less and less while the usurers take more and more. There will be no peace on earth until the working class destroys the masters and the money bags – the financiers. Private ownership of our mills and our lives must go.'

After wiping the sweat off his forehead, the speaker was off again. The crowd stood entranced. 'Not love, but hate is what matters – hatred of the capitalist class. It's madness to think that you can make a deal with the bosses. No capitalist is going to give up a good thing without a fight. The bosses have to go.'

Mr Shad was now vigorously beating one hand against

the other. 'Only when the capitalist class has been over-thrown' – here he struggled with an imaginary object and threw it to the ground – 'only when we have robbed them of the ability to exploit others, can there be true social justice. All power to the people!' he ended.

The spell broken, the crowd stirred. Here and there, there was a gentle rumble of approval. Among us, any man who could hold a crowd like that was respected.

Mr Shad struck me as a man who really believed what he was saying. He was ready to die in the people's cause. Except for the policeman, who stood to one side, a lamp on his belt, impassively watching, and making a note, I'm sure most of the audience felt as I did. The meeting ended with Mr Shad singing the 'Internationale':

> Oh, comrades, come rally,
> For the last fight let us stand,
> The Internationale,
> Unites the human race . . .

It filled me with hope. We were going to fight and win a better life.

In a subdued tone, as if they weren't quite sure if they could get away with it – and with an eye on the policeman – two or three others sang with him. To one side, several youths, the worse for drink were singing the parody of 'The Red Flag':

> The people's flag is palest pink.
> It's not as red as you might think.
> We've been to see, and now we know,
> They've gone and changed its colour so.
> While cowards flinch and traitors sneer
> We'll go on drinking bitter beer . . .

I had hoped to speak to Mr Shad when he was through, but he deliberately ignored me. His eyes said 'piss off!' He quickly furled his flag and was lost in the crowd.

The following Saturday morning I encountered him once more in the reading room. I could hardly believe that this was the same fellow who had held the crowd spellbound in the town square. He crossed the room to speak to me.

'Keep clear of me on the streets and on the square,' he warned in a low voice. 'Recognize me only here. Elsewhere it is dangerous for you to be seen with me. Capitalist repression is growing. Moseley's Black Shirts will appear in the square any day. When you're older you can make up your own mind about communism.' (The British Fascist Movement had been launched in October 1932 by Sir Oswald Moseley.)

That Saturday morning, with Mr Shad as my tutor, I began my education in political economy. Every Saturday thereafter, almost without fail, he arrived and fished books out of his deep pockets. He also gave me a glossy magazine depicting life in Russia. We knew that bringing books into the reading room was forbidden. We sat at a table in a corner with our backs to the other readers, talking in whispers. Chiefly he whispered and I listened. He first went over the *Communist Manifesto*, explaining its inner meaning. I was overwhelmed by it. Why hadn't I heard of it before? It was almost a hundred years old. How right Marx had been to say that the working class had nothing to lose but its chains. Anybody who lived at the bottom of the heap in Blackburn knew that.

Mr Shad was a born teacher. Whenever I got lost – as I often did – he started all over again. He had infinite patience, infinite generosity.

What I found difficult to swallow was his need to hate the bosses. He wanted me to hate with all my mind and all my heart. Grandmother Bridget had taught me not to hate. Hate will rot you, she'd said.

'Must we really hate the bosses?'

'You can't fight evil without hating it. Tell me, do you hate sin and the devil?'

'Oh, yes.'

'If you had the chance to kill the devil, would you?'

'Oh, yes.' I hadn't forgotten the statue of St Michael fighting the devil at St Peter's School.

'Well,' he concluded, 'the devils are the bosses; they won't go away peacefully. Rotten societies have to be toppled. That's what history is all about.'

For several months, I met Mr Shad every Saturday morning in the library. Like grandmother Bridget, and Mr Peek, he seemed honestly concerned with my education. I looked upon him as my teacher. He aroused in me an interest in what was going on in the world. Now and again he gave me a copy of the communist newspapers, the *Daily Worker*, or the *Young Worker*, but he didn't push them onto me.

The only person to whom I said anything about Peter Shad was Harold Watkins. My Saturday morning meetings in the Public Library I decided to keep to myself. One Sunday night Harold went with me to hear Shad. One moment we were waiting for him, the next moment there was the box, the lamp, the flag and the speaker. People quickly gathered; you could almost feel the growing rustle of attention. He started quietly, so that we were forced to listen carefully. As he warmed to his subject, a new note entered his voice. The voice grew in pitch and volume until it echoed from the surrounding buildings. With the speech done, and the questions answered, Mr Shad disappeared as mysteriously as he'd come. He simply melted into the crowd.

Harold marvelled at him. The look in his eyes told me that he was just as spellbound as I. There was magic in Shad's words. He got our blood up. We believed him when he said that Russia was a worker's paradise: that it was the only country in the world where no one went hungry, where no one was out of a job, and where no one could exploit the workers for profit. His stories about the Russian workers' paradise turned our heads.

We believed him when he said that the Russian Revolution was a great light beckoning the workers of the world. We believed him when he said that the revolution was coming in Britain. We believed him when he said that the world couldn't wait until capitalism died of its own weaknesses; it had earned the sentence of death and should be got rid of. We believed him when he said that religion was 'the opium of the people.' He was so eloquent, so persuasive, that we couldn't do anything else but swallow everything he said – hook, line and sinker. Not for a moment did we worry about how the revolution would be achieved. We didn't ask him and we wouldn't have thanked him for the details. It was the vision that mattered.

I knew Mr Shad for quite a while, yet there was a side of him about which I knew nothing. I'd no idea where he lived. He always left the library before me. By the time I'd got to the door, he'd gone. He never mentioned a wife or children. The only thing I knew about him was that he didn't sleep well. He talked about becoming a weaver in Brazil.

I don't know whether he ever reached Brazil. The last I saw of him was during a brawl on the square. He had predicted that Oswald Moseley's Blackshirts would turn up and they did. Having tried to deafen him with their shouts, the Fascists suddenly seized his flag. Shad fought back and was knocked to the ground. Most spectators backed away. The struggle for the Red Flag ended with Peter Shad in possession of a bare flag pole. Apart from the shouting, the affair was all over in minutes. The communists were simply swept aside.

As Mr Shad got to his feet, a policeman arrested him for 'disturbing the peace.' I had seen the same copper at many meetings. There was a struggle in which Shad must have lost self-control, for he struck the officer across the face with the flagpole. With witnesses present, that was lunacy. The policeman could have struck him, but it was a criminal act to strike back. The moment the officer released his grasp, Shad swung round and disappeared in the crowd. Peter Shad had become 'a fugitive from justice.'

A warrant was issued for his arrest. It startled me out of my clogs when I saw his picture in the paper under the name of Arthur Cray. Why had he called himself Peter Shad when his name was Arthur Cray? Or was it? Harold and I puzzled over the matter so much that we didn't know what to think. Try as I might, I could not think badly of him.

I was left in no doubt what the reading room librarian thought of him. 'Born trouble maker, I'd say,' she whispered primly. 'Tell them anywhere. Good riddance. You needn't think I didn't notice you two plotting and planning in the corner there – breaking all the rules. I thought several times of having you thrown out. From now on you'll have to watch your step.'

I went to the square the next night to see if I could learn anything from those who used to sing the 'Internationale.' No one appeared. Peter Shad (or Arthur Cray) had left my life as mysteriously as he had entered it.

A man was found drowned in the canal about this time. It was in the paper. They said he had protruding eyes. No one claimed the corpse. Could it have been Peter Shad? I sat with the paper in my hands in the corner of the library where I had first met him and wondered. I became so curious that for several weeks I went on trying to find one or other of the faces that I'd seen alongside Shad on the square. None of them ever showed up. Where Peter Shad had stood with his Red Flag, the Fascist Black Shirts now gathered.

<hr />

Shad's disappearance left Harold Watkins and me in a quandary. We were lost without him. His talk of the Russian Revolution had fired us up. As there was nothing for us in Blackburn, we decided to write to the Russians and offer to go to Russia as weavers. All the things that Mr Shad had told us about, and that we'd seen in the Russian magazines that he'd given us, we'd go and see for ourselves. I couldn't weave as well as Harold – I was at that time working at the brick works – but provided we could work together as a team, we'd manage. I trusted Harold, we'd grown up together. I knew he wouldn't let me down.

But then came the problem: how does one write to the Russians? I sought the advice of the librarian. Her spectacles jumped off her nose when I whispered, 'How can I get in touch with the Russians?'

'The Russians?' she whispered, frowning. 'In heavens name, what would a good Blackburn boy be doing writing to the Russians? Don't you know they're godless atheists!'

'I'm just curious,' I whispered, guardedly. 'I want to learn what's going on.'

'Curiosity killed the cat,' she hissed.

Had I gone on and told her that Harold and I intended to go to Russia, she would, I'm sure, have fainted dead away.

As there was no Soviet Embassy in Britain at the time (the British had accused the Soviets of spying) she gave me the address of the Russian Trade Legation in London.

It was one thing to get an address, another thing to know what to say. Harold and I anguished over our letter for some time. Clumsily, my first effort began 'Dear Sirs,' which Harold thought ridiculous.

'Communists don't call each other "dear" or "sir".'

I substituted 'Comrades,' which pleased him. He also took out my reference to Peter Shad. Eventually we agreed to send the following note:

Comrades,

We are two unemployed Blackburn weavers. We are both skilled, fit, and in our teens. We believe in the Russian Revolution and want to share it with you. Can you find us a job so that we can come to Russia and see it for ourselves? If you will write to the above address, we are free to come any time.

Fraternally,
Harold Watkins,
William Woodruff.

Very deliberately, we stuck a stamp on the envelope and took it to the main post office. A great change came over me as I slipped the envelope into the black mouth of the red letter box. All the way home we talked about what might happen. Would the Russians write or would somebody come in person? How would we get there? Well, that was up to the Russians. Anyway, we were determined not to turn back.

We never heard a word. Peter Shad's dream of a great and glorious new life in Russia was denied us. Perhaps the letter was removed from the mail by the police, or both the Russians and the police had more important things to do.

———◁◦▷———

With our Russian options closed, we gave more thought to our political futures. Not long after Peter Shad had disappeared, and our Russian venture had died, I decided to join the Youth Labour League. With a 'red' scare on in Britain (there'd been one earlier in 1924–1926 when a number of communists had been sent to jail) it wasn't the time to join the Communist Party, which had been in existence in Britain since 1920. Anybody who put Russia before Britain was run down. Even in the trade unions, those suspected of being a bolshie were rooted out.

Harold and I took every opportunity to hear the important politicians who spoke in town. Blackburn square is where I heard all the best speakers of the land. MacDonald, Snowdon, Henderson, Clynes, Thomas and Churchill all spoke there. Some like MacDonald, Snowdon and Clynes were intensely religious. They were always saying God this and God that. I'm sure none of them had read Marx.

One night I listened to Winston Spencer Churchill. The audience was belligerent from the start because of the role he had played in breaking the General Strike in 1926. He was a bald-headed figure standing on a box, wagging an admonitory finger at the crowd. 'Hang on to India,' he advised. 'Take no notice of that little fakir, Gandhi.' We knew he was talking rubbish. Even those of us whose living depended on it had the common sense to realize that we couldn't go on ruling hundreds of millions of Indians. We didn't agree with his intention to hang on to Ireland, either.

Gandhi and Churchill seemed to follow each other around. In 1931 Gandhi spent three days visiting the Lancashire textile industry. He was a little, bespectacled, ascetic figure, with a white shawl and a homespun loincloth, skinny legs and clumsy wooden sandals. He was greeted warmly. The antiquated condition of the Lancashire textile industry did not escape him. 'The machinery in the Bombay and Ahmadabad mills,' he said, 'is one hundred per cent more efficient.'

Eager to make my way in the labour movement, I began to make speeches on the square for the Labour Party. At first the speeches only lasted a couple of minutes, and I was told what to say. With Blackburn streets full of unemployed, and things getting worse every day, there was no shortage of topics and audiences. I talked about the dole, the slump in the basic industries, and the need to tax the rich.

I found public speaking unnerving. The moment I got on the box, I became tense. A five minute stint had me running with sweat. Harold was much better at it than I was. His speeches were more compelling. My maiden speech was attended by an audience of two, one of them a wild, half-clothed figure who kept shouting that the Day of Judgement had arrived. His interruptions grew louder, the longer I spoke. 'For God's sake, shut up, you silly little bugger,' he finally shouted right in my face. Sunday night audiences on Blackburn square were even more aggressive. Hecklers roughed me up in no time. Their purpose was to get me rattled. I had been warned that if they did, they'd chop me up into little pieces. They made no allowance for age.

I couldn't have survived these ordeals had I not had the help of Elsie Briggs, whom I met at one of these meetings. She swore that I was the worst speaker she'd ever heard, and that she was going to improve me or die.

Elsie Briggs was a spinster in her thirties, who lived round the corner from us in Polly Street. She was a small woman dressed in black. I never saw her face clearly because she wore a cap pulled down over her eyes. Her mouth was puckered around a pipe, which she smoked incessantly. She was one of the few spinners in town who seemed to be able to hang on to a job.

Her widowed father ran a fruit and vegetable shop in one of their downstairs rooms. I cannot imagine what the old man made out of it. There was one other member of the family, Charlotte – also a spinner – who was a couple of years younger than Elsie. She was disfigured by smallpox.

Elsie began her coaching by standing me before a stained, body-length mirror in her bedroom. I was told to address a circle she had drawn above the mirror on the wall. Throwing my arms about, I repeated the short speeches which she had written for me, and which I'd memorized while cycling home from the brickworks. In these speeches, politics were incidental. All she cared about was elocution.

I didn't get halfway through any of them because she never let me. 'It won't do! It won't do!' she'd interrupt, while blowing smoke in my face. 'I won't own you on the square if you talk like that. You sound like a gobbin. You'll be lucky if you're not lynched.'

Elsie was pure Lancashire: blunt, aggressive and sarcastic. She could also be grim and ironic. She was not the slightest bit interested in whether I liked her or not. She treated me as if I were daft. Life with Elsie was hell.

'Start again!' she commanded in a deep mannish voice. 'Look at your hands! Face the crowd! Take that silly grin off your face. You've nothing to grin about.' The punching and kneading never stopped.

I wondered if she wasn't trying to torture me. There was a touch of sadism in Elsie Briggs. Yet when she removed her black cap and I could see her grey eyes, I saw only loneliness. Charlotte swore that her sister had a heart of gold. She might have had, but I didn't see any evidence of it. Not once did I see her smile. No wonder her father threw me a look of sympathy whenever I entered the shop. I hope Elsie didn't treat him as she treated me.

One night, I complained to Charlotte. 'I'm thinking of chucking it, Elsie is inhuman.'

'It's the war. Elsie's never been the same since her bloke got killed on the Somme. That's why she wears black. I wouldn't chuck it if I was you. She needs you as much as you need her. Why drop it now when you're improving? I know she says you're only middlin', but, secretly, she thinks you're coming on real gradely.'

Charlotte was right. If I hadn't been improving, I wouldn't have put up with Elsie. But I was getting better. I wasn't as good as Harold, or as assertive as Peter Shad had been – probably never would be – but I was getting that way.

Whenever I spoke on the square, Elsie Briggs took up a position right in front of me, puffing on her pipe, umbrella in hand. She revelled in the heckling I got. The more I was ribbed, the more some crank in the crowd annoyed me, the more she cheered. The involuntary movements of her head and shoulders told me that she was enjoying every minute. Yet there was a point beyond which criticism of me was not allowed to go. At that point Elsie would turn upon my tormentor, umbrella raised.

Elsie's torture didn't stop Harold and me from building all kinds of dream worlds in Britain, as previously we'd built them in Russia. 'You know, Billy,' he said to me one night after listening to one of my speeches, 'I've been thinking about you. When I become Prime Minister, I shall appoint you as Foreign Secretary.' Harold had a droll humour, but I knew he was serious. I was impressed. As an expression of thanks, I bought him a black pudding on the way home.

Chapter XXII

The Bitter Years

When I left school in 1930, and began to look for a full-time job, half the workers of Blackburn were on the streets. The entire output of the Lancashire textile industry had been halved since 1914. Because it depended upon the export trade, our town was hardest hit. The number of workers in the mills in 1930 had shrunk to a tenth of what it had been before the war. The poor were not only going hungry; they were pawning their bedding for a meal. Some of them finished up on straw and sacking, their 'bed of sorrows.' A diet of fish-head soup and haddock was all that kept many of them going. The medical journal, *The Lancet*, reported that people in the depressed areas of Blackburn were literally dying of starvation. The birth rate declined; the infant mortality rate was higher in Lancashire than in the rest of the country. The maternal mortality rate rose. Things must have been desperate because the money lenders thrived. Sickness wasn't feared for sickness' sake, but because of the threat of destitution.

Throughout the spring and summer of 1932, there were pitched battles between unemployed workers and the police in London, Manchester, Birkenhead and Glasgow. In Belfast demonstrators had been shot and killed. In Rochdale the army had been called out. Street fights were common. In desperation, the unemployed decided to make a direct appeal for help to parliament and the king.

In the fading light of a wintry afternoon at the beginning of October 1932, Harold Watkins and I watched a column of ragged hunger marchers form up to begin the long trek from Blackburn to London. We had joined the crowd in the town square to give them a send-off.

'We're goin' to tell t' king that we need work and food,' one of the marchers told us. 'You'll see, 'e'll understand. Once 'e knows what's 'appening in Lancashire, matters will be put right, there's no doubt. After t' king, we'll tell parliament. The guvernment will sit up when they 'ear from us. It isn't going to be easy. But who cares if it puts matters straight again, eh?'

Just before their departure the Blackburn contingent was joined by a small group from Jarrow, which had missed the main Northumberland, Durham and Teeside contingent going south through Yorkshire. With the light fading, the Jarrow men, each with a blanket over his shoulder, came marching into the square with a springy step. Some had ordinary walking sticks, others carried ash rods. Most were young. Although they'd been on the road several days, their faces were still bright. They wore cloth caps and mufflers. Their belongings hung on their backs. The Blackburn people gave them wedges of bread, steaming tea and tator-hash. I helped to pour the tea. While they ate, a fellow with a banjo sang:

I'm a four loom weaver as many a one knows;
I've nowt to eat and I've worn out me clothes.
Me clogs are boath broken and stockings I've none.
Tha'd scarce gie me tuppence for a' I've gotten on.

Owd Billy o't Bent he kept telling me long,
We might have better times if I'd nobbut howd me
    tongue.
Well I've howden me tongue till I near lost me
    breath,
And I feel in my heart that I'll soon clem to
    death . . .

Our Margaret declares if she'd clothes to put on,
She'd go up to London to see the great mon,
And if things didna alter when there she had been,
She swears she would fight wi' blood up t' th' een.

I'm a four loom weaver as many a one knows;
I've nowt to eat and I've worn out me clothes.
Clogs we ha' none nor no looms to weave on,
And I've woven myself to t' far end.

The Jarrow marchers had never been so far from home.
The idea of going to London had fired them up. 'Nothing
between here and London can be worse than what we're
already going through,' they said. Three-quarters of Jarrow's
labour force was out of work. Some had been out for years.

Despite all the talk of hunger marchers being nothing but
communist riff-raff, these men were a good-natured, law-
abiding lot. I doubt there was a revolutionary among them.
Some of them had just been to church to receive communion before setting out. They'd fasted all day before receiving the Host.

In the late afternoon the Blackburn and Jarrow men formed
up together. They seemed a bit clumsy and shy at getting into
line. Someone ordered the column forward. With their heavy
boots and laced-up clogs ringing on the cobblestones, the
marchers moved off. They were going to march all night. The
fellow at the end of the column waved his lamp.

'Good luck!' we shouted.

After little more than a month they were back, thinner

than ever, their blankets and their boots and clogs worn out. London had wanted to get rid of them, and had sent them home by train. The police had seen them off. The London labour movement didn't have the resources to feed every fellow who took it into his head to talk to the king. We greeted them at the station and heard their story. In London, they had repeatedly been run down by the mounted police. It had been like a battlefield. They hadn't seen the king, or Ramsay MacDonald the Labour prime minister, or anybody of any consequence. They'd been fobbed off at every turn; promised all kinds of remedies.

They told us that there'd been big meetings in Hyde Park and Trafalgar Square at which contingents from all over the north – including the women's contingent from Yorkshire – had participated. Labour members of parliament had addressed them and poured oceans of praise upon them. They'd said that thanks to the hunger marchers, the complacency of the government would now be broken. The marchers could return to their homes, knowing that something would be done to give them food and jobs. The speakers had promised to work night and day. A manifesto had been approved calling upon the government to abolish poverty and provide work. A million-signature petition was to be presented to parliament. In the end, nothing was done. Bitterest pill of all, the police had seized the petition.

It didn't surprise me to see the marchers come home again. Peter Shad had hammered it into our heads that Pilgrimages of Grace get nowhere. It was bargaining from weakness; the weak get nothing, he'd said.

Harold Watkins and I were in a teashop in Bank Top when the hunger marchers from Northumberland, having spent a night in Blackburn, went by on their way home. Their clogs and boots pounded the snow into a dark slush. Fragments of paper-thin ice filled the gutters.

'Like the rest of 'em, they've been banging t' head against a brick wall,' Harold said, jerking his cap in the direction of the marchers. 'They look licked.'

'What do you expect? They've been shoutin' so that some-body would hear 'em. Better than sufferin' in silence.'

'Nobody gives a damn about the weak shouting. When will people learn?'

'These poor devils 'ave a real grievance, Harold.'

'Of course. They wouldn't have marched all the way to London if they'd 'ad a job and their bellies were full. You'd have never heard from 'em if they'd been getting three meals a day. They felt helpless, with nothing to loose. For all the notice that was taken of 'em, they might as well have stayed home and marched round the park. Some of them got a broken head for their troubles. The toffs don't give a damn. They don't know what we're putting up with, and if they did they wouldn't care. Lancashire's no longer part of England. So much for "This blessed plot, this realm, this earth, this England," that we learned at school.'

'You've got a point, Harold. Paper says there are two Englands: one with an unemployment rate of six per cent, the other with sixty.'

I thought of my own family. I'd had years to think about them. The Watkins family was the same. They were all hard workers, all law-abiding. None of them were feckless, or habitual drunkards. Their needs were extremely simple. Yet, no matter how much they worked and saved and schemed, their lot got worse. Even if they got a job, it would be sure to die on them before they'd had a chance to pay off their debts.

'What do we do, Harold?'

'I don't know. I do know that hunger marches aren't going to make any difference. It's not a genuine grievance they need; it's power. Anybody who goes on a hunger march, carrying a petition that "humbly prays" is asking for trou-ble. Somehow they've got to get power in their hands.'

'How?'

'Turn the toffs out of parliament and put the workers in. We've got to send our own man. Bradford did it nearly thirty years ago.'

'But the workers vote for the toffs. They won't vote for their equals. Lancashire voted overwhelmingly for MacDonald when he deserted the workers for the bosses in 1931. You know what happened when we pushed Pat Murphy as our Labour candidate.'

'As long as the workers go on doing that, they're going to go on marching like those poor, pinch-faced sods out there.'

It says a lot for the Lancashire unemployed that they didn't revolt. They certainly had grounds for it. Some of them had been out of work for almost a decade. Many of them felt unwanted, of no use to anyone, living in vain.

Some of the things happening in the industrial areas of Britain in the 1920's and 1930's were not only wrong, they passed all understanding. Government aid through the dole seemed to be deliberately aimed at breaking the spirit of anyone who was proud, thrifty, honest and upright. How could anyone 'genuinely seek work' when there was no work to seek; or accept a Means Test, which seemed designed not only to lower an already low standard of living, but also to break up family life – the only thing some of the poor had got left. Some of the regulations were mean and villainous, if not downright cruel. Hardship could be borne; meanness and cruelty had to be fought.

There was no end to the madness. Blackburn was a town that at one time had clothed much of the world; yet in the worst years of the depression we didn't have enough clothing to cover our backs. We Blackburnians bought Japanese shirts and cottons at half British prices because we didn't have enough money to buy our own products.

Blackburn was close to some of the richest coal seams in the world, yet because we couldn't afford coal, we were reduced to burning cinders. We stuffed miserable little perforated cans with coal dust, which we burned in our hearths during the coldest days and nights. The family sat over them like a lot of crows. Refusing to put up with the cold, we stole the wooden railings of the rich. We wrenched them away, one after another as we went by, and stuffed them under our jackets. Whole fences disappeared. Special guards had to be mounted on coal shipments. Any railway truck full of coal, left standing overnight in the railway sidings, was empty by morning. Local cinemas advertised warmth not films. For threepence you could keep warm, be entertained, and forget the bleak world outside.

The system was inhuman. So inhuman that it could throw people out of work on Christmas Eve, casting them off like old clothing, or give them a cheap bottle of sherry as a reward for fifteen, thirty, forty or even fifty years' work in the mills. My father brought such a bottle home. He put it on the kitchen table and – with the rest of us – sat and stared at it. Then, without a word, he picked it up, opened the kitchen door, and flung it against the alley wall. There must have been factory owners – other than Terence Peek – who felt a social obligation to the workers and to the industry, but in all my sixteen years in Blackburn I didn't know one. My family knew as much about the factory owners as they knew about our landlords – nothing. Pounds, shillings and pence, not human relations, dominated our lives.

Meanwhile newspaper advertisements were persuading the rich to take Union Line cruises to Madeira, First Class £20, Second Class £15; and to buy bed-side phones with extension cords; 'Why Get out of Bed to Answer the Phone?'

No wonder that the bottom dogs were brought up to sing:

> It's the rich that gets the pleasure,
> It's the poor that gets the pain.
> Ain't that a blinkin' shame . . .

Cotton made unbelievable fortunes for some people in Britain, but not for the working class. At one time, the Lancashire spinning town of Shaw was said to be 'the richest town in England.' But they measured it by millionaires to the square mile. Fat lot of use that is to the working man.

Perhaps things were not quite bad enough for revolution. Perhaps, as Mr Peek believed, revolution wasn't in the British workers' blood. He used to say if the workers wanted a revolution, they'd have to import it. Muddlers and tinkers don't make revolutions. Perhaps because poverty in Britain was so highly localized in Wales and the North of England, it could be contained. Perhaps the dole helped to save the country from upheaval. Perhaps religion helped. Strong non-conformists and Roman Catholics don't sit well with communism. No matter how bad things got, the British did not become a people of guns and armed risings. Except among the toffs, there never was widespread talk of the workers seizing power by force. The workers were too law-abiding for that. Fiery extremists, such as Peter Shad, who really did believe in pulling the mighty down, were called 'reds' or bolshies and kept out.

One thing that did help to turn the country away from violence was the way in which the poor helped each other through the hard times. No wonder we sang, 'It's the Poor what Helps the Poor.' There was a lot of pitching in, a lot of making do and a lot of pluck. Too little has been made of working-class solidarity and community spirit. It wasn't the dole that saved Britain from revolution, it was the nature of the British working class. The British toffs will never know how lucky they were.

Moreover, the workers didn't revolt as Peter Shad had told them because they didn't live in his world of blood and fury. The poor are by nature meek. It took a lot to get their blood up. It took even more to get them out onto the streets. The beatings they'd had since 1920 had undermined their confidence. They thought of life as a bit of a muddle that would sort itself out in time. Not least, they didn't revolt because they never lost hope. Even the poor devils I'd known in the Nab End lodging house didn't lose hope. For a Lancashire man or woman to lose hope was to lose life. As indeed they did. The number of suicides rose. Sometimes they took their life only hours after being laid off. "'Ead in t' oven' was most commonly used.

I refused to believe that the dire conditions in which we lived were, as Sister Loyola used to say, 'an act of God calling for heroic fortitude and passive endurance.' Nor did I believe that material poverty was spiritually cleansing. Material poverty was no more a virtue to me than spiritual poverty. Peter Shad had taught me not to swallow the 'act of God' business, or to suffer in silence. Those ideas were put abroad by the toffs to keep the working class down.

Our choice was either to overthrow the system as Shad had urged, or escape from it altogether. Harold and I had tried unsuccessfully to escape to Russia. We'd also talked about emigrating to Fall River where my father's brothers lived. But the fare was beyond us. Failing Russia and America, we decided to escape to London. The more we thought about London, the better it seemed. But where would we find a job in London? Mr Dimbleby had talked about helping me. But he had produced nothing tangible. With no other options open, we waited and stagnated. Everything in Blackburn hung like wet washing on the line, dead. It was like waiting for a storm.

Meanwhile we Lancastrians neither revolted nor whined. Instead, those who could, took to the fields and the hills. Things weren't so bad when it was getting warmer and summer was at hand. Some of my best days in Blackburn, before I got the job at the Darwen Brick Works, were those when I was unemployed. Provided I got something to eat, I could wander about all day. I didn't have to get back for anybody. Nobody owned me. There was no work tomorrow; no clocking in. There were times when we even laughed at our plight. As Gracie Fields, our Lancashire comedienne, used to say, 'It's so bad, luv, laughing is all that's left.' It is hardly surprising that we sang and tap-danced the American song:

I can't give you anything but love, Baby,
That's the only thing there's plenty of, Baby,
Dream a while, scheme a while,
You're sure to find happiness, and I guess
All those things you've always wished for,
Gee, but I guess I like you looking swell, Baby,
Diamond bracelets, Woolworth doesn't sell, Baby,
Till that lucky day, you know darn well, Baby,
I can't give you anything but love.

Little wonder that I should have decided to try my luck elsewhere. As things got worse and worse, Harold and I finally made up our minds to leave.

———◇———

In the spring of 1933, Mr 'Sharabang' Fisher married Mrs Beatty. Mr Fisher's ailing wife and 'Up-and-at-em' Beatty had both died in 1932. There had always been a close connection between the two families. With a complete invalid on her hands, Mrs Beatty had been relying on Mr Fisher for years. He had done all the fetching and carrying. Old 'Up-and-at-em' had just faded away. He'd been in that basket dribbling for the best part of fifteen years. His mind had never left the trench in France where Mr Fisher had picked up what was left of him so long ago. We thought it wonderful that Mrs Beatty could at long last live a fuller life. They were married at St Philip's and the reception was at St Philip's Hall where my gang used to steal meat pies. It was a crowded wedding followed by a really good send-off.

The joy of the Beatty-Fisher wedding was marred by the death of Mr Peek. I learned of Mr Peek's death by chance long after he had been buried. Chain-smoker that he was, he had accidentally set his bed alight and had died from burns. He didn't finish his book – the book that was to save the world. I was so appalled with the news that I felt I must sympathize with Roger, who by now had lost both parents.

Agnes Peek had lingered on for a year or so after her attack of tetanus and then had died of other things.

I was on the point of returning to Livingstone Road when I learned that, following their father's death, the Peek children had left town. That was the last I heard of them.

I took my leave of Rosie Gill in a manner that neither of us had expected. One evening, shortly after the Beatty-Fisher wedding, Rosie Gill was rushed to the infirmary with acute appendicitis. While I was visiting the Gill house to inquire about Rosie, a nurse came in and told Gill that following surgery somebody had given Rosie fish and chips and that she was dangerously ill. Mr Gill and I hurried to the hospital. He was beside himself. With me trying to keep up with him, he barged past everybody at the hospital who got in his way. 'Here, hang on! Where do you think you're going?' the nurses called after him.

When we got to the ward a commotion was going on. There were doctors and a priest around Rosie's bed. Nurses were running in and out with slop basins and towels. There was a strong smell of methylated spirits. One of the doctors was taking Rosie's pulse. The priest was administering the Last Sacrament. I'd stood by a number of Catholic deathbeds in my sixteen years. I knew that in the fifth chapter of James it is said: 'Is anyone sick among you? Let him bring in the Priests of the Church; and let them pray over him, anointing him with oil in the name of the Lord . . .' I knew what it meant. With tears pouring down his face, Mr Gill made the sign of the Cross.

Rosie lay like a corpse, her eyes dead and staring. Her lips were blue; her body was drenched with sweat. Her long, curly hair lay tousled across the pillow. Her faded amulet of Mary and Christ crucified – the one she'd shown me years before – rested on the sheet. There had been times when I thought something might develop between Rosie and me, but it hadn't. We were always running in and out of each other's houses and meeting at dances, but we knew without saying it that we wouldn't be anything closer than good friends.

As I stood and stared at the scar on her left temple, it all came back, flooding my mind. I remembered how we'd been fooling around in the Ribble one summer's day in our early teens; and how Rosie had finished up bashing her head on a rock at the bottom of a water hole. I got her out of the Ribble as she'd got me out of the Darwen earlier – dripping with blood. Somehow I'd managed to get her over the bridge into Ribchester, where Rosie's blood-stained towel, which I'd wrapped around her head, caught the attention of a policeman. He took us to a doctor who stitched up Rosie's wound. Then, without so much as by your leave, the policeman and his mate collected our bikes from the high bank of the river and, with Rosie, Bess and me quaking in the back of the police car, wondering what on earth was going to happen to us, drove us back to Blackburn. They were nice all the way. Poor old Gill almost swallowed his teeth when we drew up outside his front window – the one which still displayed a bowl of 'Virginia fresh tobacco.' I pushed my bike home afterward puzzled. I'd no idea that the police could be so kind. It changed my view of them.

Now Rosie was lying at death's door. The doctors and the priest, all of whom knew Willie Gill, moved aside as he bent over his child. Rosie made no response to his quiet pleadings. The older of the two doctors beckoned Mr Gill away from the bedside. With a hand on Willie's shoulder, he began talking to him quietly. I caught snatches. 'It's too late . . . You'll have to face it . . . It can happen at any moment.' One of the nurses began to draw a curtain around Rosie's bed. All I could think of was Rosie helping me out of the Blakewater river when I'd been thrown in head first. I wished I could have rendered comfort unto her in her last moments, as years before she had rendered it unto me. Instead, I stood there helpless, holding on to the weeping Willie Gill.

Rosie died a few minutes later. She was just sixteen.

I knew she was gone when I saw the nurse cover Rosie's face, and the priest beckoned us to begin the 'De Profundis.'

'Out of the depths I have cried to Thee O Lord,' the priest began almost before we had time to take up our positions at the foot of the bed. I wasn't sure that Willie was going to respond until I heard his faltering, 'O Lord, hear my voice.' He spoke like a child, lips trembling, too afraid to be heard.

One of the nurses quickly followed: 'And let Thine ears be attentive to the voice of my supplication.'

And so in hushed tones, with the priest leading, we went on together until the end: 'May she rest in peace, Amen.'

Several times I'd stood with mother and her work mates while Patrick Murphy had said the same prayer for a dead mill-hand. Whether you make the appeal among silent looms or in a hospital ward makes no difference.

I took Willie Gill home. As he stumbled through his doorway, he turned and placed a hand on my shoulder.

'They've killed my child, Billy,' he sobbed.

Chapter XXIII

Good-bye, Lancashire

At long last, having talked the subject to death with Harold Watkins, I made up my mind to leave Lancashire and go to London. I decided to risk my chance by going to Mr Dimbleby's friend, Mr Dent at the Bow Bridge Iron Foundry, with a letter of recommendation from Mr Dimbleby. Better to make up my own mind than have the Brick Works make it up for me.

As the time for my departure approached, I became more and more excited. I'd been promised a ride in a lorry from Manchester to London by another friend of Mr Dimbleby's, Mr Tomkins. It would cost me five shillings instead of the twenty-five charged by the railway. Failing the Bow Bridge Iron Foundry, I'd look for work somewhere else in London. Provided I could find a job to hang on to, Harold would join me in about a month's time. After that we'd fight it out together.

My going to London was not only a matter of finding a job, it was a matter of adventure. I used to stand at the railway level-crossing close to Polly Street and watch the trains chugging their way south. As I leaned over the gate, I wondered what the people of the south were really like. Were they like us? With Betty Weatherby in London, I had a compelling reason to go and find out. Meanwhile I was afraid that somebody would learn of my plans and stop me from going. Only Mr Dimbleby at the brickworks, my sisters Jenny and Brenda and Harold knew that I was leaving. I didn't tell the Latham's. I knew Madge would be against my going off on my own. I decided I'd write to them as soon as I'd landed a job in London.

At this time, Harold had become the Blackburn agent of the ACDO laundry soap company. It was a little job with big aspirations. He drove a motorcycle three-wheeler with a plywood box at the back shaped like a block of soap with the words MIRACULOUS, ACDO LAUNDRY SOAP, painted all over it. He was going to hang on to this job until he could join me in London.

Harold's parting gift to me was a day-long trip through the Trough of Bowland. We took two girls with us with whom we'd clicked on the 'chicken run' the week before. The 'chicken run' was the way to meet girls. Harold and I had walked backward and forward on a parade out Whalley way until we had 'clicked.' Clicking meant that the girls had responded to our greeting and that they were prepared to stop and talk. These two girls were game enough to come with us for the lark. They turned up with cheery faces.

We rode in Harold's delivery van. Harold sat up front with goggles and gloves revving up the engine. With the moustache he'd begun to grow, he looked dashing.

'Does your boss know we're taking his bike?' I asked, as the two girls and I climbed into the windowless trailer.

'He does and he doesn't.'

'What do you mean, he does and he doesn't? You're not risking your job to give us a treat, are you?'

'Now there you go again, Billy, taking the blackest view. Who's to know? This van is too small to be seen.'

'But Harold, it's the only block of soap on three wheels on the road.'

My fears for Harold's future were not lessened when I learned from a chance remark later that the ACDO company was also paying for the petrol.

Once we got under way, Harold shouted and pointed at what we were meant to see. 'Look at those trees! Have you ever seen a cliff like that! What a wonderful view of the lake!' Although it was impossible for the girls and I to see anything, being thrown about in the trailer, we took everything in our stride, laughing all the way. We laughed when we had to get out and push the bike up the steep fells. We laughed when we noticed that our hands and clothing smelled of ACDO soap. We didn't know which was worse: the fumes from the bike or the smell of soap. We laughed harder still when we ate meat pies we'd bought at Clitheroe that had a decided ACDO flavor.

After much shouting from the girls and myself, Harold stopped and we unravelled ourselves and got out of the soap bubble to see the sights. Not even the cramp in our legs stopped us from appreciating the beauty of the Trough of Bowland on a clear day. Sitting on the grass, with our backs against the trailer, we marvelled at the great vistas, at the seeming limitless expanse of the high moors and the windy fells – ridge after ridge with not a sign of human habitation. We watched the light, fair-weather clouds scudding in from the Irish Sea. We heard the curlew's lonely cry and the tumble of the streams. We smelled the lemon-scented gorse. We were exhilarated by the heights and by the air. This was the Lancashire I would remember when choice and fate had carried me far away: a great expanse of wild hills and moorland brooding against the sky; a land of vivid green valleys and beckoning dales; the blue haze of distant fells with strands of water shining in the sun. Even after the gas works, the railways, and the steam-driven factories had done their worst, the north of England would always remain for me a wild, lovely place.

And then, on full throttle, we were off again, bouncing and rattling up and down the dusty, winding lanes, through half-sleepy villages with thatched cottages, grey-stone churches and solitary spires pointing into the bright summer sky. Several times we had to stop for a shepherd and his flock. The bleating tide of bobbing black and white heads swept around us and held us in its grip. The smell of sheep and dust settled on us like a heavy mist. It took a couple of collies to get us free.

<hr />

I took leave of mother the next day without telling her what I was up to. I was afraid that there would be a scene and she would attempt to stop me from going. After all, I was the last of her brood to fly away. Mother had a way of knowing what was going on. Unlike father, who lived in another world, there was a bond of understanding between us. We didn't have to declare our love. The hug I gave her told her all she wanted to know. Poor Maggie, she was always having to deal with people who ran away: her husband, her daughters, her sons. Running away seems to have been a recurring theme with the Woodruffs. But then, it was also true of the Kenyons; Bridget and Maggie had both run away. Questing seems to have been in the blood of both families.

I didn't think father would be interested in my departure, so I didn't say anything to him either. Not that there was enmity between us. His silence at times may have been hard to bear, but it was something that we'd got used to. It wasn't that he just stopped talking, or didn't want to talk to us. It was more gradual than that. He just drifted off into a world of his own: of work, flowers and birds. It was a happy disengagement from the more immediate matters going on around him. I respected him for what he was: an honest and a courageous man. I don't think he feared anything, not even hunger or death. He was quite content to plod along as a member of the 'lower orders' as long as the 'upper orders' left him alone. If he held a grudge against anyone, we never heard of it.

At least he set me the example of being a good worker. All he wanted was a fair day's pay for a good day's work. After returning from the war in 1918, he never sought money for money's sake; he never took an unearned pound; he never earned much beyond what he needed to survive. His sights were not high – he had become almost devoid of ambition; ambitious people worried him; he thought that in scrambling after their own self-interests they were likely to damage all those around them. To the end he remained a plain and a poor man.

I had felt for him as I watched the cotton industry collapse under his feet. More than any of us, he had believed that it would never die. Mother said that it had been his secret wish that Dan and I should be weavers alongside him. It was not to be.

Although I didn't have a job to go to, and had neither friends nor a place to stay in London, Jenny and Brenda did nothing to dissuade me from leaving. I could tell from her eyes that Jenny was not as sure as Brenda about my going to London, but her doubts and fears remained unspoken. Both my sisters promised to explain to mother what I was up to when I had gone. I promised to write.

Elsie Briggs was the last person I said good-bye to. There was no emotion or sentiment about our parting; we just shook hands.

She turned aside when I tried to thank her. 'You're a bit better speaker than you were,' she said. I guardedly agreed.

She knew I was much better; but she didn't want to take credit for it.

'I'm sorry I won't be the best speaker in Lancashire. I know that was your goal.'

She gave me the only smile I'd ever seen on her face. It warmed me through. 'It's best that you should go. There's nothing here for you. Go and show London what you can do.'

'Thanks, Elsie.' I gently lifted her cap and, dodging her pipe, gave her a peck on the cheek.

Worst of all was the parting from Bess. It was the only thing that brought tears. Brenda was to care for her. Brenda and her husband Dick were fond of the dog, and I knew that Bess liked them. Harold promised to bring Bess to London when he joined me. It had been my original intention to take Bess with me. 'You must be out of your mind,' Harold had said, 'taking a dog when you don't have a bed. What are you thinking about? First get your bed; I'll bring the dog.'

I was persuaded. It was all arranged. When I said goodbye to her, Bess looked at me with unforgiving eyes and whined.

———◦———

Harold saw me off at the station for Manchester. From that station, first built in the 1840's, Blackburn cottons had been sent to the whole world. It was quiet and looked run down now. It was the station to which my family had come on their return from America in 1914. With thousands of other Blackburn men, my father had gone to war from the same platform, and had come home again, gassed. From here I'd made my trips to Bamber Bridge, to Little Blackpool and Big Blackpool. From where I stood Jenny and Gordon had gone off on their honeymoon. A year ago, I'd met the ragged hunger marchers here on their return from London.

There was a drizzle about. I wore a cap, a coat and rough trousers. I had toyed with the idea of buying my first hat, but considering my resources had decided against it. My worldly possessions, including my two pairs of overalls and my only suit – the suit I got for Jenny's wedding – I carried in a small, battered cardboard suitcase. The suit had been let out as far as it would go, and was still a bit short in the arms and legs, but it would have to do. Also in my bag was a pullover, a shirt, socks, a face cloth, soap and a razor.

Despite Madge Latham, who had introduced me to under-clothing, I wore and took no underwear. With other odds and ends, my pockets contained my worldly wealth, five pounds, a watch, a comb, a handkerchief and a knife.

Neither Harold nor I said much on the platform. There were unusually awkward pauses. I couldn't think of anything interesting to say and I was glad when the train came and we shook hands and said good-bye. I waved to him from the window. The engine gave a shrill whistle, there was a puff or two of steam, the carriages lurched forward and slowly slid out of the station. I was off. Tat-tattat, tat-tattat the wheels went. I looked through the rain-streaked window at streets and buildings and smoking chimneys that I knew so well. I should have been excited, instead I felt sad – as sad as the clouded, melancholy sky.

It was dusk by the time I found Mr Dimbleby's friend in Manchester. I had been told to be at a garage by the central bus station not later than six, and to ask for Mr Tomkins. It was ten minutes from the hour when I hurried into the cavernous depot.

As I entered, a bundled figure of a man, wearing a box-like cap, a muffler and a coat that reached down to his boots, left a little office in one corner and walked toward me. He had a blank, scrawny face.

'You the young 'un for London?' the bundled figure asked, eyeing my valise.

Putting on a bold look, and trying to sound older than my sixteen years, I said I was.

'Well then,' he went on – ignoring my 'are you – er – Mr Tomkins?' – 'don't muck abaht; jump in, we've got a long way to go.'

As he didn't tell me whether he was Mr Tomkins or not, I henceforth thought of him as Mr Bundle.

I put my suitcase in the back of the lorry among crates of machine parts, and clambered into the cab. It smelled of petrol. It was unbearably warm. However, the great hole in the canvas above the door on my side told me that I'd better enjoy the heat while I'd got it. Mr Bundle took some time to adjust the controls, then he got out and swung the starting handle at the front, at which the engine sprang into life.

Shortly after six, with a blaring of the horn, we rumbled from the garage in the direction of the London Road. At first, Mr Bundle's constant crashing of gears and screeching of brakes unnerved me, but I got used to it. I also accustomed myself to his explosive sneezes. 'Oh, oh, oh,' he'd call out before shaking the cab with an 'atchooo!' I feared that he would lose control of the wheel, but he didn't. Instead, we clattered, rocked, and sneezed our way past the groaning trams into the open countryside.

Curled in my corner, trying to avoid the gale now blowing through my side of the cab, I continued to watch the headlights as they ran before us, piercing the gloom. Periodically, other vehicles danced toward us out of the night, filling our cab with a blinding light. Now and again I saw the skeleton of trees in the background, the hazy lights of towns.

It was just as well that Mr Bundle remained silent, for I had enough on my mind. As I watched the road, all kinds of thoughts raced through my head. I was overwhelmed at the idea of going all the way to London. For a sixteen-year-old who had hardly been out of his town, London seemed a long, long way. When I thought of Bess or mother, I was overcome with a great sadness. Only when I was on the London road did I realize that I should have brought Bess with me. I shouldn't have listened to Harold. I'd allowed myself to be talked into the idea. I'd betrayed Bess. I felt like bursting into tears.

At that moment Mr Bundle followed a sneeze by pointing through the windscreen. 'See that?' I looked. 'For London,' he said. It was the London train, a long string of lights slipping across the dark valley floor before us.

'More comfortable like that.'

'Oh, yes,' I agreed, a catch in my voice.

'Tha mustn't take it badly,' he said, glancing at me. 'If tha falls flat on thi face in London, tha can allus cum 'ome 'gin wi' me.'

'Tha kind.'

The truth was that now that I was running away I had lost the desire to do so. While I didn't feel like jumping out and running back, had there been a steady job, or a steady girl to run back to, I might have done.

There must have been periods in Lancashire's history when it was possible to live a fairly contented life as a weaver without having to look elsewhere for a living. But that had not been my experience. The Lancashire I had known was a long story of broken work and broken pay; of being over-worked or having no work at all; of being paid so badly that the whole family had to work or nobody ate; with only a narrow margin separating us from sinking altogether. I was sixteen when the hunger marchers returned to Blackburn. I had lived through the worst years Lancashire was to endure. By then I didn't need anybody to explain to me, as Mr Peek had done, that the Lancashire cotton industry had been dealt a fatal blow. I had no job to go back to. Best I could hope for was pick-and-shovel work. I either sought a better living elsewhere, or I lived from hand to mouth, forever paying 'something off,' forever 'carrying over,' forever worrying where the next meal was coming from – as the rest of my family did. London was the lure, but I might not have gone there had hard times and Betty Weatherby not made up my mind.

My great-grandfather Arne had come to Lancashire when the name of Blackburn was about to be known world-wide. Now the Lancashire cotton industry was dying – as was our pride and our loyalty to cotton. An industry that treats its workers, especially its defenceless women and children as inhumanely as cotton textiles had done, must die unsung. All my life I have been puzzled why we Lancastrians should have been so good at inventing machines, at starting an industrial revolution that transformed the entire world, yet so bad at human relations. In my whole sixteen years in Lancashire I had heard nothing but 'us'n' and 'them.' The gulf dividing capital from labour was never bridged.

It didn't cross my mind that in going to London I might be jumping from the frying pan into the fire. The obvious dangers accompanying my mad-cap scheme didn't penetrate my thick head. I never thought of discomfort or danger. The fact that I had no idea where I would sleep the next night, or the one after that, added spice to the adventure. Somehow the solution to all my problems would be found at the end of the road that lay before me. I was blindly optimistic of the outcome.

I didn't hold it against anybody that I had to go. Because of what grandmother Bridget had taught me, I didn't hate anybody for it. I envied, but I can't say I ever hated the rich. That is one conversion Peter Shad had not succeeded in making.

Least of all did I blame Lancashire, the county of my birth. Regardless of the fact that Lancashire had not offered me much of a living, I was proud to be a Lancastrian, especially to be a Blackburnian. Blackburn was not just another Lancashire town; Blackburn had been the greatest weaving centre in the world. It had been the pioneer, the seed-bed of inventions in power weaving. It was unique. East Lancashire had developed the greatest concentration of manufacturing industry there had ever been. Without the textile industries of Lancashire and Yorkshire there would have been less 'Rule Britannia' in the world.

Whatever else Lancashire had denied me, it had left me with a love of individual liberty and freedom. Lancashire had given me the liberty to run as wild as I wanted. I had always had the freedom to run from dark streets and alleyways into the open rolling countryside. Liberty and freedom were in the bones of my people. Lancashire folk might be rough and ready, but they were never servile. Servile people didn't take it upon themselves to walk out as I was doing. At least Lancashire had left me free to reject my birthplace.

My heritage was joyful as well as bleak. I knew not only the squalor of a factory town, I also knew the unforgettable beauty of the surrounding fields, moors, hills and rugged fells. I shall never forget the long, joyful summer days playing on the banks of the Ribble; the hectic winter flights down icy hillsides on homemade sleds, or the happy hours spent flying a linen kite in the ever-present wind. These things are rooted in my mind, they are part of my blood. More than anything else, it was the river, the rushing streams, the wind, the hills, and the moors that made me what I am. They are with me for ever.

As a Lancashire boy running wild, I'd never known boredom. There had always been something to do. I had never had the time or need to ask, 'who am I?' I was a weaver's son, somebody close to the bottom of the social pile; somebody who could not evade reality; somebody who had been brought into daily contact with the conditions of labour; somebody who had been blessed by constant challenge: the challenge of poverty, the challenge of making do; even the challenge of a harsh climate and a cold north wind.

There was nothing dishonourable in all this. Hard times had bred resourcefulness and self-reliance. I knew by experience how to take setbacks. I also knew that nobody owed me a living. I took it for granted that in life I'd have to shift for myself. Lancashire schools hadn't taught me much. What schooling I had received was deplorable. But I had at least been taught common sense and how to survive; I wasn't quite the greenhorn I looked and sounded.

No, all things considered, I was lucky to have been born and reared in Lancashire; doubly lucky to have been born poor.

'Tha leaving Lancashire,' my friend said, as he slammed in the gear. 'Cheshire's at top of 'ill.'

'Good-bye Lancashire,' I said, a frog in my throat . . .

BEYOND
NAB END

To the memory of Leo O'Hea and
Alexander B. Rodger to whom I owe so much

Chapter I

To London

'Tha's started to shave, I 'ope,' Mr Bundle shouted, as the lorry ground its way up the hill that led from Lancashire to Cheshire. I think he'd begun to worry about me. I nodded and offered him a cigarette. His smoking added to the fog. 'Not right that tha should go to Lundun on thi own.' He sneezed. 'How old art tha?'

'Sixteen.' It was the summer of 1933.

'Tha too young to be goin' off like that. Can't think what's got into thi 'ead. Can't think . . .' Drugged by fumes and weariness, I fell asleep.

Several hours later I woke to the rattle of the engine. I was cooked at the front and frozen at the side. It was still dark. Our headlights danced on the road.

'Where are we?'

'Midlands!' Mr Bundle drew his gloved hand across the glass.

All I could see was the shadow of wayside trees, the veiled lights of towns in the distance, and approaching cars, which burst out of the darkness in a glittering stream – a bright flash, a muffled thump and they were gone. Now and again the moon broke through. I'd never been so far from home; it made me catch my breath. There was no going back now; I'd gone and done it.

The cold air blew through the torn canvas at my side. I pulled my cap down hard, tightened my muffler, and rolled myself into a ball.

I woke with a start when Mr Bundle crashed to a lower gear and pulled off the road. The truck shuddered to a halt before a wayside café.

We scrambled down, stamped our cramped legs, and made our way across the parking lot. Some drivers were cranking up, ready to leave. Moths jittered around the swaying bulb above the door.

The smell of sausages and mash hit us as we entered. A row of dim lights hung over oilcloth-covered tables. There was a rumble of talk. Through a cloud of tobacco smoke, dim figures shuffled across the worn linoleum. Pictures of boxers stared from the whitewashed walls. In a corner a blanket-covered driver lay snoring. I took off my coat.

At the counter a fellow in a brown apron slopped out tea from a dented urn. Rock buns and 'doorstep' ham sandwiches were stacked on glass trays. Mr Bundle put a bun on my plate. I offered a penny to pay for his tea. 'Nay, tha'll need that when tha gets to Lundun.' He pushed the coin back with a grubby finger.

Spilling tea from our mugs, we joined several others hunched over a food-splattered table. They had tired faces; some still wore caps and mufflers.

''Ello, 'ow do, Ernie? Fancy seein' thee.'

I thought it exciting to join a group of night-riders shovelling bangers and onions with HP sauce at two o'clock in the morning.

'Who's young'un, Ernie?'

'Dick Whittington.' Mr Bundle opened his coat and pushed his cap to the back of his head. 'Goin' to Lundun to make his pile, 'e is.'

'Where's t' cat? Dick Whittington 'ad a cat.'

'In t' lorry. Worn out, cat is.'

They burst out laughing.

'Just as well t' lad's using 'is wings afore 'e gets a ball and chain.'

They scraped their forks and slurped their tea.

'Watch out, young'un, London's full of thieves, cheats, tricksters and tarts.'

> Beware of the damsel modest and meek
> She eats thirteen faggots and nine pig's feet.

They thumped the table, shoved each other, and rattled the cups and plates.

———◇———

Half an hour later, Mr Bundle and I stubbed out our cigarettes, said 'Goodnight' and made for the door, buttoning up our jackets as we went.

'Don't forget to send us a bob or two, nipper, when yer becomes Lord Mayor of Lundun,' one of the men shouted after me.

'Oh, no.'

'Not bad sods.' Mr Bundle sneezed. 'All they need is a good night's sleep. 'Ope weather 'olds up.'

As we crunched across the stones, spots of rain began to fall. While Mr Bundle fought with the starting handle, I climbed into the cab and slammed the door. I was almost asleep by the time he got in.

When I came to, it was daylight. Heavy clouds filled the sky. We were part of an endless column of cars and lorries heaped with cargo going south. I sat up, hardly able to believe that I was part of it all.

'Watford Junction,' Mr Bundle mumbled. 'No rain.'

Watford meant nothing to me. We rattled on.

By the time we'd reached a place called Hendon, the people

of London were up and doing. They hurried along the pavements or stood in long queues at bus stops. I was astonished at the way they pushed past each other as if they were running a race. Instead of clogs and shawls, the women wore frocks; the men wore suits, and polished shoes – even ties. Many carried an umbrella. I'd always wondered what southerners looked like. Well, here they were all around me.

'Wot dost ta think?' Mr Bundle shouted, gesturing at the people and the tall buildings.

'Champion!' I felt a glow of excitement.

'I suppose that's what tha's cum for.'

'Aye.'

He stubbed out his cigarette.

<hr>

Later that morning we pulled in close to a bus stop in a crowded street. 'Tha'll get thi bus to Bow from 'ere,' Mr Bundle said. As I got down, I studied the road. They'd said in the North, 'The streets are paved with gold.' It looked like ordinary tarmac to me. I wondered what my family would think had they been able to see me in the middle of that busy London street with the crowd rushing by. Shafts of sunlight burst through the clouds.

I knew that having got to London, everything would change for the better. *The Wonderland of Knowledge* – which I had in my bag – assured me that those who ventured forth would win. Where would I have been without that book, which I had read and reread since I was six? The fate of England did not yet hang on my words, but it was only a matter of time before it would.

'Good luck, young'un,' Mr Bundle said. Kindness filled his eyes. With the engine still running, he scrawled an address on a bit of paper. 'Tha must cum 'ere if tha gets lost like. It's all t' same if tha broke. I'll get thi 'ome agin.' He handed me a florin. I protested. 'Tha goin' t' need it,' he persisted. 'Anyroad, ah'll sleep better if tha keeps the two bob.'

'I'm not goin' to fall flat on mi face,' I bridled.

'Tha might.' He got down and fished out my suitcase from under the tarpaulin.

He wrung my hand, squeezed my shoulders, sneezed into my face and was gone.

As the lorry disappeared, I suddenly felt lost. What was I to do now?

After a few minutes, a red double-decker bus approached. I tightened my grip on my suitcase.

'Bus for Bow and Stratford?' I asked the man in the queue before me.

'You betcher, come olong wi' me.' We found a seat together. He guessed that I was a northerner. I told him that I was going to an important job at the Bow Bridge Iron Foundry, that I was well on in Labour politics, and that I eventually intended to become a Member of Parliament. The excitement of the long journey and the fluster of getting to London had loosened my tongue.

Judging me by my cardboard case rather than by my boasting, the stranger smiled. 'Tahr's over there.'

'Fancy seeing that,' I answered. Everybody in England knew about the Tower. Dreadful things had happened there. Henry VIII's wife, Anne Boleyn, had lost her head in t' Bloody Tower.

When we reached Bow he pointed to a modest house. 'George Lansbury's,' he said. I knew that Lansbury was the leader of the British Labour Party. 'Saint 'e is, 's a fact. Trouble with George is 'e lets 'is bleedin' 'eart lead 'is blinkin' 'ead.'

We drove past a long brick building. 'Bow Bridge Iron Foundry,' he said. With its black roof and closed iron gates it looked as forbidding as a Blackburn cotton mill. Its three stacks stood smokeless.

'Yer gits orf 'ere,' called the conductor, his finger on the bell. I collected my belongings, said goodbye to my friend, and went to the end of the bus.

'I'll watch out for yer in t' piper,' he called after me.

'Tha kind.'

The bus pulled in against the kerb. I stepped down into a

milling crowd. 'Friday street market,' the conductor shouted. 'Mind yer don't git yerself killed.'

No sooner had I put my foot on the pavement than I was swept along by a human tide. Holding my suitcase before me as a shield, I was pushed along past stalls piled high with old shoes and hats, eggs, chickens, oranges, cabbages and meats. Everyone yelled their wares at me as if they had been awaiting my arrival.

While I was looking around, a young ragamuffin plucked at my sleeve. He had a mop of black hair. His coat was split from top to bottom on both sides. He took a white pup out of his pocket and held it under my nose. It didn't look like any pup I'd seen before. 'A bob,' the urchin said, 'come on, let's see if you're a gint – a bob.'

With one hand on my case and the other on my money ('Dick Whittington, you'll be robbed the moment you arrive, you will,' the lorry drivers had warned), I fled the dog and the boy. 'Wot's a bob?' the lad bawled after me, 'Gimme a tanner.' I dodged behind a bicycle pushed by an old gentleman in a tall hat, and ran through the traffic across the street. The ragamuffin and another urchin chased after me.

───◦───

It must have been fate that led me to cross the street, for at the other side, in front of the Talbot pub, I ran into a little barrel of a woman with a pot of beer under her shawl. She almost knocked me over.

''Ere, look whe' yer gowin' young un. Yer nearly lorst me bleedin' wallop. Wot you bleeders want?' she demanded of the two urchins.

'Nuffink, lidy,' they said, pocketing the pup and turning tail.

The woman wore a man's velvet trilby pulled down over her eyes and ears. It was decorated with a large wax flower and a stiletto hatpin. Battered and limp-crowned, it had a defiant look. From neck to knee she was wrapped in a black woollen shawl. Her dark, rough skirt reached down to a ridiculously large pair of men's shoes. They were cracked and looked as if they had never seen a brush.

Fat-faced, with little black sharp eyes, glistening jowls, and a button of a nose, the woman studied my case. 'You lorst?' Her eyes ran over me.

'Not lost. Just looking for a bed. Know one?'

There was a thoughtful silence.

''Ow's 'alf a kip?' She shifted her pot of beer.

'Better than none.'

'Fast bird you are. Come on and I'll show you what you've won.'

I followed the heavy figure round the pub corner into a dim, narrow street marked 'The Cut'. At the other end, shutting out the sky, was a grey gasometer. ''Ome sweet 'ome,' she said as she lifted the latch of the first cottage.

Stepping across the threshold, I entered a low-ceilinged corridor, which led to an ill-lit living room. There were several chairs, a cluttered table and a rocker. Bald patches marked the plaster walls. In a corner, hanging over a low window was a canary in a cage. 'That's Dick,' she said. 'Give us a song, Dick.' Washing hung before a low fire; cracked oilcloth covered the floor. There was a rotting smell.

She put her beer on the table, ignoring the cockroach that scurried away, and proceeded to show me around. The cottage was a two-up, two-down affair, such as I had known in Lancashire. Beyond the living room was a poky kitchen with a sagging ceiling. It had a small table, a coal-cooking range, a gas ring, a cracked mirror, a pile of unwashed dishes, and a bucket filled with dirty laundry. A smell of burned food hung in the air.

Beyond the kitchen was the toilet. The narrow backyard was crammed with a mountain of machine parts, rusty engines, metal bars, gratings, tubes, and nuts and bolts. There was hardly room to get by. The pile looked as though it might collapse. 'All fall dahn,' the woman croaked, as she gave a flick of her fingers across her throat.

A miry alleyway lay farther on; colonies of beetles lived

in the cindery mud. The whole area reeked of toilets and dust-bins. We heard snatches of laughter from the boozer next door. Beyond the pub was the angry rumble of the road.

When we reached the front room, the woman fell silent. Her shrewd eyes watched me. I took in the room at a glance. There was a single bed, a chair and a pisspot. On a high wooden stand in the corner stood an aspidistra. The cracked walls were held together by layers of bulging wallpaper. Aged oilcloth covered the slanting floor. A bare bulb hung from the ceiling. A radio could be heard through the wall.

'No extra charge for the music,' she grinned.

A lace curtain covered the lower half of the dirt-streaked window through which came a feeble light.

What held my attention was the bed. It was a single iron bedstead covered with threadbare blankets. The half-bed she had promised had shrunk to a quarter. She read my thoughts. 'Ben at the top, you at the bottom. A good kip.'

I felt the bed. The mattress was as hard as rock, the pillow was lumpy.

'Fifteen bob a week with grub,' she said, as if the question of my tenancy was settled. 'Five bob dahn, a week's notice to quit on either side. If yer keeps the window shut, yer'll find it stuffy. If yer opens it, yer'll get the gasworks. Ben 'as it shut.' She didn't mention that to the smell of gas should be added the smell of stale beer, as well as the smell of perfume from Yardley's factory in the next street.

'Looks all right,' I lied, as I peered through the window at the abandoned Church of the Nazarene opposite. Hesitantly, I fished out five bob and put them in her eager hand. I'd stay until I could find something better.

'Must be yer lucky day,' she said, tucking the money into her clothing. 'I've always said it, some people is born lucky.' We shook on it. Her hand felt sticky. 'Wot's yer nime? Mine's Tinker.'

The five shillings must have gone to Mrs Tinker's head, for she hustled me back to the kitchen and made me some bread and jam and a cup of tea. She put hot water on the dead tea leaves and swished the pot around. It tasted stale. The sandwich was gritty, but I was hungry.

Between gulps of beer, Mrs Tinker told me about her family: her husband Bert, her daughters Sarah and Maisy, and her son Ben. Parents and daughters slept in the two rooms upstairs. 'My "pot and pan" works on the river. 'Eavy work, Bert 'as, enough to kill 'im.' She took another gulp, wiping her mouth with the back of her hand. 'Sarah's twenty and Maisy's eighteen, them works at Bryant and May's match factory in Bow. Workers loses their jaws doin' that. They calls it "phossy-jaw", 'orrible 't is. Ben's twenty-two, 'e works for a wrecker in Stratford.'

I wondered how so many people could have so many jobs and so little to show for it.

Settling down, my landlady drew a small leather bag from deep inside her skirt. She untied the string and shook a heap of little polished stones on to the newspaper covering the table. She rubbed them with the corner of a dirty dishcloth. 'Well?' Her bright eyes quizzed me. 'More 'en you can count. Wot are them? Guess.' She took another swig of beer.

I rubbed one of the stones between thumb and finger, then another. I didn't know what they were. 'Stones?'

'Stones . . . of course them's stones. Wot else? Wot I arsks yer is wot kind o' stones?'

A heavy silence hung between us.

'I don't know.'

'Gallstones, you dummy! Mine! A record!'

I just stared.

''Struth,' she exploded, gathering up her treasures. 'Wasting my time you is. You're the kind of bloke wot gets no 'appy in anyfink.' Swearing loudly, she tucked the bag inside her skirt again.

When the rest of the family came in that evening they took my presence in their stride. Evidently I was not the first lodger to rent part of Ben's bed. Yet I was the first to come from so far away. Maisy exploded in laughter at my accent, "Ark at 'im; off 'is chump 'e is.' It was the first time anyone had laughed at me like that and it hurt. The two girls were small, though what they lacked in build they made up for with quick wit and deft talk. Their nails and faces were painted.

Later we had supper together. Although I was hungry, I managed to control my appetite lest Mrs Tinker should take alarm and raise her price. Fifteen shillings was all I could afford, and that depended on my getting a job.

As we ate, I studied my landlord. He was a tall, muscular man with a long sliding jaw, protruding cheekbones, grizzled hair and a clipped moustache. He surveyed me cautiously with one eye. The other was covered with a black shield. 'The war,' he said. He wore an old navy suit with a faded anchor on the breast pocket, a blue roll-neck pullover, and – even at table – black rubber galoshes up to his knees.

The pile of scrap metal in the backyard was his pride and joy. 'Come in 'andy one day. There's gotta be a war.'

'Die in our bleedin' beds, we will,' his wife grumped.

The moment Ben came in my heart sank. He was a hulking gorilla of a fellow with tousled hair, work-begrimed arms and a tattooed chest. He had the oddest pointed ears, but no neck. He spoke with an unmanly voice. I worried how the two of us could possibly fit into his narrow bed.

After supper, I followed Ben to his room. I sat on the chair, while he stuffed a rolled blanket between the bed and the wall to give us another inch or two. He'd obviously done it before.

'The thing yer've got ter watch is if yer jumps out the bleedin' bed on to t' floor yer'll go right through it; the floorboards are rotten. Look behind t' aspidistra. That's where Mum 'ides 'er beer. Knock it dahn and you'll go straight through t' bleedin' window. The old man is sumfink shockin', 'e is, about beer in t' 'ouse. She'll get 'er 'ead punched in if 'e finds it.' It explained why the room smelled like a brewery.

We climbed into bed, he was at the top, I was at the bottom. 'Can't beat it 'ere,' he kept saying, tucking the blanket under his chin. Using my coat as a pillow, I tried to keep my feet off his face. Before falling asleep, I asked him about his job.

'I smash stones . . . wiv a sledge 'ammer.'

I wondered whether the stones he broke hadn't broken him.

I got up that first Saturday morning without waking Ben. After a hurried breakfast of an egg, bread, tea and tinned milk, I put on my cap and went in search of the Bow Bridge Iron Foundry I'd seen from the bus. The chimneys were still idle; the iron-barred windows were thick with dirt; stunted patches of sooty grass grew against the high walls. The tall gates were chained and locked. My pulse quickened as I tried one gate after another.

'Shut Sat'day! Short time,' a passerby called.

That was all I needed to cheer me up. Factories on short time are not looking for workers. The foundry began to take on a hostile look.

With nowhere else to go and nothing else to do, I went in search of the Thames. Every northerner who comes to London wants to see the Thames.

For an hour or more, I walked down warren-like streets, past squalid alleyways and dank courtyards festooned with lines of washing. The gloomy dwellings seemed to go on and on for ever. Ragged children stopped their dancing to turn and gape at me. Some people peered from basements, others sat at open windows in their shirtsleeves. Knots of men idled at street corners. I saw a Chinaman and a Negro, and some swarthy people wearing red turbans. I'd never seen so many different faces. In one street I came upon a Temperance speaker who pointed an accusing finger at me. 'Drink is the devil's brew,' she cried. I moved on quickly. Only in a church-yard did I see grass and trees. When I got lost the Cockneys put me straight, though they did so in an offhand manner.

Eventually, I made my way round a high wall and came to a causeway overlooking the largest river I'd ever seen. The tide was rippling across the mudflats; slimy stakes stuck out of the water; rusting cranes stood against the grey sky. Excited, I made my way to the edge of the water, where I sat on some stone steps to eat my sandwich. Fort-like docks stretched as far as I could see.

Moored barges linked together with rope creaked and groaned at the rising tide. Screaming gulls fought over swill on the oily surface. An old straw mattress floated by, surrounded by pieces of driftwood. Farther out, steamers and tugs boomed, piped and whistled; a graceful sailing barge went by loaded with bricks. It had one tall mast with a patched sail and a tiny mast at the stern. There were so many ships that I wondered where they all came from and where they were going.

Much later, I left the Thames and began to make my way back to Stratford. As I walked, I knew I'd done the right thing in leaving Lancashire. Unlike the North, which had suffered a stroke and was dying, London was vibrantly alive. In Blackburn it had been pointless to look for a job. London offered hope. What I saw wasn't the London Harold Watkins and I had listened to on the radio – Saturday-night bands forever going *boom-ta-da-da-boom*, tinkling glasses, and happy voices calling across crowded dance floors – but it was the most exciting place I'd ever seen and I intended to hang on to it.

It was early evening when I arrived back at The Cut. Ben Tinker was shambling off down the street in ill-fitting clothes. 'Do yer want some beer and jellied eels?' he asked. I declined.

That night, I luxuriated in his bed. He woke me up in the early hours of the next morning smelling to the moon. In minutes he was sleeping like a log. With my head at the bottom, I kept the odour of Ben's beer and eels at bay; but there was still the smell of his feet.

———◦———

'Well I'm blessed,' Mr Tinker said the next morning, when I told him that I was about to take a bus to the City. The way he looked at me suggested that to go to the City simply for pleasure was unforgivable.

Ben, who was still in bed, took his dad's view. 'Never bin, an' hain't goin' now,' he said, pulling the blanket over his head. ''S fact.'

I caught a red double-decker bus at the corner. My face pressed against an upstairs window; I stared through the smoking chimney pots into the bright sky. My head and heart were full of expectations.

Westminster Bridge was humming with life when I got there. Cars, buses and trams were rushing by. There was an endless stream of people – all dressed up and many of them talking in languages I had never heard before. Boats hooted on the river below. The buildings were so high that I had to crane my neck to see the top. *Boom, boom, boom* went Big Ben, a stone's throw away, tolling out ten o'clock to the City and the world. I'd heard it on the radio, but that couldn't match the real thing. The sound hung in the air even after the booming was done.

With a map the bus conductor had given me, I walked round the outside of the Houses of Parliament and Westminster Abbey. I knew that the Houses of Parliament were the heart of England and the British Empire – nay, of the world.

In Downing Street I missed seeing Ramsay MacDonald, the Prime Minister, by five minutes. That was something worth writing home about. Buckingham Palace had a flag on top, but you could hardly get near it because of the crowd. Soldiers on horseback, complete with trumpets, swords, tall black fur hats and shining breastplates, had difficulty getting by. After the Palace, I visited Nelson's Column in Trafalgar Square, where a cloud of pigeons flew around me. I made my way to St Paul's Cathedral, and then to the Old Bailey. One look at the scales of justice hanging above its entrance was enough. How many times had I read in *Thompson's Weekly* about judges doffing black caps and sentencing poor people to death there. That was something else I'd have to write home about.

All that day I rushed from one thing to the next, almost forgetting to eat the bread and jam sandwich Mrs Tinker had given me. The more I saw, the more I wanted to see. It was late by the time I reached Piccadilly Circus. Coloured lights, shiny cars and double-decker buses filled the street. Shop windows displayed every luxury. I saw people in real evening dress getting in and out of taxis. How different from Blackburn it was!

Tired out, I finally returned to Stratford. Sarah had saved me some supper. The Tinkers didn't say much. When I began to tell them about the wonderful things I had seen, they gave each other queer looks, which made me feel uncomfortable. I thought Ben might have been more sympathetic, but by the time I got to bed he was snoring.

———◦———

At seven-thirty the next morning, with washed face and clean overalls, and with my straw-like hair sticking out from under my cap, I climbed the stairs to the office of the Bow Bridge Iron Foundry. The three chimneys were belching thick black smoke. The bright sun made the building look friendly. All the gates were open; people and lorries were coming and going. In my hand was the crumpled letter of introduction from Mr Dimbleby at the brick works in Darwen, Lancashire, to Mr Dent. As I knocked on Mr Dent's glass-panelled door, I became hot around the collar. The longer I stood there, the more worked up I got. The banging and thumping in the foundry below shook the windows.

Eventually a plumpish, middle-aged woman answered my knocking.

''Oojah want?'

'Mr Dent.'

'Won't be 'ere for 'alf an 'our. What's your business, anyway?'

'Private,' I said, pushing the letter back inside my overalls. I hadn't come all this way to be put off by a secretary. 'I'll be back at eight,' I called as I made for the stairs. I was so nervous and moved so fast that you might have thought the building was on fire.

'Better few minutes before,' she shouted after me. Her tone was friendly. There's one thing I thought, as I went down the steps two at a time, there is a Mr Dent; he's not dead or gone to Australia.

I spent the next half-hour pacing up and down the street carrying on an imagined conversation with Mr Dent. The people who passed me must have thought I was crazy. 'Yes Mr Dent, no Mr Dent,' I practised. I knew that the upcoming interview was vital to both Harold Watkins and me. 'Billy,' Harold had said when I was leaving the North, 'Billy, when you meet that London chap, you've got to nail him. For God's sake, don't let him get away. He's our only hope.'

Just before eight, with office workers pushing past me, I knocked on Mr Dent's door again. The plumpish woman greeted me. 'Wait and I'll try to fit you in, dearie.' Encouraged by the 'dearie' bit, I walked up and down the corridor until a small, bent figure carrying a briefcase and umbrella, whom I presumed to be Mr Dent, brushed past me. He entered his office and shouted for the secretary. Everybody in the building shouted because of the din. Doors banged, people came and went. I wondered if I would ever see either of them again. You could tell it was Monday.

Thirty minutes later I was still waiting. It didn't bother me; I'd been brought up to wait. I watched the tea urn being pushed from room to room, hoping that someone would offer me a cup. They smiled, but there was no tea forthcoming. I was just about to sit cross-legged on the floor when the 'dearie' woman popped her head round the door and asked me to come in.

She sat me opposite her boss, who didn't even look up. He was a grey-haired man, with a strong face. He wore a striped shirt with rolled-up sleeves and braces. His great unkempt moustache contrasted with his stiff, celluloid collar and glittering tiepin. Steel-rimmed spectacles sat on the end of his nose; a cloud of cigarette smoke hung above his head. He wasn't anything like the photograph that Mr Dimbleby had shown me.

Against the door stood a hatstand with a trilby, a jacket, and an umbrella. There was dust everywhere. The desk, the windows and the pictures of foundries on the walls were covered with it; so was the carpet and the black cat asleep on a chair. There was a strong smell of burning.

Clutching my letter and my cap, I watched Mr Dent as he shuffled his papers. Every now and again he would talk to himself or use the telephone. His tone was always brisk and aggressive – and loud, because of the *thump, thump, thump* of the drop hammers below.

Just when I'd begun to wonder whether I was going to have to sit on the edge of that chair for the rest of my life, Mr Dent looked up and fixed me with a stare. 'Yes?' he demanded brusquely, as if I'd just arrived. I handed him Mr Dimbleby's letter. He opened it with a knife and read it slowly. I watched him closely. Instead of questions such as 'And how is Mr Dimbleby?' or 'When did you arrive?' (the answers to which I'd rehearsed in the street), he shouted, 'Christ!' and put the letter down as if it had burned his fingers. 'Get Charlie,' he called to the secretary through the open door. My heart sank. His voice sounded cross. As I waited, Harold Watkins' anxious face passed before my eyes. ('Billy, for God's sake, nail him!')

It was a relief when Charlie Bobbit the foreman arrived to end the painful silence. I liked Charlie Bobbit from the start. He was as round as a ball. A brown dustcoat covered him from top to toe. He had twinkling eyes and wore a crushed bowler above his soot-smudged face. A short-stemmed pipe stuck out of the side of his mouth. He nodded affably to me, picked up the teapot and poured the last drop of tea into Mr Dent's empty cup. Only when he had drunk the dregs did he speak up.

'What's doin', 'Arry?'

Mr Dent nodded at me. 'That silly bugger Arthur Dimbleby has gone and sent this lad on spec.' He handed Charlie the letter. Draping himself over a chair, Charlie read it and then looked at me. I felt hot under his gaze.

'No warnin', 'Arry?'

'Months ago I heard from him . . . didn't reply because there were no jobs. Standing our own people down, we were.'

'Lost a lot of good sods.'

'Dimbleby could at least have rung. I'll give him what for on the blower later. He's a bloody fool to put a youngster out on a limb like this.'

Charlie turned to me. 'When did you get here, son?'

'Friday.'

'Could you go back?'

'I've nothing to go back to.'

'Any friends in London?'

'No.'

'Where are you living?'

'I found half a bed in The Cut near the canal in Stratford.' Our conversation was interrupted by the phone ringing. 'What can I do about it?' Mr Dent shouted into the phone. 'What do you mean? . . . No I won't shoot myself.' He slammed the phone down. 'What do your folks do?' he asked me, as if the phone had never rung.

'Cotton workers, with no jobs.'

'The trouble with you northerners is that you think that jobs in London are two-a-penny,' Mr Dent said, speaking to the wall.

The secretary entered with some letters to sign. Unnoticed by the others she caught my eye, placed her finger under her chin and raised her head. I got the message: keep your chin up. She'd been listening through the open door.

'Ever worked in a foundry?' Charlie asked.

'No, but I'm a quick learner,' I answered, a note of desperation in my voice. I could feel Harold Watkins prodding me.

There was a long silence while Charlie removed his bowler and wiped his brow.

'Well?'

'Well,' answered Charlie, 'you can either send this little bugger back to where 'e's come from, or . . .' here he paused, 'for Arthur's sake, you can 'elp 'im out for a couple o' weeks while 'e tries to find a better 'ole. We've drunk a lot of beer with Arthur Dimbleby, we 'ave.'

'What are they going to say in the shop? And what about the Union? We're on short time. And what would the chairman say?'

'Nobody's goin' to know nothin', unless you shout it from t' bleedin' roof.'

For a few moments Mr Dent nursed his pen. He then turned to me. 'Count your blessings, young man, that Mr Bobbit didn't die coming up the stairs. He'll put us all in the workhouse, he will, before he's done.'

'Worrygut!' Charlie grinned.

And so it was settled. They'd let me hang on for a week or two while I searched for something else. I'd get one pound a week for which I thanked them. Cap in hand, I followed Charlie down the stairs. Mr Dent looked unhappy, but the secretary smiled as I left.

———◇———

When I reached the foundry floor, I wondered why I'd tried so hard to get there. The air was stifling; everything breathed fire. 'A soddin' place occupied by lunatics,' shouted Mr Bobbit. Welders' torches sizzled and flared; black leather belts hummed up and down; stamping machines and drop hammers shook the building; clouds of steam and smoke rose from bubbling pits of red molten ore; half-clad, black-grimed shadowy figures flitted about. 'Sand rats,' said Bobbit. In the rafters, sparrows flew. As I looked on, my eyes watered; dust clogged my nose and throat. I feared I was about to choke.

—◇—

By the end of the day, I was trembling with fatigue. My face was plastered with mud, the armpits of my shirt were black with sweat; my trousers were wet from the steam. To save the bus fare, I walked to Stratford. I needed the fresh air.

I reached the Tinkers on the point of collapse. Stripping to the waist, I cleaned up at the kitchen sink. It was the only place to wash. Having struggled to stay awake through supper, I fell on Ben's bed. He had to sleep at the bottom that night.

The next week was a test of endurance gauged by the foundry hooter. From seven-thirty until five, with an hour off at midday, I worked harder than I'd ever done. Shovelling sand and fighting trolleys with lives of their own left me so exhausted that I didn't know which day of the week it was. When I wasn't shovelling sand, or pushing a trolley, or carrying ladles, forceps, tongs and hammers, I was cleaning up after somebody else. Clay, water and sand became second nature to me – so too did burns and blisters.

Every day was a battle to get up, work and sleep. I learned to breathe while being roasted. I also learned to take a cursing when I did the wrong thing. Praise was unknown. Flopping down on Ben's bed at night was the only escape from the battles of the day. The screaming of injured metal drove everything else out of my head. Going to the tap for a drink, or to the toilet for a smoke were the only ways to relieve the pressure. I remembered the look of exhaustion I'd seen on my brother's face when he was a foundry worker years before. It had never occurred to me that I would find myself in the same boat. Time became a blur. I was engaged in a struggle in which I dared not fail.

I'd have been out of a job had I not won the friendship of Charlie Bobbit. Every now and again he let me off for an hour to chase other jobs that were being offered locally. My efforts were a waste of time and bus fares. For every job there were a dozen applicants. When I told Bobbit that I hadn't got the job, he'd remove his pipe, shrug and say, 'She'll be right tomorrow.' But tomorrow came and I still hadn't landed anything. I suppose Bobbit delayed throwing me out because I was working my hide off.

At the end of the first week I didn't need anyone to explain to me the need for the Sabbath – a day of rest. I wrote post-cards to my sister Brenda, my friend Harold Watkins, and Mr Dimbleby at the Darwen Brick Works. I knew that Brenda would share my card with the family.

Chapter II

A Different World

Once I'd adjusted to the pace at the foundry, I woke each morning with a new feeling of adventure and excitement. Life began to have meaning again. Had Ben not warned me about the rotten floor, I'd have jumped out of bed.

Mr Tinker's shout, 'It's four bells,' made me hurry to breakfast. After that I joined the endless flow of vehicles and people going westwards towards the City. There were no pedestrian crossings on Bow Road. Sometimes I dashed across; other times the traffic was so dense that I had to wait. I loved the excitement and the danger of it all. I accepted the turmoil of city life as I accepted the cloud of sulphur on the foundry floor – without thinking. To stay in London, I was prepared to put up with anything.

<hr>

After each gruelling day at the foundry, I'd tramp back to Stratford. It was a blessing to reach The Cut, clean up at the sink and sit down with the family for some food. Of the Tinkers, Sarah soon became my favourite. She was the giving type. She was decent and never did me a wrong. She had a suitor with the improbable name of Widge, of whom she was very fond. 'It's as if sumfink nice 'ad 'appened every time 'e cums in,' she would say. Widge was an ordinary fellow with a low forehead and heavily lidded eyes, who carried on a conversation by jerking his head. Yet his heart was in the right place; his eyes said so. He used to come every Friday night to court Sarah against the wall in the dingy area between the front door and the living room. There was nowhere else. They used to push and scramble so hard against the wall behind which I was trying to sleep that it was a relief when the lovemaking reached its climax and the wall stopped bulging against my bed. Without fail, the affair would be repeated the next night.

Sarah was the only Tinker with ideals. With Widge, she was determined to escape from The Cut. Her ambition was to start all over again in the countryside where she could bring up a family 'in t' fresh air'. She wanted a garden where her children could play – even if they had to live in a caravan. Anything was better than spending the rest of her life making matches. I did so want her dream to come true. With tears in her eyes, she used to say that she wasn't asking for anything to which she wasn't entitled; whereas I knew she was asking for the moon. Widge and Sarah were really good people. The trouble was that they were poorer than the proverbial church mouse.

Sarah's sister Maisy was all for herself. She wore a thick layer of mascara and used so much powder on her face that it used to flake off and fall in her food. Her idea of heaven was to go to the Troxy on Commercial Road on Saturday nights with some bloke who was prepared to stuff her with chocolate, ice cream and oranges. For those few hours she lived the life of the screen. When she came home she'd dance about the living room taking off the stars she'd seen. The Troxy was where we all went to dream. It relieved us of the drabness of our surroundings. In other people's hopes, loves and hates, we saw ourselves.

Reality was to return to The Cut and get involved in a Tinker fight. One night Mr Tinker threw a dreadful tantrum. Once the "Arf a mo, shut that, missus' phase had begun, the battle was on. The girls ran upstairs; Ben and I took refuge on our bed. After several minutes of bloodthirsty howls, Mrs Tinker gave such a scream that her daughters came running. Ben remained completely unmoved, except for having a good scratch.

I didn't like Maisy. Her darting eyes were always watching me. Once when I came home she was the only one there. She offered to wash the dirt off my back at the sink. I was surprised at her sudden helpfulness; I was even more surprised when she tried to wash my thighs. I felt her hands against my skin; they were hot and clammy. Repelled by her, I grabbed my towel and made for the door. She never forgave me. After that, I avoided being in the house with her alone. I would wash my back and below the waist on a Sunday morning when everybody else was asleep. Sarah feared that her sister was out to devour me; she watched us like an old hen.

I not only became daggers drawn with Maisy, I also had to watch my step with her mother. When Mrs Tinker wasn't nagging her husband, she was nagging me about the dirt I brought home. I was using too much soap and hot water. I would gladly have walked out on her had I been able to. But what was on offer for fifteen shillings was as miserable as the Tinkers. I put up with the awful conditions because I had to.

Food was the greatest trial. Mrs Tinker might claim that she'd bought "arf a shoulder o' mutton and pertaters', but the meal didn't even faintly resemble mutton or potatoes. It was a gala occasion when she took to her bed and Sarah cooked. Whenever I had pennies to spare, I bought food on the street. The parcels of buns and shortbread that my sisters sent helped me to get by.

Mrs Tinker's idea of housekeeping was not very ambitious. The kitchen sink was always covered with grime. The bugs, which dropped down the walls with the noise of grains of sand, were worse, though in fairness, she would have had to burn down the house to defeat them. She had no sense of smell. I would come back from the foundry at the end of the day to find Ben's window shut and the stench of the unemptied pisspot under the bed unbearable. Yet I hated her emptying the pisspots in the morning. She'd stick her thumb in all of them, and then make breakfast.

One of the reasons why Mrs Tinker could not smell urine was that there were so many other smells in the house. The smell of beer was awful. I never knew any woman drink such quantities; I think it was where my fifteen shillings went. She always had a jugful hidden behind the aspidistra in Ben's room. There was also a sour, earthy smell, which was worse after rain. The house was always damp and cold.

The Cut was a cul-de-sac. At dawn, while scrambling to get dressed, I watched my neighbours pass my window on their way to work. Like myself, they went off to poorly paid jobs. They were hardened by poverty and misfortune. 'Got to tike wot yer finds,' they'd say. Some laboured at the gasworks, others on the docks as stevedores, riggers, ballast-heavers, or winchmen. There was also a chimney sweep, who cycled past wearing a tall hat, carrying his brushes. One little woman never passed without having to run back – I suspected a pot left on the stove. Sometimes I'd watch children skip and jump. They were small for their age and intense. 'Punch and Judies [school inspectors] catches 'em and makes 'em go to school,' said Ben. If I had the light on, the odd gawking face would peer in. Stark naked, I would gawk back at the two eyes frozen to the glass. I would see our neighbours again when they returned at night, flitting by like bats. On Saturday nights they would spruce up and head for the pub. Though the majority were steady, sober people, there were always one or two who returned drunk.

In time I became part of the street. I knew who was sick, who was not speaking to whom, who had illegitimate babies, and who was queer in the head. I knew who had died. You stood in your doorway when the cortège went past.

I got to know our next-door neighbour, hollow-cheeked, watery-eyed Mrs Wheeler, a little better than most. Her radio against my wall was always turned up to get maximum effect. She was a drinking companion of Mrs Tinker's. Unrestrained by my presence, she would go into all the seedy gossip of the street. She had a passion for making a story larger than life – 'filling in the corners' she called it. She never imparted a spicy titbit without prefacing her comments with, 'Wot I'm abaht to tell yer must stiy within these four walls.'

Sustained by 'the spot of tiddly', Mrs Wheeler was convinced that she would 'larst a loiftoim' – which was more than could be said for her family. Her husband and son had worked as wreckers. They'd lived a cat-like existence demolishing buildings all over London. She told me how her menfolk had stood and talked on top of a chimney before taking it down brick by brick. A high wind never bothered them. Other times they'd used dynamite. That's where the Wheeler skill came in.

Having avoided accidents for a long time, their luck eventually ran out. Peter tumbled off a wall and finished up in a wheelchair; his father fell off a factory chimney. The street duly gave him a funeral full of dignity and respect. In this the Cockneys were like the poor of the North: they loved to squander on a funeral. Death was something special.

The Nicholls farther down the street worked on the wrong side of the law. The old man and two of his older sons had done time for what Ben called 'dippin'' or 'shoot-flyin''. The younger members picked the pockets of ladies; the more experienced picked the pockets of gentlemen. They looked perfectly respectable. Mr Nicholls boasted a gold watch chain and a sovereign across his waistcoat, but those presumably were not his. I'm sure they thought their thieving was honest work. 'Too many wicked people abaht,' Mr Nicholls used to say. Whenever a 'grasshopper' (a policeman) went past my window, the odds were he was on his way to the Nicholls.

'Good neighbours, that's what the Nicholls is,' old man Tinker used to say. 'They keeps a large family goin' without askin' no one for nuffink. Keeps 'is family out of the insti-tooshun, 'e do. And gentle they is. Tikes yer watch or yer wallet without ye knowin' it. Down on gamblin' and drink they is too.'

I'd never run into people like the Nicholls and I didn't know what to make of them. I'd come from a community that condemned stealing, regardless of the circumstances. Later, when I learned about the wild, homicidal bullies who terrorised London's underworld, I came to think of the Nicholls as relatively harmless.

The richest woman in The Cut was Pearly Lilly, an attractive blonde, who by plying her profession as a 'bride' among the nobs of the West End, earned more in a night than any of us earned in a week. 'Oh my word, rich she is,' said Mrs Tinker enviously. 'Would like to see the inside of 'er purse, I would.' Pearly Lilly was not ostracised as she would have been in the street where I was born. In The Cut people talked to her like they would to anybody else. She was the only one who could afford to come home in the early hours like a queen in a cab all to herself. Now that for us was living it up:

> See her riding in a carriage,
> In the park and all so gay;
> All the nibs and nobby persons
> Come to pass the time of day.

I used to contrast Lilly's attractiveness with the grimy face of her slovenly old mother.

Pearly Lilly was preferable to Mrs Bindy, who had a large number of children, but no husband. Where the husband had gone to, not even Mrs Wheeler knew. The woman was a professional beggar. The children could take off a blind or crippled child, as mute and pious as could be. I gave an involuntary shudder every time I saw her setting out with her brood.

———◇———

I was shocked at the waywardness of some of my neighbours. I'd been brought up with a strict code of ethics; revival Methodism had drummed into us the difference between right and wrong. In Blackburn the Sabbath was a day of prayer – the trains did not run, and shops and cinemas were closed; even whistling was frowned upon. I had an awful sense of guilt the first time I went to see a film on a Sunday; it spoiled the show.

In Stratford, Sunday was deafening: children screamed, newspaper boys shouted 'piper!', radios blasted, and the Salvation Army band blared at the pub corner, accompanied by the crash of tambourines:

> Here we suffer grief and pain
> Here we meet to part again
> In Heaven we part no more
> Oh, that will be joyful.

I don't wonder that some churchmen preferred to make their conversions in Africa or in the West Indies. Only the tough ones remained in the East End trying to guide and guard their flock.

Sunday was the day I went exploring. I'd never seen so many colourful little shops – they were strung across the district like beads on a string. Everything was available to those with money. You couldn't walk down a street without somebody trying to sell you something: "'Ere y' are! Tyke yer chyce!' Street vendors offered fish and chips (wrapped in greasy newspaper), roasted chestnuts, 'taters – all 'ot!', black puddings, pies, sausages and muffins, ice cream and soft drinks. Raw oysters were eaten on the spot with vinegar and pepper. With or without money, people swarmed. They were like floodwater, filling every space. I used to wonder where they all came from and where they went at night.

What the Cockneys lacked in physical strength – they seemed to be small and narrow-chested – they made up for with nimble wits. Whereas Lancashire men might go to pieces because they were on the dole, unemployed Cockneys laughed it off. They didn't moralise about being without a job. Another one would be sure to turn up, or family and friends would provide. A man could hire a 'cock sparrow' and push a barrow selling fruit and vegetables, or play a mouth-organ or a concertina, or buy a box of chalks and become a 'screever'. I never went out without seeing someone on his hands and knees 'makin' skitches'. Portraits of the King were mixed with those of the dapper Prince of Wales and favourite racehorses.

'Griddling' at street corners was open to anyone with a good voice. There was a fellow in The Cut who swore that 'Sins are wot piys. If yer tells 'em 'ow wicked yer've bin and 'ow yer fell dahn, and 'ow yer now tikes up yer Cross dily – and sings 'ymns about redemption – they'll fill yer 'at.'

In spite of the excitement of urban life, I never lost my love of the countryside. Victoria Park in Bow was the only large piece of open ground easily accessible to me. The avenues planted with trees, the green turf, the rustic bridges, and the swans and boats on the lake – all these things were wonderful. One could even find a songbird there among the swarms of sparrows. The drawback was the crowds – especially at weekends. If the weather was fair, bodies lay thick on the grass and covered the benches. One couldn't move for them. Yet nobody grumbled. People were only too happy to sit or lie in the open air, while the children ran wild. They didn't seem to notice the traffic rushing by outside the railings. On my first visit I was surprised to see people swimming in such a dirty lake.

I not only missed the countryside, I missed the people I'd left behind. As the weeks passed, I became homesick. Loneliness took as much out of me as the heavy work I was doing. At the foundry I couldn't talk because there was so much noise; at the Tinkers' I'd only Sarah to talk to. Conversation with Ben consisted of a few well-meant grunts. I never discovered what went on in his head. He had no idea about the world in which he lived; his expectation of life was the next meal. I cannot believe that no one had mentioned Jesus Christ to him. 'Caw!' he said. 'I've never 'eard of 'im.' Even when he opened up with me, I had difficulty following him, his mind went off at all angles. ''S fact,' he kept saying, staring at some point above my head. I became convinced that he didn't know what he was saying. The family treated him as a kind of cuckoo clock that sounded off at regular intervals, but did not need an answer. They thought him a bit 'loopy'.

I don't know what I'd have done without the letters from home. They affected me like water splashing on a parched plant. Harold Watkins' letters were marvels of hope. 'We'll go a long way in politics,' he wrote. 'Don't forget that when I'm Prime Minister, you'll be my Foreign Secretary.' That's what he'd promised, and Harold kept his promises. I didn't breathe a word of this to anyone.

My parents never wrote. My mother couldn't write, my father didn't think it necessary; nor did my brother Dan. I dropped everything to read letters from my sisters. Jenny wrote about her son and that her husband Gordon had got a job painting again. It saddened me for days to learn from Brenda that my dog Bess had run away the day after I left Lancashire. I knew that she was trying to find me. I felt terrible about it; we'd been inseparable. I knew at the time that in leaving her I was doing wrong. To my sorrow, I never heard of her again.

To ease my loneliness I started to look for Betty Weatherby, my north-of-England sweetheart, who'd been sent to school in London after her family discovered our romance. My love for her was still strong; often at work I'd catch myself daydreaming about her. I went to Stratford Public Library and asked a librarian to help me find her. She looked at me queerly: 'There are dozens of women's colleges in London,' she shrugged. Heartaches and loneliness weren't her business.

———◦———

To my delight, Harold wrote one October day to say that he had left the ACDO soap company in Blackburn and was about to join me in London. A cousin of his in west London, who had migrated from Lancashire some months before, had offered him shelter until he could get on his feet.

I met Harold at Euston Station two weeks later on a cold, blustery Saturday afternoon. I'd never been in a big London railway station before and I found it gloomy and bewildering. I had to fight my way through crowds going to Wales, Scotland, Ireland and perhaps America. I wondered where they'd got the money.

I could hardly contain myself when I saw Harold coming down the platform with our bikes and a load of luggage. He would have brought Bess if he could have found her. Except for a luxuriant moustache, he was just as I'd left him. We couldn't help giving each other a hug. We even had a cup of tea and a bun at the station restaurant to celebrate. While we drank, I listened to his news from the North. He spoke of our families, the Rovers football team, and the depression that still gripped the town. He thought us lucky to have got away.

Sharing the luggage, we then cycled to Harold's cousin in Southall, fifteen miles away. There had been a light snowfall earlier and there was black slush about. Like a couple of country bumpkins we were oblivious of the cars and lorries hooting their horns while trying to pass us; those who cursed us, we cursed back. It never occurred to us that it would have been better for everybody had we taken a train. That would have cost money; to pedal a bike cost nothing but time and energy and we had plenty of both.

It took us a long time to reach Southall, and almost as long to find Harold's cousin, Jack Connor. We found him in the middle of a new, treeless, muddy housing estate where every house looked exactly like every other. They were so small, so raw, so thin that the locals called them 'hen huts'. The estate was full of migrants from northern Britain, Wales and Ireland. A corner had become the preserve of a small coloured group. No one knew whether they had come from India or the Caribbean, or both.

Mr Connor's 'hen hut' was packed with Lancashire migrants, most of them young men like ourselves who had come to London to make their fortune. Some had been so desperate that they'd cycled all the way. There were so many bodies that it was almost impossible to move from one room to another. People slept on collapsible cots or on the floor; planks of wood on bricks served as tables. At least these people weren't strangers to each other, as was the bewildering crowd of faces in the streets. 'If you put on a new suit here, nobody would notice,' one of them said. Some of them would have gone back to the North, had they had a job to go to.

Harold's roguish-looking cousin met his mortgage payments by everybody pitching in. Not that Mr Connor stayed awake at night worrying about it. A natural gambler, he seemed quite happy to have signed away his future earnings. He slapped his head and roared with laughter at the idea of a crippling thirty-year mortgage. 'We'll go to prison? Will we heck!' He was probably as poor as he had ever been, but now for the first time in his life he had electric light, hot and cold water, a bath, a gas stove, a flush toilet, a new galvanised dustbin, and an unconscionable debt he could never hope to repay.

Mr Connor survived by working as a dishwasher in a high-class restaurant on the outskirts of Southall. He brought home the leftovers and shared them with the others. Sometimes his boss gave him the used flowers, which brightened up the house.

I spent only one night in the 'hen hut'. As it was the week-end and pointless to go looking for work, we talked and sang and laughed together until late. Harold and I slept in a corner covered with an old curtain.

On Sunday afternoon I cycled back to Stratford. Before leaving, we agreed that as soon as Harold could find a job, we'd meet in the City for a night on the town. I got home late in the evening, half dead. Against Mrs Tinker's protests, I put my bike in Ben's room next to the aspidistra. Unless I was to leave it in the street and have it pinched, there was nowhere else I could put it – the backyard was full. I couldn't afford to lose anything as precious as my bike.

About a month later I had a letter from Harold. 'I've landed a job as a weaver in a fly-by-night place in west London. If you're willing, I'll fit you in alongside me. We could live at Connor's place until something better turns up.' As I was still hanging on to my job at the foundry through Bobbit's kindness, and other jobs were not to be had, I agreed at once. I knew that Mrs Tinker would be happy to see me go. Harold also said that now that he had a shilling or two, the time had come for me to show him the sights of London. We agreed to meet on a Saturday morning in two weeks' time at the Marble Arch. He would tell me about the weaving job then. He also said that he had news from Blackburn about Betty Weatherby. My heart skipped.

As agreed, we met at the Marble Arch a fortnight later. We were both dressed up in suit, shirt and tie. The weather was cold but sunny.

The first thing I asked him about was Betty Weatherby. 'She's at St Anne's, a girls' college near Berkhamsted. I've looked it up. We could cycle there from Southall and give her a surprise.'

It didn't occur to us to pick up a telephone and call: I'd never used one, neither had Harold.

We spent the whole day seeing the sights. Food we got from street vendors. When Harold saw the Houses of

Parliament, and Big Ben, and Buckingham Palace, and No. 10 Downing Street, and all the other things I tried to squeeze in, he was just as excited as I had been. 'By gum!' he kept saying. The more we saw, the farther we went, the greater our mutual sense of accomplishment. We went on hour after hour, never tiring. We were not awkward rustics any more; we were two special young northerners who were seeing the largest city on earth.

As soapbox orators, we were eager to visit Speaker's Corner in Hyde Park. We found a dozen speakers. The first fellow was able to communicate with the dead. The next one wanted to get rid of the British in India. Alongside him was a wild character quoting great chunks from the Bible, who said that our end was near. He was drowned out by hecklers. The last fellow in the row was a chap with a bowler hat, who offered us an emaciated brown-yellow cat. 'Now I arsk yer, gints, 'ave yer ever seen an animal treated as badly as this? Wot is England cumin' to?

———<o>———

With the coming of evening, we made our way to the Lyons Corner House at the Marble Arch. We wanted to listen to Harry Roy's famous band. What we'd listened to in Lancashire on the radio – the blare of the band, the rattling of cups, the scraping of chairs and the tinkling of glasses – we'd now see for ourselves. Despite the cold, we joined the queue; we weren't going to walk away from the high point of our night out. We felt privileged to be able to queue up outside a restaurant that claimed 'We never close!' What would Blackburn think of that?

While we were waiting, Harold talked about his weaving job. It was in a sweatshop managed by a Hungarian who spoke no English. The pay and working conditions were poor, but it was a job. I could join him in a couple of weeks if I'd take the risk. I said I'd come as soon as he gave me the signal.

After standing for ages, we made it inside and were overwhelmed by the lights and the glitter. Feeling that everybody was staring at us, we followed a waitress to a table with gold chairs. The table was so small that our knees touched. Hair shining, Mr Roy turned and smiled at us as we sat down – we might have been royalty. We were so close to him that we could have shaken his hand.

On the table were white napkins, silver cutlery, a bowl of flowers and a starched tablecloth that almost touched the floor – there were even free matches. A chandelier hung above our heads. We waved to the mirror at our side. After all the walking we'd done that day, we couldn't wait to eat.

Our high spirits lasted until we saw the prices on the menu. I nudged Harold's leg. 'We're going to have to wash dishes,' I whispered.

'Oh hell, Woody, this is not the people's palace, it's a toffs' restaurant.'

I looked around at the other diners who were happily stuffing themselves. The prices hadn't put them off – they were so busy eating that they had no time to applaud the band, as Harold and I did.

We eventually ordered a cup of tea and a bun. It was either that or walk out, and we had queued and queued. Of course it was ridiculous to eat a bun under a chandelier with our movements reflected in a mirror in the presence of the famous Harry Roy, but that is all we could afford.

We ate the bun crumb by crumb. 'Non so fast,' Harold kept saying. We sipped our tea as if it was boiling hot. The waitress looked hostile, her frantic hand signals to someone at the entrance made us think she was calling the police. Only Harold's ordering another round stopped her whisking the dishes away. We had taken a lot of trouble to get here, and we refused to take flight.

We ate our second bun as we had eaten our first: crumb by crumb, while enjoying the band. We were so close to a gypsy with a violin that he seemed to be playing just for us.

Only when we had had our fill of entertainment did we

leave a modest tip and flee. We were less nervous in getting out. We knew we would not be coming back for a long time.

At least we'd seen the real thing. As we left we heard Harry singing:

> Somebody stole my gal,
> Somebody stole my pal,
> Somebody came and took her away,
> She didn't even say she was leavin'. . .

A week later – in search of Betty Weatherby – Harold and I cycled to Berkhamsted in Hertfordshire. Harold had worked out the best route, and had drawn up a map. We brought capes against rain and, as it was November, pullovers, scarves, mittens, and woollen caps. We also carried sandwiches and a flask of tea. Harold had bike tools, spare tyres and tubes. We planned to reach St Anne's before noon. By our reckoning, having spent an hour with Betty, we'd turn around and get back to Southall shortly after dark. I would spend the night there, leaving at four on Monday morning to get to Bow in time for work. A wild scheme, but then I was in love and had just turned seventeen.

The day broke cold and clear; the wind had died down. Once away from London we travelled through a lovely hilly countryside with fields and woods stretching into the distance. There were no factory chimneys or coal pitheads to spoil the view. We kept to the back roads, where the wintry fields lay bare.

Stopping only to eat and drink, we cycled through wooded, park-like valleys. After the flatness of east London it was exciting to struggle up the chalky hills and go helter-skelter down the other side. Our curiosity was aroused by a weathered stone cross in the centre of a ploughed field; we felt for it the reverence due to age. In past times, the plodding peasant would have said a prayer there. In one village we stopped to look at an impressive Elizabethan mansion through a hole in a thick yew hedge. Mostly we hurried on.

Sometime during the morning we fell in with a cyclist near St Albans who was out for a day's ride. He was a pleasant fellow who led us through picturesque lanes and byways that we could never have found for ourselves. Sometimes he would point out an important estate or country view. Being a Hertfordshire man, he was aghast at our ignorance of Hertfordshire's vital role in the making of England. To hear him tell it, this was the most important county in the entire realm. Before leaving us at Hemel Hempstead, he gave us directions to Berkhamsted: 'On the Roman road to Wendover, by Tring and Lilley Hoo.' At Berkhamsted we cycled past a castle, low stone houses crouched outside its gate. Beyond the town were stands of beech trees with smooth grey bark and widely branching roots. Through a break in the trees we caught sight of manicured fields alongside an extensive gorse common. A golfer was playing in the distance.

Our final directions came from a man who was watering two white horses. 'Take the first left at the end of the forest,' he said. 'The college is a mile farther on, standing on a hill. Can't miss it.' Both of us breathed a sigh of relief. Our legs were beginning to give out.

We came upon St Anne's at the edge of a great expanse of trees. It was a long sandstone building standing in a quiet park, with a bell tower above the main entrance. Ivy climbed the embattled walls and wound about the leaded windows. Crows were settling in the trees, their cawing echoing through the woods. As we approached, a bell began to toll. One . . . two . . . three. We were shocked how late it was. We parked our bikes and climbed the steps to the front door where several well-dressed young women stood talking.

We were greeted inside by a middle-aged woman who must have seen us arrive. 'Can I help you?' she asked.

'Yes, I would like to speak with one of your students, Betty Weatherby.'

There was a long moment of silence.

'Please come this way and I'll see what I can do.' She led

us into a panelled waiting room, which despite the season was full of the scent of flowers. Excusing herself, she went in search of the Mother Superior.

Turning my cap in my hands, I watched her go down the corridor. Mysterious candles flickered in the distance, there was a statue of a kneeling monk saying endless prayers in stone.

'We've made it, Woody,' Harold whispered a little nervously.

'Yes,' I answered, more nervous than he.

Before I could stop him, Harold got up and made for the door. 'I'll wait outside.' Wondering what I would say to Betty, I continued to fumble with my cap.

A few moments later I heard steps. The middle-aged woman was returning, accompanied by a black-robed nun in her late sixties. Her penetrating glance intimidated me.

'This is Mother Superior, she will speak to you about Miss Weatherby.'

The nun took a seat and pointed to another chair. A small ivory cross dangled from her wrist. She seemed in no hurry to speak. I thought it better to tell her who I was. 'I know,' she said. I wondered who had written to her about me.

For several moments we sat together, silent and impassive.

'I am afraid I must tell you that Miss Weatherby is no longer here.'

I caught my breath. 'Not here?'

'No, she left for France two weeks ago.' The voice was gentle and warm.

'France?' I stammered.

'Yes.'

'Is she coming back?'

'No. That is all I can tell you.'

Without realising it, I suddenly found tears coursing down my face. I stared at the floor too embarrassed to speak. I found it hard to suppress my tears and a disgrace to shed them.

The nun leaned toward me. 'You need to learn patience, my child, you are very young.'

I shook my head, hurt.

'Don't shake your head like a goat. God knows what He's doing, you'll see.'

Brushing my face with my hands, I got to my feet and slowly made for the door. It seemed pointless to stay any longer.

'How did you get here?'

'We cycled from Southall.'

'Do you intend to return to Southall today?'

'Yes.'

The nun joined me at the door. 'You cannot possibly cycle so far today. It's half past three and the weather is threatening. You'll have an accident.'

'We are using the back roads.'

'Then you'll get lost.'

'Didn't get lost coming.'

'No, that's because you rode in the light.'

'We have no choice. We have to go to work tomorrow.'

There was a silence between us. I made a gesture for her to pass through the door.

'If you insist on cycling through the night you must have some hot food before you go.'

'You're very kind.' I was more upset than hungry.

She accompanied Harold and me to the kitchen and gave orders to serve us a meal.

'God keep you,' she said as she left.

When I told Harold what had happened, he was as bewildered as I. 'Sorry we came on a fool's errand, Woody. Better make tracks home. It's almost four.' We ate in silence. I felt crushed.

We came out of St Anne's to be greeted by a cold, strangely leaden sky. There was a foreboding murmur in the wind. Dead leaves swirled against the college wall and the odd flake of snow was falling. A robin sang his plaintive tune.

We put on our capes. By the time we'd reached the golf links they were blanketed with snow and the wind was quickening. In the forest the trunks of the trees were turning white; the puddles were beginning to freeze over. Smoking snow spun around us; starlings flew low seeking shelter. Save for the raucous cries of crows, the forest was hushed. The falling snow made it seem later than it was; house lights appeared in the gathering gloom. The air grew colder.

Eyes half shut, we cycled against the wind keeping our worries to ourselves. The main thing was to get back to Southall.

An hour later the ground and roofs of the houses were covered with snow; there was a whistle in the wind. As night fell, the shrouded world around us disappeared. The small round patches of light from our lamps preceded us. Even the petrol stations were shut. I had the sensation of marking time – of cycling on the spot in a white, empty world.

With our hoods pulled down over our foreheads and our mufflers wrapped tightly around our faces, we pushed on. Our wet capes swished, our tyres crackled and crunched. Now and again the wind blew the capes over our heads; our mittens froze to the handlebars. Wreaths from a nearby cemetery flew by. Gradually the truth struck home: we were alone in the middle of a blizzard, adrift in a frozen sea.

With every mile the snow became heavier and colder, the wind stronger – it lashed our faces and our legs. Desperately we continued to struggle forwards, one behind the other, taking turns to lead, never once going straight. Our shouting was lost in the wind. There were times when there was no trace of the road and the snow was too thick to cycle, we found ourselves slipping and sliding all over the place. We lugged our bicycles from one snowdrift to another with great clods of frozen snow sticking to our boots. We were too busy fighting the elements to fight each other, though tempers flared.

Too exhausted to go on, bent before the wind, we took shelter behind the trunk of a giant elm. Huddling close for warmth, we ate what scraps of food we had left and drank the flask of hot coffee the nuns had given us. Our breath frosted our mufflers.

'Ah'm tellin' thee,' panted Harold, as he gulped down the hot coffee, 'we maun be gormless to be out here.' Icicles hung from his moustache and his eyebrows.

The coffee saved us from collapse. Even with it we had to get back on to our frozen saddles quickly, for our bodies were losing heat. 'Whatever else, we must keep going, we maun't fall asleep,' Harold warned. We went on, hardly conscious of our direction, averting our heads at each blast, closing our eyes against the needles of snow, gasping for breath. It hurt to breathe. I thought the howling wind vindictive: it pounded me as if I'd done it some wrong. It was all I could do to retain a grip on the handlebars. One moment my hands seemed frozen, the next moment they felt on fire. My body ached to stop and rest; my mind told me that we must go on.

Much later we realised that we'd been riding in a circle. We were too exhausted to cry. By then we had reached the end of our tether and were living in a disconnected world. We should of course have gone and knocked on somebody's door and got somebody up – provided that we could find a door, which we couldn't. Had we known where to find a police station we would have gone there, but there was no one to ask. We hoped that a police car might find us stranded in the blizzard. None did. Several cars, covered with a thick crust of snow, glided past us during the night, but they evidently had more important things to do than rescue two lunatics stumbling about in the storm. The truth is we were too stubborn to seek help: having got ourselves into a pickle we'd somehow get ourselves out. Heads down, we pushed on, fighting against the bitter elements.

Hours later, we emerged from the storm to see the outlines of buildings slowly taking shape. In the distance the lights of London were reflected against the clouds. The more we struggled toward the lights, the more they seemed to recede. The last hour seemed like a lifetime.

It was after midnight when we reached the outskirts of Southall – seven hours later than we had planned. We were chilled to the bone and hardly able to move. We needed all the will we could muster to keep going. When eventually we reached the Connors' house and got off our bikes, great lumps of ice and snow fell from our clothing. Once indoors, we undressed mechanically. Muscles I never knew I had ached all over me. 'Next time tha goes courtin',' said Harold, standing in his shirtsleeves and watching me with frosted eyes, 'tha goes on thi own.' But he said it in jest. It took a gallon of scalding tea and a hard rubbing-down to put back a semblance of life into us. Tired to the point of being drugged, I fell asleep feeling that I had just run a great race.

After only three hours of sleep from which I had to be shaken, I staggered about getting dressed and left Southall for Stratford at about four. Groggily at first, with screwed-up eyes, I pushed on through the frozen stillness and the dark. The saddle of my bike was cold and hard, the chain was stiff. After what seemed like another endless journey, I reached the foundry by seven-thirty – glad for once to get back into the furnace-like heat. That day the papers were full of the blizzard – the worst in decades, they said. They never mentioned us.

About a month after returning from St Anne's, Harold and I celebrated our first Christmas away from home. I gave him some cigarettes, he gave me five small cigars. I'd been in London five months, Harold had been there three, and neither of us had much to show for it. To cap it all, Harold had lost his weaving job on Christmas Eve. The weaving shed in which we were both to find a living had shut its doors for good. The Hungarian had vanished. That put a damper on our spirits that not even the convivial Mr Connor could dispel.

Yet neither of us doubted that eventually things would take a turn for the better. We were too young to know what we ought to have been worrying about. Regardless of the obstacles we faced, we looked upon London as the place to be.

Harold and I saw in the New Year of 1934 together. We were full of faith in a boundless future.

Chapter III

Hard Labour

Instead of staying at the Bow Bridge Iron Foundry for a couple of weeks, I stayed there for more than two years. I obeyed the siren when it commanded me to work and I obeyed the siren when it commanded me to stop. The thump, thump, thump of the machinery and the rattle of the overhead cranes numbed my senses. Bobbit continued to pay me one pound a week and to use me as a dog's body: 'The sods have to have somebody to kick,' he said. He knew I didn't intend to stay. He was right. I didn't want to work there for the next five years, with the risk of being thrown out when I became entitled to a man's wage. So many people yelled at me that I'd no need to think for myself.

What a relief it was to be sent out occasionally with a crew to install the foundry's metal work. I could watch the sky, see the trees, hear the birds, and feel free. All I had to do was to give a hand, brew tea and run errands. Alas, such occasions were few. When the job was done, we'd all trail back to the dirt and the din on the foundry floor.

At the outset, the foundry had seemed chaotic. It took some time for me to learn that there was order behind the chaos: ovens, cranes, furnaces and coke bins, as well as the piles of sand and loam, pig iron and charcoal had their proper place. It all made sense once you knew how the foundry worked.

The nerve centre was Bobbit's office, whose dirty bay window projected a few feet into the shop. He used his office chiefly to go over blueprints with Mr Simpson, the draughtsman. Bobbit was the first to arrive in the morning, the last to leave at night. I cannot imagine how the business would have functioned without him. Sometimes I'd catch a glimpse of Mr Dent taking important people round the floor. I never knew who owned the place or for whom I worked. Bobbit ruled my world.

The next most important man to Bobbit was Mr Simpson. He was the fellow who turned ideas into blueprints. He was always dressed in a suit and tie; his hair glistened with oil. His office was next to Bobbit's and was also protected by glass. He worked with slide rules, drawings and tiny blocks of steel to measure things. On the few occasions when I entered his office, he was always pleasant. Yet to my astonishment, I saw him pick up his telephone one day and smash it to bits. He hit an iron pillar with it until there was nothing left. I never saw such a mad act. Then he stood there scratching his head looking puzzled. I thought it was the nature of the job that made him do it, but Bobbit said it was his wife. Eventually, Mrs Simpson was asked to stop calling – the phone smashings were costing the foundry a mint of money. The problem was that he was a chronic womaniser. I once heard him trying to catch a woman on the telephone, it was like a fellow fishing for trout.

Mr Harding the storeman, a gaunt, tall man with a shock of white hair, also had his strange ways. He was forever moaning; every time I visited the stores there was something wrong. 'How are you Mr Harding?' I'd ask in an attempt to cheer him up. 'It's worse, much worse,' he'd mutter throwing his hair back. 'I've got to leave this bleedin' place before it's too late.' What 'it' was I never found out. I told one of the moulders what Harding had said. 'Silly bugger 'as been like that for twenty years. Tryin' it on, 'e is. We ought to drop a crane on 'im.' Bobbit always prefaced his remarks to Harding with, 'I know you're dying, Tom, but . . .' As far as I know, Mr Harding remained as fit as a fiddle until he retired.

At the noon break we'd sit around on the foundry floor and tell stories, laughing as we ate – some of the fellows wolfing the food down in great gobbets. In summer we'd squat outside against the foundry wall among the heavy traffic to get a breath of fresh air. Having eaten, we played cards or tossed coins on to a line drawn in the dirt. We always talked horses; we knew which horse had won the moment the news arrived on the phone – the winner was shouted from the office door. It's just as well I didn't have money to gamble.

Sometimes the laughing and joking would give way to blows. Woe betide anybody who strayed into another moulder's space. Tempers would flare. 'Turn it up! Pack it in!' Bobbit would bawl as he ran to intervene. As a last resort he'd call upon two workers with massive shoulders and gnarled hands, who together had the strength to settle any argument.

Some fights were renewed behind the foundry wall at night. I only went to one and that was enough for me. It was between Standing and White. Both were in their mid-thirties. I knew Standing because he lived close to The Cut. He was a nice sort of bloke. White was taller than Standing, but Standing was heavier. Bared to the waist, they seemed well matched. I don't know what the argument was about, but the two men were determined to settle it with blows.

The ring was a flattened cinder pad, lit by the lamps on the outside walls. The spectators – a fight always raised a crowd – stood in a larger ring, some of them in deep shadow. There was no referee; a fight went on until one of the men was knocked out or surrendered. Kicking with heavy boots was forbidden; that could lead to death. Bets were placed. In the background was the roar of traffic. Cigarette smoke hung above the crowd.

The fight began calmly enough, with each man looking for an opening. They held themselves like professionals and knew how to shift their position to gain a tactical advantage. Sparring and feinting, they concentrated on breaking down the other's defence. Now and again there was a thud to the body or a crack to the jaw, followed by cheering from the crowd.

Standing was the more aggressive and nimbler on his feet. He did the driving. In comparison, White was slow. Yet he was skilful in evading the other's fists, although not for long. Soon, Standing landed a terrific uppercut. The blow, followed up by a quick left to the body, sent White careening into the crowd. Shouting encouragement, his workmates pushed him back into the fight.

White didn't need pushing. Face bleeding and in a flaming temper, he hurled himself at his rival. Before Standing could fall back, White had delivered several blows to the body and a right to the mouth. For a moment, Standing staggered and fell to his knees. When he got up he was bleeding from the mouth. With a crushing blow to the head, White felled him again. 'Give it 'im 'Arry!' the crowd howled.

By now both men had puffed-up faces, bloody chests and red knuckles. White's lightning attack had made Standing wary. For some time he was content to trade blows, hitting and getting out of the way before White could react. The thud of ringing punches, the harsh gasping for breath and the shuffling of feet went on. It was drowned only by the cheering.

Suddenly, Standing hit White on the side of the head. Before White could recover, he hit him again across the eyes. Hands to his head, White reeled to one side and fell. Standing stood over him ready to punch him into submission. There was a tremendous commotion among the crowd. White's supporters yelled at him to get up.

It would have been better for everybody if White had stayed

where he was, but he didn't. Like a drunk, he staggered to his feet, only to be knocked down again. Fighting with a cold anger, Standing hit him when and how he pleased. No sooner did White get up than he was battered to his knees again. His eyes were swollen and his nose bled. He no longer knew what he was doing. Staggering about like an idiot, he fell across Standing in an effort to protect himself. I wanted to run in and stop the fight, but I knew better than to try; the crowd wouldn't have stood for it.

With appalling monotony, White staggered to his feet, tangled with his opponent, only to be knocked down again. Had the crowd not intervened eventually, Standing would have had to kill White to stop him getting up. I thought this bare-fisted way of punching somebody to a jelly was horrible, and I never went to a fight again.

Some months later, I came across Standing having a row with a coal-cart driver who had been beating his horse. 'Yer should be 'ung fer such savagery,' Standing yelled at the driver. I came away thinking about what he'd done to White.

Fortunately, fights usually ended with a few bruises and goodwill between the contestants. Like the metal they poured, moulders' tempers flared up, burned out and died.

After a year, I got a rise of five shillings and was given a steady job as a 'helper' to a moulder. Whether I liked it or not, I was now a 'sand rat'. I was assigned to George Edwards, a good man and a good moulder with years of experience behind him. Edwards was a tall, well-built fellow with a furrowed face, grey hair, shrewd brown eyes and freckled hands. Under his overalls he always wore a plaid shirt. I began to learn about moulds and the priestly cast of moulders. I watched him as he constructed gates and rises to feed the moulds and keep the metal flowing. He taught me about the chemistry of metal – 'mysteries of the craft' he called it. I learned about carbon, silicon, phosphorus, sulphur and manganese. In time I could talk about cheeks, joints, copes, combs, pigs, sows and drags with the rest of them. Edwards taught me not to take short cuts. 'Don't be 'asty; bide yer time,' he'd say. 'Let 'er go steady loike.' I once told him about my political ambitions. 'Aha, um,' he said. I'm sure he looked upon my talk of socialism as blasphemy.

I became one of a four-man team: George Edwards, Reg Leary and Syd Bates, the other helper who was about my own age. Mr Leary was younger, and slim compared with Mr Edwards. He had fair hair, delicate features and unusually blue eyes. He had a habit of staring at you for ages without blinking. He was the only one among us with tufts of hair on his cheekbones. Unlike Edwards, who rarely spoke his mind, Leary was bluff to the point of aggression. 'What the hell are you standing there for? Put the bloody rods down and bugger off.' I learned not to inflame his hot temper.

Syd Bates was a bully who liked to brag about his sexual conquests. Every Monday morning he'd narrate the lascivious details of his weekend exploits. I couldn't help but doubt that this slack-mouthed fellow with a bad complexion could have been such a Romeo.

One day when we were alone his bullying became too much. 'You can go to hell,' I said. He took a swipe at me. Fending him off, I tripped and landed my fist in his face; I felt the crunch of bone. With his nose bleeding, he staggered and fell. For a moment or two he lay there motionless, his eyes rolling grotesquely. Anxiously, I helped him to his feet. Mr Leary returned at that moment. 'Caw, you don't 'arf look seedy, Syd,' he said. He then took the two of us by our hair, banged our heads together and left us. After that Bates and I got on well.

As helpers, Syd and I started our day by removing the previous day's castings. Sometimes it was forty-eight hours before the castings cooled. We then shovelled and riddled the sand for the next pattern. With long-handled spades we spread the sand and broke it up to give it a fluffy texture. It was the moulder who pressed the pattern into the wet sand, rammed the sand around it and withdrew it prior to pouring. He worked with a shiny trowel and a tool called a rammer. His fingers told him when the sand was firm enough. Too dry, it would crumble; too wet, it would cause the metal in the mould to bubble. Only the moulder could judge its consistency; he did so by taking a handful of wet sand and squeezing it. The way Edwards pulled his face and pursed his lips while making the decision reminded me of a tea taster. Sand, I discovered, could be the queerest thing.

The molten metal – spluttering and blazing – was then poured into the mould. Once you started pouring you couldn't stop until the job was done; you couldn't pour according to whim; nor could you take your mind off the process – not even to admire the rainbow colours produced by the fiery metal. Casting was an exact art demanding split-second timing and control – especially when pouring with the help of an overhead crane. It was the moulder who decided when the glowing cascade – too dazzling to look at – would be poured, and when to stop. We helpers handed him the vent rods, but it was he who decided where the gases would escape when the metal was poured.

I learned that everything in moulding must be done right the first time. Even jarring a mould or causing a draught could ruin it – as could steam, air or pockets of impurities. Every mould had a life of its own. 'Hain't it a beaut?' Mr Edwards would say. A 'beaut' had a sound, clean, smooth surface. Workers would admire a particularly good casting as if something new had appeared in the world – their faces glowing with a sense of achievement and gladness. A 'sod' was a casting that was warped or distorted; the metal was not sufficiently tensile and had cracked under strain. Some 'sods' had too many blowholes, cracks, lumps and swells to rescue them. Others might be straightened out. There was always a feeling of tension and drama in the air until a good clean casting emerged. If it did, we'd troop off to the lavatory for a smoke, and at night to the boozer for a beer.

I used to love the visits to the Crown and Anchor – there

was always lots of beer, leg-pulling and companionship. Nobody drank like foundry workers. Some of them drank all their earnings. No matter how much we imbibed, we knew it would be sweated out of us the next day: people who work in a steambath don't have any trouble with alcohol. I suppose the prospect of a beer or two at the end of the day helped us to put up with the gruelling work.

Pouring metal was always dangerous, hence the face-guards, the leg-pads, the heavy gloves and the heavy boots. Workers were always tripping over things, scorching their clothing, cooking their feet, or banging themselves on moulds and machinery. Freshly poured metal might look like crusty bread straight out of the oven, but it could roast, scald, blind or cripple in seconds. I never stepped over the golden stream as the moulders did. Put your foot in there and it was gone. It took a 'sand rat' to survive.

Being shut up all day in an inferno, mostly on my feet, often squatting to get relief, was hard going. I survived because I indulged in what Bobbit called 'daydreaming'. I watched what I was doing, but often my mind was elsewhere. Yet I did eventually have the satisfaction of seeing what my sweat had helped to create. Out of the chaos at Bow Bridge came an unending stream of metal products. Some were useful things like pipes and boilers; others were lace-like works of art. All were known for their quality. The work of the Bow Bridge Iron Foundry can be seen to this day on the bridges over the Thames.

———◇———

One day, Syd Bates took me to join the Transport and General Workers' Union. A trade union was the only thing my father had ever joined, so I thought I owed it to him. For somebody who had only his labour to sell, I knew I'd be better off in a union; everybody in dockland knew that.

I went to my first meeting on a Monday night. It was in a ramshackle room in a fusty old building on Bow Road. I told the secretary, who was sitting at a blanket-covered table, that I'd like to join. He shook my hand, told me his name was Albert Eastead and dusted cigarette ash off his suit. Pushing a ledger aside, he helped me to fill out a membership form. I paid my dues. He lit another cigarette, shook my hand again and called me 'brother'. I knew that the first principle of trade unionism was that all men are 'brothers'. 'Tyke a seat,' he said.

Clutching my card, I joined Syd and several others on a bench. There were about twenty of us – two of us from the foundry. I was the youngest.

Mr Eastead called the meeting to order and introduced me. There was a murmur of approval; I felt the searching eyes.

The meeting began and one item after another fell to the secretary's chant: 'Do I have a motion?' 'Proposed.' 'Seconded.' 'So moved.' 'Questions?' 'All those in favour say "aye".' 'To the contrary?' 'Motion carried.' When the members couldn't make up their minds, he would urge, 'Git on, can't stiy 'ere all night.' It bothered me that the 'brothers' were so wishy-washy.

We then heard reports. A bearded man spoke of a meeting he'd been to on unemployment. 'For the fust toim in six years, the number of unemployed is dahn.'

This was greeted by jeering and clapping. 'The figures are cooked. Go and look at the unemployed on the streets!'

Another member had been at a meeting to consider the growing threat of the Black Shirts. 'Oswald Mosley is using the same tactics as fascists in Germany and Italy. 'E wants to persecute Jews and communists, like they do there.'

'What did the meeting decide?'

'Nuffink.'

There was more laughter and clapping. The speaker shuffled uncomfortably and sat down.

A young man sitting next to me jumped up and yelled, 'While you're laughing, the bastard Black Shirts are opening a branch office two streets from here. The way to stop 'm is to go out now and bash 'm. That would teach 'm.' There was a passionate wildness about him that was exhilarating. He was so intense as to be intoxicating.

Everybody sat up.

'Who's coming with me?'

Syd Bates signalled with his eyes for me to keep my head down. An embarrassed silence filled the room, the secretary hid himself behind a veil of smoke. There were no takers.

The youth looked around, 'I'd chuck the lot of you, that I would,' and stormed out.

The discussion continued as if he had never spoken. I didn't know what to think. George Lansbury had said that fascism was being exaggerated. I'd met fascists in Lancashire but they'd been looked upon as a mad fringe. I didn't want to go out and bash fascists, but I did feel that something should be done.

I walked back to my lodgings that night asking myself how on earth Labour could win an election when the workers didn't know what they wanted and couldn't agree. Was socialism going to finish up with nothing but words?

At work the next day I told Syd that the meeting had struck me as dead. He laughed. 'The trouble with you, Woody, is that you think London has been waiting for you to get 'ere. We're in the union because it helps us to get better pay. We're not in it to get a broken 'ead and change things. Forget about a world socialist commonwealth in which all men are "brothers". The communists and the chapel-socialists will never agree among themselves.'

———◇———

A week later, after my next branch meeting, I talked with the young man who had proposed bashing the fascists. Syd had already told me that he was a communist. He was small and angular with a round, clean-shaven face and a pair of thick-lensed spectacles. He earned his living from a back-breaking job in the rag trade. His name was Peter Levine.

'You didn't get very far last week.'

'I despair of this crowd. They won't do a damned thing.'

I waited for him to go on.

'Anyway, what are you doing here? You're not a Cockney.'

'I'm from the North.'

'Were you in the Labour Party up there?'

'Yes, I did a lot of speaking. I hope one day to represent the party in Parliament.'

'You've got a nerve. You won't get to Parliament from here. Cockneys don't take to outsiders. They're scared you might be another northerner going to do them harm like Ramsay MacDonald. The party will never get on as long as they fight among themselves. Everybody should join together in a popular front. It's our only hope.' When Peter said 'popular front', his eyes flashed.

It didn't take me long to learn that the trade union 'brothers' thought him an extremist who deserved watching. Afraid of communist subversion, the official trade-union line was to keep the communists out.

Chapter IV

Back to School

One day in a crowded underground train I found myself staring at a notice from the London County Council. Stuck between advertisements for Brylcreem and Watney's beer, it looked out of place.

> Do you want a better job?
> Education is the key.
> Join a London County Council night school.
> There is one in your area.

As the train rattled on, the light alternating between the tunnels and the bright sunshine, I wondered if this education business wasn't worth a try. A little of it could hardly do any harm. I didn't want to remain a labourer in the foundry for the rest of my life. Much as I liked Bobbit, I was stuck with a job without any prospects. Grandma Bridget had said that 'larnin'' was the key to all doors. 'The one with the most knowledge has the longest reach,' she used to say. It was ironic coming from her: with all her 'larnin'', she'd finished up in the workhouse.

By the time I reached my destination, my mind was made up. I'd take a look at this night-school business. There was a school only minutes away from the foundry in Denbigh Road, off Bow Road. I'd seen the students coming and going with their books.

The next night after work, I waited my turn before the supervisor of admissions. He gave the impression of having had a long day. I told him I'd seen the poster in the train. Stubbing out his cigarette among a pile of dead stubs, he nodded in a way that told me he had heard it all before.

'What schooling have you had?'

'Elementary.'

He explained what the school offered for people like me. I became so enthusiastic that I wanted to register for everything.

'First do the three R's,' he advised.

He then turned to money matters. He asked about my earnings, about my family and about myself. Retiring into a cloud of smoke, he played with some figures on his blotter. 'Nobody's going to ask you for anything. Books too will be supplied.'

I enrolled there and then; I filled in the forms and was given vouchers for books.

Back on the street, I wondered what on earth I'd got myself into.

<hr />

Three nights later I attended my first English class. Apprehensive, I sat at the back. The teacher was Miss Hesselthwaite, an elf-like, bespectacled spinster. She wore a tightly buttoned grey jacket and skirt, and laced-up black boots.

I fell under Miss Hesselthwaite's spell from the start. She taught me the magic of words. 'The active tense is the stuff of good writing,' she would say in a gentle voice. 'Write clearly, the right words in the right order. Don't use unnecessary words: not "it is my understanding", but "I understand"; avoid vague language like "could, should, might, maybe" – they weaken your message.'

Several nights later, she criticised my first one-page essay as 'unbecoming'. She rewrote it on the blackboard, killing most of its adverbs and adjectives on the way. She corrected me in such a gentle way that I wanted to go to any length to please her. It became a matter of honour.

Henceforth most of my nights were given to 'larnin''. I used to get away from the foundry at about five-thirty, race to The Cut, wash my hands and face, get a quick meal, and go to night school still wearing my overalls.

Miss Hesselthwaite taught me how to use words, and Mr Charlie Duke taught me to enjoy literature. He was a small tweed-wrapped, pipe-smoking fellow. Wet or fine, he would make the journey through the dark streets on foot with his books in a knapsack on his back. Mr Duke regarded the make-belief of fiction as one of the greatest consolations known to the human race. He only recommended classics. To be approved by him a writer had to be long since dead. He knew the works of Sir Walter Scott, Henry Fielding and Charles Dickens by heart. He introduced me to Honoré de Balzac. 'There's a man who makes his characters live,' he said. I liked Balzac; he described people I knew. Mr Duke read so movingly that he carried us off to a different world. Even a whisper from him could fill the room, he could have been playing a flute. It was the sound that moved my heart.

The books he recommended fired my imagination and quickened my pulse. I read them in all sorts of places and at all sorts of times; completely absorbed, I would become involved in the unfolding of the story. I wasn't the only one in the world who had had to struggle and who was down on his luck. I couldn't work out the plots fast enough, and took everything I read as gospel truth. Not that I enjoyed everything. Jonathan Swift's *Tale of a Tub* I thought dull and said so. 'Greater men than you have thought differently,' Mr Duke reproached me. In his light a classic was inviolable.

The third R that the supervisor of admissions had wished on me was arithmetic, taught by Mr Westerman. He was a good teacher and I'm sure knew what he was doing – numbers poured out of him – but his subject never stirred me. I knew all the basics from having been a newspaper boy with George Latham, the newsagent on Revidge Road, Blackburn. He used to say, 'We're businessmen, Billy.' Logarithms, calculus and algebra I thought an abomination. I shall never know why writing and reading possessed me, while arithmetic left me wooden. Anyway, I did my best and did well in exams. But as soon as I could, I dropped arithmetic and gave more time to writing and reading.

I was seventeen when I went back to school. It was the autumn of 1934. At the foundry they thought I was tackling something of little value; the Tinkers thought I'd gone 'batchy'.

Learning aroused my curiosity and imagination. There was wonder in it and adventure – an entirely new way of looking at life had opened up. My desire to learn became so great that I could hardly wait for the next class. I progressed by leaps and bounds because I was doing what I wanted to do. My mind was unworked, fertile soil.

Not everything was plain sailing. I had to do my homework under a poor light in Ben's room with Mrs Wheeler's radio blaring through the wall. I'd been tossed off the corner of the living-room table because I was in the way of the three women. They thought it odd for a healthy young man to be bothering with books. Mr Tinker didn't interfere, he invariably disappeared behind his newspaper and stayed there without saying a word.

At night school I met and was befriended by Alex Hargreaves, a small intense fellow, about my own age. He had brown eyes, slicked hair and the beginnings of a moustache. He was studying finance and accountancy and was contemptuous of my studying literature. We used to share breaks between classes and make our way home together. I thought him very clever.

—◇—

One night when I was returning some books to Miss Hesselthwaite in her back-street lodgings where I often visited her, she suddenly put her knitting down and looked at me as if she was seeing me for the first time. 'You did so well in your exams, have you ever thought of going to a university?'

'Goodness, gracious, no.'

'Well, I hope you will.'

The idea of becoming a scholar could not have been farther from my thoughts. It made me feel slightly giddy. Other than Grandma Bridget all my forebears had been labourers. A mental abyss separated the likes of us from universities. All I knew about Oxford and Cambridge was that they rowed against each other on the Thames.

At the end of the year Dr Cord, the principal, sent for me. Like my sister Brenda before me, I had shone in examinations. He asked me about my subjects, my family, and what I hoped to do with my life. My telling him that I hoped to become a Member of Parliament caught him off balance. 'I'd like to continue my education,' I confessed. When compared to working in a foundry, the idea attracted me; learning had opened up an entirely new world for me.

I went back to my classroom feeling that the principal was a bit flummoxed by the kind of fish he'd caught, but was definitely out to help me.

Prompted by Miss Hesselthwaite, I began to attend a Workers' Educational Association (WEA) evening class in world affairs, held once a week by Reg Sorenson, MP for West Leyton. We met in a little room over a shop in Westminster. He used to come to us straight from Parliament on foot, lay his briefcase aside, take off his hat and overcoat, and plunge in.

It was an unforgettable experience to listen to such an

articulate, stimulating teacher. His jumping from country to country widened my horizons immensely. He described the circumstances in which Lenin, Mussolini and Hitler had come to power; he told us about the Japanese occupation of Manchuria. I had no idea where Manchuria was, but invading it seemed the wrong thing to do. He also spoke of the turmoil in India, Ireland and Palestine. He was convinced that a war between the democracies and the dictatorships was inevitable.

Another night he dealt with the socialist writers Sidney and Beatrice Webb, who had been to Russia and had described conditions there in their book *Soviet Communism, a New Civilization?* I had bought a copy of the book very cheaply at my last trade union meeting. For many of us, the Russian example had become the only hope for the working class. While the structure of capitalist society was breaking down, Russia was forging ahead in trade and industry. At least, that is what they led us to believe.

The Webbs were food and drink to young socialists who couldn't swallow Marx. We were captivated by their simple answers. They painted a glowing picture of the society we ought to build. From them we got our belief in the nation-alisation of industry as a panacea. Their *History of Trade Unionism*, which was also distributed through the unions, defined the object and purpose of trade unions as compris-ing 'nothing less than a reconstruction of society by the elim-ination from the nation's industries and services of the Capitalist Profitmaker'. The book confirmed what many of us already believed: that private enterprise was a predatory animal that had to be tamed.

I was so worked up about the Russian experiment that I took my turn shouting the Webbs' ideas from a soapbox in front of Poplar town hall.

<hr />

One Sunday morning I woke up to find that there was no Ben in bed. As far as any of us could reckon, he'd gone off on Saturday night for his beer and eels and had vanished. We started a search for him. My fear was that he'd fallen into the canal.

The truth was almost as bad. When I got home from work on the Monday evening, the coppers were all over the house. All the Tinker family looked grey. Before I could get my dinner, I was bundled into Ben's room where I was questioned by a plain-clothes detective. He wanted to know who I was, where I'd come from, where I worked and what my relations were with Ben. He ended up asking me more questions about myself than about him.

'What has this got to do with Ben Tinker?' I eventually asked.

'Ben Tinker is being held in Pentonville on criminal charges.'

'What charges?'

'Of being in possession of a deadly weapon – a revolver – and of discharging the same at the police with intent to kill. A most serious charge, you will agree.' His eyes searched my face.

I was speechless. Ben . . . firing at the police! There was something wrong.

'That's not the Ben I know. He wouldn't know one end of a revolver from the other. His head doesn't work that way.'

'There was a robbery in Stratford on Saturday night. We arrived to find the accused standing outside the premises hold-ing a gun. He'd been drinking. Shortly before we arrested him, a shot was fired. After he'd sobered up he confessed to everything. "That's me," he said, as I read out the charges. Full of regret, he is. Wonder he wasn't killed. It should be a lesson to you.'

'I still don't think it could have been Ben. It's beyond him to plan a break-in.'

'The evidence against him is overwhelming.'

The detective wrote everything down in a book. He said he would return the next evening for me to sign a statement. He also said that I might be called as a witness for the defence.

His parting shot was, 'I don't suppose you were with Ben Tinker that night, by any chance, were you?' For a moment I felt a chill. There was no telling what Ben had said.

'No,' I answered.

The copper smiled stiffly and left.

A couple of nights later, after I had signed the statement, we learned that the minimum sentence Ben would get would be five years. The Tinkers took it badly. Mr Tinker asked me if I'd go with him to see Ben to cheer him up.

Come Saturday, Mr Tinker and I visited Ben. We had a long wait in a dreary room with peeling walls. We sat on a bench facing people who looked lost and who kept a still tongue about their troubles.

Eventually, with a warder listening, we spoke to Ben through a wire screen. He was glad to see us. He looked well, and was scrubbed clean. I think he was enjoying his turn of fate: it was a rest from stone-breaking. I thought for a moment he was about to say, 'Can't beat it 'ere,' but he didn't. He asked for nothing and made no complaints. We'd been told not to discuss the circumstances of his arrest. I'm sure he didn't realise that he was in deep trouble. We said we would return.

About a month later, on condition that he underwent psychiatric treatment, Ben was discharged. His case didn't go to trial. He would have agreed to everything had they tried him. I suppose the authorities eventually got the measure of the man: given his mental condition, he couldn't have fired and hit a building, let alone a police officer.

Ben went back to his stone-breaking, and his Saturday-night feasts of beer and jellied eels.

Chapter V

From Stratford to Bow

It was the grand finale of a dreadful day at the foundry. I'd started back to the Tinkers late; the traffic was awful; to cap it all, a cloudburst almost washed me away. I eventually reached Ben's room looking like a drowned rat. Nothing else can happen now, I thought, as I parked my bicycle in the corner.

Fate decided otherwise. I bumped into the aspidistra stand, sending Mrs Tinker's hidden jug of beer crashing to the floor. Horrified, I watched a brown tide flow across the oilcloth. I forgot that I was wet through.

Mr Tinker put his head round the door. 'Yours?' he demanded, pointing at the beer, his one eye flashing.

'No, no,' I faltered, trying to mop up.

I heard him ask Mrs Tinker the same question. Their voices rose one above the other. Suddenly, something hit the wall. Battle was on. It was one of the rowdiest fights I'd heard.

The next morning Mrs Tinker burst into my room before I had time to get up. She had a black eye.

'Yer can sling yer 'ook,' she yelled, slamming the door.

Where could I sling my hook to? I worried.

I was still worrying when I went to night school that evening. Appalled at the prospect of my being thrown into the street, Alex Hargreaves, my night-school friend, promised to speak to his stepmother. He was as good as his word. The next evening he took me to his home in Addington Road, Bow.

I was impressed by the great stone houses, with their wrought-iron railings and large front steps. Closer up, they didn't look so good: stonework was cracked, windows were stuffed with rags and paper, chimney pots were broken. The scraps of garden at the front were covered with weeds and littered with junk. Dogs and cats wandered about.

To get into Alex's house we had to squeeze past a great oak hallstand. 'Must have cost a mint,' I said, admiring the intricate carving, the mirrors and the china figurines.

'Got it for a song in Petticoat Lane. Look at the worm-holes. It's been stuck here for years; can't get it any farther. How's this for more junk?' He threw open two glass-panelled doors. Sagging chairs and couches, lace-covered tables, worn rugs, knick-knacks, and large, chipped Persian vases filled the rooms. 'These are the "best rooms". Used only at Christmas,' he said, shutting the doors.

At the end of the hall an impressive staircase with a carved handrail wound its way upward. We went downstairs, our fingers trailing over the smooth wallpaper, grey with people's hands. Generations of masters, mistresses and servants had worn the staircase hollow. Voices and laughter reached us from below.

In the living room, Mrs Hargreaves greeted me. I recognised her; I'd seen her stocky figure at Bow Labour meetings. Her cheeks were as pink as a girl's and her grey hair was pulled back in a bun. Alex's stepfather sat by the fire. One glance at him told me that he was very sick. 'I'm the fellow whose train is going out,' he said, shaking my hand. Everybody talked to him as if he would be returning to his job as a street sweeper the next day.

I was introduced to Alex's stepbrothers Chris, Denny and Bernie, and his stepsister Carol: they had all been adopted by Ma Hargreaves when they were infants. They were now in their twenties and looked alike. Finally I met the two lodgers, Milton and Dick.

Dominating the room was a picture of a smiling, close-cropped soldier. This was Nick, the Hargreaves' only son, who had perished at Ypres in Flanders in 1916. He looked so full of fun that I expected him to wink at me. Woven into the fabric upon which the picture was mounted were the words: 'The War To End All Wars'.

A large cupboard ran down the length of the outside wall. Above it was one small window that looked up to the weed-filled garden. It was open a crack to allow flies to escape. Someone tapped on the glass and grimaced through the grating.

Avoiding any preliminaries, the Hargreaves offered me a whole bed and full board for the same money I was paying at the Tinkers. 'It won't profit us, but it might 'elp yer,' Mrs Hargreaves said. I couldn't believe my luck.

Tired of sleeping with Ben's feet in my face, I jumped at the offer. I went straight back to The Cut, said goodbye to Mr Tinker, Sarah and Ben, grabbed my few belongings and fled.

'Didn't like the looks of yer from the start,' Mrs Tinker flung after me as I went through the door. Her conduct severely tested my belief that there is a residing virtue in the working class.

On my return to Bow, I was taken in tow by Emily Tracy, the Hargreaves' daughter, a tall, thin woman in her thirties, who showed me round the house. I was to share a bedroom with Milton, Dick and Alex on the top floor, the old servants' quarters, which had been divided into three rooms, all painted a faded green. I stowed my belongings under my bed, which stood in a corner against the sealed window. A black stocking filled with sand on the window ledge kept out the cold. A bed to myself with clean sheets – I'd come up in the world.

Chris, Bernie and Denny occupied the middle bedroom. It had a skylight. Their door stood ajar to let in air. Carol slept in a windowless converted storeroom at the end of the corridor. It was suffocating in there and smelled of stale cheese.

As we walked down Emily pointed out the family bedrooms, which were above the two unused 'best rooms'. There were two indoor toilets.

Halfway down the stairs I was introduced to Emily's husband Clem Tracy, who had just rushed in past the hallstand. He was small in stature, had bright eyes, and a face that looked like a polished apple. After shaking hands with me, he dashed upstairs.

'Clem is forever in a rush,' Emily sighed. 'He works in the laboratory at Poplar general hospital.' I learned later that he was good at giving injections and would sometimes help his father-in-law out if he got into trouble over the weekend.

I soon settled down to the Hargreaves' routine. After a hurried breakfast of tea with tinned milk, two rashers of bacon, one pale fried egg, tomatoes and as much bread and margarine as we could eat, all of us, except Mr and Mrs Hargreaves and Emily, rushed off to work. We snatched a wrapped bread and cheese sandwich off the hallstand as we went through the door. Cut and prepared by Emily the night before, the sandwiches were stiff and stale by lunchtime.

Except on Saturday and Sunday, the family reassembled at night for the evening meal. We ate what was put in front of us or we went hungry, but the food was so much better than at Mrs Tinker's that I never complained. Dinner done, some would go out for the night, the rest played shove-ha'penny or Wilkie Bards (cards). Most nights Alex and I would do our homework in 'the best room at the back'. Before going to bed, we held post-mortems of the day's dog and horse races. This is where Mr Hargreaves came into his own, gasping out the name and odds of the horse we should follow. We started the day with 'What 'orse are you on?' Emily organised the bets with a bookie who had a pitch on the pavement in Bow Road. I never heard of a copper intervening. Later on, in 1938,

Pa Hargreaves won me a princely sum on an American horse called Battleship.

No one in their right mind ever missed the Hargreaves' Sunday dinner, which was eaten at noon when the men came back from the 'rub-a-dub' (pub). There never was any alcohol in the house: 'The scourge of the poor,' old man Hargreaves used to say with a sigh, though I noticed his moral rhetoric stopped when whisky was about. The meal was a feast of roast beef, several vegetables and, strangely enough, lots of Yorkshire pudding. On Sundays we all sat down clean and washed, the week's grime behind us. Pa Hargreaves always ate alone by the fire. When he'd finished his soup he'd fish in his pocket for his false teeth to eat the beef course. The meal always ended with rice pudding and a cup of tea.

Sunday dinner was much more important than Sunday church, which only Dick attended. Dick was the one who really believed in God. He belonged to a queer sect over in Poplar who thought that all religions were equal. The rest of us were either unrepentant pagans, or God-fearing Christians who didn't go to church. Most of us were comfortable in our disbelief – so comfortable that we never discussed it. Dick's 'You don't ask the question that matters: what is the purpose of life?' didn't interest us.

The Hargreaves household was a happy one. We knew we were happy, which is half the battle. Not that life was all laughter. Occasionally there'd be a crackling of lightning and a crash of thunder. One moment there'd be peace, the next there'd be a roaring fight going on, with everybody leaping to their feet and leaning across the table shouting. With Pa Hargreaves calling, "Arf a mo. 'Arf a mo,' and the dog barking, and Ma Hargreaves yelling, 'What kind of socialists are you?' the battle would rage on.

But, with the exception of Alex, whose nature was unforgiving, verbal blows were soon forgotten. Most of us had come from worse conditions and were glad to have found food, shelter and companionship. We had somewhere to eat and sleep. It was enough for me that I didn't need to go on the dole or into the street to beg. Compared with the Tinkers, life at the Hargreaves' was very good.

Mrs Hargreaves had dedicated her life to helping the poor. It was her sense of commitment that gave her the energy to work endless hours, day after day, as a member of the town council. I was surprised by the activities she could squeeze into a single day. The Juvenile Court and the Public Assistance Committee took most of her time. She also worked with local orphanages and shelters for women. Her idea of Utopia was England with the worst abuses against the poor left out. 'Socialism,' she'd say, 'means no more wars, no more want, no more wickedness.' Homeless children and the condition of the old saddened her most. What she couldn't understand was why a supposedly all-merciful God didn't do something about it. 'Either 'e don't exist, or 'e don't care,' she concluded.

Pacifism was her strongest cause. I don't think she'd ever recovered from losing her son Nick. The tenderness and affection with which she mentioned his name told me that she had lost her greatest love. ''E went to France believing that 'e was doin' the right thing. 'E came 'ome on leave, disgusted. 'E said, "The war is the biggest sodding lie, Ma. There can't be a God." I knew when 'e left that 'e wouldn't come back, and 'e didn't.'

Emily looked after everything and everybody in the house. She even made my bed. She was rarely still except during a game of cards at night. Her brother's death, her father's suffering and her childlessness all weighed heavily upon her – she had a gaunt appearance, which her cropped hair made worse. Gone were the days when she and Clem had danced in the Palais de Dance in Mile End Road. We used to say that Emily was stronger than any man – she had to be.

Fortunately she could always rely upon Clem. He was so able that we always said, 'Leave it to Clem.' He made the decisions for the household and saw them through. He never seemed to relax, even when playing cards, he'd get up and walk about. He would rush home at five, wash, eat and if the weather was fine, potter in the back garden until the light failed. He never looked up when he was out there, and he didn't welcome visitors. His crops of vegetables and flowers were prodigious. Most of them he sold to the hospital.

It took longer for me to become familiar with the four siblings: Chris, Carol, Bernie and Denny. They were small, wiry creatures, with eyes set too far apart. At first I couldn't tell one from the other. Chris, with his protruding Adam's apple, was the oldest. Everybody liked him because he was good-natured and kind. He worked with Clem at the hospital and was the tail on Clem's kite.

Chris's brother Bernie was a combination of rascality and goodness. He was a porter at the hospital and turned everything that happened there into a farce. They tolerated him and his ever-rasping cough because they knew – as I didn't – that he was dying of tuberculosis. His emaciated face and flushed complexion should have alerted me to that. Later, Emily confided to me that Bernie had been married, but that his wife had taken off with a gypsy pedlar. Perhaps Bernie's clowning was meant to conceal his sorrow and his need for love.

The younger brother Denny puzzled us all. He kept to himself. Strangely enough, he was the only one who had a regular 'Judy' (girlfriend).

Carol was brittle and had no time for the lodgers – Milton, Dick and me.

Thanks to Ma Hargreaves' political influence, and the victory of Labour in the local elections, Clem and all five adopted children had jobs in local government. Nobody threw a fit of conscience about it.

———◁◦▷———

During the week we were in bed by ten-thirty. Ma Hargreaves, Clem and Emily were the last to retire, bringing Pa Hargreaves with them. Milton, Dick, Alex and I usually ended the day yarning and smoking upstairs. There was always something to laugh about before going to sleep. The football rivalry of Tottenham, West Ham and the Arsenal was our standby. Because of the shortage of space, we stuffed our clothing between the bed and the wall. Occasionally, garments slipped on to the floor and were dragged around the house by Emily's dog.

Sometimes before going to sleep, I would sit up in bed and stare at the lighted windows below. I used to wonder what was going on under all those glistening roofs. With a mist, the scene could be magical. Occasionally, a storm crashed down – flashes of lightning lit up the sky; gale-strength winds rushed past the house shaking it fiercely.

Dick's bed was next to mine. He was a tall, powerfully built, fair-haired youth with a face that could have been carved out of stone. Scars ran down his back. His right arm was tattooed with a snake. He had the largest hands, which he was forever opening and closing to make a fist. Energy came off him in sparks; everything about him was wild and passionate. His piercing blue eyes could flash with anger. We all feared his temper. 'I wouldn't start anything wiv 'im, if I was you,' cautioned Emily. Sometimes I'd see his long knife lying on his bed.

In his late teens Dick had arrived at the London docks from Pitcairn Island. His only possession was a locked tin box that he kept under his bed. I didn't know that Pitcairn existed until I met him. In a strange English he would some-times talk to us at night about his birthplace: about the wind, the cliffs and the crashing surf, and about sunsets more beau-tiful than any of us had ever seen. I think it helped him to cover up his self-consciousness and his innate nervousness.

'London's a dark hole,' he once said, 'full of mouldy mist. Everything is swallowed up by buildings, smoke and fog. Everybody's a stranger.' Sometimes I thought of him as a great fish that had become stranded on the mud banks of the Thames. The astonishing thing was that he couldn't swim.

He told us there were no beaches at Pitcairn, only cliffs hovering above a heaving, pitiless sea.

One night I asked him why he had left.

'Simply happened. I wanted to know what was beyond.'

Because of him, we knew all about the mutiny on the *Bounty*, and Captain William Bligh long before we saw the film. Fletcher Christian was one of his forebears.

Dick intended to make his fortune, sail back to Pitcairn, find a wife and raise a family there. How his dream could be fulfilled on a starvation wage as a knock-about on the docks was beyond us. Yet it almost came true.

Every Tuesday night several of us would go over to the Hackney Wick Greyhound Racing Track and place a bet or two on the dogs. The place was always packed. Coarse-looking men stood about handling thick bundles of pound notes. You wondered where all the money came from. It was enough to turn your head.

I had so much on in those days – night school, union meetings and homework – that I rarely had time for the races. When I did go I loved everything about it: the vast arena, the banks of faces, the restless crowd, the pageantry and the races themselves.

Noses pressed against the wire, the dogs scrabbled and whined until the hare flashed by and the gate of the traps flew up. There followed thirty seconds of bedlam while the dogs raced round the track, leaping the hurdles, neck to neck. The yelling and shouting only stopped when the hare had gone to ground and one of the dogs was declared the winner.

One night Dick struck it rich. We watched in awe as he recklessly threw back into the next race every penny he had won. He dashed about like someone possessed; there was no stopping him. We brought him home that night in triumph with thousands of pounds in his pockets. When he piled his winnings on to the table, everything in the house stopped. Pa Hargreaves even stopped gasping for breath. Ma Hargreaves just stood there, hand over mouth. Only Clem, who worked for the bookies, had ever seen so much money. What comfort it gave us to run our fingers through the piles of one, five and twenty pound notes. The wonder is we didn't pinch some of them.

'Dick,' gasped Pa Hargreaves, raising his shaking hands, 'you must never go near the track again.' There were tears in his eyes. 'You can go 'ome to Pitcairn now. Your luck is in, boy; you're a free man. Find a ship and go.'

Everybody agreed, but Dick had other plans. He'd tasted blood and was not to be put off. Against our pleading, he went back the next racing night with a shoebox full of money under his arm. 'He's dotty,' Pa Hargreaves despaired.

Dick came home that night richer than ever. We couldn't believe our eyes. Like a madman, he shovelled the pile of bank notes from one end of the table to the other, shrieking. He'd had a few drinks, and his speech had become incomprehensible. His face glistened with sweat, his distended nostrils twitched with excitement. Between hiccups, he shouted that he loved us all and embraced us one after the other. He even danced with the dog. Each time he calmed down, he counted his money again, placing it in stacks. This time Pa Hargreaves said nothing. Instead, he held out his steel-rimmed spectacles and rubbed them closely. The following day Dick bought himself some coloured silk shirts and a pair of the wildest red velvet corduroy trousers. We roared with laughter when he put them on.

The next racing night, except for the Hargreaves, Emily and Milton, who opposed betting, we were all at the track. For one night I skipped night school. Even Clem joined in. If Dick could make a fortune, so could we – all we had to do was to follow him. We were too poor not to want to take advantage of his miracle.

Alas! On the third night Dick lost heavily. So did we. 'I hope you're not angry with me,' he said as we came home.

After that, he went back night after night, determined to renew his lucky streak. Three weeks later he was broke, self-tormented and self-destroyed. Shorn of money and pride, he walked out with his tin box on his shoulder and was never seen again. 'God 'elp 'im,' muttered Pa Hargreaves. We could only think that he had slipped back into the shadows of the docks from which he had come. It was odd how much we missed him. To cheer us up, Emily used to say that anybody as handsome as Dick would be sure to find a nice, rich widow. But we didn't believe her. Often in the bedroom, especially on a starlit night, we'd talk about Dick and wonder if he'd found his ship. It was curious that the only one in the house who believed in God should have been deserted by Him.

<hr />

Milton, a quiet courteous middle-aged bachelor, was as steady as Dick was wild. His steadiness was reflected in his round boyish face, wise eyes, and the perfect proportion of his brow, nose, cheeks and chin. His sleek brown hair was still unmarked by grey. He was the best-groomed among us: without fail, he shaved every day. He didn't drink, smoke or swear; he never got worked up. Heavy showers and dirty pea-soup fogs seemed to wait until he was safely indoors. Where he'd come from nobody knew. If they asked, he looked at them with a slow, watchful stare. He took no part in family rows and refused to discuss politics or religion. I think there was great kindness in him, but he didn't like Emily's cocker spaniel and he avoided women. He reined us in if the sex talk became offensive at night. He always struck us as a bit squeamish, the one way to turn his stomach was to squash a bug on the wall in front of him.

Furled umbrella in hand, Milton left the house at precisely the same time every weekday dressed like a banker. ''Ere comes a swell,' we used to say. 'He's probably just a button-hole maker,' said Clem. We never found out. With a neatly folded newspaper under his arm, Milton returned at exactly the same time every night. On approaching the front door he would take his watch out of his waistcoat pocket. 'Always-on-time-Milton' we called him. We set our watches by him.

One night in the bedroom, Alex started needling him for

being an 'old maid' and to our astonishment Milton exploded. For half an hour words poured out of him. He revealed that he had once lived a licentious life soaking up the drink. His family had cut him off. He'd lost his job and become a drifter. Half mad, he had been committed to an asylum. After a year, he emerged a different man – one who would fear alcohol for the rest of his life.

We never teased Milton again. Behind that façade of calm was an extraordinary vulnerability. For the first time we understood the meaning of the words chiselled into a piece of wood above his bed:

> With midnight always in one's heart,
> And twilight in one's cell,
> We turn the crank, we tear the rope,
> Each in his separate hell.

Later in life whenever I was close to going over the edge, it was the memory of Milton that pulled me back. I could not forget his warning: 'Don't take to drink.'

''E was lucky, 'e was,' Emily said. 'But 'e's afraid of falling back into the pit from which 'e's crawled.'

The fourth person in our bedroom was Alex. He was kind to me, but difficult to live with. He had been abandoned as an infant on a bench in Bow. Instead of being grateful to Ma Hargreaves for adopting him, Alex held it against her that he should have been cast with the poor.

They were daggers drawn over socialism. 'You and your like are a no-good rabble with too much power,' I heard him say to her one day. 'You're ruining Britain. You're handing out money to people who've already made up their minds to be helpless and destitute. All they want is to sit on their backsides.'

She was too simple and kind to handle him. ''E'll be the death of me,' she'd say.

'Couldn't whimper when we took 'im in,' the old man grieved. 'Now 'e's breakin' our 'earts.'

Clem would have thrown him out but for Emily, who forgave Alex all his faults. They'd grown up together and her affection for him was unconditional.

Highly intelligent and motivated, Alex set himself to capture what he thought was his proper place in society. Money was central to his plans and he proceeded to acquire it. At night school he studied accountancy. 'It's where the numbers are,' he'd say. 'Numbers is money.'

Alex clung to his cherished gentility. Every Saturday and Sunday morning, weather permitting, he headed for the West End, armed with a cricket bat or a tennis racket. After playing tennis or cricket with the nobs he presumably had his weekly bath there.

Milton, Dick and I used the public baths on Roman Road. Apart from the occasional bather who spat on the floor, the baths were fairly clean. They were hosed down before you stepped in. There was unlimited hot water and no restriction on time. Thanks to the Labour government, they were cheap (threepence for a bath; sixpence with soap and towel). We carried on a shouting match from cubicle to cubicle. To lie back in hot water and bawl and laugh was exhilarating.

———◇———

Carol gave us the shakes one night when she walked in with strangely shining eyes and announced that she was going to get married. She must have been wanting to tell us for days for it all came out in a rush. For a moment we were struck dumb. We'd never heard of Mike, the would-be groom. The next day Ma Hargreaves showed us a letter from a nurse telling us that Mike was in hospital dying of cancer. The young fellow was too ill to reach the altar. Carol was not put off by what anybody said. She intended to marry her bloke.

Except for Pa Hargreaves, we all went to the town hall to witness the marriage. Nobody dressed up, not even the bride. We hadn't met Mike and we didn't like what we saw. He was on his last legs: he had a sunken face, his clothing hung on him like a scarecrow and he talked as if he'd just run up a long flight of stairs. He'd given up his job as a mug-faker (photographer) months before. It bothered us that Mike didn't seem to have anybody there from his side. The tenderness Carol showed him was more like a mother's than a bride's.

The happy couple spent two days at Southend on their honeymoon, after which they took up residence in Carol's storeroom on the top floor. I thought they might have set up home in one of the 'best rooms', but they didn't. I used to wonder whether there wasn't something sinister about those rooms.

A week later Mike collapsed. Whenever he tried to get out of bed he fell over. For two months Carol excelled herself as wife, nurse and cook. She ran up and down the stairs as if they didn't exist. She gave all her time to him. What little savings she had, she spent on buying the best food, nobody could convince her that love and diet alone do not a cure make. She flew off the handle when Mum suggested that all the money she was spending wouldn't help. She never lost the stubborn will to go on.

'I can get 'im back into 'ospital,' Ma Hargreaves suggested. 'That's something I can do.'

But Carol wouldn't budge. If Mike was going to die, he was going to die in her care at home. She was so defiant that we thought it best to keep out of her way. 'Let 'er be,' said Mum, weeping.

We did what we could to cheer Mike up. Not that it was easy. It pained him to talk and his coughing fits left him breathless. His brow and dishevelled hair were always drenched with sweat. His face darkened, his eyes dimmed; he seemed all skull. Although Carol kept cleaning him up, there was always dried foam on his lips and flecks of blood on his chin. His bedside table was a mess of medicine bottles, cotton wool, slop basins and crumpled towels. As his agony grew, he became difficult to handle and much more demanding. It was easier on all of us when his mouth fell open and his voice became a feverish whisper. Eventually he became too sick for us to visit.

In time, his wheezy breathing could be heard throughout the top floor: it sounded like a cow in labour. It was astonishing that a dying person could make such a din. We had to shut our bedroom doors and put up with the fog to get a night's sleep.

Early one morning I woke and listened for the bellowing. There was none. Other than the gritty scraping of somebody's feet passing down the corridor, everything was quiet. Carol, a bride of two months, was a widow.

Mike's death taught me something about the special circumstances in which two people will come together and pledge their troth. Carol lost, but not before she had given us an example of self-sacrifice, faith, hope and charity. Mike was the only person who ever gave her life meaning.

For a couple of days Mike's coffin stood in the 'best room at the front'. Except for those of us in the house, nobody came to see him. When I tiptoed in to say goodbye, Carol was sitting by his head in silence. The room was as still as the grave. Mike lay there, his face a frozen mask. His cheek and chin bones stuck out; his ears seemed uncommonly large; his hair was flat and lifeless; his hands, folded across his front, bore little flesh.

Later, we all went out and had him buried. It was a miserable funeral in wind and rain, not July weather at all. We walked in pairs behind the black-plumed, horse-drawn hearse, Mum and Carol leading. Each blast of wind threatened to tear our umbrellas out of our grasp. Several ragged-looking pallbearers followed. Here and there a passerby nodded or raised his cap, or made the sign of the cross. Some thought we were burying old man Hargreaves. 'No,' we called, 'not 'im.'

We were met at the cemetery by a pair of gravediggers wrapped in wet sacking and a priest soaked by the slanting rain. The mound of wet earth gave off a mouldy smell. In the distance rooks sat on gravestones, watching. The bottom of the grave was full of water, its surface peppered with rain-drops. It seemed wrong to bury anybody in a puddle; and in such a polished, expensive coffin, too. The only thing right about Mike was that he had been insured.

Ignoring the wind and the pouring rain, the priest spoke of death as 'coming to us all'. He talked about the 'last trump and the resurrection and the life. Out of death comes life.'

His remarks were lost on me. All the resurrection and trump business made no sense: Mike was dead, none of us thought we'd ever see him again. Yet there had to be more to life and death than a rain-soaked cemetery.

The coffin was lowered into the water with a splash. On the lid was a bunch of anemones, which Carol had put there. We all took a lump of wet earth and threw it in. Bent double, the gravediggers did the rest. The wind shook the evergreens and wet us still more.

As I left the graveyard, I decided that death and funerals were not for me. I felt there was something awful about Mike lying in the wet earth.

After the funeral, Carol sat among us mute and expressionless. She was insensitive to what was going on, recognising no one, scarcely seeming to breathe. Sad lines etched the corners of her mouth. Everything about her – from her dress to her unkempt hair – suggested that she was about to go to pieces. It took time before Mum got her to eat properly. 'You won't do Mike any good by dying.'

It was just as well that the Hargreaves took their summer holiday a week after the funeral. It wasn't much of a holiday – three weeks in the fields of Kent picking hops – but it took them from a sad house. They'd picked hops during August and September for as long as they could remember. Lodgers and neighbours who could get away also went; Clem arrived with a hired lorry into which they all climbed.

Ma Hargreaves' brother Len, his crushed mopstick wife Sheila and their daughter Miranda, came along too. Miranda was a big-breasted, brown-eyed beauty with a mane of shining chestnut hair done up in a thick, smooth braid. It was the first time I'd seen her and I was struck by her beauty. Her red lips were full and sensual. She was wearing blue overalls and a nebbed cap with artificial daisies around it. I learned later that her real name was Daisy. She'd seen the name Miranda in a magazine and had liked it, and kept it.

Miranda's father Len was a scarlet-faced fellow and an outstanding drinker. Perhaps that's why he liked to pick hops. He was fat to the point of being interesting. Long, sickly faced Sheila, who loved to tell you her troubles, was always worrying that Len would drop dead in the house and that they would not be able to get his coffin out. I watched as they levered him aboard the lorry.

Pa Hargreaves went along too. Nobody thought it odd that they should take a rattling skeleton with them. 'If 'e 'as to die, 'e might as well die in t' fresh air,' Ma Hargreaves said. Bleary-eyed, crumpled cap on his head, he sat in the back on a collapsible chair covered with a blanket. He preferred the lorry, where he was surrounded by relatives and friends, to going by train or bus. Everybody cheered when the lorry started. I waved to them until they were out of sight.

Several weekends later I took a special bus from Poplar town hall directly to the hop fields. I arrived at night. A light smoke hung above the fields. The paraffin lamps and the campfires made it look like an army bivouacked in the bush.

Moving among the scattered huts, I found the Hargreaves family eating hot beans and pork around a rough table. Pa Hargreaves was propped up in a deck chair. They greeted me warmly and gave me a plate of food. After cleaning up, we played cards. From across the field we heard people calling and the sound of an accordion. The moon hovered among the clouds.

The next morning I went hopping. It was like entering an impenetrable jungle. The plants were entwined around wires supported by tall poles. We moved through the maze pulling down the bines and picking the silky, sticky, yellow-green hops as we went. We were paid by the bushel. Most pickers earned ten to twelve pounds each for three weeks' work –

sunup to sundown. From our wicker baskets the hops were poured into large sacks, which were carted away to the cone-shaped oasthouses where they were spread out to dry. Later they would be pressed and sent to the brewery. The picked field was like something the locusts had left behind.

The job was relatively easy, and we talked and sang as we went:

> Where have you been all day,
> Henry, my son,
> Where have you been all day,
> My beloved one?
> In the fields of nature, in the fields of nature.
> Make my bed, I've a pain in my head,
> And I want to lie down.

That night Miranda and I wandered off from the camp-fire into a hop field. It was full moon and the smell of the hops was heavy. We'd hardly sat down when Chris tapped me on the shoulder, 'Ma wants you to play Wilkie Bards with the rest,' he said darkly. Had a dragon appeared at that moment and devoured him, Miranda and I would have cheered.

I was sorry when my weekend was over and I had to take the bus back to Poplar.

The Hargreaves returned after three weeks with rosy cheeks, freckled noses and sunburned hands. The fresh air and sun had done wonders for them, especially for Pa Hargreaves. He came home full of beans.

———◦———

Several months after Mike's death, Denny was cast off by his girlfriend Bonnie, who went off and married a brawling drunkard. Denny and Bonnie had had an on-off relationship for some time and we all thought him much better off without her. But that was not how he saw it. He became extremely nervous, flaring up over trifles and finding fault with everybody. He was forever telling us that one day he'd get away from us all. Without us knowing it, he must have been fighting a dark fate.

One night Clem came rushing into the house, passed the hallstand, and went slap-bang into Denny's legs swinging in front of the glass-panelled doors of one of the 'best rooms'. Wearing his Sunday suit, Denny was hanging from a rope tied to the balustrade at the top of the attic stairs. He was quite dead when Clem cut him down. His body had been removed by the time I got home. Several heavy-coated policemen were there. It sent a chill down my back when I stumbled into the darkened house and was told the news.

Nobody ate that night. We spoke in whispers. Old man Hargreaves kept blowing out his cheeks; Ma Hargreaves sighed and dried her eyes with the corner of her dress; Chris, Bernie and Carol wept for their brother. Dry-eyed at Mike's funeral, Carol cried her eyes out for Denny. Strange people came and went. We knew Denny had had woman trouble, but it had never occurred to any of us that he would kill himself. Chris told us that the night before Denny died he had rushed into the bedroom as if he intended to say something, but had left without saying a word. He left neither note nor money.

We all had to pitch in to bury Denny, whether we liked it or not. Without insurance – suicides don't get insurance money – we could only afford the bare bones. Chris and I were in charge of the finances and we had a lot of trouble making ends meet. I don't know what we'd have done had someone not put us on to a cut-rate funeral parlour in Poplar. It was a mean little place with two flashing signs in the window: 'The Complete Inexpensive Funeral Service' flashed one. 'The Dignified Death', flashed the other. In the circumstances, the gravediggers also promised us a discount. Because it would have cost us too much to pretty him up, the coffin lid was kept on.

For a day or two Denny lay in the 'best room at the front',

candles and all. The black trestles on which the coffin rested had been included in the price.

We buried him in a corner at the end of the cemetery in unconsecrated ground. He was on his own next to the gravediggers' hut and the empty flowerpots, only a thick hawthorn hedge prevented him from slipping into the canal. It was a beautiful spring day with the sun warming the land and the sparrows chattering. A gentle breeze ruffled the trees.

A black-veiled stranger joined us at the graveside. It was Bonnie. 'We made the rope and he used it,' she sobbed to a shocked Ma Hargreaves. Carol covered her face and wept.

The preacher didn't do as well for Denny as he had done for Mike. He dwelt on the need for God's mercy and eternal rest. 'There is no such thing as death,' he ended. Well, Denny looked dead to me.

I joined Clem in his garden that evening. We sat silently on the bench together. I'd never known him to sit still for so long. He was like a pricked balloon. Although it takes a lot to surprise a Cockney, Denny's death had taken the wind out of him.

Emily always held a grudge against Denny for having hanged himself in her house: 'Right there against our front door. For Gawd's sake, why couldn't 'e 'ave 'ung 'imself at Bonnie's? 'Umiliating, that's what it is.'

———◄○►———

The memory of Denny hung about the house for a long time, saddening us all. Only gradually did we get back to our normal routine. One morning about dawn I heard the phone ring. Emily answered. 'Yes Ruth . . . no Ruth . . .' There was a muffled conversation, after which Emily dressed quickly and dashed out of the house on 'an errand'. She returned shortly afterwards with a large parcel. There was more telephoning. Close-mouthed neighbours and friends arrived during breakfast and were closeted with Emily. A little shame-faced, with bundles under their coats, they left the house as quickly as they'd arrived.

Later, one of Emily's secret packages provided me with a new suit, which was altered the same day by a Jewish tailor in the next street. From Ruth came shirts, underwear, ties, socks and Sunday shoes – all at giveaway prices, pennies instead of shillings, shillings instead of pounds. For the first time in my life I wore a silk singlet and silk underpants. I felt a different man.

Everybody was casual about the arrangement, least said, soonest mended. I raised the matter with Miranda. 'Stolen,' she said. 'Pinched at night and sold to lucky devils like us before sunup.'

'Does Ma Hargreaves know they're knocked off?'

'Don't be silly,' she tittered. 'Next thing you'll be telling me you don't want the bleedin' stuff. You get the lolly while someone else gets nicked for it. What more do you want?'

Who Ruth was and where she lived I never found out.

If Ma Hargreaves supported these shady deals, she didn't do it for money. When I came to know her better, I realised that she was a kind of Robin Hood. Her ethic was to help the poor, even if it meant stretching the rules. With a religious passion she believed that life was a wrong that had to be put right: 'It's no sin to steal, if it's not for yourself or from your own.' Her concern was suffering, not sin. 'We was poor,' she'd say, 'but we was 'onest.'

Chapter VI

Finding My Way

I used to accompany Ma Hargreaves to the meetings of the Labour Party in Bow. One night she introduced me to George Lansbury, whom I had admired for years.

"'E's a Lancashire weaver's son,' she said, "'oo thinks 'e knows 'ow to run the country.'

Lansbury greeted me as if I was someone important. I felt his great warmth. He was a tall, heavy old gentleman with a broad brow and a fine head of white hair, some of which straggled down the sides of his face. His blue-grey luminous eyes were smiling. He looked at peace with himself. His double-breasted, blue-serge suit was buttoned up. His bowler hat and his clipped white moustache conveyed a sense of being in charge.

I knew he was one of Britain's leading pacifists. In World War I he had refused to carry arms. When visiting Russia in 1920 he had disagreed with Lenin over the use of force. He opposed rearmament. The basis of his teaching was love. It is not surprising that he should have risen when he did;

poverty, anti-feminism, militarism, imperialism and colonial-
ism – all of which he fought – were rampant at the time of
his rise. War was his greatest fear. Chapel-reared, he had a
passionate religious conviction that the application of
Christian principles would save the working class and the
world. He challenged my disbelief in a Christian solution. I
was captivated by him.

Lansbury was not the only one who feared another capitalist war. One Saturday morning at the beginning of 1935,
my trade-union friend Peter Levine told me about an anti-
war film that was to be shown in a Poplar cinema. He told
me to keep the meeting to myself and to arrive without attract-
ing attention.

I wandered into the crowded cinema at the given time.
Peter was already there; we sat together. The lights went out;
the hubbub ceased. After several minutes, the film had made
its point: we were there to learn how to bring the government down in case of war. We were shown how to disrupt
communications and bring munitions factories, electricity, gas
and water works, docks and railways to a standstill. Given
the will, one could wreak havoc with wire-cutters and a span-
ner. The film also told us how to infiltrate the military to
prevent them firing on the workers. Finally, it showed how
to organise a general stay-in strike. The idea of overthrow-
ing the British government stunned me. This was 'incitement
to disaffection', for which you could go to jail.

No one at the meeting took responsibility for the film. When
it was over we dribbled out in ones and twos as unceremoniously as we had dribbled in, with an eye open for the coppers.

Sedition was heady stuff to Peter. He said the film had been
made in Moscow, from where we got all our Russian propaganda. Glossy magazines showing how good things were for
the masses in the Soviet Union had persuaded Harold Watkins
and me to volunteer to go to Russia as weavers years before.

Throughout the 1930s, the challenge of fascism in the East End grew. Against Labour's pacifism, the fascists preached the cult of the warrior; against Labour's divisions they demanded unity and absolute obedience to their leader, Oswald Mosley; in place of Labour's vacillations, they promised decision and authority. The Black Shirts made no threat to private property or capitalism. In 1931 Mosley had resigned from the Labour Party. He abandoned socialism and international brotherhood for a policy of 'Britain first'.

With their bands and flags, the fascists began to parade in the East End, where half the Jewish population of Britain lived:

> Onward Black Shirts! Form your legions,
> Keep the flag for ever high.
> For a free and greater Britain
> Stand we fast to fight or die!

The Cockney response was:

> Hitler and Mosley, what are they for?
> Thuggery, buggery, hunger and war!
> Two, three, four, five,
> We want Mosley, dead or alive.

The deteriorating economic situation and the growing flood of German Jewish refugees into Britain gave the fascists a rallying point. They claimed that Britain was being overrun by the Jews. By 1934 all grievances were being blamed on them. In Stepney, Shoreditch, Hackney, Poplar, Bow and Bethnal Green the Jews became alarmed, especially after hooligans smashed Jewish shop windows in Mile End Road. They feared that they were about to be subjected to the same brutal treatment as Jews in Germany.

'Stay away from the fascist meetings,' Ma Hargreaves warned me, 'you are only providing them with publicity.' The official trade union and Labour Party policy was to ignore them. This was asking too much of young people like Levine and me; we couldn't fight fascism by pretending it didn't exist.

Out of curiosity Peter and I, and a crowd of 15,000 others, went to the fascist rally at Olympia Hall, White City, in June 1934. Slogans about the meeting had been going up in the East End for weeks. Along with hundreds of opponents we managed to get into the hall with forged tickets. Outside thousands of shouting and booing anti-fascist demonstrators fought with foot- and mounted-police. As we entered the brightly lit hall, I looked back on the surging crowd with its banners and flags. Snatches of the Internationale and the Red Flag could be heard. The air was full of passion and uproar.

Inside the hall, columns of black-shirted men and women stood guard. One felt the suspense and the air of expectancy.

We had been there about twenty minutes when there was a general stir. Orders rang out; the spotlights were swung to the entrance, where flag-waving supporters were greeting Oswald Mosley. He looked insolent and self-assured. His dress reminded me of the Italian fascists and German Nazis I had seen in newsreels. He made his way to the platform, which was ringed by Union Jacks and fascist flags. I had to concede that he was one of the most striking figures I had seen on any platform.

He had hardly begun when the loudspeaker wires were cut. The cry 'Down with Mosley!' was taken up in different parts of the hall. The searchlights swung to the fights between demonstrators and stewards. Some people made for the doors. Until the last protester was thrown out the atmosphere was chaotic.

The wires repaired, Mosley began again. Striding up and down, he called for a renewal of British life. It was a Hitler-like performance: the angry glances, the contemptuous stare, the pointing, stabbing finger. He'd spoken for about ten minutes when another uproar broke out. The speaker stood silent while the second batch of protesters was ejected. On and off, the disturbances continued for the best part of two hours.

Suddenly Peter jumped up and began howling at Mosley. Before I could pull him down he was seized, punched, kicked and carried out. I picked up his spectacles off the floor. When I reached him in the corridor, he was still fighting and getting the worst of it. Without his glasses he could hardly see. As I forced my way to his side, I was punched for good measure. Peter had come for a fight; I hadn't, and I resented being knocked about.

I got Peter to a First Aid post to have his cuts and bruises treated. His face was a mess for weeks. He could thank his lucky stars it was not worse. The papers said that truncheons, knuckle-dusters, razors and iron bars had been used. With bruises to show for it, I vowed never to sit next to him at a fascist meeting again. Miranda thought me out of my mind to have gone at all.

In September 1934 I attended another fascist rally in Hyde Park with Harold Watkins, with whom I was always in touch. This was one of the few times we had been able to get together. We never saw Mosley. The police kept the fascists and anti-fascists well apart.

It was wonderful to be with Harold again. He was working in a timber yard at Southall. I expected him to be frustrated with all the setbacks he'd had since coming to London, but he was his old bright self – convinced that everything would work out in time. We were both going to night school now and exchanged news. One way or another we were going to get an education.

Peter Levine was my first Jewish friend. He guided me through the maze of East End politics. He showed me how Jews were active throughout the east London trade-union movement and the Labour Party. 'Action is our life,' he said.

I had never lived among Jews before. I sensed a current of

envy and resentment of them among the Cockneys. Because the Jews dressed differently, sometimes spoke a different tongue, and kept themselves to themselves, the Gentiles thought of them as foreigners in a way that was not true of a migrant such as myself. To the Cockneys they were Yids or Jew boys. We were Goys. As long as one side did not try to lord it over the other, Goy and Yid got on well together. Clem Tracy worked for the Jews at the dog track at Hackney. 'They pay well,' he said.

One night after Peter and I returned from a meeting, I was looking at a book in his bedroom, the state of which reflected his habitual untidiness. We would sit until midnight sometimes telling each other how we would change the world. Peter was watching me from the bed where he was lying, hands clasped behind his head. 'Woody, why don't you join the Communist Party?' he suddenly asked. I could tell from his calculating look that his question was premeditated. I knew enough about Peter to realise that if I answered 'Why not,' I'd quickly become a card-carrying member.

Instead I said, 'I'm not a revolutionary. I don't share your apocalyptic vision. Nor am I sure that God is dead.' At heart I was an evangelical and humanitarian pacifist like Lansbury. It was the pacifist streak in me from my mother's side, the Kenyons. 'I don't want to go round bashing people. I don't see why I should go round bashing people if communism is – as you keep telling me – inevitable.'

'You're squeamish,' he answered. 'The working class can only improve its lot through the strike – by violence. Appealing to a sense of justice or humanity, or even long-term capitalist interests, is futile.'

'Employers can be persuaded.'

'Rubbish!' His voice was rising. 'Power is the only thing the bosses take stock of. Do you imagine that things can go on as they are? There has to be revolution. You can't tinker with the system; you have to dig it up by the roots. I don't know who is the more naïve: you with your belief in democratic persuasion, which simply means replacing one group of capitalists with another, or Lansbury with his "Blessed are the poor" business. You both have to learn that those who control the means of production control everything else. We want action, not dreams.'

I didn't answer his tirade.

He did not hold my rejection of his offer against me. On the contrary, he did everything he could to help me in the labour movement. Neither Peter nor anyone else ever asked me again to become a communist.

There was another reason why I didn't take up Peter's offer to join the Communist Party. Only a week before, I had attended a lecture in Poplar town hall given by Father Leo O'Hea. The labour movement had given the meeting its blessing. O'Hea was one of the few priests whose ministry lay with the poor. As an Irishman, he was particularly friendly with the Catholic Irish leaders of the East End. Ma Hargreaves had praised his strength and sincerity.

His topic was 'The Social Problem'. He gave a good talk, saying that neither communism nor fascism was the answer to our problems – Christianity was. Despite the length to which he went to tell us why that was so, I came away unconvinced. Yet he'd said enough to increase my doubts about a communist solution.

Actually, I was struck more by the person than by the speech. He was tall and straight, with a granite-like face heavy with experience. His deep-set grey eyes were sympathetic. His firm mouth and aquiline nose expressed strength. He had a natural manner and a clear, powerful voice. He gave the impression of being good and godly without being remote.

I told Peter I'd been to O'Hea's lecture. 'Do you know him?'

'He's like all Jesuits, dark and sinister; all that incense swinging and candles stuff . . . He sings the same song as Lansbury, only worse.'

Italy's invasion of Abyssinia in 1935 provoked a crisis in the British labour movement. It forced us to ask ourselves what we were going to do about aggression in international relations. It was a moment of truth both for the Labour Party and its leader George Lansbury.

Through the efforts of Albert Eastead, my trade-union secretary, I became a delegate to the Thirty-fifth Annual Conference of the Labour Party held in Brighton between 30 September and 4 October 1935, where policy toward Italy was to be threshed out.

The issue before the conference was whether the Labour Party should support the imposing of sanctions against Italy for its aggression against Abyssinia. As leader, Lansbury was confronted by a dilemma: if he agreed to the use of force against Italy, it would contradict the pacifism he had stood for in the past; if he didn't agree it would undermine the League of Nations and the idea of collective security, which the party endorsed.

Lansbury – still the most loved of all the Labour leaders – began the meeting by admitting that it wasn't logical of him to accept the obligations of the League, while refusing to use force to uphold them. Yet, as a true pacifist, he could not support the League in using force. In the past he had met the problem of his pacifism either by keeping quiet or, as leader during the past four years, doing the best he could for the party as a whole. 'It was inconsistent of me,' he said. 'I have always been inconsistent. Life demands it.'

The assembly may not have agreed with Lansbury, but it was obvious from the applause that the audience admired his honesty and piety.

Ernest Bevin, head of my own Transport and General Workers' Union, spoke next. A skilful, ruthless trade-union leader, Bevin had risen through the ranks and was steeped in the power struggle. Everybody knew that he despised and distrusted Lansbury's misty preaching.

In an irritable tone, Bevin told the audience that they should not be influenced by sentiment or personal attachment to Lansbury, whom he accused of being irresponsible and contradictory. 'Lansbury's attempt to serve two masters – his own conscience and party policy – is dishonest. The labour movement is being betrayed.'

Although there was a confused murmur of protest against Bevin's fierce attack, the audience didn't need persuading that Lansbury was in the wrong. Making no allowance for his age, for the service he had rendered the party, for his recent accident and the death of his wife, Bevin proceeded to destroy him. The conference voted overwhelmingly in favour of sanctions against Italy, and later for armed deterrence to back it up. Lansbury's leadership of the Labour Party was ended. I opposed the use of force over Abyssinia as Lansbury did. But then Lansbury was old and should have known better. I was young and my sense of rightness was typical of the pacifist and anti-militarist stand of many of my generation. I felt wholly right. Time would prove me – and I think Lansbury – wholly wrong.

————◇————

Several weeks later the Poplar Labour Party gave a party for Lansbury on his retirement. Ma Hargreaves got me an invitation. It was a small affair made up of East Enders and one or two visitors, including Father Leo O'Hea, whom I had heard lecture. Lansbury said a few words. 'I've come home,' he ended, wiping away a tear with the back of his hand. Ma Hargreaves thought the old man was delighted to be out of office. ''E's a saint,' she said. ''E should never have been persuaded to accept the leadership. It was 'is greatest mistake. 'Is stepping down don't make the slightest difference to us. We'll always love 'im.'

She introduced me to O'Hea, who had heard of me through her and Albert Eastead. 'They expect great things of you,' he said. He asked me about my work in the foundry. We spoke about Bevin's criticism. 'The important thing,' he said, 'is that Lansbury's resignation marks a turning point in Labour's attitude towards foreign policy. Bevin was right in insisting on uniformity. In foreign affairs, Labour must speak with one voice.'

Looking at me intently, he asked: 'What are your own plans?'

'I hope one day to become a Labour Member of Parliament.'

He smiled.

'My immediate concern is to get an education. My wildest dream is to go to a university.'

'You'll do what God intends,' he said, as if the matter was settled. 'God will reveal to you what you should do and which way you should go.' Until then I hadn't thought that God was involved. 'Learning,' he went on, 'is of less importance than what you do with it. If you intend to become a leader, you must know how to act. I'll put you in touch with an old friend of mine, Mr Philip Stone, who might help you with advice.'

I thanked him and we said goodbye. Father O'Hea left the meeting, tramping in with his heavy boots. There was a loneliness about the retreating figure.

A week or two later I received a letter from O'Hea's friend Philip Stone. The envelope had Pan Am printed on it and it was crisp and new. My name was typed in capitals; I might have been somebody important. He invited me to dine with him. It was the first written invitation to dinner that I'd ever received.

We met in the City at an expensive restaurant, where I was addressed by the waiter as 'Sir'. I was spiffed up in a new shirt and tie, and a suit that Emily had got from Ruth. I remember it was the day King George V died. The doleful sound of guns could be heard in the distance.

Mr Stone was a middle-aged man with eyes full of laughter. He was an affable host. Just as well that he was, for the amount of cutlery and china on the table made me nervous. I noticed him looking at my hands. He was more astute than I realised. I discovered that he was an executive of the Pan American Airline.

After dinner he offered me a cigarette. He smoked his own

in an elegant cigarette holder. He asked about my work in the foundry.

'Father O'Hea tells me that you have hopes of going to university?'

'I do. The trouble is that my qualifications are not good enough. I've already been rejected by the London School of Economics.'

'Unless you can be excused entrance examinations, you don't stand a chance of getting in.'

'What about the Central Labour College in London?'

'All you will get there is class-war propaganda.'

'What about Oxford?'

'The university proper will not accept you. Your only chance of going there is to be admitted to either Ruskin or the Catholic Workers' College, which is run by Father O'Hea. Both offer a two-year course for working men and women who give promise of becoming leaders. Ruskin was founded by three American admirers of John Ruskin. The Catholic Workers' College was founded by Father Charles Plater.'*

'Are the colleges part of the university?'

'They are and they aren't. Their students cannot graduate in the university. Nor can they wear a gown. In all other respects they are members of the university.'

'I find it baffling.'

'So does everybody else.'

'Does one have to be a Catholic to go to the Catholic Workers' College?'

'The crucial question is: are you the kind of person who will eventually put a university education to good use in the labour movement?'

The next night I wrote to both colleges. I also wrote to Harold Watkins, telling him what I was doing.

*The Catholic Workers' College changed its name to Plater College in 1965.

I had further meetings in the East End with O'Hea. Christmas 1935 came and went. Eventually I had a request from O'Hea to write a ten-page essay on 'Why I joined the Labour Party'. Stone had forewarned me that he used it as an entrance examination.

I wrote the essay in Ma Hargreaves' 'best room at the back'. She encouraged me in every way. 'It's one of the things I regret, never 'aving 'ad an edication.'

'My joining the Labour Party,' I began, 'was an act of protest against the social conditions of my childhood. I have not forgotten the armies of unemployed and the utter demoralisation of my father and those around us as workless month followed workless month. If the Tories are responsible for Britain's decline, as I think they are, then I must fight to replace them with Labour.'

I went on and on, talking glibly about Labour's mission to end exploitation, unemployment, ignorance, and war and want.

Having sweated endlessly over several drafts, and chewed several pencils in the process, I went up to Bow Road and posted the essay before I changed it all again.

The next night I visited Miss Hesselthwaite. She knew nothing about Ruskin or the Catholic Workers' College. 'Get to Oxford, no matter what,' she said. 'There's no telling what might happen to you there.'

After Miss Hesselthwaite I talked to Reg Sorenson, my WEA teacher. 'Go and be educated,' he said. 'The labour movement needs men like you.' He undertook to write testimonials for me and advised me to accept whichever college offered me a place.

He thought I'd be wise to get the help of Harry Graves, an East End politician. I already knew him as a leader in Labour circles and I'd been to his house several times. He was a bachelor. I called him and arranged to meet him at home the following Thursday at seven in the evening.

When I got there nobody answered my knocking. Finding the door unlocked I wandered in, and continued to wander until I came upon two naked figures on a couch. It was too late to turn away, nor would my feet respond. Rigid with fright, I was frozen to the spot. The lovers couldn't believe their eyes when they saw me. We just stared at each other – bewildered. I wondered why they hadn't locked the door. That was the end of any help I would get from Harry Graves, I thought. Wrapping a towel around himself, he prodded me to the door. He had forgotten all about my appointment.

I didn't dare tell the Hargreaves. A thing like that would have been blabbed all over the East End in a day.

When I met him a few days later, neither of us mentioned our last meeting. It might never have happened. He willingly wrote a testimonial for me; he helped me ever after. I was beginning to discover that life is very strange.

Finally I had a long talk with Peter Levine. 'You're crazy to think of going to Oxford, Woody,' he said. 'Oxford is for the nobs. They know nothing about the class struggle. The only worthwhile education is one governed by Marxist ideas. For that you have to go to the Central Labour College.'

—◇—

Some time before I dined with Stone, I had seen a notice of a vacancy for a job as an administrative assistant with the Thames and Lea Conservancy Board. The job attracted me. I knew the rivers; I lived within a stone's throw of the Lea, and I liked the idea of working out of doors. Compared with the foundry, the terms of the appointment were regal. I told Bobbit that I was applying for it. 'It's the gint's job that I've been looking for all my life,' he laughed. With nothing to lose, I sent in my application and forgot all about it. Weeks later, to my surprise, I was called to the head office of the Board at Brettenham House, Lancaster Place, the Strand.

Wearing my best clothes and speaking my best English, I arrived on the day, at the time stated. There were two other shortlisted candidates. We took a written test in the sunlit boardroom at the top of the building, sitting on red leather chairs. Everything about the room, including the long,

521

polished oak table with its pewter inkpots, was tasteful. Except for the rumble of traffic on the Embankment below, all was quiet and orderly. I looked out across the Thames, above the treetops and Cleopatra's Needle to the south bank of the river and thought what luck some people had to be able to work in a place like this.

Although I had trouble with the arithmetic, I was saved by the one-page essay on the Thames. I'd read an article on the Thames in the train that very morning. When the examination was finished the other candidates and I sat about and waited.

Eventually the door opened and I was called before the board's second-in-command, Mr Charles Ives. He interviewed me, and then the other two candidates. I waited. After an hour or so Ives came back for me. He spoke encouragingly and took me to the chairman's office. Sir William Desborough, a benign, white-haired gentleman, wasted no time on me. It was obvious that Ives was making the appointment anyway, and that I was his choice. 'Are you one of the Woodruffs who operate the wharf at Wapping?' was Sir William's last question. A fine pickle, I thought. If he is a friend of the Woodruffs of Wapping, I'm in; if he hates them, I'm out. 'No,' I answered, 'no connection whatever.' 'Thank goodness,' he said, dismissing me. Perhaps because I knew Oxford was in the offing and I was relaxed, I got the job.

I returned to Bobbit and told him of my success. 'I knew you'd come good,' he grinned, wringing my hand. 'Fust ryte.' That night, with much beer and many toasts, I celebrated my success in the pub.

———◇———

Before leaving the foundry a week later, Miranda and I went on the works' beano to Southend. We joined the foundry men and their families on the embankment near Westminster Bridge, with Big Ben tolling nine o'clock and the traffic eddying and swirling about us. Everybody was dressed to kill.

Miranda was wearing a chic leather beret and an expensive black leather coat that had 'pinched' stamped all over it. We were in high spirits and up to every kind of trick. It's amazing what a day off will do to folks. These were different people – there was no cursing, everybody smiled and showed off their children.

We boarded the steamer at Westminster Pier, larking and joking as if we were going to America. We cheered when the steamer hooted and cast off. We joined a great concourse of vessels making their way to the sea. We passed under Tower Bridge and all the other bridges on our way to Wapping and Limehouse. Some of the workers waved to relatives on shore. Beyond the Isle of Dogs we steamed past moored ships from the ends of the earth. All around us were cliffs of warehouses, power stations, gas works and refineries and factory chimneys; everybody on shore was scurrying about trying to make a living. It gave us a feeling of superiority to stand back and watch other people work. We were breaking loose.

After leaving the city and the crowds behind we floated on a quieter stretch of river, past ancient wharves, green fields and a few trees, and felt better for it. Farther down, the shore was marred by ugly petrol storage tanks looking like giant silver mushrooms, and higgledy-piggledy buildings from which flashed advertisements for gin, whisky and beer. There was a bar on board and Miranda and I took time off from staring at the ships and the shore to show that we were really enjoying ourselves.

It was low tide when we reached Southend. You could smell the salt, the fish and the fresh air. It was all space. We faced a vast expanse of mud and a crowd of other holiday-makers eating ice cream. As the mud looked so forbidding, everybody flocked to the pier, the longest in the world, lined with shops. At one booth there was a wooden effigy of a man who bore a surprising resemblance to Bobbit. I'm sure it was meant to look like him. 'Tyke a pot shot at 'im,' the barker yelled, handing us the wooden balls, ''ee can't 'it yer back.' Miranda and I did.

You needed eyes at the back of your head; cheats were everywhere. The gold watch Mr Harding the storeman bought for two shillings and sixpence was tin. 'Lor lumme, matey, yer aht awf a crown,' was all he got when he took it back. We drank heavily and gorged ourselves on seafood and vinegar. No one outdrank Mr Bobbit.

Later we wandered along the front, past lodging houses, squinting into shop windows. We listened to the barkers at the fair and the boatmen on the beach, and had a donkey ride against the incoming tide. With the sun setting we heard a military band. Afterwards we sat on deck chairs and pretended we were at Monte Carlo. Miranda thought she was.

The fresh air must have done us good because at the end of the day the foundry workers, some a little far gone, sang their way back up the river. Other steamers were coming up on the tide. Accompanied by an accordion, we sang such favourites as 'My old man said follow the van, and don't dilly-dally on the way . . .' and 'Nelly Dean', and 'Down at the Old Bull and Bush'. You can't stop a Cockney singing. Bobbit led us and was on his feet till the end.

From the great bend of the Isle of Dogs, all through Cockneyland, Miranda and I danced, while others spread themselves on the benches and slept. She would have been happier had the boat turned around and we had danced all the way back to Southend. The closer we got to home, the more the lights blazed: on the river a confusion of green, red, amber and white colours glittered. It was magic to sail under the bridges with all the illuminations reflected on the water. Crawling across London Bridge was an unending line of car lights. From shore, signs winked at us extolling the benefits of Schweppes Tonic Water, Gordon's Gin, Haig's Whisky and Wrigley's Gum – 'Keeps you alert'. Lit up, Big Ben and Westminster looked just like fairyland. Before we disembarked we all stood and held hands while Bobbit led us in singing 'Auld Lang Syne'.

All that remained was to dodge the rumbling traffic and

catch the District Line with its draughty carriages and its advertisements flapping in the breeze. Exhausted, with our arms around each other we pretended to sleep. When we got out at Bow Road, we passed the same fellow whom we'd seen strumming on his banjo when we set out that morning. With a charcoal-covered face and a few pennies in the cap at his feet, he was still playing at the kerb with the traffic roaring by. I took Miranda home.

I stayed in touch with Bobbit for years, never forgetting his decency. I can't imagine what might have become of me had he not shown me such sympathy in my early days in London.

———⟨○⟩———

The following Monday, I put on a suit, collar and tie and reported at Brettenham House for duty. My hours were from nine until four – a great change from the seven-thirty to five in the foundry. I started late enough to avoid strap-hanging in the Tube.

I began by working under Mr Ives, who taught me how the Board worked, how to communicate and how to use my time. Later I would learn about actual operations on the rivers. He was the first man I'd met who set me an example of reticence and reserve. I needed it. I never knew him to raise his voice.

'Did you shout for me?' I asked him one day on entering his room.

'I may have called, Woodruff, but I certainly didn't shout.' That put me in my place.

Often he would reply with one word. I found myself imitating his demure 'indeed' and 'really'. I began to use 'doubtless' and 'rather' on the telephone and felt better for it. Ives was always well groomed, efficient and considerate of others. I could not have had a better boss; the chemistry between us was perfect.

After being appointed, I never spoke to Sir William again.

I came to like him and respect him, but only from a distance. He would have been surprised had he known that at lunchtime I occupied his chair in the boardroom. I ate my sandwiches looking out over the Thames; I thought it a shame for such a beautiful room to be unused. It pleased me that Sir William's chair could spin round and round. There were times when I imagined myself facing the members of the Board. 'The meeting will come to order,' I would silently call, raising Sir William's gavel and peering at the shining expanse before me. Having made sure I left no crumbs, I would then walk along the tree-bordered Embankment from Cleopatra's Needle to Westminster Bridge and back. Always I was accompanied by a procession of trams, buses, lorries, carts, cars and people.

There followed three extraordinarily happy months. For weeks I simply couldn't believe that my job was real. I thought I'd wake up and find it gone. After the foundry, the conditions were unbelievable. No din, no dirt, no danger, no straining, and a clean office to myself. I had guaranteed holidays, guaranteed sickpay, and a guaranteed pension. Morale at the Board was high. Conduct was beyond reproach. Nobody said, "Ey you!' 'Stop jawing!' "Arf a mo!' or 'Wot's doin'?'

Ma Hargreaves and the rest of the family couldn't believe my luck either. Overnight, my weekly income had jumped from twenty-five to fifty shillings. I could afford to buy a daily newspaper, which I read like a proper bureaucrat going to and coming from the office. The workers used the trains several hours before us and we toffs sat there later with washed faces and starched shirts, feeling very important and self-satisfied. Clem worked out to a penny what my pay would be in ten years' time, and how much I would get when I retired. He thought I'd gone barmy when I told him I'd still go to Oxford if I got the chance. No Cockney gave up a job like that. Only Ma Hargreaves and Alex supported me.

Getting the Water Board job was the cause of my first big row with Miranda. With the extra money she thought me a good prospect for marriage. But until then there had never been a suggestion of marriage in our relationship. We'd been too poor to talk about it. Besides, our lives pointed in different directions – I wanted to get an education and go into politics; she had no interest in politics. Happiness to her was having more money to spend, especially on pleasure. If the toffs could go to glittering balls, why couldn't she?

To talk about the possibility of giving up the Water Board for Oxford made her madder still. 'Oxford is not for the likes of us,' she said. I ended the argument with her the only way I could: 'If I get the chance to go to Oxford, Miranda, I'm going to take it.' Oh, how she raged!

———◇———

Miranda almost got her way. One Saturday we went on a trip up the Lea. It was a hot summer's day. I did the rowing, she steered. We'd hired a large boat with canvas awnings, which could be let down if it rained. Miranda was looking her best. She was wearing bejewelled sandals, a pair of Bermuda shorts and a cotton shirt tied at the waist. It was so loosely buttoned that her breasts were more outside the shirt than they were in.

About noon, we pulled over and fastened the boat to a willow tree. The fields were ablaze with wild flowers; black satin cows, tails swishing, eyed us. A great silence prevailed; nobody else was in sight.

Reaching out for an oar that had got loose and was in danger of floating away, I was suddenly given a push from behind which landed me in the water. While I struggled and spluttered, Miranda sat on the cushions rocking with laughter. I didn't think it funny at all.

Back in the boat, with Miranda still in fits, I tried to get my sodden clothes off, watching her over my shoulder because I knew she was capable of pushing me in again. I dropped the awning on the riverside for privacy and when I turned to get my towel, Miranda was standing there before me naked. Her hair was down. She slid her hands around my neck and gently pulled me to her. I was overwhelmed by the sight and smell of her nakedness. 'I love you,' she said, her voice liquid and soft. Holding each other, we sank on to the cushions. She tossed her thick hair over my head.

Only when it was too late did I realise that I'd forgotten to put on the condom Chris had given me. I fished in my clothing for it. 'Don't put that bleedin' thing on,' she said, pulling me back on to the cushions. The outside world ceased to exist.

Miranda was as tempestuous about making love as about anything else. She could not have enough. When I fell back on to the cushions exhausted, she slid over me sinuously until her mouth, legs, arms and breasts held me down. My exhaustion soon fled.

Eventually even she was satisfied. We dropped the awning on both sides, curled up under our towels and slept. When I awoke, I saw the light through the strands of Miranda's hair. The angle of the sun had changed, it was late afternoon. All I could hear was the lapping of the water against the boat, the drone of insects, the chink of a blackbird and the sound of a boat engine far away. I shook Miranda. 'It's getting late, we'll have to go.' She responded by embracing me again.

All the way back she lay on the cushions and purred like a cat.

It was dark when we returned the boat. Wearing my wet shirt, pants and shoes, we walked to Ma Hargreaves', where I changed into my overalls and then took Miranda home. She clung to me at the door. Her mother's penetrating voice called from the kitchen: 'Bring 'im in!' Miranda giggled and tugged at me, but all I wanted to do was to go home and sleep.

I woke on Sunday morning much before my usual time. The others were fast asleep. Daylight was approaching. As I studied the ceiling, I worried about what had happened the day before. Would Miranda become pregnant? I'd had plenty of warnings about her from Chris, which I'd ignored. For the first time it struck me that making love to Miranda – or to anyone else for that matter – could be perilous. I wasn't ready to have a family and was uncertain of my love for her. The more I lay there, the less I liked my predicament: ecstasy had turned to worry. I didn't dare tell Chris I hadn't used his condom.

In the following weeks I went on worrying. If Miranda were pregnant, as she hoped, I'd have to marry her. That was the code. 'We can always live with Mum,' she said. Living with Mum was the last thing I wanted. Luckily, as it turned out, I was spared.

After that, I did my best to avoid Miranda. I didn't trust her, or myself. 'Look,' she said. 'We don't have to get wed now if you don't want to. If you're worried about a child, I can use some pessaries Mum gave me.' I sensed a note of desperation. I already knew about those particular pessaries from talk among the lodgers. An East End company made them. If they didn't work and you complained, they sent you a book called *Bringing up Baby*. I hoped *I* wouldn't get stuck with having to bring up a baby.

One day in the middle of summer I picked up the letters from behind the front door to take them downstairs, and saw a letter addressed to me with the Oxford postmark. My spirits rose, I was so excited that I turned the envelope over and over in my hands. I didn't open it until I'd run back upstairs to my bedroom. It was a short letter from Father O'Hea, but it was all I wanted to hear: I could go to Oxford – the Catholic Workers' College had offered me a place! The financial assistance of the London County Council would be helpful, but O'Hea would take me with or without their help. He needed to know my response quickly.

I read the letter two or three times before running downstairs to show it to Ma Hargreaves. She might have been my mother the way she hugged me: 'Wonderful! Billy, I can't tell you 'ow 'appy I am.' I detected a tear. When Clem came home that night he was incredulous at the thought of my giving up the Water Board job. 'You've got to be mad,' he said. 'Only a madman would exchange books for cake. One day, when it's too late, you'll realise that books are for blockheads.' ''S right,' said Chris. 'Can't eat books.'

The next day I used Ma Hargreaves' phone to call Ruskin College. I spoke to the secretary, asking if he might let me know where I stood with my application. I was to learn that educational bodies don't make that kind of decision on the telephone. He advised me to take O'Hea's offer while it was going. Remembering what Miss Hesselthwaite and Reg Sorenson had said about a bird in the hand being worth two in the bush, I committed myself to O'Hea. It was one of the best decisions I ever made.

I dropped a note to Philip Stone. He wrote back congratulating me, and saying how fortunate I was. I also wrote to Brenda. She answered at once on a postcard. 'Lucky you, luv.'

It remained for me to tell Charles Ives. Not wanting to burn my boats, I put it off for several days. He was genuinely disappointed when I told him; so was Sir William. It helped that they were both Oxford men. The Conservancy Board was hundreds of years old; no doubt it would struggle on without me. Uppermost in Ives' mind was whether I'd take up rowing. As an old rowing blue he was always telling me what a fine sport it was, and how I'd benefit from it. To please him, I said I would certainly try. Our harmonious relations continued until the day I left and we parted good friends. It was a privilege to have worked with such a man. Even though my stay at the Water Board had been brief, it had strengthened my self-confidence and given a tremendous lift to my ego. I wasn't about to ride in triumph in the Lord Mayor's coach, but in joining the Water Board I'd come a long way. It taught me that – regardless of the odds – I could win through.

Miranda was speechless for days at my decision.

In July 1936, two months before I went to Oxford, General Franco rebelled against the legitimate Popular Front Spanish government. The long-awaited death struggle between fascist and anti-fascist forces, which Peter Levine had been talking about for ages, had begun. Germany and Italy at once identified themselves with Franco, the Soviet Union with the Republic. Britain and France remained neutral.

In his WEA lectures, Reg Sorenson was on about Spain all the time. He showed us how Spain had become divided between the forces of the Right and the Left: between the military, the monarchists, the large landowners and the Church on the one hand, and the socialists, the communists and the anarchists on the other. Anybody looking for a cause – romantic or heroic – had now found it.

The Spanish Civil War was a moment of truth that affected us all. Until then most of us Labour activists in the East End had not given a thought to Spain. Why bother about a country so far away? Two communist East End garment workers, Sam Masters and Nat Cohen, were the first to organise a British group of volunteers, which eventually became the International Brigade. Peter Levine was one of their first recruits. 'You must come to Spain, Woody, it's a chance to hit back. Oxford can wait,' he said.

It caused me to examine my conscience about pacifism all over again, but ultimately I was too much of a pacifist to follow Peter, and he should have known that.

I saw him off at Waterloo Station. He was to meet up with other volunteers in Paris and from there go on to Spain. It was a sad parting. Peter had been a good friend.

Chapter VII

To Oxford

The day of my departure to Oxford in September 1936 arrived all too soon. I was close to tears when I said goodbye to Ma Hargreaves. The whole family stood at the door shouting their good wishes. Miranda and Bernie came as far as Paddington Station to see me off. Miranda was dressed to kill in a smart, brown costume. You'd never have guessed she was a factory hand. 'If Oxford throws yer out tonight, we'll pick yer up tomorrow,' Bernie said, beating my shoulder. Miranda made up for her silence by giving me a hug.

I was nineteen and in the highest spirits. The prospect of a sixty-mile journey through the English countryside, rushing to a place I'd only dreamed of, filled me with excitement and a sense of freedom. Once more, I was gladly venturing into the unknown.

As the empty train began to rattle and twist its way out of the station, I waved goodbye through a cloud of steam. Three years earlier, when I had run away from northern

England, the idea of my going to Oxford University would have been preposterous. Now the absurd was happening. I had no fears of the future. I was convinced that if I worked hard I would win through.

As I stared through the window, I fell to thinking about Miranda. I was glad we were parting. Our relationship had become very unsettling to me; I felt I was being pursued. Only the week before, she'd come unexpectedly upon me in one of the Hargreaves' 'best rooms', where I had been working alone. She was wearing a red dress with big white buttons down the front. Before I had time to get up from the table she had thrown her hands around my neck and kissed me. 'How much do you love me?' she asked. I put my hands on her thighs; she was not wearing panties. Suddenly she lifted her dress until it sat on her shoulders. Despite all my good intentions to avoid her, we embraced passionately and sank to the floor. Almost when it was too late, I withdrew, coming all over Ma Hargreaves' 'best rug'. 'Shit!' Miranda said, and went off in a flaming huff. Embarrassed, on hands and knees I tried to clean up the mess with my handkerchief.

I came out of my daydream as the train approached Reading. The sunlit river, hills and meadows captivated me. The September weather was holding up. All the time I'd been in east London I'd never lost my love of the land. Now I was rattling across the open country as if I owned it. I saw trees and fields and woods and hills and animals as if for the very first time. I remained glued to the window until the train slid into Oxford, where I caught my first glimpse of the university's towers. It was a week before term.

I surrendered my ticket at the gate and made my way out of the station. As my bag was light, I decided to walk to the Catholic Workers' College.

As I went along, I became conscious that I had reached a quieter, cleaner and more confident world. There were no crowds of noisy cloth-capped workers, no dirty gutters. I saw no beggars, no slums, no barrowboys, no screevers, no gridlers and no long procession of lorries. There was a light, expectant mood in the air. Compared to Bow Road it was like being in church. In place of factory chimneys there were college spires; in place of workshops and warehouses there were great stone-fronted colleges with manicured lawns. In the sunlight, the stone looked golden. Trees, shrubs and flowers lined the streets. The private houses were built on a grand scale. They had a settled, comfortable, orderly appearance. For me Oxford was love at first sight.

Half an hour later I was standing in front of No. 1 Walton Well Road, the Catholic Workers' hostel. It was a four-storeyed, self-assured Victorian dwelling, with a large entrance and four great bay windows overlooking the street. Fronted by elegant wrought-iron railings, the building conveyed a feeling of strength and spaciousness.

I was greeted by the matron, Mrs Padmanabha, a buxom woman who led me up a wide staircase past a print of Titian's *Madonna and Child* to one of the bedrooms at the front, which I was to share with another student. I then joined other students in the common room downstairs. The room extended all the way from the bay windows at the front to a large window overlooking an extensive wooded garden at the back. Shadows from the trees flittered over the colourful loose-covered couches. The walls were covered with books. A fire burned in the grate. Later I reported to Father O'Hea in his office. It was a packed, well-used room smelling of tobacco.

At tea, I was introduced to my roommate Jim Foggerty, a coal miner from New Silksworth, County Durham. Jim was the most handsome of men. He was of medium height, muscular, brown-eyed, with delicate features. He had a down-to-earth quality. He spoke his Tyneside dialect with a shy, gentle voice, which took me days to get used to.

We were both delighted with our bed-sitting room overlooking the street. Light flooded through the bay windows. It was a much larger room than the one I had shared with three others at Ma Hargreaves'. The furniture was simple; there was nothing polished or off-putting. There was so much space that the room seemed empty, even after we had unpacked. The bathrooms and toilets were steps away. We could have a bath every day if we wanted to. To us it was luxury.

To my surprise, my ears picked up the rhythmic blows of a drop hammer. I was told that there was an iron foundry beyond the back garden; the hostel had once been the foundry owner's house.

Sometime before supper, Jim and I took a short walk to nearby Port Meadow, through which the Thames flowed. The Thames was much cleaner here than in the East End. Slowly our eyes took in the trees, the river, the towpath and the endless grassland lost in a distant mist. The still-ness of the scene was overwhelming. We heard only bird-song and the sound of distant bells. Later, we learned that flooding had preserved Port Meadow down the ages. It was this unspoiled countryside that I had yearned for in London. Eyes closed, I reached out to the enormous unoccupied space. I could breathe again. I went to bed that night feeling very much at peace.

The day after our arrival, Father O'Hea brought us together in the common room. There were ten of us: eight men and two women. All of us had working-class back-grounds. Foggerty was a miner. The other six were a weaver, a bricklayer, a docker, a clerk, a factory hand and a railway man. They ranged in age from their late twenties to late thir-ties. Some of them were married. I was the youngest. Several had been unemployed for long periods. The women, Miss Dempsey and Miss Humphries, lived in lodgings elsewhere.

The principal began by introducing Mrs Padmanabha, who talked about the running of the place. The house followed the university practice of not locking doors within the hostel. The front door would be locked at eleven at night. She asked us not to drink in rooms; there was a pub opposite the college and another next door.

O'Hea then explained the purpose of the college. 'Education for leadership is our goal,' he said. 'You are here because of your origins and experience. I look on you as "the spark in the clod". There is no better way to develop that spark than to spend two years here. The influence of even a small group who wants to do something socially useful can spread far and wide. Oxford itself started from small beginnings. I hope that your coming here will eventually help those from whom you have sprung.

'In the next couple of days, I shall give each of you the names of your tutors and their colleges. After that it is up to you. Books, lectures, essays and term examinations are matters settled between student and tutor. Tutors will advise on lectures. Although lectures are not compulsory and only loosely connected with examinations, I think it would be foolish not to take advantage of them. It is not every day that one can listen to some of the brightest minds in Britain. Those of you who stay for a second year will be required to sit for the university's diploma in economics and political science.

'It will not be easy for you to change from using your hands to using your heads. You are going to have to learn how to argue with pen and ink. The university will make no allowance for your deficiencies, whether in assimilating or analysing material, or in reading or writing. There will be no factory hooters to tell you when to begin and when to stop. The university never stops. You will be constantly lured from your work by lectures by speakers of world renown. To try to take in everything would be adding to your already heavy burden. In past years some students have been unable to keep up and left. You'll have to get used to working with the middle and upper classes, which will be an education in itself.'

He explained that the academic year was divided into three eight-week terms: Michaelmas (October–December), Hilary (February–March) and Trinity (April–June). Vacations were for catching up with reading. As our scholarships only covered term work, we'd have to find a living between terms.

'However hard it is going to be,' he ended, 'I can assure you that the effort is worthwhile. For the past seven hundred years students have benefited from coming here. You must take the university on trust. You have a great challenge and a great opportunity; what you learn here you will never lose.'

A day or two later O'Hea took us on a tour of the university. We all rode bicycles. For several hours we visited college after college. Our last stop was the magnificent hall of Christ Church. I returned from the tour with a blurred vision of ancient, weather-beaten buildings with leaded-glass windows, of proud spires, of silent quadrangles, of emerald-green lawns with borders of colourful blooms, and of elaborate steep-pitched vaulted roofs with dormer windows. I saw Oxford that day as I would never see it again.

———◇———

My first week of term stood me on my head. I didn't know what I was doing. Joining a flood of students wearing caps and jacket-length, sleeveless black gowns with streamers flapping in the wind, I raced this way and that; I pedalled furiously from lecture to lecture. Not having matriculated, I had no right to wear a cap and gown and I did not like being stopped at the entrance to a lecture room for not wearing one. It gave me the feeling of being an intruder.

A good deal of the lectures' content was beyond me. At nine o'clock one morning I listened to a professor extolling the virtues of the Renaissance (whatever that was). He couldn't say enough about the Renaissance having given vibrancy and energy to the whole of Western civilisation. At ten, in the same room, I learned from another that in discarding the dogma of Original Sin, the Renaissance had blurred the lines of Western thinking. He blamed it for all the faults of Western society and held it responsible for the worst aspects of the present-day mechanistic, secular civilisation. What was I to think?

Accustomed to working with my hands, I was overwhelmed by the amount of thinking and writing I had to do. And I had to do it on my own. I was used to following orders or working with a crew. Here, no one ordered me about; nor did anyone give me help. I think there was a conspiracy to deny it. If you didn't know what to do, you had no right to be there. Tutors spent no time on the intellectually lame. Had I not fallen under Oxford's spell, I would have fled.

The first tutor I visited was A. B. Rodger, dean and tutor in History at Balliol College. I was wearing a tie. As I crossed the quad, bells tolled. I wondered what was in store for me. In answer to my knocking, I received a bellowing response to enter. I stepped into a large, book-lined study. The ivy-framed windows looked out on to a quadrangle swarming with students. Lamps burned overhead and on the tables. A heavy-bodied, middle-aged man of medium height stood with his back to the fire. He was wearing a tweed jacket, grey flannel trousers and a plaid shirt. His flushed face and large, bald head, which was cocked quizzically to one side, gave the appearance of a bulldog about to bite. At one end of the mantelpiece was a wedding picture of the man I faced. 'Yes,' he said fiercely, squinting at me over his half-moon spectacles.

'I'm Woodruff.'

'Ah, yes, Woodruff,' he answered, sceptically. 'So you want to do some work, do you?' He ignored my outstretched hand.

'Yes,' I said cautiously. I had made up my mind that the bulldog was not going to bite. As bidden, I sat down on the edge of a chair.

'Done any history at an upper level?' he asked, shaking the loose change in his trouser pocket.

'No, sir.'

'None?'

'No.'

'Where did you go to school?'

'Blackburn, Lancashire.'

'When did you leave school?'

'At thirteen.'

'Thirteen,' he repeated, staring at me in a bemused way, while whistling under his breath.

'What do you hope to do in life?'

'To be a Labour politician.'

He rattled his coins some more.

'Tell you what,' he said, his eyes challenging mine, 'why don't we break the ice with a paper on the Enclosure Movement of the eighteenth century . . . you know . . . when a lot of people were chased off the land . . . Material and moral loss of the poor, etc. You might not think so, Woodruff, but it has a lot to do with what has been happening in Russia lately.'

Although I knew a little about the collectivisation of agriculture in the Soviet Union, I hadn't the slightest idea what the English Enclosure Movement was. 'Yes,' I agreed, my voice breaking.

'Well, that's settled,' he said, striding about the room, shuffling papers as he went.

I sensed he expected me to leave. I didn't dare – I either spoke up now or I was lost. 'Where might I find the details?' I ventured.

'Details, details?' he started, as if it were improper of me to ask. 'Well, you might look at Slater and Beresford, and Fisher and Johnson for a start,' he said grudgingly. 'If you look at them, you'd better look at the Hammonds, and Cole, and Fay, and Prothero.'

I scribbled names down in my notebook as fast as I could. He seemed puzzled and a little put out when I asked him for the authors' initials and the titles of the books. I didn't dare ask him which parts of the books I should read.

By now I wasn't even talking right. How on earth was I going to find eight books, read them, and produce an essay in a week's time? 'Will it be necessary to read all eight volumes?'

'Gracious me, no, Woodruff,' he boomed. 'You'd be mad to. You don't read books, you gut them; it's the gist you're after. If you feel that an author has nothing important to say, drop him. You'll get to the nub of things pretty quickly, you'll see. Anyway, you won't find half the books I've given you. There are other students preparing essays, you know.' Smiling, he waited.

My face must have registered consternation.

'Even looking for a book you can't find will teach you something, Woodruff.' He whistled under his breath again, shuffled his papers, and indicated that I should go.

I stayed. I had to – I was desperate. 'How long do you expect the essay to be?'

'Well, Woodruff, that depends on you, doesn't it? Some do it in ten pages, others with nothing to say, dawdle it out to twenty. The standard rule is to start at the beginning and to go on till the end. You're a sensible fellow, Woodruff, I'm sure you'll know when you've reached the end.'

While I gathered my papers to go, he gave me some advice on lectures. 'You might try Rowse . . . everybody does. Good on Tudors. I'd look in on Clark too, while you're at it. Sound on the seventeenth and eighteenth centuries is Clark. What you are after is the gist, remember.'

I really was not listening. I was wondering why he was recommending Rowse and the Tudors when the Tudors preceded the dates of my examinations. I thought he must have made a mistake and I said so.

'Ah,' he answered, smile on lips. There was a pause while he whistled some more. 'Woodruff, you have not come to Oxford to take examinations, you have come to learn. The whole purpose of Oxford is learning.'

I stared at him, bewildered. How on earth was I supposed to recognise the 'gist' he talked about. To ask him, I realised, would be a reckless thing to do. Flight was the only wise course.

Mumbling my thanks, I made for the door. As I stumbled out into the quad, I wondered how I was going to cope. Dazed, I made my way past the porter's lodge into the street. I jumped on to my bike and rushed off in search of the recommended volumes, to gut the 'gist' from them.

Later that day I visited my economics tutor, Dr Eric Dowdell of St John's. I found him sitting by the fire. He had expected me and did not get up or turn towards me when I entered the room. With a wave of his hand he indicated where

I should sit. His tone and dress were sombre. This time I didn't even try to shake hands. Compared with Rodger he seemed a younger, frailer, quieter body, devoid of eccentricities. For some minutes he questioned me about my background and my knowledge – if any – of economics. Addressing the fire in a quiet voice, he then set me a topic: 'What are the primary factors of production?' He provided me with an endless list of books, advised me to attend James Meade's lectures at Hertford College on economic analysis and policy, and waited for me to leave. Not once had he looked me in the face. Only when I was leaving did I realise that he was blind. No one had mentioned it.

It remained for me to see G. D. H. Cole at University College whose lectures I would attend and with whom I would work closely in my second term on the theory and practice of trade unions (labour movements). I'd heard of him long before I came to Oxford. I knew him as the leading labour theoretician and historian. I was also curious to meet an academic who had written detective stories. I was already familiar with his *The Common People*, and *What Marx Really Meant*, and knew that he was opposed to revolutionary methods.

I found Cole in his rooms. He was a tall, austere figure, well and neatly dressed. He was a friend and supporter of O'Hea, and had expected me. I knew from the first moment that I was in the presence of a most informed and penetrating mind, and that I was fortunate to be there. Again, there was no shaking of hands. In fact he hardly emerged from a deep leather chair. I expected him to ask me about my experience as a foundry worker, but he didn't. He stuck to his topic, going off like a gun. I felt that he was not as happy with people as he was with books; he talked like a book. Avoiding digressions, he talked about labour movements and gave me a reading list. Not another word.

As he talked, my attention was drawn to his hands. Since my arrival in Oxford I had been fascinated by people's hands. Unlike the scarred, shovel-like hands at the foundry, Oxford hands were delicate-looking, with long, bony fingers.

Cole's signal for me to leave was to put his head into a book.

———◇———

Oxford at the start was an unending race, which absorbed me from morning till night. In the mornings I was at lectures, in the afternoons I looked for the books needed to write the essays. Nights I spent preparing my papers. Rarely did I get to bed before midnight; nor did my roommate Jim.

For the first time in my life I was challenged to think. I was no longer an ox under a yoke. I had never known such freedom, even if it was the freedom to drown. At least I was working for myself.

I must have lost ten pounds during those first frantic weeks. I didn't seem to have a second to myself. The idea of going for a walk was out of the question. Snatching a nightly pint of beer with Foggerty in the smoke-filled Golden Hart opposite was all I managed. Smoking seems to have been my only recreation; my consumption of tobacco doubled. There wasn't even time to get my hair cut. The only way I could cope was to rise at five and study the whole day. I had never worked so hard, that was the truth.

The fiction was that no one exerted himself. Undergraduates pretended to toss off work in a nonchalant manner. I don't think the women students were as blasé, but the idea of success without visible effort was widespread among the men. I would have gone hungry had I tried that at the foundry. Workers knew that life was work, and were proud of it. Toffs, I discovered, had a different code: kill yourself, but don't mention it and don't show it.

In contrast to the hammer-and-tongs-way of the working class, the atmosphere of the university was peaceful and orderly; life moved along in a discreet and gentlemanly way. I'd never known so many people going out of their way to be polite. The first time I was addressed as 'Sir' in Oxford, I felt two inches taller. Public-school manners were in charge; rules on study were lax; rules on conduct were stern. Honour mattered; character mattered; but conduct mattered most of all. No one got rattled; no one was rude; no one bawled. Resentment against us working-class students who had managed to scale the walls of privilege was about, but it was muted. The aristocrats rarely snubbed anyone on grounds of class; the middle class was too industrious to waste time discussing it.

No matter how stressful those first weeks were, I could always escape to the hostel. I was at ease there among my own kind. Class support was important to us, the presence of each of us supported and reassured the others.

Life at the hostel followed a simple routine. The day began with Father O'Hea banging away in the cellar, raking out and stoking the boiler. With crashes and thumps enough to waken the dead, and oblivious of the fact that we were trying to sleep, he shovelled the coal like a proper stoker. We always knew when he was through: the shovel would be dropped with a clang, the furnace door thrown to with a crash. We called him the 'boilerman'. Reluctantly, we admired his strength. He would then take an ice-cold bath in the bathroom on our landing. For some reason, he always left the door open. I agonised every morning until he took the last of three plunges – I felt for him in his spluttering and coughing. Why his bath water had to be ice-cold, I never worked out. The rest of us were delighted to be able to have a hot bath.

Father O'Hea rang a bell at seven for Mass. I never went down to the chapel without being moved. Life was magnified in that unadorned room. The stark simplicity of the altar heightened its effect. We might have been in a cathedral, with the prayers and responses rising to the vaulted roof. As I watched the candles flicker, I was amazed that the turning of bread and wine into the body and blood of the Saviour could take place in such a humble setting. I know that the service brought meaning to the lives of the other students; it made sense of their existence. Christianity after all was a religion of hope – addressed to the poor and the downtrodden.

I shared in the worship, though I could not share my companions' commitment. Sometimes during Mass my attention would wander and I would find myself studying the feet hurrying past the cellar window, or the face of a stray dog looking in.

Breakfast, at which the principal read *The Times* and *The Daily Herald*, and no one took any notice of anyone else, was at eight. One rarely talked to the other students until dinner at one, or supper at seven. Every meal was superb. The day ended with O'Hea going upstairs to his small bedroom under the roof. It was usually long after midnight, long after the last bus had ground its way past our window.

At Oxford I felt I was in a world into which I did not naturally fit. I had little in common with the urbane, privileged schoolboys who had come up from the public schools. More class-bound than I, they struck me as being very young and immature. They knew little about the real world. They were always overdoing it a bit – a bit too languid, a bit too indifferent. It was an entirely new experience for me to meet youths of my own age, who told me in an affected tone of voice how they were 'awfully happy', or for whom things were 'too stunning'. Every time I sounded my flat northern vowels, I pronounced my difference. I stood out in speech, dress, emotions, tastes, manners – even the way I ordered a drink – and movements. My lack of schooling was most evident. I was an outsider, with a deep-seated feeling of social inferiority.

Regardless of their immaturity, the intellectual self-confidence of these students surprised me. With their lightning plays on words and an easy assumption of nonchalant superiority, they knew much more than I, and they knew it effortlessly. Nor did they tiptoe about as I did; they walked about as if they owned the place, which they did.

I may have been a fish out of water – insecure and sometimes laughed at for my gullibility and my accent – yet I was in no doubt about the advantages of my new life. I'd never lived in a society in which people could afford to do nothing but sit and stand around, read books and linger over coffee, eat and drink their fill, and talk – especially talk. Words were the legal tender. I was amazed that nobody thought it unusual, and that the university had got away with it for so long.

Still, with all these frightening beginnings, Oxford conveyed to me a sense of security, permanence and order. I didn't need to bow and scrape. The clocks I saw and the bells I heard were there for my pleasure, not to repress me. If I pleased, I could ignore them and I wouldn't lose a penny or go hungry. For the first time in my life I was not living from hand to mouth. I didn't have to worry where the next shilling was coming from, or whether I was going to be thrown out of a job on to the street. I bought on credit. I didn't have to stand in queues and wait my turn. Gentlemen did not wait their turn.

After Blackburn and the East End, it seemed unreal that I should live in a town as beautiful and as mellow. The only towns I had known were dirty-brick ugly. In awe and wonder I studied the buildings, the clean sky, the verdant fields and the river. The beauty of the place grew on me and as it did I came to love its every nook and cranny. Many was the night I stood outside the Camera captivated by its dome against the starlit sky. I came to know the splendour of Magdalen, Christ Church, New College and Merton, all of them 'miracles in stone'. I marvelled at the tranquillity of the cloisters of New College, and the peace of the Botanic Garden, the gardens of St John's, and Merton's 'Mob quadrangle' – all of them oases of peace. To attend evensong in Christ Church Cathedral or New College Chapel was an unforgettable experience.

It was equally unreal to listen to lectures in Christ Church

Hall on a wintry morning, with a great log fire crackling in the hearth, the light flickering through the windows of the tall vaulted bays and the past looking down at me from the portraits on the walls. Not even the icy bench on which I sat or the freezing table on which I took notes deterred me from appreciating the magnificence of my surroundings. When the beams of the immense timbered roof were raised, English colonists were founding the New World. I felt in them the spirit of another age. What other students took for granted, I regarded with awe. The red-cheeked, long-legged girls added immeasurably to the scene.

Oxford's sense of history seeped into me through my pores. Wherever you went you breathed the past – which gave meaning to the present. On visits to Balliol I hurried across the spot where Bishops Ridley, Latimer and Cranmer had been burned at the stake during the Reformation. At five minutes past nine Great Tom of Christ Church tolled 101 strokes, representing the number of students when the college was founded in the sixteenth century. It signalled the closing of its great iron-studded doors. Perhaps it was mystique, perhaps a spell, but I felt privileged to be there.

———◇———

Somehow or other I came to terms with lectures and tutorials; I wrote my first essays. Rodger of Balliol criticised my essay on the Enclosure Movement with 'Good *Daily Mail*, Woodruff,' which I knew was a nice way of saying it was journalism. He then elaborated: 'You're looking to history for easy answers, Woodruff – to confirm your idea of right and wrong. You're another clever Dick condemning the past for being shortsighted. What generation has ever looked beyond the end of its nose?'

Having knocked all the wind out of my sails, in a few spellbinding sentences, he proceeded to show me where I'd fallen down and what was required of me.

Dr Dowdell's comment on my first paper was, 'Thank you,

interesting' ('interesting' meant you might pass, 'very interesting' meant you were coming along fine). With a sniff he
gave a masterful résumé of the kind of paper I should have
written. Neither Rodger nor Dowdell needed to tell me that
I was out of my depth. Had I been able to sit around and
become introspective, I suppose I might have despaired. What
saved me was my sense of purpose. I had to succeed. What
immature schoolboys could do, I could do. I remembered
Miss Hesselthwaite's warning that the beginning would be
hard. It was.

But it got better. The quirks of tutors gradually ceased to
bother me. Although I was unable to toss off essays – for me
each one was an ordeal – I began to reap the benefits of the
tutorial system, where knowledge is shared rather than used
as a stick to beat the student. I learned how to benefit from
the coaching of distinguished scholars. Teaching was para-
mount. 'Never write a book, Woodruff,' Rodger used to say
to me, tongue in cheek. 'If you do, make sure it is a slim
volume. There are already too many books.'

The trick was to stay wide awake, ready to catch the sprats
of wisdom thrown offhandedly in your direction. It called for
intense concentration and a heightened appreciation of the
subtle, rarely repeated digressions and idiosyncratic, sometimes waspish anecdotes. Let your mind wander for a second
and you were lost.

By a solid effort rather than intelligence, I made sense of
the books I was told to study. My working-class colleagues
called them 'the big books'. I avoided chasing books by studying in the Camera, the reading room of the Bodleian Library;
this way books were brought to me. I was there when it
opened at ten and, except for meals, lectures and tutorials,
stayed until it closed at ten at night. It meant that Foggerty,
who didn't mind when others barged in on him, could have
our room to himself. The sound of drop hammers coming
from the back of the building did not disturb him as it did
me.

If I worked late at the Camera, the pubs would be shut and

Foggerty and I would drink a beer in our room. Against all regulations we kept a box of warm beer under his bed. Sometimes Jim played his harmonica: the beer and the music smoothed us down.

The Camera reading room was as silent as the grave. A respectful hush prevailed. Staff members spoke in whispers; coughs and sneezes were admonished with one *sh-sh*. If flirtations took place, they were silent and unseen. There was a sense of greatness and challenge about the place. Those who sat there were not just any old flotsam and jetsam, they were readers for life at one of the oldest and greatest libraries in the world. They were sitting where famous men had sat. I knew that the students around me, however languid, were among the brightest in the country. Their superiority was infectious. When the dreaded time of 'Schools' came at the end of my course, it was with these that I would have to compete.

I followed Rodger's and Dowdell's advice and attended the lectures by A. L. Rowse, G. N. Clark and James Meade. I took few notes. Rowse drew a great crowd. Peacock-like, he was brilliant and colourful. Clark was magisterial. The doors of his lecture room were locked when he entered on the stroke of ten and were kept locked until he was done. I think this was to prevent his listeners from running away rather than to preclude latecomers from getting in. Meade was the most stimulating. Unlike Dowdell, who dealt with economic theory as an end in itself, he was concerned to use theory to improve public policy. There was always a moral element in Meade's thinking. He had everything in his favour: youth, good looks, knowledge, intelligence, modesty, good manners, human sympathy, wit and energy. His enthusiasm was infectious. Yet, surprisingly, he usually had a small audience – so small that often a lecture became a seminar. I had the good sense to stay silent.

The lectures given by the famous Father Martin C. D'Arcy, university lecturer in Moral Philosophy and Master of Campion Hall, introduced me to an entirely new field of knowledge. Brow furrowed, gown rustling, eyes focused on his toes or half-closed as in a trance, D'Arcy would often stop his pacing to study the floor or the ceiling in search of the exact word to express his meaning. Meanwhile I was suffocated by his 'oughts', 'ifs', 'buts' and 'howevers', which floated above me like a dense cloud. Having grasped what he was saying, I was thrown off when he questioned what I thought we had already agreed upon. I was also thrown off by the way he kept the dogma of Original Sin up his sleeve. He left us in no doubt about the limitations of human nature. He was fond of quoting Immanuel Kant: 'Out of the crooked timber of humanity, nothing straight was ever made.' Fat lot of good that was to someone like me who intended to rebuild the world.

I never managed to get a handle on his subject. In a foundry I knew what I was doing; with philosophy everything hung on a verbal thread. His discussion of topics such as 'What is the Good?' or 'What is the true end of man?' or 'What is truth?' left me floundering. This constant worrying about doing the right thing sounded unnatural to me. The people I'd come from just *did* without 'feelosophising'. The working class didn't have time to reflect whether or not they'd done the right thing. They either followed the rules or lost their job and went hungry. It amazed me that I could stand around discussing the 'moral imperative' and get three meals a day. I listened wide-eyed as D'Arcy turned his words inside out and upside down. His crowded audiences loved his brilliance, his wit and his word play, but I have to confess that he was wasted on me.

I don't know what he would have said had I told him that the clothes I was wearing had been obtained from a 'fence'. D'Arcy's philosophy didn't seem to me to have much to do with life in east London.

I understood the lectures of Father Lewis Watt from Heythrop College on Catholic Social Doctrine much better. An ex-lawyer, Watt was as lucid as D'Arcy was vague. A crisp little man in a black suit, with a convict haircut, a pale face and a pinched nose, he never wasted a word or a second. There was no 'iffing' and 'butting' and wandering around the room looking for the right word. He stood stock-still and shot his points at you as if they were bullets.

In a short space of time Watt taught me a great deal about Marxism, totalitarianism and the state. The danger of Marxism, he used to say, is that it is temptingly simple. He considered it a half-truth. While all the other great religions (he called Marxism a secular religion) dealt with the secular and the sublime, with life and death, Marx dealt only with life. In place of the Marxist doctrine of class war, Watt advocated cooperation based on Christian charity and recognition of the dignity of labour. Not that he refused to give Marx his due. He considered Marx's protest against the social conditions of the time and his grandeur of conception admirable.

Watt also introduced me to the papal encyclicals *Rerum Novarum*, On the Conditions of the Working Classes (1891), and *Quadragesimo Anno*, On Reconstructing the Social Order (1931). The aim of both encyclicals had been to close the gap between the Church and the working class. In modern industry the worker had become a replaceable part, tied to the machine and the clock.

Watt could not only handle the grand sweep of history, but as a lawyer he could handle the details. He introduced me to the teachings of Thomas Aquinas on private property: 'It is one thing to have a right to the possession of money, and another thing to use money as one wills.' Property implied a function. I hadn't heard of Aquinas, but I had heard of the nineteenth-century French anarchist Proudhon who had declared, 'property is theft'.

On returning to our room, Jim and I would sometimes debate the points brought up by D'Arcy and Watt. We found ourselves holding different views. I think I must have been a complicated person compared with him. For Jim everything was simple and clear. There was a self-assurance about him that I lacked. To Jim, faith in God was everything. Peter Levine had lamented my lack of faith in communism; now Foggerty was lamenting my lack of faith in Christianity.

'I can't love God as you do, Jim,' I told him. 'I am not religious. I recognise Christ's passage across history as of extraordinary importance, but my mind is torn by difficulties and contradictions. I don't understand what is meant by eternity. I don't need a God to tell me that hatred is evil and love is good; that tolerance is preferable to intolerance; that to help the poor is right; and that to ignore the misery of the poor is wrong. These things I know from experience and feeling. I'm unable to take things on faith. Instead, I want to get to the heart of things. I want to look everything and everybody straight in the face. I want to see things as they are. The freedom to think like that is surely one of our most precious freedoms. My attitude does not arise from stubbornness or false pride, Jim, but from downright spiritual confusion.'

'You want to know everything, Billy, and you can't.'

'Why can't I?'

'Because there is a door in life beyond which you can't go; there are things that you cannot see and touch. There are things that are too big for you and must be left to God.'

'What are these things?'

'I don't know, except there wouldn't be life without them. That's where faith comes in. You can never define love or beauty, yet you know they exist. You're in a bad way, Billy, you're questioning the word of God. If the world has meaning it must have a mind. I think the mind that directs life is God. God is inscrutable. You must trust God. Find Him, Billy, before it's too late.'

'How am I to find Him?'

'You can only find God through grace. "Seek first the kingdom of God which is within you."'

'I've done it and He doesn't answer.' Jim didn't realise how much I felt the weight of my own inner doubts and conflicts.

'Stop thinking of yourself as somebody special. If you

approach God with your heart and not with your head, He will answer. God's grace is like a moonbeam. It will find you:

> Amazing Grace! How sweet the sound
> That saved a wretch like me!
> I once was lost, but now am found,
> Was blind but now I see.'

My trouble was that I believed in this life on earth; I believed in things that I could see and touch. Jim believed in the unseen and the eternal. To him the Lord God was a kindly father and everything more or less fell into its right place.

'Follow your conscience and do the decent thing,' he ended.

I gained some relief from my spiritual problems by attending debates at the Student Union and the Labour Club. The pacifism of certain speakers sat well with me. Although there were more conservatives and liberals, the socialists made the most noise and gained the most attention. To my surprise, some students had suddenly discovered a new loyalty to 'the people' and 'the masses'. Their efforts were bent on climbing down rather than up. According to them 'the masses' were doing wonderful things; ordinary people were wiser than their leaders.

Outside of Ruskin and the Catholic Workers' College, I don't think I ever met a genuine socialist at Oxford. What I did meet were intellectual socialists who had a negligible effect on the life of the masses. They were all head. They collected working-class experiences as others might collect stamps or butterflies. We working-class students called them 'pretend socialists'.

Instead of worrying about 'pretend socialists', I extended my friendships elsewhere. I started going to Ruskin's Friday-night hops (the dance halls in town were out of bounds), where Foggerty sometimes played the piano. For an hour or two I took my brain out of my head and put it in my feet. The difference between Ruskin dances and those elsewhere in the university was that at Ruskin you danced and danced;

elsewhere, you stood around and talked and talked. When it was time to go, instead of playing the National Anthem, Jim used to bang out the Red Flag, smiling. Few of us intended to live and die beneath it, but we sang it anyway.

O'Hea's way of turning us into civilised human beings was to subject us to the cultural evenings put on by two dear old ladies who lived in a large, sepulchral house in south Oxford. Each week we would straggle after him to visit them.

Dressed in silk and buttoned up to the chin, our hostesses greeted us as if we were returning prodigal sons. They'd spent the whole week preparing for the occasion and fussed over us until we were seated on their unhappy-looking Victorian chairs.

The elder of the two ladies played the piano. Mozart sonatas were her favourites. As she played the same pieces week after week, we became familiar with them. She always finished with a final flourish of her hands. She would then stand, eyes sparkling, and bow with great dignity as if it were a London concert. We stood and clapped. We would not have dreamed of hurting her feelings. Her sister read Shakespeare sonnets. With great dramatic gestures, she lived every line.

The last word said, the last note sounded, we were served supper fit for a king. The fine china looked out of place in our hands. Our fairy godmothers were always astonished at our appetites. I used to wonder what they thought of us: their easy-going chatter left us tongue-tied. Foggerty was the charmer because he could talk about music.

I'm convinced that our unfamiliar appearance and speech brought light into their lives. I can only hope that they thought us worth the trouble they'd taken.

When I could find time, I wrote to my family in Lancashire and my friends in the East End. There was talk of my father finding a job with Rolls Royce in Derby. I also kept in touch with Harold Watkins. Both my sisters had set up their own homes by now and were busy raising a child – Brenda a daughter, Jenny a son. Bobbit, who wrote encouraging notes, but declined my invitation to visit Oxford with a 'not bleedin' loikly', told me that the foundry was still 'a sodding place occupied by lunatics'. Miranda wrote loving notes. Her greatest worry, I think, was that I might become religious. Miss Hesselthwaite and Ma Hargreaves always cheered me up. Although more people were finding jobs, they told me that conditions in east London were still bleak. Hunger marchers were still pouring into London.

On a quick visit to Bow at the beginning of October I didn't see Miranda, but I did meet my old trade-union secretary, Albert Eastead, who had become mayor. 'Didn't realise there was so much bad abaht,' he said cheerfully. ''Ardly time to get a pint.'

<hr>

The clash of secular ideologies and the growing menace of war were never far from our thoughts. Sir Alfred Zimmern, who occupied the Montague Burton Chair in International Relations, was a political oracle who opened our eyes to the world scene. He was stocky, with a large head; his bright eyes peered through thick lenses. 'The problem of our survival,' he stressed, his finger stabbing the air, 'lies more in the foreign than in the domestic sphere.' He was convinced that a confrontation between the liberal Western democracies and the fascist states was only a matter of time. The world was arming to the teeth; another Great War threatened.

With war clouds gathering in Europe (the British government had ordered forty million gas masks) it didn't take much for him to persuade us. As a constant visitor to the continent and a strong supporter of the League of Nations, he always had first-hand knowledge of the growing political crisis. He used to say: 'If children can decide how they will act together, why can't we?' I was surprised one day in 1937 to see Heinrich Brüning, the ex-Chancellor of Germany, enter the lecture hall with him. Brüning's picture had been in all the papers, there was an air of distinction and authority about him. I sat directly in front of him while he expressed his worst fears of Hitler and national socialism. I came away impressed, but hardly surprised that such a civilised, gentlemanly person had been outmanoeuvred by the Nazis.

Zimmern also dealt with the emerging nations in Asia and Africa. Although he usually left his audience to make up its own mind – 'you either support the colonial peoples in their struggle for independence, or you support the colonial powers in putting down the national movements . . . which?' – his sympathy with colonial peoples in their struggle was manifest.

After lectures Zimmern would invite discussion. He was interested in my origins and found it fascinating that a foundry worker should be attending his class. Yet he poured cold water over many of my favourite ideas. My belief in a world socialist state was a nonstarter with him. 'A dream,' he said, 'and not even a beautiful dream. If the problem of international relations concerned our ability to move sacks of potatoes about, we'd solve the problem tomorrow. Moving human beings about and obtaining mutual understanding between them is, however, a problem of an entirely different order. Neither international socialism nor international capitalism can bring about world unity. World systems, whether we like it or not, go against the grain of human nature. Those who try to build a heaven on earth fail to understand human psychology.' He also poured cold water on my idea that socialism was the alternative to compulsion. 'You wouldn't get far in the world without compulsion,' he said. 'Society needs government and government needs power. Without power you have anarchy.'

Zimmern's lectures may not have improved my examination chances, but they provided me with a wonderful education.

The coming of examinations took my mind off world affairs. I'd worked hard during the past eight weeks – perhaps too hard. I was hanging on by my teeth, but I was sufficiently confident to believe that I would get by. In the examinations I did the best I could. I came away neither elated nor depressed. I would not know the results until the beginning of the next term.

To celebrate, the students at the hostel swept the furniture aside and put on a dance, to which many Ruskin friends came. Our 'orchestra' was a gramophone.

The last thing I did before leaving for the Christmas vacation was to have a long talk with O'Hea. He thought I was settling into the new life very well. He had heard nothing but good about me from my tutors, and expected I'd do well in the course and get a great deal out of it. I never mentioned spiritual problems, nor did he. He had a wonderful way of not intruding into one's private life. Except for going for a walk up the river with him now and again, he had left me entirely to my own devices. There was nothing petty or mean in the man, nothing slipshod. Behind the gentle, outward appearance lay a shrewd mind and great inner strength. After eight weeks, my trust in him was complete. No one who knew him doubted his integrity, or his vocation. He devoted his weekends to the spiritual needs of inmates of a prison in the Reading area, or to workers' meetings elsewhere in the country. I was not surprised that the Church allowed him the scope it did.

O'Hea was a doer as well as a thinker. He taught by example. I once witnessed two students arguing about whose turn it was to carry the buckets of coal upstairs. Without a word O'Hea picked up the buckets and carried them himself. The way he carried them, they might have been full of air.

One had to think twice before accepting an invitation from O'Hea to go for a walk. For him, a walk was a test of endurance in which hedgerows, streams, brambles and bogs were ignored. He went through them like a buffalo. He was the only man I knew who could walk past a bull and keep the conversation going. One day I was about to cross a field with him. A bull was bellowing at the other end. As it came towards us, I vaulted over the fence. 'Look out,' I shouted. O'Hea took not the slightest notice. Instead he continued to study the birds through his binoculars; he seemed oblivious to the lowered head and lashing tail. I had visions of him being carried away on the horns. Not at all. The bull halted some yards away, confused; eventually it wandered off. I caught up with O'Hea several fields later. He never said a word.

I left Oxford to share Christmas with my parents in Derby, where they had resettled after leaving Lancashire. I intended to spend the next six weeks at home studying. It was a happy homecoming after three years away. I found my parents well. Mother, now grey-haired, stretched out her hands to greet me. My parents could not understand what I was doing at Oxford, or what Oxford meant. But whatever I was doing was evidently better than what I had been doing, and that's all they cared about. My suggestion that they should visit me there embarrassed them. Mother cared only for her new house. It was smaller than the one in Livingston Road, but for her it was the ship that had come home. Father was either at work or nursing plants in his greenhouse. Because Britain had begun to rearm, he worked day and night helping to make Spitfire fighter planes for the Rolls Royce Company. My people no longer knew the penury they had known in Blackburn. They had money to spare. Even so, I'd got so used to them being poor that I would not have dreamed of imposing additional expenses upon them.

Late on the afternoon of my arrival I went for a long walk in the snow-covered countryside. It was a bitterly cold December day. I was out for several hours and went to bed that night exhausted. I woke in the early hours in a high fever, unable to breathe. My face was on fire, I had intense pain in both lungs. The sheets were wet with sweat. Somehow I roused my parents. Realising that they were facing something quite abnormal and perhaps dangerous, father went out into the sleety night to fetch a doctor. I have a vague memory of his arrival. He diagnosed pleurisy and advised my immediate removal to the central hospital in Derby; neglect could cause suffocation. My parents objected; they had not lost their fear of hospitals. The physician agreed to return in an hour and if there was no improvement, I would either be admitted to hospital, or he would refuse further responsibility for my care. Fortunately my temperature had fallen by the time he returned, so I was left in bed at home, where he visited me on and off for the next three weeks. All these things I learned later. At the time, other than the look in my mother's eyes, I had little idea what was happening. Encased in a hot mud poultice, all I could do was to lie there and feel sorry for myself.

Sometimes when the hours grew long I felt that I was swimming in a still lake in which I was sinking and rising again. I heard the ticking of the clock, a timid bird pecking at the window, muffled sounds and voices coming from the kitchen. I watched the sun's rays going around the room. I heard the sound of Christmas bells and shouting in the street. I had no visitors, for I knew no one in Derby.

As I improved, I listened to the radio. There were reports of the Spanish Civil War. I thought of Peter Levine. The war made me face up to the weakness of my convictions: what kind of a pacifist was I? I was beginning to suspect that I was too self-willed and too self-centred to be a true pacifist. There was a combative streak in me.

After several weeks I tired of sorting out my own and the world's problems and turned to reading. Once I was up to it, I did nothing else but read. When I got tired of my university texts, I drew upon a list of books, which Charlie Duke had given me when I left the East End. Mother ferried books to and from the public library. I was a glutton, devouring one volume after the other.

Eventually the time came for me to return to Oxford. Still

feeling wobbly, I paid a last visit to the doctor. After being indoors for so long, the fresh air and the street noises were unfamiliar. He told me to keep my mud waistcoat on for several weeks. 'You probably fell ill because your body and mind have been subjected to too much stress. Regardless of the work you have to do, you must set aside part of every day to get out of doors into the fresh air. At this point there is not very much I can do for you that you cannot do for yourself. If you follow my advice, you will make a complete recovery.'

Chapter VIII

Second Wind

My return to Oxford for Hilary Term 1937 was like coming home. I came out of the railway station glad to be back. Although it was a wintry afternoon with trampled leaves and some snow about, I walked to the hostel. My footsteps crunched on the frozen pavement and I arrived in Walton Well Road glad to escape from the cold. Appetising smells came from the kitchen; everything was scrubbed and clean. We might have been her own children the way Mrs Padmanabha welcomed us back.

I joined Jim Foggerty upstairs. He had spent his vacation working down the mine. To catch up with each other's news we went for a walk on Port Meadow, where a heavy mist covered the river.

The next morning I woke to the murmur of voices and the tinkle of the altar bell. The foundry whistle blew at the back of the house.

I spent an hour that morning with the principal going over my first term's papers. He was pleased with my progress. My assignments for the new term were labour movements with Cole, political science with Richard Price, and Rodger and Dowdell for further reading in history and economics. I'd already decided to attend Zimmern's lectures. His recently published *The League of Nations and the Rule of Law* had impressed me.

Once term began my life was dominated by writing essays. Every one remained a trial. There were times when I was overwhelmed by the sheer volume of material; I had never heard of some of the ideas tutors threw at me. I could only keep up by cutting back on sleep. Reading essays was no easier than writing them: by page three of my first paper for Price, I found myself whispering in a strange, husky voice. I couldn't believe that I was mouthing such wild ideas in such an idiotic way.

My first tutorial with Cole was on the socialist movement in Britain. 'Socialism here,' he began, 'is different from that on the continent. It places greater emphasis upon evolutionary rather than revolutionary methods.' Hardly pausing for breath, he then surveyed the history of the labour movement. 'Do you have any questions?'

'Yes,' I said, for I was not afraid of Cole, 'I notice that you say little about the class war. Is the idea dead?'

Again he went off like a gun – his tongue racing to keep up with his thoughts. 'The idea of class warfare was the invention of Marx. It was the product of the Industrial Revolution with its factory system, its wage labour, and its growing proletariat. Marx held that everything is primarily economic. In real life everything gets mixed up. I do not underestimate Marx, he had a formidable mind, but his talk of class warfare is unconvincing. Labour's problem is class unity.'

Overwhelmed, I could hear him rushing on. 'British workers have not followed Marx, because they do not like theory. Socialism here grew like topsy, undefined. What's more, almost all of our early labour leaders were devout churchmen. They sought respectability.'

I listened to him, wide-eyed and open-mouthed as he went

on and on, until someone banging on the door told me it was time to go.

Price, with whom I had an appointment immediately after Cole, was known as a holy terror. My friends looked at me pityingly when I mentioned where I was headed. 'Well, all the best,' they said, wringing my hand.

On entering his study I found a strange little fellow sitting with his legs tucked under him. He reacted to my entry like a cat disturbed from its favourite spot. He had an effeminate voice. His hands were so white and so fine that I was mesmerised by them. He wasted no words.

'You Woodruff? Come in, find a seat,' which was impossible without moving stacks of books and papers. Giving me no time to get out pen and paper, he outlined my assignment: 'Using Rousseau's *Social Contract* as your text, write a paper on the theme that man is by nature good and is only corrupted by the development of civilisation. The object of the exercise,' he said, rubbing his head, 'is to get you to say something intelligent about the nature of society and its origins. Good day.'

He gave me a look that defied me to stay. I was completely overcome. I croaked 'Good day,' and fled.

As I dashed out of Price's room another victim stood waiting at the door. 'Moody?' he queried.

'Don't linger,' I advised as I escaped into the quad.

In the weeks that followed I did a number of essays for Price: 'Summarise Hobbes' political theory'; 'Criticise the work of John Locke'; 'Do you agree that Machiavelli's *The Prince* is a primer on self-interest?'

For Price there always had to be an answer. I thought him brilliant. The drawback was that he took a sadistic delight in throwing mental fireworks into your lap, and watching your reaction: 'The innermost principle holding society together is the very opposite of reason,' he said during one tutorial. 'Right? Hume says so.'

No sooner had I got over that hurdle than he delivered another blow. 'How can a statesman remain faithful to his principles as long as other statesmen are trying to undo him? Machiavelli says he can't. What?' Any remaining sign of life in me only encouraged him to add to the torment.

'Why bother with political science to decide what we should do? The Marxists argue that it will happen anyway; the non-Marxists put their trust in a dictator or the market system; the true Christian leaves it to God; many think that fate decides everything. What need is there for us to do anything? What?' Many's the time he made my collar tighten.

After being raked over three times, I no longer knew or cared 'What'. In my haste to get out of the room, I knocked over a pile of books. Back on my bike, I fell to wondering what the Price household was like. I'm sure there wasn't a Mrs Price. How could there be when he never smiled? Perhaps he had a dog. What?

———◇———

I got on well with Dowdell, with whom I did a half-term's work, but thought he lived in an impenetrable world. I never got to know what he was really like. He had a way of lapsing into a preoccupied silence, which made me feel tense. He was devoted to teaching, but seemed so lonely. Perhaps that is why O'Hea dragged him across bogs and ditches to listen to the song of migrating birds. It was just as well that Dowdell was blind to the bulls and other perils which he faced in O'Hea's company. I thought it preposterous for two fully grown men to stand up to their ankles in icy water discussing the finer points of a bird's call.

Sometimes when I was early for my tutorial I would wait for Dowdell by the fire. On the mantelpiece a clock patiently ticked the time away. Silently the door would open. Having greeted me solemnly, he would cross the room to take a seat at my side. He knew where I was sitting. I knew he was wary of me, wariness entered the room with him like a mist.

That term I wrote papers for Dowdell on value, capital, competition and monopoly, rent, wages, interest and profit. He believed in the virtue of free-market capitalism, relying upon Adam Smith's 'hidden hand' to automatically direct self-interest to a higher good. I told him what free-market capitalism had done to my birthplace. He made a quiet response and left it at that. I used to think him cold and bloodless; at first I thought him asleep. Not likely – he never missed a point. He had a remarkable capacity for committing to memory everything I'd said. Looking back, I was lucky to have had such a foil to my socialist arguments. It made me think.

Of all my tutors, Rodger was my favourite. I did several essays for him that term. He taught me that history is always alive and can be thrilling. It did me good to visit him. He was always vibrant, self-assured, expansive and exciting. For other tutors I had great respect; for Rodger I had affection. A happily married man, he seemed to live in the best of all possible worlds, doing precisely what he wanted to do.

He had the knack of summarising what we had discussed in a few short sentences – short enough that I could grasp their meaning. His explanations were rapt and vivid; he understood the nuances of words and used them like fine tools. 'You are immature, Woodruff,' he would chaff. 'All socialists are. You are sensible of the past only in so far as you want to change the present. You think the past can be chopped up like a piece of meat; that you can measure it; that everything is known; that there is no mystery. The past is not a clearly discernible rung on a ladder leading towards some future Utopia. Your vision of the future is not based on the past, but on odd things going on in your head.'

I always came away from his rooms having learned something. He was forever questioning me, forever forcing me back on my own thinking. 'Mustn't treat you like an empty bucket waiting to be filled, must we, Woodruff?' He brought home to me the extent to which the Great War had been a watershed in world affairs. He also challenged the Marxist idea that history is a science. 'To generalise about matter is one thing, to generalise about human beings is another.'

I would sometimes quote one of the sources he had given

me. 'Yes, yes,' he'd reply. 'Stone does say that, but what do you think? Use your common sense, man.' I found being asked to think (when previously no one had ever had the slightest interest in what I thought) an overwhelming experience. I always knew when he was becoming exasperated: he would gently turn his wedding picture to the wall. His hands grasping the mantelpiece, he'd mutter: 'That's not so, my boy; that's not true, my boy.' Later, 'my boy' would become 'old boy'. His tone of voice was always warm.

Rodger was a big man; there was nothing petty or mean about him. He was more a patrician than an intellectual. With all his learning, he never lost sight of everyday life. One summer's day I turned up for my tutorial without my essay. I confessed that for once I'd played truant and had spent my time canoeing up the river. His response was immediate: 'Oh, I say, sensible fellow, sensible fellow, Woodruff. Not often we get weather like this. I wish I could have joined you.' To me, he was one of Oxford's great personalities.

<hr>

In my second term I was still an outsider looking in. I didn't have the college tie or blazer to be accepted as one of the crowd. Some mannerisms – however minor – I never mastered. To attend receptions where we balanced cups and plates on our knees and indulged in loose chatter was an ordeal for me. I couldn't use a saucer without making it rattle. The silver sugar tongs went berserk when I touched them. I had the same trouble with the cutlery at formal dinners. The first time I was given a finger bowl I stared at it incredulously.

I was helped to overcome my awkwardness by Hans Thiel, whom I found one day on Ruskin's staircase addressing a group of students. '"Pretend socialists" are mingy little people with sniffish, superior middle-class ways,' I heard. I stopped to listen. He gave me a friendly nod and continued. He might have been a professor the way the others hung on his words. His manner of speaking had an uncanny, penetrating force.

After he had finished, I was introduced to him. He was dark-featured, of medium build, and about my own age. His thoughtful face and shining eyes intrigued me. There was an air of mystery about him. As he talked, he kept running his long, nervous fingers through his thick, black hair. Repeatedly, he adjusted his spectacles.

I discovered that Hans Thiel had an incisive mind and the quickest flash of wit. He loved the intellectual pleasure of conversation. He was so eloquent that he usually led the discussion, interjecting a bright quip whenever anyone paused in answering him. His family had fled from Germany and his parents were living in New York, but he rarely talked about his past and I never probed. We were both birds of flight: he from German anti-Semitism, I from poverty. We became friends.

Perhaps Hans overcomplicated his life by trying to know everything, but had he not done that I'm sure he would have died of boredom. He was interested in revolutionary socialism, but I knew at heart that it was the last thing he wanted. His socialism was intellectual.

He was at his best when relating some dashing irony about university life. Gossip was his tonic. He loved to tell tales of back-stabbing among the dons. He was full of fun – fun serious, fun farce. He'd go to any length to cause a commotion among the stiff-lipped academics.

One day he persuaded three of us to dress up as women and float past the sunbathers at Parsons Pleasure. As we approached in our punt, I saw what looked like a heap of sea lions gathered on the bank. Sleep hung over the still bodies. A whole island of male nudes sunbathing shocked my working-class feelings. Even the free-living Soviet people kept their pants on.

We were almost alongside them when one of the nudes stirred, looked at us with a disbelieving eye, and raised the alarm. With a great shout, white tails bobbing, the sea lions took to the water. Doubled over in laughter, we lowered our parasols and drifted by.

Until I met Hans I didn't realise that I had been worrying unnecessarily about studies and examinations, and that the immense effort I was making was rather bad form. He thought that my flitting from lecture to lecture was lunacy. With quicksilver brilliance and great sophistication, he assured me that there was absolutely nothing to worry about; university work was quite manageable. He scorned the worker's talk of 'big books'. For him it was all so effortless. He didn't stay up all night finishing essays. I envied him his self-confidence.

Hans loved to socialise. Whereas I was reluctant to attend receptions (especially as I was still wearing the thick, itching mud plaster), he would saunter off and hold his own, gliding in and out of functions like a bird. Neither people nor occasions intimidated him. While I was dropping saucers, he would be directing the conversation.

One sunny day, instead of having tea in his rooms, he insisted that we carry the teapot and cups and plates and knives and sandwiches down the street and picnic on Worcester College lawn, which beckoned invitingly from his window. 'But Hans,' I said, 'we're not members of Worcester . . . and such things are not allowed.' Five minutes later, my protests swept aside, we were eating tomato sandwiches on Worcester's precious lawn.

'Mustn't be inhibited, Woody,' he said as he basked in the sunshine and drank his tea in royal style. 'Wouldn't do.'

Hans was good for my ego and my studies. If I met him in the street with a pile of books under my arm, he'd stop and advise me what to throw away. 'Absolute rubbish this one,' he'd say, taking a book off my stack. 'Can't imagine why he recommended it.' Yet close as our friendship became, there were times when our interests differed. At Friday night hops at Ruskin, I never saw Hans dance. He preferred to stand and talk. I never saw him in football or cricket garb. Rowing would have been an abomination. Exercise for him was lying in a boat floating down the river. His idea of a walk was going from bookshop to bookshop.

———◇———

Some weeks after returning from vacation, I decided that it was time to remove the mud waistcoat that I had been wearing since my illness at Derby. By now it was thoroughly stuck to my skin and the itching was damnable. The choice was to soak it off bit by bit, or wrench it off in one go. With Jim hanging on to the end of the dressing, I counted one, two, three, and pirouetted across the room. The effect left me speechless; I had to sit on my bed to get my breath back. I was convinced that Jim was not only holding the dressing, but my skin as well.

Having got rid of my straitjacket, I began to play football. It was one of the things I did really well; I had been playing football since I was four. I played so well that colleges used to borrow me if they were a man short – all I had to do was change my jersey. I preferred to play centre-half, which allowed me to wander all over the field.

The game was played for the unadulterated joy of playing. At best you might have a man and his dog watching, or a crowd of three or four who had nothing better to do. A game fought in a frenzy of energy, regardless of weather, was what lumbering youths like me needed. Afterwards, we'd stand about – physically exhausted, half-dressed – discussing the match. Few were brave enough to take a freezing cold shower in a little draughty hut called a pavilion. After downing a shandy (half beer, half soda), we'd leap on our bikes, and disregarding the rain, pedal furiously back to a hot shower. Football helped me to be at ease with the toffs. They were not all head, as I had thought at first.

———◇———

As the vacation approached, Jim invited me to his home at New Silksworth. 'Nothing fancy, but it will give you a chance to see how coal miners live.' It sounded exciting and I accepted.

Term work finished, Jim and I took the train to the North. We set out early in the morning, travelling through a damp, cold countryside, and reached New Silksworth at dusk.

The Foggerty family received us with great warmth. Jim's father had died of silicosis years before. The rest of his family were soft-spoken like Jim. There were so many people in the house that I wondered where I'd sleep.

I'd hardly been made to feel at home when two of his brothers came in from the mine. They cleaned up in a tin bath before the fire. That evening we all sang around the piano. Oh, how a mining family can sing! Later, as if it were the most natural thing in the world for eight to sleep where there was only room for four, we all found a corner.

At dusk two days later I walked with Jim and other miners down a narrow country road to the pithead. In the distance screeching buckets were tipping slag on a pyramid of waste. At the pithead the miners put their pipes, matches and cigarettes into lockers, and changed into rougher clothes. We were given Davy lamps. We then mounted a steel stairway and made our way past miners and coal tubs to the shaft. We crowded into a packed, narrow cage like herrings in a barrel. It smelled of sweat and dampness and danger. The gate fell, fastening us in.

With no warning we suddenly dropped like a stone into the earth. For a moment I thought I'd lost my stomach. Had the cable snapped? My companions showed no concern; they continued to mutter to each other, while glistening cables, slimy beams and flashing lights shot by. Two thousand feet down there was an awful jolt, which made me think that the cage was rising again. A dusty burning smell filled the air.

We stepped out into a low main road. The grime-covered dayshift stood waiting to go up. A strong draught of air came from rattling ventilating machines. At a signal we climbed aboard a line of empty coal tubs headed to the coalface under the sea. After about a mile Jim waved for me to get off – the din was so great that speech was impossible.

Entering a gallery we stumbled forwards along a rough, wet track. The only lights were the Davy lamps and the lights on our helmets. Without my helmet the wooden beams would have felled me. Foggerty was able to move with his head down, yet see where he was going. As I staggered after him, wondering how much farther, I had my first feelings of claustrophobia. Ominous cracking noises came from the beams above my head. My back, neck and thighs were aching. The glamour of going down a mine was beginning to fade.

At the coalface Jim joined his team, leaving me to watch from a distance. Through the coal dust I saw a shadowy group of men. Some wore only clogs and kneepads. The temperature was over 80° F. In the flickering light the men looked tough. I watched them break up lumps of coal that had just been cut and blasted out of the wall. New holes were drilled and explosives inserted. Everyone took cover. There followed a tense moment of waiting. The signal was given and with a crash that stunned me, down came a seam of coal. As soon as the dust settled miners dashed in to prop up the roof with pitprops as thick as a man's calf. They worked as a team; each knew what to do. I wondered how a gentle dreamer like Jim could do such Herculean work.

Sometime during the night the pandemonium stopped and I was offered a little food that I washed down with cold tea. Jim introduced me to his mates. They nodded; they probably thought I was a nuisance.

After seven-and-a-half hours I groped after Jim down the endless galleries to the railway. There was no conversation on the way up. The men stood like sheep in a pen.

Light was coming when we reached the top. The air was sweet. As we shuffled out of the cage, the day shift shuffled in. We changed our clothes, handed in our equipment, gargled to rinse out the coal dust, and fell in with a stream of miners trudging across the bleak landscape. An east wind blew in from the sea.

Back in the house we stripped to the waist and, kneeling over a large tin bath in front of the fire, took turns washing. I cleaned Jim's back; he cleaned mine. It took several days to get rid of my aches and pains.

The next day Jim and I cycled to Hadrian's Wall, the north-west frontier of the Roman world, and explored its earth-works. I'd heard so much about the wall as a child that I was thrilled to see its ruins. The ruts of Roman chariot wheels were still there.

After several days I said goodbye to Jim and his family and took a train back to Oxford, stopping off for a night at Derby to see my parents. Jim went back down the mine. I left behind a courageous, generous, light-hearted people.

—◦—

Before Trinity Term began I spent a month reading in the Camera. I stayed with Mrs Padmanabha, who lived next door to the hostel. My savings and the money from the LCC schol-arship kept me going. I was happy to forget that 'Schools' would come in June. There were times when I slipped away from my books to lie on flowered lawns with rose scent in the air and have tea, or sleepily sunbathe at Parsons Pleasure, or doze over endless cricket matches in the sunshine in the Parks, with bees in the grass and muffled bells sounding far away. What bliss to paddle a canoe to the Trout at Godstow, to linger over a beer and talk and watch the fireflies; how wonderful to dance in bare feet on lawns in moonlight with soft music coming through open windows; how easy to venture out into the enchanted Cotswolds, returning with the stars; and have enough shillings to rattle in your pocket to pay your way.

No wonder I loved Oxford. I was completely captivated by it. I loved it for what it was: a great centre of learning; I loved it for the challenge it presented; I loved it for the free-dom and the wonderful life it offered; I loved it for the oppor-tunity to enrich my life; I loved it for the teachers who had accepted me and who tried to help. They would never know what it meant to me. My only fear was that I would wake up one day to find that I was back with Charlie Bobbit at the Bow Bridge Iron Foundry.

I loved Oxford so much that I finally discarded my stolen clothes and bought a tweed jacket and grey flannel trousers like any respectable undergraduate. Before doing so, I pondered which was the more ethically correct: to wear clothing that I knew had been stolen, or to buy clothing with money for which I had not worked.

———◇———

Trinity Term begun, I worked hard at my studies. Somehow or other everything was beginning to come together. I also played hard. I rented a canoe called *Ruby*, which I regularly paddled to Godstow or Kings Lock. There I stripped off and swam. It was pure animal pleasure. 'You's a silly, bloody fool you is. You'll break your bloody neck, you will,' the lock-keeper bawled as I dived into the roaring water which flung itself over the weir into a rock-studded pool. Deaf to all caution, my body shot across the bottom like a trout. There are moments in life, like diving off a weir gate, which you never forget. Youth and spring together invite madness. I wallowed in the bliss of being alive. In those days God was everywhere. Every morning, while Jim was in chapel, I cycled to Port Meadow, stripped off and swam with the swans as my companions. Only those who have bathed in the crowded lake in Victoria Park would know the joy.

———◇———

Springtime is the time at Oxford when visitors fall from the sky. Dear Miss Hesselthwaite came from Bow. I met her at the station, found her a place in a house on Walton Street for the night, and spent the whole day with her going from college to college, and dining her out. She wore a starched print frock, a new hat with red glass cherries and a flowery scarf. She must have thought that the sun was stronger in Oxford than in London, for she held a parasol in her white-gloved hand. A few days before, she had seen the new king and queen in their gold coach on their way to the coronation at Westminster Abbey. Oxford had celebrated with dancing and champagne. She was thrilled at everything, and said all the right things to the people we met. What surprised me was that she said them in a superior tone of voice that I'd never heard before. She was thrilled to see the places where C. S. Lewis taught. She was familiar with *Dymer*, Lewis' book-length poem. She was so honest and good, so pleased at everything that was happening to me, that I felt like having a good cry when she left. 'Do well, Billy, for Bow,' she called as the train drew away.

The Mayor of Poplar, my old trade-union leader Albert Eastead, also paid me a visit. He arrived at the hostel in a shining limousine. ''Is 'Oner' was sitting next to his liveried chauffeur. O'Hea knew him well and was delighted to see him. From the letter that had preceded the mayor, I knew he was pleased to find an excuse to take a day off. 'Blimey,' he said, on getting out of the car, 'you 'ave become a toff, Billy.' I noticed the blue pouches under his eyes, his slight stoop and his shortness of breath. But he struggled on around the university and was interested in all I showed him.

When I introduced him to anybody of note, he'd invariably say the wrong thing in the direst Cockney accent. He answered Rodger when talking about Hitler with: 'If yer arsks my opinion [I honestly feared he would say 'old cock'], there's gonna be a war. Ye can't ply arahnd wiv people like 'Itler. Not 'im, not 'alf. 'E needs turning off, 'e do.' Eyebrows raised, Rodger had the good sense not to incite ''Is 'Oner' any further.

Late that afternoon ''Is 'Oner's interest in Oxford colleges began to wane. 'Look 'ere, Billy,' he said, mopping his brow, 'hedication is ahl right, but hain't it time we wets our whistle?'

''S right Albert,' the chauffeur agreed.

I prayed that the mayor and his chauffeur would not wet their whistles too much on their way home.

Harold Watkins also came as term was ending. He was still working in a woodyard. He came all dressed up wearing a starched shirt and a suit and shiny shoes. He had the same jolly eyes; his teeth flashed white under his dark moustache. He stayed at the hostel so that he might be closer to O'Hea and me. It was as moving to have Harold with me as it had been to have Miss Hesselthwaite. He and I had been together since we were children. For old times' sake, we drank and talked about the past most of the day and night. It was all nostalgia. We went into fits of laughter when we talked about the time we went looking for Betty Weatherby in a blizzard, and wondered what would have become of us had we gone to Russia. He had no news of Betty and little news of Lancashire. As we walked through the colleges, he marvelled at university life. 'Nobody working and three meals a day, Billy! You've arrived.' I introduced him to all the right people, to try to encourage him to get in, but he never did. It would have been wonderful if we could have been at Oxford together. He would have worked hard and done well. Harold was a good man, right down to his heels.

There was a note of sadness at our parting. Would we meet again, and in what circumstances? It was obvious that our lives were drifting apart. Unspoken, we both wondered how I had got to Oxford while he'd failed. We swore everlasting friendship. 'Billy,' he said, clasping my hand, 'Ah'll tell thee sumthin'. It's for thee own good. When tha famous, don't forget me or where tha's cum frae. Tha can get that in thee noddle.' My hand wilted in his clasp.

───◦◦───

And then one morning, unawares, came the dreaded thought of examinations. Gracious! How many weeks were left? How cruel that one could not go on enjoying the spring! I knew that failing was not an option. I'd no job to go to; I had to pass. So back to the Camera I went, back to the books; further dancing on lawns in the moonlight would have to wait.

———◦———

One evening, on coming back from the Camera, I found a note from the principal asking me to see him. I went to his office and, late as it was, found him at his desk.

'What do you intend to do during the long vacation?'

'I have no plans. I haven't given any thought to it.'

'How would you like to spend the summer at the Ecole Sociale at Louvain University in Belgium?'

'What language do they speak in Belgium?'

'Flemish and French.'

'I don't know either.'

Ignoring my remark, he went on. 'A group of students from the Ecole Sociale are about to make a study-tour of the industrial centres of Belgium, Luxembourg and north-west Germany. The experience would be valuable, and it would help you to make connections abroad.'

I knew nothing about Belgium, except that my father had fought there. Although I had seen the word Louvain in learned articles, I didn't know that it was an ancient university. Later I discovered that O'Hea had studied there. 'What about money and how will I make myself understood?'

'The money can be worked out between Louvain and Oxford, the languages are your worry.'

'When do you want my answer?'

'Now.'

I took a deep breath. 'I shall be very happy to go, and am most grateful.'

'You've made the right decision,' he said returning to his papers. 'I'll provide you with details later.'

I was just about to leave when I blurted out a bit shame-facedly: 'I don't have enough money to keep me going until September.'

O'Hea was like Hans Thiel, nothing ever stumped him.

There was a perfectly simple way of doing everything.

'There's a man named William Cockerill,' he said, 'who was at Oxford a hundred years ago. He founded an armament industry and, among other things, the Cockerill Shipping Line. Their headquarters are in Liège, where the business started, but they have offices everywhere. There's one in London whose address I'll give you. Write to them, tell them who you are, and what your plans are. They'll put you on the continent and take you off without any trouble. Won't cost you a penny. It's something the founder thought would be a good idea for Oxford men. It's still done. I heard of someone getting a passage to North Africa the other day.'

I began to think of magic carpets.

'As for pocket money, there are half a dozen sources. Look up the ice-cream people, Tom Wall's. They're very generous to students like you who want to travel. Yes, I think Tom Wall's will do. Better get on to it tonight; there's not much time left.'

'No, there isn't.' I left in a daze. Going to Europe had been beyond my wildest dreams Yet here it was all settled – in minutes. It was overwhelming. O'Hea and I had discussed sums of money equivalent to my annual wage at the foundry.

I returned to my room and told Foggerty about my windfall. His first comment was that the principal must have felt pretty sure that I was going to pass my examinations. I thought so too. We toasted my luck with a glass of warm beer.

I wrote to the Cockerill line and to Tom Wall's. It bothered me to write to strangers for money. Any money I'd ever had, I'd had to work for – which I'd been brought up to believe was the right and proper thing to do.

Everything worked out as O'Hea had said. Cockerill sent me a card and a letter. The card was addressed to the Captain of the *Ghent*, which would take me from Tilbury to Antwerp. The letter told me to write to them in Hamburg for my return passage. Tom Wall's sent me a cheque almost by return mail. I studied that cheque for a long time. It was stiff and crisp and new. I'd never received money like that. I'm sure Tom Wall's knew what they were doing, yet the amount worried me, especially as I hadn't earned it. Ever after that I bought Wall's ice cream.

I also obtained my first passport. Its arrival at the hostel caused quite a stir. Foggerty and I thought its embossed golden lion, unicorn and crown most impressive. Imagine His Majesty requesting the whole world to allow me 'to pass freely without let or hindrance and to afford [me] such assistance and protection in [my] travels as may be necessary'. I didn't think anyone, least of all the King, would go to that trouble on my behalf. And for a mere seven shillings and sixpence.

Meanwhile I kept my nose to the grindstone. The examinations came and went. By luck, or industry, or both, I could not have done better. Rodger wrote across my papers: 'This would get a First in PPE' (Politics, Philosophy and Economics). O'Hea gave me the scripts to read for myself. He offered no praise. Foggerty passed, much to my joy, which meant we'd be together again in the autumn. He told me his plans were to spend the summer down the mine.

To celebrate the end of examinations, a group of us drank our way across the town. We started at a pub in North Oxford and downed a half-pint at every pub all the way to Magdalen Bridge. The thirst I had acquired as a 'sand rat' stood me in good stead. Foggerty and I were the only two sober enough to walk across Magdalen Bridge and take a drink at the pub at the other side. Our friend Thiel was nowhere to be seen.

The next day, dim-eyed, but excited and joyful at the prospect of my first sea voyage, I took the train to Tilbury to join Cockerill's freighter *Ghent*. I called in on the Hargreaves, but kept well away from Miranda – to whom I'd not written for a long time. I carried my very first pair of pyjamas in my bag.

I smelled the sea the moment I got out of the train. I found the *Ghent* tied up among a huddle of masts. Sailors were leaning over the rail. The ship was a scarred, battered workhorse of the seas. A wisp of steam rose from the funnel, the hatches were battened down.

I presented my card to the captain. He was a tall, bearded Scot with the beaked nose of a hawk. He was not pleased to see me or his company's card, and addressed his comments to his stubby pipe. The founder's intentions notwithstanding, students and other free riders were an abomination to him. Having assigned me a cabin, he waited for me to leave.

Disregarding the sullen reception, I went looking for my cabin. It was a tiny cell containing the bare essentials: bunk, seat, hand basin and a porthole. There was a smell of engine oil and burned soup. A lifejacket hung on a hook. I put my suitcase under the bunk and went up on deck. Darkness was falling.

Beneath a damp, leaden sky I watched the seagulls fighting for food. I knew that Romans, Saxons, Danes and Normans had been at Tilbury before me. Vikings had come to plunder. The fear of the Spanish Armada had run through its streets. Hunters for spices, gold, souls, fame and adventure had passed this way.

I was brought down to earth by a sailor who sidled up to me. 'So you're a student, are yee?' He eyed me in a jaundiced way. '. . . from Oxford?'

I said I was.

'Ah weel,' he went on, 'there's no tellin' what some people will do for a livin'. You are a good sailor?'

'I've never been to sea.'

'The pity,' he laughed. 'There's a storm brewing in the Channel and the old man has decided to sail on the night tide. He's at his best when water is coming over the gunnel. He has the record with Cockerill, he has, for the number of ships he's lost. We'll reach Antwerp about sunrise.'

My sense of adventure was coming under serious attack.

An hour or so later, the same sailor brought a large bowl of onion soup and some bread to my cabin.

'There's a poker game going on below deck,' he said as he laid out my food. 'I'll come for you if you wish.'

I said I did wish. Having eaten, I joined three others in a smoke-filled cabin at the stern. They all had weather-beaten faces. There was lots to drink. I didn't touch it; my face was swollen from the excesses of the previous night.

The speed with which they started to take my money scared me. I could see myself getting off the ship naked. I had to work myself into a lather to win it back. At cards my East End training stood me in good stead; I was not the dimwit they took me for.

While we were playing, the engine-room bell rang; boots clattered along the deck. With a slow rhythmic dipping movement and only the slightest suggestion of a roll, the *Ghent* glided out to sea. The night was quiet, the sea calm. For me, it was a moment of disbelief. Born on an island, I was sailing out into the world, as many of my forebears had done. Before turning in, I went on deck. I felt as free as a bird.

———◇———

With a crash that sounded like the end of time, the storm struck soon after midnight. I woke to thunder and a howling wind. I felt my bunk rise, only to drop to the floor again. For a moment I didn't know where I was. I struggled out of my cot and clung to the bulkhead. I put on my lifejacket. Knees bent against the heaving floor, I lurched to the porthole and looked out. An angry, white-capped wave rolled towards me; there was a blinding flash of lightning. I saw leaping mountains of water and shivered with cold. Every time the bow came crashing down, the ship groaned with me. I hoped that those on board knew what they were doing.

That night I was sicker than I thought it possible to be. When I was not clinging to the taps with my head over the basin, I was lying on my bunk contemplating the merits of free travel on the Cockerill Line. Exhilaration had left me. I vowed never to drink my way across Oxford again, or to eat onion soup. Exhausted, I fell in and out of sleep as the *Ghent* pitched wildly. The waves pounded against the porthole. I thought they would never stop.

The ordeal ended when we reached the shelter of the Scheldt. Since the sixteenth century this river had been used by the fleets of the world. The noises of the wind and the sea died away. I went on deck as soon as I could get myself together. The dawn was pale, grey and cold; lights flickered at the mouth of the river; a pilot came aboard. The shore loomed like a shadow; low clouds roiled across the land. Our prow divided the water into two curved sheets. Our engines beat more confidently now that the sea had been left behind.

Fifty miles later I caught a glimpse of the spire of Antwerp Cathedral soaring above the city. Its bells rang across the land. The *Ghent* shut off steam and glided to its berth. Ropes plopped into the water and were made fast; the shuddering stopped. We'd arrived. Moored ships and tall warehouses stretched as far as the eye could see. With a protesting creak the gangplank was lowered.

Feeling that it would be spurious to thank anyone for such a dreadful voyage, and reluctant to meet the captain again, I gathered my belongings, cleared customs with a Belgian official who came aboard, and staggered on to the quayside. The stamping of my passport restored my self-esteem. I had become an important person whose movements uniformed foreign officials took seriously.

I found a small dockside café and took a seat. For the first time in my life, I was on foreign soil. What a difference the crossing of a strip of water made. People looked different, talked another language, and drove on the wrong side of the road.

I ordered a strong cup of coffee. The proprietor detected the smell of onion soup. 'S'il vous plait, Monsieur . . .' (beyond that I understood not one word). Using his hands he wafted me to a little white-painted iron table outside. A parrot perched on a ring by the door screeched as I passed. To my surprise he squawked in French. I wondered what 'Merde! Merde!' meant.

Everything on the quayside was wet from the storm. I pulled my clothes tight around me in the freezing morning air as I drank my coffee and ate a miserable piece of flaking pastry called a croissant. No wonder we British believed that everything at the other side of the Channel was inferior. I was much too exhausted to take delight in having reached another world.

Chapter IX

Spreading My Wings

After another cup of coffee, I began to take an interest in my surroundings. Gulls wheeled overhead, sea water slapped and sucked against the quayside. The deep bass sounds of a foghorn filled my ears. The overhead cranes were busy swinging freight ashore.

After breakfast, I took a tram to the railway station. The train to Brussels departed with a feminine shriek. We slid across pasture land intersected by canals; parks, sleepy villages, cows and lumbering carts, all wrapped in the mist, slipped by. Later the sun broke through.

In Brussels I made my way to the youth hostel of the Jeunesse Ouvrièr Chrétien (Young Christian Workers) on Boulevard Poincaré. A lively young man, who introduced himself as Jean Doeraene, welcomed me. He was the secretary of Abbé Joseph Cardijn. He was delighted to have the opportunity to speak English. I was given a sleeping cubicle, open to all and sundry, and had a shower. While helping me to wash the onion-soup stains from my clothes, he told me that the Jocistes (whose aim was to bring the Christian gospel into working-class life) had played a militant role in capital-labour relations since the French sit-down strikes in 1936.

Later that morning, Doeraene took me on a whirlwind tour of the city. I have a dim recollection of churches, palaces, parks and triumphal arches – enough to last a lifetime. The pace was killing. I tried to say in French, 'Let us sit down under the trees and rest.' He probably didn't understand a word. Desperate, I looked up the word for hangover: I wanted to tell him I had a hangover and that I needed to go a little slower. The dictionary said *gueule de bois*. I decided to skip that one. Instead I raced after him. By lunchtime, the conducted tour had become a blur.

Our tour ended at the Luxembourg Gardens among flower beds that stretched for acres. We were lost in admiration of the roses when a young couple stopped arm in arm alongside us. Without one word of 'by your leave', the young man took out his penis and watered the roses. It caught us both by surprise. I was all for the workers of the world uniting, but not to piss on the roses.

———◦———

The following afternoon, I took the train to Louvain. After a good deal of hunting I reached the Ecole Sociale, where I was met by the director, Pater Perquay. To my embarrassment he kissed me on both cheeks.

Pater Perquay was a tall, white-haired Dominican priest in his late fifties, who spoke English in a deep Flemish voice. He was the soul of hospitality. He was quick to tell me that I had come to what at one time was the outstanding university of Western Europe. We drank a cup of coffee together, after which he insisted on showing me the college. I almost had my hand shaken off by the students to whom I was introduced.

Later, he took me to my room – a spacious, airy study on the ground floor that looked directly on to a canal with water lilies. Beyond were vegetable gardens and fields. A wood crowned the horizon. Although I still had to learn about the swarms of mosquitoes that would descend upon me at night and the pungent smell of 'night soil', which would greet me each morning, the arrangement seemed admirable. Through the open windows I could hear a carillon.

I sat next to Pater Perquay at dinner that night. While nuns, wearing white, starched headdresses, served us, he told me about the destruction of the university and the town in the Great War. Belgium had endured four years of German occupation. I was more concerned with the fact that I was eating horsemeat for the first time. As I was the only Englishman, the other students looked upon my arrival as a heaven-sent opportunity to try out their English. I had to fight every step of the way to speak French. After dinner we sat about in the common room. There were about twenty students there. Their greatest worry was the growing threat of war. Most of them had done military service, and were subject to immediate recall. At Oxford, war was a subject of conjecture; at Louvain it stared you in the face.

The next day, interspersed with endless cups of coffee, a couple of students showed me the university. The library had a soaring tower with a famous carillon. I saw the statue of Erasmus who had taught here; also a treasured copy of Thomas More's *Utopia*. Later, I was taken to classes. I learned little, but it gave me the chance to see Louvain's famous lecturers in action.

A couple of weeks after my arrival, our tour began. Our bus, when it arrived, did not inspire confidence, nor did Denis the driver. With a cigarette clenched between his yellow teeth, he looked a sad gnome.

Our journey took us south-west to Mons on the largest coalfield in Belgium. Every town we passed through had its memorial to those who had fallen in the Great War. From Mons through a flat countryside, we went eastward to Charleroi, centre of the Belgian iron industry.

As I stood among the showers of sparks and watched the workers toil, I couldn't help wondering how a 'sand rat' could sweat his guts out and be paid very little for it; whereas if you studied workers – as I was doing – you did very well. The farther one got away from working with one's hands – the work that made the wealth of nations, that gave us our daily bread – the better off one was. I had been brought up to believe that hard manual work paid – it didn't. None of the men I was looking at would come to be known individually; they'd play almost no role in forming the opinion of their age; yet without them our world could not continue.

From Charleroi we rattled eastward to the Liège-Seraing area on the banks of the Meuse, the heartland of Belgian industry. Here the night sky was lit by the eerie glow of blast furnaces, and coal and iron dust filled the air.

Ominous preparations for war met us wherever we went. In Liège we saw a machine that produced a rifle a minute. The finished rifles came off a moving belt faster than they could be handled. Production went on round the clock. Paradoxically, at one Belgian plant they were busy shipping crude iron to Germany by the trainload to make more weapons, to make . . .

On the wharf at Seraing, I came across a bronze statue of John Cockerill, son of the Oxford student William Cockerill, the English mechanic who had helped to turn Belgium into one of the workshops of the world, and on whose ship I had sailed from Britain.

Wherever we went, reinforced steel and concrete mounds and dragon's teeth tank traps scarred the countryside. I had never seen fortifications like that in England. Our defences were at sea, or built in somebody else's land.

The irony of studying the means of killing people during the week, and the treasures of Western art at weekends was not lost on me. We were the heirs of a very strange world.

———◇———

The racket of our engine echoing through the hills, we bounced through the narrow wooded valleys of the Ardennes. With nerve-racking regularity, Denis would halt the bus on the hills and struggle to find a lower gear. We would all breathe a sigh of relief when, amid the howls of the clutch, we were jerked forwards again.

We finally reached the city of Luxembourg perched on a rocky plateau. We stayed for several days and visited towns with unforgettable names such as Dudelange, Differdange, Rudange and Dommeldange. In 1937 Luxembourg was benefiting from rearmament and was considered an economic miracle. There was only one man unemployed there, or so they said. He was dusted off and brought before us when we visited the Minister of Labour. He was a jolly fellow in his fifties who enjoyed the role he was playing.

One day we lunched close to the German border. Through binoculars, we could see the frontier post at the top of a white-gravelled road. I took on a wild bet with the Belgian students that I could sprint to the German village of Roth, buy some German beer and sprint back again before the bus moved on. Bets placed, I left to a cheering start.

Once started, I began to have second thoughts. The road was steeper than I had thought, and I could not get a grip on the stones. Except for the buzz of insects and my own heavy breathing, no sound broke the withering heat. Knowing that my progress was being watched from above and below, I refused to turn back.

By the time I reached the checkpoint, my face was burning and I was drenched with sweat. The border guards concealed their thoughts with a curt 'Heil Hitler.'

'Good day,' I choked.

'Wo wollen Sie hin?' one of them said, as he studied my passport.

'I want to go to Roth to buy two bottles of beer.'

'Warum?' they demanded, eyebrows raised.

'I want German beer.'

They looked suspicious.

'Wo ist Ihr Gepäck?'

'I don't need any bags, only beer.'

While one of them consulted the regulations, the other fixed me with an unblinking stare. I sensed that he thought me a dangerous idiot.

Slamming the book shut, the first one took up his stamp and struck my passport a powerful blow. 'Gehen Sie,' he ordered, pointing to the door.

Gladly, I ran down a long hill to Roth. Using sign language, I purchased two large bottles of beer from a startled shop-keeper, then, clutching the bottles, I ran back to the two Germans at the top of the hill.

With a wooden stare, they told me that the beer could not be exported to Luxembourg without paying duty. But I had spent my German marks. One of them read out something in German. He was strangely serious, as if he was dealing with a smuggled bomb rather than smuggled beer.

'Basta,' he ended.

For a moment I was flummoxed. Did I have to surrender the beer? Had I run through all that heat for nothing? I could hear the Belgians laughing. The Germans looked as if they might laugh too.

Excusing myself, I left the hut and sat down among the wildflowers outside. With the two men watching, I drained both bottles. There was no regulation against that.

A little unsteadily I got to my feet and asked them to stamp my passport again. They looked at me angrily.

Clutching my passport and the two empty bottles, I stumbled down the hill to the bus and amid whoops and cheers I clambered aboard. Concealing his impatience, Pater Perquay studied the empty bottles. 'Holy Mother of God!' he said.

My passport and the empty bottles were passed from hand to hand. I revelled in my triumph. Although I had not returned with the beer in the manner intended, I had won the wager;

594

my slightly drunken state confirmed that. 'Sauvage anglais,' said Denis, starting the bus.

---◄◦►---

Before leaving Luxembourg, Pater Perquay spoke to us about Germany and the 'new order' that governed it. He talked about the use of cameras, of guarding our tongues and not going off on our own. He left us in no doubt about his own disquiet. Nazism, he feared, threatened to create a godless state: slowly but surely the Nazis were divorcing the Church from the people, the children from their parents, and the nation from God. For evil men to triumph it only remains for good men to stay silent. For refusing to compromise their conscience and their soul, many Germans were now languishing in concentration camps. A few months earlier in March 1937 the encyclical *Mit brennender Sorge* (With Deep Anxiety) had been smuggled into Germany and read from every Catholic pulpit. In the encyclical the Pope denounced the Nazi doctrine of race and blood.

After the Roth incident, I think Perquay worried about me. 'You English,' he warned, 'are a happy-go-lucky people with a sense of humour; the Germans are not, especially when they are in uniform. You have a lot to learn, my child, be prudent.'

Perquay would never know the effect his few words of caution had upon me. In a flash I realised what Father D'Arcy had been talking about in his lectures on moral philosophy. 'What is the Good?' 'What is the true end of man?' he had asked, and it had all gone over my head. Now I realised that there had to be a Good – a right and a wrong way – independent of the exigency of the moment, independent of the political regime in power, independent of time. Man is a moral being and he has to make choices. D'Arcy had not been in the clouds after all. I had. He had been dealing with a real problem; a problem that was now costing people their lives and their liberty. I spent much of the rest of that day turning

595

these things over in my mind. It was like catching a fever.

From the moment we reached Trier with its Roman ruins, we were conscious of having reached a different country. The impression grew as we drove along the Mosel to Koblenz, where I first caught sight of the Rhine.

The countryside was so beautiful that I took time off to send coloured postcards of ancient towns and castles to family and friends. (My sister Brenda's reply awaited me when I returned to Louvain. It read: 'Have you robbed a bank?')

Compared with Britain and Belgium the atmosphere in Germany was almost euphoric. There was a brightness and a vibrancy about everything: a feeling of strength and pride. The post-war anarchy and humiliation of Germany were a thing of the past. The note of exhilaration conflicted with Perquay's grim warnings.

The Ruhr Valley throbbed with industrial power. There was a bitter smell of iron dust in the air; sombre clouds of smoke and steam hung over the region like a fog; blast furnaces glowed at night. A depressed area in 1933 when the Nazis came to power, the region now worked round the clock. The Belgian students were awestruck; it did nothing to lessen their fears.

The ugliness of the towns was deceiving. Alongside the smog and dirt were parks and forests, and lakes where we swam. We often sat in beer gardens eating sauerkraut and a vast variety of sausages and black bread. We learned to sing, 'Trink, trink, Brüderlein trink.' Some of the towns were renowned for their choirs, orchestras and museums. The Gothic towers of ancient churches rivalled the factory chimneys. Moats and ramparts were there to prove that there was hardly a town that hadn't been beleaguered at some time or other. The houses huddled together behind the walls like sheep. The only walled cities I knew in England were Chester and York, and that was because of the Romans.

For a week and a half, we visited industrial plants in Dortmund, Bochum, Wuppertal and Duisburg. People did everything they could to make our visit a happy one. Our arrival at Krupps coincided with that of the company's directors. They got out of their limousines wearing long black frock coats and tall silk hats; it looked like a meeting of funeral directors. Our bus was shunted aside until they had entered the building. I thought it fitting that such a group of sombre crows should direct one of the largest armament plants in the world.

The first thing I noticed on entering Krupps' main building were poster-size photographs of Hitler and other Nazi leaders on a visit to the plant. Armament manufacturers, like bankers, have to be humoured. A senior official formally welcomed us, clicking his heels and bowing. He reminded us that Krupps had been occupied by French and Belgian troops (emphasis on the Belgian) between 1923 and 1925.

On our last evening in Essen, we were addressed by a gently spoken party functionary who came to our lodgings to extend the best wishes of the state. Starting with 'Heil Hitler,' he stressed the need for cooperation between the youth of all nations. He went on to extol Germany's strength, pride, virtue and invincibility. Under Adolf Hitler the Germans had realised their age-old dream: the creation of a unified state. Their only wish now was to live in peace. In coming to power, Hitler had placed the peaceful cooperation of nations above all other aims. He reminded us of the pledge given by the Führer on the Fallen Warriors' Day in 1936 that he would never sacrifice the flower of the German nation in war. 'It is not for you to *die* for your country,' Hitler had declared, 'but to *live* in a country worthy of your love.' The speaker ended with a plea for peace.

I'm convinced he honestly believed every word. No questions were invited; none were asked. After a hush, Pater Perquay thanked him on our behalf.

The next morning we heard that Japan, with whom Germany was cementing relations, had begun an undeclared, all-out war against China.

And then our trip was over and we were back in the rattling, wheezing bus headed for Aachen on the frontier. The visit had made a deep impression on us. Nobody on the bus criticised the German people who had been so generous; nobody denied the exhilarating feeling that we'd felt throughout our tour; nobody doubted that Germany was a most civilised country. What we feared was the brutality of the regime. The persecution of minorities and opponents could not be talked away.

Our thoughts were best summed up by one of the students: 'We are Athenians,' he said, 'returning from a visit to Sparta.' There was little humour in Sparta and even less tolerance.

The debate about Germany continued after we returned to Louvain. Each of us had his own version of how the future would reveal itself. The hope of the rule of law prevailing in international relations was being shattered daily in Spain, Ethiopia, and now in China. Crude power was taking over the world.

During the remainder of my stay in Belgium I visited the homes of students across the country – from the flax fields of Flanders to the valley of the Meuse. Always I was asked the same question: 'Will there be war?'

Meanwhile, I did my best to study the books I had brought with me. Staring at the fields beyond the canal outside my window, I also tried to improve my French with the help of a Hugo *Teach Yourself* book. Occasionally, I'd continue to work at my open window until the long, graceful shadows had yielded to darkness and a pale and mystic moon.

At the beginning of September I met up with Jean Doeraene, the young man I had met in Brussels. Together we went on a two-week cycling tour of the Ardennes. We took a train from Louvain Station late one morning on a fine summer's day. Our destination was a low, blue ridge on the horizon. Hour after hour, our train creaked its way into the hills. The higher we went, the colder it got; we finally wrapped ourselves in our blankets. Steam misted the windowpanes. We were still rattling along when the sun set behind us among blood-red rays.

We finished up hours late, half-dead, in the pitch-dark, on the platform of an abandoned railway halt called Quarreux. The station was the nearest point to the Jociste youth hostel we were headed for and trains stopped on request. We watched the dwindling red light of the departing train rocking into the gloom. Its whistle sounded lonely and sad.

We didn't know where we were, or how we could get to the youth hostel. The platform was covered with nettles; the building – abandoned for the wind to batter and the rain to beat – was collapsing from lack of repair. All around us was a dense forest with a strong resinous smell; somewhere below us a river rushed by; a low mist lay among the trees; there was no moon. We gazed at our bleak surroundings and bedded down where we stood.

'This will test les Anglais,' Jean said, as he took out his groundsheet and blanket. Reluctantly, I followed suit.

Half an hour later the cold forced us to get up. We stamped about to restore circulation. Desperate, we removed the hasp from the waiting-room door and lay down on the benches inside. We'd hardly put our lights out when we heard a pattering of little feet. Warily, we stared into the darkness.

I woke to rats rustling among my kit. Light filtered through the dirty windows and the cracks in the walls. We got our things together and, guessing at the route, entered the forest. The land was hushed and grey. My spirits were a little better than they had been the night before. As we pushed our bikes, sometimes climbing over fallen trunks, the greyness changed to green.

We eventually located the youth hostel by its smoke. It was a remote cabin, buried in a wood of silver birches and pines. It had about it an air of wanting to remain hidden. Breakfast was being cooked; we were given a warm welcome.

It is amazing what a hot drink and food can do to make the world seem a better place.

The hostel contained a bench, a table made from local pine, a Dutch tiled stove with logs stacked against it, and several cots. The table had been scrubbed so often that it was milky-white. Candles and paraffin lamps were the only light. Everyone helped with housekeeping and log splitting. The pervading smell was one of wood smoke and bodies.

When the sun had gone down and the hills had risen huge and dark, we sat around a crackling campfire – the light flickering on our faces, the smoke sometimes blowing in our eyes – singing and telling tales, disregarding time. For the hardy, there was a homemade swimming pool filled with ice-cold water. The less hardy could share a tin bath with water heated on the stove. Except for those who washed first, the colour of the water went from grey to black.

If the weather was good, Jean and I cycled along narrow winding roads to isolated villages. En route, I was given a lecture on the Ardennes, most of which I promptly forgot. Sometimes we'd have to push our bikes up the long, silent grades. Exhausted, we would lie on our backs in the velvet grass against the sun-warmed earth, listening to the hum of insects. We picnicked by gurgling streams, feasting on bread, cheese, onions and apples. One day we stood and watched a solitary hedgehog crossing a lonely country lane. We'd sit in bright sunshine on a stone bridge and lose ourselves in the water's flow. With a hawk hovering almost motionless overhead, a partridge leaped from the grass with a startled whir. With the shadows becoming night and darkness creeping through the hills, we'd return to the hostel, mosquitoes singing in our ears, our handkerchiefs full of mushrooms

Gritty porridge and mushrooms were the staple diet. We boiled the mushrooms and ate them with salt and pepper, or cut them to bits and fried them in butter with garlic and onions. Everyone except me seemed to know where to find them, and how to distinguish the poisonous from the wholesome, the tasty from the bitter. Jean was a connoisseur. There was always speckled trout. At the end of the day our bodies ached with weariness. I seldom had time to study the knot-filled ceiling above my cot before falling asleep. You don't notice mosquitoes when you're worn out.

I usually rose early to watch the dawn – my senses have always been most aware of beauty at first light. The morning dew gleamed on the trees like pearls. I revelled in the cloudless sky, the sun touching the hills, the pine-scented air, and a lark making its tireless chant. I was entranced by the countryside in its summer garb: I watched the hills changing colour in the different light, the river hurtling and foaming, and the trees bending in the breeze. I caught a glimpse of red deer bolting for cover.

At day's end, pools of shadows and the sun's rays faded among the trees. A long twilight and a reddened sky gave way to a hushed blackness. The nightingales sang. Occasionally, planes flashed across the sky reminding us of another, more urgent world.

On our last night around the campfire, with an improbably large yellow moon rising over the hills and a ring of young faces turned to the flames, we talked about the coming war in which we probably would have to fight. It was a still night with the hills settled into silence. Before turning in, somebody began a lullaby; the rest of us took it up:

Ferme tes jolis yeux	Close your pretty eyes
Car les heures sont brèves	For the hours are brief
Au pays merveilleux	In the wonderful country
Au beau pays du rêve.	In the beautiful country of dreams

Ferme tes jolis yeux	Close your pretty eyes
Car tout n'est que mensonge	For everything is but an illusion
Le bonheur est un songe	Happiness is but a dream
Ferme tes jolis yeux.	Close your pretty eyes.

After singing it several times Jean and I said goodbye to the others. I left the fireside lost in thought. While I was moved by the singing, I rejected the idea that the whole adventure of life was false and that only in sleep was there relief.

'What do you think?' I asked Jean.

He shrugged. 'Leave it to God,' he said, turning away.

—◦—

We rose at dawn to catch the only train halting at Quarreux that day, silently creeping out of the hut before the last star had faded. Around us the world was hushed. Capped by the morning mist, the brown hills slept. We took a short cut across a field to the station, leaving a track of black footprints. We climbed from a cold platform into an even colder train.

Our train creaked its way downhill through fields of marigolds and cowslips. We returned to the plains with our senses sharpened, our eyes and ears keener, and our range of feelings widened. We were bursting with good health. As the day wore on and the cold mist melted from the land, we ate the blackberries we had picked the day before. We had come across great thickets of them and had pulled them down and gobbled them hungrily by the handful until the juice ran from our chins.

—◦—

From Brussels I went with Jean to his home in the village of Bois d'Haine for a weekend visit. The countryside was tinted with autumn colours. Jean's fiancée Julienne Olivier, a petite, attractive girl wearing a Brussels university cap, met us at the station. She called me Guillaume. She was accompanied by her aunt; chaperoning was *de rigueur*. Whenever we went for a walk in the countryside, the aunt always trailed us.

On Sunday morning we went to church and returned for a midday feast to Julienne's sprawling family farm outside the village. It was the first time in my life that I had been treated as the guest of honour, and I found the warmth of it overwhelming. Relatives had come from miles around.

When Jean and I arrived, we were greeted by a jolly, noisy gathering. A long dining table and benches ran down the room; a selection of wines lay on the table in wicker baskets. After introductions, we were offered an apéritif and were soon jostling and shouting with the rest. At one end of the room women were cooking among a cloud of steam. Julienne and her mother constantly ran from guests to ovens. Close to the entrance, a man played a fiddle. All the windows were open and the shutters were thrown back.

Before the feast, Monsieur le Curé said grace. After a delicious vegetable soup the real eating and drinking began. Just when I thought the meal was done, we started all over again – each dish greeted with a cheer. We ate shellfish and duck and veal and vegetables and puddings and savouries and blackberry tarts and cheeses and nuts and fruits and goodness-knows-what else. You either met the challenge of the next dish or felt the shame. Everyone gave the impression that they intended to sit there eating and drinking for days.

As course followed course, talk and laughter became more excited; faces reddened. Between drinks, the fiddler played. Like the others, I loosened my tie and unbuttoned my jacket. I was intrigued by the way the men would light up their pipes between courses, or chat with each other at the open windows, or even wander off and come back again. It was like going to a long play at the theatre where one was allowed to go out at the interval to recover. The women chatted to each other, trying to exchange years of gossip in a single afternoon. The children ran about uninhibitedly; the infants were passed around the room.

At the end of the meal, Jean suggested that I should offer a toast of thanks. I responded as best I could in halting French. Either the company had ceased to be discerning, or my eloquence had improved with wine; whichever, my toast brought prolonged applause and a whole stream of other toasts. Jean got up to toast my health and obtained from me a pledge that I would return to Flanders. For each toast it was compulsory for me, as the guest of honour, to consume twice the amount that other people were drinking. At least that is what happened. I began to wonder when all the conviviality would end – I knew I couldn't keep up much longer.

After the guests had gone, Jean and I staggered out of the house and threw ourselves down under the branches of an apple tree, where we slept until the shadows fell.

By now the two of us had become firm friends. It was hard for me to say goodbye to him in Bois d'Haine and make my way back to Louvain.

◦

At the beginning of October, with the earth a little cooler and the summer fragrance gone, I parted from my friends in Louvain with the greatest regret. They gave me a send-off by taking me out on a drinking spree, and as a parting gift they gave me a German bicycle lock I had admired. It was far superior to anything we had in Britain. Fixed to the frame of the bike, it threw a bolt across the spokes; it was extremely effective in putting off bike thieves. Later on I could always identify my bike with it.

'My child, I think war will come,' Pater Perquay said as he hugged and kissed me farewell. 'I shall pray for your safety. I think Hitler will drag the German people and us into the pit. I don't believe the League of Nations will make the difference. What is everybody's business is nobody's business.'

Once more I travelled from Antwerp on a Cockerill vessel down the Scheldt. We went slowly in the evening light, trailing smoke, the silver river ruffled by a breeze, the water whispering at the bow. For the moment I was conscious of a shining, sensuous world. I remained on deck as we passed through the shadowed dunes, the sun-tipped spire of the cathedral receding behind us. Westward the sky glowed red.

The echoing notes of the carillon could be heard long after Antwerp had disappeared into the night. With each peal of the bells the hush of night deepened; there was goodness in the moment. The world was at peace; heaven was on earth and we were at its centre. Time was suspended.

The captain of this ship could not have been more hospitable. With much yarning and laughter, we drank our way to Tilbury. For one night, I forgot all about the threat of war.

I reached Oxford at the beginning of Michaelmas Term, with some ice-cream money still in my pocket. I was glad to be back, and aware of the great debt I owed O'Hea, Perquay, the Cockerill shipping line and Wall's ice cream. My north-of-England conscience reminded me that while my fellow students at the hostel had been working, I'd been having the time of my life. I felt a touch of guilt. I wondered if I should salve my conscience by returning the unspent money to the ice-cream company.

◄○►

I returned with greater self-confidence and a much broader outlook than I had had when I set out. Above all, I recognised the universal nature of Christianity. A Mass in Germany or Belgium was the same as a Mass in Oxford. Going abroad had enlarged my imagination and my knowledge of French and German. I came home to England's odd-shaped fields and winding roads realising how lucky Britain was to be an island. How peaceful it was compared with the continent. Yet I no longer saw it – as I had done since childhood – as the strongest country on earth. While Germany was self-assured, officious and bold, Britain seemed to be faltering. Germany couldn't find sufficient labour to do all the jobs it had to do; millions of people in Britain were still out of work.

My travels had played havoc with my pacifism. What I had seen and heard had convinced me that the Nazis were bent on aggression; and the same could be said for the

605

Japanese who were now pillaging China. How much longer, I asked myself, could I afford to be a pacifist?

But I returned to an Oxford untroubled by the threats of war. People like me, who came hurrying back from Germany with a note of alarm in their voice, were called prophets of doom. My companions had no time to discuss that clown Hitler.

Chapter X

An Old Hand

Oxford, when I had set eyes on it a year ago, had been love at first sight; now it was love enduring. The fears I'd felt then had long since passed. Superior voices and Oxford airs still jarred me, but I no longer felt my separateness, or had to clench my teeth or watch my temper. When I heard the endless peals of Big Tom, I knew I had come home.

Foggerty and I were glad to see each other. We had a beer to celebrate. We now occupied the other large bedroom at the front of the hostel – why we should have occupied the best rooms for two years was something we didn't enquire into.

While I had been enjoying myself on the continent, Jim had been mining coal. 'I've never known anything else,' he said.

Thanks to O'Hea and Rodger, I was directed to all the right tutors. By now Rodger had become my mentor and I was careful to follow his advice. He had a way of smoothing out bumps without fussing. I settled down once more at a desk in the Camera, did my tutorials, and attended the lectures I wanted to hear.

After Louvain, with its stuffy afternoons spent in smoke-filled cafés and students' rooms, I was happy to get back to football, swimming and canoeing. The work-hard, play-hard Oxford regime suited me better, and I got more work done. While the soft autumn air continued, Foggerty, Thiel and I would sometimes cycle to the low-beamed parlour at the Trout at Godstow and have a bite of food and a drink, which is what people had been doing there since the twelfth century. While the water rushed over the weir, we talked about life and its tangled human relations.

The threat of war was never far from our talks. Although my hope for peace was beginning to fade, it had not faded enough for me to join the Officers Training Corps. Those who did would be commissioned on the outbreak of war. I was too much of a pacifist to take their advice. Hans and I stayed out because we were anti-military; Jim stayed out because mining was a reserved occupation. We'd been brought up in an age that was appalled by the staggering losses of Ypres, the Somme, Verdun and Passchendaele. Our fathers' generation had been fooled and betrayed. A great many of us believed that the military had botched the Great War, and that the politicians had botched the peace. If we didn't watch out, the old men would sacrifice us next. We didn't agree with Winston Churchill that war with Germany was inevitable. With his scaremonger views, he was in the wilderness, isolated and unpopular. But as time passed, the odds of war grew. 'Our frontier,' said Lord Baldwin, 'is on the Rhine.' Many of us wondered whether we would have time to finish our studies.

———◦———

I kept the growing tensions in international relations from interfering with my life by indulging in a good deal of outside reading. I didn't respect the dictum: 'You should read what you're told to read, and keep your nose out of books that don't concern you.' With Thiel pointing the way, I discovered Thucydides and Herodotus, Livy and Tacitus. I found the Bible, the Koran and the Bhagavad Gita. I also read the Jewish Book of Psalms. With the exception of the twenty-third Psalm, 'The Lord is my shepherd . . .' I was appalled by them. 'Why are they so full of horror and violence and vindictiveness?' I asked Thiel.

'To remind us of terrible times.'

I bought used books at a shilling a time, and consumed the works of Swift, the Brontës, Hardy, Ruskin, Wells, Shaw, one after the other. They greatly enriched my life. Rodger encouraged me to read Macaulay, Green, Gibbon and Hume. Gibbon I found ironical; Hume was too dour. I couldn't swallow the idea that we could never prove something to be valuable or right. I thought that reason guided emotions and not the other way round. Everything Rodger recommended stirred my imagination, which is what he intended. The appeal of history, he kept saying, is imaginative. Perhaps that's why I loved history. A manual worker has an inborn antipathy to theories – as I discovered when doing economic theory – but shows no reluctance to use his imagination.

I have to thank Thiel for introducing me to the Old Vic. 'Come with me, Woody, you lack sophistication; can't let studies interfere with a renaissance in the theatre.' The West End plays were a long way from the 'penny readings' I had heard as a child. If I had any reservation, it was that too few of them dealt with the problems of the masses.

In November 1937, my old East End friend Peter Levine paid me a visit. Invalided out of the Republican Army in Spain, reality for him was that he no longer had a right hand. I'd already been told about it and I couldn't help wondering what might have happened to me had I gone with him.

He got out of the train full of life and greeted me warmly.

Neither of us mentioned the missing hand, but for a moment it made our meeting awkward. Although the weather was mild, Peter was wearing heavy clothing. His face, which looked older and thinner, still showed its customary pain of commitment. He wore a Trotsky-like beard and a coarse cap; his spectacles were of the cheapest kind. I thought that something abstruse had crept into his face since I last saw him: it had hardened. As he gripped my shoulder with his good hand, I caught a glimpse of the old fanatical fire in his eyes. He could have been a member of the Soviet Politburo.

I introduced him to O'Hea, whom he had once called 'dark and sinister'. Talking about old times, we wandered about the town, eating and drinking as we went. I remembered the day in Poplar when he had invited me to join the Communist Party; I wondered if he was about to try again.

Without a word being said, I could see that the beauty of the university was lost on him. His mind and his feelings were elsewhere. He spoke with great passion, as he always had done, of the uselessness of intellectualism. He regarded Oxford as a citadel of class privilege aimed at perpetuating a social order that benefited the rich. 'Vacuous, feeble people,' he said viciously, 'too tired to lead. It's this herd that is bringing the country to its knees.' He didn't give a damn if he was overheard. I listened to his bitterness with impatience. I'd never known him quite so censorious.

After a year at the university I was willing to adapt traditional institutions to a new setting. Why sweep away a centre of learning that expressed so well the ideals of order, harmony, proportion and beauty? I couldn't help thinking that with Peter as vice-chancellor the university would be a bleak place.

That afternoon Peter spoke before the Labour Club; communism was respectable at 'Red Oxford'. The club had been infiltrated by the Communist Party and the Young Communist League, especially since the outbreak of the Spanish Civil War. The talk was a Peter performance, full of sacred fire. He described the heroic resistance of the Loyalist troops in Madrid. 'But for Russian tanks, Franco would have entered Madrid in October 1936.' He didn't hesitate to tell his audience that almost all of the British volunteers of the International Brigade were working class.

'Spain is the dress rehearsal for a worldwide conflict between socialism and fascism. The British labour movement should stand up and demand "Arms for Spain". Labour's opposition to conscription is utter madness. Sooner or later you'll all have to fight. Pacifism means abandoning the world to tyranny. Weapons are the crucial factor in the saving of the world.' Krupps would have agreed with him.

He finished to great applause. The students were on Peter's side – this fellow, we thought, is talking about the war he's fought. Yet Peter had his critics. One student accused him of depicting the war as part of a contest between good and evil. Another complained that Peter had led us to believe that the Republicans were united, which they weren't. They were killing each other. Someone else thought that the Soviet Union was being painted in too good a light. Its intrigues and growing influence in Madrid had provided Franco with an excuse to intervene. Peter was so spiritually exalted with his crusade against Franco that he was not open to argument. In answer to a question, he accepted the murderous purging by Stalin of leading Russian communists as completely above board. He refused to believe reports of atrocities committed by the socialist republican government of Spain.

The meeting was an eye-opener for me. I didn't realise that there were so many ifs and buts about the conflict. I saw the Spanish Civil War, as Peter still saw it, as black and white; right and wrong. I don't suppose Peter would have gone off and lost his hand had he not seen it like that. He had risked his life because he had had a vision.

We went for a beer after the meeting. Making no allowance that Peter was a guest, Thiel went after him hammer and tongs. It was an experience for Foggerty and me to listen to two brilliant people arguing from different sides of the barricade.

'Communism is not out to save the working class,' Thiel argued, 'it's out to use them. Your loyalty does not lie with the British working class but with the Communist International and Russia.'

The two became so heated that they did not even take time off to drink their beer. 'What is the difference,' Thiel asked finally, 'between a Nazi and a communist tyranny? They are both tyrannies.'

Peter was not slow in answering. 'One tyranny, if you must call it that, represents the masses, the Nazi tyranny represents the few.'

'Those two spoiled my beer,' Foggerty later complained.

Peter and I met again the next day. No matter how hard I tried to avoid it, we started arguing with each other. 'The nobs have captured you,' he interrupted me, as he strode restlessly about my room. 'They'll turn you into a bourgeois intellectual, you'll see; you're going to be as effete and ineffective as the rest. You're no longer one of us.' He stopped his pacing to look out of the window as if he were expecting someone. Then he was off again.

'You don't know what you are talking about,' I shouted. 'You won't listen. I can't stand it any longer.' What I wanted to say was: 'You frighten me, Peter. You have become so concerned with the struggle that you have lost sight of the ideal with which you and I set out. You've stopped talking about people, except to say that the people must not rule; the revolutionary minority must rule, of which you leave me in no doubt you are one. When you imply that inhumanity can be excused on the grounds of class war, we must go our separate ways.'

I learned later that Peter returned to Spain as a political advisor. In 1939 I spoke with someone who swore he had seen him in Moscow; he had had no difficulty in identifying a fellow without a hand. After that there was silence; no subsequent inquiry succeeded in finding him. He must have been liquidated in one of the communist purges by someone more dedicated and ruthless than he.

Peter's certainty about a coming world tragedy haunted me after he'd gone. A nice pickle I'd be in if he was right: I'd either have to go to jail as a conscientious objector, or I'd be sent to the front. Either way, it would be the end of Oxford for me. He'd been so cocksure that I expected a declaration of war to appear on the newspaper placards every time I went out. It was a relief when leaving the Camera at night to read that 'Lightning wins Aintree at 20 to 1', or that Jean Batten had flown from Australia to London in five days, eighteen hours. As long as the horses kept running and Jean Batten kept flying, I felt safe.

———◦———

I don't know what Peter would have said had he seen me a week later. To my surprise, the girl who sat opposite me in the Camera slipped a note across the desk, inviting me to dinner.

I spiffed myself up and, clutching a bunch of flowers, climbed the staircase to her rooms at the appointed time. Everything went well: the meal, the drinks, the conversation and the candlelight. The room was pleasantly warm. What more could I ask, I wondered?

I soon found out. Dinner done, the girl opened the window 'for a breath of fresh air'. Up went the window, out went the candles. The room was plunged into darkness.

'I say,' a voice reached me from the dark, 'isn't this all too jolly?'

There followed a tense silence during which I did not come up to scratch. I behaved miserably – I struck a match.

Since then I've never seen candles blown out with one puff without thinking of that wonderful girl.

———◦———

In mid term I had a visit from Ma and Emily Hargreaves. They came off the train carrying umbrellas and handbags.

615

Their hair was curled, they wore floral dresses, loose jackets, large straw hats and fancy shoes. I don't know how much robbery had gone on to turn them out like that. Mum's cameo of a swan was pinned to the centre of her bodice. I hugged them both. They hadn't changed a scrap.

'How are you, Mum?'

'I've still got me 'elth an' strenf.'

'You talks like a nob, Billy,' said Emily.

I made an impressive start by taking them by taxi to the lodgings I had rented for them.

Their reaction to Oxford was like my own a year earlier – they thought it unreal. They couldn't get over the beautiful buildings, the empty streets, and the colour people had in their cheeks.

The first night we dined at the Mitre, where I'd reserved a table for three with candles. The second night we dined with O'Hea at the hostel. He liked to fuss over people from the East End.

He talked with Ma Hargreaves about her work. He scolded her for opposing the building of air-raid shelters in Poplar.

'Only encourages war,' she argued.

'But if you're wrong?'

'Well, we'll sing "Hain't it grand to be bloomin' well dead".'

Later that night, she talked to me about the Hargreaves family. 'Clem an' Chris are still at the Poplar 'Ospital. If war comes, they'll go to an 'ospital in Cambridge. Clem 'as made sure that if 'e 'as to jump 'e'll be given a good place to jump to. Carol is still in 'er old clerical job.'

I asked about Miranda.

'She's 'avin' a stormy affair with Milton. Much better if it 'ad been you. I'd always 'oped it might be. Miranda's dad 'as died. It was the wallop that dun 'im in. They 'ad trouble getting 'is coffin out of the 'ouse. Bernie too 'as died. The TB did it. 'E was the family clown till the end.'

Alex – my old night school mate – had married a widow and lived in a penthouse in the West End. He was prospering in some shady financial business. He'd done what he'd set out to do: he'd left the working class behind.

I worried about Ma Hargreaves after she'd gone. Like Lansbury, she seemed so fixed in her views about pacifism. She was ignoring the growing menace of the fascist powers. In her daily life she was down to earth; in politics she could be in the clouds.

———<◇>———

To my intense surprise I came home one night to find Miranda sitting in my room. She had come uninvited and unannounced. She could not have come at a worse time. She was provocatively wide-eyed and beautiful. She wore a yellow jacket and skirt, silk stockings, high heels and a wide-brimmed straw hat. Her hair straggled out in an enchanting way; around her neck was an imitation gold chain. Anticipating problems with the principal (female guests did not go upstairs), I immediately found a room for her in Walton Street.

I soon discovered why Miranda had come. She'd hardly got settled than she reached for me and snuggled her head against mine.

'I think we should get married,' she said. She kissed me gently and looked deep into my eyes.

It took several moments for me to get hold of myself. I was too confused, I'd thought that my going to Oxford had made a clean break between us. Common sense told me that marrying Miranda would be a disaster.

She bit her red lips as she awaited my answer. The street noises faded away. There was a great quiet between us. Only our eyes were joined.

'Miranda, it would be wrong of me to marry you. We are good friends, we've meant a lot to each other, but we are not life partners. If I married you it would end up in my making you unhappy.' I dared not say that the university atmosphere would choke her to death.

Tears filled her eyes. 'I wish you knew 'ow much I love you. Don't you love me just a little?' She put her head on my shoulder and held me close. Passion and pity nearly did me in.

'Of course I love you Miranda, but that's different from marrying you. Try to understand me. We love each other but we live in different worlds; it would be a lie to think anything else.'

'You only see your own world, you do. You think I'm set in my ways, but I'm not. I've got a good 'eart, I 'ave.'

'Of course you have. I don't want to try to change you. Be yourself. Stay as you are.'

'What you're saying is that I'm no longer good enough. You've become a nob, Billy. You've no time for a working girl like me. I can understand you wanting to get rid of me.' She burst into tears.

'Miranda, I'm not a nob and never shall be. My being at Oxford has nothing to do with my liking you or not. Let's not hate each other whatever happens.'

'Why don't you just say I'm not good enough, and 'ave done with it. I'd understand that; it would be 'onest.'

I tried to console her, but she shook me off, exclaiming, 'You're a no-good nob.' Tears ran down her face; her make-up became a dreadful sight. I felt guilty, it was terrible to see her like that.

The next two days were spent sorting out our relations. My work had to go to the wall. It was an exhausting experience during which I had to struggle repeatedly not to be unkind. I wanted to smooth away all anger and hurt, but no words fitted. The more we talked, the less we understood each other. Eventually we saw the futility of it all and lapsed into silence – what was there to talk about? We were both in a daze.

Miranda left on the morning of the third day. She had seen almost nothing of the university. It was a strain to look at each other, so awkward were our feelings. I thought it cruel that our friendship should end this way. It was hard for both of us until the train pulled out. I must confess that as I watched it disappear, I felt relief.

It was shortly after Miranda's visit that German refugees began to arrive at the hostel. They talked with O'Hea in his office. I noticed that he shut his door. They were always hungry, always downcast and always in transit – an hour or two and they were gone with their worldly possessions under their arm. Apart from introducing us to the visitors, O'Hea was tight-lipped about them. He had strong connections with the German labour movement and was saddened at the refugees' plight. 'Heads will roll, heads will roll. For some, vengeance is sweet,' were his only comments.

As 1937 gave way to 1938 the drumbeats of war grew louder. From this point on there was no stopping Hitler. On 4 February 1938 he assumed sole command of the German armed forces; on 12 March, while the French government was in complete disarray, German troops entered Austria. By uniting Germany and Austria, Hitler had violated the Treaty of Versailles. Britain and France breathed fire and smoke; the League condemned the Anschluss, but nothing was done. What could be done? Ninety per cent of Germans and Austrians were cheering. Another nail had been driven into Europe's hope for peace.

Two days after the Anschluss, Winston Churchill rose in the House of Commons to warn Britain of Hitler's aggressive plans. Terrifying forecasts had been made about the overwhelming superiority of the Luftwaffe. Anthony Eden, also critical of Chamberlain's policy, resigned his post as foreign secretary and joined Churchill in the wilderness. 'We are heading,' he said, 'for a universal tragedy that will engulf us all.'

I offset my growing worries about the worsening world scene by playing cricket in the Parks. Although I hadn't played cricket before, I took to it at once. War or no war, I bought white trousers and white boots. My sister Brenda knitted a pullover of the right colours and away I went. There must have been something about cricket that suited me because I excelled at it. It thrilled me to clout the ball with all my strength. Yet it was a nob's game, played low-key.

I loved bowling most of all. What a thrill to get the feel of the ball while rolling up your sleeves and taking stock of the batsman and the field. What joy to run up to the wicket with the right pace, skip and a jump. How wonderful on reaching the stumps to throw your body right back, point your left shoulder at the batsman, shoot out the left arm to the full, and then come through with the right arm, hurling the ball with enough strength to blow the batter and the wicket away.

What peace later on to lounge about in the sunshine in the outer field, while chewing on a stalk of grass and waiting for a catch or the last over. What fun to listen to the spectators calling, 'Run, run man. Make a single . . . Oh I say, well stopped . . . lovely!' Cricket taught me a great deal about the adaptability of my fellow countrymen. It also tested my courage. Anyone who can face a fast ball on a bumpy pitch with the sun in his eyes can face anything.

———◦———

I cannot refer to the Parks without feeling embarrassed. A terrible thing happened to me there one day. Coming out of a crowded lecture at Keble, I saw a young cleric jump on my bike and pedal away. My bike was old – I'd bought it for ten shillings – but it was my only transport. While all Oxford bicycles were old and looked alike, I knew it was mine because I recognised the German lock that my Belgian friends had given me. It was the only bike in Oxford with a lock like that.

'Excuse me!' I shouted after the cleric as he passed through Keble's gates. 'Excuse me! You've taken my bike!'

He pedalled away harder than ever.

I ran after him. 'I say,' I called as I caught up, 'you've made a mistake!'

He gave me a frightened look.

I either had to let him go or do something drastic. I chose to do something drastic. Almost out of breath, I gave him a hard push that sent him and the bike flying into the gutter. Wheels spun around, books and papers littered the street.

It is hard for anyone to appreciate how I felt when I discovered that the bike was *not* mine. I didn't know where to look, or how to begin to apologise. No words fitted my predicament.

Uttering a string of 'terribly sorrys', I helped the poor fellow to his feet and dusted him down. He stifled a groan. I recovered his possessions, while he watched me with injured, fearful eyes. I knew he was looking upon me as a dangerous lunatic.

I pointed to the lock on his bike. 'I thought I was the only one in Oxford with such a lock.'

'I bought it on a visit to G . . . G . . . Germany,' he stammered.

The wonder is I wasn't sued.

During the Easter vacation of 1938 I kept the promise I'd made to Jean Doeraene and went on a cycling tour of Flanders. I wanted to see the places my father had talked about, such as 'Wipers' (Ypres), Dixmude, Poperinge, Menin and Passchendaele – places where countless British soldiers had died in the Great War. That war was like a cloud above my head when I was young. There was no escaping it. My father had gone to war out of idealism and adventure, and had come home cynical and disgusted.

I took the train to Tilbury, where I crossed to Antwerp.

My passage to the continent was provided by the Cockerill Line, my pocket money by my friends in the ice-cream business, Tom Wall's.

Everybody said that April was the wrong time to cycle in Flanders, but I went anyway. I didn't worry about the weather – after cramming books for eight weeks, I needed to get out in the open air, my energies needed release. I didn't give a thought to where I would sleep, or what I would eat.

I spent the first night with Jean Doeraene and his parents in Bois d'Haine. He'd offered me the use of his bike. The next day I packed my belongings on to his old-fashioned machine and cycled back to Antwerp via Malines. It was a bad start; it rained all day and I was wearing all the waterproof garments I had brought.

I saw the unfinished spire of Maline's thirteenth-century cathedral through the drifting rain long before I got there. I arrived alongside busloads of chattering school children. I had come because Jean had insisted that I should see Van Dyke's famous *Crucifixion*. Standing before it, I was as spellbound as the wide-eyed children whispering at my side. I saw the pierced feet and hands, the sorrowful face and the blood-besprinkled head beneath its crown of thorns. I forgot Thiel's criticism of Van Dyke: 'Lacks vigour and authenticity. Your time will be better spent with Rubens.' This was not just another Crucifixion. It was *the* Crucifixion. It caused something embedded in my soul to come alive. That was the moment in my life when I decided that more important than form or design or colour in art was mystery. Van Dyke conveyed to me Christ's pain, agony, suffering and death as I'd never felt them before. I also felt Christ's victory over evil. I stared for a long time at the Cross, which I knew was the symbol of my civilisation, and I came away moved by the painting's timeless, universal appeal.

From Malines I cycled across a land veiled in a thick mist. By the time I reached Antwerp again it was night. I found the youth hostel and was glad to eat and sleep.

The next day, to the sound of cooing pigeons, I climbed

the endless, narrow staircase, past enormous bells, to the top of the cathedral tower. I watched the birds coming and going from their nests in the stonework; I looked down on clustered roofs, the docks, the harbour, and the shimmering Scheldt stretching away in the sunlit distance to the sea. 'God made man, the Scheldt made all else,' was the local saying. I was not deceived by the calmness of the scene. I knew that the city had endured the ravages of the Dutch, the Spaniards, the French and the Germans. Time and again, violence and death had swept past the cathedral's doors.

A favourable wind blew me out of Antwerp and set me on the road to Ghent. Rain stood on the horizon like smoke. It was good to be in the open countryside again. On lonely roads, I made my way through village after village, past cottages covered with budding apple trees with lime-washed trunks, past gardens with the first crocuses and tulips, past fields planted with flax, and along poplar-lined canals, where twittering swallows dipped merrily. In the fields lambs played, in the hedges hawthorn bloomed. All breathed the new life of gentle spring. Here and there I came across linen mills. In earlier times migrant Flemish weavers had enriched England.

There were potholes and puddles all the way, which I bumped in and out of in the best of spirits. Without the tools and spare inner tubes Jean had given me, my travels would have come to a halt. In the villages, I feasted off bread and honey or bread and apple jelly, or bread and poached eggs. I ate one of the best omelettes I have ever eaten in a village post office.

Sometimes I'd stop at an inn. I made myself understood by body language, or English, or broken French. At one place I met a craggy little fellow, who wore a frock coat and a sailor's cap. I had to shout to make him hear. He not only insisted on paying for my drink, despite the hubbub in the inn, he insisted on singing 'It's a Long Way to Tipperary'. His face shone as Caruso's might have done. I clapped – I didn't dare say that I hadn't recognised one word. The peasants nodded their round heads and grunted their approval – they thought me daring for having crossed the Channel. From the inn I went to the church across the way, where a cold stillness prevailed. I found a knight and his lady resting in stone. Outside, old moss-covered gravestones leaned against the wall or nodded together in the long grass.

I enjoyed cycling alone. That way I was free to go where I would. The rhythmic pedalling encouraged me to sing. The flatness of the land was in my favour. The rain was part of the grey landscape and there were moments when it would pretend to let up. The birds didn't mind it, nor did I. Indeed, once I was wet to the skin I took a reckless delight in getting wetter.

The people on the road were invariably kind. In asking directions of peasants who knew no English – for I often got lost in a tangle of lanes – I became expert at matching my facial expressions and gestures with theirs. People would shake my hand in a country lane and jabber as if I were a local youth. They'd drop what they were doing to show me the way.

One day, while the bells pealed joyfully, I followed a straggling, sombre-clothed procession into a church. I sat in a back pew and listened to hymns. The next morning, my curiosity to know what was going on in another village church trapped me in a christening ceremony. Before I could extricate myself, I was shaking hands with relatives who indulged in a plethora of kisses, which the cold English find so hard to bear. Henceforth I kept my curiosity in check.

The next day I ran into a village fair with its wheezing hurdy-gurdy. The roundabout was mounted on a cart and rotated by hand. It brought great joy to the children. I dallied to watch a wrestling match. As night fell a bonfire was lit to commemorate some poor wretch who had been burned for witchcraft four hundred years before; there was a metal plate in the square to prove it. Her crime, they said, was to have consorted with the devil. Amid showers of sparks and the crackle and roar of the fire, we held hands and solemnly moved round the pyre. I thought it a bit odd that someone who had been a witch should have become a martyr.

I came to Ghent on a fine morning with the sun shining on its roofs. As I arrived, a carillon was playing Bach's 'Jesu, Joy of Man's Desiring'. In contrast to the grey countryside, the town was full of flowers; begonias were cultivated there by the million. That night I joined a dance on the square; I had no choice – everybody joined in with gusto. I didn't know the movements, but it didn't seem to matter. Across the square, mocking our jollity, was a moated castle with a most dreadful collection of instruments of torture which I had seen earlier.

I left Ghent early on a fresh spring morning, with the dawn's pale light shining through the wayside trees. A brisk wind blew me along the road. It was late and quite dark when I passed through one of the gates into Bruges. Attracted by noise in the square, I became entangled in a torch-light procession headed by the local firemen, their brass hats flashing light, their faces red with wine. Everyone found my predicament humorous.

Bruges was a friendly, medieval town. The river and the canals mirrored old houses, bridges and windmills. Chimes rang out from the twelfth-century belfry. I visited the Gothic town hall. In one of the churches I saw a miraculous relic of drops of blood of the Saviour; it had been brought back from the Holy Land in the twelfth century. People came from near and far to worship.

I was given shelter for two nights in a church. An unfriendly housekeeper served dinner in a cold, whitewashed room behind the altar. On the second night, a young farm labourer joined me. His face was as rough as his hands and his smock. He couldn't believe that I had nothing else to do but cycle about for pleasure, stopping and starting as the mood took me.

We were given a small dented enamel pot containing what I presumed was coffee. My meal was just sufficient to get me through the night. My companion ate several slices of bread with a little margarine: it was all he could afford. I tried to share my food with him, but he would not hear of it. We slept in a draughty room where the window rattled all night.

The next morning I left early for Ostend. Having dawdled en route, I reached its line of broken dunes in the late afternoon. I met an elderly couple and asked directions to the youth hostel. When they heard that I was an Oxford student, they adopted me on the spot. Against my protests, my bike and I were almost carried back to their house, where I was offered a feast. Piling food on my plate, they said they were paying back a war debt to Britain. During dinner they described the Germans' attempt to reach the Channel ports in 1914. To halt the Germans, the marshlands of Belgium had been deliberately flooded. Indescribable suffering had taken place; Ostend had become a large mortuary. Their own lives had been in peril.

'Will the nightmare of those years be repeated?' they asked. Not wanting to spoil a wonderful evening, I painted the most optimistic picture of the future I could and I'm afraid they believed every word.

The next morning they protested when I proposed going on to Ypres. I had to agree to stay another day, in which they took me by car along the coast to Zeebrugge and to Dunkirk in France. The next day, by which time I had stopped protesting, we went on a picnic.

After three days we walked out together to the Dixmude road and said goodbye. If I had listened to them I'd have let them take me by car on a conducted tour of the battlefields. I looked back to see those two lovely old people standing by the side of the road waving. I was to see them once more, in the summer of 1939.

I cycled across a countryside that was completely laid to waste during the Great War. On reaching Dixmude I was struck by a cloudburst so fierce that I fled to the nearest farmhouse for shelter. Battered by the slashing rain, my wheels swishing through the deluge, I reached the door amid dreadful thunder and lightning. As there was no answer to my frantic knocking, and no cover above my head, I tried the latch. The door opened with a loud creak on to a dark hallway; I stepped inside and called out. To my horror a mastiff, the size of a small donkey, sprang at me with bared teeth. I fell back, slammed the door behind me and overwhelmed by fear, leaped on to my saddle and cycled away frenziedly through the deluge . . . regardless.

From Ypres I visited the various battlefields. Between 1914 and 1918 the whole area had been bitterly contested. All the towns had been reduced to rubble. After twenty years life had returned; the villages and the towns had been rebuilt; bells were heard across the countryside again. The repairs to the cathedral and the Cloth Hall in Ypres were almost completed. Soon the scars of war would be effaced. What could not be effaced were the war cemeteries containing the remains of thousands upon thousands of husbands, sons and brothers – all of them, including the enemy, comrades in death. The pitiful, serried ranks of white crosses spoke of the desolation of war.

Flanders is a land haunted by past hatreds and tragedies. My father had struggled in the mud here before being gassed in the third battle of Ypres. Nick Hargreaves, whose picture hung in the basement in Bow, had died here. The sea of graves was an overwhelming sight. There was nothing like this in England. Had the dead risen and joined in a deafening scream, I could not have been more overwrought; nothing expressed so poignantly the madness of war. These men had been the best that Europe had to offer. Our entire civilisation had been impoverished and permanently impaired; reverence for life had never been the same. If 'little men' led us after 1918, it was because bigger and better men were buried here. I began to understand the phrase 'the Lost Generation'.

On my first night in Ypres I went out to the British War Memorial at the Menin Gate. The rain fell in sheets at either end of the tunnel-like building. There was not another person in sight. A hundred feet above my head was an arched roof. Mist filled the air. I stood my bike against the kerb. Inscribed on the lighted walls were the names of more than 58,000 men: 'Here are recorded names of officers and men who fell in the Ypres salient but to whom the fortune of war denied the known and honoured burial given to their comrades in death.' I thought of Bunyan: 'So they passed over and all the trumpets sounded for them at the other side.'

What I wanted to express was inexpressible. I followed the names down the street, gazing at an endless tragedy. For a moment I felt that there were thousands and thousands of eyes looking down at me, asking me why they had had to die and what I was going to do about it. My mind did not respond. I felt intense sadness. How horrible, I thought, for life to end with a little name on an endless wall in an empty, mist-filled street.

I was just about to leave when two muffled-up civilians rode up on bicycles. Standing their bikes next to mine, they took out their bugles, removed their caps, and on the stroke of nine sounded the Last Post. The sad notes, echoing against the high vault and the cold stonewalls, contained all the sorrow that mankind had suffered since the beginning of time. In two minutes the buglers had come and gone, leaving me alone with the dead. No longer conscious of the rain, I cycled back to my lodgings across the Ypres salient, past endless cemeteries, wondering how such madness could have occurred.

On leaving Ypres the next day, I came across a stone marker: 'Here the invader was brought to a standstill.' The cost was a staggering million lives. No wonder that so many of my generation were pacifists. As I stood there among the fields of dead, I thought there had to be another way. I recalled the words:

> Take up our quarrel with the foe:
> To you, from failing hands we throw
> The torch; be yours to hold it high.
> If ye break faith with us who die
> We shall not sleep, though poppies grow
> In Flanders fields.*

* *In Flanders Fields*, Lieutenant Colonel John McCrae (1872–1918).

I took shelter from a downpour against a barn in Courtrai. All around were wet, ploughed fields. Hearing a rattling above my head, I looked up to see a macabre collection of rusted helmets, rifles, bayonets, shellcases and gun parts all hanging on wire and blowing about restlessly in the wind. German tin hats were mixed with British. They had been dug up by the farmer.

Before leaving Courtrai, I saw a plaque in a Flemish church which read:

Leven is weven	Life is weaving
En sterven	And dying
Is zijn stuk	is to give your work
Aan God afgeven	to God

After three weeks I returned Jean's bicycle to him at Bois d'Haine. How wonderful it was to have his family's hospitality showered upon me: for a couple of days I was thoroughly spoiled.

———◦———

I returned to Oxford from my solitary tour knowing myself a little better. My travels had brought home to me the great richness as well as the periodic insanity of Western civilisation. Flanders was my first lesson in art. It was also my introduction to death on an unimaginable scale.

Flanders taught me something about the turbulent nature of religious faith and heresy, and the extent to which they had helped to shape the past. The effect of the Reformation in England was not to be compared with its effect in Flanders. To my generation all things were possible to science; in an earlier age all things had been possible to faith. I now appreciated to what extent the Cross had been the symbol of an age when nothing mattered as much as the saving of a soul.

———◦———

Back at Oxford, Flanders quickly faded before the threat of final examinations for the university diploma in economics and political science. I worried if Trinity Term would be my last. My two years were up, yet I desperately wanted to stay. Life was rich, it had meaning. 'Let's see how you come out of "Schools",' Rodger said, 'then we'll talk.' Thiel was his usual calm self, but he had more options. I needed to excel and was determined to do so.

The only way I could affect the future was to work. Apart from an early morning swim, I sacrificed everything to study. I became antisocial. For the first time I had emotional highs and lows. I did not answer mail. Even though there was trouble brewing in Czechoslovakia, I spent little time reading newspapers.

I was not the only one to become antisocial at the hostel. Nothing concentrated our attention as 'Schools' did. The tension grew as the dreadful days approached. After I'd put out my light and gone to bed, Fog was still hunched over his books. He ended his day on his knees at the side of his bed. His silent prayers conveyed a feeling of rare purity. I felt my inadequacy. Yet there were times when I could almost touch the God he was worshipping.

In the end my orderly planning of revision came to nothing. I discovered that time before 'Schools' is not ordinary time: sometimes the day was gone before it had begun.

The madness ended one morning with Fog and I cycling to 'Schools', dressed in dark suits, wearing the mandatory white shirt and white bow tie. Given a tall hat, Fog could have passed for a duke.

With sixty to seventy others, we finally faced neatly tied bundles containing writing paper and examination questions. Each candidate was identified only by a number. At a given signal we untied our bundles, looked at the paper and began to write. To the merriment of the room, one student stood up and slowly swallowed his string. I envied his light-heartedness.

I slogged away for most of that week and part of the next.

One after another, the papers in economic theory, modern economic organisation, the economic history of England, political science, political history and organisation, and labour movements came and went. I didn't think any paper was easy, and there were times when I wondered what on earth I was writing. At night I sometimes regretted what I had written. Fog and I supported each other, coming and going together, having a couple of beers at the end of the day, getting ready for the next bout, and doing our best to forget the errors we had made. Even in my sleep I kept answering questions.

And then the last day came and the last paper was done. We looked at each other meaningfully as we left the 'Schools', took our bikes out of the racks and quietly pedalled away. In a week's time we would know the results.

———<o>———

With O'Hea's blessing, Fog and I had decided that instead of sitting about waiting for the results, we would spend our last week running wild up the river. We both had the right shoulders for prolonged canoeing. We had no set plans. We might get as far as Lechlade, even Cricklade, near Thameshead, the disputed source of the Thames. We'd see. We carried a small tent. There was always food available at the locks, or at the occasional pub. At worst, there were plenty of fish in the river to keep us alive.

The day after exams we were paddling my canoe *Ruby* towards Godstow Lock. It was June and the weather was warm. We had been under strain for so long that it was a relief to escape into the open air, especially to escape on to the river, which conveyed a sense of adventure. A faint mist was rising; the rippling water sparkled in the sun; a gentle breeze ruffled the reedy, flowered banks; a lark high above Port Meadow heralded a new day. Rhythmically we paddled through lakes of light, with fish leaping and nervous moorhens trotting briskly on the water.

Finding our pace we paddled through Port Meadow, dotted with pasturing animals, to the ruins of the Godstow Nunnery at Wolvercote, 'built by Editha ye Prioress in the year 1138 and dedicated in honour of ye Virgin Mary and St John ye Baptist'. On our left were the Wytham hills.

Sometime during the morning I realised we had company in the canoe. Every now and again a field mouse would appear from nowhere, run across our feet, examine the baggage, squeak and disappear again. While I had been doing examinations the mouse had made a home in the lining of my boat.

Enticed by peanuts, the mouse adopted us; it enjoyed the voyage every bit as much as we did. Often it sat and preened itself on the baggage until drowsiness overcame it and it took shelter in one of my shoes, which I had kicked off. At night it used the ropes to scramble ashore. Often we glimpsed the glitter of its eyes in the firelight. We thought we might lose it to the land, but it would appear in the canoe the next day. Fog and I became very fond of it. We called it Midge.

For the next three days we steered through endless water meadows, the water reflecting the sky, the sunlight catching our paddles. Our course was generally westward, but the river's twists and turns meant that we pointed in every direction. Each minute brought a fresh view. Each night we searched for a bank, not too high, not too low, and tied up against a willow tree. Having pitched our tent and fastened it down, we stuffed ferns or dry grass under our ground sheets to level the ground and make it softer. We hung the kettle above the fire, and fried the day's catch of fish. The stars shone, the bats flitted about, the river glittered in the moonlight. After eating and talking lazily, we bedded down in our tent on the sweet, clover-smelling earth. Around us the trees and bushes huddled together and slept as soundly as we.

Each day we woke to the crowing of cocks and the barking of dogs. From the woods a cuckoo called; a chorus of birdsong greeted the new day. The fish rose, the rabbits played outside their burrows on the gravelled bank, long-legged herons stalked along the water's edge. A light mist rose above the long wet grass.

Some afternoons during those endless summer days we tired of paddling and our rambling conversation, and threw ourselves down in the shade in a drowsy world to sleep. On waking we'd silently and dreamily listen to the voice of the river and watch the odd sluggish cloud drift by. It was enough just to stare at the ever-moving water and wonder. Around us were peaceful meadows with daisies, buttercups and poppies, flitting butterflies and glassy-winged dragonflies. Wild ducks flying low cut the water with their feet. To me it was joyful. To Jim, who spent so much of his life digging deep into the earth, it was heaven.

In the locks, the gushing, roaring water lifted *Ruby* up the shining walls. To rise in a lock on a summer's day is a magic ritual, which carries you into another world.

With the meadowlarks singing and the river heavy in the heat and insects flying about, we paddled on. Cows studied our passing with drowsy eyes; we greeted fishermen cast in stone; a distant grey church tower rose out of the tall grass. Between the dipping of our paddles, we exchanged a smile with lovers on the bank, answered the wave of a hand from a passing boat, and followed the course of a barge horse straining on a taut rope dripping rain. We met barges bright and barges dingy. Occasionally, we heard the hiss of a haughty swan, the slow majestic flapping of a heron's wings, ducks squawking by shaded banks and the mellow call of the thrush. At night there was the sound of laughter and music on water, and pub talk between darts and draughts about 'Itler and Czechoslovakia.

On Sunday morning we stepped from the sunlit river into the dark interior of a moss-covered village church to hear Mass. Corn sheaves stood in a corner, the relics of a harvest festival.

We turned around at Lechlade; beyond, the river was too shallow. To reach the bank we had to walk the canoe up the current through a mass of vegetation. We had our last swim there, the reeds clinging to our arms and legs. Lechlade's church steeple stayed with us long after we had left.

A strong headwind slowed our homeward pace. The water hissed against us like a cold rain; small waves lapped our prow. We were thoroughly tired by the time we reached Godstow's high arched bridge. Arriving a day late, we docked our boat as the sun's last rays were flickering across Port Meadow. We also brought Midge back home.

The first thing we asked for at the hostel were the examination results. Yes, they had them. Fog and Thiel had passed. I had been awarded distinction. Speechless, we grasped each other's hands. I felt an indescribable satisfaction. I had set my heart on doing well. The results ended any self-doubts I may have had. Yet all things considered, Fog's was the better performance; he had spent half his time working down a mine. O'Hea was tight-lipped, but I could tell he was pleased.

That night a crowd of us met on Port Meadow to drink and sing songs to the moon. Thiel joined us, with the detailed results of our examinations. We were puzzled how he got them, but nothing ever stumped Hans. In the early hours the police escorted us back to our colleges, but not before we had held hands with them and sung 'Auld Lang Syne'.

In the next day or two the hostel emptied. For Fog and I the time for parting had come. 'I shall always pray that you may remain in the safekeeping of God, Billy,' were his last words. It was wonderful to have known such a man; though there were times during our two years together when I had longed for him to fly off the handle. He taught me serenity, and that man has a soul that gives life to the body, and that the soul, unlike the body, is immortal. He taught me to give as well as to take. I don't know what I'd have done without him.

On the last day, we all pitched in to buy Mrs Padmanabha a new handbag. The Catholic Church will never know how much they owed to that wonderful Protestant matron.

Having no job to go to, I found temporary shelter at a house in Walton Street where I'd rented rooms for visitors before. I wrote thank-you notes to all who had helped me during the past two years. In response to my note Rodger invited me to tea at his home. He asked me what I intended to do. I told him that the only thing I really wanted to do was to enter the university and graduate in the School of Modern Greats: Philosophy, Politics and Economics. 'You're on a fairly straight course, Woodruff,' he said. 'Take Modern Greats, go to the Bar in London, become a barrister, and I predict you will make a fortune in labour litigation. You have the ability to grasp quickly the essential features of matters quite strange to you. You are a natural for labour.' So that I might do all these things he offered to write a letter to Mr E. M. Rich, the chief education officer at the London County Council.

That night I telephoned Ma Hargreaves and gave her my examination results and told her that I wanted to stay on to take a degree. I also told her that Rodger was writing to Rich, whom she knew. I didn't ask her to pull any strings at the LCC. I knew she would do that without asking.

Not long afterwards I was surprised to receive a note from Mr Rich himself. There was an impressive seal on the stationery. He asked me to call his secretary for an appointment. I did. A few days later I was standing outside County Hall in the heart of London. The size of the building intimidated me. The entrance was overrun with people. I told one of the clerks that I had come to see Mr Rich. 'Oh you 'ave, 'ave you?' he said huffily, as if I'd asked to see the Pope.

'This young gint's come to see Rich,' the clerk said turning to one of his superiors.

''E 'as, 'as 'e?' The senior approached me. 'U got han appointment?'

'Yes,' I answered, producing Rich's personal note. 'My appointment is at eleven.'

'Oops-a-daisy, so you 'ave. Wonders never cease. George, take Mr Woodruff to Mr Rich's office at once, get a move on.'

After that it was, 'Yes, sir, no, sir, three bags full, sir.' George whisked me to the office of the great man and I found myself sitting at a long table facing Mr Rich. His secretary sat next to me.

Mr Rich was a courteous man with piercing grey eyes. 'I've heard so much about you, Mr Woodruff, that I wanted to see you for myself.' He took a moment to congratulate me on my examination results. 'What do you hope to do next?' Resting his hands on the table, he waited for my reply. I repeated what I had said to Rodger. Gracefully, yet always to the point, he questioned me about my background and my studies. I had the uncomfortable feeling that he was reading my mind. The two men began to exchange notes across the table. I wondered why they didn't speak up. I was tempted to look over my neighbour's shoulder to see what he was writing.

The exchange of notes eventually ceased. 'Mr Woodruff,' Mr Rich said, turning to me, 'I'm afraid that there is no major London County Council scholarship to Oxford for which a person like you can apply.'

My heart stopped.

'However, provided the university will allow you to matriculate, I think I can persuade my committee to meet your special needs.'

My heart started again.

'We need to create an adult scholarship – a senior adult county scholarship for people like you.' Somewhere in the room I could hear Rich's voice. 'If you will let me have Oxford's acceptance, I shall convey the committee's decision to you as soon as I can.'

He asked if there was anything else I wished to discuss. I said I thought not. We shook hands. I made for the door.

'Mr Woodruff,' he called as I was about to leave. 'If in due course you graduate and are looking for a job, I hope you will come and see me again.'

I said I appreciated his kindness and I certainly would return.

'Good luck!'

Once out of the building, I stood for a moment on the embankment trying to get my breath back. I was so happy, I could have somersaulted down the pavement or jumped into the Thames. I looked across the river at the House of Commons. Everything was going the right way, all I needed now was acceptance by the university. I walked away as if striding on air.

I had to rush back to Oxford after my interview, but I called Emily Hargreaves the next day and asked her to tell her mother all that had gone on at County Hall.

Following Rodger's advice, I applied to the university to be accepted as a candidate for the degree in Modern Greats. I also petitioned to be excused Responsions (the entrance examination) and Pass Moderations (the examination at the end of the first year). I wanted to bypass the school work I had not had.

The outcome of my petitions was a compromise: the university accepted me as a student and waived Responsions. Beyond that they were not prepared to go. A custom that had been built up over hundreds of years was not going to be changed because a queer frog had jumped into their pond. Fit in or fall out was the gist of the ruling. I had no choice. Somehow I'd have to get through Pass Mods. 'Half victory, half defeat, Woodruff,' Rodger said with pursed lips. 'Stability has become rigidity.'

I informed Rich of the university's decision. I was on tenterhooks now to know if I was going to get a scholarship. No good the university accepting me if I was broke. A week or so later I received a letter from County Hall telling me that I had been awarded an LCC Senior Adult County Scholarship for the year 1938–39. Its renewal depended upon my performance. I'd got myself so worked up about the scholarship that all I could do was to collapse in a chair and keep reading the letter. I simply couldn't believe it.

With money in the bank, I turned to finding a college. I should have consulted Rodger. He would have found a place for me at Balliol. But from here on I felt obliged to look after myself. After consulting Thiel, I joined St Catherine's Society in St Aldates. Its great advantage was that although I was required to eat dinners in Hall, I could live out.

I was interviewed by the Dean of St Catherine's, W. G. Kendrick, and by the Censor, the Reverend J. V. K. Brook. There was an incredulous look on the Dean's face when, having intoned 'Education,' I answered, 'Elementary school, sir, some night school, and the Diploma in Economics and Political Science with distinction.'

'Do you know any Latin or Greek?'

'No.'

'Do you speak any modern language?'

'A little German and French. I spent the summer in Belgium and Germany.'

He rested his chin on his fist and studied me. 'And you propose to take Pass Moderations in one year?'

'I hope to.'

'Well,' he sighed, 'you've got a cheek, I'll say that for you.' There was a strained pause. 'No one to my knowledge has ever done it without having had a secondary education, but I see no reason why you shouldn't try. I look forward to hearing what the Censor says.'

After climbing the narrow spiral staircase, I entered the office of the Reverend John Victor Knight Brook, and sat before him on the edge of a chair. 'Woodruff, Woodruff,' he kept saying as he ploughed through a stack of papers. He'd been interviewing students all morning and his face was beginning to show the strain. His collar was digging into his neck.

Having read my application, he placed his spectacles on the desk, drew his lips together and fixed me with a stare. His eyes were kind; I felt I was in the clear. But there was a long, uncomfortable pause during which he continued to eye me. I felt my colour rising.

'You know, Woodruff,' he said, picking up my application form, 'I can't for the life of me understand why people like you want to come here.'

I was devastated. I must have looked crushed. It was the only time at Oxford that anyone had really hurt my feelings. We looked at each other. Neither spoke. There was a cold stillness. Had I deluded myself in getting mixed up with the toffs, I wondered. Surely, he couldn't believe that I should be excluded from the university because I was working class! Didn't he understand that it was lack of knowledge that had always kept us back?

Eventually I stammered some kind of reply.

'Oh well,' he said rising, 'we'll see how you get on.' He reached across, offering his hand. I touched his fingers for a moment and left. I never spoke to the Reverend Brook again. It was a cold reception, but I knew that I had been admitted.

To console myself, I went out and bought an undergraduate cap and gown.

Chapter XI

To Germany Again

That afternoon I burst into O'Hea's office with the news that I had been accepted by the university. If he was pleased, he didn't show it. Instead, he picked up a letter lying before him.

'I was thinking about you,' he said. 'Are you interested in returning to Germany? I've just received this letter from friends of mine, the Wolfrath family. I'm sure they will put you up for the rest of the summer if you want to go. They have a son about your age.'

For a moment, his change of topic knocked me off balance. I tried to show interest.

'Professor Zimmern has a very close friend at Bonn, Erwin Fritsch, professor of international relations. Why don't you audit his seminar. Zimmern will arrange it for you.'

At O'Hea's suggestion I went and talked to him. A week later, on a calm sea, I sailed from Tilbury to Hamburg; from there I took a train to Bonn.

Using what German I possessed, I asked my way to the

Wolfrath's house. I rang the bell; a woman opened the door a crack and peered at me. While I was spluttering out in German who I was, she continued to stare. I wondered if I'd come to the wrong house. I was so confused that I forgot to bow. After some moments she opened the door. 'We were expecting you,' she said in a subdued tone. On arrival in Louvain a year earlier I'd been hugged and kissed on both cheeks. Not here in Bonn. Not until I had been received formally by Herr and Frau Wolfrath, and we had sat down to coffee, did our relations thaw. He was a small, rounded, thick-necked man, who worked at the Rathaus. She looked and dressed as if there had been a death in the family. They were both in their early fifties.

I met their son Ludwig several days later when he came home on leave from the Arbeitsdienst (Labour Service). He was in uniform. He was a little younger than I, tall, thin and as intense as his mother. He had a beaked nose, an olive skin, brown eyes and curly hair, of which he was inordinately proud. Educated in England, he spoke perfect English; until the Nazis abolished dual nationality, he had travelled back and forth on his British passport. I thought him a complex character and was ill at ease with him.

He introduced me to Professor Fritsch, a small, middle-aged scholar with the sharpest eyes. After talking about Zimmern, he mentioned that he had lectured at Oxford in 1937. It's as well that Ludwig was with me that day because Fritsch spoke so quickly that I could hardly follow him. I worried about what I would get from his seminar. I did not see Ludwig again during the rest of my stay.

Once a week I went to Fritsch's seminar, which was completely over my head. I would have drowned but for the help of the other students. Yet my German improved by the day.

The students were a light-hearted lot – despite the fact that two-and-a-half years of their time had been taken up with military and labour service. I joined them in outings to Bad Godesberg, or to picnics in the countryside. We also canoed on the Rhine. I was amazed at the risks they took canoeing among the large ships. There was always a drink and a song when the day's paddling was done. Indeed, there were times that summer when life could not have been better.

The crisis over Czechoslovakia in the summer of 1938 ended all that. I walked into the student cafeteria one day to get my breakfast to be told by a couple of English students that Britain had put all its defence forces on twenty-four hour alert. France, Germany, Poland and Czechoslovakia followed suit. All men under the age of sixty-five were forbidden to leave Germany; food supplies and transport facilities were conscripted by the government. The threat of war played havoc with our studies. Anxiously, we stood around discussing our options.

The Czech crisis was the point where we young people lost our innocence; it ended the carefree outlook of our youth. I began to question whether my idealism was adequate enough to deal with the realities of the deteriorating world situation.

As the news worsened, the atmosphere at the Wolfraths grew more intense. Whenever we talked politics we first closed the windows. We avoided talking seriously in the presence of the maid. Frau Wolfrath was always cautioning me. 'Vorsichtig sein, Wilhelm,' she would say, finger on lips. To relieve her worries, she would sometimes sing at the piano. Her shrill voice unnerved me, but I always applauded when she'd finished. It was expected.

Herr Wolfrath began to put on a double act. In one act he was a member of the old guard, admirer of the Kaiser, survivor of the battles of the Somme and the Marne, and enemy of the Nazis. In the other he was a 'good party man', the district collector of scrap metal, the maker of speeches, the admirer of the 'Führer', the one who never forgot to give the right salute. 'Heil Hitler,' he would call to a departing guest, 'and don't forget to shut the gate.' As a civil servant he had to buy *Der Stürmer* whether he liked it or not. Frau Wolfrath despised the Nazi paper and used to destroy it the moment it came into the house. 'It is incautious to do that,' somebody warned her, and thereafter the paper was prominently displayed in a neat pile for visitors to notice.

I once had occasion to meet Herr Wolfrath in his office in the town hall. 'Make sure you give the Hitler salute when we meet,' he warned me. 'People will be suspicious if you don't.' I really didn't have much choice – above the town hall entrance was an enormous sign: 'Hier grüßt man nur Heil Hitler.'

As I got to know Frau Wolfrath better, I came to appreciate her unease. I learned that on the death of her first husband in London, where she had lived for years, she had returned to Germany with her son and married again. In 1933, the year of her second wedding, Hitler had come to power. Since then she had known nothing but trouble. Under the Nazi racial laws, her son Ludwig, born in London of a Jewish father, had been debarred from studying medicine. 'I never dreamed that a son of mine would be persecuted in Germany for his blood,' she told me.

The local dentist and his family, the Bettermans, whom I got to know through the Wolfraths, shared their fear of the Nazis with me. Willi Betterman was a huge, moon-faced sceptic. He was called 'der dicke Mann'[*]. He spoke German slowly, which helped me. If we got stuck, his English was passable. Sometimes, when he was talking about things better not heard, he would cover his mouth with his hand, which gave a furtive expression to what he was saying. We used to eat at his club and talk in a corner. Every speck of uneaten food was taken home. 'Self-sufficiency in Germany is a dream,' he said.

More serious conversations we exchanged on a bench in his garden.

'How do you explain Hitler's popularity?' I asked him one day.

'Look at what preceded him,' he answered. 'The Germans brought him to power because they were sick of street fights, sick of labour unrest, sick of having no job, sick of a useless

___
[*] the fat man

currency, sick of hunger, sick of profiteers, sick of communists, sick of corruption, sick of democracy that didn't work, and sick of being trodden on by France and Britain. They thought Hitler couldn't make matters worse. At the outset he didn't, he made things better. He put an end to hyperinflation, unemployment and the destitution of the post-war years. Street fighting was stopped; law and order were restored. He also denounced Versailles – a treaty that had accused Germany of sole guilt for the war and burdened us with a tribute that we couldn't possibly pay. This boosted Hitler's popularity. He reoccupied the Rhineland because the Rhineland was German. He brought German-speaking Austria into the Reich, because that's where it wanted to be. Believe me, Hitler's record is a success story. No one is going to throw out a winner. For most Germans, he is a hero, a man of action, the wished-for Führer sent by Providence. Who knows what lies ahead?'

There was a long silence between us.

'The price of all this,' Herr Betterman went on, 'is tyranny. Anyone who opposes Hitler is silenced; all sense of justice is lost sight of in the Nazis' determination to stamp out opposition. Every item of news here is doctored: the only items you can rely on are those the Nazis denounce. You don't dare raise your voice: the Jews and anyone who raises his voice are deprived of their legal and social rights. The number of people to whom I can speak openly has become less and less.'

'None of this is known in England.'

At the end of September, while I was still in Germany, Hitler, Chamberlain, Mussolini and Daladier signed the Munich Agreement. Czechoslovakia was stripped of its Sudeten territories – Hitler's last territorial claim in Europe had been met, or at least we thought so. Chamberlain vouched for it.

I was back in London on 1 October 1938 when Chamberlain returned from Munich. The Western world had marched to the brink of war and had marched back again. Sanity had prevailed. Mr Chamberlain's statement on his return to London: 'I believe it is peace for our time . . . peace with honour,' left us drunk with relief. 'Peace for our time,' we called to each other in the streets. The crowds cheered and sang. No. 10 Downing Street was mobbed. A lot of us forgot our previous opinion that Chamberlain was a blinkered old fool. The war that every country in Europe feared had been avoided.

With other students, I got on top of a London bus and sang my way through the streets. Where the bus was going didn't matter – we'd won a respite. Next day all the churches thanked God for our deliverance; in Westminster Abbey the crowded congregation sang, 'Now Thank We All Our God'. 'Never has the power of prayer been more obviously and gloriously vindicated before our eyes,' proclaimed the Dean of Westminster.

In time, Chamberlain would be blamed for the Munich Agreement. It became known as appeasement. The truth is we were all responsible; we were prepared to agree to anything to allay our fears. Everybody except Churchill and a few others wanted a peaceful solution as much as Chamberlain did. We cheered him when, in our name, he had avoided war. Only later, when the Munich Agreement turned sour, did we accuse him of betraying our trust.

Chapter XII

War Clouds Gather

I returned to Oxford for my third academic year in October 1938. At long last, I stood with other students in cap and gown before the Vice-Chancellor at the matriculation ceremony. It was a sombre affair. He addressed us in Latin, telling us that we were now members of the university. As our names were called, amid the doffing and donning of caps, we each stepped forward to receive our certificate.

> Oxoniae, Termino Michaelis AD 1938,
> Die XXII, Mensis Oct.
> Quo die comparsit corum me
> William Woodruff

If only Grandmother Bridget had been there.

I had found rooms with the Tates family on Botley Road, close to Wytham Wood. The university regulations required me to rent a sitting room and a bedroom. Fortunately, I could now afford it. The Tates were a wonderful family, consisting of Mr Reg, Mrs Minnie, a son Reg Jr and a daughter Charlene. The only problem was Minnie's endearing habit of tidying up after me – I could never find a thing.

My day began at seven-fifteen when Reg brought me a cup of tea. He was such a happy man that I was convinced he would live to be a hundred. With the tea came the headlines from the BBC, which he had just heard downstairs. Then came the gossip: Reg worked at a store in town and always lingered to share the previous day's catch, his laughter shaking the room.

Breakfast was at seven-thirty; it was the only time we were together. I preferred eating with the family to eating alone. Minnie shuffled about the dining room in her dressing gown and curlers serving gargantuan portions of eggs and bacon, toast and marmalade. I think it was her ambition to increase our individual weight to the 250 pounds she carried.

By eight-thirty, except for Minnie, we'd all gone off to our different jobs. To get to the university I rode my bike. I ate lunch with student friends; dinner I had in Hall at St Catherine's. Each night I looked down the rows of fresh-faced youths sitting at long, polished tables; I saw the play of light on cutlery and glassware; I heard the nightly grace: 'Benedictus . . .' The ritual was so secure, so certain, so civilised. If Oxford taught me anything it taught me to respect tradition. 'Tradition is the dead hand of the past,' I had shouted from soapboxes, without knowing what I was talking about.

What struck me most when I first began dining in Hall was the waste of food. It came as a shock. These people were not only eating without having worked for it; they were wasting what was put in front of them – food was often pecked at. At the workers' hostel meals had always ended with polished plates.

My belief that I could catch up on seven years' secondary school work in one was plain arrogance. I soon found out that preparing for Pass Mods was formidable. They seemed like a barrier to ensure that I couldn't graduate. Yet I had to respond to the challenge or leave. 'Security is mortals' chiefest enemy,' said Shakespeare.

The support I got made all the difference. Dean Kendrick found the best tutors for me and planned my strategy. He advised me to take French and Political Economy in Hilary Term, and Latin and Constitutional Law and History in Trinity. Wilfred Kendrew at St Catherine's was my tutor in Latin. He was first class. If he thought that it was impossible for me to learn Latin in so short a time, he never said so. The 'set' book was *Agricola et Germania* by Tacitus; I was also required to do translations from 'unseen' texts, usually drawn from Livy, Caesar, Ovid and Vergil.

Kendrew knew what was going on in my head. 'You are not wasting time, Woodruff, in trying to meet some ridiculous requirement of the university. You are being given a chance – nay, the privilege – to learn about a civilisation whose achievements were unrivalled in the history of the West.' Having let that sink in he went on: 'Rome is the base on which you are standing. If you want to know about lasting greatness in thought and deed, you must study Rome. Latin provided the Catholic Church with a universal language. It's also the language of medicine. When you speak Latin you speak to the world. It is not a dead language.'

With Kendrew's words ringing in my ears, I got down to work. Every morning as I shaved, I learned the verbs and nouns I had pasted on to my bathroom mirror. In cycling to the university I would recite: 'I'm a bo, I'm a bis, I'm a bat,' or something else I needed to memorise. Kendrew poured Latin grammar into me until I choked. The experiment of trying to make a Latin scholar out of a foundry worker fascinated him.

Studying Latin was the toughest mental assignment I had faced until then. There was no other subject that I started out hating and finished up being grateful for having had the chance to study.

Help with French came from Miss Hugo, a friend of O'Hea's. She was sixty-ish, almost blind, and read with a large magnifying glass. She lived in a rambling house beyond Magdalen Bridge with her brother, a devoted churchgoer, whom she regarded as 'un peu malade de la tête'. As a teacher she was devastating. 'Dites après moi: un, deux, trois . . . Again. Encore une fois. Encore. Encore. Encore . . .' After an hour's mental pummelling, I didn't know where I was. 'That's enough for today,' she would end.

She expected me to study French and only French, twenty-four hours a day. Responding to my ignorance with true Gallic élan, she instilled in me a love of the language. The great thing about Miss Hugo was that she believed in me. She got so excited about my growing ability to translate the 'set' book, Alexis de Tocqueville's *L'Ancien Régime*, that she often rewarded me with a cup of tea. Whenever I asked her or O'Hea who was paying for my lessons, they would reply, 'It has been arranged.'

———◇———

Certain things I refused to sacrifice to the daily madness. I continued to play football and cricket and go canoeing in my precious *Ruby*. Time lost to sport during the day I'd make up by working late at night. On Thiel's insistence I regularly went with him to the theatre. 'We'll make a gentleman of you yet, Woody.' We had an understanding: I'd take time off for the theatre if he helped me with French and Latin.

I was able to work hard and play hard because I was blessed with abundant energy and excellent health. Vitality was the key to my success, and I was in love with life. Without tiring, I worked longer and longer hours as my first examinations approached. When they arrived in March 1939 I sailed through the papers with ease. Thanks to Miss Hugo, I did so well in French that I found myself outside 'Schools' going over the 'unseen' paper with a group of students who had been studying it since they were thirteen. The paper was about a French circus, it was full of Gallic humour. Later that day I went over the paper with Miss Hugo, who clapped her hands repeatedly. 'Merveilleux! Merveilleux!' The 'set' book I'd almost memorised, so that gave me no trouble. Thank goodness for my memory.

Arriving one morning a few minutes late for my tutorial with Rodger, I found the student who usually preceded me still sitting there. The week before, we'd exchanged glances as we passed each other at his door. Rodger thought her very bright. She was one of his favourite pupils. I thought her darkly enchanting, but a little mysterious. Now, she looked pale.

'Be a good fellow,' Rodger boomed as I entered his study, 'and take Miss Bradington for coffee. She needs cheering up.' The request must have caused me to raise my eyebrows. 'You'll fill the bill, my boy, don't worry.' There was a rattling of coins. 'I'll make up the hour later.' Miss Bradington's gentle protests were ignored.

I must have stared at him strangely. Not like Rodger to turn his students pale, I thought. 'Nothing to do with me, my dear boy,' he shrugged. 'We all feel off colour at one time or another.' With Miss Bradington still protesting, he ushered us through the door.

There was an embarrassed silence between us as we crossed the quad.

'Well,' I said, 'it's typical of Rodge, I must say.'

'He was only trying to be kind. I'm perfectly well now and I hope you will not bother about me any more.'

'What do you mean, "not bother", I've got to bother. You know Rodge as well as I. Next time I see him he's going to ask me how many lumps of sugar you took.' She laughed.

We went to one of the cafés in the Cornmarket. I did my best to be social, as I'm sure she did, but our conversation fell flat. To make matters worse, she was a pebble-in-the-mouth type – beautiful manners but no warmth. Grudgingly, I noticed her flawless features, her rose-pink lips and her excellent taste in clothing.

After she insisted on paying, I walked her back to Somerville. I left her at the entrance, where she thanked me formally. I said I hoped she would soon be well and turned away, ready to forget her.

After that I seemed to be bumping into Margaret Bradington every time I went out. I saw her as she left her tutorial with Rodger; she smiled at me across the room at lectures. One day we walked across Port Meadow; on the way back we were holding hands.

She'd turn up in her car when I was playing football and haul me to my lodgings with my bike strapped on the back. She was ever considerate, supremely unpretentious. Her car was a Sunbeam deluxe, all polish, leather seats and real oak panelling. She couldn't believe that I'd never sat in such a car. Later, we saw the Cotswolds together. As the weather warmed, we went up the river. She handled a canoe as well as I. We swam in the weirs with the joy of two wild otters. The lock keeper kept up his shouts: 'You'll break your bloody necks, you will.' She was a real tomboy, and that's how I treated her. I used to come up through the water beneath her and topple her over with my back – she loved it. She shared my intense love of life; as long as we were two boys having a rip-roaring time, everything was fine.

Gradually a bond of affection grew up between us. It seemed that we'd both found the person we'd been looking for: despite our different upbringing, we had so much in common. She couldn't get enough of my tales of Lancashire and east London; poverty was something she studied. She became my tutor in English and continental literature.

Everybody expected us to get engaged. We didn't for the simple reason that deep down Margaret Bradington didn't want to get married. There was a strange spirituality about her that went beyond her devout Catholicism. Although she was wonderfully affectionate to me, she had a vocation – an inward vision – to give herself to more than me. Having spent some years with her family in India, she had what I called the 'Indian bug'. Perhaps because of Gandhi, she'd always wanted to return to help the poor of India. Why not the poor of Britain, I asked. My question was pointless; India drew her like a magnet. In going to India Margaret sought self-realisation. I owed it to her to stay silent.

One day she took me to tea with her family who were staying at the Randolph. I met a group of aristocrats who outwardly could not have been more gracious. Margaret introduced me to her father, who had the bearing of a retired general, regular army, Indian-frontier type. He was affability itself. 'My dear boy, my dear boy,' he said as he took my hands, 'Margaret has told me all about you . . . Interesting, most interesting.' He kept saying this to himself, while studying me with a keen eye. I was not deceived – however warm his grasp, his half smiling eyes said, 'What on earth are *you* doing here?' I turned to Lady Bradington. She had Margo's slender build, the same sweet face. She received me kindly, but gave the impression of being confused. Only our fingers touched. 'Charmed, charmed,' she murmured, but her eyes betrayed her: 'My God,' they said, 'there's a Hottentot on my lawn.' Margaret looked on sympathetically.

I had enough common sense to realise that to marry into the Bradingtons would have been like going over to the enemy. The importance of class was written on their faces. They belonged to the class who owned; I belonged to the class who worked. The barriers separating us were too wide. Had I joined this family of delightful snobs, I would have died from suffocation in the first three months.

In any event, I was too proud to think of marrying Margaret. I couldn't imagine living on her money. It hurt enough that she would never let me pay for anything. 'For me it makes no difference,' she would say. She was the only person in my life to whom money did not matter. One of the first things she bought me was a silk dressing gown for which

I had no use. I learned that a private income can give self-assurance and self-respect.

Margaret Bradington graduated in the summer of 1939. Shortly afterwards she made plans to leave for India.

We spent our last evening together, as Margaret had planned, at Bourton-on-the-Water in the Cotswolds. She drove across the peaceful countryside at great speed, with the warm night air rushing in through the open windows. With the light fading, we came to a hotel in a small park, where she told me her family often came. From the moment we entered, it was all bows and scrapes. Our table was ready against a window that looked out on to a river and trees. The water was the colour of dull silver, the trees were charcoal black, not a breath moved the leaves. Patches of hair-like mist rested on the banks. The muted notes of a piano came from an adjoining room. Margaret wore a long, low-necked, deep-blue dress of moiré silk with puffed sleeves; across her shoulders hung a white mohair shawl. Her silky hair was held back by a blue velvet ribbon. I thought she looked very beautiful.

She had arranged the meal before we arrived. It was exquisitely prepared and served. We had trout washed down with hock, followed by a steak grilled over a charcoal fire. The meat, she said, required burgundy, so we had burgundy. We ended the feast with fruit and pastries, cheese, coffee and brandy. I was allowed to smoke my pipe. By now we were a little red in the face and I wondered how we were going to get back. She had imbibed a bit much, I couldn't drive – despite all her efforts to teach me.

Margaret paid the bill without flinching. I'd have had to work for several months to pay it. We drove back to Oxford across a moonlit landscape. The countryside was wrapped in sleep; the first bats had begun to flicker. I thought it a magically beautiful night. This time she drove slowly, lost in thought. Although we'd chattered all the way there and through dinner, it didn't seem right to chatter all the way back. There are times when silence is the tie that binds. I knew better than to talk about India.

She dropped me off at my lodgings on Botley Road at about midnight. 'A topping evening,' she said. I promised to give her a hand in getting away the following morning.

By eleven o'clock the next day we'd got all her bits and pieces out of her rooms into her car. After paying her bills and handing in her keys she joined me outside. She was wearing a velvet hat, a leather jacket, which went with her dark features, and a blue skirt. Her people were expecting her for lunch, after which she was taking a train to Liverpool. We gripped each other's shoulders as she made to get into the car. I had a feeling that there was nothing real about what we were doing – it was a play I'd seen at the theatre. Whatever it was, it brought us both close to tears.

'God keep you, William,' she whispered through the open window. She always called me William. 'And thanks for the wonderful times we've had together.'

'God keep you too, Margo.' We kissed, her face touching mine tenderly. There was a wave of the hand as she moved off down St Giles. I stood waving back, and thinking of the first time I had taken her to coffee and why I hadn't made a last try to keep her. Then I climbed on to my bike and pedalled away aimlessly. Our joy had become pain.

I heard from Margaret after her arrival in Calcutta where she was working with a group of nuns ministering to the poor. It was a long letter in which she described the immense beauty and the overwhelming poverty and ugliness of the city. For the first time she was living life intensely. She sounded very happy and, much as I missed her, I was glad for her sake.

Meanwhile the June examinations had come and gone. I got by with Latin because of the coaching I had received. Also by then I had grown to love the language and had worked hard on it. I think I could have stood up in the examination room and recited great gobs of the 'set' book.

In passing Pass Mods, Dean Kendrick thought I might have

created a precedent. 'I say, Woodruff, you surprise me. I honestly thought you'd come a cropper. Well done, very well done.'

'Knew you'd do it,' Rodger said. 'Sensible fellow, Woodruff. Now it's on to the degree. No more roadblocks. Nothing to stop you.' O'Hea gave me a silent, pensive look over his spectacles. Thiel and I drank too much that night. Reg Tates had a hard job waking me the next morning.

A few days later the LCC renewed my scholarship for the coming academic year 1939–40.

———◇———

While I had been going out with Margo and studying to get through Pass Mods, the world had been falling down about our ears. Japan continued its conquest of China. There were clashes between the Japanese and the Russians in Manchuria. There were growing threats to Western empires in the East. The situation in Palestine and Northern Ireland was worsening – IRA bombs exploded in many parts of Britain. In March 1939, while I was struggling with examinations, Hitler had seized the rest of Czechoslovakia. Nothing changed Britain's attitude to Hitler as much as this did. He had broken his word to both Britain and France – you could feel the sudden growth of anti-Hitler sentiment in the streets and in the pubs. The British were conscience-stricken. Public anger exploded; our faith in Chamberlain was reversed.

No matter what reasons Hitler gave, after March 1939 he was disbelieved. Any hope of reconciliation between Britain and Germany died. There was a sea change in the country's attitude toward pacifism and conscription: students no longer debated whether they should fight for King and Country, but whether they would have to fight this year or next. Rearmament was no longer a dirty word.

Hitler had gone on to denounce the Anglo-German Naval Treaty and the German-Polish Non-Aggression Treaty. No day went by without Hitler rattling the sabre at Poland. The bone of contention was the Polish Corridor (created by the Versailles Treaty in 1919) that separated Germany's West from Germany's East Prussia. Also in dispute was the ancient German town of Danzig – now under League of Nations control. From Spain came an announcement that General Franco's victorious government would join the Axis Anti-Comintern Pact, which meant in effect that Spain had allied itself with Germany, Italy and Japan. 'Are there not signs of a return to the Dark Ages?' the Archbishop of Canterbury asked. The changes came so quickly, one after the other, that I was left confused. Whatever hopes for peace had been raised at Munich the year before were now dashed.

Forced by public anger, in April 1939 Chamberlain's government made it specifically clear to Hitler that if he went to war with Poland he would find himself at war with Britain. This time there was no prevaricating. The power that had dragged down Napoleon and the Kaiser now prepared itself to confront Hitler. Britain even held talks with the Russians, about whom the British had the greatest suspicion. Physically and mentally the United States was too far away to be of any consequence.

Meanwhile the distant rumble of war grew louder; the movement of soldiers and military equipment filled the highways of Britain. While I was doing the final day of 'Schools' in June 1939 a mile-long military convoy rumbled up the High. Step by step, Britain moved towards the brink; with inexorable momentum we were being drawn into war. Appeals for peace were made by Washington and the Vatican. Unlike Thiel, I still clung to the belief that we would be spared. No one, I figured, would be evil enough, or mad enough to start another world war.

<hr />

Despite the darkening scene, I had already made plans to return to Bonn in the summer of 1939. O'Hea knew about it. A week before I was due to go, I had a call to come and see him. He asked if I would deliver an envelope to the Wolfrath family. It contained a British passport for Ludwig, who was in hiding – a fugitive from the law. 'There is no danger in delivering the envelope,' he said, 'but you might wish to think about it.'

I knew enough English history to know that the Jesuits were not good at cloak-and-dagger tactics. In the English Reformation Jesuit spies had come to England from the continent seemingly to become martyrs. Many a doomed missionary, confined to the priest holes of England, had ended up being burned alive at Smithfield. I was not seeking martyrdom.

'What about customs and passport control?' I asked.

'That depends. Normally the train you get on at the Hook will take you straight to Cologne. My information is that you might have to change trains and go through immigration and customs at Kaldenkirchen on the frontier.' He pointed to a map. 'If that happens you will be met by a porter who will take your suitcase and your coat containing the envelope.'

'How will I know him?'

'He will approach you as soon as you arrive. He will wear a metal disk on his blouse with a No. 6 on it.'

'How will he know me? What if he is not there?'

'He will know you and he will be there. That is all I can tell you. He will see you through all the formalities and will put you and your baggage on the train to Cologne. By then the envelope will have been returned to your coat.'

'And what do I do if I don't get the envelope back?'

'Simply forget it and continue.'

Studying timetables, we discussed the undertaking. I didn't think it dangerous. Entering and leaving Germany had always been plain sailing. I agreed to collect the envelope immediately before my departure. To me it was a chance to help someone O'Hea thought ought to be helped. I knew better than to discuss with Thiel what had occurred, he thought me mad for going back to Germany anyway. As I cycled to my lodgings, it occurred to me how O'Hea could be so sure that the German porter would recognise me. He had recently taken an end-of-term photograph of me in the garden behind the hostel. I wondered at the time why he was taking it. I'd been most uncooperative.

The next day I continued my preparations to leave. This time I didn't bother the Cockerill Line or Tom Wall's. I could afford to pay my way.

The last thing I did was to take some flowers to Miss Hugo and thank her for her pains. She wasn't used to being given a bouquet and received it awkwardly. I think she wondered why on earth I was going to Germany instead of France. 'Quel dommage!' she murmured.

I embarked at Harwich on the day that the British call-up of conscripts began. The ship had few passengers. Early the next morning I disembarked in Holland and took the train to Germany. Very few British people accompanied me. As O'Hea had feared, the train stopped at Kaldenkirchen and we were asked to alight. Surrounded by other passengers and their luggage, I had not gone far before I was met by a middle-aged porter plainly marked with a No. 6. The way he came up to me left me in no doubt it was the right man. Taking my valise and coat, he led me through customs and passport control. The whole thing only took a few minutes and was too quick for worrying. I crossed the platform and found a seat on a train to Cologne. The porter put my luggage on the rack, my coat on the seat beside me, took his tip, touched the neb of his cap and left.

I felt inside my coat pocket. The envelope was there. How foolish of me to have got myself worked up over nothing. I resisted the urge to break open the envelope and study the passport. O'Hea had said that it was an English passport prepared with great care. I presumed it was made out in the name of Ludwig's father, Steiner. It certainly couldn't have been made out in the name of Ludwig Wolfrath – deserter.

As the train pulled out, I settled down to read some newspapers I had brought with me. Eventually the compartment emptied. The last to leave was a brewer who knew a little

English. The worse for a few drinks, he talked about the German sky, the German landscape and the German sun – he couldn't say enough about the wonders of his fatherland.

On approaching Cologne, I heard the door slide back. From behind my newspaper I assumed that someone was entering the compartment and went on reading. But the door did not close; the air from the corridor continued to blow about my legs. Curious, I peeped over the top of *The Times* and looked directly into the bespectacled eyes of a uniformed member of the Sicherheitsdienst. I knew I was in serious trouble.

'Engländer?' the man challenged me, his cold eyes holding my stare.

'Ja,' I murmured, doing my best to feign indifference.

'Wo fahren Sie hin?'

'Bonn.'

I thought of the envelope in the coat lying beside me. My mouth went dry; I became frozen to the seat. O'Hea and I had not rehearsed this scene.

I waited for him to make the next move. The train rocked gently from side to side, the officer blocked the door. The silence was unbearable.

After a long, wringing pause, he stepped into the compartment. My heart jumped. I thought he was going to arrest me. Instead he reached for my newspapers.

'Geben Sie mir die Zeitungen,' he commanded.

I couldn't give him the newspapers fast enough.

Having gathered the last sheet, he stepped into the corridor, gave me a sardonic look and went off with the papers under his arm. I sat back exhausted. I felt he might return, or that I would be taken into custody in Cologne. Nothing of the sort happened; on leaving the train there was no sign of the security police.

Even so, my heart pounded until I reached the Wolfraths. Frau Wolfrath opened the door before I had time to ring. Unlike my first visit, there was no stiffness between us. With great concealed relief, I handed over the envelope. I didn't tell her how glad I was to be rid of it. She thanked me. I told her about the Sicherheitsdienst officer on the train and she became worried that I might have been followed.

The three of us sat down to supper. Inevitably, there was a Kartoffelsalat: everything was becoming pinched, they said, but potatoes were plentiful. They both looked under strain. They told me that Ludwig had gone underground. While marching along a country road with a platoon of the Arbeitsdienst, Ludwig had made a joke about Hitler. Without a moment's hesitation the fellow behind him had brought his spade down on Ludwig's head and knocked him unconscious. In fear of his life, Ludwig had fled his unit.

I spent most of my time that summer in Bonn. I had a room in a house in Ermichelstrasse, close to the university. I attended Professor Fritsch's seminar again, but I never succeeded in piercing his worried exterior. There was no familiarity, no invitation for me to visit his home.

I was allowed to come and go at the Wolfraths as I pleased, but my visits were rare and always brief. Ludwig was not there, nor was he mentioned. Whoever came to the house looking for him was given the same answer: they didn't know where he was. Frau Wolfrath spent long periods staring out of the window as if she expected her son to suddenly appear at the gate. On occasions she'd burst into tears for no reason at all. During one of my visits I was told that the police had been to the house demanding a list of visitors – of whom I was one. The news left me uneasy. To get your name on lists was not advisable.

The general atmosphere of uncertainty and fear got on my nerves. I didn't need Frau Wolfrath's constant warnings to keep out of trouble. I became doubly careful to whom I spoke and what I said. Like everybody else, I became adept at dodging and weaving in conversation. I learned what to say to whom; I took seriously the idea that somebody was listening. Letters coming from England, or from Margaret in India, always had a tape across them saying that they had been opened by the censor. From my going into Germany almost to my coming out I avoided writing letters. O'Hea had told me not to. After Margaret's first letter from Calcutta, I asked her to write to my college.

During the summer I visited the old cynic Willi Betterman again. He had acquired a Nazi party badge, which he wore in his coat lapel. He took me several times to dine at his club. He told me that some weeks earlier a group of drunken Nazis had marched in, stamped about as if they owned the club, and drowned out everybody else by bawling the 'Horst Wessel Lied'. Some members had collided with each other getting through the doors; others had refused to panic.

He told me that he no longer went to the Netherlands. He had been a courier, illegally carrying German currency in his rectum. On his last trip someone on the train had warned him to turn back. He did. It saved his life: he had watched someone less fortunate being seized and dragged away.

One day he led me up a long staircase at the club. He walked slowly as if he was about to reveal a mystery. At the top he threw open a door and stood back. I looked in. Directly opposite was an impressive portrait of the Kaiser with the inscription: 'Hoch lebe der Kaiser'. He shut the door and shuffled downstairs again.

'What are the odds on peace?' I asked him.

'I've given up hope. The stage is set for war. It only needs one more confrontation between Hitler and the French–British alliance to bring the European house down. Hitler is intent on war, especially against Poland. Armes Deutschland!' he muttered. 'Sometimes I think the Germans are a fated people. We triumph only to fail.'

<hr />

Despite growing tensions, there were times that summer when I could not have been happier. I fell in with the same wonderful group of students that I'd known the year before. Full of high spirits, we forgot the Nazis; we shut our minds to the persecution of dissidents and to the possibility of war. Instead, we talked and sang and drank and cycled and forgot the Polish Corridor. Whatever was reprehensible about Germany didn't concern us. It concerned those others, whoever they were. We didn't arrange our lives according to someone's desperate predictions. We didn't even hear the warnings. We wanted to believe that all was well.

And so the band played on and on and the Führer was in charge and it was a wonderful summer. There was merry-making at the university and in the town. There was a week of festivals with fireworks and searchlights playing on the river and the fountains, and dancing and boat parties and *Gemütlichkeit* with delightful companions. But the silly talk about atrocities against Germans in Poland, which screamed from the newspaper headlines every day, refused to go away. I found it impossible to close my ears to the growing rumours of war – not least because the possibility of war kept intruding.

I became friendly with a young married couple, the Müllers. Richard Müller was a gifted young scientist who was not good at clicking his heels. I was visiting them one day when they were preserving beans: they put beans and salt in a barrel and then we took turns treading them down with washed feet, rather like pressing grapes. As I took my turn, I thought they were preserving an incredible amount for one winter – they already had a barrel of sauerkraut. 'Might be a long war,' Richard said. While I was in the cellar I could not help noticing box after box of spark plugs. The cellar was full of them. I could not imagine what he wanted them for. He had no car. 'We'll barter them for bread.'

After we'd finished with the beans, we went to his mother's house for 'Kaffee und Kuchen'. While the others were in the garden, the white-haired old lady showed me her bankbook. 'As you are an Engländer,' she said hesitatingly, 'perhaps you'll be able to tell me what has happened to the savings which Herr Müller and I had in the bank. All they can tell me is that they have vanished. But how can so much money saved over so many years disappear? Herr Müller never understood; I think it killed him.'

Embarrassed, I looked at the book. It recorded a fortune in marks saved before the Great War. There was no mystery about what had happened to it: like so many others, the Müllers had lost their savings in the hyperinflation of the 1920s. I was too shocked to explain to Frau Müller what her family must have tried to do many times. I was relieved when the young Müllers returned from the garden and the woman squirrelled the book away. I wondered if she hadn't lost her mind.

⸺◇⸺

A couple of days later a young priest with whom I had become friendly visited me in my lodgings. We had often met to discuss politics. 'Will there be peace,' I asked him as he was leaving, 'now that the Czech problem has been resolved?'

'No, Hitler is bent on conquest in Poland. He's determined to bring war down on our heads.'

When I met the priest again he asked me if I would come to talk at a meeting that a friend of his, a professor of philosophy, was arranging. Only students who could be trusted would be there. I accepted the invitation without thinking.

On reaching the meeting I was introduced. I had seen the professor before, but had never spoken to him. I recognised some of the students who were scattered about the room; they sat silently with watchful eyes. A lamp in the corner was lit, the curtains were drawn. Frau Wolfrath's 'Vorsichtig sein, Wilhelm' echoed in my head. I could see her finger on her lips. 'Psst! Maul halten Wilhelm.'

I thought I was the one to speak, but to my surprise the professor preceded me. He talked mainly about Germany's woes. 'What a scapegoat Germany has been,' he ended. 'The world press, controlled by international Jewry, has maligned the Third Reich. The Jews would not be persecuted had they not brought their troubles upon themselves. They insisted on a separate identity which created a state within a state. Their power in the media, finance, business and the professions was out of all proportion to their numbers.' He went on and on with me standing there.

The first thing I said when it came my turn to speak was that the British no longer trusted Hitler. 'He gave his word that he neither wished nor intended to annex Austria: he broke it. He gave his word after Munich that he had no further territorial claims: he broke it. Britain will declare war if Germany attempts to conquer Poland.'

As the night wore on the professor and I reached an impasse. Tempers flared. His taut face and indignant eyes made me regret ever having come. Both of us – whether in English or German – kept using the same phrases: 'That is not the point,' 'That is not what I said.' I thought it pathetic that a sincere German and an equally sincere Englishman, both of whom hated war, were unable to find the means to avoid it. I could tell from his face that it was purposeless to prolong the debate any longer and I said so. In a choked voice, his hand emphasising and beating time to his words, he ended: 'If war comes, my sons will be proud to fight and die for Germany.' Curiously, not once did either of us mention America.

The meeting ended with the priest thanking us both. I shook hands with the professor and left. Only in the corridor were the students prepared to talk.

—◦—

I decided finally that war was imminent at a mass rally in Düsseldorf where Hermann Göring was to speak. I'd become friendly with the university barber and he invited me to go with him. Once more I ignored Frau Wolfrath's warning not to get mixed up in Nazi meetings.

When we reached Düsseldorf the railway station was filled with a wildly excited crowd. Special trains and buses had brought people in from all over the Rhineland. The streets

669

were packed with a heaving, pushing human mass. With the barber's son riding his father's shoulders, we made our way to the town square. Every window overlooking the square was occupied; every roof had its bands of Hitler youth. Hysteria swept through the crowd like electricity – you could hear it crackle. Long black, white and red swastika flags draped every building; hundreds of lighted torches blazed. My friend and I eventually found a place on the far side of the square encircled by a forest of flags. The podium was too far away to see clearly. We saw bodies moving about, we could hear Göring's heavy voice on the loudspeakers, but for all we saw of him, he might as well have been in Berlin.

Göring's approach was direct and brutal. His appeal was emotional. It was as if he was sending out flashes of lightning and the audience was the lightning rod. Every declaration was followed by delirious, thunderous: 'Sieg Heil! Sieg Heil! Sieg Heil!' In a voice that rang with conviction, he declared that Germany's hour of trial had come.

As the speech continued, Göring introduced a strident note that threw the audience in all directions. On and on he went, his voice getting heavier and heavier, his pace quickening to a crescendo.

An hour later he reached his peroration. He became more and more heated. He appealed to patriotism. A certain rough eloquence possessed him. And then, quite suddenly he stopped. His last words were greeted with half a million people shouting: 'Sieg Heil! Sieg Heil! Sieg Heil!' Pandemonium reigned. I was shaken; I'd just heard the most emotional harangue of my life.

The din continued until the sinister rattle of kettledrums broke across the square. A hush fell on the crowd, thousands of arms rose. 'Hand hoch, Wilhelm,' my companion whispered, a note of anxiety in his voice. I raised my right arm. I hate to think what would have happened had I not done so. I looked up at the barber's infant son on his father's shoulders. His tiny arm was raised like mine. There followed the 'Horst Wessel Lied' and 'Deutschland, Deutschland über alles'. The singing must have been heard for miles.

The dignitaries gone, we found ourselves inextricably locked in a swaying, surging sea of humanity, which had no thought of going home. We were swept out of the square by this great human tide. Once more I feared that I might be separated from the barber. The whole thing had become scary.

We remained part of the cheering, turbulent mob for at least another hour; only when the great wave had spent itself were we able to extricate ourselves and make for the railway station. We took turns carrying the child who had long since fallen asleep. And as I walked down the street with the infant on my back, I noticed the moon had emerged from the clouds. Through all the turbulence, it had remained serene and unaffected.

The meeting in Düsseldorf banished any doubts I had about a coming war. Back in Bonn, I wrote to my parents telling them to buy food.

A week later, we were shaken by the news of the non-aggression pact between the Russians and the Germans. Hitler had seized the initiative again; mortal enemies had become allies. In Bonn most Germans thought the pact would ensure peace – Poland would have to capitulate.

I asked the young priest what he thought of it. As always he was dangerously outspoken. 'Why shouldn't Russia and Germany make a pact?' he answered. 'Both countries were outlawed in 1919 and drew together; both are without principles except naked power; both are led by tyrants; both are militaristic and intolerant. They think that the Western democracies are rotten.' He paused and studied his hands. 'They will take us into the dark night, but they will not prevail.' Such talk would have brought imprisonment had he been overheard. I feared for him.

<hr />

Not long after the signing of the Moscow–Berlin pact, I received an urgent message from the Wolfraths to come at once. I went and was told that Ludwig was going to try to flee to Britain the next day. Despite their denials, the Wolfraths had hidden and hung on to their son as long as they dared. They were now concerned to get him out of the country before it was too late. The idea was that I should take him to O'Hea, who had promised to help him. Ludwig was expected to arrive before dawn.

'Pack and return at once,' Frau Wolfrath said. 'Leave the travel arrangements to us.'

Their note of urgency did not surprise me. I'd already ignored three warnings sent by the British Consul in Cologne telling me to leave. Other foreign students had long since gone. Only that morning my landlord in Bonn had pleaded with me to go: 'Es macht mir Ärger daß Sie noch hier sind. Wenn Sie noch einen Tag länger bleiben werden mir die Fenster eingeschlagen. Man hat mich gewarnt.'* I didn't want to be around when his windows were broken. I had already felt a coolness towards me by certain students; some were becoming hostile. I didn't need persuading.

In a mad scramble, I went back to the university, packed up, paid my bills, said goodbye, and rejoined the Wolfraths that afternoon. I didn't go out of my way to take my leave of Professor Fritsch, I thought it might embarrass him.

While Frau Wolfrath busied herself preparing her son's luggage – suitcase and contents all English – I cycled to a neighbouring village to tell the maid not to come the next day. I had delivered similar messages before. I was told to say that the Wolfraths had decided to visit friends. When I reached the village I called at the post office to mail cards to England.

'Sind Sie Engländer?' the man asked as he studied my cards. 'Ja.'

'Gibt es Krieg?' He regarded me earnestly. How many times had I been asked, will there be war?

'Ja,' I answered. Ting-a-ling went the doorbell as another customer entered. Not another word was said.

---

* 'I'm in trouble because you're still here. If you stay another day they'll smash my windows. I've been warned.'

As I continued my ride I couldn't help noticing a stillness lying across the land: a note of expectation was in the air. Was it the hush before the coming storm?

The maid was not at home but her brother was. I'd met him before and thought him a crank. I was always repelled by his swaggering. He was a Nazi and had a blind hatred of all things foreign. He detested the English. He was startled when he opened the door, especially when I didn't respond to his 'Heil Hitler.' He suddenly grasped me by the collar.

'Was machen Sie noch in Deutschland, Engländer? Ich werde Sie anzeigen.' I wasn't afraid of him calling the police. His dull face was contorted by anger. There was danger in his eyes.

'Mach das,' I said brusquely. With all my pacifism, I was conscious of a desire to bash him on his silly head. Thank God I didn't. Eyes blazing, his face grim and iron-hard, he went on about English spies. Feldmarschall von Brauchitsch was to make an important speech on the radio that night; war would follow. The way he gripped my neck and kept making accusing wags of his head at me seemed to imply that I was responsible for the whole thing.

Having delivered my message, I struggled to escape his grasp. He was holding both lapels of my jacket and would not let go. I had a horrible dread that he was going to hang on to me until war was declared. I could see him dragging me to the police station.

Eventually I broke his grip and fled on my bicycle. He spat after me. I couldn't help thinking how stupid it was of Frau Wolfrath to have sent me there. Perhaps it was an excuse to get me out of the way while they discussed things they didn't want me to hear. When I got back, she didn't show any fear that the fellow might raise a hue and cry. 'Danger does not come from those who fly into a rage,' she said. 'It's the silent and the meek you have to watch.'

The rest of the day and night was unbearable. None of us went to bed, instead we sat and worried whether Ludwig would come home in time. We could only hope that he would not be trailed, and that the house was not being watched. Frau Wolfrath rarely left her seat by the window.

Towards dawn a tired, worried-looking Ludwig arrived. He made us all jump with his scratching on the windowpane. He didn't say where he'd come from, or how he'd got there. I thought he'd aged since I saw him last. There were emotional scenes; Frau Wolfrath wept. Ludwig thanked me for the passport. 'Don't forget that I am now called Steiner.' I knew that to help a fugitive was to share his crime, and that the penalty for desertion was death. Yet I felt no peril. No one could trace the passport back to me, and I knew that the Wolfraths would not betray me.

After breakfast, it was decided that Ludwig, his mother and I would take different routes to the railway station. I was the first to leave, at about noon. I shook the hands of Herr and Frau Wolfrath and of Ludwig. 'Auf Wiedersehen,' they said. I wondered when that would be. For a moment there was a painful stillness between us, then I picked up my valise and climbed into a taxi.

Our movements had been worked out to the last detail. I was not to recognise Frau Wolfrath or Ludwig again until we reached the Netherlands sometime that afternoon. It was a grey day; the town was going about its business. The people I saw looked subdued. I stopped en route to buy my father a pipe with a coloured tassel and a removable grate for the ashes.

'Gibt es Krieg?' I was asked once more.

'Ja,' I answered, collecting my change.

Shortly after I reached the station, Ludwig's mother arrived. After her came Ludwig. We all sat apart. In the distance a radio was playing military marches. Endlessly long troop trains slowly made their way past us going westward. The trains must have travelled through the night because the soldiers were lying in heaps, asleep.

At Cologne we sat and waited for the train to Kaldenkirchen and the Netherlands. The time for departure came and went. No train. After an hour Ludwig began pacing the platform, his open English coat hanging limply on his narrow shoulders. From time to time he glanced at his English gold watch; Frau Wolfrath looked as though she was about to cry. Other passengers became equally tense.

'Try the ticket office,' Ludwig whispered as he passed me, watch in hand.

I went and asked. 'Das weiß ich nicht,' the ticket man said, snapping the window back into place. Obviously, I wasn't the first to ask.

'No one knows,' I whispered to Ludwig.

'Try the man in the signal box, he's sure to know.'

So I went to the end of the platform and climbed a narrow iron ladder leading to a little door. The troop trains rumbled below.

'Entschuldigen Sie bitte,' I said as I entered the box, 'wann kommt der Zug nach Holland?'

The man turned his back on me and rubbed some grease on a switch lever. I tried again, raising my voice against the clatter of the trains. 'Entschuldigen Sie, kommt der Zug nach Kaldenkirchen und Venlo?' The man continued to grease the lever. I got the message and left.

'He won't answer,' I told Ludwig who was anxiously peering up the line.

Ten minutes later the train arrived and the few passengers got aboard. There was only one open coach. Foreigners had long since been ordered out by their governments; Germans no longer had the freedom to cross frontiers. We sat apart, complete strangers. The atmosphere was tense.

After a further delay the guard blew his whistle. Our journey had begun. We overtook a packed troop train lumbering along on a parallel line, then our train was shunted into a siding to allow other military trains to pass.

Two hours later, we threaded our way out of the siding and headed for the border. I watched Frau Wolfrath and Ludwig out of the corner of my eye. No turning back now. Through the windows I saw weekend allotment gardens; Nazi flags flew defiantly above the roofs of the tiny cabins.

The train came to a halt at Kaldenkirchen. There were more officials on the platform than there were passengers on the train. Frau Wolfrath left the train with several others. She muttered something in a choked voice as she passed her son. Someone entered the coach to announce that passengers for the Netherlands should remain seated. All formalities would be completed on the train. We sat still in embarrassed silence.

Through a curtain of steam, I watched Frau Wolfrath as she crossed the platform and sat down on a bench with her back to a wall. Now and again she fished into her bag for a handkerchief to wipe her eyes.

After a few minutes German frontier officials came aboard working their way from one passenger to the next. I took out my papers and waited my turn.

'What have you been doing in Germany?' an official asked me, thumbing through my passport.

'Having a good time.' He knew that I had been a visiting student at Bonn. He was just about to say something else when we were startled by a distraught-looking man in his fifties, who bolted past us and ran through the open carriage door. We watched silently as he fled across the railway sidings with policemen and dogs after him.

With furtive glances at the door, my interrogator took up his questions where he had left off.

'Why didn't you leave earlier? The British consulate in Cologne told you three times to leave.' He stopped talking and squinted at me.

He was right. It surprised me that they should have assembled such detail.

'I was enjoying myself too much.'

The official didn't reply. He thumbed through my papers.

After the longest pause, he stamped my passport. 'Gute Reise,' he said stiffly, with what might have been a smile. He moved on to the next passenger. There were other officials who questioned me about currency and baggage, but I knew I'd survived the crucial test.

Without making it obvious, I now turned my attention to

Ludwig. He seemed to be producing all kinds of papers from his wallet. All I could hear was a rumble of voices speaking in English. Two Sicherheitsdienst officials were working on him. They were also going through his luggage, which they had not done with mine. Outside, Frau Wolfrath, hands clutching her bag, watched every move. She didn't look as if her heart was in her mouth, but it must have been.

The questioning of Ludwig went on and on. I worried if the name of Steiner would hold up. I wondered if the passport and the papers – which were being handed from one official to another – would survive their scrutiny. Every moment I thought that they were about to escort him off the train.

I gave a great inward sigh of relief when the officials finally stamped Ludwig's papers and left. My respect for Ludwig rose. I had obviously underestimated him: one had to be very smart to get past that hawk-eyed crowd.

For the next half-hour we sat in the empty station. I pretended to read a German newspaper, but my eyes would not follow the print – I was too nervous. The mournful howl of a dog in the distance didn't help. What is going on? I wondered. Are they checking up on Ludwig by phone? Except for Frau Wolfrath, the platform was empty and quiet. I knew that neither of us was safe until we had crossed the river Maas and reached Venlo. I did not look in Ludwig's direction. I'm sure he was feeling worse than I.

After what seemed like an eternity, the coach suddenly lurched forwards, jolting as it passed over the points. I heard the clank of the couplings. Puffs of steam flurried over our window. I could have cheered. Frau Wolfrath did not wave; nor did her son. They both sat quite still.

A few minutes later the border came into view. Tortoise-like, giving haphazard jerks, the train trundled across the bridge into the Netherlands.

Ludwig was the first to get off. Falling on his knees, he kissed the ground. Then he hoisted me into the air. He was radiant with joy.

677

Before boarding another train for the Hook of Holland we stood and watched the German train jerk its way back towards the frontier. It would be a long time before a train passed that way again.

At the Hook we boarded a crowded ship. Lights shone on the masts of other vessels at the quay. The radio told us of the appeals for peace made by the British government and the Pope: 'Once again a critical hour strikes for the great human family . . .' President Roosevelt had appealed to the King of Italy to mediate. I stayed on deck until the shore gang cast off, severing the last links with the continent. The ropes hit the water with a burst of spray. A bell rang; the engines started. A flutter in the bowels of the ship told me that we were under way; the water stirred into slow ripples at the stern. To the sound of gongs and shouted orders, with the water moving past us quietly in long, swelling waves, we slid away from the lights of the land to the encompassing darkness of the sea.

It was a rough crossing. Ludwig found some friends in the first class who were also fleeing Germany and abandoned me. His leaving me on deck was not appropriate, but I didn't mind. I had the company of three pretty English girls who'd been wandering across Europe together, and hadn't the slightest idea that war was imminent. They'd never stayed in one place long enough to hear from a British consul. They'd been wakened the previous night by police in their hotel in Nürnberg and unceremoniously escorted to a train, which rushed them across Germany into the Netherlands. The only thing they regretted was that the mad flight to safety had not been done on horseback. As far as they were concerned, it had all been 'terribly ripping'.

I was disturbed during the night by a ship's siren that silenced all other sounds. It had a sinister note. I rushed to the rail to see a German steamer sailing directly ahead of us towards the English coast. Minutes later, the ship broke course and turned back in the direction of Hamburg. Not a good sign, I thought. I didn't sleep much more that night.

At four-forty-five on the morning of Friday 1 September, while we were approaching Harwich, Germany attacked Poland. World War II had begun. As our ship sidled up to the dock and made fast and the vibrations and movements in the water stopped, I noticed that the buildings along the quayside had been camouflaged. The town was still wrapped in the darkness of night, still unaware that war had come.

I dropped Ludwig off at the hostel. O'Hea didn't think there was anything remarkable about our both being there. I hesitated to mention the trouble I'd had with the Sicherheitsdienst officer on the Cologne train, for fear that he might ask why I hadn't brought the fellow back with me.

In the early hours of 3 September I took a fast train from Oxford to my parents in Derby. The government had already begun to exercise emergency powers. School children were being evacuated from London. The blackout of Britain had begun. England had girded for war.

Chapter XIII

The Enemy at the Gate

I arrived at my parents' house shortly after eleven on the morning of Sunday 3 September 1939. My mother came to the door, her eyes frightened. 'Chamberlain is declaring war against Germany,' she said. That the events of 1914–18 were to be repeated was too much for her.

I reached the radio in time to hear Chamberlain's closing words: 'It is the evil things that we shall be fighting against – brute force, bad faith, injustice, oppression and persecution – and against them I am certain that the right will prevail.'

Angered at Czechoslovakia's fate and Germany's brutal attempt to conquer Poland, the British could hardly have done anything else but declare war. Many wanted it: they were tired of Hitler; they were glad that the deceit had ended and the life-and-death struggle had begun. Month by month our country had slid down the slippery slope that led to war, while we acclaimed each new calamity as a step towards lasting peace. Now reality had intervened. My friends in Germany had become my deadly enemies.

Later that day King George VI spoke to Britain and the Empire: '. . . For the second time in the lives of most of us we are at war. Over and over again we have tried to find a peaceful way out of the differences between ourselves and those who are now our enemies. But it has been in vain . . . We can only do the right as we see the right, and reverently commit our cause to God.' Because of his stammer, it was as much of an effort for us to listen to him as it was for him to speak.

That night I heard the wailing of British air-raid sirens for the first time. I listened for the bombs and the anti-aircraft batteries. We'd been led to believe that with the declaration of war the bombing would begin, but it was a false alarm. When the all-clear had sounded, I tossed and turned in bed deciding what I should do. For hours I lay there, first on my back, then on my side, wide awake, listening to the night sounds. Should I stick to pacifism, or take up arms in defence of my country? My feelings towards Nazism had hardened: Hitler was a fanatic who had no real concern for peace, truth or sincerity; he was leading the German people and us into the abyss. He obviously intended to go on using force until somebody stopped him. I felt that he ought to be stopped, even if the heavens fell.

By dawn my mind was made up. I looked out of the window on to a grey day. To fight was the lesser of two evils. I would arrange my Oxford affairs and join up.

In a night I had grown from youth to man. I understood myself better than I had in a long time. Patriotism had become more important to me than pacifism. I was not eager to be a soldier – I was concerned with resisting aggression – but to fight in self-defence I thought justified. The idea of justice – of doing the right thing – possessed me. I had a cause.

I went down to breakfast. Mother never mentioned the war.

'Did you sleep well?'

'Of course.'

While I ate, she told me what was happening to the rest of the family. Other than mother, all my family was now on war work. I was afraid that she would ask me what I intended to do, but she didn't. She asked me silently with her eyes instead.

Before leaving, I told her that I had business to do in Oxford and that I'd be back soon. She shrugged her shoulders as if to say, 'You don't have to tell me. I know what you're about to do.' I knew that my father had told her something similar when he'd gone to join up in 1914. I think she was too sad to cry.

I returned to the railway station through the silent rain. The people in Derby were as subdued as the people in Bonn had been: the same worried look, no flag-waving, no hysteria.

At the station, I bought a newspaper. It had a banner headline: BRITAIN AT WAR. A liner had been torpedoed off the Hebrides; theatres and cinemas were to close; car lights were to be dimmed; factory sirens silenced; cars were to be immobilised at night; machine-gun emplacements had been set up at Buckingham Palace gates; the French Army was preparing to invade Germany.

The ticket office window was taped with strips of brown paper against blast; sandbags were stacked against the wall. A large new sign greeted me: IS YOUR JOURNEY REALLY NECESSARY? I thought it was. I walked past a military guard who had been posted in the night.

The train was packed. The atmosphere in the compartment was as heavy as that of a funeral cortège – everyone sitting in their private worry. In hours, the tone and moral climate of Britain had changed. The talk in the train was dreary. It was all about the blackout, air-raid precautions, anti-aircraft balloons, guns and scrap iron. Trenches were being dug in the parks, gas masks were being distributed. People were volunteering for Red Cross work and fire service.

Mother had given me a letter from Harold Watkins. He'd joined the RAF. Back in Oxford I went to their office in New Inn Hall Street. Disorder reigned. I was not the only one wanting to join the air force. I volunteered for Bomber Command; I wanted to be a rear gunner in a Wellington bomber, and I hoped I might be with Harold.

'We don't have the planes,' they said. 'We'll call you when we do.'

685

Later, under a university scheme, I switched to the army, which deferred my call-up until after my examinations in June 1940.

Following my visit to New Inn Hall Street I ran into Harold Wilson on the steps of University College.

'I've just volunteered,' I said. 'What are you going to do?'

His reply startled me. 'I've been called to higher things.'

I suppose I jumped to conclusions, but his eyes were upraised, he did have a hand on his heart, and his face expressed pain.

'I didn't know you had trouble with your heart, Harold.'

'Nothing wrong with my heart, Woody, I've decided to join Bill Beveridge.' (Sir William Beveridge was head of University College.)

'Doing what?'

'Studying the five giant evils: war, sickness, ignorance, hunger and unemployment.'

I was perplexed; perhaps he was pulling my leg. I thought of Harold during the war. He had joined the economic section of the war cabinet. In 1945 he became a member of Attlee's government and later Prime Minister.

After talking with Harold Wilson I collected my mail from St Catherine's. I was excited to see a letter from Calcutta, though I thought it odd that the writing was not in Margo's hand. I opened the letter in the street outside the college. It told me that Margaret Bradington had died from typhoid fever a month earlier. The news left me stunned. For a moment I didn't see or feel or hear anything: there was a giant hush. When I came to, I was leaning against the college wall, holding the letter. All I could think of was Margo diving off the weir gate, arms outstretched.

Separated by class, by money, by vocation and by distance, we were now separated by death. What was the rhyme and reason of it all? For a long time I simply refused to believe that she was dead. Nothing mattered any more. I remembered the lullaby I'd sung at Quarreux three years earlier: that happiness is a mirage, life an absurdity.

I conveyed my condolences to her family but received no reply.

--◇--

Oxford in wartime was Oxford in disarray. The old, steady, peaceful place I had loved so much was no more. Tutors had gone to war, or were preparing to do so; Rodger was in air force uniform. Fellow students were getting ready to go to France. By 12 September 1939 the first British contingent had crossed the Channel. Ruskin College and the Catholic Workers' College had been requisitioned for war use.

On the steps of St Catherine's I ran into a student I knew. He had just been commissioned as a second lieutenant. For a moment I didn't recognise him, he looked a different man. As he turned round for inspection, his peaked officer's cap and his shining belt, brasses and insignia dazzled me; so too did his large revolver. His chest was wider, his face glowed with pride. 'No more exams for me, Woody,' he said. He called the little stick under his arm his swagger-cane.

I was so struck that I stood and watched him as he swaggered up St Aldate's on his way to France and God knows where. He went with the excitement of a child going to the seaside.

Thiel thought my volunteering an act of madness. 'You're impatient to get yourself killed.'

I took refuge studying in the Camera, coming out at night to creep about in the blackout, which lasted from sunset to sunrise. Only the odd flashlight pierced the gloom.

At the outset of the war the massive bombing of Britain did not take place. Instead, Poland was overrun by Germany and Russia in a month, after which there was a lull. The expected attack of Germany on the Western front did not materialise; except at sea, war seemed suspended. Until April

1940 we called this the 'Phony War'. Britain and France waited for Hitler to make the next move. Meanwhile, we bombed Germany with propaganda leaflets and sang 'We're gonna hang out the washing on the Siegfried Line'. Many of the evacuees from London and other major cities took advantage of the lull to go home again. From Oxford, those without the train or bus fare walked for three days along the Thames' towpath until they reached Westminster.

Gradually the university adjusted to the changed conditions. Students who were excused military service until June 1940 were given the option of taking a shorter war degree. I opted for this.

I took the army's physical examination. 'Put out your tongue, say "Ahhh" . . . Take a deep breath . . . Any serious illnesses? . . . None . . . You'll do.'

I tried to get down to work, but I didn't have my heart in my studies any more. My determination to excel had gone. I realised that having joined up I might never see Oxford again. I kept busy by force of habit, but I was limping and shuffling instead of striding. I didn't go up the river, after Margo's death, it didn't seem right.

Every day brought new disasters at sea. In September 1939 the aircraft carrier *Courageous* was torpedoed. In October the battleship *Royal Oak* was sunk in Scapa Flow. Hitler offered his peace terms and was rebuffed by both Britain and France. In November the losses of British merchant shipping were becoming insupportable. The USSR, having conquered half of Poland, attacked and defeated Finland. In December the German battleship *Graf Spee* was scuttled at the mouth of the Rio de la Plata.

One day I was sitting with Rodger in his study when I happened to see a list of names above his head on the wall. Below it were the words 'Dulce et decorum est pro patria mori'. Students I'd known were already dead, the college's first casualties. I was shocked – one of them I'd known really well. He'd joined the navy; he'd been one of the toffs with whom I'd been so ill at ease when I first came to Oxford.

A troubled Christmas, which I shared with my parents, came and went. They were silent about my joining up. Now that I was committed, both kept their thoughts to themselves. The war was the recurrence of a bad dream.

George VI made his first halting Christmas broadcast to the nation:

> And I said to the man who stood at the gate of the year:
> 'Give me light that I may tread safely into the unknown.'
> And he replied: 'Go out into the darkness and put your
> hand into the hand of God. That shall be to you better
> than light and safer than a known way.'

All of us felt helpless in the face of the unknown.

———◇———

Shortly after Christmas 1939 I cycled the eighty miles from Oxford to Cambridge to visit Ma Hargreaves who, with Emily, Clem and Chris, had been evacuated from Bow. I found them living like country squires in a large requisitioned house in the countryside. Clem's foresight had paid off. I think he had traded on his mother-in-law's prestige. In a world at war, he felt entitled to all he could get. I thought the house was ideal: all conveniences including heating. There was a good pub within easy walking distance, a flourishing village institute, a district nurse, and a bus to take them into Cambridge. Clem thought me mad for having joined the army. 'You're supposed to be the one with a "loaf of bread" [head].' The way that Mum and Emily looked at me, I knew they thought I was about to share the fate of Nick Hargreaves.

Mum was the only one who still called herself a pacifist. I thought her a tragic figure. All that she had secretly feared had come to pass. She didn't know what to do; and now that Lansbury was ill and her husband dead, where to turn. She had been on tiptoe to see the coming Jerusalem, instead of which she was witnessing a new hell.

689

The news they gave me from the East End was sad. London was being bombed. Old friends in Bow had been killed; youths we had known had been mobilised; families had been broken up. We talked about Alex. 'He's belly-up,' said Mum. 'Lost 'is own and 'is wife's money. She stood behind 'im until the end, but 'e treated 'er badly. Fought with 'er until the day 'e left. Chased by creditors, 'e's gone into 'iding with the army in the Middle East. Miranda 'as walked out on Milton and taken 'er baby with 'er. 'Er life 'as become a bit of a mess. Milton 'as gone back on the bottle. Carol is still at Poplar Town 'all. She 'as grey 'air loik a woman twenty years older, and refuses to dye it.'

It wasn't a pleasant visit and I was glad to begin the journey back. Mum's eyes filled with tears when she gave me a final hug.

I fell in with another cyclist on the way back to Oxford, but the current spy scare reduced our conversation to a stale patter.

◦

The 'Phony War' ended in April 1940 when Germany invaded Denmark and Norway. Britain fought briefly in Norway, but retreated at the end of that month.

One day, about this time, I was going to a tutorial in Christ Church when I happened to look up at the girl who was coming down the wide oak staircase. My heart stopped. The girl approaching looked like Betty Weatherby – an older Betty, but unless I was mistaken, it was her.

'Excuse me,' I stammered, as she made to pass me. 'Are you Betty Weatherby?'

She flicked the prettiest brown eyes at me and smiled. 'I'm afraid not. I'm Kay Wright.' The flash of her teeth added to her charm. I detected a northern accent.

'Look,' I dared, 'I'm sorry to stop you like this, but I thought you were a girl I knew years ago in Blackburn.'

She gave me a long, friendly, wordless stare. I could see

she was blushing. 'I hope you're not disappointed.' Her voice was sweet, her eyes merry. 'I come from a village north of Blackburn in Westmorland.'

'Well, we have something in common. Can I take you for coffee?'

'But what about your work?'

'It can wait, I hope.' She thought that was very funny.

——◇——

We sat over coffee as we told each other what we were doing in life. Wisps of silky brown hair protruded from beneath the scarf knotted under her chin. All her features formed a harmonious whole. I thought her beautiful. There was not a shadow of affectation in her. I told her that I was taking Modern Greats. She told me she had recently graduated from Glasgow University, and was now in her first job at the Oxford County Agricultural Board. She had been consulting with an agricultural scientist in Christ Church.

Neither of us could conceal our joy at having met. We both talked at once, interrupting each other. I could have sat there all day gazing into her smiling eyes.

After ages of talk, we rode our bikes along St Giles and Woodstock Road to Kay's lodgings in Warnborough Road. I was introduced to her two dolls, one a rag doll called 'Joy', the other a colourful clown called 'Sorrow'. Having got there, Kay couldn't think of any reason why we should be there, so we got on our bikes again and cycled to the Botanic Garden. We forgot what we should have been doing. I had never seen the garden so beautiful, or felt the air so fragrant. Why hadn't I noticed it before? There must have been other people there but I cannot remember seeing a soul. Come to think, there was no one in the street either, I saw only Kay's happy face.

Late in the afternoon we went to her office near Carfax where she handed in some kind of report. We went somewhere for dinner; it didn't seem to matter where we ate or what we ate as long as we were together. After dinner I took

Kay back to her lodgings. I sensed how nervous we both were on entering her rooms. We suddenly became tongue-tied. She opened her mouth to say something but there was no sound. For a moment we did nothing but stare into each other's eyes. We had fallen in love. I don't know how long we stood clinging to each other – long enough for me to tell her that I loved her. I didn't dare tell her that I was about to go to war.

I cycled back to my lodgings in Botley Road late that night and thought only of Kay. Something had happened in our lives with aptness and finality – something I knew was wholly right, so right that I was prepared to believe that it was intended.

We spent the whole of the next day canoeing on the river. We felt utterly free. Our love was like nothing else on earth, everything willed it: the river, the trees, the clouds. Everything shared it: the people we met, the gardens we sat in, the birds that sang. Our love had made everything complete and one; it brought to us beauty and meaning. If only the music we heard would last for ever. That night we saw *The Wizard of Oz*. On our way back to Warnborough Road, we light-heartedly skipped to the tune of 'The Yellow Brick Road' along St Giles. The world's worries were far away; we were wild and childish, with all thought driven from our heads.

Henceforth we were rarely apart. The university didn't exist; the Agricultural Board didn't exist either; only the two of us existed in our dream world, and in our love the two of us were united. On May Day 1940, long before six o'clock, I woke Kay by throwing stones at her bedroom window. Muffled up against the cold, we climbed the steps of Magdalen Tower. There, while the bells pealed, we greeted the sunrise by chanting a Latin hymn into the wind. We breakfasted in a punt on the Cherwell. We sang together in the boat:

> Bliss was it in that dawn to be alive
> But to be young was very heaven.

That night I told Kay that we would have to part in June.

Our dreamtime ended nine days later, on 10 May. I was lying in bed at the Tates, staring at the apple blossom pressing against the window. In Wytham Wood a cuckoo called. I found myself humming the tune Kay and I had sung the day before:

> Sumer is icumen in, Lhude sing cuccu!
> Groweth sed, and bloweth med,
> And springth the wude nu.

There was a bang on the door. Reg appeared. 'Get up,' he said. 'The King wants you.' For the first time he wasn't smiling. There was no tea.

I was shocked. 'What is it Reg?'

He handed me the newspaper. The Germans had invaded Luxembourg and Belgium and were racing towards the Channel ports. The British Expeditionary Force (BEF) had left France and entered Belgium to halt the German advance; the continent was aflame.

I jumped up, had a little breakfast, collected Kay, and together we went to Thiel. We found him glued to his short-wave radio tuned to the Netherlands. We heard the Dutch stations tracking the German planes bombing Rotterdam. Fighter planes were strafing the streets of The Hague. The air was full of wild voices. This was the real thing; people were getting killed. It was the only time I'd ever seen Thiel's eyes large with tears – the clockwork man wound up for life had become very human. I'd often wondered what went on behind those eyes. I knew his family had been scattered. With the bombing of the Netherlands, the dam had burst; the carefree period of his exile had ended.

Later that day Churchill became Prime Minister. Only Churchill could meet the hour and the peril. MacDonald, Baldwin and Chamberlain had gone. Five days later the Dutch surrendered.

Thenceforth, hour-by-hour, blow-by-blow, Britain, France

and Belgium tried to stem the German tide. To no avail – lines of defence were pierced one after another. In ten days the Germans were at Abbeville, Calais and Boulogne. I wondered what was happening to Jean Doeraene and the students I'd met at Louvain and Quarreux.

On 26 May a service of intercession was held in all the churches for our troops across the Channel. We hadn't the vaguest idea what was happening to them, but we could at least pray for them.

Kay and I were coming down the river in *Ruby* one peaceful Sunday morning at the end of May when we saw what looked like a sea of human beings – thousands of them – pouring on to Port Meadow. As we drew closer, we were told that they were survivors from Dunkirk, who'd been brought from Dover by train. It was in all the newspapers and on the radio. Saved by a miracle – the sea had remained calm throughout the evacuation – the major portion of Britain's fleeing army had been brought home.

We moved among the bedraggled and exhausted survivors listening to their tales. The ordeal through which they had passed was reflected on their faces, some of them were unspeakably weary. The speed of the German attack had overwhelmed them. Some had been rescued from the sea several times. Their uniforms were torn and dirty, their boots cracked; their eyes were hollow from lack of sleep; two weeks' growth of beard was on their chins; they were hungry and thirsty. They were a brave but sorry-looking lot.

A week or two later Paris fell. The invasion of Britain was imminent. Not since the Norman invasion of 1066 had Britain faced the prospect of fighting an aggressor on its own soil. Our change of fortune left us dazed. Hitler called upon Britain to surrender. 'We shall never surrender,' answered Churchill. There would be no surrender, no appeasement, no panic. Never had Britain rallied to a leader's words more than it did during those dark days. For a brief moment in our history, oratory closed our ranks. In June, Mussolini ('that Jackal' said Churchill) entered the war on Hitler's side.

The crisis revealed us to ourselves. In the white heat of those perilous days our resolution, our sense of goodness, hope, commitment, patriotism and service intensified. With the enemy at the gate, any wound of class and national divisiveness was healed. Britain spoke with one voice; indecision was replaced by certainty and action: Britain would fight on. We were proud to be standing alone, and we were not going to be licked by Hitler or anybody else.

Kay and I dashed about as if everything was normal. We didn't express our fears and doubts. Having found each other, our only concern was to get married before we were parted.

While all this was going on, early one morning in June 1940 I went across to Thiel's place to have breakfast with him. The breakfast was on the table; his lodgings looked as if he'd just stepped out. There was the usual disarray: newspapers and books stacked to the ceiling, jazz records on the floor, clothes on the bed. His landlady didn't know where he'd gone. I sat and waited. Eventually I left.

Unknown to any of us Hans had been taken into custody early that morning and interned as an 'enemy alien'. I found out only by chance. Ferdie Smith, the college secretary at Ruskin had bumped into Hans and his escort on a crowded London railway station. It was a shock to lose him that way. No goodbyes.

While this nightmare was unfolding, I was trying to prepare for 'Schools': whatever happened, I was not going to leave Oxford shabbily. The morning of 'Schools' came. I did the best I could, and well enough. (It would be six years before I could return to graduate.)

The days before my leaving Oxford weighed heavily upon me. Kay knew I had to go. But with the sword of parting above our heads, we kept on pretending it was not so. Yet the days passed and then the hours and then it was time to say goodbye. The last night we spent together in

Warnborough Road – a candle flickering, the breeze moving the creeper against the open window. We tried to forget tomorrow, it was all a bad dream that would pass in the night. Perhaps an earthquake or something dreadful would happen. There might be peace. I said silly things such as not to worry, and that it wasn't the end of everything, and that I'd see her soon, and that the odds were that we'd remain together for ever. We were young; we were determined to have nothing to do with reality. We buried our heads in each other's shoulders and cried silently with joy. We swore no one would part us. Outside, the nightingales sang.

But then the dawn came and with it reality. It crept through the window and told us to get up. We dressed and went into the street. A column of army ambulances was making its way through the town. Heavy of heart, we passed Worcester College, whose walls now seemed grey and streaked with damp, and made our way to the railway station and on to the crowded platform. Trains came and went. Everybody, it seemed, was either going to war or coming from it. We weren't the only couple saying a sad farewell; tears were plentiful. When my overcrowded train arrived it hissed clouds of steam. Kay stood outside the carriage window with glistening eyes. With everybody pushing and shoving, and people running backwards, and forwards, on the platform shouting about seats, I asked stupid questions such as, 'How will you get back to Warnborough Road?' She remained silent, not trusting her tongue. Our clasped hands remained firm until the engine broke our grip. As the train slid away I looked back to see a small, lonely figure waving to me. The wind was blowing her dress, and her soft, brown hair.

It's said that if you live with beauty you fail to appreciate it. I appreciated Oxford and Kay until the last moment – until the waving figure and Oxford were no more.

Chapter XIV

The Years the Locusts Ate

That night I slept in a bell tent with eleven other recruits at a barracks at Devizes in the west of England. With our feet against the tent pole, we were like sardines in a can. I wore drab denims; my head had been shaved. Supporting my makeshift pillow were the heaviest boots I'd worn in years. Feeling like a parson who'd strayed into the village pub, I talked about Oxford and my reluctance to join the OTC.

'Ox, mite? Aren't you on the wrong bus? Ox nobs are officers. Does yer mean to say, mite, that yer passed up a bleedin' bed and a batman to live in a tent wiv us?'

'Look,' I answered, 'forget everything I said. I'm here because I dipped into somebody's petty cash box.'

That seemed to satisfy them and they never questioned my credentials again. 'Yer all right, mite. Yer one of us. We'll 'elp yer go strite.' The irony of having to be specious to get back into the working class was not lost on me.

Henceforth I was one of them, laughing my heart out,

699

nodding my head, closing my eyes and ears to what I found hard to bear – especially the foul language.

They had every reason to be curious about me. Out of a thousand recruits there were only two university men, myself and Edward King, a Cambridge classics student, who had also neglected to join the OTC. He was a bright fellow with a mad glint in his eye. The hard conditions, the tempers of the drill sergeants and the intellectual poverty of army dialogue gnawed at him. Wisely, he hid his feelings behind grins and silence. He and I used to wonder how we had got ourselves into such a pickle where education didn't matter one jot.

The trouble was that we had read too many books and heard too many lectures, especially ones extolling Western civilisation's vital contribution to the widening of individual freedom. In the army you did what you were told; to think was to ask for trouble. We were in fact prisoners of thought. While we discussed the finer points of Nazism and fascism, or Greek or Roman history, the other soldiers were content to scrub their mess tins, polish their brasses and make sure they'd got the drill right. They had a feeling of duty and sober resolution, which, despite all our education, we lacked. I envied their unselfish, simple outlook. It moved me when they practised marching and counter-marching outside the tents at night.

Before the summer of 1940 was out the Battle of Britain was well under way. Bombs fell on London almost daily. Havoc struck the East End. Recruits from Cockneyland came back from leave mourning their dead. They told dreadful stories of monstrous fires that had engulfed everything and set the Thames alight. Often when news of relatives' deaths arrived, a soldier would throw himself down on to the grass and weep. Everybody was sympathetic, knowing that it might be his turn next.

Edward King and I felt that we'd both been short-changed by the military. I suspect my fate had been decided during the interview with the Oxford University Joint Recruiting

Board. I should have kept my mouth shut about my pacifism. But with A. D. Lindsay, Master of Balliol, in the chair, I felt I had nothing to fear in speaking out. I'd been taught to speak out. I thought that I would be sent to an Officers Training Unit. At least I thought they would make use of my knowledge of German and Germany.

Time proved me wrong, I was taken down a peg. His Majesty the King sent me a postal money order for seven shillings and sixpence so that I could get to boot camp. Once there, it was too late to protest.

After four weeks of boot camp, I was promoted to corporal. I held my rank for seven days. While walking down a street one day, I heard 'Corporal! Corporal!' I looked round and saw an officer threshing the air with his swagger-cane. I crossed the street hurriedly and gave him one of my best salutes.

'Have you stopped saluting officers?' he spluttered.

'No, sir.'

'Then why didn't you salute me?'

'I didn't see you, sir.'

'Are you without eyes?'

A knot of people was collecting.

'I've saluted so many officers today . . . I was bound to miss one.'

An old lady tittered: 'Take no notice of him, luv, he's just showing off.'

Embarrassed that he was becoming an object of ridicule, the subaltern took my name and hurried off to do as much harm as he could. I lost my rank.

How Edward King laughed as I picked the stripes and the threads out of my tunic sleeves.

The separation from Kay gnawed at me so much that I climbed the camp wall before dawn one Sunday morning to go to Oxford. Edward King covered for me. A car soon picked me up; those who still had cars were glad to help a lone soldier. The real danger was running into the military police, they were out in force. The country was awaiting invasion, and all leave had been cancelled.

When I arrived at Kay's lodgings, the landlady, being a romantic type, insisted that I should take Kay's breakfast upstairs. Having knocked like a maid on her bedroom door, I entered, juggling a tray with breakfast for two, a tin hat, a gas mask and a rifle. We had a whole day before us that we might never have shared. We were overwhelmed by our richness.

I returned to the camp by the same route in the dead of night, careful to avoid the trigger-happy guards who occasionally took potshots at nonexistent Germans coming over the wall.

Every Sunday after that I disappeared to go to Oxford. Only once did my scheme falter. I was tramping along an empty country road back to camp late at night, when a car pulled up. 'Want a lift to Devizes?' the driver shouted. I quickly jumped in. Only when I had slammed the door shut did I realise that I was sitting next to a drill-sergeant from the camp. Of all the stupid things I might have done, this was the worst. I'd managed to get myself caught red-handed. I could either throw myself out of the car or be arrested at the barrack gates. I sweated at the choice.

The sergeant's amiable conversation only added to my discomfort. He was ten years my senior and a civilian recruit like myself. He lived halfway between Oxford and Devizes. By the looks he gave me now and again, he must have thought me strangely tongue-tied. My mind was on other things.

Before we reached the camp, I decided to confess. 'Sarge, I don't have a pass. I came out over the wall.'

I expected the car to stop with a sharp jolt, but it kept going.

'Why would you want to do a daft thing like that? Could land you in clink.'

'My girl's in Oxford.'

He didn't reply for some time. The engine knocked away. 'Look,' he said eventually, 'I haven't heard a thing you said. I'll drop you off before the barracks. If you get your bloody head blown off going over the wall, that's your business.'

'Thanks, Sarge.' I blew out my cheeks and sat back. There was a long pause.

'Listen,' he said as he dropped me off. 'If you're as mad next Sunday, come to my house before ten and I'll bring you back. I need to flee too.'

His help was important, his sympathy even more so.

At the beginning of July, while the Germans were bombing London, my unit was doing manoeuvres on Salisbury Plain. One day the 'enemy' made inroads into our positions; the next day we flung him back. It was all done in the best of spirits, though it was largely a waste of time.

After several days my interest had fallen to zero. How much better everything would be, I thought, if I were with my own true love in Oxford. It wouldn't do for everybody to think like that – there'd be no manoeuvres – but then not everybody was in love. Whether I stayed or took to my heels would not make the slightest difference to the outcome of the 'battle'. Chaos was so widespread that I wouldn't even be missed. While I was wondering how best to get away, I met a motorcycle dispatch rider who was willing to swap roles with me for the day. He didn't mind riding backwards and forwards all day in the back of a truck.

Of course there was a risk about my madcap scheme: the military police were always looking for fools like me. But that was a risk I'd have to take.

The next morning I was on a motorcycle tearing down country lanes, past mile-long military convoys. With crash helmet, goggles, gloves, dispatch bag and the motorcyclist's long coat, I looked the real thing. In two or three hours, I thought, I'll be in Oxford. The faster I went the more the army urged me on. At the speed I was going, they presumed that I was carrying top-secret dispatches upon which the fate of the 'battle' turned. The military police gave me the right of way. It's just as well they didn't know that all that was in my bag was a bread and cheese sandwich.

Oblivious of fate, I pushed on with greater speed. Everything went well until I began to overtake a column of tanks on a narrow road alongside a river. Suddenly the road swerved sharply to the right across a high-arched stone bridge. There was a tank in the middle. As I struggled with the brakes, I caught a glimpse of the narrow gap between the tank and the stone parapet. There was a dull thud as I slammed into the gap. I was thrown on to the stones and heard a muffled voice calling down a long tunnel: 'Don't touch him! Don't touch him! Leave him alone!'

I woke up in St Hilda's College, which had become a hospital for head injuries. Ironically, Kay lived in the next street. One of the first things I recognised when I came to was a crushed helmet lying with my possessions on the floor. My head was bandaged, as were my left leg and arm.

I spent most of that day with doctors, nurses and X-ray technicians. They told me that the helmet had saved my life and I had been spared from broken bones. Except for a few bruises and cuts and a slight dizziness, I thought myself in the best of health, and said so.

It was eventually decided that I was fit enough to be returned to my unit. My appeals to be allowed to visit Kay in the next street were not heard. 'Let's go!' my officer escort said, pointing to a car at the kerb. 'Don't you know there's a war on?' I looked in the direction of Kay's lodgings and sighed. Did I know there was a war on!

Edward King had a wicked grin when I told him what had happened. 'Pure Aeschylus,' he said. 'In Greek drama there is a law of inevitable justice whereby every wrong brings its own punishment; one's sins are always found out.'

Nobody bothered about me, or the bike, or the accident

again. But American photographers had been taking pictures of the tanks crossing the bridge at the moment that I made my spectacular entry. My flying through the air was grist to their mill and photos of me landing on my head on the cobbles were distributed by Movietone News throughout Britain and America. They used a dreadful caption, something like 'Rider lays down life in defence of Britain'. An odd way, I thought, of describing my going courting.

———◇———

Later that summer I returned one Sunday night from Oxford, where I had been on forty-eight hours of leave (this time legitimate), to find that my entire unit had vanished. As I approached the entrance to the disused factory where we had been billeted, I waited for the usual harsh cry of: 'Halt, who goes there?' Instead silence reigned. Bewildered, I wandered into the empty building. Only one feeble light burned; there was not a soul about. Except for the scratching and squealing of rats, there was no sound. Hanging from the ceiling of the long, empty barracks was a solitary duffel bag – mine. The men I'd known might never have existed.

I went out and stared at the moon and wondered what on earth had happened. With my duffel bag over my shoulder, I reported to a neighbouring barracks. They knew as much as I did about where the others had gone.

[In 1948 I met a man on the London underground who recognised me and told me what had happened to my comrades years before. While I had been in Oxford my unit had been mobilised and shipped in great haste via Bristol to meet a crisis in Singapore. They had arrived in time to become prisoners of the Japanese. Most of them died working as slave-labourers on the Rangoon–Bangkok railway: the bridge over the Kwai. King had been one of them. As I climbed the wet concrete steps from the underground to the street, I could hear Private Edward King, scholar of Cambridge, laughing at some joke as we walked along the footpath of the canal at Devizes. I'm sure he kept a brave heart until the end.]

———◇———

In the autumn of 1940, I was posted from Devizes in the West Country to the 45th Infantry Division defending Clacton-on-Sea on the south-east coast. With reinforcements from all over Britain, the division was dug in opposite the Dutch and French Channel ports.

At Clacton we lived a day-to-day existence, wondering when the enemy would come. We lay down each night not knowing what fate would bring. We had aerial photographs of the Germans massing at the other side. There would be no retreat, our Order of Battle forbade it. So we sat behind the beach and waited and waited and cleaned our rifles and watched the water rise and fall and wondered when the Germans would strike. We prayed that the foul weather would continue.

In 1588 the 45th had faced the Spaniards. Sir Francis Drake was its patron. Our emblem was *Drake's Drum*:

> Take my drum to England, hang et by the shore,
> Strike et when your powder's runnin' low;
> If the Dons sight Devon, I'll quit the port o' heaven,
> An' drum them up the Channel as we drummed
> them long ago.*

The only Germans we saw were dead Germans washed up on the beach, and the daredevil observer pilots who daily photographed our positions at chimney-top level.

We waited for something to happen. Nothing did. The winter tides came in and went out again relentlessly. The wind howled at us from the sea. One grey, wet, cold, dreary day

* *Drake's Drum*, Sir Henry John Newbolt (1862–1938).

followed another. We began to feel that it might be a good thing if the Germans did come.

That Christmas, Kay and I travelled north to stay with her widowed mother in the village of Temple Sowerby in Westmorland. Kay's sister Mary joined us from a college in Wales. Their brother John was at sea. Everyone did their best to make it a happy Christmas. We took walks together through the snow-covered fields, but we never succeeded in throwing off the worries of wartime. While I was there, we heard that John's hospital ship had been bombed and sunk off the coast of France, but that he had been rescued.

After getting back to my unit I had a note from Harold Watkins, who was with Bomber Command two hundred miles away. He thought I'd like to know that Betty Weatherby had married a navy officer and had left Blackburn to live in Surrey.

———◦———

Much of 1941, spent at Clacton, is a blur. The army did all the things it could think of to keep us busy – exercises, training, inspections, route marches – but morale among the men remained low. We'd been sitting staring at the sea for too long. I wrote to Kay daily; her letters sustained my spirits. Sharing a few days' leave in the spring, we decided to get married. Other than my two-shillings-a-day army pay, I had no means of supporting a wife, but it didn't seem to matter. Treasuring the gift of life, we did what we thought we should do as lovers – become one. 'You're being rash,' friends cautioned, 'wait until the war is over.' We thought rashness the most wonderful thing in the world. Besides, tomorrow might be too late.

As Kay was a Protestant and I was not much of anything, we were married in September by Father O'Hea in a brief ceremony in St Augustine Church, Oxford, before the closed altar gates. Kay and I had both kept in touch with O'Hea – he had become a father figure to us. Other than family, there were few people at our wedding. I was in uniform; I had been commissioned as a second lieutenant two days earlier. A radiant Kay wore a close-fitting blue costume, with a tiny hat perched on the front of her head. The best man, a friend in the army, had come straight from manoeuvres in camouflage battle-dress, wearing enormous boots. As her father was dead, her brother John gave her away.

It was the bare bones of a ceremony: no flowers, no candles, no incense, no singing, no bread and wine. There should have been no organ either, but the organist was a soldier too and he waived the rules. His organ thundered out to an almost empty church.

Looking at us over his spectacles as if he was seeing us for the first time, O'Hea gently led us through the ceremony. I could hardly believe my ears when he said, 'I now pronounce you man and wife.' He gave us his blessing.

Kay's mother had come to the wedding. She had arrived on the same train as my mother and my sister Brenda. They were wearing new fox furs around their necks – now that we were at war everybody had jobs, and money to burn. I thought the foxes looked sad but said nothing. Socially, the two mothers were miles apart, but they did their best for our sake.

We received lots of telegrams, including one from Harold Watkins, one from Jim Foggerty, who was back in the New Silksworth mines, and another from Miss Hesselthwaite of Bow. Hans Thiel wrote from the Isle of Man, where he was interned as an 'enemy alien', saying that to marry at this time was crazy.

The reception was at Reg's and Minnie's in Botley Road. We broke all the rationing regulations. There were lots of toasts and speeches and laughter. The fear of a German invasion was forgotten. We were wished 'A long life and much happiness.' I had to say a few words, which I found difficult. I excused myself: 'My problem is that I haven't been married before,' and that seemed to please everyone, including O'Hea. When the time came for us to leave, Kay hugged her mother; together they cried.

We said goodbye to O'Hea, who was also about to leave Oxford. He held my hands on parting, something he'd never done before. There was a touch of anxiety about him – he might have been a loving father saying goodbye to his son. He had had such hopes for me, and had acted so unselfishly on my behalf, only to lose me to war.

Kay and I had a three-day honeymoon in a country inn near Henley-on-Thames. Three days is not a long time, but it is a long time when you are living every moment. At night aircraft droned overhead. Lying in the grass on our backs the next day, we watched a dogfight. Following the thud of guns and rattle and pop, the German plane fell to earth; a parachute drifted across the sky.

On the fourth day I returned to Clacton-on-Sea. It was a grim journey in darkened trains, through the London underground, choked with people. I had left Kay behind in Oxford. I hoped she would be safe there.

Although none of us knew it at the time, it was quite purposeless for me to return to defend the shore of Essex. Germany had invaded Russia in June 1941 and by September was fully committed to war on its Eastern front.

In October, as the threat of a German invasion lessened, the 45th was moved inland; I was posted to the 24th Guards Brigade at Addington on the outskirts of London. The blessing of going to London was that Kay and I could occasionally meet. We would rent a hotel room for two or three hours. Even to spend a day together sitting on the grass in Hyde Park was bliss.

Early in 1942 my brigade was ordered to Scotland as part of the First Infantry Division. Before leaving I received a call from the adjutant of my battalion.

'You are to join the battalion in Ayr as "C-A-P-T".'

'What does that mean?'

'You don't know what that means? It's PT. It means that

you will be the chief physical training officer.'

'What on earth has physical training to do with me?' I felt hurt.

'Not ours to question why, dear boy, but to do or die. Don't take it to heart. You're not being dumped. You'll find that it will work out to your advantage. I'm only sorry to see you go.'

Two days later, I marched into the office of my new commander. 'Second Lieutenant Woodruff reporting for duty, sir.' I gave the best salute I could muster.

'Get out of here, Woodruff, and get yourself properly dressed. Don't you know you have been promoted to Captain?'

'No, sir. I don't. My friends have played a trick on me.'

Not to this day do I know who kicked me up the promotion ladder.

As 1942 wore on it was rumoured that we were going to North Africa. We were given a week's embarkation leave. I left for Oxford to join Kay. Her face was full of joy when I walked in on her. 'You're about to become a father,' she whispered. I reached out for her. As we held each other, I'd never felt so close to her.

We lived the week to the full: during the day we travelled in her car on her job in the countryside; at night, we were holed up together in her lodgings. The week passed as a day might pass, and we were parted once more. In tears, we agreed to use the code word 'Hope' when I had orders to sail.

When I reached Scotland again, I expected to find that some of the men, especially those who had gone home to Ireland, had not returned from leave. I was wrong. No one complained about being shipped out to Africa, nobody stopped to ask. We lived in a trance, while others arranged our lives.

To keep us busy, we were given commando training. The War Office couldn't have men standing about doing nothing. Regularly, on dark nights, we were trucked out to the inner fastnesses of the moors, where we were left without food, shelter or blankets to shift for ourselves. I'm sure it was excellent training in survival, but I'd never felt so miserable.

One night, against regulations, I took the quilted radiator cover off the truck in which I was riding. I had a cold coming on and I didn't want to lose my Christmas leave. No sooner had I bedded down in the freezing heather with the cover wrapped around me, than we were ordered to fall in and march. In addition to fifty pounds of kit, I had to carry the heavy cover, which I'd promised the driver to bring back. By dawn I was exhausted and running a fever. I left Scotland that morning to be with Kay who had gone to join her mother in Temple Sowerby.

The day-long journey was a haze and I reached Kay on the point of collapse. By the time I'd recovered from my fever, Christmas had come and gone, my leave was finished and I was on my way back to Scotland.

One morning in early January 1943, our brigade was told to parade in battle order. In endless khaki columns we marched through the streets of Ayr to the railway station. Our journey to the real battlefield had begun. Our long column hardly got a glance from passers-by. A train took us to the Clyde where our convoy waited to sail to North Africa. This was something I'd never envisaged when I joined up to defend England.

Before going on board, I phoned Kay and told her, 'Hope.' We both wept.

In June 1943 in Tunisia, I received a decoded message that read: 'Mother and son well.'

For the next three years I was tossed about in Greece, Crete, North Africa and Italy. I had so little control over my destiny that I might have been fighting anywhere. Disorder, disruption, slaughter and chaos were my lot. There were times when I felt that we'd been sent on a damn-fool mission. Witnessing the killing and dying, I wondered about the sanity of those responsible for our strategy. I fought for two-and-a-quarter years in Italy to reach what Churchill called 'the soft underbelly of Europe'.

These were the longest years of my life. To this day their pattern is indiscernible. They were years in which I had a different sense of reality, time and self. The ordeal lasted so long that its overwhelming sorrow and rage and cruelty threatened my essential humanity. Bitterly, I discovered that the essence of war is man's inhumanity to man. Life was discontinuous and fragmented; death and disease thinned our ranks. The roll call was never the same; the certainties of yesterday were not worth discussing. Eventually, I came to look upon war as a giant absurdity. It took twenty years before I was able to purge myself of the nightmare in my book *Vessel of Sadness*.

Kay and I used to say that these were the years the locusts ate. In the first five years of our married life we had five weeks together. For the rest, we waited and waited and waited while our heartache grew. Our only link were the little blue airmail forms, carried by angels we used to say, into which almost daily, year after year, we poured our love. The war ate up the marrow of our bones. How long will the war last? we kept asking each other. Love was our hope and our strength, it was a candle forever burning in the window of our life. Without hope – hope that was renewed a thousand times – we might have despaired. How many times in those dreadful days in the Mediterranean did I think of home and wife and child? I had someone to live for, someone to love. Through the hardest times they sustained me. By 1945 I no longer pleaded with God for grace to know Him; I pleaded with Him to stop the war.

Chapter XV

Afterword

In January 1945 my unit was sent from Italy to Greece to stop the Greeks from killing each other in their civil war.

However, I contracted typhoid fever and ended up lying on the floor of a bare room in a burned-out building in an Athens square. It was ironic that having escaped death in battle, a microbe should bring me down. I was left where I fell. There was an epidemic and the hospitals were full. For two weeks I saw only an army doctor who visited me each day and sat cross-legged on the floor. 'One for you, and one for me,' he'd say as he fished two bottles of cold beer out of his bag. He brought me extra blankets; I watched him through fevered eyes. No one else came. There were footsteps outside, but that was all. The long dark nights and the silence of the room oppressed me. I lay there thinking of Kay and our child and waiting for the dawn. During the day, I studied the walls and the ceiling. Sometimes the sun caught the shattered glass of the window lying on the floor. I might have been buried alive.

One morning in May 1945, I was wakened by a Greek band playing in the square below. A crowd was cheering. The war that would never end had ended. Elated, I got up and opened the door of my cell. On the other side was a skull and crossbones. Unsteadily, I made my way down the corridor, back to life.

———◦———

Now that the war was over, I expected to go home. Instead, I was shuttled about from transit camps in Greece to transit camps in Italy, awaiting transport. In June I was sent with thousands of others to a camp outside Bari in southern Italy. Each day we were going home; each day only a handful got away by air. The 'first in, first out' bunkum didn't count when there were no ships and no trains. Had we known how long we would be trapped there, we would have torn the place down on arrival. The war done, the British Tommy became a piece of unfortunate baggage that needed to be repatriated. We called ourselves 'The Forgotten Army'.

To lessen the soul-destroying boredom, I began to pick up the shattered pieces of my pre-war life. Wherever I could I wrote and renewed the friendships I'd known before the war. I learned that Bow and Poplar had been devastated by bombing: half of Poplar had been levelled. From the East End I learned that the Tinker family had perished in the 'blitz'. The Hargreaves' old home in Addington Road, Bow, was a pile of rubble; all that remained of George Lansbury's house in Bow Road was a door blowing in the wind. Blessedly, he had died a few days before the German onslaught, and was spared the depths of wickedness that the war revealed.

Ma Hargreaves had died in north London. She had intended to throw herself back into social work once the war was over, but was never given the chance. They said that the war had killed her, that its brutality had undermined her strength. Clem, Emily and Chris were planning (or at least

Clem was planning) to retire to a cottage in Devon. Like so many others who had fled east London, the Hargreaves never returned to their old haunts.

Alex Hargreaves survived the war. He'd got rid of a great deal of his hostility fighting the Germans, and he'd won a Military Cross. While I was waiting to go home outside Bari, he was already back in business in London. His first wife had divorced him and he had remarried. He had switched his allegiance from the Conservative to the Labour Party and had been swept into power by the landslide Labour victory of 1945. He charmed the masses as a Member of Parliament and they loved him. Alex was going to go a long way.

Miranda, my old girlfriend, had been killed in the ambulance service during the bombing of London. The news left me sad for days. Miranda's 'I've a good 'eart, I 'ave' rang across the years. Alex had adopted the little girl she had left behind. Some said Alex had always loved Miranda; I had thought that long ago. On the surface, he'd always appeared egotistical, but at the bottom he'd been a mixture of compassion and hostility.

No one had any firm news of Milton. In an attempt to get himself killed he had joined a bomb disposal squad. Some say he survived the war. If he did, he disappeared in the post-war maze.

Carol Hargreaves was still working for Poplar Council. She hadn't remarried. While Poplar was being flattened all around her, she'd taken in the homeless and helped out with the anti-aircraft batteries in Victoria Park. She never knew again the joy she had known when caring for her dying Mike.

Harold Watkins had died in a bombing raid over the Rhine. I grieved Harold's passing, as I grieved that of Ma Hargreaves and Miranda. Harold and I had grown up together. I felt that life had not treated him fairly. By then I knew that life rarely does.

Hans Thiel – with whom I had kept up a correspondence – had become a tutor at Oxford. He had spent the war there after returning from detention on the Isle of Man. He was still a bachelor. 'When are you coming back?' he wrote. He invited me to join him.

Jim Foggerty had spent the war down the mine and in public service. He had married and was busy raising a family. He had become a miners' leader – a far more important person than either Thiel or myself. Britain was safe with men like Foggerty in charge.

Wonder of wonders, Oxford had remained untouched throughout the war. O'Hea, Rodger, Dowdell and Cole were back in their caps and gowns. O'Hea wrote to say that he was looking forward to going on where he'd left off in 1939. With the overwhelming victory of Labour, he thought he would have more support in educating working men and women.

My old landlord, Reg Tates, whom I'd expected to live to be a hundred, had died of a heart attack, and Minnie was inconsolable.

All the members of my own family had remained well and safe during the years I had been away. My sisters had gone from war work back to their homes. My brother had worked as a labourer in a factory and brought up a wonderful family. My father, having spent almost seven years helping to make fighter planes, was unemployed again.

Of my Belgian friend Jean Doeraene there was no news. [I finally ran him to earth in Nivelles in 1974. Julienne, his wife, answered my knocking. 'Je suis Guillaume,' I said, as if thirty-five years didn't matter.]

Ludwig Wolfrath survived the war. In 1939, with O'Hea's help, he had gone with a new name and yet another passport to continue his medical studies at Dublin University. Returning to his lodgings one night in 1940 he had been horrified to find a letter from the German Embassy addressed to him, by his real name: the Gestapo had caught up with him. In mortal danger, he fled to British Belfast. In 1944, with his studies completed, he became a physician at a London hospital. His parents were alive and well.

As a diabetic, Willi Betterman had died during the war for want of insulin.

By August, the men in the Bari camp could stand the waiting no longer. They decided to build a train from the wrecked equipment lying on the railway sidings, and the idea was taken up with enthusiasm. It gave them a purpose and tested their ingenuity; it eased the dull ache of endless separation from home. They had all the skilled men they needed. In days, they'd set about scavenging and cannibalising every bit of railway equipment they could find, and soon, with heavy lifting gear provided by Italian wrecking crews, a skeleton of a train began to take shape.

One day, while working in the railway marshalling yard, we heard on the radio that an atom bomb (whatever that was) had destroyed Hiroshima. Some men cheered and then went back to work. After six years we'd become callous. To us, the atom bomb was just another bigger bomb. No one stood around discussing the moral implications of using it; no one was conscience-stricken. Besides, it was the Yanks' war, not ours. The fall of Hong Kong and Singapore at the beginning of the war had affected us much more. It had been mind-boggling that Britain should have been defeated by Japan.

I also learned for the first time about the holocaust of the Jews. I found it hard to believe. Until 1945, those of us who fought at the front had no inkling that the Jews were being systematically killed off in the countries under German control.

At the beginning of December 1945, seven months after the war had ended, our train was ready to roll. Looking like a travelling circus rather than a victorious army, we pulled out

719

of Bari station on a cold, windy day. Muffled to the ears, we peered through the wooden slats that had been nailed across the shattered windows at the cheering soldiers who were left behind. We never wanted to see Bari or Italy again.

There were ten of us to a compartment: two lying on the rebuilt racks above our heads, the rest of us sitting in the wooden troughs that had been bolted to the frame. The Italians had pillaged everything else. There was little heating. At night, our candles were put out regularly by the wind blowing through the cracks, but we were going home. Nothing else in the world mattered. Some food we took with us, most we scrounged from military depots on the way.

For two weeks our train picked its way across war-torn Italy to Brig on the Swiss frontier. The Swiss officials were reluctant to let us in, they said they'd never heard of us. We stood in the snow and eventually came to a compromise: we could cross into France, but we must use a Swiss locomotive and we must not stop at any station. That I suppose is why we stopped at Geneva for at least thirty minutes, while the populace ran up and down the station steps shouting, 'Good luck, Johnny, good luck!' Some tried to shake our hands through the wooden slats. We had hoped for chocolate.

We reached Dieppe in time to watch our troop steamer for Newhaven sail away. In a ragged line, we shouted and howled after it; we even fired our rifles into the air, but it didn't return. After some discussion, the order was given to fall in. We were to march to a transit camp on the outskirts of Dieppe to be deloused. The order was ignored; the men sat down sullenly and would not move. In six years I had never seen British troops refuse to obey, but I did then. As the sergeant-major's voice rose higher and higher, ordering the soldiers to get into line, I smelled trouble. I knew that restlessness had been growing in the ranks. These men had been too long in battle, too far from home. It had taken years to get this far and they weren't going to miss the next ship.

'What on earth are you shouting for, Sergeant-Major?' the colonel-in-charge asked as he walked towards us on the pier.

'The troops have just mutinied, sir.'

'Mutiny, Sergeant-Major? Mutiny, you say? Well for God's sake, don't stand there shouting, get some tea!'

———◇———

From London I took the overnight express to Scotland. As a major, I had been given a seat in a first-class compartment. I sat next to a Member of Parliament, who complained that the war had given him ulcers. He was lucky that I was too exhausted to tell him what the war had given me. Not having been deloused at Dieppe, I felt no remorse when he started scratching.

Kay met me at Carlisle station. She was wearing a dark brown winter coat and a hat edged with fur. Red-cheeked with the cold, she could not have looked more beautiful or more radiant. Yelling, I fought my way through the crowd to reach her. We fell into each other's arms. I thought my heart would burst. The pushing, shouting crowd and the steaming train did not exist. We laughed and cried and trembled with our arms around each other. Our reunion was the vision I'd seen in all the restless, terrifying moments of war. It brought a strange, almost frightening happiness. All the way home to the Eden Valley, I kept having to stop the car so that we might tell each other of our love.

On reaching Temple Sowerby, I was overcome by the stillness. The village was wrapped in snow; blue smoke curled above the roofs; the summit of Cross Fell gleamed in the distance. I stood and watched the rooks returning to the trees around the church. Nothing had changed.

The son I'd never seen was running about, shouting when my mother-in-law opened the door. He was dressed in a red woollen roll-neck pullover and grey trousers. With Kay's eyes wide with delight, I put my hand on our child's head. I felt a universe. I saw the fresh, bright face, the fair hair, the fine skin, the blue eyes and the wondering innocence of his gaze. His eyes mirrored everything. For me, it was a timeless moment, a bottomless depth of bliss.

'And whose little boy are you?' I asked.

'What's in your bag?' was the reply. I pulled out a poorly made rubber ball, a cheap, unpainted, wooden Pinocchio, both of which I had obtained in Milan. 'What else?' Kay's mother looked on with moist eyes. For him and me it was a shy beginning.

My son watched as I deloused myself standing naked in a tin bath on the cobbles in the cold backyard. With him still babbling at my side, I then soaked all my cares away in the bath upstairs. Later we decorated the Christmas tree, hung the stockings and set out the candles. When darkness fell, we greeted the carol singers at the door.

I slept badly that night; I was unused to sleeping in a bed. In two-and-a-quarter years in Italy, except in hospitals, I'd slept in a proper bed only twice. But beds didn't matter; what mattered was that I no longer heard men shrieking in their sleep. For the first time in years I was at peace. It was a time of rebirth and renewal.

———— ❖ ————

In going to war, I had followed what I thought was the truth, regardless of the outcome. In support of my beliefs, I could not have offered more than my life. I came home years wiser; war had revealed the core of life to me.

I came home devoid of the political ambitions I had had when I set out. Much to other people's surprise my aspirations to become a leader in public life had died on the battlefield. Apart from voting for Labour in the transit camp in Bari, I took no part in the landslide Labour victory of 1945. The war had taught me to distrust political myths and grand panaceas. The small things in life had taken on a new intimacy; so had the heart. Before the war I had talked about building a new civilisation, at the end I knew how fragile civilisation is. All I wanted was the peaceful, private family life the war had denied me.

I came home stunned and remained stunned for some time. Finding my way back to my true self was like waking up from a six-year sleep. It took a long time for the memory of other men's deaths to fade.

Note on the author

In 1946 William Woodruff renewed his academic career in Oxford. In 1950 he was awarded a research fellowship by the Bank of England, which allowed him to write his first book. In 1952 he went as a Fulbright Scholar to Harvard University. He remained in the United States from 1953 until 1956 as a professor at the University of Illinois, after which he moved to Australia to head the Department of Economic History at the University of Melbourne. Since 1966 he has been at the University of Florida in the United States. Visiting professorships have taken him to the Institute for Advanced Study, Princeton; the Free University, Berlin; Waseda University, Tokyo; and finally, in 1978, back to Oxford to St Antony's College. He retired in 1996, a distinguished world historian.

William Woodruff has published over ten highly acclaimed books, including *Vessel of Sadness*, a novel based on his World War II experiences in the Italian Anzio campaign; *Paradise Galore*, an allegory; and *Concise History of the Modern World*, which is in its fourth edition.

William Woodruff has seven children: two sons by his first marriage to Kay and, following Kay's death, a daughter and four sons by his second wife Helga, to whom he was married in 1960.

SHADOWS OF GLORY

William Woodruff

Arnold College, Oxford. When Sir George Kemp returns to his old university to celebrate the launch of a new barge, he can't help noticing a photograph on the wall: the 1939 rowing team, of whom George had been the cox.

Sixty years earlier had been a heady, intoxicating time for George and the crew: Alex Haverfield, the handsome, natural leader; Charley Bradbury, a Scotsman with communist leanings; Roger Blundell, light-hearted and mischievous; Bill Clark, a naval cadet; David Evans, the mathematical genius who talked in riddles; Max Elsfield, rude-tongued and fabulously wealthy; Tony Markham, a landed aristocrat with luck on his side; and Pat Riley, the charming but mysterious Irishman.

But with conflict inevitable, the nine friends find the Dreaming Spires giving way to the nightmare of modern war: George, joining the RAF, is increasingly worried about his German love, Johanna; Roger, fighting in France, doubts he'll ever see his fiancée Gloria again; and David, facing romantic dilemmas, is becoming ever more reckless and brave . . .

General Fiction
Abacus
0 349 11689 X
978 0 349 116891

VESSEL OF SADNESS

William Woodruff

'A remarkable book indeed, bringing us close to the huge
face of war glaring, mad' J. B. Priestley

Italy, 1944 – this is the setting of one of the most convincing
and quietly magnificent stories about man and war that has
ever been written.

They were young when they left, and jolly. They sang as
they sailed down the Clyde, westwards, towards the sun-
burnished hills of the Mull of Kintyre. As the light faded
across the water, one of them climbed the rigging and
waved to a lonely figure standing on a mound by the
shoreline. They didn't know where they were going. They
didn't really care. They didn't want to fight. They hardly
knew what the war was about. But they went, together,
singing, to what lay before them.

Here, distilled from the experiences and observations of the
author, who served in Italy in the British infantry, is the
story of those who fought and died at Anzio.

'Excellence that sets it above the routine of memory.
William Woodruff has put these things down with
vividness, honesty, and a complete lack of emotional
posturing' *Sunday Times*

General Fiction
Abacus
0 349 11811 6
978 0 349 11811 6

A CONCISE HISTORY OF THE MODERN WORLD

William Woodruff

William Woodruff's magisterial history has a particular
resonance in today's world; for it is a history of the last five
hundred years, of the ascendancy of the West over the older
empires of the East. The rise and expansion of the West
began with the messianic zeal of Christianity asserting itself
over the Muslim world, something that, half a millennium
later, is being revisited through the use and abuse of that
crucial element of statecraft – power. For as much as this is
a study of history, it is also a portrait of that power and
how it has shaped our contemporary world.

We cannot hope to understand the present, contends
Woodruff, without knowing about the past. And, with
broad and boldly illuminating brushstrokes, he paints a
vivid picture of the past half-millennium and the scope,
significance and speed of the changes the West has effected.

After five centuries, contends Woodruff, the pendulum is
swinging back towards the East. The baton once wielded by
the European imperialists in their frenzied drive to 'save the
world' has been seized by America and is pointing east to
Islam, the world's fastest-growing religion, and to Asia, the
new powerhouse of the great nation states.

Learned and lucid, *A Concise History of the Modern World* is
also pertinent and provocative. Rather than an excavation of
the past, it is an assessment of our history as both
companion to the present and architect of the future.

History
Abacus
0 349 11837 X
978 0 349 11837 6